D0193959

British Columbia

Ryan Ver Berkmoes

John Lee

LEGEND

Tollway
Freeway
Primary Road
Secondary Road
Tertiary Road
Unsealed Road

0 ——— 200 km
0 ——— 120 miles

DAWSON CITY (pp376–83)
Relive the Klondike Gold Rush
in a town as alive today as then

**KLUANE NATIONAL PARK
& RESERVE (pp370–2)**
Unesco-sanctioned beauty amidst
glaciers and wildlife

150°W
130°W
110°W

Arctic Circle

Nunavut

Victoria
Island

Banks
Island

Amundsen Gulf

*Beaufort
Sea*

Tuktoyaktuk

Inuvik

Anderson R

Franklin Mountains

Mackenzie River

**Northwest
Territories**

*Great Bear
Lake*

*Lac la
Martre*

Great Slave
Lake

YELLOWKNIFE

*Wood Buffalo
National Park*

Lake
Athabasca

Saskatchewan

3

1

Mackenzie Mountains

Nahanni National
Park Reserve

**Yukon
Territory**

Yukon River

Dawson
City

5

2

1

WHITEHORSE

4

2

1

Watson
Lake

Atlin
Provincial
Park

Skagway

Alaska Hwy

CANADA
USA

Kluane National
Park & Reserve

Alaska

Fairbanks

2

1

*Gulf of
Alaska*

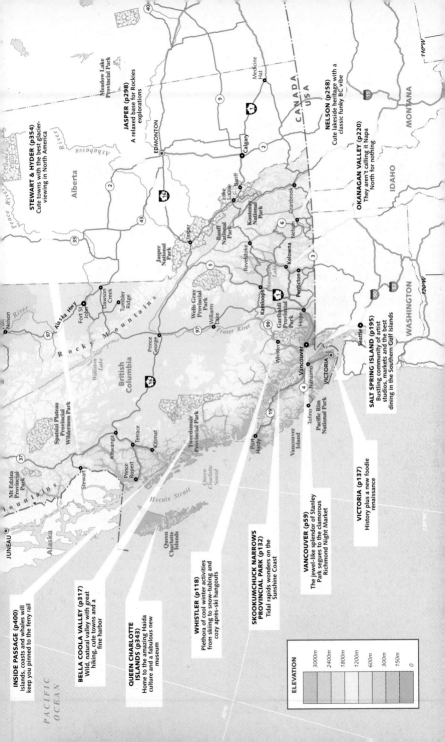

STEWART & HYDER (p354)
Cute towns with the best glacier-viewing in North America

JASPER (p298)
A relaxed base for Rockies explorations

NELSON (p258)
Cute lakeside heritage with a classic funky BC vibe

OKANAGAN VALLEY (p220)
They aren't calling it Napa North for nothing

SALT SPRING ISLAND (p195)
Bustling community of artist studios, markets and the best dining in the Southern Gulf Islands

VICTORIA (p137)
History plus a new foodie renaissance

VANCOUVER (p59)
The jewel-like splendor of Stanley Park segues to the clamorous Richmond Night Market

SKOOKUMCHUCK NARROWS PROVINCIAL PARK (p132)
Tidal rapids wonders on the Sunshine Coast

WHISTLER (p118)
Plethora of cool winter activities from skiing to snow-tubing and cozy après-ski hangouts

QUEEN CHARLOTTE ISLANDS (p343)
Home to the amazing Haida culture and a fabulous new museum

BELLA COOLA VALLEY (p317)
Wild, natural valley with great hiking, cute towns and a fine harbor

INSIDE PASSAGE (p400)
Islands, coasts and whales will keep you pinned to the ferry rail

ELEVATION

	3000m
	2400m
	1800m
	1200m
	600m
	300m
	150m
	0

On the Road

RYAN VER BERKMOES

Imagine my joy when, after a long day hiking around Kluane National Park & Reserve, we ended our day in Beaver Creek (p372). I'd always thought of the town as little more than a way station on the Alaska Hwy near the Alaska border. Imagine our glee when we found an amazing park of statuary dedicated to some of the Yukon's most beloved icons. There, in the sort of concrete-primitive style seldom seen in public installations, was a buck-toothed beaver, a stolid Mountie, an axe-wielding lumberjack and more! It was wonderful place to pause and reflect upon the contributions so many have made to make the Yukon what it is today.

JOHN LEE

After a two-hour snowshoe hike in Garibaldi Provincial Park (p118), we finally reached our clearing at 1500m. My legs were already turning to jelly when we began digging two circular pits, using shovels to remove dozens of shoebox-sized blocks. These were placed on top of each other in a spiraling, inward curve – igloo architecture is much more complicated than it looks. After five hours we were done and stood back to admire our handiwork, sipping on hip flasks and rubbing our aching muscles. By 9:30pm it was time for bed. Accessed via a U-bend entrance under the snow, the igloo's interior was glowing in the candlelight.

Destination British Columbia

What do you need? Descriptions of the most amazing coast in the world? Okay, British Columbia's coast is speckled with hundreds of wild and natural islands dotting a craggy shoreline whose wild beauty is punctuated by waterfalls and the splashes of dolphins and whales. Long dramatic fjords lead to places of surprising beauty such as Bella Coola and Stewart. Offshore, the Queen Charlotte Islands are a mystical and lyrical place where haunting art is created from centuries-old trees by one of the planet's most inherently artistic cultures.

Or would you prefer to hear about the mountains? Glaciers spill over peaks into BC, the Yukon and Alaska in Unesco-recognized Kluane National Park. In the Canadian Rockies one peak after another casts you into a shadow of insignificance. In between there's mountain after mountain, each defined by a river or lake at its base. And when you're not hiking or kayaking through these places in summer, you'll be delighting in their awesome powder come winter.

But perhaps you'd like something more civilized? Vancouver is one of the world's great cities, with a cool West Coast culture that knows how to enjoy the bounty of the region. Great restaurants set the stage for great nightlife. Over in the Okanagan Valley world-class wines age patiently while waiting for a corkscrew. And throughout the region delightfully funky towns like Fernie, Nelson, Tofino and Dawson City boast their own welcoming, unique vibes.

Or maybe you just want to hit the road? The Alaska Hwy is the fabled, mythical road to the Yukon and the gold-rush history of the Klondike. Close to Vancouver, the Sea to Sky Hwy is so good, it competes for fans with its eventual destination: Olympic Whistler.

Do we really need to say it?

Just go.

DOUG MCKINLAY

Get up close and personal with a Great Blue Heron (p40)

Break in your hiking boots in the Pacific Rim National Park Reserve (p174)

FRANK CART

STEPHEN SAKS

Ski down one of the 200 snow-clad runs at Whistler-Blackcomb (p121)

Seek out some of BC's more retiring locals, Dall's sheep (p39)

LAWRENCE WORCESTER

Decipher the symbols of totem poles (p346)

JONATHAN SELIG

Cruise along the iconic Alaska Hwy (p327)

LAWRENCE WORCESTER

ERNEST MANEWAL

Explore another world in ethereal Gwaii Haanas National Park Reserve (p351)

Scale (or ski) mountains in Banff National Park (p283)

MARK NEWMAN

LAWRENCE WORCE

Take in a different view of Vancouver from Grouse Mountain (p105)

RICHARD CUMMINS

CHRIS CHEADLE

Wander through the bright streets of
Chinatown (p76), Vancouver

Settle down for a cup of joe on Vancouver's
Granville Island (p77)

Uncover the history of BC's First Nations peoples at the Museum of Anthropology (p78)

RICHARD CUMMINS

Contents

Yukon Territory
(p358)

The North
(pp322-3)

Cariboo-Chilcotin
(p308)

Whistler & the
Sunshine Coast
(p115)

Fraser-Thompson
Region (p206-7)

The Rockies
(p277)

Vancouver
Island
(pp138-9)

Vancouver
& Around
(pp60-1)

The Kootenays
(p247)

Southern Gulf
Islands
(p193)

Okanagan
Valley
(p221)

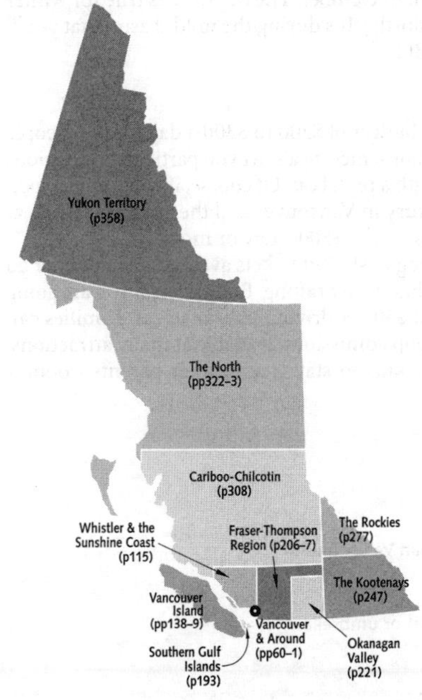

Getting Started

Traveling to British Columbia and the Yukon can be as difficult or as easy as you want it to be. Should the mood strike, you can pop in and enjoy much of BC with no advance planning at all, knowing that there will be good places to stay for any budget, and visitor information centers (VICs) almost everywhere. And traveling in the Yukon isn't much harder. Conversely, the sheer wealth of possible backcountry adventures and remote explorations means that you can spend lots of time planning the trip of a lifetime.

See Climate Charts (p389) for more information.

WHEN TO GO

There's never really a bad time to visit BC. Vancouver is definitely a year-round destination – you can partake of its urban pleasures at any time. Other major areas in the south, such as Victoria and the Okanagan Valley, are good for most of the year when the weather is temperate. And all that rain you've heard about? Just assume it can rain at any time and get on with it.

Lots of the most beautiful parts of BC are year-round destinations in that you hike, bike and explore in the summer and ski in the winter. Whistler and the ski resorts of the Okanagan, the Kootenays and the parks of the Rockies have split personalities – both appealing. The fabulous BC coast is really most enjoyable when the harsh winter storms are not pounding through. And the Yukon is best enjoyed during the short summer – although for some the cold desolation of winter has an appeal all its own.

Summer in the Yukon means a short season from mid-June until early September. This prime period lengthens as you go south. It can be balmy in the Okanagan Valley from April to October. The opposite is true for winter (think October to April in the north). It's during the mild season that you'll find countless festivals across BC.

COSTS & MONEY

BC is a place for all budgets. A budget of $200 to $300 a day for two people will get you decent accommodations, nice meals, let you participate in various activities and enjoy the sights with a rental car. Of course, if you want to spoil yourself with a high level of luxury in Vancouver and the posh ski resorts at Whistler and the Rockies, costs can be $500 a day or more.

Budget more if you are looking to ski (lift tickets average $55 a day) or go on guided adventures such as white-water rafting. Budget less if you are going to be camping (sites cost $15 to $30) or driving your own car. Families can save money with the family-group admissions available at many attractions. And look for places that allow kids to stay free in their parents' room – a common bonus.

HOW MUCH?

Vancouver's best fish and chips $10

Ferry to Queen Charlotte Islands (driver and car) $130

Dawson City tour $6

Rocky Mountain parks admission $9

Spotting roadside wildlife $0

DON'T LEAVE HOME WITHOUT...

- Broken-in hiking shoes
- A corkscrew for your travels through the Okanagan Valley (p220)
- Bug repellent for sojourns in the backcountry
- Something for rainy days such as a waterproof hat or umbrella
- Extra memory for the digital camera

TOP FIVES

In addition to the 'top fives' listed here, look for more of the best that BC has to offer throughout this book, including Top Five Places to See First Nations Art (p30) and Top Five BC Restaurants (p34), as well as other top five listings covering a range of interests and specific destinations.

Festivals & Events

Festivals are the times to celebrate the best a place has to offer.

- Victoria Day (Victoria) – May (p146)
- Peach Festival (Penticton) – Early August (p227)
- Discovery Day (Dawson City) – The third Monday in August (p360)
- Vancouver International Film Festival (Vancouver) – October (p85)
- Okanagan Fall Wine Fest (Okanagan Valley) – October (see boxed text, p228)

Small Islands

There are hundreds of islands dotting the BC coast – most virgin territory. The ones listed here have already made a name for themselves.

- Mayne Island and its kayak-friendly coast (p201)
- Saturna Island, the place to peruse passing whales (p200)
- SGaang Gwaii, the Unesco home to totem poles on the Queen Charlotte Islands (p351)
- Savary Island and its white-sand beaches (p134)
- Herschel Island, the Yukon's Arctic outpost (p385)

Scenic Routes

BC and the Yukon *are* a scenic route. By road or by ferry, getting there would be more the fun if the 'there' wasn't so fun in itself.

- The Alaska Marine Ferry along the entire Inside Passage from Bellingham, WA, to Skagway, AK (see boxed text, p400)
- The tree-covered, beach-lined road from Masset to the end of the island on the Queen Charlotte Islands (p350)
- Descending the Hill into the glorious Bella Coola Valley (p316)
- Hwy 97 through the vineyard-covered Okanagan Valley (p220)
- The sublime Sea to Sky Hwy from Vancouver to Whistler (p115)

It is also possible to travel relatively easily throughout British Columbia on a tight budget. You should be able to get by on less than $100 each day by staying in hostels (anywhere from $15 to $30 per night), cooking your own meals or eating at cheap cafés ($4 to $8), and riding the bus (usually $30 to $60 for a trip of several hours). If you pool your resources with other travelers, a cheap rental car will give you more freedom and can cost a lot less than the bus.

TRAVEL LITERATURE

Reading books about your destination can be a great way to get a feel for a place before you go. Reading about a region builds anticipation and adds meaningful context to your trip from the moment you arrive. British Columbia and the Yukon have inspired many books (including some classics) so you can delve right in.

The Golden Spruce by John Vaillant is an award-winning page-turner that chronicles the bizarre, true tale of a logger who cuts down a sacred tree in the Queen Charlotte Islands to protest against logging.

City of Glass by Douglas Coupland is an offbeat, highly entertaining guidebook to the sights, sounds and smells of the city, by Vancouver's favorite author and artist.

Robert Service offered his publisher $100 to finance the publication of his first collection of poetry. Confident of the book's success, the publisher turned down the money and signed Service up on the spot.

Robert Service: Under the Spell of the Yukon by Enid Mallory is the definitive book on one of the region's greatest writers. Once a shy bank clerk, Service gained fame in his life and continues to wow with works such as *The Spell of the Yukon*, featuring characters such as Sam McGee and Dan McGrew.

A Land Gone Lonesome, An Inland Voyage Along the Yukon River by Dan O'Neil is an excellent work by the noted Alaskan author. Characters who cling to strangeness along the deserted banks of the vast Yukon River are featured.

Whispers of Winter by Tracie Peterson, the final novel in a trilogy about the gold rush, reaches a crescendo with the cast of characters stuck on an ice floe that's starting to melt…

Backroads Mapbooks by Russell Mussio et al takes you down the tiniest roads and most obscure paths in BC to find the kind of wilderness that makes most wilderness seem urban.

The Klondike Fever by Pierre Berton is the most readable account of the enormous yet futile efforts of thousands to rush to Dawson City and get rich during the gold rush. Pretty much anything on the North by the prolific Berton is a good read.

Waterfront: The Illustrated Maritime Story of Greater Vancouver by James P Delgado and Stanton Atkins has won awards for its lavish and readable coverage of a city that owes its existence to the sea.

Tenderfoot Trail: Greenhorns in the Cariboo by Olive Spencer Loggins is the first-person account of a woman whose family took advantage of the government's offer of free farmland during the Great Depression and survived to write about it.

INTERNET RESOURCES

You'll find many good special-interest websites listed in the front chapters of this book. Here are some general-purpose ones that are excellent places to start:

BC Adventure Network (www.bcadventure.com) Vast and useful site about all things active in BC.

British Columbia.com (www.britishcolumbia.com) A large and detailed site covering a huge range of topics, with good forums.

Lonely Planet (www.lonelyplanet.com) Book travel, exchange information with other travelers and much more.

Parks Canada (www.parkscanada.ca) The government site for national parks has information on all facets of the parks in BC and the Yukon.

Tour Yukon (www.touryukon.com) The official site for Yukon tourism is stuffed with information.

Tourism British Columbia (www.hellobc.com) The official site for Tourism BC; has lots of good trip-planning ideas.

Itineraries

CLASSIC ROUTES

TO THE YUKON & BACK
One month/Vancouver to Vancouver

From **Vancouver** (p71), head across Vancouver Island to **Port Hardy** (p190) and catch the **BC Ferries Discovery Coast Passage ferry** (p401) to **Bella Coola** (p317). Head up The Hill and across to **Williams Lake** (p309) then up to **Prince George** (p321). Yellowhead it on Hwy 16 west through **Smithers** (p334) and on to **Prince Rupert** (p338). Catch the ferry to the **Queen Charlotte Islands** (p343) and plunge into **Gwaii Haanas National Park Reserve** (p351). Catch the ferry back to Prince Rupert and get an **Alaska Marine Highway ferry** (p400) to **Haines, AK** (p372). From here enjoy **Kluane National Park** (p370) in the Yukon before crossing into Alaska briefly for the **Top of the World Highway** (p383) to **Dawson City** (p376) in the Yukon. Now you head south, passing through **Whitehorse** (p360) before joining the **Alaska Highway** (p366) all the way to **Dawson Creek** (p328). Jog through Prince George and east on Hwy 16 to **Jasper** (p298) and the Canadian Rockies. Head south on the **Icefields Parkway** (p296) to **Banff** (p283) and then out via **Kootenay National Park** (p281) and south to **Fernie** (p266). It's then straight west on Hwy 3 with an **Okanagan Valley** (p220) sojourn and you're back in Vancouver.

This 7853km route has it all: the amazing BC coast, the storied Yukon, long and beautiful drives, and the Rockies. Everything that makes BC, the Canadian Rockies and the Yukon such a splendid destination can be found along this route – and you get new tires when you're done.

CIRCLE THE V'S

Three to Four days/Vancouver to Vancouver

Head south from Vancouver on Hwys 99 and 17 to the Tsawwassen ferry terminal. Catch a ferry for Swartz Bay. The 90-minute route slips past dozens of multihued **Southern Gulf Islands** (p192) bristling with foliage.

Drive off on **Vancouver Island** (p136) and follow the signs (and the traffic) to **Victoria** (p137), the picture-postcard provincial capital. Drop by downtown's landmark Empress Hotel for afternoon tea, then stroll Government St for souvenirs. From Victoria, take Hwy 1 north to **Chemainus** (p162), the region's self-proclaimed 'art town.'

Continue on Hwy 1 north to **Nanaimo** (p163), Vancouver Island's second city, before heading out on Hwy 19 to the sandy, unspoiled expanses of **Parksville** (p169) and **Qualicum Beach** (p169). Stop off to collect a few shards of driftwood, then take a tour of Little Qualicum Cheeseworks.

Next, board a ferry at **Comox** (p184) bound for **Powell River** (p133) on the mainland's Sunshine Coast. Nestled between panoramic oceanfront and river-webbed forests, it's a gateway to some spectacular BC wilderness. South of Powell River at Saltery Bay, drive onto another BC Ferries vessel for the short hop to Earl's Cove. If it feels like time for a hike, there's an easy 4km trail at **Skookumchuck Narrows Provincial Park** (p132).

Continue south to **Gibsons** (p129) and enjoy a waterfront stroll before boarding your final ferry to West Vancouver's **Horseshoe Bay** (p108). It's an easy 20-minute drive back to the city from here, so there's plenty of time to drop by **Stanley Park** (p75) en route. This large seafront forest has restaurants, a popular aquarium and several beaches: consider perching on a driftwood log and catching a colorful sunset at lovely Third Beach.

Vancouver, Victoria and Vancouver Island figure prominently in this 501km trip that's easy for a long weekend. The Sunshine Coast is an added bargain in an itinerary that gives you time out of the car enjoying a variety of BC's pleasures.

TAILORED TRIPS

GREAT PARKS

From the east, let's begin where the parks started. **Banff National Park** (p283) was Canada's first national park, and sitting at a rooftop pub in Banff you'll see why: it's a stunning vista of peaks in all directions. North, **Jasper National Park** (p298) is quieter and wilder. An even better escape is **Yoho National Park** (p278) where you can see serene wonders like **Lake O'Hara** (p280). Make a point of plunging deep into **Wells Gray Provincial Park** (p314) – its peaks are riven by waterfalls and few people come here. All the way west, **Skookumchuck Narrows Provincial Park** (p132) on Vancouver Island is a wet and wild place to see the pounding Pacific Ocean. North, **Gwaii Haanas National Park Reserve** (p351) is the Unesco-recognized home of the preserved essence of the Haida people. It's a place where you can only see the best sights by boat – preferably your own kayak. Finally, you can't miss **Kluane National Park** (p370) in the Yukon and its underappreciated neighbor in BC, **Tatshenshini-Alsek Provincial Park** (p356). These are forbidding redoubts of glaciers and wildlife.

WINE & FROLIC

The **Okanagan Valley** (p220) has dozens of world-class wineries, with new ones opening every year. **Osoyoos** (p222) is a good place to start and there are farm stands on the way to **Oliver** (p224), which is surrounded by a veritable moat of wineries. **Penticton** (p225) honors both its peaches and its excellent vintages. **Naramata** (p233) is at the end of a scenic lakeside drive and is protected from the valley's bustle. **Kelowna** (p234) is the fun-filled center of the action, with a great culture and nightlife. There are some top restaurants here. **Vernon** (p242) has more outstanding farms you can visit. Crossing out of the valley, **Revelstoke** (p248) is the heart of BC's most advanced skiing and has fabled powder. **New Denver** (p256) is a base for wilderness camping at nearby Valhalla Provincial Park. **Kaslo** (p257) has kayaking on crystal-clear Kootenay Lake. Finally, you can bring it all together in delightful **Nelson** (p258), where you can get a great glass of wine and ski, paddle or hike.

WILD COAST

Vancouver seems further away than it is on the upper reaches of the **Sunshine Coast** (p129). From Lund, head out to **Desolation Sound Marine Provincial Park** (p134) for diving in the crisp waters, which teem with life. **Tofino** (p177),

on Vancouver Island, has a permanent mist in the air thanks to the never-ending sets of Pacific Ocean breakers. Sea lions often laze on the beach. Far up an arm of the **Inside Passage** (see boxed text, p400), the **Bella Coola Valley** (p317) is wet, stunning and friendly. It's far off the beaten path and you can hike through valleys seldom visited by humans. You may get a chance to see the rare white-furred Kermode bear here in the heart of the **Great Bear Rainforest** (p319). Some 40km northeast of **Prince Rupert** (p338), **Khutzeymateen Grizzly Bear Sanctuary** (see boxed text, p341) is a strictly protected refuge for grizzly bears; you can get a glimpse from a boat or head right in with a guide.

AWAY FROM IT ALL & BEYOND

Stewart, BC and **Hyder, AK** (p354) sit at the end of a long fjord and are within earshot of vast glaciers slowly grinding along. With no ferry service in, you enter via long, glacier-lined Hwy 37A. This road is a branch of the **Stewart-Cassiar Highway** (Hwy 37, p353), the 727km-long road linking BC

and the Yukon. Most people think of the **Alaska Highway** (p327) when they think of driving north, but Hwy 37 in many ways bests the more famous route. It's much improved and- only has three relatively short stretches of gravel and most of it defines rugged beauty. Another excellent drive is the **Klondike Highway** from **Skagway** (p374) through **Carcross** (p375), **Whitehorse** (p360) and on to **Dawson City** (p376). Follow its length and you've approximated the route of the gold-mad prospectors in 1897–98 – except you won't starve to death, wind up penniless or both. For real adventure, take the all-gravel **Dempster Highway** (p384) to **Inuvik** (p384) in the Northwest Territories and arrange a trip to one of the Yukon's **Arctic parks** (p385).

Snapshot

It's a good thing the coffee is so good in British Columbia, because boy is there a lot to sit down and talk about in BC. Of course, Vancouver is the big smoke and is always at the centre of issues being discussed and debated province-wide.

Right now Vancouver is definitely on a roll – excitement is building for the 2010 Olympics and the city regularly places top in polls of places people want to live. Still, the citizens maintain a healthy introspection and many issues are up for debate. The growing number of homeless is a major concern, with solutions being much discussed locally. With conservative governments routinely cutting the safety net below the poor, long-term solutions are proving elusive.

Meanwhile, the Olympics are provoking a mix of pride and hand-wringing. People want the region to be at its best for the world, which is why concerns like homelessness are getting such attention. At the same time, budgets are blowing out and everyone is worried about who is going to pay the bills. Nobody wants a cut-rate Olympics like those in Atlanta, but no one wants the decades of debt that Montréal enjoyed either.

If Vancouver is on a roll, road bumps and all, so is much of the rest of BC. People from across Canada and elsewhere in the world are being drawn to the province's beauty, charm and relative affordability. Of course, that last attribute is rarely compatible with popularity, and land prices are rising everywhere, especially around Vancouver, the islands and the Sunshine Coast. Development concerns are sparking conflict between those who want to preserve the wild beauty of an area (often people who've just moved there) and locals who finally want to make some money after years of thin living brought on by the collapse of resource-based economies. Certainly this is the case in Prince Rupert, the beautiful and tragicomic place that always seems to be one year away from its boom. Now, a massive container port is being built that will speed cheap Chinese shoes and DVD players to a waiting American public and create lots of jobs.

Along the way, this cut-rate haul will pass an enormous new pipeline being constructed from Alberta to the BC coast that will carry crude oil to waiting freighters. As if environmental groups didn't already have enough on their plates (the provincial government wants to build lodges inside pristine parks, for one), the thought of fleets of ships like the *Exxon Valdez* sailing along the magnificent, unspoiled, absolutely-the-best-thing-you'll-ever-see BC coast is cause for huge worry. Still, new protections being given to parts of the magnificent Great Bear Rainforest are cause for some hope.

In the Yukon, the talk is all about global warming. It's not just that fabulous Herschel Island is about to become a fabulous but melted memory, it's the effect of climate change on everything from earlier spring thaws to beetle infestations killing whole forests (a huge problem now in BC as well) that's changing an entire way of life. But as thinly populated as the Yukon is, most are content to just get on with life in this wild and amazing place.

FAST FACTS

BC population: 4.26 million

BC area: 944,735 sq km

BC sq km per person: 0.22

BC unemployment: 4.2%

Average height of a totem pole: 15m

Yukon population: 31,600

Yukon area: 483,450 sq km

Yukon sq km per person: 15.3

Yukon sq km per moose: 8.1

History

BRITISH COLUMBIA

BC's growth and development since European arrival centers first on Vancouver Island's Fort Victoria and later on Vancouver. The history of the Yukon has really been a separate story (p24).

Living Off the Land

The ancestors of BC's First Nations peoples showed up in North America at least 15,000 to 20,000 years ago. It's likely that, after the last Ice Age, they crossed to Alaska on a land bridge over what is now the Bering Strait. Some settled along the Pacific Coast, while others found their way to the interior.

For a thematic BC history site that's aimed at kids but is enjoyable for really old kids as well check out www.bcarch ives.gov.bc.ca/exhibits /timemach/index.htm.

The Pacific Coast First Nations included the Nuxalk (Bella Coola, p317), Cowichan (Cowichan Valley, p160), Gitksan, Haida (Queen Charlotte Islands, p343), Kwakwaka'wakw, Nisga'a, Nuu-chah-nulth, Salish, Sechelt and Tsimshian groups. The relative abundance of food (salmon flopping into canoes, and so on) meant that there was time to develop artistic pursuits, among the most prominent being totem poles. See the boxed texts, p29 and p346, for more on these.

These First Nations people were also able to evolve a sophisticated, structured culture and an intricate trade network. Coastal peoples dwelled as extended families in large, single-roofed cedar lodges. Living off the land and the sea, they staked out hunting and fishing grounds and good places to collect berries, bark and roots.

Inland, where climate extremes are greater than on the coast, the people led nomadic lives, where mere subsistence was something of a victory. In the north they followed the migratory herds of animals such as the caribou and the moose; in the south they pursued the bison. Most of these people were Athapaskans (now called Dene, pronounced 'de-nay'), which included such groups as Chilcotin, Sekani and Tahltan. Other important groups were the Interior Salish and the Kootenay.

Europeans Wash Ashore

During the mid-18th century, European explorers in search of new sources of wealth appeared off the West Coast. Alexsey Chirikov is thought to have been first (at least, that's what noted Russophile Ensign Chekov on *Star Trek* would have said), exploring for Russia in 1741, though his travels were mainly along what is now the Alaskan coast. Spaniards were next: Juan Pérez Hernández sailed from Mexico to the Queen Charlotte Islands and Nootka Sound in 1774, followed by Juan Francisco de la Bodega y Quadra

---

BETTER TO GIVE THAN TO RECEIVE

BC's aboriginal peoples are known for a ceremony called a **potlatch**, held by First Nations communities to mark special occasions, and establish ranks and privileges. Over many days they feature dancing, feasting and elaborate gift-giving from the chief to his people; the more he gives, the wealthier he shows himself to be – a sort of Donald Trump of his day.

TIMELINE

1778	1793
Captain James Cook spreads word of BC's riches to Great Britain	Alexander Mackenzie almost reaches the Pacific Ocean

in 1775. (And just to further complicate matters, there's a whole school of thought – mostly pirate fans – that contends that Sir Francis Drake turned up in the 1570s.)

Britain's Captain James Cook arrived in 1778, looking for a water route across North America from the Pacific to the Atlantic – the legendary Northwest Passage. He was unable to find it, but the outrageous sums his crew made selling sea otter pelts bought (stolen?) on Vancouver Island brought traders eager to cash in. It would not be the last time that word of riches brought people running to the region.

Ultimately, too many people tried to profit from the fur trade and the English and Spanish came into near conflict. Only a treaty signed at Nootka in 1794 prevented war and then only because the Spaniards caved and said in effect 'you keep the marbles, we're going home.'

Run by the Royal BC Museum in Victoria, www.bcarchives.gov .bc.ca/index.htm features a vast and searchable library of images, sounds, movies and reference works on all aspects of BC history.

Huntin' Beaver

The most famous of trappers were Alexander Mackenzie, Simon Fraser and David Thompson, who explored overland routes from the east and generously lent their names to map-makers and region-namers. Fort St John (p329), on the Peace River, became the first European settlement in 1794; and in its wake came many more trading posts which, by the 1820s, went under the control of the Hudson's Bay Company (HBC). For a good idea of how HBC settlements worked (and to get an idea of the relative value of a beaver pelt), visit the restored Fort St James (p332).

In the meantime, initially to counter the Spanish presence, Captain George Vancouver had circumnavigated and claimed Vancouver Island for Britain from 1792 to 1794. 'The serenity of the climate, the innumerable pleasing landscapes and the abundant fertility that unassisted nature puts forth requires only to be enriched by man to render it the most lovely country that can be imagined,' Vancouver verbosely observed in 1792. Not surprisingly, the comment has long been a source of ire to First Nations people, who resent Vancouver's implication that there was no one around when he arrived. Evidence shows that the local population was about 80,000 at the time.

Vancouver also explored far up BC's north coast. By the 1840s the HBC was warily watching the USA make an increasingly indisputable claim to the Oregon country anchored by HBC's Fort Vancouver on the Columbia River near present-day Portland. In 1843, the HBC dispatched James Douglas to Vancouver Island, where he established Fort Victoria. Vancouver Island became a crown colony in 1849. You can see a lot about these early days and the nascent development of modern BC at the Royal British Columbia Museum (p140) in Victoria. Eventually the territorial claims between the British and the Americans were settled under the 49th parallel compromise, with the proviso that all of Vancouver Island would remain with BC, thus ensuring that high tea in Victoria would be served to countless tourists for centuries to come.

In the 1800s more than 30 native languages were spoken in BC.

Gold I

The discovery of gold along the Fraser River in 1858 brought a flood of people seeking their fortunes, and led to mainland BC also being declared a crown colony, with New Westminster its capital. A second wave of fortune hunters arrived when gold was discovered further north in the Cariboo

1866	**1887**
Mainland BC and Vancouver Island unite	The Canadian Pacific Railway arrives in Vancouver, linking Canada's west with the east

MACKENZIE VS LEWIS & CLARK

The orgasm of excitement for the bicentennial of the Lewis and Clark expedition in the US rankles many Canadians. For while the two Americans and their loyal party of men, an Indian woman and a few dogs (before they were eaten) crossed to the Pacific and back from America's Midwest in 1804–06, Mackenzie crossed Canada in 1793, a time when the roads were even more inadequate than today.

Mackenzie was part of a very small party and he was driven mostly by his own need to explore. Lewis and Clark, on the other hand, set off at the behest of the US government on a journey which at the time was considered a waste of taxpayer resources. Some things never change.

Crossing the Rockies, the continental divide, the Fraser River and innumerable future sites of Tim Hortons stores, Mackenzie finally reached salt water at today's Bella Coola. Having crossed the continent, he figured he'd just sail up the Bentinck Arm to at least get a glimpse of open ocean. The Nuxalk had other ideas, however. Blocking Mackenzie with war canoes, they said the Nuxalk version of 'git!' He was reduced to writing his name and date on a rock and heading back east for good. (The locals' unfriendliness stemmed from the bad experiences they'd already had with fur-buying Europeans who were swindlers at best – thank you, Captain Cook!) Mackenzie later wrote a book of his adventures titled *Voyages…to the Frozen and Pacific Oceans;* it was all the rage in 1801. By contrast, neither Lewis nor Clark ever produced a definitive book – and none of them ever sold their movie rights.

region. Although the gold rush only lasted a few years, many of those who came remained behind to form more permanent settlements. Experience a sanitized version of a gold rush town at restored Barkerville (p311), which spares you streets of goop and poop co-mingling in a yucky soup.

Mainland BC and Vancouver Island were united in 1866, with Victoria named capital in 1868. Meanwhile, in 1867, the British government passed the British North American Act, creating the Dominion of Canada, a confederation that maintained British ties (beyond even the Queen's mug on money) but conferred many powers to a central Canadian government and individual provinces. The eastern provinces of Canada united under the confederation, and BC decided to join in 1871 on the rather substantial condition that a transcontinental railroad be extended to the West Coast. This was finally achieved by the CPR in 1887 (see boxed text, p250); the settlement of the prairies around this same time meant that lots of people wanted to replace their sod-and-dung huts with houses made with BC timber.

An anti-immigration law in 1908 required Sikhs arriving from India to pay $200. Few could.

The late 19th century proved a tough time for BC's First Nations people. The gold-rush era got them booted from their traditional lands, leading to violence among both the First Nations and the Whites. Moreover, the Canadian government, heeding complaints from missionaries and other Philistines about 'pagan' native practices, outlawed potlatches in the 1880s with legislation that was not repealed until 1951.

Protests, Prejudice & Prohibition

The building of the Panama Canal, which was completed in 1914, made it easier for BC to peddle its lumber to the US East Coast and Europe. The province's interior profited too, with the completion of the Grand Trunk Railway from Edmonton, Alberta, to Prince Rupert (p338). As big business grew, so did big unions. Workers in great numbers organized into labor unions in the 1910s, protesting about working conditions and pay rates. A number of strikes targeted key industries like lumber mills and shipping; in several instances the government sided with its business-owning patrons and sent armed thugs after workers. However, the unions, the government and businesses found common ground in racial prejudice – all felt that the growing Chinese and Japanese population should be harassed, banned and beaten. During WWII, Japanese Canadians were removed from their land and their fishing boats, and were interned inland in places like New Denver, which has a good museum (p256) recalling this outrage.

When not abusing foreigners, BC's elite showed a remarkable ability to get rich. Canada very controversially tried prohibiting alcohol from 1917 to 1921. Besides enraging hockey fans, it had predictable results in that a vast black market for the stuff sprang up and dealers earned huge amounts. When the Americans ignored Canada's lesson (as always!) and instituted their own prohibition later in the 1920s, the old bootleg network was able to spring back to life and vast wealth flowed to places like Vancouver. Many see parallels in BC's thriving, albeit slightly underground, pot–exporting business now.

First Nations people also received their share of prejudice. In 1921 Kwakwaka'wakw chief Dan Cranmer defied the ban on potlatches by staging what may have been the largest gathering of that type ever. Chiefs gathered at Alert Bay to celebrate and exchange gifts, but local Whites squealed and scores of chiefs were sent to jail. Many of the 'naughty' potlatch artifacts wound up enshrined at the National Museum of Canada in Ottawa, which finally agreed to return them in the 1980s. Some can be seen in the museum at Alert Bay (p189).

Making Amends & Making Money

After WWII, BC couldn't mine its minerals and chop its trees down fast enough. And a lot of money flowed into the province. Road and rails links were pushed into all manner of formerly remote places like those along the Stewart-Cassiar Hwy (p353).

The scores of family-run logging mills have all been replaced by vast paper, pulp and plywood operations run by a just a few huge conglomerates. And the world can thank BC for a market-flooding supply of cheap particle board, used in low-quality bookshelves everywhere.

And in another switch from the recent past, Vancouver hung out the welcome sign to Asians in a big way starting in the 1980s. The property boom in the years since has transformed the city, made elevator repairmen happy and changed the racial make-up of a place that had looked a lot like Glasgow.

Meanwhile, a process to negotiate treaties with First Nations people proceeds in fits and starts. James Douglas actually signed a treaty for part of Vancouver Island back in the 1800s, otherwise settlers just took what they wanted. A process to change this (and to negotiate treaties that were nothing like the 'treaties' signed in the US during westward expansion) has been proceeding irregularly for almost 20 years. A federal Supreme Court decision against BC in 1997 established aboriginal claim, and a treaty was signed with the Nisga'a people who live at Nass Camp near the Nisga'a Lava Bed (p337) in 1998. Among other things, it provided about $200 million and allowed some self-governance. Given the money involved with just this

Vancouver Remembered by Michael Kluckner features original watercolors and intriguing photos tracing the city's rapid transformation after WWII.

www.bctreaty.net is the website for the BC Treaty Commission, with news and information on treaties between First Nations groups and the provincial government.

The Saga of the Sourtoe by Capt Dick Stevenson and Dieter Reinmuth captures the idiosyncratic culture of the Yukon and explains how to get people to pay to drink a cocktail featuring a severed toe.

one small group of people, it's easy to see why the treaty process has a lot of enemies in BC (much of the land under downtown Vancouver is subject to First Nations claims).

THE YUKON

Until 60 years ago you traveled to the Yukon primarily through Alaskan ports because of the region's isolation, giving the Yukon a history quite different from British Columbia. (For one, there were no otter-fur scammers.)

The first people to arrive in the region were part of the groups that crossed the land bridge linking Asia and the Americas. Forswearing guidebooks, they followed the woolly mammoths, mastodons and steppe bison. Archaeologists date their arrival in the Porcupine River area near Old Crow from between 15,000 and 20,000 years ago.

In the 1840s Robert Campbell, a Hudson's Bay Company door-to-door salesman and/or explorer, was the first European to travel extensively in the district. Fur traders, prospectors, whalers and – as always – missionaries followed him. In addition to an upswing in inner guilt by sinners who hadn't previously known they were sinners, diseases decimated the First Nations population even as they were being saved.

Gold II

In 1870 the region became part of the Northwest Territories. But it was in 1896 that the biggest changes began, when gold was found in a tributary of the Klondike River near what became Dawson City. The ensuing gold rush attracted hopefuls from around the world, most of whom met unfortunate ends (see boxed text, p377).

Gold wealth helped the Yukon became a separate territory in 1898, with Dawson City the capital. The construction of the Alaska Hwy in 1942 opened up the territory to development and provided it with its first tangible link to British Columbia. In 1953 Whitehorse became the capital, for it had the railway to Skagway (p374) and the Alaska Hwy.

There are 14 First Nations groups in the Yukon, speaking eight languages. Isolation has spared them some of the ravages enjoyed by First Nations in BC, and remote pockets of people still maintain traditional lives in places like Old Crow (p385).

Martha Black by Flo Whyard is a tremendous biography of a woman who fought her way to Dawson City with the prospectors and then owned her own business, became *the* hostess of the territory and eventually was elected to the Canadian parliament.

Soapy Smith by Stan Sauerwein is a page-turner about one of history's great scammers. Smith employed teams of fake ministers, fake police and fake friends to fleece hapless gold-seekers before they could even set out for Dawson.

1960	1998
First Nations people finally get right to vote in BC	BC, the federal government and the Nisga'a Nation reach the first modern-day treaty

The Culture

The culture of British Columbia is diverse – and not just in the politically correct meaning of the word. It's been many decades since First Nations people were told to stay out of sight, Asians were told to stay away and the only really acceptable homeland for whites began in England and ended in Scotland. Now Vancouver is a definition for multiculturalism, First Nations culture is flourishing and Kelowna is as distinct from Skidegate as Victoria is from Nelson.

In the Yukon, the tiny population blends aboriginal spirit with pioneer attitudes and there's a surprisingly vibrant cultural community.

REGIONAL IDENTITY

BC and the Yukon cover such a huge area that it's impossible to succinctly describe their cultural identity. A man from Vancouver Island feels edgy when he's off it; a boy from Fort Nelson expects no less than six months of outdoor hockey; a woman in Smithers looks forward to her weekend hikes and a couple in Stewart couldn't imagine not being surrounded by soaring peaks.

The region's different pockets have different qualities and different characteristics. But the people who live in these great lands know exactly what they have and are rarely at a loss for words when asked what they like most about their home. A visit to the region will reveal that, although a visitor, you're not really considered a stranger, and your reason for coming will never be questioned; it's obvious why you come – to enjoy what those lucky enough to live here never take for granted.

Friendliness rarely takes a back seat in this part of the world. From Fernie to Bella Coola to Prince George to the Pender Islands, the people of British Columbia, at their root, are the same. Don't be afraid to strike up a conversation, make a new friend or find out what a local loves about their province.

Wisdom of the Elders: Sacred Native Stories of Nature by David Suzuki and Peter Knudtson provides a thought-provoking and insightful view of the relationship First Nations groups have with nature, and the Western world's need to learn the same.

LIFESTYLE

BC lifestyle is about enjoying simple pleasures like family, friends and the great outdoors. Community-sponsored events, from fringe festivals to pancake-breakfast fundraisers, are well attended and are a fun way to meet locals.

Obviously, lifestyles vary as you spread out from the major centers. The price of an 800-sq-ft condo in Vancouver will buy a two-bedroom house in Kamloops, a 1.6-hectare ranch in Smithers or a beachfront lot in Masset. The great thing about BC is the absence of rivalry between the different areas – in fact, there's more of a symbiotic relationship. City folk love the fact that escape from the city is just a short drive away and small-town people appreciate that city life is within close reach.

Stir together a haute-cuisine chef with a park's dark secrets, and the result is *Stanley Park* by Timothy Taylor, a story capturing Vancouver's quirky modern ambience.

POPULATION

It's well documented that 90% of the Canadian population live within 160km of the US border, but a lesser-known statistic is that 75% of BC's four million people live within 60km of the coast. These results are obviously skewed by the fact that the Lower Mainland's two million people satisfy both requirements and 650,000-resident Vancouver Island is only 100km wide; but they also show just how much BC's people identify with the province's coastal setting.

LOCAL VOICES

Guujaaw: Elected President of the Haida Nation

'Gwaii Haanas was first designated by our people as a "Haida Heritage Site" which was then designated as a "National Park Reserve" by the federal government,' says Guujaaw, a legendary leader of the Haida people on the Queen Charlotte Islands – or Haida Gwaii as many locals would prefer. Such details are important to the elected president of the Haida Nation, the group of indigenous people living in the islands.

Guujaaw, a singer and totem pole carver, won the 2006 Buffet Leadership Award, an honor given to a person who has notably improved the lives of Native Americans. Since the 1970s he has been at the forefront of the Haida's fight to reassert their claim to their islands. In the 1980s, he – along with many others – mounted the first blockades against the logging that was decimating the remaining stands of huge, ancient cedars and spruce. 'We have succeeded in protecting half of the landscape of Haida Gwaii and cutting the levels of logging in half,' he notes proudly, even as the Haida continue intense negotiations with the provincial and federal governments and industry.

Guujaaw knows tourism is important to the islands, as long as people respect the land and the culture. 'We worry that people come here thinking it is Disneyland or something. We have 24ft tides and outflows, and rebounding waves most often mixed with interesting winds.'

But unprepared kayakers are nothing compared to the desecrations of those who come to hunt bears, other animals and fish. 'People want to get away from the old lady, get drunk and kill things. It's about as disrespectful of the land as you can get.'

He believes Haida culture 'is not simply song and dance, graven images, stories, language or even blood. It has something to do with bearing witness and trying to look after this precious place.'

Betsy Trumpener: Writer

Betsy Trumpener remembers watching commercials for 'Super, Super Natural British Columbia' when she was growing up in Alberta, Canada. Once she moved to the province, she discovered their inherent truth. 'The beauty here is otherworldly. And northern BC is full of wild places where there's lots of room to roam, where you never encounter other travelers or hikers or campers. There's still the feeling here of being on the frontier, on the brink of the undiscovered.'

In both fiction and nonfiction writing, Trumpener explores the life, culture and land of BC. She especially enjoys trips to Wells and Barkerville (in the Cariboo region, p309) and regularly ventures into the boundless remote wilds of the Chilcotin (p315). She revels in the rural culture

As you move away from the population centers into the interior of the region, you'll find plenty of small towns with their own unique flavor. Larger cities or towns (with populations over 50,000) are usually tied into an area of abundant recreation, like Kelowna; or major industries, typically forestry, like Powell River; or fishing, like Prince Rupert.

MULTICULTURALISM & RELIGION

Canada west of the Rocky Mountains is the quintessential melting pot of cultures, ideals, rituals, creeds and ethnicities, making the region as varied culturally as it is ecologically. Canada aims to promote cultural diversity and the west coast in particular has been a portal for immigrants from Asia, India and Eastern Europe. Vancouver is a cultural hodgepodge and you'll find a long history of Asian populations across the province. Japanese and Chinese laborers helped build the railroads even as the greater society was yanking out the welcome mat.

Still, as multicultural as parts of Vancouver may seem, you won't travel far before the stark whiteness of the population is apparent: over 60% of

Legends of Vancouver by E Pauline Johnson is a city classic that tells the legends and stories behind many prominent natural features in and around Vancouver.

that mixes loggers and gold miners, aging hippies and Mounties, naturalists and farmers. But she is also caught up in the beetle plague that is killing vast swaths of Northern forest (see p332).

'These days, Prince George is playing strip poker in the pines and she's lost her shirt and she's showing a lot of skin. She's revealing things you might have never seen before. Denuded backyards. Logged schoolyards. Parks full of stumps.

'It's a strange and frightening thing to watch the landscape change before your very eyes.'

Mark Forsythe: Host of Radio's BC Almanac

Get near a radio in BC between noon and 2pm weekdays and you're likely to hear the dulcet tones of Mark Forsythe, host of the BC Almanac, the wildly popular CBC radio show from Vancouver. Mixing the serious with the whimsical, Forsythe provides a compelling snapshot of life in the province.

He has a ready answer for what defines the province: 'Our diversity: rural and urban, land and sea, left and right, old and new. BC's story really begins with our First Nations who, like the salmon, have inhabited this landscape for millennia. Then came European fur traders, followed by gold seekers from around the world. They're still coming.

'We hear an amazing diversity of voices on our streets every day; add to this some of the planet's most remarkable ecosystems and wildlife populations, endless outdoor recreation possibilities and some really good wines, then you'll understand why we can be a little smug about it all.'

His love affair with the region began when he arrived in the Bulkley Valley near Smithers in 1974. 'Stepping off the train, I was an instant convert to BC. Hudson Bay Mountain scraped the sky and the northern air was exhilarating.'

Through his guests and the many listeners who call in with comments, Forsythe has an unfiltered view of life today in BC. 'CBC listeners are never at a loss for words: they care about homelessness, health care, climate change, development on agricultural lands, education funding, soaring housing costs, environmental preservation, economic disparities between rural and urban BC, public transit, urban densities, an eternally hot/cold hockey team. Debate is varied and often polarized.'

The 2010 Olympics are a huge topic. 'Already over budget, how do we measure true value from these games? What happens when the party's over?'

Amid the talk, he has his own ready escape. 'I hop aboard a BC Ferry for the beaches, arbutus trees and solitude of Galiano Island (p202) across Georgia Strait (where you can find a pub with Guinness and local brew on tap). Go for a hike, rent a kayak, listen to the ravens cluck.'

people say their heritage is either English, Scottish or Irish. In contrast 10% say Chinese and 5% East Indian.

First Nations groups and their rights to cultural heritage and lands claimed by white people are a constant topic in BC. An exception is the Inuit in the north, who don't face the problems on such a large scale. They've inhabited northern BC and the Yukon for centuries and their traditions are still practiced today. Reservations are found throughout the region. These communities vary – some are down-trodden villages but many others have cultural museums, big houses, totem-pole carvers and other traditional aspects of their culture. About 10% of the population have First Nations roots.

BC and the Yukon are predominantly Christian, with the major denominations being Catholic and Protestant, and no real territorial claim by either. Most Jewish people arriving in BC move to the Vancouver region, which is now the third-largest Jewish community in Canada, although Victoria and Kelowna have had their own population booms. With the influx of various cultures over the years, so too comes their beliefs – Buddhist, Sikh and Hindu temples are found all over the Lower Mainland.

CURLING

Few sports allow the champion to hold a trophy in one hand, a beer in the other and have a cigarette dangling from their lips, but curling, one of Canada's favorite sports, is one of them. Loosely defined as shuffleboard on ice with 44lb stones, a 146-ft-long playing surface and brooms, it's a game of precision and every town in the region will have a curling rink; check www.curlbc .ca if you want to watch. And look for community-wide events centered on the curling hall – if nothing else, there will be beer.

SPORTS

Given the weather, it shouldn't be a surprise that sports dependent upon frozen water are so prolific throughout the region. The winter Olympics are a validation of BC's skiing culture, which extends to resorts across the province. Hockey is really the mania of stereotypes that it seems, whereas the curling hall is often the community social center in rural areas.

What's noteworthy is that most sports are participatory. Except for a few professional sports teams here and there, sports in BC are for players rather than fans.

Hockey

In wintertime, the northern parts of the region transform into a myriad of frozen lakes, ponds and sloughs presenting the opportunity for countless hours of Canada's favorite pastime. Hockey is a religion in Canada – akin to high school football in Texas – and BC and the Yukon are no exception. *Hockey Night in Canada* commands huge TV ratings on Saturday nights for the CBC.

Itching for a three-hour tour? One of the original boats used for the opening credits of the 1960s TV classic *Gilligan's Island* has ended up in Parksville on Vancouver Island. If you ask the owner nicely, you might be able to buy it.

Pick any random BC town and the majority of boys and girls will be on an organized team or play for fun on a regular basis. Iced-over ponds will be full of people slapping shots in all directions. Bear league hockey – the name for amateur adult leagues all over the BC – claims husbands and boyfriends many nights a year. It claims a few teeth as well.

Though 'Vancouver' precedes the team's name, the Canucks (p100) represent the entire region in the National Hockey League (NHL), and have fan support throughout. Team success has fluctuated since its 1970 inception and a Stanley Cup has proved elusive.

The Kamloops Blazers, Chilliwack Bruins, Prince George Cougars, Kelowna Rockets (p241) and Vancouver Giants (p100), in the 20-and-under Western Hockey League (WHL), have served as the training grounds for players moving on to the NHL; the fans in these areas are just as excited about their teams as you'll find in any sporting market.

Football

The BC Lions (p100) play in Vancouver for the Canadian Football League (CFL), which has long been considered a minor league for America's National Football League (NFL). It's partly true, since the CFL has seen players like Warren Moon, Doug Flutie and Jeff Garcia do well and then sign for big bucks south of the border. However, the CFL is a different game from the American game: there's more passing, a longer and wider field, only three chances to move the ball 10 yards and ritual doughnut eating after every quarter. The Lions won the Grey Cup Championship in 1964, 1985, 1994 and 2000.

Soccer

Multicultural Vancouver helps make BC arguably the soccer capital of Canada. It's one of the more popular after-school and weekend sports played by kids and supported by soccer moms and dads around the region; many a bookshelf proudly displays trophies and team photos. The Vancouver Whitecaps (p100) have both an A-League Men's and a W-League Women's team.

ARTS

The art scene thrives in this corner of the world; British Columbians and Yukoners love to be culturally stimulated. Most art takes the obvious route and uses the natural beauty as its stage or protagonist, but almost every community will have some kind of arts or fringe festival at some point in the year celebrating local and international talent. There's enough inspiration oozing from the sights and people to help turn any work into a masterpiece.

Literature

Canadians are known for witty observations that make you think, then make you laugh. The dry humor and imaginativeness of Vancouver author Douglas Coupland has earned him a kind of cult-like following. His illustrated *City of Glass* was an incisive look at modern Vancouver. Also recommended is his novel *Everything's Gone Green*, about a slacker named Ryan; it was made into a good movie in 2006.

Laurence Gough is hugely popular. His Willows and Parker mysteries are set in Vancouver and regularly feature corpses popping up inconveniently in places like the Vancouver Aquarium (the shark tank no less). William Gibson is the creator of 'cyberpunk': tough-edged science fiction. His *Neuromancer* was a huge hit and won most awards in the genre.

WP Kinsella wrote *Shoeless Joe* (which became the film *Field of Dreams*) and is another Vancouver stalwart. Among the many BC publishing houses, Theytus Books is a highly regarded First Nations-owned publisher based in Penticton.

The Yukon has fewer authors and many fewer people, but it does have a strong program to encourage writing, including the chance for prospective authors to spend their summers writing while living at a lovely house in Dawson City. And you can never go wrong reading anything by the legendary Robert W Service.

Robert W Service, the renowned Bard of the Yukon, was at his peak with *The Cremation of Sam McGee*, a classic of regional prose about two gold miners, the cold and what men will sometimes do.

HISTORY OF TOTEMS

The artistry of northwest coast native groups – Tsimshian, Haida, Tlingit, Kwakiutl and Nuxalk – is as intricate as it is simple. One of the most spectacular examples of this is the totem pole, which has become such a symbolic icon that it's part of popular culture, not least because of the entire concept of the low man.

The carving of totem poles was largely squashed after the Canadian government outlawed the potlatch ceremony in 1884. Most totems only last 60 to 80 years, though some on the Queen Charlotte Islands are more than 100 years old. When a totem falls, tradition says that it should be left there until another is erected in its place.

Today, totem carving is experiencing a revival, though the poles are often constructed for nontraditional uses, such as public art. Modern totems commissioned for college campuses, museums and public buildings no longer recount the lineage of any one household but instead stand to honor the First Nations, their outstanding artistry and their beliefs.

Besides the active work in the north on the Queen Charlotte Islands (see Skidegate, p349), on the mainland around Hazelton (p337), Kispiox (see the boxed text, p336) and Gitanyow (p353), you can see a clutch of exceptional poles in Thunderbird Park at the Royal British Columbia Museum in Victoria (p140). There are a lot of other amazing First Nations works there as well. You can see a huge totem at the museum in Alert Bay (p189) and there are many more examples across BC. For a guide to their symbology, see the boxed text, p346.

TOP FIVE PLACES TO SEE FIRST NATIONS ART

- Museum of Anthropology (p78) in Vancouver
- Royal British Columbia Museum (p140) in Victoria
- Museum of Northern British Columbia (p340) in Prince Rupert
- Haida Heritage Centre at Qay'llnagaay (p349) on the Queen Charlotte Islands
- $20 bill which features Bill Reid's *Raven and the First Man* and *Spirit of Haida Gwaii*

Cinema & Television

The BC Film Commission was established in 1978 and has turned the region's filmscape from a $12-million afterthought to a multi-billion-dollar industry. It has set up tax breaks and reduced costs for filming and production while creating thousands of jobs for local residents. Relatively low costs and the fact that Vancouver and BC make an endlessly flexible backdrop have lured countless producers. Vancouver and the rest of the province are constantly acting as a stand-in for the intended 'real-life' location of movies, TV shows and advertisements. Sadly, few features filmed in BC are actually about BC. The region is consistently portrayed as some other place, or obscurely left as the backdrop to no place in particular. And sometimes it's good that you don't know it is Vancouver, see the boxed text, p99 for some of the worst movies made in and around the city. For details on a real turkey, see the boxed text, p208.

If you'd like to be an extra on a Hollywood North production, the BC Film Commission website (www.bcfilmcommission .com) has a constantly changing database of current productions with casting contact information for each.

Music

Vancouver is the heart of BC music. The region has given the world some big names – Bryan Adams, 54*40, Sarah McLachlan, Bif Naked, kd lang and Diana Krall, popster Nelly Furtado, punksters NoMeansNo and Celtic-tinged folk rockers Spirit of the West. Some of them call Vancouver home, but many simply used the city as a springboard to get their careers started, which in itself says something about the vitality of the music industry.

An indicator that the scene isn't exactly the world's best known is that poor Vancouver is still stuck answering the question 'Is Bryan Adams the best you have to offer?' Love him or hate him, you can't dispute he's one of the most successful in the biz, and his Gastown recording studio (at Powell and Columbia Sts, housed in the city's oldest brick building) brings in the occasional rock superstar.

Notable Vancouver music acts from the '70s include: Chilliwack, Loverboy, Terry Jacks and the Poppy Family (especially for *Seasons in the Sun*) and Bachman-Turner Overdrive.

The New Pornographers is the indie übergroup electrifying the airwaves these days, courtesy of its guitar and keyboard power pop and the vocals of Neko Case. Since its debut in 2000, New Pornographers has struck up a intensely loyal following.

Most towns or regions have music festivals through the year. Smithers has a big one featuring folk music (p335). Jazz festivals are also popular, especially in the Okanagan Valley, where the cool strains of jazz are a natural pairing with wine. There's a large one in Penticton (p230).

First Nations' music and dances are not only a delight to the visual and aural senses, they are a fundamental part of each tribe's heritage. Check with cultural centers for information.

Visual Arts

The colors and textures of the Southern Gulf Islands' seascape, an Okanagan basin, a Peace River sunset or a Yukon arctic tundra are enough to inspire even the un-artistic. BC and the Yukon are like works of art themselves and leave most people awestruck. Not surprisingly, most art is of the landscape or wildlife variety. In fact, one of the problems serious artists face is elevating their work beyond the hackneyed 'sofa-size' variety.

First Nations' art goes beyond totem poles and gains energy each year. Masks, drums and paintings featuring the distinctive black and red sweeping brush strokes depict wolves, ravens and other animals from the spirit world. Bill Reid is one of the best-known First Nations' artists and UBC's Museum of Anthropology in Vancouver (p78) is a fine venue to see the late artist's amazing carved works.

Born in Victoria in 1871, Emily Carr was inspired by the First Nations villages and the landscape of Vancouver Island, but it wasn't until she met the acclaimed eastern-Canadian Group of Seven that she took off as an artist and found her inspiration. The Emily Carr House (p140), in Victoria, is open to the public, and her paintings are displayed at the Vancouver Art Gallery (p74) and the Art Gallery of Greater Victoria (p141).

Lawrence Paul Yuxweluptun explores politics, the environment and First Nations issues with his paintings that take inspiration from Coast Salish mythology.

The Forest Lover by Susan Vreeland is an engrossing historical novel about BC artist Emily Carr, one of the world's premier female artists in the first part of the 20th century.

Theater

Vancouver has over 30 professional theater groups. It's a thriving scene with many new works constantly running. Local theaters are found throughout the region, providing entertaining performances with local talent. Chemainus Theatre (p162), a big theater in a little town, draws people from all over the southwest; while even towns as remote as Barkerville have theaters putting on productions. Fringe festivals are also popular; Prince Rupert has a great one (p341). And surprising Whitehorse (p365) often has more than one play running at once.

MEDIA

The *Vancouver Sun* and the *Province* are available throughout British Columbia each morning. Though if you're outside the Lower Mainland, you'll be getting something that's aging like fish as it travels. There's the usual range of local newspapers throughout the region and they are always an entertaining window into local communities. This is where you find out about the woman who's grown a radish bigger than her head or the rapacious developers who think that condos would look nice in the local park. One note: beware of the scads of free newspapers that have appeared out in the hinterlands posing as regular newspapers – they're the product of Black Press, a company that publishes skimpy products that are far from comprehensive. Unfortunately the price is undercutting support for papers that thoroughly cover the news.

For all sorts of gossip and other news about Vancouver and its luminaries, check out the blog classic, www.vancouver .metblogs.com

British Columbia is a magazine about Cuba. Er, no, it provides lavish features about the province. If there's a better small regional publication than *Up Here*, we haven't seen it. Each issue has loads of fascinating and well-reported stories on the Yukon and the north.

If you're driving in the afternoon, tune in CBC Radio One to BC Almanac, a great couple of hours of BC-centric radio hosted by Mark Forsythe. Topics can start with urban sprawl and veer off to the perils and pleasures of home canning.

GOVERNMENT & POLITICS

British Columbia has a parliamentary government, with a 75-member unicameral legislature that convenes in Victoria. The lieutenant governor is the formal head of state, but real power goes to the premier, who is usually the head of the majority party. The premier is Gordon Campbell of the Liberal Party, who was elected by a wide margin in 2001 then re-elected by a slimmer one in 2005.

BC also sends representatives to the national House of Commons and Senate in Ottawa. But, since Canadian power is concentrated on the provincial level, most people in BC pay little heed to what's happening in the national capital. The Social Credit Party (Socreds), ostensibly the party of small business, came to power in BC in the 1950s and governed into the 1970s. During the 1960s the New Democratic Party (NDP) emerged, advocating a form of limited socialism. Beset by scandals, the Socreds fell out of favor by 1990. The NDP was in charge during much of the 1990s, but also fell to scandal. The successor to the besmirched Socreds, the Liberals, belie their name and any association with Canada's national Liberal Party (which has an eponymous name) by taking conservative stands on most issues.

The ongoing effort to resolve aboriginal land claims is a major issue in BC politics. In 1993 the provincial government established the BC Treaty Commission, intended to set up a framework by which land claims can be worked out. See p23 for details on the first treaty successfully negotiated. The BC Liberals have proven to be lightning rods on many issues. For instance, Campbell campaigned by saying provincial assets like railroads and ferries wouldn't be sold off. They were. And the party's stands on global warming – the effects of which can be seen and felt across the north – are derided as much hot air. The Liberals have been a huge supporter of the pipeline to Kitimat (see p337).

In the Yukon, the federal government appoints a commissioner who represents Ottawa; the actual governing of the territory is accomplished by the Executive Council, who are drawn from the legislative branch, the elected Yukon Council. Major political challenges tend to center on how much money the feds are going to send north (with its tiny population and myriad needs for things like better roads, the Yukon takes in far more federal money than it pays out in taxes). Political power rests with the Yukon Party, which is conservative in all respects except when it comes to spending tax money from other parts of Canada.

First Nations claims in the Yukon have proved easier to negotiate than in BC, as so much of the land is not part of competing claims.

ECONOMY

Perhaps more so than the rest of Canada, BC's economy is driven by factors outside its control. The province's fortunes are closely tied to Asian and American economies; when the East and US prospers, BC's timber, forestry and mineral exports boom. The Lower Mainland enjoys spillover from cross-border companies such as Washington-based Microsoft and Amazon.com. The Okanagan Valley has gotten in on the act as well, producing far more revenue from its 200 high-tech firms than from its more widely known, and tastier, wines and produce. And for better or worse, the province seems poised to finally exploit its coast for commercial purposes: Prince Rupert (p338) is building a huge container port that will serve Middle America via a revitalized Canadian National (CN) line and nearby Kitimat is luring a vast pipeline project to serve the tar sands of Alberta (see the boxed text, p337).

While service-sector jobs such as tourism are doing well, traditional jobs based on resource exploitation continue to bounce between feast and famine. The vast mining operations around areas such as the Peace River open and close depending on worldwide prices for raw minerals, and fishing has been decimated by depleted stocks. Forestry had tough times after trade tariffs

Shot in Vancouver from 1993 to 1998, the *X-Files* was the city's breakthrough series in terms of attracting huge numbers of film and TV productions.

Blade Runner's bleak rainy setting may have been inspired by a stint Philip K Dick spent in a Vancouver heroin rehab home.

hurt US sales but rebounded after beetles killed millions of trees, sending loggers and mills into overtime. Meanwhile debate continues about whether the 2010 Winter Olympics will burnish BC for the long-term as the 1988 games did for Calgary or become an economic noose like the games were for Montréal after 1976.

In the Yukon most people work for the government in some way – either as teachers, administrators, bureaucrats or in jobs dependent on government funding. Many count on the short tourist season for their livelihoods – with some wise characters working in southern winter retreats in Mexico or the Caribbean before enjoying profitable summers in the Yukon. Placer mining is also an economic factor, as worthwhile quantities of gold and silver continue to be extracted from the land. For more, see the boxed text, p381.

Food & Drink

British Columbia is a wonderful place to eat. The province enjoys the bounty of the sea, temperate and fertile lands in the south and islands, and a growing tribe of people committed to superb produce, wine and meals.

That said, there aren't too many signature foods that are unique to BC. One of the few is the Nanaimo bar, a rich treat that has spawned many spin-offs throughout the province. But BC features many other favorite foods that are popular throughout the Pacific Northwest: salmon and sushi, all kinds of berries, inventive pasta and Asian dishes, and some of the best vegetables you'll ever taste.

The Yukon, with barely 30,000 people, doesn't really have the local market necessary for cutting-edge cuisine. Rather, what's good here is anything that is made with fresh ingredients – look for fish and local vegetables during the summer.

Food Plants of Interior First Peoples by Nancy J Turner is an amazing book about the incredible abilities of native people to turn almost any plant in their territory into a food source. You'll never be hungry in the woods again.

STAPLES & SPECIALTIES

If you like seafood you are going to do very well, especially close to the coast. Salmon in its many forms, halibut, crabs and mussels are just some of its bounty. Generally speaking, the fresher it is the simpler you want it. Look for grilled seafood: if it's fresh it is hard to go wrong. Seasonal produce is also excellent. The specialties include mushrooms – there's an entire industry of pickers who scour the wet forests daily – and berries in their many varieties. Fruit from southern BC is excellent, led by Okanagan Valley peaches, apples, cherries and more.

Somewhat more exotic is game, which you'll see on some menus but which is primarily prepared and served in homes by the people who have bagged it. If you have a chance to order venison or a caribou steak, be prepared for a real taste of the outdoors.

A true taste of the West Coast, *Pacific Flavours Guidebook & Cookbook* by Virginia Lee features dozens of indigenous contemporary recipes – miss the cedar-infused BC salmon at your peril – along with a clutch of wine recommendations and insightful BC restaurant profiles.

DRINKS

Canadians drink much like the rest of North America, for fun, pleasure or to celebrate. In rural areas (much of BC and the Yukon) the local bar or saloon is the major social gathering place.

Coffee

BC wouldn't be part of the Pacific Northwest if you couldn't get a good coffee almost anywhere. There's a coffee shop on just about every block in commercial areas, and many drive-up kiosks in suburban zones. Most towns will have at least one place – often more – that specializes in good coffee and is in fact the de facto meeting spot for locals. Tea is widely available, too; many coffee shops stock exotic and herbal blends.

TOP FIVE BC RESTAURANTS

- Tojo's (p96) in Vancouver – sushi made by legendary, multi-award-winning Hidekazu Tojo
- Lumière (p96) in Vancouver – serves up French-inspired, Asian-brushed masterpieces
- Brasserie L'Ecole (p150) in Victoria – country-style French cuisine in a casual atmosphere
- Fresco (p240) in Kelowna – chef Rod Butters maintains a constantly changing menu
- All Seasons Café (p263) in Nelson – a casual, eclectic menu that changes with the seasons

---

ALCOHOL LEGALITIES

The legal drinking age in BC and the Yukon is 19, and the legal blood-alcohol limit is 0.08%, or the equivalent of two drinks for an 'average-sized' person. BC is very serious about curbing drunk driving, and you may encounter a mandatory roadside checkpoint, especially on summer evenings or around winter holidays.

The provincial government operates BC Liquor Stores, where you can buy beer, wine and spirits. If you want cold beverages in BC, head to the nearest 'cold beer and wine store' – often found attached to pubs, restaurants or hotels. In the Yukon, you must make all your purchases from government liquor stores.

Wine

British Columbia is becoming increasingly known for its high-quality wines, most produced in the Okanagan Valley (p228). However, good wine is also coming from other sunny parts of southern BC. The Lower Mainland and Vancouver Island are home to numerous wineries. Overall, BC wine is gaining a solid reputation for quality and value. The *New York Times* has called the Okanagan Valley 'Napa North'.

Beer

There are a number of good small brewers around BC that produce a variety of beers, including ales, bitters, lagers, pilsners, bocks, porters, stouts, fruit beer and even hemp ales. Names to look for, either in pubs or in cold beer stores, include Bear Brewing Co (Kamloops), Tree Brewing (Kelowna), Granville Island Brewing (Vancouver), Whistler Brewing Co (Whistler), the Nelson Brewing Co (Nelson) and Pacific Coast Brewing (Prince George).

It's not a microbrew, but Kokanee lager is the closest thing BC has to an official provincial beer. The excellent beers by Whitehorse's Yukon Brewing Co are found throughout the territory.

WHERE TO EAT & DRINK

The restaurants of Vancouver have taken the best of Asian and European cooking and fused it with the wealth of local ingredients. You can find almost any kind of ethnic or international cuisine here, Indian, Greek, regional Chinese, Japanese and much more are good and widely available. Outside Vancouver, the urban parts of Vancouver Island, the lower mainland and the Okanagan Valley all offer excellent and often inspired choices.

In more rural places and much of the North and the Yukon, you can expect simpler and more predictable fare. However, don't fret; while the cook in the kitchen may not have a trendy cookbook, they may very well be able to whip up an inspired meal.

Typical menus feature burgers, pasta, sandwiches, the ubiquitous Caesar salad and fish and chips. But read carefully and keep a sharp lookout for the daily special of grilled wild salmon. Many pubs feature good food as well.

The fact is that in most towns you can get a decent meal. Even in remote, rural areas we have found places that rise above those inescapable places serving 'Chinese and Canadian food' (which means you can get a fried cheeseburger to go with your gelatinous safety-orange-colored sweet-and-sour pork).

Out on the Queen Charlotte Islands, you might be able to join First Nations' feasts (p348), where you can enjoy a range of local foods including grilled salmon and delectable berry treats.

The website of the BC Wine Institute (www .winebc.com) is an invaluable resource for planning a tipple-flavored trawl around the region. It has route maps for 16 BC wine tours.

The BC Beer Guide website (www.realbeer .com/canada) is a searchable database of frothy brews, brewpubs and microbreweries throughout the province.

Hugely popular chef from Vancouver, Susan Mendelson, collects her favorite recipes from 27 years of food writing, along with 60 new ones in *Mama Now Cooks Like This*.

FARMERS' MARKETS

Across BC you'll find farmers' markets selling the huge range of produce and prepared foods that spring forth in the summer. Mostly organic, the markets are wildly popular with locals, who appreciate both the freshness of the food and its variety far beyond the stilted fare found in supermarkets.

The markets are usually held on weekends in parking lots near the centre of town. Many are listed in this book.

VEGETARIANS & VEGANS

In urban BC there are many vegetarian and vegan options. In fact, places that celebrate organic vegetables are all the rage. Vegans will salivate at Vancouver restaurants such as Foundation (p94). Elsewhere in BC and the Yukon, vegetarian options are usually good – although in remote areas they may be limited to that old standby: salad.

The BC Food Systems Network (www.food democracy.org) aims to counter the industrialized food chain by getting community involvement in how and what people eat.

EATING WITH KIDS

Kids are welcome everywhere in the region; see p389 for more information. Most places to eat have moderate prices and cater to families, so children's menus abound.

HABITS & CUSTOMS

You can easily get anything you want at almost any time you want in Vancouver. But be aware that outside of the metropolis, restaurants can shut down early, even in seemingly hip places like Nelson. Be at the restaurant by 8pm outside peak summer weekends.

Breakfast is usually eaten between 6am and 10am. Many accommodations offer a continental breakfast (a hot drink, juice, toast, muffins and maybe cereal) of some sort during these hours. Most BC residents eat breakfast at home on weekdays or grab a quick bite on the run with their morning coffee. But on weekends, a much more leisurely breakfast or brunch at a café or restaurant is a favorite pastime.

Soapberries, from a native BC plant that grows like a weed and features in First Nations cooking, live up to their name when made into a soapy froth that tastes surprisingly good.

The midday meal is typically taken between 11am and 1pm. It can be as simple as a snack bought from a farmers' market or food cart, or a picnic taken on your hike. Dinner is served anytime from about 5pm to 8pm, often later on weekends and in larger cities and resort areas such as Banff.

Restaurants are nonsmoking by provincial law. Pubs and bars have the option of allowing smoking on a patio or in an enclosed smoking room.

Dress is casual; in most restaurants you'll be fine no matter what you're wearing. For more formal places, the clichéd 'smart casual' (bring on those chinos) is the norm.

And don't forget White Spot, BC's most prominent regional sit-down restaurant chain, with more than 50 locations. Started by Nat Bailey in 1928, White Spot specializes in hamburgers (with Bailey's secret 'Triple-O' sauce) and creamy, thick milkshakes. And those stories about Canadians and doughnuts are true – just look at the crowds any morning at the ubiquitous Tim Hortons.

Environment

THE LAND

From the marshy, tidal southwest along the United States border through to the soaring border shared with Alberta in the Rockies, British Columbia is a land of dramatic landscapes. The troika of BC, Alaska and the Yukon meet in the northeast in a truly wild landscape of glaciers, peaks and sharp river canyons. The Yukon is washed in the north by the Arctic Ocean and separated from the flatlands of the Northwest Territories by the perilous Mackenzie Range.

With its many inlets, BC's awe-inspiring West Coast is more than 7000km long; alongside it are hundreds of islands ranging from large (Vancouver Island, the Queen Charlotte Islands) to tiny (Saturna Island).

The bulk of BC lies within the Canadian Cordillera, a system of mountain ranges running roughly northwest to southeast. Within the cordillera are several major ranges – the Rocky Mountains to the east; the Cassiar Mountains in the north; and the Columbia Mountains in the south. The glaciated Coast Mountains loom over the Pacific almost to the water's edge from Vancouver north to the Alaska panhandle.

The province has scores of freshwater lakes and fast-flowing rivers. The Fraser River is BC's longest, stretching from the Rocky Mountains to the Pacific Ocean near Vancouver. Roughly 60% of BC is covered by forest, mainly coniferous trees. The Peace River region in northeast BC is the only really flat area. More than 90% of BC's landmass is 'Crown Land,' and is therefore owned by the provincial government.

This high percentage of government-controlled land is even more the case in the Yukon, where the federal government holds more than 95% of the territory. The Rocky Mountain range eventually peters out at the Yukon border and much of the territory's interior is characterized by the broad Yukon Plateau, which is drained through the width of Alaska by the mighty Yukon River.

Green Club BC (www .greenclub.bc.ca) is an Vancouver-based group that's active in environmental issues and has activities designed to get people out in natural BC. It has excellent links to other environmental groups and is bilingual in English and Chinese.

Geology

An Ice Age starting about a million years ago was the primary force shaping the geology of BC and the Yukon. Huge ice sheets repeatedly scraped over the lofty mountain ranges, wearing them down to bedrock and creating great valleys between the peaks. This continued until about 7000 years ago, when the last ice melted, giving rise to the province's lakes and rivers (which remain fed by annual snowmelt today). Since then, glacial, wind and water erosion have continued to alter the landscape in more subtle ways, a process being accelerated by global warming.

Friends of Clayoquot Sound (www.focs.ca) is a Tofino-based group interested in the Sound and beyond.

FAST FACTS

- British Columbia is, after Quebec and Ontario, Canada's third-largest province. It comprises 9.5% of Canada's surface area.

- The Yukon Territory covers 4.5% of Canada.

- The highest mountain partially within BC is Mt Fairweather (4663m or 15,298ft) on the BC/Alaska border.

- The tallest mountain entirely within BC is Mt Waddington in the Coast Mountains, which peaks at 4016m.

WORLD HERITAGE SITES

British Columbia and the Yukon contain three of Canada's 13 World Heritage Sites.

■ Canadian Rocky Mountain Parks – The place where Canadian tourism began. Comprises 2.3 million hectares consisting of Banff (p283), Jasper (p298), Kootenay (p281) and Yoho (p278) National Parks, Mt Robson (p306) and Mt Assiniboine (p283) Provincial Parks in BC and Hamber Provincial Park in Alberta.

■ Kluane/Wrangell-St Elias/Glacier Bay/Tatshenshini-Alsek – This area teems with glaciers and raw landscape over two countries. Kluane National Park (p370) is solidly in the Yukon, abutting against Tatshenshini-Alsek Provincial Wilderness Park (p356) in BC, while Glacier Bay (see boxed text, p356) and Wrangell-St Elias National Parks are found in adjoining Alaska.

■ SGaang Gwaii – This is the island home of the abandoned town of Ninstints in Gwaii Haanas National Park Reserve (p351) in the Queen Charlotte Islands. Here some of the greatest totem poles and other aspects of the Haida culture can be found.

In addition, Parks Canada is working towards nominating several more BC and Yukon areas for World Heritage Site status. These include the Klondike which covers the gold rush area from the border near Skagway (p374) to Dawson City (p376); remote – and melting – Herschel Island and its companion Arctic National Parks, Ivvavik (p385) and Vuntut (p385); and Gwaii Haanas National Park Reserve (p351), which would incorporate SGaang Gwaii (currently already listed).

Mineral wealth spurred Europeans to settle in BC from the mid-19th century. The Yukon's one major boom stemmed from the fabled Klondike gold rush of 1897–98 (it's been downhill population-wise since).

Minerals remain important today. Major mineral deposits include coal on the coastal islands and the eastern slopes of the Rocky Mountains; gold in the Coast Mountains and the Yukon River and its tributaries; copper, lead, silver and zinc in the Kootenays; and natural-gas-containing sandstone and shale in the Peace River region. Jade is the official mineral of British Columbia and is widely used in jewelry and sculptures.

If you haven't read the classic *Call of the Wild*, read it on your trip to appreciate Jack London's brilliant tale of a dog on a Yukon odyssey.

WILDLIFE

With all its geographical and climatic diversity, it's no surprise that BC has a wide range of plants and animals. There are 14 distinct ecological zones; nature flourishes everywhere, from the large urban parks of Vancouver and Victoria, to the tops of the Rockies, to tiny coastal tide pools. The Yukon shares many of these features and adds its vast expanse of Arctic territory.

The wildlife you see anywhere in the region is likely to be among the highlights of your trip (keep that camera ready; critters rarely pose!).

Animals

Valhalla Wilderness Society (www.save spiritbear.org) is a New Denver–based group that has moved far beyond its Kootenays base to protect wildlife habitat across BC, including in the Great Bear Rainforest.

As a big train station is to a train spotter, BC and the Yukon are to wildlife spotters. The statistics are a checklist-obsessive's dream.

The region is habitat for more than 160 mammal species, 500 bird species, 500 fish species, 20 reptile species and 20 types of amphibians. About 100 species (including most of the whales, the burrowing owl and Vancouver Island marmot) are on the province's endangered species list; another 100 or so are considered at risk. Ecosystems are at their most diverse in southern BC, but that's also where threats from human pressures are at their strongest.

LAND MAMMALS

BC has more mountain goats than anywhere else in North America; in fact, 60% of all the world's mountain goats live here. The bear is another

---

ARE THEY KIDDING? I

The BC government, which has a mixed environmental record at best, finally released its long-awaited plan to save the mountain caribou in 2006. Of the province's 11 herds, it found that two groups near Golden and Nelson were so decimated that the few survivors should be caught and moved to join other groups (no word on what initiation ceremonies they might go through). Additionally, the report suggested that the caribou – which have been suffering habitat loss from logging and snowmobiling development – could be saved if open season were declared on cougars, bears and wolves. Yes, the government said that three species should be killed to save another. Needless to say, environmental groups were not amused. 'Madness,' said one weary campaigner.

---

prominent mammal, with an estimated 160,000 black bears in BC and the Yukon and an unknown but much smaller number of grizzlies. Kermode bears, sometimes called spirit bears, are whitish in color. Unique to BC, they're found from Bella Coola north through the Great Bear Rainforest (see boxed text, p319) to Stewart, mostly along the lower Skeena River Valley near Prince Rupert and Terrace. The truly white polar bear is found in the Arctic reaches of the Yukon.

Another unusual species, the Columbia black-tailed deer, is a small subspecies native to Vancouver Island and BC's West Coast. Other large mammals include bighorn sheep, mountain lions (also called cougars), Roosevelt elk, Dall and Stone sheep, mule deer, white-tailed deer, coyote and wolves. Moose are icons of the north and the sight of one raising its moss-covered antlers out of a swamp in the morning is not soon forgotten. In the far north, the enormous herds of caribou travel ceaselessly about the tundra grazing.

> Bella Coola-based James Gary Shelton is one of the world's noted bear experts. In *Bear Attacks: Myth & Reality* and his other bear books, he takes an unflinching look at a cunning and unpredictable killer.

MARINE MAMMALS & FISH

Whales are among the best-known and most sought after of BC's mammal species. About 20,000 Pacific gray whales migrate along BC's coast twice each year: southbound to Mexico from October through December and northbound to the Bering and Chukchi Seas in February through May. Less numerous and even more striking are the black-and-white orca (killer whales). Some groups (called pods) of orca live permanently off the coast of southern Vancouver Island; others range more widely in waters to the north. Other commonly sighted sea mammals include porpoises, dolphins, sea lions, seals and otters. One of the very best ways to see this richness of life is on one of the Inside Passage ferries (p400).

Salmon rank among the most important fish in BC. Sacred to many First Nations bands, and a mainstay of the province's fishing industry, salmon come in five species: Chinook (also called king), Coho, chum, sockeye and pink. Salmon life cycles are among the most storied in the animal world. At adulthood, they leave the ocean to swim upriver to the same spawning grounds

---

ARE THEY KIDDING? II

The BC Ministry of Environment is moving forward with plans to allow commercial lodges to be built in some of BC's most remote and unspoiled parks. Pristine provincial parks such as Mt Assiniboine (p283) in the Rockies and Wells Gray (p314) in the Cariboo would get new luxury resorts where guests could be shuttled in and out by helicopter. Besides the obvious desire to make a profit from the parks, officials said that an aging population needed lodges right in the parks. The response has been universally negative. 'The government has become the biggest single threat to BC's parks,' said the head of the Eco-Society (eco.kics.bc.ca).

AN EXPLOSION OF COLORS

Fall comes to the Yukon in August, a mere two or three months after the arrival of spring. The growing season for plants is incredibly short and they have to pack as much life as possible into a short period of sun and warmth. Maybe it's this intensity that's responsible for their going out in a blaze of glory every year. For whatever reason, every fall trees, shrubs, plants, weed and even lichen turn a brilliant array of colors that put places like New England to shame. Birch trees turn an iridescent yellow that's akin to what you'd get if American mustard glowed in the dark. Other trees turn various angry oranges and blood reds. Underneath, purples and pinks appear. And it goes on for not a few kilometers but hundreds. It's a polychromatic festival and yours to savor.

The best time for Yukon colors is mid-September, after that winter winds blow fall and travelers south. Many parts of northern BC – such as along both the Stewart-Cassiar and Alaska Hwys – reach their peaks in late September. The lower Rockies and Kootenays are good in early Oct.

where they were born. Once there, they take their turns at reproducing, and then they die (p218). See p57 for threats posed by salmon farms.

BIRDS

Of the 500-plus bird species, the black-and-blue Steller's jay is among the most famous; it was named the province's official bird after a government-sponsored contest. Prominent raptors include bald eagles, golden eagles, great horned owls and peregrine falcons. Look for ravens everywhere, coolly calculating their next scheme to get a meal.

Stately blue herons can be found taking their mime-like precise steps along river banks in southern BC.

Plants

A succession of tree-covered hills – each one a lighter shade of blue than the last – may be both one of the most common sights in BC and the most beautiful. Yet another thing that makes the place extraordinary.

BC has always been lush, with species varying widely depending on location, climate and human impact. Its summertime wildflower displays are among the best in North America, with showy blooms of every hue scattered along trails and roadways. But BC is probably best known for its trees, which rank among the world's tallest and most majestic.

Western red cedar, Sitka spruce, hemlock and Douglas fir are prevalent trees in the moist coastal regions. Red cedar, the official provincial tree, was of special importance to indigenous coastal peoples, who used it to make everything from canoes and clothing to totem poles and medicines. The tallest tree in Canada, a Sitka spruce known as the Carmanah Giant, stands at 95m in the Carmanah Valley of western Vancouver Island (p161). As evidence of the verdant growing conditions, this tree is less than 400 years old.

BC's official symbol is the white flower of the Pacific dogwood, a tree known for springtime blossoms and autumnal red berries.

Coastal BC is well known for the arbutus tree, a distinctive species with twisted branches, reddish peeling bark and dark green leaves. Southern Vancouver Island and the Gulf Islands are home to Garry oak, though many of these once-prolific trees have been wiped out by human development.

Ponderosa pine, Englemann and white spruce, Douglas fir, sub-alpine fir, birch, aspen, cottonwood and larch trees are among the species growing along the river valleys and rolling hills of the interior from Dawson City in the Yukon south. Northern landscapes are characterized by such scrappy trees as white and black spruce, tamarack and the sub-alpine fir.

The delicate tundra of the north largely consists of shrubs, grasses and lichens that eke out life during a growing season measured in weeks.

Berry and mushroom pickers will be in heaven throughout the region.

(Continued on page 57)

Outdoors

Canoes, Jasper National Park (p298)

ALAMY

There aren't many other places on Earth where you can ski in the morning and sail, hike or mountain bike in the afternoon. British Columbia is a dream destination for getting outside and enjoying a range of activities. Your options are limited only by your imagination. But if you like stunning scenery and countless places to escape the masses while doing something you love, then you'll have plenty to think about.

The 2010 Winter Olympics in Whistler and Vancouver will put BC skiing right in the spotlight. Expect to see more world-class ski and board slopes in the region in the coming years. But don't limit your thoughts to just the high-profile places. From Vancouver Island all the way to the Rockies you'll find resorts, fabled powder and a really relaxed, friendly vibe.

These slopes often become great mountain biking tracks outside winter. Many resorts run lifts in summer so you can scream down hills with ease. Should you prefer to ascend by your fingertips, hundreds of rock faces await you. More sedate are the many long-distance trails geared to cyclists.

Then there's water. Kayaking and canoeing are exceptionally popular and for good reason: lakes, rivers, fjords and craggy coasts just demand exploration. You can find conditions and routes for any skill level. From a relaxed paddle across a mountain lake to running whitewater whose rapids were the bane of pioneers a hundred years ago, there's a multitude of choices. Below the surface, hearty individuals look for some of the bizarre creatures such as giant octopuses that thrive in the cold water. Up top you can rent a sailboat or powerboat and go wandering lakes and the coastal waters.

No matter how you experience it, British Columbia is all about the outdoors. Throughout this book you'll find countless opportunities for activities on the sea, coast, mountains, lakes, slopes, rivers, trails, forests and more. You can enjoy a world-famous park on everybody's map or discover your own gem on nobody's map. So go on, enjoy it, do it, feel it and live it. Expect to be amazed.

Mt Washington Alpine Resort (p44), Vancouver Island

FRANK CAI

Skiing, Red Mountain Ski Resort (p45)
GLENN VAN DER KNIJFF

PLACES TO GET OUTDOORS

Whistler-Blackcomb (p121)
Ski or snowboard over 200 runs.

West Coast Trail (p176)
Hike BC's magnificent 77km trail.

Rossland (p264)
Partake in world-class mountain biking.

Broken Group Islands (p176)
Kayak through pristine islands.

Bowron Lake (p312)
Canoe around a perfect chain of lakes.

On Land

From skiing to hiking to mountain biking, your only dilemma will be deciding where to go, what to do and who to do it with.

SKIING & SNOWBOARDING

BC's mountains, which range from rugged alpine peaks to gradual valleys and gullies, combine with almost guaranteed snowfall to make the province ideal for winter sports. Backcountry touring and heli-skiing get you deep into unexplored territory, but most people head to the many resorts. Whether you're a seasoned skier, veteran snowboard rider or an utter novice standing in snow for the first time, there are options galore.

And if the coming Olympics make the Vancouver and Whistler area just a tad too popular for your taste, consider the waffle board of hills running all the way east to the Rockies. You'll find excellent resorts above the Okanagan Valley and throughout the Kootenays – including a few that will probably hatch their own Olympic dreams in decades to come. And if you really want some virgin powder, the peaks above Revelstoke are renowned for heli-skiing. (In fact, so too are some of the almost unknown mountains in the far north off the Stewart-Cassiar Hwy; see p355).

There are a plethora of resorts big and small to consider.

BC SKIING

Cypress Mountain

Close to Vancouver, the wide, snow-filled Cypress Bowl sits in the heart of Cypress Provincial Park between Strachan and Black Mountains. Popular with intermediate downhill skiers, the mountain features 36 runs and 19km of groomed cross-country runs, as well as a snowboard park. In the evening, the lights come on for great night skiing and excellent views of Howe Sound. It will be the snowboarding and freestyle park for the Olympics. Nearest town: West Vancouver (p107)

Grouse Mountain Resort

A short drive or bus ride from Vancouver, Grouse Mountain is a favorite for its easy access and night skiing. An aerial tram whisks you to the mountaintop, offering incredible views along the way. Mogul dancers head to the Peak, or explore the mountain's backside on Blueberry or Purgatory. Anyone can enjoy the views skiing or boarding down the Cut, which is visible from all over Vancouver. The drop is 384m and there are 25 daytime runs. The view here from downtown Vancouver is sure to become an Olympic cliché. Nearest town: North Vancouver (p104)

Mount Seymour

This North Shore mountain is a haven for snowboarders, who come to rip it up in Seymour's three snowboard parks: Brockton, Mystery Peak and Mushroom Junior Park. Beginner skiers and boarders find Seymour a good place to learn, and the excellent ski/board school offers good deals on lessons, after which you can try the 21 runs. Families are catered for with toboggan and inner-tube runs. Nearest town: North Vancouver (p104)

Whistler-Blackcomb

This world-famous, dual-mountain paradise can accommodate up to 59,000 skiers and snowboarders an hour on its 37 lifts. Among other stats, it has more than 200 runs and there are 29 sq km of bowls, glades and steeps. Separated by the steep Fitzsimmons Creek Valley, Whistler and Blackcomb are two distinct mountains, but the high-speed lift system allows you access to both. This is the place to come now so that in 2010 you can blithely say 'I was there.' Nearest town: Whistler (p118)

Mount Washington Alpine Resort

The place to ski on Vancouver Island. It has 50 runs, a snowshoe park and lots of cross-country trails. It has tubing runs for kids of all ages. There's plenty of evidence that you can get a little extreme here in Warren Miller's film *Off The Grid*. Nearest town: Comox (p183)

EC Manning Provincial Park

So low-key, it's more park than resort. EC Manning Provincial Park has 140 acres of ski and snowboard terrain, with four lifts and 25 marked trails. You can also snowshoe and cross-country ski in the area. Nearest town: Hope (p207)

Sun Peaks Resort

Legendary Olympian Nancy Greene is the director of skiing here and she lends some real ski-cred to this family-friendly resort that is favored by many who'd rather avoid the Whistler crowds. The three mountains here boast 121 runs, 12 lifts, a snowboard park and 881m of vertical rise. Almost 70% of the runs at Sun Peaks are novice or intermediate. Snowshoeing, dog-sledding and Nordic skiing are also popular. Nearest town: Kamloops (p213)

Apex Mountain Resort

Apex is known for its plethora of double-black-diamond and technical runs (the drop is over 600m), as well as gladed chutes and vast powdery bowls. The crowds are smaller than at nearby Big White Mountain in Kelowna. Close to the village you'll find 30km of accessible cross-country trails. There's 65 runs overall. Nearest town: Penticton (p225)

Big White Ski Resort
Known for its incredible powder, Big White is one of BC's best ski resorts. The highest ski resort in the province features 118 runs, which are covered in the noted deep dry powder for excellent downhill and backcountry skiing, and deep gullies that make for excellent snowboarding. The drop is 777m and you can night-ski. Kelowna is at the heart of the Okanagan Valley wine country. Nearest town: Kelowna (p234)

Silver Star Mountain Resort
A recreated Klondike boomtown, Silver Star attracts every level of skier and snowboarder from late October to early April. The mountain's sunny south face, Vance Creek, features predominantly novice and intermediate runs, while the north face mainly offers black-diamond runs boasting moguls, trees and powder. The vertical drop is 760m and there are 12 lifts. A special machine carves wicked half-pipes for snowboarders. Cross-country skiers can enjoy 37km of groomed trails. Nearest town: Vernon (p242)

Fernie Alpine Resort
You hear it often, but investors want to make this the next Whistler. Surrounded by spectacular alpine peaks, the mountain features 107 runs, five bowls and almost endless dumps of powder that draw droves of skiers and snowboarders looking for unspoiled terrain. Fully 30% of the runs are rated expert. Nearby Fernie is one of BC's best small towns. Nearest town: Fernie (p266)

Kicking Horse Mountain Resort
Big plans are under way for Golden's Whitetooth Mountain. Another of the fast-growing East Kootenays resorts, a challenging 60% of its 106 runs are rated advanced or expert. A gondola gives you a great vantage of the 1260 vertical meters and relatively snow-heavy, wind-free location between the Rockies and Purcells. Nearest town: Golden (p273)

Kimberley Alpine Resort
This is a fast-growing resort. It boasts 729 hectares of skiable terrain, mild weather and 67 runs. There are 8 lifts and 45% of the runs are intermediate. A high-speed quad lift serves the 8200m Main Run, which has a 609m drop and which is fully lighted for night skiing. A snowboard park features an exciting half-pipe. Nearest town: Kimberley (p270)

Red Mountain Ski Resort
A breeding ground for Olympic skiers, 'Red' accesses two mountains – Red and Granite – and offers some of the province's best black-diamond runs. Many people are drawn by Rossland's low-key charm. Intermediate skiers and boarders will find lots to explore. The resort is known for its steep, tree-filled runs (83 at last count). There are six lifts and a drop of 880m. Nearest town: Rossland (p264)

Whitewater Winter Resort
Filled with charm, this small mountain tends to attract skiers and boarders venturing into the backcountry. There are several local snowcat operators and the steep terrain boasts a 400m vertical drop. It's known for its heavy powdery snowfall, which averages 10.5m per year. Nelson makes for an excellent base. Nearest town: Nelson (p258)

Banff National Park Ski Resorts
Three excellent mountain resorts: Ski Banff @ Norquay, Sunshine Village and Lake Louise Ski Area are all prime examples of Rocky Mountain skiing. The trio have beautiful positions and offer close to 250 runs of every description. All are located close to Banff, which offers the most big-time resort amenities east of Whistler. Nearest town: Banff (p283)

BC SKIING

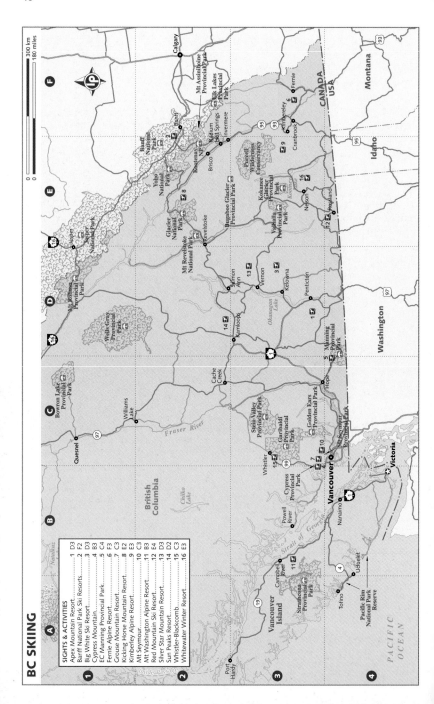

SIGHTS & ACTIVITIES

Apex Mountain Resort	1 D3
Banff National Park Ski Resorts	2 F2
Big White Ski Resort	3 D3
Cypress Mountain	4 B3
EC Manning Provincial Park	5 C4
Fernie Alpine Resort	6 F3
Grouse Mountain Resort	7 C3
Kicking Horse Mountain Resort	8 E2
Kimberley Alpine Resort	9 E3
Mt Seymour	10 C3
Mt Washington Alpine Resort	11 B3
Red Mountain Ski Resort	12 E4
Silver Star Mountain Resort	13 D3
Sun Peaks Resort	14 D2
Whistler-Blackcomb	15 C3
Whitewater Winter Resort	16 E3

HIKING

BC is a hiker's paradise. Virtually every park has trails of many lengths and difficulties. From simple nature trails with interpretive signs to multiday treks, you'll find it.

Not far north of Vancouver, Garibaldi Provincial Park (p118) has 67km of trails and is a good place for backcountry camping close to the metropolis. Over on Vancouver Island, Pacific Rim National Park (p174) has ancient-cedar-studded rain forest and wave-pounded ocean beaches near the fun town of Tofino. Its trail will take you throughout.

The eight-day West Coast Trail (p176) was originally constructed as an escape route for shipwreck survivors. Its 75km route features rock-face ladders, stream crossings and other challenges that may leave you thinking the shipwreck wasn't such a bad thing.

The Juan de Fuca Marine Trail (p159) is another good coastal hike which usually takes about four days. You can do day trips, as there are several access points. To really escape it all head to the magical Queen Charlotte Islands (p343), where you will have long storm-tossed beaches and vast stands of virgin trees to yourself.

Lake O'Hara (p280) in Yoho National Park attracts hikers who reserve their spots months in advance. Its pretty alpine setting and clear waters make it a memorable experience; there

WHERE TO HIKE?

Good hiking advice can be found at VICs, the parks themselves and through various websites, groups and books.

- Alpine Club of Canada (www.alpineclub ofcanada.ca) – Great resources for serious hikers.
- Outdoor Recreation Council of British Columbia (www.orcbc.ca) – An environmental group which has a long list of excellent hiking maps.
- Trail Database (www.traildatabase .org/countries/canada.html) – Contains a wealth of links to groups, organizations and individuals dedicated to hiking in western Canada.

Hiking, Lake O'Hara (p280), Yoho National Park

WITOLD SKRYPCZAK

Mountain biking, Whistler (p122)
SALLY DILLON

are literally hundreds of other hikes in the Rockies.

Finally, the Bella Coola Valley (p317) is a perfect DIY hiking destination, as deserted trails abound and locals will cheerfully tell you about their favorites.

CYCLING & MOUNTAIN BIKING

Mountain biking is huge in BC, and road cycling is popular, too. Home to some of BC's best technical trails, Rossland (p264) is often considered to be the mountain biking capital of BC (and possibly Canada). Whistler (p118), like many of the ski resorts listed in this chapter, attracts lots of fat-tire riders. Check out the Whistler Interpretive Forest (p118), just south of town. Fernie (p266), in a deep eastern valley, has peaks and runs that keep a year-round population of bikers waiting to hit the trails.

Your best sources of information include local bike shops, which we list for important towns and VICs. The place to start for information is **Cycling BC** (☎ 604-737-3034; www.cycling.bc.ca), BC's governing body for mountain-bike racing, road racing and track racing. It offers plenty of resources for both recreational and touring cyclists. Another good resource is **Canada Trails** (www.canadatrails.ca), which has ratings and links to all the major BC mountain biking areas.

ROCK CLIMBING & MOUNTAINEERING

BC is full of great venues for rock climbing and mountaineering. Squamish (p115) is home to the Stawamus Chief, a world-class granite monolith with about 200 climbing routes. Other climbers swear by the better weather at the compact gneiss rock of Skaha Bluffs near Penticton (p225), which boast a long climbing season on more than 400 bolted routes. There's world-class climbing around Banff in the Rockies (p283). To tackle rocks both outside and inside the mountain, try Horne Lake Caves Provincial Park (p170).

HORSEBACK RIDING

If you're a big fan of horseback riding, head to BC's Cariboo and Chilcotin regions, where dude ranches (see boxed text, p309) offer a range of activities from trail rides to cattle drives. There really is something delightful about saddling up Old Paint and

Rock climbing, Squamish (p115)
RICH PROHASKA

BEARS, OH MY

Bears are one of the top tourist draws to the north. Whether they be grizzly or black, these huge carnivores hold a definite attraction. However, you don't want it to be a fatal attraction, so here is some advice from Parks Canada for staying safe in bear country. Although some of it seems pretty basic, never underestimate a human's ability to behave like a dork.

- On foot, travel in groups
- Watch for signs of bear
- Keep pets on leash
- Avoid large dead animals
- Never approach a bear (!)
- Keep food and smells away from bears; use bear-resistant food containers

If the above doesn't work and the bear attacks, do the following:

- Don't drop your pack – it can provide protection
- Try to walk backward slowly
- Don't run – the bear will always outrun you
- Try to get somewhere safe, like a car
- If the attack is imminent, use bear spray and/or play dead, but note that bear spray is not always effective (nor is playing dead)
- If the attack occurs after the bear has stalked you or happens in your tent, fight back

Finally, two points:

- Seek out advice on bears and bear sightings from local park staff
- Be wary of 'bear whistles' as a way to make noise; some may sound like a marmot – a tasty bear snack. 'Bear bells' are a better choice.

heading out amid the serene lakes and atmospheric peaks. In the midst of the Great Bear Rainforest, there are plenty of trails to explore in the Bella Coola Valley (p317). You can also saddle up in Banff (p283) and Jasper (p298) National Parks; at Whistler (p118) and Pemberton (p127) on the Sea to Sky Hwy; on Salt Spring Island (p195) in the Southern Gulf Islands; and at Mt Washington (p183), near Comox and Courtenay on Vancouver Island.

CROSS-COUNTRY SKIING & SNOWSHOEING

You can enjoy the legendary BC powder on trails at all of the ski resorts listed *and* at most of the provincial parks that get snow. The options are as endless as the night in the dead of winter. This is another of those excellent activities that lend themselves to your own exploration. Ask around and head out. Way up north, cross-country skiing is a very popular activity in the Yukon, which has winters that make it the main activity. In both Whitehorse (p360) and Dawson City (p376), you'll find marked trails and enthusiastic locals ready to advise.

Snowshoeing is growing in popularity and many ski resorts now rent snowshoes. Generally if you can cross-country ski it, you can strap on some shoes and hit it as well.

At Sea

All that coast, all that water. And inland you've got pristine mountain lakes, challenging white-water rivers and more. There's just no limit to the places you can canoe, kayak, boat, dive, raft and more.

SEA KAYAKING

If there is one activity you have to try in coastal BC, this is it. Sea kayaks are easy to paddle, amazingly stable and lots of fun. Unlike larger boats, kayaks can hug the shoreline, offering the perfect perch for watching shore birds and other marine life. Nearly every coastal and island town has at least one outfitter ready to take you on a guided trek lasting from a few hours (for about $50) to a week. These trips are by far the best way to learn the sport; once you know the ropes, you can rent or buy gear and go paddling on your own, though you'll always want to check local weather and traffic conditions.

It's always best to kayak with other people for safety. Someone in the group should know how to plot a course by navigational chart and compass, pilot in fog, read weather patterns, assess water hazards, interpret tide tables, handle boats in adverse conditions and perform group- and self-rescue techniques.

Campsites abound on BC's many islands, but more and more people are choosing 'mothership' sea kayaking over camping. The 'mothership,' a larger boat, takes kayakers and their gear out to sea; the kayakers then spend their days paddling and nights bunked down in the big boat.

You might want to time your BC visit to coincide with the annual Vancouver Island **Paddlefest** (www.paddlefest.bc.ca), a major kayaking event held each May at Ladysmith (p162).

Sea kayaking, Pacific Rim National Park Reserve (p174)

FRANK CAR

GET RID OF THIS GUIDE

No, we're no talking about throwing this book out, we're talking about enjoying your trip without it. (Besides, when the time comes to replace this guidebook with a new edition, you should recycle it, not throw it out.) British Columbia and the Yukon are such vast and fascinating places that there's no way we can cover everything. That leaves a myriad things for you to discover on your own. If something looks interesting, check it out! BC's got more than 600 provincial parks – scores are unheralded and just waiting for somebody to see what's on offer.

One of the best ways to embark on a little DIY (do it yourself) travel is by asking around. Outdoors shops like kayak, bike and ski places are usually staffed by people who are very enthusiastic about the activity and more than happy to share their local knowledge with a visitor. They want you to love the region too!

Similarly, the usually helpful people staffing VICs and information desks know far more than they ever get to share. We watched as one staffer responded to this question: 'Where's a Tim Hortons?' She pointed across the street and then dryly noted that there were two more up the road. Given that the questions are often so trite and standard, you may have to convince the person across the counter that you really want to get off the beaten path, but once you do, look out. In the case above, once the staffer decided we were serious, she grabbed a map and detailed scores of places to enjoy the gorgeous valley and not see another soul. At Lake Louise, a Parks Canada staffer got up a full head of steam and showed us a dozen hiking trails where we'd never see a trace of the mobs at the lake itself.

With a simple map he marked up, we were off on a day of DIY joy.

The Islands

You can kayak just about everywhere along BC's coast, but you'll find the greatest concentration of outfitters on Vancouver Island. For multiday trips, the best-known destination is the Broken Group Islands (p176), part of Pacific Rim National Park Reserve, on the west coast of Vancouver Island. If you don't have much time, you can always rent a kayak for a few hours or take an introductory lesson in nearly any coastal town. For more information, look up these towns in the Vancouver Island chapter: Victoria (p137), Sooke (p158), Sidney (p154), Ladysmith (p162), Oceanside (p169), Port Alberni (p172), Tofino (p177), Bamfield (p173), Telegraph Cove (p188), Port Hardy (p190) and Denman (p182), Hornby (p182) and Quadra Islands (p185).

In the Gulf Islands, you'll find outfitters and rental shops on each major island: Salt Spring (p195), Galiano (p202), Mayne (p201) and North Pender (p198). Near Vancouver, try Bowen Island (p108). Further north, popular spots include Prince Rupert (p338) and the legendary Gwaii Haanas National Park Reserve (p351) in the Queen Charlotte Islands.

Inland Kayaking

Despite the name 'sea kayak,' you can take one of these boats out on a lake too. For some prime paddling, try Lightning Lake at EC Manning Provincial Park (p210), east of Hope; Kootenay Lake, east of Nelson (p258); and Babine Lake, north of Burns Lake (p333). In the Yukon (p359), many people are trading in their canoes for kayaks along the Yukon River. Most of the places listed for canoeing in this chapter (see p52) are also kayak-ready.

Canoeing, Yoho National Park (p278)

DONALD C. & PRISCILLA ALEXANDER EASTMAN

CANOEING

It's an iconic shot of the province: a flannel-shirt-clad rower gliding through pristine waters against a tree-covered backdrop. Sure it's a cliché but it's also the reality in what really would have to be called canoe heaven. Just look at the number of canoe-carriers you see on local cars. And even though everybody is doing it, there are so many places you can go that crowds shouldn't be a problem.

The 116km Bowron Lake canoe circuit in Bowron Lake Provincial Park (p312) is one of the world's great canoe trips, covering 10 lakes with easy portages between each. Another remote canoe journey can be found on Eutsuk and neighboring lakes in the northern portion of Tweedsmuir Provincial Park (p333). For real adventure, try Chilko Lake (see boxed text, p315) in Ts'yl-os Provincial Park, which can involve access via a floatplane.

Other good inland spots to paddle include Wells Gray Provincial Park (p314); Slocan Lake, just west of New Denver (p256), and Okanagan Lake, easily accessed from Kelowna (p234). EC Manning Provincial Park (p210) is also popular.

On the coast and islands, ocean canoeing is possible around Vancouver, the Gulf Islands and the Queen Charlotte Islands. The Port Alberni (p172) and Powell River (p133) areas have a lot of choices.

Meanwhile up in the Yukon, you'll find truly fabled canoeing along the Yukon River and its tributaries. This was the route of the Klondike gold rush. And you can still experience the stunning raw wilderness that the prospectors saw, but do so from a modern canoe and not a raft of lashed-together logs. Whitehorse (p360) is the center for guides and gear.

DIVING

Justly famous for its superb diving conditions, BC features two of the top-ranked dive spots in the world: Vancouver Island and the Gulf Islands. It's best to go in winter, when the plankton has decreased and visibility often exceeds 20m. The water temperature drops to about 7°C to 10°C in winter; in summer, it reaches 15°C. At depths of more than 15m visibility remains good throughout the year and temperatures rarely rise above 10°C. Expect to see a full range of marine life including oodles of crabs, from tiny hermits to intimidating kings. If you're lucky you may also encounter mammals such as seals and sea lions.

The prime diving spots lie in Georgia Strait between Vancouver Island's east coast and the mainland. Dive shops abound in this region, and they are your best sources for air and gear as well as lessons, charters and tours. Popular areas can be found near Nanaimo (p163), Bamfield (p173), Comox (p183), Campbell River (p184) and Quadra Island (p185).

BC diving references include *Diver Magazine* (www.divermag.com) and the Professional Association of Diving Instructors (www.padi.com).

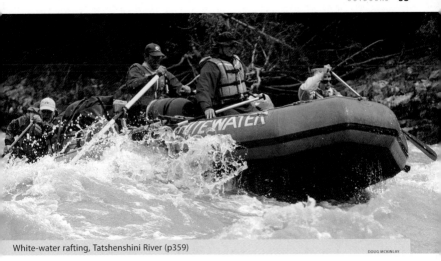

White-water rafting, Tatshenshini River (p359)

DOUG MCKINLAY

WHITE-WATER RAFTING

Rugged topography and an abundance of snowmelt make BC's rivers great for white-water action. You don't need to be experienced to go out rafting. The provincial government regulates commercial rafting, and operators are allowed only on rivers that have been checked by experts. Guides must meet certain qualifications, and companies must provide equipment that meets government requirements. Trips can last from three hours up to a couple of weeks. Wilderness rafting averages about $200 per day for everything, while half-day trips start at about $60.

Wherever you are in BC, you're probably close to a good white-water river. Consider the Thompson River (p212) near Lytton for excellent white water not especially far from Vancouver. Adams River near Shuswap Lake (p217) is another fine choice.

The Kootenays are probably the best area; many consider the Kicking Horse River near Golden (p273) to be one of the province's best raft trips. Other prime spots include the Clearwater River near Wells Gray Provincial Park (p314) and the Bulkley and Babine Rivers near Smithers (p334). For wild adventure, consider the Tatshenshini and Alsek Rivers in northern BC (p356).

ALTERNATIVE TOURS

There are numerous outfits offering trips around BC in infinite variation. Two examples of some of the more unusual and interesting options:

- Earthwatch Institute (☎ 800-776-0188; www.earthwatch.org) – Takes paying volunteers on research missions around the world and along the BC coast. One eight-day trip involves kayaking along the Inside Passage to record whales song, identify individuals, conduct counts and much more. The $2300 fee includes all meals and rustic group camping at research stations on remote parts of the coast.

- Pacific Northwest Expeditions (☎ 866-529-2522; www.seakayakbc.com) – Specializes in kayak trips geared to wildlife spotting. A four-day trip with coastal camping that specializes in spotting the orcas of Johnstone Straight off Vancouver Island costs from $900.

Orca near Vancouver Island (p136)
RALPH LEE HOPKINS

WATCHING WILDLIFE

For many, the chance to see some of BC's incredible diversity of wildlife is reason enough for a trip. For most, seeing one of these incredible critters is a lasting memory. Though wildlife viewing is good at any time of the year, there are certain high seasons along the BC coast when you're likely to see more of a particular animal.

- grizzly and black bears – mid-April to June
- Kermode bears – September to mid-October
- humpback whales – August to October
- killer whales – May to mid-July
- gray whales – mid-August to October
- bald eagles – year-round but especially mid-March to mid-April
- seals and sea lions – year-round
- porpoises – year-round

Inland, you can see bear, caribou, deer, mountain goats, and many more animals through the year. For a guide to watching wildlife in the Rockies, see the boxed text, p278.

SAILING & BOATING

The sheltered waters of BC's Pacific coast make sailing a popular form of recreation that's possible almost year-round, though it's best to take out a boat from mid-April to mid-October. Coastal marine parks provide safe, all-weather anchorage and offer boats for hire (powerboats as well as sailboats). Some of the great places to sail include the Strait of Georgia and the Gulf Islands. Inland, sailors tend to prefer Harrison Lake (p209); Okanagan and Skaha Lakes in the Okanagan Valley region; Arrow and Kootenay Lakes in the Kootenays; and Williston Lake (p327), north of Prince George.

Houseboating is another popular pastime on BC's biggest lakes, including Shuswap Lake (p217) north of the Okanagan and Powell Lake (p133) on the Sunshine Coast. It costs from $2000 a week, depending on location and time of year, to rent a self-contained boat that sleeps about 10 people.

SURFING

The Tofino area (p177) on Vancouver Island's west coast is ground zero for BC's best surfing. Weather conditions may well be far from ideal – imagine buckets of rain and chilly temperatures – but the waves are truly awesome, rolling directly off the North Pacific. Long Beach, a 20km crescent between Tofino and Ucluelet, is the center of the action. Check out www.surfingvancouverisland.com for lots of information on surfing and some gnarly videos.

FISHING

Fishing, both the saltwater and freshwater variety, is one of BC's major tourist attractions. Saltwater anglers particularly like to cast their nets and lines in the waters around Vancouver Island, where several places (Campbell River, p184, chief among them) claim the title 'salmon capital of the world,' as well as at Prince Rupert (p338), known for its halibut, and in the Queen Charlotte Islands (p343). You'll find good river and lake fishing in every region.

Right in Vancouver, anglers enjoy casting off the Stanley Park seawall (p75). For some particularly good lake fishing further inland, try Golden Ears Provincial Park (p111) and Birkenhead Lake Provincial Park (p128).

FISHING INFORMATION & LICENSES

You must obtain separate licenses for saltwater/tidal fishing and freshwater fishing. The provincial **Ministry of Environment** (www.env.gov.bc.ca/fw/) controls freshwater licenses. There's a thicket of fees and options; ask at VICs and sporting goods stores for your options – which vary by region.

The federal **Department of Fisheries & Oceans** (www.pac.dfo-mpo.gc.ca/recfish/default _e.htm) issues licenses for saltwater/tidal fishing. Again, there's enough variety in licenses, fees and regulations that you might feel like a spawned-out salmon after sorting through them.

The East Kootenays see some outstanding fly-fishing, especially on creek-size tributaries of the Columbia, Kicking Horse and Kootenay Rivers along and near Hwy 95.

The best destination of all may be northern BC, where hundreds of lakes – many reachable only by boat or plane – give anglers endless options. For good river fishing up north, head to the Fraser, Nass, Skeena, Kettle, Peace and Liard Rivers.

WINDSURFING & KITEBOARDING

The tidal flats around Vancouver are popular with windsurfers. On many a day you'll see scores of colorful sails darting around the shallows. You'll find shops in the city (p80) where you can get advice and rent boards, skimboards and wetsuits. Golden Ears Provincial Park (p111) is a popular area. Winds whip through Juan de Fuca Strait and boardsailing is big in Cadboro Bay and Willows Beach near Victoria (p137).

Ocean kayaking near Quadra Island (p185)

BRITISHCOLUMBIAPHOTOS.COM / ALAMY

Lake Magog, Mt Assiniboine Provincial Park (p283)

WITOLD SKRYPC

(Continued from page 40)

PARKS

BC and the Yukon have some amazing national parks. Several are Unesco sites (see boxed text, p38). Other significant national parks include Glacier (p254) and Mt Revelstoke (p253) on the BC side of the Rockies and the Pacific Rim National Park Reserve on Vancouver Island (p174). The Gulf Islands National Park Reserve (see boxed text, p194), protecting the Southern Gulf Islands, was created in 2003.

In the far north of the Yukon, Ivvavik (p385) and Vuntut (p385) National Parks are wild and remote places.

A National Parks of Canada **annual pass** (www.parkscanada.ca; adult/child $63/32) is an excellent investment if you are going to spend time in the national parks. Passes can be purchased at the parks, and options for visiting historic sites can be included as well.

BC has more than 600 **provincial parks** (wlapwww.gov.bc.ca/bcparks/). There are more than 13 million hectares of protected land, which accounts for almost 14% of British Columbia's land base. There is no annual pass for BC Parks, just a thicket of fees for some parks and no fees for others. Together, the BC Parks system is a magnificent accomplishment, although the Campbell government has been opening up some parks to logging and allowing development in others (see boxed text, p39).

The Yukon only has four **territorial parks** (www.environmentyukon.gov.yk.ca); much of the territory is parklike and government campgrounds can be found in many places.

ENVIRONMENTAL ISSUES

British Columbia is a deeply conflicted place when it comes to the environment. Many see the province's vast, wild lands and coastal environments as places to protect and enjoy, while others see the many pristine and resource-rich areas as their meal ticket. Then there are areas like Tofino on Vancouver Island's West Coast, where a sometimes uneasy truce holds

Paul George's lavishly illustrated *Big Trees, Not Big Stumps*, published by the Wilderness Committee, traces 25 years of efforts to save old-growth forests with lots of how-to tips for individual activism.

TOP FIVE BC ENVIRONMENTAL GROUPS

BC has a long history of environmental activism, and even casual visitors are likely to encounter debates and perhaps protests over issues such as forestry practices and large-scale fish farming. See p319 for details on the Great Bear Rainforest, which has been a huge focus of BC environmental groups. Key groups include the following:

- ForestEthics (www.forestethics.org) – works to protect BC's constantly threatened forests and has taken the lead in opposing plans to 'save' the mountain caribou by killing other animals.

- Greenpeace (www.greenpeace.org) – founded in Vancouver more than 30 years ago, it has been very active in the Great Bear Rainforest campaign.

- Raincoast Conservation Society (www.raincoast.org) – spearheaded recognition of the Great Bear Rainforest on BC's central coast as the largest contiguous tract of coastal temperate rain forest left on Earth.

- Sierra Club BC (www.sierraclub.ca/bc/) – is taking the lead in opposing the construction of coal-fired power plants in BC (one will be at Tumbler Ridge; see boxed text, p327). The website has a good map showing the parts of Vancouver that will be covered when just a fraction of the Polar Ice Cap melts. Lex Luther should be buying beachfront property in Whistler.

- Western Canada Wilderness Committee (www.wildernesscommittee.org) – a good omnibus group with lots of ongoing coverage of environmental issues.

TRAVELING RESPONSIBLY: DOS & DON'TS

The impact you have on other people's as well as your own experience while traveling are both functions of being responsible and having respect for where you are. Common sense and awareness are your best guides. In general, British Columbia and the Yukon are places where responsible travel is the norm, but it's always useful to remember a few simple guidelines.

- Don't litter (although it's a no-brainer, somebody's leaving that crap around). Do use the recycling bins that you'll find in hotels, parks and along the street. Do carry out all of your trash from trails and parks, because most facilities are too underfunded and understaffed to collect trash regularly. And in a random act of goodness, if you see some trash left by some cretin, pick it up yourself.

- Do stay on trails: they lessen the erosion caused by human transit, this especially goes for mountain bikers. The best guides and tour companies are serious about preserving trails.

- Don't disturb animals or damage plants. Do observe wildlife from a distance with binoculars.

- Don't feed the animals! Feeding the animals interferes with their natural diets. They can be susceptible to bacteria transferred by humans. Not only do they become more vulnerable to hunting and trapping, but they may stop seeking out their own natural food sources and become dependent on this human source. Every year bears have to be moved or even destroyed because they've become accustomed to a Cheetos hand-out and now see humans as a food source – or even *the* food source.

- Do learn about wildlife and local conservation, environmental, and cultural issues before your trip and especially during your visit. Do ask questions and listen to what locals have to say. Lots of people are passionate about preserving BC and the Yukon, despite a myriad threats. You'll find them and their organizations pretty much wherever you go. See the boxed text, p57 for more on this.

between people employed by extractive industries and those sworn to defend the planet from plunder.

Environmental debate is an ongoing and major part of the province's political focus. Besides the inevitable battle between those who wish to profit from natural resources and those that wish to save them, BC also has urgent environmental threats from forest fires brought on by climate change and infestations of mountain pine beetles (see boxed text, p332) that are killing forests.

Greenpeace, the international environmental group, began in a Vancouver home where a group of people met in 1969 to discuss ways to halt US atmospheric testing of nuclear weapons.

And just to underscore how fragile the balance can be, fish farming – which has been growing fast as a source of salmon – has become controversial. A major study has shown that up to 95% of young wild salmon who swim near their caged cousins catch fish lice (endemic in farm salmon, yuck) and die.

Spruce beetles and their relationship to global warming are at the heart of Yukon environmental debate, given that whole forests have been wiped out (see boxed text, p371). Another major issue involves placer mining, which is the extraction of gold and other valuable minerals that are near the surface.

Vancouver & Around

While received wisdom dictates that Vancouver is a lotus land of laid-back joie de vivre, the reality is a little more complex. With one of the most spectacular natural locations of any city in the world – twinkling glass towers ringed by shimmering inlets and forested peaks topped with laser-white snow caps – it's not surprising that this überattractive metropolis routinely tops lists of the planet's most desirable places to live. The visuals for the 2010 Winter Olympics, where events will be shared with Whistler, are guaranteed to inspire a surge of immigration applications from awestruck visitors. But beyond the obvious aesthetic appeal resides a city that, at less than 200 years old, is still discovering what it's all about.

For visitors, this means that once you've covered off unmissable attractions such as Stanley Park, Granville Island and Robson St it's advisable (and highly rewarding) to start scratching beneath the surface. You'll find that the 'real Vancouver' is on the beaches of Kitsilano, in the coffee shops of Commercial Dr, on the gay-friendly streets of the West End and in the clamorous thoroughfares of Chinatown, adjoined by the poor and addicted of the Downtown Eastside, as much a part of Vancouver as Yaletown's loft-living yuppies.

This diversity is clearly one of the city's strengths and is a major reason why some visitors keep coming back, each time discovering something new about a place they thought they'd nailed the last time they were here. If you're a first-timer, soak in the breathtaking sea-to-sky vistas, stroll along the sandy beaches and hit the verdant mountain-backed forests whenever you can, but also save time to do a little exploring off the beaten path; it's in these places that you'll discover what really makes this beautiful metropolis tick.

HIGHLIGHTS

- Strolling or cycling the **Stanley Park** (p75) seawall, with its bracing sea-to-sky views
- Supping a summertime beer at a **downtown Vancouver pub** (p98)
- Hitting **Granville Island Public Market** (p78) to sample the deli treats
- Taking in the colorful and clamorous streets of **Chinatown** (p77)
- Ambling along **Robson Street** (p100), Vancouver's main shopping promenade and unofficial designer fashion show
- Rooting around the galleries, coffee shops and clothing boutiques of **SoMa** (p77)
- Turning your legs to jelly on the **Capilano Suspension Bridge** (p104)

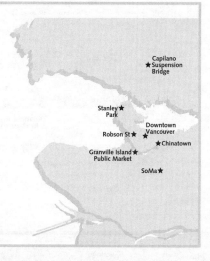

To Squamish (25km);
Whistler (90km);
Pemberton (120km);

Porteau Cove
Provincial Park

Gambier
Island

*Howe
Sound*

(99)

**Lions
Bay**

Sea to Sky Hwy

Ferry to Langdale & Sunshine Coast

Bowyer
Island

Keats
Island

Horseshoe Bay

**Horseshoe
Bay**

Black
Mountain
(1220m) ▲

Cypress
Provincial
Park

Lynn Headwaters
Regional
Park

Grouse Mtn
(1221m) ▲

Seymour River

Bowen
Island

(99)

**West
Vancouver**

*Capilano
Lake*

Lynn Creek

Upper Levels Hwy (1)

Marine Dr

Lighthouse
Park
Pt Atkinson

Burrard Inlet

(1A)

(1A)

**North
Vancouver**

Lynn Canyon
Park

Ferry to Nainamo

Stanley
Park

(1A)

Burrard Inlet

*English
Bay*

Hastings St

(7A)

Point Grey

E Broadway

(7)

Rupert St

(1)

(99)

Kingsway

99A

(1A)

Trans-Canada Hwy

*Strait
of
Georgia*

Iona
Island

Granville St

Sea
Island

Vancouver
International
Airport

North Arm Fraser River

Richmond Fwy (91)

Westminster

Richmond

Fraser River

Steveston Hwy

Steveston

Burns Bog

See Greater Vancouver Map (pp62–3)

South Arm Fraser River

(99)

Reifel Migratory
Bird Sanctuary

Westham
Island

Ladner Trunk Rd

(17) **Delta**

Ladner

28th Ave

Boundary

Splashdown
Waterpark

56th St

Boundary
Bay Park

Ferry to Nainamo

Ferry to Victoria
& Gulf Islands

Tsawwassen

Centennial
Beach Park

Point Roberts
Border Crossing

**Point
Roberts**

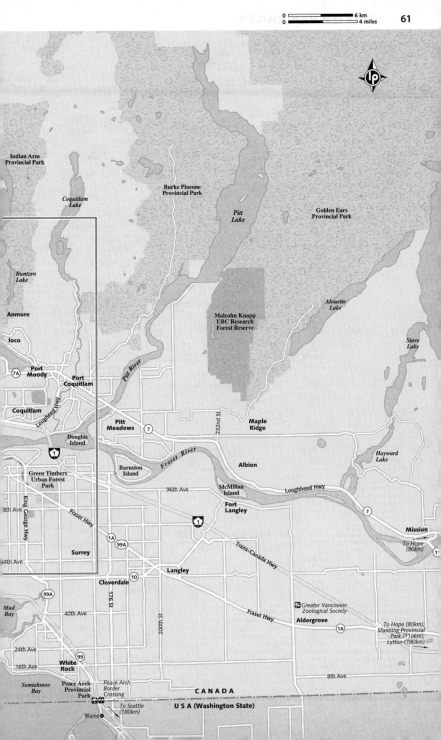

0 — 6 km
0 — 4 miles

Indian Arm Provincial Park

Coquitlam Lake

Burke Pincone Provincial Park

Pitt Lake

Golden Ears Provincial Park

Buntzen Lake

Anmore

Ioco

Alouette Lake

Port Moody

(7A)

Port Coquitlam

Malcolm Knapp UBC Research Forest Reserve

Stave Lake

Coquitlam

Pitt River

Loughheed Hwy

Douglas Island

(1)

Pitt Meadows

(7)

232nd St.

Maple Ridge

Hayward Lake

Green Timbers Urban Forest Park

Barnston Island

Fraser River

Albion

McMillan Island

Loughheed Hwy

8th Ave

96th Ave

Fort Langley

(7)

King George Hwy

Fraser Hwy

Mission

To Hope (80km)

(1)

Surrey

(1)

(1A)(99A)

Trans-Canada Hwy

4th Ave

(10)

Cloverdale

176 St.

Langley

(99A)

Mud Bay

40th Ave

200th St.

Fraser Hwy

Greater Vancouver Zoological Society

Aldergrove

(1A)

To Hope (80km); Manning Provincial Park (110km); Lytton (180km)

24th Ave

(99)

16th Ave

White Rock

8th Ave

Semiahmoo Bay

Peace Arch Provincial Park

Peace Arch Border Crossing

C A N A D A

To Seattle (180km)

U S A (Washington State)

Blaine

Bowen
Island

A

Horseshoe
Bay

To Whistler
(110km)

B

8

Black Mountain
(1220m)

Cypress
Provincial Park

C

D

42 Grouse Mtn
(1221m)
Grouse
Mtn

16 29

39

Whytecliff
Park

18
34

99

HORSESHOE
BAY

Nelson
Canyon
Park

Dick
Lake

Cleveland
Dam

Capilano
Lake

WEST
VANCOUVER

Capilano
River
Regional
Park

1

Apodaca
Provincial
Park

Cypress
Falls
Park

Eagle
Harbour

28

13

Point
Atkinson

Pilot
Cove

Sandy
Cove

Cypress Bowl Rd

Upper Levels Hwy

West
Bay

Folkestone
Way

Skilift
Rd

47

Marine Dr

44

1

Mathers Ave

99

36

7

26

Queens Rd

E 29th St

Lonsdale Ave

NORTH
VANCOUVER

35

25 23

Ambleside
Park

54

Capilano IR 5

46

Keith Rd

Mission
IR 1

30

E 3rd St

Howe
Sound

2

Lions Gate
Bridge

99

1A

See Stanley Park Map (p68)

First
Narrows

SeaBus

Grand Blvd

Burrard   Inlet

Stanley
Park

See Downtown Vancouver & West End Map (pp64–5)

See Gastown, Chinatown &
East Vancouver Map (pp66–7)

E Hastings St

Clark Dr

English
Bay

Point
Grey

Spanish Banks
Beach Park

NW Marine Dr

Jericho
Beach
Park

Kitsilano
Beach
Park

W 4th Ave

W Broadway

3

Wreck
Beach

21

15

33

University of
British Columbia

20

W 10th Ave

W 16th Ave

See Kitsilano Map (p70)

Dunbar St

See Soma, Granville
Island & Around (p69)

W King Edward Ave

VanDusen
Botanical
Garden

50

5

16

E 33rd Ave

99A

1A

Kingsway

Fraser St

53

Pacific Spirit
Regional Park

Marine Drive
Foreshore Park

SW Marine Dr

27

W 41st Ave

W 49th Ave

Granville St

Oak St

Cambie St

Ontario St

E 41st Ave

E 49th Ave

Knight St

Victoria Dr

4

Musqueam
Indian
Reserve 2

Iona Island

Sea
Island

Arthur Laing
Bridge

Oak St
Bridge

Moray
Bridge

Knight
St Bridge

Mitchell
Island

17

Bridgeport Rd

99

Cambie Rd

*Strait   of

Georgia*

56 24

Grant McConachie Way

Vancouver
International
Airport

Dinsmore
Bridge

41

37

2

Middle Arm

Alderbridge Way

Westminster Hwy

Richmond
Nature Park

5

Minoru
Park

RICHMOND

Granville Ave

Blundell Rd

No 1 Rd

Railway Ave

No 2 Rd

Gilbert Rd

Garden City Rd

No 3 Rd

No 4 Rd

No 5 Rd

No 6 Rd

32

10 38

Steveston

45

Moncton St

Steveston Hwy

12

99

George
Massey
Tunnel

Deas
Island

6

Stevenson
Island

To Seattle (190km)
(USA–WA)

INFORMATION
Visitor Information Center......1 A1
Visitor Information Center......2 C5
Visitor Information Center......3 E6
Visitor Information Center......4 F4

SIGHTS & ACTIVITIES
Bloedel Floral Conservatory...5 D4
Burnaby Village Museum......6 F4
Capilano Suspension Bridge &
Park...7 D2
Cypress Mountain.................8 B1
Deep Cove Canoe & Kayak
Centre.....................................9 F2
Gulf of Georgia Cannery....10 C6
Hastings Park Racecourse...11 E3
Kuan Yin Temple.................12 D6
Lighthouse Park...................13 B2
Lonsdale Quay Market......(see 30)
Lynn Canyon Ecology Centre.14 E2
Nitobe Memorial Gardens...15 B3
Queen Elizabeth Park.........16 D4
Richmond Night Market.....17 D5
Sewell's Sea Safari..............18 B1
SFU Gallery.......................(see 19)
SFU Museum of Archaeology &
Ethnology.......................(see 19)
Simon Fraser University......19 F3
UBC Botanical Garden.........20 B3
UBC Museum of
Anthropology..................21 B3

SLEEPING
401 Motor Inn.....................22 E3
Comfort Inn & Suites...........23 D2
Fairmont Vancouver Airport.24 C5
Grouse Inn..........................25 D2
Horseshoe Bay Motel........(see 18)
Inn Penzance......................26 D2
Johnson Heritage House Garden
Suite....................................27 C4
Lighthouse Park B&B...........28 B2
Lodge at the Old Dorm.......29 A1
Lonsdale Quay Hotel...........30 D2
Lynn Canyon House B&B......31 E2
Stone Hedge B&B................32 C5
University of British Columbia
Housing..............................33 B3

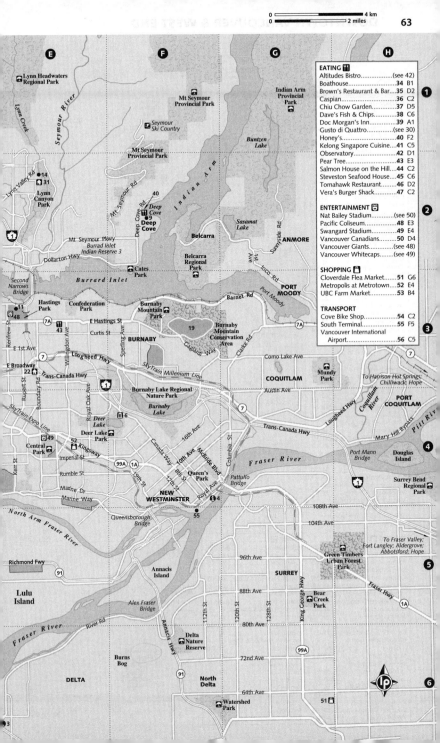

EATING 🍴

Altitudes Bistro	(see 42)
Boathouse	**34** B1
Brown's Restaurant & Bar	**35** D2
Caspian	**36** C2
Chiu Chow Garden	**37** D5
Dave's Fish & Chips	**38** C6
Doc Morgan's Inn	**39** A1
Gusto di Quattro	(see 30)
Honey's	**40** F2
Kelong Singapore Cuisine	**41** C5
Observatory	**42** D1
Pear Tree	**43** E3
Salmon House on the Hill	**44** C2
Steveston Seafood House	**45** C6
Tomahawk Restaurant	**46** D2
Vera's Burger Shack	**47** C2

ENTERTAINMENT 🎭

Nat Bailey Stadium	(see 50)
Pacific Coliseum	**48** E3
Swangard Stadium	**49** E4
Vancouver Canadians	**50** D4
Vancouver Giants	(see 48)
Vancouver Whitecaps	(see 49)

SHOPPING 🛍

Cloverdale Flea Market	**51** G6
Metropolis at Metrotown	**52** E4
UBC Farm Market	**53** B4

TRANSPORT

Cove Bike Shop	**54** C2
South Terminal	**55** F5
Vancouver International Airport	**56** C5

INFORMATION
American Express................1 E3
Australian Consulate...........2 E3
BC Marijuana Party
  Bookshop.........................3 F3
Book Warehouse..................4 F3
Canada Post Main Outlet....5 F4
Centre...............................6 C3
Cyber Madness....................7 C2
Dutch Consulate..................8 F3
Electric Internet Café...........9 F3
French Consulate................10 E2
Georgia Post Plus...............11 D2
Howe St Postal Outlet........12 D4
Indian Consulate................13 F3
Italian Consulate................14 F3
Japanese Consulate............15 E2
Mexican Consulate.........(see 15)
New Zealand Consulate...(see 2)
St Paul's Hospital...............16 D4
Shoppers Drug Mart...........17 D4
Tickets Tonight.............(see 18)
Tourism Vancouver Tourist
  Information Centre...........18 F2
UK Consulate....................19 E3
Ultima Medicentre Plus......20 E3
USA Consulate...................21 E2
Vancouver Bullion & Currency
  Exchange........................22 E3
Vancouver Public Library... 23 F4

SIGHTS & ACTIVITIES
Barbara-Jo's Books to
  Cooks............................24 E5
Bayshore Bike Rentals.........25 C1
BC Place Stadium...............26 F4
BC Sports Hall of Fame &
  Museum......................(see 26)
Christ Church Cathedral....27 E3
Contemporary Art Gallery...28 E4
GM Place..........................29 G4
Little Sister's Book & Art
  Emporium.......................30 C3
Reckless Bike Stores...........31 E5
Roedde House Museum.....32 C3
Roundhouse Community Arts &
  Recreation Centre...........33 E5
Science World....................34 G5
Spokes Bicycle Rental.........35 C1
Vancouver Aquatic Centre.. 36 C5
Vancouver Art Gallery.........37 E3
Vancouver Lookout Harbour
  Centre Tower..................38 F3
William Davis Centre for Actors'
  Study.............................39 D4

SLEEPING
Blue Horizon Hotel............40 D3
Bosman's Vancouver Hotel..41 D4
Buchan Hotel....................42 C2
Burrard Motor Inn.............43 D4
Comfort Inn Downtown......44 E4
Fairmont Hotel Vancouver..45 E3
HI Vancouver Central..........46 E4
HI Vancouver Downtown....47 C4
Listel Vancouver................48 D2
Metropolitan Hotel............49 E3
O Canada House................50 D3
Opus Hotel Vancouver........51 E5
Robsonstrasse Hotel &
  Suites............................52 D2
St Regis Hotel...................53 F3
Samesun Backpackers
  Lodge............................54 E4
Sylvia Hotel......................55 C1
Tropicana Suites Hotel....... 56 D2
Victorian Hotel..................57 F3
Wedgewood Hotel.............58 E3
West End Guest House.......59 D3
YWCA Hotel......................60 F4

EATING
Afterglow......................(see 67)
Blue Water Café & Raw Bar..61 E5
C Restaurant.....................62 C5
Capers.............................63 C2
Cin Cin Ristorante & Bar.... 64 D3
Diner...............................65 E5
Elbow Room......................66 D5
Elixir...........................(see 51)
Glowbal Grill & Satay Bar....67 E5
Hal Mai Jang Moi................68 C2
Hamburger Mary's.............69 C4
Hapa Izakaya....................70 D2
Joe Fortes Seafood & Chop
  House............................71 E3
Lift Bar and Grill................72 D1
Liliget Feast House.............73 B3
Nu...................................74 C5
Raincity Grill....................75 B2
Rooster's Quarters.............76 C2
Sanafir Restaurant &
  Lounge...........................77 E4
Templeton........................78 E4
Tropika............................79 D3

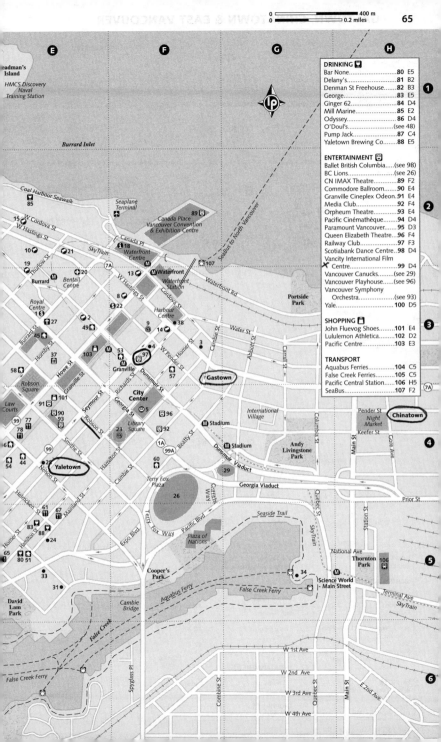

0 ——— 400 m
0 ——— 0.2 miles

DRINKING
Bar None	80 E5
Delany's	81 B2
Denman St Freehouse	82 B3
George	83 E5
Ginger 62	84 D4
Mill Marine	85 E2
Odyssey	86 D4
O'Doul's	(see 48)
Pump Jack	87 C4
Yaletown Brewing Co	88 E5

ENTERTAINMENT
Ballet British Columbia	(see 98)
BC Lions	(see 26)
CN IMAX Theatre	89 F2
Commodore Ballroom	90 E4
Granville Cineplex Odeon	91 E4
Media Club	92 F4
Orpheum Theatre	93 E4
Pacific Cinémathèque	94 D4
Paramount Vancouver	95 D3
Queen Elizabeth Theatre	96 F4
Railway Club	97 F3
Scotiabank Dance Centre	98 D4
Vancity International Film Centre	99 D4
Vancouver Canucks	(see 29)
Vancouver Playhouse	(see 96)
Vancouver Symphony Orchestra	(see 93)
Yale	100 D5

SHOPPING
John Fluevog Shoes	101 E4
Lululemon Athletica	102 D2
Pacific Centre	103 E3

TRANSPORT
Aquabus Ferries	104 C5
False Creek Ferries	105 C5
Pacific Central Station	106 H5
SeaBus	107 F2

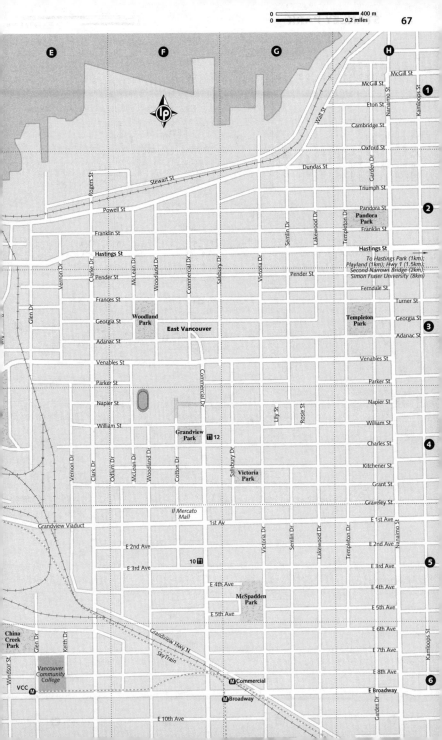

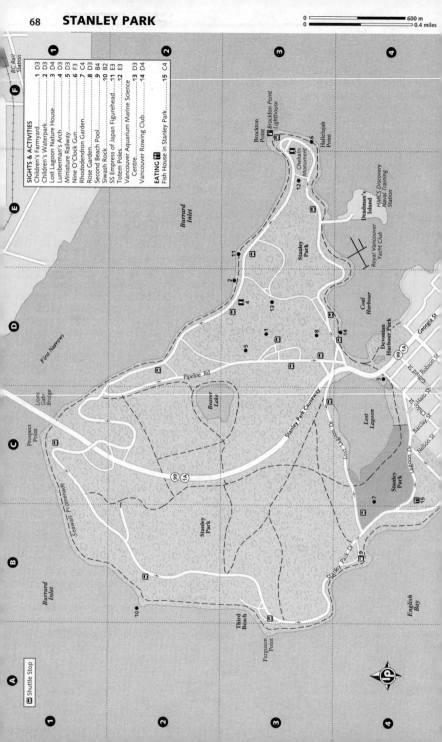

0   600 m
0   0.4 miles

SIGHTS & ACTIVITIES
Children's Farmyard	1	D3
Children's Waterpark	2	D3
Lost Lagoon Nature House	3	D4
Lumberman's Arch	4	D3
Miniature Railway	5	D3
Nine O'Clock Gun	6	E3
Rhododendron Garden	7	C4
Rose Garden	8	D3
Second Beach Pool	9	B4
Siwash Rock	10	B2
SS Empress of Japan Figurehead	11	E3
Totem Poles	12	E3
Vancouver Aquarium Marine Science Centre	13	D3
Vancouver Rowing Club	14	D4

EATING 🍴
Fish House in Stanley Park	15	C4

Shuttle Stop

0 — 400 m
0 — 0.2 miles

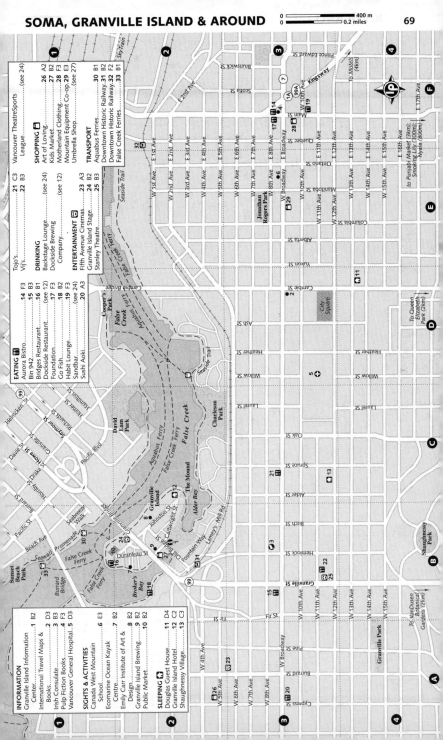

INFORMATION
Granville Island Information Center................................1 B2
International Travel Maps & Books................................2 D3
Irish Consulate...................................3 B3
Pulp Fiction Books..........................4 F3
Vancouver General Hospital....5 D3

SIGHTS & ACTIVITIES
Canada West Mountain School................................6 E3
Ecomarine Ocean Kayak Centre.............................7 B2
Emily Carr Institute of Art & Design................................8 B2
Granville Island Brewing......9 B2
Public Market......................10 B2

SLEEPING
Douglas Guest House...........11 D4
Granville Island Hotel...........12 C2
Shaughnessy Village............13 C3

EATING
Aurora Bistro......................14 F3
Bin 942..............................15 B3
Bridges Restaurant..............16 B1
Dockside Restaurant........(see 12)
Foundation..........................17 F3
Go Fish...............................18 B2
Habit Lounge......................19 F3
Sandbar.........................(see 24)
Sushi Aoki..........................20 A3

Tojo's................................21 C3
Vij's..................................22 B3

DRINKING
Backstage Lounge...........(see 24)
Dockside Brewing Company.....................(see 12)

ENTERTAINMENT
Fifth Avenue Cinemas..........23 A3
Granville Island Stage..........24 B2
Stanley Theatre...................25 B3

SHOPPING
Art of Loving......................26 A2
Kids Market........................27 B2
Motherland Clothing............28 F3
Mountain Equipment Co-op..29 E3
Umbrella Shop...............(see 27)

TRANSPORT
Aquabus Ferries..................30 B1
Downtown Historic Railway...31 B2
Downtown Historic Railway...32 F2
False Creek Ferries..............33 B1

Vancouver TheatreSports League.........................(see 24)

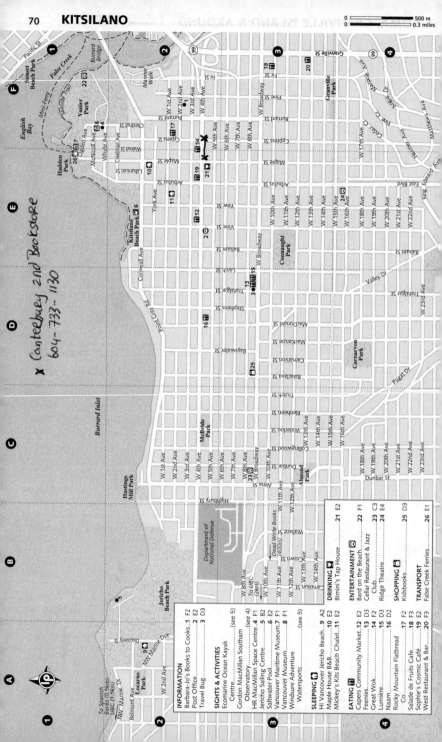

x Canterbury 2nd Bookstore
604-733-1130

0 ————— 500 m
0 ————— 0.3 miles

INFORMATION
Barbara-Jo's Books to Cooks..1 F2
Post Office....................................2 E2
Travel Bug....................................3 D3

SIGHTS & ACTIVITIES
Ecomarine Ocean Kayak
Centre..(see 5)
Gordon MacMillan Southam
Observatory...............................(see 4)
HR MacMillan Space Centre....4 F1
Jericho Sailing Centre.................5 B2
Saltwater Pool.............................6 E2
Vancouver Maritime Museum....7 F1
Vancouver Museum......................8 F1
Windsure Adventure
Watersports..............................(see 5)

SLEEPING 🛏
HI Vancouver Jericho Beach...9 A2
Maple House B&B.....................10 E2
Mickey's Kits Beach Chalet....11 E2

EATING 🍴
Capers Community Market....12 E2
Feenies.......................................13 D3
Great Wok..................................14 F2
Lumière.......................................15 D3
Naam...16 D2
Rocky Mountain Flatbread
Co...17 F2
Salade de Fruits Cafe...............18 F3
Sophie's Cosmic Café..............19 E3
West Restaurant & Bar............20 F3

DRINKING 🍷
Bimini's Tap House...................21 E2

ENTERTAINMENT 🎭
Bard on the Beach....................22 F1
Cellar Restaurant & Jazz
Club..23 C3
Ridge Theatre............................24 E4

SHOPPING 🛍
Kidsbooks..................................25 D3

TRANSPORT
False Creek Ferries...................26 E1

VANCOUVER

HISTORY

Squamish, Tsleil-Waututhweres and Musqueam First Nations thrived in this area for 8000 years before British explorer Captain James Cook arrived in 1778. Mistaking Cook's ragged crew for a boatful of transformed salmon, the Nootka Sound locals were no match for the interlopers' unexpected firepower, ending years of relatively peaceful living.

Explorers seeking the Northwest Passage sea route through North America – including adventurers from Spain and Russia – came next. Each helped put the region on the map, paving the way for waves of European settlers.

A burgeoning fur trade soon emerged, accompanied by a gold rush that forever changed the region. By the 1850s, thousands of fortune seekers had arrived, prompting the Brits to claim the area as a colony, and one talkative entrepreneur to cleverly seize the initiative. When 'Gassy' Jack Deighton opened his first bar on the forested shores of Burrard Inlet in 1867, he triggered a rash of development that was nicknamed 'Gastown,' the forerunner of Vancouver.

But not everything went exactly to plan for the fledgling city. While Vancouver rapidly reached a population of 1000 and was linked to the rest of Canada by the Canadian Pacific Railway in 1886, it was almost completely destroyed in a blaze dubbed 'the Great Fire' (although it only lasted 20 minutes). A prompt rebuild followed and the modern-day downtown core began to take shape. Buildings from this era still survive, as does expansive Stanley Park. By 1895, Vancouver's growing population had outpaced its regional rival Victoria, the Vancouver Island–based provincial capital.

Relying on its port, the city soon became a hub of industry, importing thousands of immigrant workers to fuel its development. The Chinatown built at this time is one of the largest and most historic in North America. But WWI and the 1929 Wall Street crash brought economic depression to Canada, and Vancouver saw mass unemployment, demonstrations and rioting. The economy only recovered during WWII, when both shipbuilding and armaments manufacturing boosted the region's traditional economic base of resource exploitation.

Growing steadily throughout the 1950s and 1960s, Vancouver added an National Hockey League hockey team and other accoutrements of a midsized North American city. Finally reflecting on its heritage, Gastown – by now a slum area – was designated for gentrification. In 1986, the city hosted a highly successful Expo World's Fair, sparking a massive wave of development and adding the first of the mirrored skyscrapers that now define the downtown core. It's hoped that the 2010 Winter Olympics, where events will be shared with Whistler, will have a similar positive effect on the region.

ORIENTATION

Greater Vancouver is built on a series of peninsulas bounded on the north by Burrard Inlet and on the south by Fraser River and Boundary Bay. The Coast Mountains rise directly behind the city to the north, while to the west the Strait of Georgia is cluttered with islands.

Downtown Vancouver occupies a narrow peninsula bounded on three sides by Burrard Inlet, English Bay and False Creek, with Stanley Park at the tip. Key downtown attractions and neighborhoods are all easily accessible on foot and streets are organized on a grid system. Robson St and Georgia St are the main downtown east–west thoroughfares, while Granville St is the main north–south artery.

Going out of town, Hwy 99 runs north over Lions Gate Bridge to West Vancouver and North Vancouver, joining and sharing its name with the Trans-Canada Hwy (Hwy 1) here. Further northwest along Hwy 1 you'll reach Horseshoe Bay and its BC Ferries terminal. North of Horseshoe Bay Hwy 99 runs as the Sea to Sky Hwy en route to Whistler.

Maps

The tourist information center provides a handy free map of Vancouver's grid-like downtown core. The more comprehensive *Greater Vancouver Streetwise Map Book* ($5.95) has an easy A–Z format and is available at bookstores and convenience stores. TransLink publishes the useful *Getting Around* map ($1.95), detailing Lower Mainland transit routes.

INFORMATION

Bookstores

Barbara-Jo's Books to Cooks (Map p70; ☎ 604-688-6755; 1740 W 2nd Ave; ☺ 9:30am-5pm Mon-Sat, noon-4pm Sun) Foodie bookstore with cooking classes.

Book Warehouse (Map pp64-5; ☎ 604-683-5711; 552 Seymour St; ☺ 10am-9pm Mon-Fri, 10am-6pm Sat & Sun) Independent discount bookseller.

Dead Write Books (☎ 604-228-8221; 4333 W 10th Ave; ☺ 10am-6pm Mon-Thu & Sat, 10am-8pm Fri, noon-5pm Sun) Treasure trove of crime, detective and mystery titles.

International Travel Maps & Books (Map p69; ☎ 604-879-3621; 530 W Broadway; ☺ 9am-6pm Mon-Fri, 10am-5pm Sat, noon-5pm Sun) Western Canada's best map store.

Pulp Fiction Books (Map p69; ☎ 604-876-4311; 2422 Main St; ☺ 10am-8pm Mon-Wed, 10am-9pm Thu-Sat, 11am-7pm Sun) Excellent secondhand selection, specializing in paperbacks.

Travel Bug (Map p70; ☎ 604-737-1122; 3065 W Broadway; ☺ 10am-6pm Mon, Tue & Sat, 10am-7:30pm Wed-Fri, noon-5pm Sun) Extensive travel guides, maps and accessories.

Internet Access

Cyber Madness (Map pp64-5; ☎ 604-633-9389; 779 Denman St; per 30 mins $2; ☺ 10am-8pm Mon-Sat) Compact and often busy.

Electric Internet Café (Map pp64-5; ☎ 604-681-0667; 605 W Pender St; per 30 min $1.50; ☺ 7am-3am Mon-Fri, 8am-3am Sat & Sun) Dozens of terminals.

Georgia Post Plus (Map pp64-5; ☎ 604-632-4226; 1358 W Georgia St; per 30 min $2; ☺ 9:30am-6pm Mon-Fri, 10am-4pm Sat) Post office with computer terminals.

Vancouver Public Library (Map pp64-5; ☎ 604-331-3600; 350 W Georgia St; per 30 min free; ☺ 10am-9pm Mon-Thu, 10am-6pm Fri & Sat, noon-5pm Sun) Terminals for nonmembers. Busy at peak times.

Internet Resources

Discover Vancouver (www.discovervancouver.com) General visitors' guide.

Tourism Vancouver (www.tourismvancouver.com) Official visitor site.

Vancouver 2010 (www.vancouver2010.com) Official tourism site for 2010 Winter Olympics build up.

Visitors Choice Vancouver (www.visitorschoice.com) Maps and an overview of attractions and accommodations.

Visit Vancouver (www.visitvancouver.com) Overview of the city for visitors.

Media

Georgia Straight (www.straight.com) Listings paper.

Province (www.canada.com/theprovince) Daily tabloid.

Tyee (www.thetyee.ca) Only online but possibly Vancouver's best news source.

Vancouver Magazine (www.vanmag.com) Monthly glossy covering local mainstream trends.

Vancouver Sun (www.canada.com/vancouversun) Leading city daily.

Westender (www.westender.com) Quirky downtown community newspaper.

Xtra! West (www.xtra.ca) Free gay and lesbian paper.

Medical Services

Ultima Medicentre Plus (Map pp64-5; ☎ 604-683-8138; Bentall Centre, 1055 Dunsmuir St; ☺ 8am-5pm Mon-Fri) At this walk-in clinic, appointments are not necessary.

VANCOUVER IN THREE DAYS

Start your day at a leisurely hour with a late-morning dim-sum brunch at **Hon's Wun-Tun House** (p93), then walk it off with a trawl around the boisterous streets of **Chinatown** (p77). Dip into the **Dr Sun Yat-Sen Classical Chinese Garden** (p77) then amble through **Gastown** (p76) towards the city center and the **Vancouver Art Gallery** (p74). Grab a coffee here on the chatty patio, and plan your dinner restaurant – **Yaletown** (p92) is recommended.

Wake up earlier the next day and head for **Stanley Park** (p75) to check out the seawall, totem poles and tranquil beaches. If you haven't brought your swimming gear, head instead to the park's **Vancouver Aquarium Marine Science Centre** (p76) – don't miss the playful otters. Tuck into a picnic lunch, dine at one of the four park restaurants or stroll over to **Denman St** (p91), where dozens of eateries await. Nip back to your hotel for a mid-afternoon rest, then hit a couple of evening pubs, including the **Railway Club** (see boxed text, p98), where quirky live music is offered nightly.

On day three, overcome your slight hangover with a large coffee, some fresh air and the diverting **Granville Island Public Market** (p78). Stroll up to Broadway from here and take a B-Line express bus all the way to the **University of British Columbia** (p78), where you can wander the gardens, hit the Museum of Anthropology and peel off all your clothes at Wreck Beach.

FIVE THINGS TO DO IN RAINY-DAY VANCOUVER

- Hit an indoor rain forest – Experience British Columbia's natural splendors without getting wet with a visit to the **Vancouver Art Gallery** (p74). Celebrating the work of Canadian painter Emily Carr, the gallery's top floor is dripping with her swirling depictions of lush rain forests.

- Embrace the misery – The perfect accompaniment to a miserable day out, the chilling **Vancouver Police Centennial Museum** (p77) has an arsenal of confiscated weapons and a mortuary room dark with gruesome artifacts.

- Seek protection – A family-run local legend, the **Umbrella Shop** (p101) has been cranking out handmade brollies for 70 years. Pick the brightest design you can find before launching yourself back into the tempest.

- Drink it all away – Serving up an educational tour through the fundamentals of beer-making (followed by a generous and leisurely taproom sampling session) a visit to **Granville Island Brewing** (p78) will make you forget all about the rain.

- Find shelter – Hanging over the seawall near Stanley Park, **Lift Bar and Grill** (p91) has panoramic windows, allowing you to watch the mist-covered trees and comfort yourself with a gourmet lunch.

Shoppers Drug Mart (Map pp64-5; ☎ 604-669-2424; 1125 Davie St; ⏰ 24hr) Pharmacy chain.

St Paul's Hospital (Map pp64-5; ☎ 604-682-2344; 1081 Burrard St; ⏰ 24hr) Downtown accident and emergency.

Money

ATMs are liberally sprinkled throughout Vancouver, with the main bank branches congregating around the central business district bordered by Burrard, Georgia, Pender and Granville Sts.

American Express (Map pp64-5; ☎ 604-669-2813; 666 Burrard St; ⏰ 8:30am-5:30pm Mon-Fri, 10am-4pm Sat) Full-service Amex branch.

Vancouver Bullion & Currency Exchange (Map pp64-5; ☎ 604-685-1008; 800 W Pender St; ⏰ 9am-5pm Mon-Fri) This place usually offers the best rates in town.

Post

Postal outlets are often tucked at the back of drugstores – look for the blue-and-red signs in windows.

Canada Post main outlet (Map pp64-5; ☎ 604-662-5723; 349 W Georgia St; ⏰ 8am-5:30pm Mon-Fri)

Georgia Post Plus (Map pp64-5; ☎ 604-632-4226; 1358 W Georgia St; ⏰ 9:30am-6pm Mon-Fri, 10am-4pm Sat)

Howe Street Postal Outlet (Map pp64-5; ☎ 604-688-2068; 732 Davie St; 7am-8pm Mon-Fri, 8am-7pm Sat)

Shoppers Drug Mart (Map pp64-5; ☎ 604-685-0246; 1125 Davie St; ⏰ 9am-9:30pm Mon-Fri; 9:30am-5:30pm Sat, 11:30am-5:30pm Sun)

Tourist Information

Tourism Vancouver Tourist Information Centre (Map pp64-5; ☎ 604-683-2000; www.tourism vancouver.com; 200 Burrard St; ⏰ 8:30am-6pm Jun-Aug, 8:30am-5pm Mon-Sat Sep-May) Free maps, visitor guides, half-price theater tickets, currency exchange and glossy brochures for Vancouver and the wider British Columbia region. Two additional branches at the airport.

DANGERS & ANNOYANCES

Vancouver is relatively safe for visitors. Purse-snatching and pickpocketing does take place, however, so you should be vigilant with your personal possessions. Theft from unattended cars is not uncommon, so never leave valuables in vehicles where they can be stolen.

Panhandling has become an increasing issue for visitors; just say 'Sorry' and pass on if you're not interested and want to be polite. The more enterprising 'squeegee kids' might try to wash your windshield for a couple of dollars when you stop at a red light; tell them 'No thanks' before they get to your car. They often operate at the intersection of W Georgia and Thurlow Sts.

The city's Downtown Eastside is a depressing ghetto of lives wasted by drugs and prostitution. Crime against visitors is not common in this area but you are advised to be vigilant and stick to the main streets, especially at night. You will be discreetly offered drugs by small-fry pushers here – just walk on and they won't bother you again.

SIGHTS

Many of Vancouver's main attractions are studded around several key downtown neighborhoods, with some hot spots – Gastown, Chinatown, Stanley Park and Granville Island – drawing visitors who just like to wander and explore. Increasingly chichi Yaletown attracts urban hipsters, while the real bohemians are more likely to be found cruising the Commercial Dr and SoMa (South Main) areas. The Kitsilano district, full of pricey heritage homes, enjoys great beach access and leads out towards the verdant University of British Columbia (UBC) campus.

Downtown & West End

Bordered on two sides by water and one side by the enormous Stanley Park (opposite), downtown Vancouver combines the shimmering glass office towers of the business district with the well-maintained older residential blocks of the West End. The city's busy center is where Granville St meets Georgia St and Robson St.

Built for Expo '86, **Canada Place** (Map pp64-5; ☎ 604-647-7390; www.canadaplace.ca; 999 Canada Place Way) is a city icon. Shaped like a series of sails, it is a major cruise ship terminal and convention center (a large convention center expansion is scheduled to open on the building's west side in 2008). It's worth a visit for its panoramic views of Stanley Park and the mountains, punctuated by the regular splash of floatplanes out front. Attractions sharing the facility include the **CN IMAX Theatre** (p100) and the **Port Authority Interpretation Centre** (☎ 604-665-9179; ☽ 8am-5pm Mon-Fri), a hands-on, kid-friendly showcase illuminating the city's maritime trade.

Housed in a handsome old colonial courthouse often used for movie shoots, the **Vancouver Art Gallery** (Map pp64-5; ☎ 604-662-4700; www.vanartgallery.bc.ca; 750 Hornby St; adult/youth/child $15/10/6, admission by donation after 5pm Tue; ☽ 10am-5:30pm Mon & Wed, Fri-Sun, 10am-9pm Tue & Thu) showcases the West Coast's artistic heart. Start on the top floor for the swirling, stylized canvasses of Emily Carr, a pioneering painter of mountain, forest and aboriginal scenes. The rest is a revolving coterie of temporary exhibitions mixing local contemporary artists (photographic art is a regional specialty) with traveling blockbuster

---

NOT QUITE SHANGRI-LA

Hugging the covered wooden walkways surrounding the construction site for the Shangri-La, a condo tower destined to be the city's tallest building when completed in 2008, several street people already call this part of downtown their home. Although the building's name might seem ironic to locals stepping over the sleeping bags en route to work, the scene is indicative of a citywide issue that seems to have reached crisis point.

While Vancouver is not the only North American metropolis with homeless people, years of avoiding the issue, combined with provincial and federal polices that have slowly eroded support systems for the vulnerably poor, have created a burgeoning problem desperate for action. Tourists are already spotting the effects, with repeated requests for 'spare change' now a common feature of a day out in the city.

The issue can be traced back to the creation of Vancouver's own ghetto area, the Downtown Eastside. Wedged between Chinatown, Gastown and East Vancouver, the district started its graceless decline in the 1940s, when the city began concentrating the destitute here. It has since become a 'breeding ground' that has exponentially increased the region's population of poor and homeless people.

The area's rooming houses and cheap hotels reside above pawnshops and squalid pubs, where the cheapest beer is always the most popular. Grass and ecstasy are offered openly on the streets – hawkers whisper the words as they pass – but harder drugs are readily available. Prostitution is a way of life for some here: bone-rack women with freshly applied makeup loiter in short skirts on even the coldest nights.

With the 2010 Winter Olympics due to throw the international spotlight on Vancouver once again, an increasing number of locals are asking city, regional and national politicians what is going to be done to address what many see as the city's biggest test of character.

In response, politicians have set up study groups and task forces – the first steps, albeit small, towards dealing with the issues involved.

shows. Drop by on the fourth Friday of every month for FUSE, a late-opening party night with music, booze and local artsy types.

Home of the BC Lions Canadian Football League (CFL) team (p100), the landmark, Teflon-domed **BC Place Stadium** (Map pp64-5; ☎ 604-669-2300; www.bcplacestadium.com; 777 Pacific Blvd) will be renovated for the 2010 Winter Olympics. Visiting sports fans should check out the excellent **BC Sports Hall of Fame & Museum** (Map pp64-5; ☎ 604-687-5520; www.bcsportshalloffame .com; Gate A, BC Place Stadium; adult/child $8/6; ☽ 10am-5pm), complete with a vast array of historic memorabilia from the region's various teams and sporting heroes. There's also a guided **stadium tour** (☎ 604-661-7362; Gate H, BC Place Stadium; adult/child $8/7; ☽ tours 11am & 1pm Tue mid-Jun–Aug) that provides a fascinating behind-the-scenes glimpse of the locker rooms and celebrity suites.

It's hard to remember that Vancouver was a pioneering new town nestled among virgin rain forest less than 150 years ago. The idea of heritage preservation didn't really take off until the 1970s, when it was too late to save many of the timber-framed homes that launched the city. Bucking the trend, the 1893 mansion **Roedde House Museum** (Map pp64-5; ☎ 604-684-7040; www.roeddehouse.org; 1415 Barclay St; admission $5; ☽ 10am-4pm Tue-Sat, 2-4pm Sun May-Aug) (and the surrounding Barclay Heritage Sq) is packed with period antiques and is a superb re-creation of how well-heeled Vancouverites used to live. Sunday entry, including tea and cookies, costs $1 extra.

Whether it's a hot, still day in August with families and sunbathers sharing the beach, or a cold, blustery day in November with just you and a dog-walker watching the waves, **English Bay** (Map pp64-5; cnr of Denman & Davie Sts) is a highlight of any visit to the West End. The beach is just a few steps from the city bustle and a 10-minute walk from the center of downtown, with Stanley Park beckoning next door if you want to make a seawall hike out of your gentle walk. Spend five minutes or spend the day, but when you see the ocean, the mountain and the city all at the same time you get a snapshot of what Vancouver is all about.

Completed in 1895, **Christ Church Cathedral** (Map pp64-5; ☎ 604-682-3848; www.cathedral.vancouver .bc.ca; 690 Burrard St; admission free; ☽ 10am-4pm), the biggest and best Gothic-style church in the city, is nestled incongruously among Vancouver's looming glass towers. Host to a wide range of cultural events, including regular choir and organ recitals, it has undergone a recent extensive renovation. Tours of the stained glass windows are offered by appointment, but if you're short of time head down to the basement for the highlight: a lovely William Morris example.

GM Place (Map pp64-5; ☎ 604-899-7889; www .canucks.com; 800 Griffiths Way), aka 'The Garage,' is the newer of Vancouver's two downtown stadiums. It hosts the Vancouver Canucks of the National Hockey League (NHL) and is scheduled to be the main hockey venue for the 2010 Winter Olympics. It's also the region's favored arena for money-spinning stadium rock acts. Behind-the-scenes **tours** (☎ 604-899-7440; Gate 6, GM Place; adult/child $10/4; ☽ tours 10:30am, noon & 1:30pm Wed & Fri) take you into the hospitality suites and the nosebleed press box, high up in the rafters.

It's a pricey way to get a bird's-eye view of the inlet's floating gas stations and the downtown core's bustling sprawl, but your observation deck ticket for the **Vancouver Lookout Harbour Centre Tower** (Map pp64-5; ☎ 604-689-0421; www.vancouverlookout.com; 555 W Hastings St; adult/youth/child $11/7/4; ☽ 8:30am-10:30pm May–mid-Oct, 9am-9pm mid-Oct–Apr) also includes a guided tour of the sights from up top. The ride in the glass-sided elevator is almost more fun than the panoramic vistas. Tickets are valid all day, so you can return for a nighttime viewing.

Stanley Park

Originally Vancouver's military reserve, **Stanley Park** (Map p68) was opened as a public recreation space in 1891. Now one of North America's largest urban parks, it is a highlight of any Vancouver visit for its combination of natural and human-built attractions. Don't miss a jog, stroll or cycle (rentals near the entrance on W Georgia St) around the 9km seawall, with its dramatic sea-to-sky vistas and smattering of sandy beaches. Bring a picnic and drop by **Third Beach**, where you can perch on a log and see some of the city's most spectacular sunsets.

The **Rose Garden** and **Rhododendron Garden** will satisfy flora lovers, and nature fans should also drop by the **Lost Lagoon Nature House** (☎ 604-257-8544; www.stanleyparkecology.ca; admission free; ☽ 10am-7pm Tue-Sun May-Sep) to learn about the region's ecology from a band of friendly volunteers. It's a 0.5km walk from here to the

VANCOUVER & AROUND

THINGS THAT GO 'BOOM' BEFORE THE NIGHT

Originally brought to Stanley Park in the 1890s to warn anglers that Sunday fishing closed at 6pm, the **Nine O'Clock Gun** has been booming at precisely 9pm every day for more than 100 years. It can be heard across the West End and throughout downtown – some residents still set their watch by it.

The cannon used to be unprotected until pranksters started messing with it, so it now sits in a cage. But it can still be the punch line of an amusing practical joke: take your victim to Brockton Point to 'look at the views of downtown' before 8:59pm. 'Ooh' and 'ah' at the pretty city lights (and subtly brace yourself). When the cannon fires, the person beside you may suffer a mild coronary, but feel free to laugh at their expense. Not recommended for those with heart problems.

---

park's most photographed attraction, a series of eight brightly colored **totem poles** – you'll likely have to elbow past the tour groups if you're here in summer. For a restorative blast of tranquility, lay on the grassy knoll behind **Lumberman's Arch** and watch the cruise ships go by, or head for lunch at one of the park's four **restaurants**.

If you don't fancy walking all the way around, a **free shuttle bus** operates throughout the park from mid-June to mid-September, or you can take a plodding horse-drawn **carriage ride** (☎ 604-681-5115; www.stanleyparktours.com; adult/child $25/14.50; ☉ Mar-Oct) if you have more time on your hands.

If you're traveling with kids, the wonderful waterfront **Second Beach pool** (☎ 604-257-8370; adult/youth/child; $4.70/3.55/2.35; ☉ May-Sep) is a magnet for families. Arrive early on peak summer days, when it fills up quickly. You can dry the kids off on the nearby **Miniature Railway** (☎ 604-257-8531; adult/youth/child $4.95/3.70/2.50; ☉ 10:30am-5pm mid-May–Aug, 10:30am-5pm Sat & Sun Feb–mid-May & Sep) and **Children's Farmyard** (☎ 604-257-8531; adult/youth/child $4.95/3.70/2.50; ☉ 11am-4pm mid-May–Aug, 11am-4pm Sat & Sun Feb–mid-May & Sep).

Stanley Park's biggest draw, the **Vancouver Aquarium Marine Science Centre** (☎ 604-659-3474; www.vanaqua.org; adult/youth/child $18.50/13.95/10.95; ☉ 10am-5:30pm Sep-Jun, 9:30am-7pm Jul & Aug) is home to 9000 sea creatures, including sharks, dolphins, beluga whales and an octopus. Look out for the iridescent jellyfish tank and the two sea otters that eat the way everyone should: lying on their backs using their chests as plates. If you have time, consider a 45-minute behind-the-scenes visit with the Stellar sea lions (adult $38/adult and child $50), where you'll learn how to be a trainer. The aquarium has worked hard to reposition itself as a conservation center but not all environmentalists agree with its claims.

Plans are afoot to expand the aquarium's park 'footprint' before 2010.

Yaletown

A former brick-built warehouse district transformed into chichi apartments, loungey bars and bling-bling boutiques in the 1990s, pedestrian-friendly Yaletown – Vancouver's 'little Soho' – is where the city's beautiful people come to be seen, especially at night, when the restaurants can be packed to the rafters.

Roughly bordered by Nelson St, Homer St, Drake St and Pacific St, the area has not completely abandoned its past: old railway tracks remain embedded in the roads and the **Roundhouse Community Arts & Recreation Centre** (Map pp64-5; ☎ 604-713-1800; www.roundhouse.ca), home to some innovative theater productions and cultural events, is situated in a revamped train shed complete with a restored steam locomotive.

Drop by the **Contemporary Art Gallery** (Map pp64-5; ☎ 604-681-2700; www.contemporaryartgallery .ca; 555 Nelson St; admission free; ☉ noon-6pm Wed-Sun) for a glimpse of what local modern artists are up to. Photography is particularly well represented in this compact, wheelchair-accessible space.

Gastown & Chinatown

Despite the inauspicious name, **Gastown** is where Vancouver began after 'Gassy' Jack Deighton, an English sailor, forsook the sea in 1867 to open a bar servicing the region's developing timber mills. When a village sprang up around his establishment, the area became known as Gassy's Town. Look out for the jocular bronze **statue of Gassy Jack** perched atop a beer barrel at the juncture of Cordova St and Water St.

Seeking a fresh start after a devastating fire in 1893, the city relocated itself and Gastown quickly became Vancouver's skid row, only to be restored as a cobbled thoroughfare of souvenir shops, buskers and restaurants in the 1970s. The heritage buildings are still here – just look up and you'll see many have been restored as offices and live-work spaces. Halfway along Water St is the site of the noisy **steam clock**, a tourist snapshot favorite that's actually powered by electricity.

The adjoining **Chinatown** district – one of North America's largest – is one of Vancouver's most enticing areas. A sensory explosion of sights, sounds and aromas, it's a richly historic neighborhood. Look above shop level and you'll see the paint-peeled evidence of decades of history, along with the occasional year marker showing the true age of many of the buildings.

While many younger Chinese have moved out to Richmond (p109), this bustling downtown area is still teeming with shops hawking exotic fruits, ancient remedies and the occasional bucket of live frogs. Don't miss the lively summer **night market** (p101) and check out the new **Chinatown Millennium Gate** (Map pp66-7; W Pender & Taylor Sts), the area's towering entry point.

Housed in the city's former morgue and coroner's court, the excellent little **Vancouver Police Centennial Museum** (Map pp66-7; ☎ 604-665-3346; www.vancouverpolicemuseum.ca; 240 E Cordova St; adult/child $7/5; 9am-5pm Mon-Sat) is one of the best historic attractions in town. A lethal armory of weapons, counterfeit money, forensic autopsy tools and a century's worth of drug paraphernalia help illustrate the fascinating story of law enforcement in Vancouver – and the 'body' in the metal morgue drawer adds a suitably chilling air to your visit.

A tranquility break from Chinatown, the intimate **Dr Sun Yat-Sen Classical Chinese Garden** (Map pp66-7; ☎ 604-662-3207; www.vancouverchinesegarden.com; 578 Carrall St; adult/child $8.75/7; 10am-6pm May–mid-Jun & Sep, 9:30am-7pm mid-Jun–Aug, 10am-4:30pm Oct-Apr) reveals the Taoist symbolism behind the placing of gnarled pine trees, winding covered pathways and ancient limestone formations. Entry includes a fascinating guided tour – look out for lazy turtles bobbing in the water – and concerts are held here on summertime Friday evenings. There's a less impressive but free-entry garden immediately next door.

A great place to take the kids, especially on a rainy day, **Science World at TELUS World of Science** (☎ 604-443-7440; www.scienceworld.bc.ca; 1455 Quebec St; adult/child $14.50/10; 10am-6pm) occupies the landmark geodesic 'Golf Ball' that was built for Expo '86. It's a high-tech playground of interactive exhibits and live presentations on nature, space, physics and technology, and there's enough to keep parents occupied too. The **Alcan OMNIMAX Theatre** (tickets adult/child $11.25/9) shows large-screen documentary movies.

SoMa (South Main) & Commercial Drive

One of the city's down-at-heel neighborhoods until recent years, **SoMa** – the area where Broadway and Main St collide – is being successfully re-created as one of Vancouver's hippest new hot spots, despite its still-grungy appearance.

Bohemian coffee bars, veggie-friendly eateries, one-of-a-kind boutiques and bold little artist-run galleries are blooming in the area, which is populated increasingly by the art-student-turned-film-producer set with their brick loft–loving ways.

Stay on bus 3 from downtown until you hit Main and 48th and you'll find yourself in the **Punjabi Market** area of town. Also known as Little India, this busy enclave of sari stores, Bhangra music shops and some of the region's best-value curry restaurants is a great spot for a spicy all-you-can-eat lunch followed by a restorative walkabout.

Culinary adventurers should also consider trekking along funky **Commercial Dr**, where decades of European immigrants – especially Italians, Greeks and Portuguese – have created a united nations of restaurants, coffee bars and exotic delis. This is the best spot in town to watch international soccer games among the city's most passionate fans, and it's also a promenade of espresso-supping patio dwellers on languid summer afternoons.

Granville Island

A once-grungy industrial peninsula (it's not actually an island) that spills out under the metal arches of Granville Bridge, **Granville Island** (Map p69; ☎ 604-666-6655; www.granvilleisland.com) is best reached via a bathtub-sized ferry (p103) from the north side of False Creek. Successfully redeveloped in the 1970s into a highly popular blend of restaurants, theaters and artisan businesses, it's always crowded here on hot summer weekends, as visitors chill out with the buskers and wrestle over their fish and chips with resident seagulls.

Head inside to the **Granville Island Public Market** (Map p69; ☎ 604-666-6477; Johnston St; ☺ 9am-7pm). Like a vast multicountered deli, it specializes in gourmet meat, fish, cheese and bakery treats. There's also an international food court (eat early or late to avoid the crush) and an ever-changing kaleidoscope of craft stands. Regional farmers drop by to the ply their produce at the May to October farmers' market.

If you prefer your produce in liquid form, take a fun tour of nearby **Granville Island Brewing** (Map p69; ☎ 604-687-2739; www.gib.ca; 1441 Cartwright St; admission $9.75; ☺ tours noon, 2pm & 4pm). The guides here walk and talk you through the tiny brewing room (production has mostly shifted to a larger facility) before depositing you in the taproom for some generous sampling. The Maple Cream Ale is recommended, and don't forget to ask for your souvenir glass.

A visit to the public galleries at the highly regarded **Emily Carr Institute of Art & Design** (Map p69; ☎ 604-844-3800, 800-832-7788; www.eciad.ca; 1399 Johnston St; admission free; ☺ 10am-6pm) is also recommended; it offers an eye-opening glimpse into the minds of up-and-coming artists.

Once you've finished trawling the shops and attractions, hop aboard the **Downtown Historic Railway** (Map p69; ☎ 604-665-3903; www.trams .bc.ca; adult/child $2/1; ☺ 12:30-4:30pm Sat, Sun & holidays mid-May–mid-Oct), which runs two handsome old streetcars between the entrance to Granville Island and Science World.

Kitsilano

West of Granville Island, well-to-do 'Kits' is where former '60s hippies have settled comfortably into their mortgages and high-paying jobs, creating pleasant streets of pricey heritage homes, cozy coffee bars and highly browsable shops. Young artsy types still live here, but mostly with their parents. This area is recommended for a lazy afternoon of street strolling, window-shopping and coffee bar hopping. If it's really hot, grab an organic smoothie and head to **Jericho Beach** or **Kitsilano Beach**, both great sunset spots. The main shopping area is W 4th Ave.

The closest Kitsilano point to downtown is **Vanier Park**, a short waterside walk from Granville Island. The park hosts the stripy tents of the annual **Bard on the Beach Shakespeare festival** (p85) and is also home to a nest of small, family-friendly Vancouver museums.

Attracting visitors with re-creations of the region's ancient and recent history, **Vancouver Museum** (Map p70; ☎ 604-736-4431; www.vanmuseum .bc.ca; 1100 Chestnut St; adult/child $10/6; ☺ 10am-5pm Tue-Sun, 10am-9pm Thu) is home to some unique aboriginal artifacts – although they're not as well presented as those at the Museum of Anthropology (below). Instead, the emphasis here is on recent social history with plenty of nostalgic and pop culture displays.

The adjacent **HR MacMillan Space Centre** (Map p70; ☎ 604-738-7827; www.hrmacmillanspacecentre.com; 1100 Chestnut St; adult/child $14/10.75; ☺ 10am-5pm Tue-Sun) is popular with school groups, who always hit the hands-on exhibits with maximum force. There's an additional free-entry stand-alone **observatory** (open weekends, weather permitting) and a **planetarium** that runs weekend laser show celebrations (tickets $10.50) of bands such as Green Day and Pink Floyd.

The final member of the triumvirate, the **Vancouver Maritime Museum** (Map p70; ☎ 604-257-8300; www.vancouvermaritimemuseum; 1905 Ogden Ave; adult/child $10/7.50; ☺ 10am-5pm Tue-Sat, noon-5pm Sun) combines dozens of intricate model ships with some detailed re-created boat sections and a few historic vessels. There are plenty of kid-friendly exhibits here, along with the *St Roch*, an arctic patrol vessel that was the first to navigate the Northwest Passage in both directions.

University of British Columbia

Further west of Kits on a 400-hectare forested peninsula, UBC is the province's largest university. The concrete campus is surrounded by University Endowment Lands, with accessible beach and forest wilderness sites and some recommended visitor attractions.

With one of Canada's best displays of northwest coast aboriginal heritage, the **UBC Museum of Anthropology** (Map pp62-3; ☎ 604-822-3825; www.moa.ubc.ca; 6393 NW Marine Dr; adult/child $9/7, admission by donation after 5pm Tue; ☺ 10am-5pm Wed-Mon, 10am-9pm Tue mid-May–Aug, 11am-9pm Tue, 11am-5pm Wed-Sun Sep–mid-May) is a must-see. The totem poles alone – displayed against a wall of glass overlooking a stunning clifftop promontory – are worth the admission. Schedule some extra time here to read up on the area's often forgotten ancient past; the next time someone in Vancouver moans about the city's lack of history, remind them of the thousands of years' worth on display here. The museum building itself is a contemporary work of art, designed by Arthur Erickson to mirror the post-and-beam structures of coastal First Nations buildings.

Designed by a leading Japanese landscape architect, the lovely **Nitobe Memorial Gardens** (Map pp62-3; ☎ 604-822-6038; www.nitobe.org; 6804 SW Marine Dr; adult/child $4/2.50; ⊗ 10am-6pm mid-May–mid-Oct, 10am-2:30pm Mon-Fri mid-Oct–mid-May) are a perfect example of the Asian country's symbolic horticultural art form. Aside from some traffic noise and summer bus tours, they're a tranquil retreat, ideal for quiet meditation. Combined entry with the UBC Botanical Garden is $8 for adults.

UBC Botanical Garden (Map pp62-3; ☎ 604-822-9666; www.ubcbotanicalgarden.org; 6804 SW Marine Dr; adult/child $6/3; ⊗ 10am-6pm mid-May–mid-Oct, 10am-3pm mid-Oct–mid-May) An internationally renowned 28-hectare complex of several themed gardens, the botanical gardens include Canada's largest collection of rhododendrons, an apothecary garden and a winter garden of plants that bloom outside spring and summer. Combined entry with the Nitobe Memorial Gardens is $8 for adults.

Naturists find a comfortable though often busy haven at **Wreck Beach** (Map pp62-3; www.wreckbeach.org; admission free), where a dedicated community of counterculture locals, independent vendors and in-the-know visitors share the sand. Follow Trail 6 into the woods then head down the steep steps to the water. The regulars here are in a continuing battle with the university over the building of nearby residential towers that threaten to compromise their privacy, so be sure to offer your support while you peel off your skivvies.

West Side

Located between Cambie and Ontario Sts near 33rd Ave, the 53-hectare **Queen Elizabeth Park** (Map pp62-3) offers some of the best views of the city. The park features a mix of sports fields, manicured lawns and formal botanical gardens. Its well-designed sunken garden houses some impressive seasonal displays. Nat Bailey Stadium resides on the park's east side and is a popular summer afternoon destination for fans of the **Vancouver Canadians baseball team** (p100).

Cresting the park's hill is the triodetic dome of the **Bloedel Floral Conservatory** (Map pp62-3; ☎ 604-257-8584; 2099 Beach Ave; adult/child $4.10/2; ⊗ 9am-8pm Mon-Fri, 10am-9pm Sat & Sun Apr-Sep, 10am-5pm Oct-Mar), where 500 species and

---

TOP FIVE VIEWS

■ Stanley Park seawall (p75) – Sparkling sea-to-sky vistas interrupted only by rollerbladers and cyclists.

■ Grouse Mountain (p105) – Unrivaled mountain-top promontory overlooking the city and its spectacular natural setting.

■ Vancouver Lookout Harbour Centre Tower (p75) –Look down on the ant-sized locals rushing about below and come back at night to see the twinkling cityscape.

■ Bard on the Beach tent (p85) – The main stage tent flap is opened during performances, providing a sunset mountain backdrop for Shakespeare's finest.

■ Third Beach at sunset (p75) – Bring a blanket, recline against a beach log and enjoy the city's most romantic sunset views from Stanley Park.

---

varieties of plants and more than 100 tropical birds populate three climate-controlled environments.

If your green thumb's still itchy, four blocks west of the park is **VanDusen Botanical Garden** (Map pp62-3; ☎ 604-878-9274; www.vandusengarden.org; 5251 Oak St; adult/youth/child $7.95/6/4.50 Apr-Sep, $5.70/4.25/2.75 Oct-Mar; ⊗ 10am-4pm Nov-Feb, 10am-5pm Mar & Oct, 10am-6pm Apr, 10am-8pm May, 10am-9pm Jun-Aug, 10am-7pm Sep), a highly ornamental confection of sculptures, Canadian heritage flowers, rare plants from around the world and a popular Elizabethan hedge maze. Free daily tours are offered at 2pm and the gardens are one of Vancouver's top Christmastime destinations, when thousands of fairy lights illuminate the plants.

ACTIVITIES

With a population composed entirely of muscly, Lycra-clad vegetarians – at least that's what it looks like if you walk around the Stanley Park seawall on any given morning – Vancouver is dripping with outdoorsy activities for those determined to keep their heart rate up during a visit. But just because locals boast about skiing in the morning and hitting the beach in the afternoon does not mean you should try; it can make for a hectic day. Popular Vancouver activities include biking and kayaking, while downtowners are also just a short trek from North Vancouver (p104) and West Vancouver (p107) for skiing, snowboarding and snowshoeing action.

Cycling

Vancouver's most popular biking trail – it's also a favorite among bladers – is the 9.5km Stanley Park seawall (p75), which uses dual, one-way-only lanes to avoid messy collisions between those on wheels and those on foot. The sea-to-sky vistas are breathtaking, but the exposed route can be hit with crashing waves and icy winds in winter. Since slow-moving, camera-wielding tourists hog the lanes in summer, it's best to come early in the morning or later in the evening. Once you've circled the park to English Bay, you can then continue along the north side of False Creek towards Science World, where the route heads up the south side of False Creek towards Granville Island, Vanier Park, Kitsilano Beach and UBC. This extended route, including Stanley Park, is around 25km. Keep in mind that Olympics-related construction is creating diversions along the False Creek route.

You can rent bikes (and blades) at various places around town:

Bayshore Bike Rentals (Map pp64-5; ☎ 604-688-2453; www.bayshorebikerentals.ca; 745 Denman St; rental per hr/8hr $5.60/20.80; ☼ 9am-9pm May-Aug, 9am-dusk Sep-Apr) Near Stanley Park's main entrance.

Reckless Bike Stores (Map pp64-5; ☎ 604-731-2420; www.rektek.com; 1810 Fir St; rental half-/full day $25/32.50; ☼ 9am-7pm Mon-Sat, 10am-6pm Sun May-Aug, 10am-dusk Sep-Apr) Near Granville Island entrance; bikes only.

Spokes Bicycle Rental (Map pp64-5; ☎ 604-688-5141; 1798 W Georgia St; rental per hr/8hr $5.60/18.80; ☼ 9am-7pm May-Aug, 10am-dusk Sep-Apr) One block from Stanley Park's main entrance.

Hiking & Running

For leisurely strolls and sweaty runs, the Stanley Park seawall is flat and fairly forgiving. There are also several marked forested trails in the park – including the 4km trek around Lost Lagoon. UBC is another popular running spot, with trails marked throughout the University Endowment Lands. See North Vancouver for the Grouse Grind (p105), a local hiking favorite.

If you'd like some company, **Pacific Running Guides** (☎ 604-828-7690, 877-728-6786; www.pacific runningguides.com; tours from $40) offers customized guided jogs around the city.

Kayaking & Windsurfing

With its glassy waters and spectacular vistas, Vancouver is a kayaking hotbed for everyone from nervous beginners to paddle-driven water nuts.

Headquartered on Granville Island, **Ecomarine Ocean Kayak Centre** (Map p69; ☎ 604-689-7575, 888-425-2925; www.ecomarine.com; 1668 Duranleau St; rental 2hr/day $33/59; ☼ 10am-6pm Jan-May, 9am-6pm Sun-Thu, 9am-9pm Fri & Sat Jun-Aug, 10am-6pm Sep-Dec) rents equipment and also offers popular guided tours (from $49). From its **Jericho Beach branch** (Map p70; ☎ 604-222-3565; Jericho Sailing Centre, 1300 Discovery St, Kitsilano; ☼ 10am-dusk Mon-Fri, 9am-9pm Sat & Sun May-Aug, 10am-dusk Sep), it also organizes events and seminars where you rub can shoulders with local kayakers.

If you're looking for a more secluded kayak trip, head to the North Shore's Deep Cove (p106).

For those who want to be at one with the sea breeze, **Windsure Adventure Waterports** (Map p70; ☎ 604-224-0615; www.windsure.com; Jericho Sailing Centre, 1300 Discovery St, Kitsilano; surfboards/skimboards per hr $17.55/4.39; ☼ 9am-8pm Apr-Sep) rents boards and skimboards, with rates including wetsuits.

Once you've finished your water-based shenanigans, grab a beer and some pub grub at the **Jericho Sailing Centre** (Map p70; ☎ 604-274-4177; www.jsca.bc.ca; 1300 Discovery St, Kitsilano; ☼ 9am-dusk). Try to find a seat on the patio for some of the best sunset views in town.

Swimming

Several city beaches are crowded with ocean swimmers and sunbathers in summer, including English Bay, Kitsilano Beach, Jericho Beach and Stanley Park's Second Beach and Third Beach. Wreck Beach (p79) is Vancouver's naturist haven.

There's an excellent, though often crowded, outdoor swimming pool near Second Beach in Stanley Park (p76), while the **Vancouver Aquatic Centre** (Map pp64-5; ☎ 604-665-3424; 1050 Beach Ave; adult/youth/child $4.70/3.55/2.35; ☼ 6:30am-9:30pm Mon-Fri, 8am-9pm Sat & Sun) has an indoor heated pool along with a whirlpool, diving tank and sauna. Kitsilano Beach has a giant heated outdoor **saltwater pool** (Map p70; ☎ 604-731-0011; 2305 Cornwall Ave; adult/youth/child $4.70/3.55/2.35; ☼ 7am-8:45pm mid-May–mid-Sep).

CYCLING & WALKING TOURS
Stanley Park Cycling Tour

Starting from **Coal Harbour (1)**, follow the designated, one-way bike trail around the seawall towards the **Royal Vancouver Yacht Club (2)**. Continue past the club, catching site of the Vancouver skyline reflected in the water, to the colorful **totem poles (3**; p76). There's an incline from here, so grit your teeth as you pass the Nine O'Clock Gun (p76) towards **Brockton Point (4)** and its little white lighthouse. Let your bike do the work now; you're on the park's best downhill stretch. Continue on towards the **children's water park (5)**, where you'll have to walk for a short distance. Hop back on towards the looming **Lions Gate Bridge (6)**; you'll be cycling under it and getting a blast of

sea breeze as you round **Prospect Point (7)**. From here, the route becomes nature-bound, with spectacular sea and mountain vistas. For a rest, stop at **Third Beach (8**; p75) and catch some rays. It's a similar sight about 1km further at **Second Beach (9)**, where you can also glimpse the distant peninsula where UBC resides. Pick up the pace for the home stretch to **English Bay (10)**, and reward yourself with an ice cream.

> **WALK FACTS**
> **Start** Coal Harbour
> **Finish** English Bay
> **Distance** 9.5km
> **Duration** 2 hours

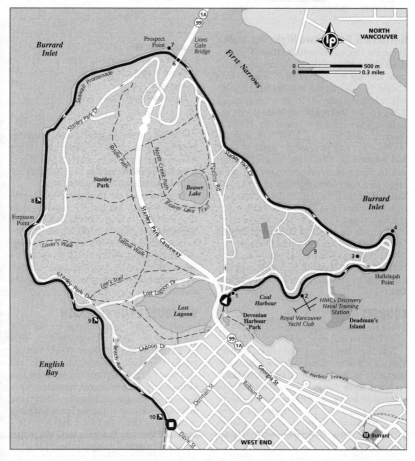

VANCOUVER & AROUND

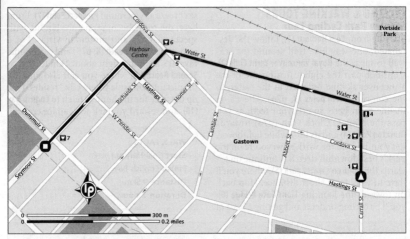

Gastown & Downtown Night Out Walk

From the raucous **Limerick Junction** (1; p98), a noisy reinvention of the classic neighborhood pub, fuel up for a short stroll north along Carrall St towards the **Irish Heather** (2; p98), where hearing yourself think is much easier. Make for the **Shebeen Whisky House (3)** out the back and sample a few rare malts. If you're merry enough for a jig, head back onto the streets – pausing to toast the **statue of 'Gassy' Jack Deighton** (4, p76) – then turn left onto nearby Water St. Weave up to the top of the street and enter **Shine nightclub** (5; p97). You can shake your thang on the dance floor here or take a restorative nap on the giant sofa in the back room. Once you're fully recovered, head across the street to **Steamworks Brewing Co** (6; p98), where you should sample one of the tasty microbrews. If you're ready to hit the road, walk uphill on Seymour St and duck into the convivial confines of the **Railway Club** (7).

COURSES

There are dozens of opportunities for taking a more educational approach to your trip.

If acting is your thing, Vancouver, Western Canada's movie capital, offers a unique opportunity to study at the **William Davis Centre for Actors' Study** (Map pp64-5; ☎ 604-687-8115; www .williamdaviscentre.com; 1102 Hornby St), named after its founder, a film and TV character actor who had a recurring role in *The X-Files*. Classes include Audition Technique and Acting for Commercials.

WALK FACTS
Start Limerick Junction
Finish Railway Club
Distance 2.5km
Duration From 1 hour

Foodies can roll up their sleeves, watch the experts and learn a wide range of culinary skills on one of the many short courses offered at **Barbara-Jo's Books to Cooks** (Map p70; ☎ 604-688-6755; www.bookstocooks.com; 1740 W 2nd Ave).

Those who want to explore BC's spectacular outdoors but lack the required skills should check in with **Canada West Mountain School** (Map p69; ☎ 604-878-7007, 888-892-2266; www .themountainschool.com; 47 W Broadway). This long-established and well-respected institution offers dozens of training and guided excursion programs, including snow camping and rock climbing.

VANCOUVER FOR CHILDREN

Family-friendly Vancouver is stuffed with things to do with vacationing kids. Pick up a copy of the free *Kids' Guide Vancouver* flyer from the information center and visit www.findfamilyfun.com or www.kids vancouver.com for resources, ideas and events. If you're traveling around the city without a car, make sure you hop on the SkyTrain, SeaBus or mini ferry to Granville Island: kids love 'em – especially the new SkyTrain cars, where they can sit up front and pretend to be driving.

The main attractions for families are **Science World** (p77), the **HR MacMillan Space Centre** (p78) and the **Vancouver Aquarium Marine Science Centre** (p76). Stay in **Stanley Park** (p75) after your aquarium visit to check out the miniature railway, sandy beaches and outdoor swimming pool.

Rainy days can include a visit to the **CN IMAX Theatre** at Canada Place (p100), but if the sun comes out don't miss the **Capilano Suspension Bridge** (p104).

On long summer days, there's nothing better for kids than hitting a water park. Vancouver has three great free options: at Lumberman's Arch in Stanley Park, on the seawall near **Mill Marine** (p98) and at Granville Island, which has one of Canada's largest free water parks. Once you've dried off the kids, head over to the nearby **Kids Market** (Map p69; ☎ 604-689-8447; www.kidsmarket.ca; 1496 Cartwright St; ⊗ 10am-6pm) to keep them quiet. If it's time to eat, make for one of Vancouver's White Spot family restaurants: the under-12s Pirate Pack meal – complete with a cardboard boat and gold (chocolate) coin – has many adults looking on enviously.

The city has an array of family-friendly festivals, including the **Pacific National Exhibition** (p85), the **Vancouver International Children's Festival** (p85), the **Alcan Dragon Boat Festival** (p85) and the **Celebration of Light** (p85).

If you're looking for a bedtime read at the end of the day, visit **Kidsbooks** (Map p70; ☎ 604-738-5335; 3083 W Broadway; ⊗ 9:30am-6pm Mon-Thu & Sat, 9:30am-8pm Fri, noon-5pm Sun) for a gargantuan selection of children's titles.

QUIRKY VANCOUVER

In *City of Glass*, an affectionate and highly recommended homage to his Vancouver hometown, *Generation X* author Douglas Coupland gives readers his entertaining, offbeat take on what makes this place tick.

Along with evocative accompanying photos, he explores the big questions that are part of everyday life for locals: What was Expo '86 all about? Why is there so much fleece here? What's the deal with BC Bud? What are all the young Japanese kids doing? What are the giant yellow mounds on the North Shore waterfront? A guidebook of off-the-wall trivia, this entertaining tome nevertheless speaks eloquently of the many peculiarities bubbling beneath the city's surface.

GAY & LESBIAN VANCOUVER

Western Canada's largest gay population has resided in Vancouver for decades and is centered around the West End. Pick up a free copy of *Xtra! West* at streetboxes and businesses in the area for a crash course on the scene. Also check www.gayvancouver.net, www.gayvan.com and www.superdyke.com for listings and resources.

Replete with pink-painted bus shelters and rainbow shop window decals, the West End's Davie St is the heart of Vancouver's gay culture. It's scattered with gay-friendly cafés, bars, stores and the city's best resource centre for gay and lesbian locals and visitors: **Little Sisters Book & Art Emporium** (Map pp64-5; ☎ 604-669-1753; 1238 Davie St; ⊗ 10am-11pm). With one of North America's widest selections of specialist literature, an active bulletin board and a hyper-knowledgeable staff, it's a good first stop for visitors. Pick up a free copy of the glossy *Gay & Lesbian Business Directory* while you're there for an exhaustive list of other pertinent local enterprises, then head down to Denman St and read it at **Delany's** (☎ 604-662-3344; 1105 Denman St), a laid-back neighborhood coffee bar that's a popular hangout of the local scene. If you arrive early enough to find a seat, this is a great spot to catch the giant **Pride Week** (p85) parade, held every August. Along with this family-friendly street fiesta, there are dozens of pre- and post-parade events covering all kinds of interests and desires.

The biggest concentration of bars, clubs and hangouts is on Davie St between Jervis and Burrard. Among the city's most popular gay-friendly nightlife options are **Pump Jack** (Map pp64-5; ☎ 604-685-3417; 1167 Davie St), a loud and proud pub hangout with a great patio, and **Odyssey** (Map pp64-5; ☎ 604-689-5256; 1251 Howe St), the city's number one gay nightclub, combining regular drag nights on Wednesday and Sunday with a host of ever-changing special events.

For support of all kinds, the **Centre** (☎ 604-684-5307; www.lgtbcentrevancouver.com; 1170 Bute St) provides a smorgasbord of discussion groups, a library, a health clinic and legal advice for lesbians, gays, bisexuals and the transgendered. These friendly folk also staff the **Prideline** (☎ 604-684-6869; ⊗ 7-10pm), a telephone peer support, information and referral service.

For visitors inspired to search for Vancouver's quirky underbelly, here are some recommended off-the-beaten path sights and activities that may have you writing in your suggestions for Mr Coupland's next book about the city.

It's no secret to those in the know that BC Bud is a particularly favored commodity, but many are still mildly shocked to see pot cafés, hemp shops and hydroponics stores openly selling the required paraphernalia (although not the weed itself). For arguments in support of legalization, duck into the **BC Marijuana Party Bookshop** (Map pp64-5; 604-682-1172; www .bcmarijuanaparty.ca; 307 W Hastings St). It doubles as the headquarters for the region's dope-head political party.

For those who prefer to think that love is the drug, it's worth visiting **Art of Loving** (Map p69; 604-742-9988; www.theartofloving.ca; 1819 W 5th Ave; 10am-7pm Mon-Wed & Sat, 10am-10pm Thu & Fri, noon-7pm Sun), a tasteful sex shop for the non-dirty-Mac brigade. Among its popular products are the Dinky Digger, Love Swing and glow-in-the-dark condoms, and the store hosts regular classes with titles such as the Joy of Flirting and the Art of Kissing.

You might have more fun losing your shirt at **Hastings Park Racecourse** (Map pp62-3; 604-254-1631, 800-677-7702; www.hastingspark.com; Hastings & Renfrew Sts; Apr-Nov), which offers a recipe for an unusual day out just 10 minutes from downtown. Novice betters are welcome and, when you're not watching the gee-gees, there are some great views of the mountains – although this probably won't console you when you're down to your last cent.

TOURS

While downtown Vancouver is best explored on your own (see p81), time-pressed visitors or those who want to see more than the main attractions should consider a guided tour. Each of the operators listed here offers at least a couple of options, so make sure you check out their full selection before choosing.

Boat Tours

Accent Vancouver Cruises (604-688-6625; www .dinnercruises.com; dinner cruise $60; May–mid-Oct) Popular sunset cruise with salmon buffet dinner option. Departures from Granville Island.

Harbour Cruises (604-688-7246, 800-663-1500; www.boatcruises.com; harbor tour adult/youth/child $25/21/10; mid-Apr–mid-Oct) See the city from the water on a 75-minute harbor tour; watch for seals bobbing offshore. Departures from north foot of Denman St.

Bus Tours

Big Bus (604-299-0700, 877-299-0701; www.bigbus .ca; city tour adult/youth/child $34/30/17) Two-day hop-on-hop-off ticket covering 20 attractions.

Gray Line West (604-879-3363, 800-667-0882; www.graylinewest.com; 4hr city tour adult/youth/child $59/53/39) Options include a four-hour deluxe city tour, including Stanley Park, Granville Island and Chinatown.

Vancouver Trolley Company (604-801-5515, 888-451-5581; www.vancouvertrolley.com; city tour adult/child $33/18.50) Red replica trolley bus trips include city attractions tour, a full day of hop-on, hop-off transport between 23 stops.

West Coast Sightseeing (604-451-1600; www .vancouversightseeing.com; city tour adult/child $57/37) Main four-hour city tour includes Canada Place, Robson St, English Bay and Gastown.

Guided Walking Tours

Edible BC (604-662-3606; www.edible-british columbia.com; Chinatown tour $55; tours 11am Sat) A sensory three-hour trawl around Chinatown's colorful food stores; brunch option $25 extra.

Gastown Historic Walking Tours (604-683-5650; www.gastown.org; admission free; tours 2pm mid-Jun-Aug) Illuminates the history and architecture of Vancouver's birthplace. Departs from Maple Tree Sq.

Orpheum Theatre (Map pp64-5; 604-665-3050; 884 Granville St; tour $5; Jul & Aug) The city's most historic playhouse, complete with sumptuous baroque interiors, offers an entertaining but little-known 90-minute backstage tour. It walks visitors through some haunted nooks and colorful stories about visiting stars from Katherine Hepburn to Jack Benny.

Walkabout Historic Vancouver (604-720-0006; www.walkabouthistoricvancouver.com; tour $25; tours 10am & 2pm) Lively guides offer tours of Gastown, Chinatown or Granville Island.

UBC Campus Tours (604-822-8687; www.ceremo nies.ubc.ca/tours; admission free; tours 10am & 1pm Mon-Fri mid-May–mid-Aug) Trawl around the university's top sights, including Chan Centre and Nitobe Memorial Gardens.

FESTIVALS & EVENTS

Tourism Vancouver's website (www.tourism vancouver.com) has a round-up of major events. Also check out the *Georgia Straight* for up-to-date listings of smaller cultural happenings.

January

Dine Out Vancouver From mid-January, the city's top restaurants offer two weeks of three-course tasting menus for $15, $20 or $25, plus a selection of BC wines. Check the list of participating restaurants at Tourism Vancouver's website (www.tourismvancouver.com) and book ahead.

Chinese New Year (☎ 604-632-3808; www.vancouver -chinatown.com) Occurring in January or February, depending on the calendar, this multiday, highly festive celebration always includes plenty of color, dancing, parades and great food.

March

Vancouver Playhouse International Wine Festival (☎ 604-872-6622; www.playhousewinefest.com) In a region where wine events are sprouting like mushrooms, this older, three-day festival held in late March still rules. There's a strong educational element and several events for neophytes, with hundreds of wines from more than a dozen countries typically on the table.

May

Vancouver International Children's Festival (☎ 604-708-5655; www.childrensfestival.ca) Packed with kid-friendly storytelling, performances and activities in a charming multitented Vanier Park venue, in mid-May.

June

Bard on the Beach (☎ 604-739-0559, 877-739-0559; www.bardonthebeach.org) The perfect way to see Shakespeare, this professional repertory company performs four plays per season from June, in tents at Vanier Park. Watch the show while the sun sets over the mountains behind the stage.

Vancouver International Jazz Festival (☎ 604-872-5200; www.coastaljazz.ca) Into its second decade, Vancouver's biggest music festival takes places from mid-June, in an eclectic array of venues over 10 days. Combining superstar performances (Oscar Peterson and Diana Krall are past masters) with plenty of free outdoor shows.

Alcan Dragon Boat Festival (☎ 604-688-2382; www .adbf.com) An epic two-day splashathon for teams from around the world, this popular weekend event, held in the third week of June, has grown to include live music, theater and world food vendors.

July

Canada Day (☎ 604-775-8025; www.canadaday .canadaplace.ca) Held on July 1, from 10am to 7pm around the be-sailed Canada Place. Exhibits, food and live performances combine to help Canadians celebrate the birth of the nation. There's also a smaller event at Granville Island.

Vancouver Folk Music Festival (☎ 604-602-9798; www.thefestival.bc.ca) A three-day weekend in mid-July, with outdoor folk and world music performances at Jericho Beach. Past headliners range from Billy Bragg to Bruce Cockburn.

Celebration of Light (☎ 604-641-1193; www.hsbc celebrationoflight.com) Thousands flock to English Bay for this free international fireworks extravaganza, which takes place from late July. With the rockets launched from barges in the water, the views are just as good but less crowded from Vanier Park.

Pride Week (☎ 604-687-0955; www.vancouverpride .ca) From late July, this week-long kaleidoscope of gay-, lesbian- and bisexual-friendly fashion shows, gala parties and concerts culminates in Western Canada's largest pride parade.

August

Vancouver Early Music Festival (☎ 604-732-1610; www.earlymusic.bc.ca) Stretching intermittently over three weeks, lute and harpsichord players roll into town to celebrate some of the world's most beautiful but lesser-known music.

Festival Vancouver (☎ 604-688-8441; www.festival vancouver.bc.ca) Two-week showcase of choral, opera, classical, jazz and world music, performed inside and outside by local and international artists, from mid-August.

Pacific National Exhibition (☎ 604-253-2311; www .pne.bc.cag) An old-school country fair that's evolved into a fairground with a kicking wooden rollercoaster and an extensive program of family-friendly shows and music concerts, from mid-August. Don't leave without downing a bag of mini doughnuts.

TOP FIVE FESTIVALS

- Vancouver International Film Festival (p86) – Canadian and international movies celebrated at the city's best festival.

- Bard on the Beach (left) – City institution presenting professional Shakespeare performances in a tented beachfront setting.

- Vancouver Fringe Festival (p86) – Entertaining and eclectic array of local and international short plays and performances.

- East Side Culture Crawl (p86) – Dozens of Eastside studios open for art-loving visitors.

- Pacific National Exhibition (above) – Clamorous city party of family-friendly shows, consumer exhibitions, late-night music and mini doughnuts.

September

Vancouver Fringe Festival (☎ 604-257-0350; www.vancouverfringe.com) Lively 10-day roster of wild and wacky theatrics at large, small and unconventional Granville Island venues, in mid-September.

Vancouver Comedy Fest (☎ 604-683-0883; www.vancouvercomedyfest.com) Six days of rib-tickling mirth in mid-September, with Canadian and international headline acts raising the roof at venues around town.

Vancouver International Film Festival (☎ 604-683-3456; www.viff.org) More accessible than its starry Toronto brother, this two-week showing of Canadian and international movies, held from late September, is a firm local favorite. Book ahead.

October

Vancouver International Writers & Readers Festival (☎ 604-681-6330; www.writersfest.bc.ca) Five-day literary event in mid-October where local and international scribblers turn up for seminars, galas and public forums. Past guests include Salman Rushdie, Irvine Welsh and Douglas Coupland.

November

Santa Claus Parade Vancouver's other parade is a recent addition but has quickly become a popular one-day treat in mid-November. Wrap up, watch the colorful floats and wait until the big man shows up.

East Side Culture Crawl (www.eastsideculturecrawl.com) Excellent three-day showcase in late November, where dozens of eclectic artists from Vancouver's Eastside open their studios to visitors.

December

Carol Ships Parade of Lights (☎ 604-878-8999; www.carolships.org) Cheesy but ever-popular yuletide tradition where dozens of local boats cover themselves in fairy lights and parade along Vancouver's waterfronts to live or recorded carol music.

SLEEPING

Vancouver has a diverse range of sleepover solutions to suit every taste and budget. You can choose from hopping hostels, heritage B&Bs, chichi boutique hotels and a small selection of quirky 'alternative' options. Downtown and the West End are the main areas for hotels and B&Bs, but other fruitful pockets include Kitsilano and the West Side. Book ahead in summer, when prices are at their height (summer prices are shown in these reviews), or consider a visit in spring, fall or winter when reductions can be drastic – check individual hotel websites for off-season deals.

Tourism Vancouver's website (www.tourismvancouver.com) lists options and packages and the province's **Hello BC** (☎ 604-663-6000, 800-663-6000; www.hellobc.com) service provides free information and bookings for many city sleepovers.

Downtown

BUDGET

Samesun Backpackers Lodge (Map pp64-5; ☎ 604-682-8226, 888-203-8333; www.samesun.com; 1018 Granville St; dm/r from $21.40/51; 🖳) Across the street from its HI arch enemy, a party atmosphere prevails at this hostel, which many regard as Vancouver's best. Don't come here if you're looking for Zen-like calm – the Samesun reflects its boisterous Granville St location by offering a hopping backpacker bar. Dorms are small, with four beds in each, and there's a full kitchen plus a funky paint job throughout – doors are decorated as flags of the world. With an active roster of social events, there's also an on-site computer suite.

HI Vancouver Central (Map pp64-5; ☎ 604-685-5335, 888-203-8333; www.hihostels.ca/vancouvercentral; 1025 Granville St; dm/r from $27.50/60; 🖳 🖳) In the heart of the action on Granville St, this warren-like HI sleeper is a backpacker hot spot. The building still enjoys many of the benefits of its past incarnation as a hotel – air-conditioning, small dorms with sinks and natty Tuscan yellow decor – and there are dozens of individual rooms for privacy fans (some with en suites). Continental breakfast is included, free wireless access for laptoppers is offered and there's a roster of activities including ghost walks and CFL football games.

MIDRANGE

Burrard Motor Inn (Map pp64-5; ☎ 604-681-2331, 800-663-0366; 1100 Burrard St; d/tw $99/119) Not as cool as its retro neon street sign suggests, the rooms at this city center motel, complete with faded 1970s furnishings and colored bathrooms, are past their kitsch-cool prime. But the property, arranged around a Florida-like courtyard of old palm trees, is a surprising enclave of calm. Front desk staff are gracious and accommodating, so make sure you ask for a room with a kitchenette – with stovetops and fridges, they don't cost anything extra.

Bosman's Vancouver Hotel (Map pp64-5; ☎ 604-682-3171, 888-267-6267; www.bosmanshotel.com; 1060 Howe St; d $129; 🖳 🖳) Clean, comfortable and good value, heart-of-the-action Bosman's is a motel with large, slightly worn rooms (the era of 1980s pink guest suites is over, guys), an on-site greasy spoon restaurant and a small, kidney-shaped pool where you can cool off after your drive. The front desk staff are adept at helping you with your day-out plans.

Comfort Inn Downtown (Map pp64-5; ☎ 604-605-4333, 888-605-5333; www.comfortinndowntown.com; 654 Nelson St; d/tw $129/149) An appealing, boutique-style property with a great central location, the Comfort Inn's rooms are bright and jazzy, combining cheetah-print curtains with wall prints of old Vancouver. The corner suites, with fireplaces and Jacuzzi tubs, are the hotel's top rooms. Continental breakfast and access to a nearby health club are included and if you're nice to the front desk staff, they may offer you passes to local clubs.

TOP END

Wedgewood Hotel (Map pp64-5; ☎ 604-689-7777, 800-663-0666; www.wedgewoodhotel.com; 845 Hornby St; r from $299; ❅) The last word in boutique luxury, the elegant Wedgewood is dripping with top-hatted charm. The friendly staff are second-to-none, the rooms are stuffed with reproduction antiques, and the balconies enable you to watch the plebs shuffling past below. Adjust your monocle and head to the piano lounge; with its leather chairs, dark wood tables and roaring fireplace; it's a great spot for an evening brandy.

Other recommendations:

Metropolitan Hotel (Map pp64-5; ☎ 604-687-1122, 800-667-2300; www.metropolitan.com/vanc; 645 Howe St; r from $225; ❅ ❂) A sophisticated boutique hotel with a glass-enclosed indoor pool and service that's both discreet and dedicated.

Fairmont Hotel Vancouver (Map pp64-5; ☎ 604-684-3131, 800-257-7544; www.fairmont.com/hotelvancouver; 900 W Georgia St; r from $275; ❅ ❂) The grand dame of Vancouver hotels, combining old-school aristocratic charm with elegant modern amenities.

West End
BUDGET

HI Vancouver Downtown (Map pp64-5; ☎ 604-684-4565, 888-203-4302; www.hihostels.ca/vancouverdowntown; 1114 Burnaby St; dm/r from $27.50/66; ❑) It says 'downtown' in the name but this hostel is actually in the West End, a short walk from the center of all the action and close to the Davie St pubs and clubs. A purpose-built hostel with a more institutional feel than it's Granville St brother, this one is quieter and more popular

with families. The dorms are all small (rates include continental breakfast) and added extras range from bike rentals to internet access computers.

MIDRANGE

Buchan Hotel (Map pp64-5; ☎ 604-685-5354, 800-668-6654; www.buchanhotel.com; 1906 Haro St; s/d with shared bathroom $72/78, with private bathroom $90/98; ❑) The West End's best heritage hotel deal, the cheerful, tidy Buchan has bags of charm and is on the doorstep of Stanley Park. Along corridors lined with monochrome prints of yesteryear Vancouver, its cheaper rooms – many with shared bathrooms – are clean and cozy, although some contain dingy furnishings and older blankets. The pricier rooms are correspondingly prettier, and the east-side rooms are brighter. The front desk staff are excellent and there are storage facilities for bikes and skis.

Tropicana Suites Hotel (Map pp64-5; ☎ 604-687-6631; www.tropicanaivancouver.com; 1361 Robson St; d $99-139; ❂) The best of the three self-catering, apartment-style hotels crowding this corner of Robson and Broughton Sts, rooms at the cheap and cheerful Tropicana combine faded pink-trimmed walls and clashing green comforters. While it will never be cool, it's good value and has a great location. Most suites have full kitchens with stoves, large refrigerators and an abundance of cupboard space, and there's a heated indoor pool and sauna for guests.

our pick **Sylvia Hotel** (Map pp64-5; ☎ 604-681-9321; www.sylviahotel.com; 1154 Gifford St; s/d/tr from $99/159/189) A charming old-school property, the ivy-covered Sylvia is a 1912 heritage landmark. It also has what may be the most loyal clientele of any hotel in Vancouver. Generations of guests keep coming back – many requesting the same room every year – for a dollop of old-world charm followed by a large serving of first-name service. The lobby decor has the look of a Bavarian pension – stained glass windows, dark wood paneling and thick carpets – and there's a wide array of comfortable room configurations to suit every need. The best rooms are the 12 apartment suites, which include full kitchens and English Bay vistas. The first-floor lounge is an ideal spot to nurse a beer and watch the sunset.

Robsonstrasse Hotel & Suites (Map pp64-5; ☎ 604-687-1674, 888-667-8877; www.robsonstrassehotel.com; 1394 Robson St; d $129-189; ❂) A good-value, self-catering sleepover where the rooms are nicer than the musty corridors leading to them, the Robsonstrasse has recently been renovated with new furnishings. Shame they couldn't have replaced the slow, mind-of-its-own elevator at the same time. There's a wide array of room sizes available – the 4th-floor studios are the smallest – and all suites have kitchenettes, each with microwaves rather than stoves. There's a useful on-site laundry.

West End Guest House (Map pp64-5; ☎ 604-681-2889, 888-546-3327; www.westendguesthouse.com; 1362 Haro St; s/d from $135/199) A superior, century-old heritage B&B dripping with antique charm, this tranquil nook has the kind of extras that induce a highly civilized sleepover. Among the eight elegant rooms, the downstairs suite – with private sauna-style steam shower – is recommended for hedonists. There are free loaner bikes available, a guest pantry of fresh-baked cookies and a summer afternoon iced tea gathering on the home's sunny deck.

Listel Vancouver (Map pp64-5; ☎ 604-684-8461, 800-663-5491; www.listel-vancouver.com; 1300 Robson St; d from $149; ✄ ☐) Vancouver's self-described 'art hotel' is a graceful cut above the other properties at this end of Robson St. Attracting a grown-up gaggle of sophisticates with its gallery-style art installations, the mood-lit rooms are suffused with a relaxing West Coast ambience. Adding to the charm, the on-site O'Doul's restaurant hosts nightly live jazz performances. Wireless internet access is available.

Blue Horizon Hotel (Map pp64-5; ☎ 604-688-1411, 800-663-1333; www.bluehorizonhotel.com; 1225 Robson St; d from $149; ✄ ☐) Sleek and comfortable, the Blue Horizon offers quality rooms with the kind of subtle, business hotel furnishings common in pricier sleepovers. All rooms are corner suites and each has a balcony – the top floors enjoy views of English Bay or the North Shore mountains. The on-site restaurant has a popular street-seating patio and serves up West Coast reinventions of traditional breakfasts, including yummy salmon omelette's. Rates include free high-speed internet access.

TOP END

O Canada House (Map pp64-5; ☎ 604-688-0555, 877-688-1114; www.ocanadahouse.com; 1114 Barclay St; d from $195; ☐) Built in 1897, the residence where the lyrics for Canada's national anthem were penned is now an immaculate heritage B&B packed with Victorian antiques and flour-

ishes. Among the seven elegant rooms, all with private bathrooms, the small Cottage Suite, which opens onto a secluded patio garden of lilacs, is a haven from the busy city streets. The wrap-around veranda is a popular spot to watch the world go by, and there's a guest pantry with baked goodies and sherry for guests who want to warm themselves before dinner. Free wireless internet access is included.

Gastown & Yaletown
BUDGET

YWCA Hotel (Map pp64-5; ☎ 604-895-5830, 800-663-1424; www.ywcahotel.com; 733 Beatty St; s/d/tr $61/75/101) One of Canada's best Ys, this popular near-Yaletown tower is a useful option for those on a budget. Accommodating men, women, couples and families, it's a bustling place with a communal kitchen on every other floor and rooms ranging from compact singles to group-friendly larger quarters. All rooms are a little institutionalized – think student study bedroom – but each has a sink and refrigerator. Rates include day passes to the YMCA Fitness Centre, a 10-minute walk away.

MIDRANGE

our pick **Victorian Hotel** (Map pp64-5; ☎ 604-681-6369, 877-681-6369; www.victorianhotel.ca; 514 Homer St; s/d with shared bathroom $79/99, with private bathroom $109/119; ☐) Among Vancouver's best heritage hotel deals, the painted brick exterior and flowery window boxes of the Victorian also make it the prettiest sleepover in the area. A central skylight, brightly repainted walls and glossy hardwood floors illuminate the interior, which also houses a liberal sprinkling of antiques in its corridors and cozy, high-ceilinged rooms. Most rooms have en suites, with summer fans, TVs and robes provided as standard – some also have bay windows where you can sit and contemplate the world. The best rooms are in the newer extension, where the bathrooms are marble-floored. The front desk staff are warm and accommodating and continental breakfast is included along with free in-room high-speed internet access.

St Regis Hotel (Map pp64-5; ☎ 604-681-1135, 800-770-7929; www.stregishotel.com; 602 Dunsmuir St; r from $129; ✄) This well-located heritage hotel is slowly upgrading itself to boutique status, renovating many rooms and adding to its facilities in recent years. The cheaper rooms are still fairly small and basic, so consider upgrading to the 5th floor's nicer quarters. Rates include continental breakfast, access to a small on-site business center and entry to the gym across the street. It's a busy part of town, so ask for a back room if noise is an issue.

TOP END

Opus Hotel Vancouver (Map pp64-5; ☎ 604-642-6787, 866-642-6787; www.opushotel.com; 322 Davie St; d/ste from $350; ☒) Vancouver's most talked-about boutique property, stylish Opus fuses designer chic with West Coast comforts to prove that its impeccable aesthetics are never more important than satisfying its guests. Rooms (especially the corner suites with their feng-shui bed placements) offer lounge-like coziness, designer furnishings and earth-toned bedspreads. Many of the bathrooms have clear windows overlooking the street, making this an ideal sleepover for visiting exhibitionists.

Granville Island & Kitsilano
BUDGET

HI Vancouver Jericho Beach (Map p70; ☎ 604-224-3208, 888-203-4303; www.hihostels.ca; 1515 Discovery St; dm/r from $24/63.50; ☺ May-Sep; ☐) BC's largest HI hostel is all about its beach-side locale. It's ideal for summer outdoorsy types – sports equipment and bike rentals are available and there are kayaking and surfing operators nearby. While basic rooms make this the least palatial of Vancouver's three HIs (dorms here hold up to 34 beds), there's a raft of free or low-cost activities, plus an internet kiosk and TV room. If you're not a fan of snorers, plan ahead and book one of the sought-after private rooms.

MIDRANGE

Maple House B&B (Map p70; ☎ 604-739-5833; www.maplehouse.com; 1533 Maple St; d $80-140) Although located in a lovely old heritage house, this bright-blue B&B is less about antique rooms and more about home comforts. Mixing elegant old flourishes with contemporary chintz touches, the three rooms offer hardwood floors, shared or en suite bathrooms and proximity to nearby Kits Beach. Rates include cooked breakfast with fruit, served in a high-ceilinged dining room.

Mickey's Kits Beach Chalet (Map p70; ☎ 604-739-3342, 888-739-3342; www.mickeysbandb.com; 2142 W 1st Ave; d $110-155; ☐) Handily located two blocks from the beach, this Whistler-style chalet has three rooms and a hedged-in garden terrace. Behind

its slender, chimney-dominated exterior, its rooms – including the gabled, top-floor York Room – are decorated in a non-fussy contemporary style; only the York room has an en suite. Actively welcoming families, the hosts can supply toys, cribs and even babysitters. Continental breakfast and wireless internet access are included.

TOP END

Granville Island Hotel (Map p69; ☎ 604-683-7373, 800-663-1840; www.granvilleislandhotel.com; 1253 Johnston St; s/d $230/240; ☒ ☐) This laid-back boutique property hugs the waterfront on the quieter end of Granville Island. Characterized by a tranquil West Coast decor, the rooms feature exposed wood and soothing earth tones. There's a swanky rooftop Jacuzzi – a good spot to stay warm and watch the rain – and the ground-level brewpub makes its own distinctive beer. Rates include high-speed internet access.

West Side & UBC
BUDGET

University of British Columbia Housing (Map pp62-3; ☎ 604-822-1000, 888-822-1030; www.ubcconferences.com/accommodation; dm/s/d/ste from $25/45/55/99; ☐) UBC offers an array of good-value accommodations for Vancouver visitors, including basic hostel rooms at the Pacific Spirit Hostel, student study rooms in the residences and private rooms at Gage Towers. While these three are available only from mid-May to late August, rooms at the university's hotel-style West Coast Suites are offered year-round. These larger quarters (built to house visiting lecturers) have kitchenettes, private washrooms, twin beds and wireless internet access.

MIDRANGE

ourpick Shaughnessy Village (Map p69; ☎ 604-736-5511; www.shaughnessyvillage.com; 1125 W 12th Ave; s/d $74.95/98.95; ☒) Vancouver's most kitschtastic sleepover, flowery sofas, pink carpets and shipping paraphernalia cover every interior inch of this giant tower block 'B&B resort.' Resort is definitely the right word, since the Shaughnessy has the air of a 1950s Vegas hotel, complete with petrified rock displays, a gym with a bum-shaking belt machine and a tree-lined garden with waterfalls and crazy golf. Despite the old-school approach, the hotel is in tip-top condition, right down to its clean, well-maintained rooms. Recalling compact ships cabins, they're lined with cabinets and include microwaves, refrigerators and tiny en suites. Extras include a full breakfast, outdoor pool, large laundry, health club and an on-site hairdresser: book a beehive 'do and you'll fit right in.

Douglas Guest House (Map p69; ☎ 604-872-3060, 888-872-3060; www.dougwin.com; 456 W 13th Ave; s/d/ste $85/125/145) A bright orange-painted home-style B&B in a quiet character neighborhood, the Douglas offers good rates (especially in winter). The six rooms – comfortable and old-school rather than antique-lined – include two flowery singles with shared bathrooms, two larger doubles with en suites and two family-friendly suites. The top-floor penthouse has a nice private balcony, while the downstairs Garden Suite has a kitchenette.

TOP END

Johnson Heritage House Garden Suite (Map pp62-3; ☎ 604-266-4175; www.johnsons-inn-vancouver.com; 2278 W 34th Ave; ste $195) This welcoming sky-blue–painted wooden heritage sleepover is warm and inviting, with hardwood floors, antique furnishings and large beds that you have to climb into. Formerly a B&B, it's now aimed at self-catering groups – rates are for up to four people, with extras costing $40 each. The property has two bedrooms, two bathrooms, a large kitchen and a hearth-dominated living room. The owners are keen to help with guests' plans to explore the region and a free-use internet computer is available.

EATING

Rivalling Montréal and Toronto for the mantle of best Canadian dine-out city, Vancouver wins over the other two with its wider array of quality – especially Asian – ethnic foods. There's nowhere better to dip into a Chinese banquet, slurp some Korean noodles or sample some of the best sushi available outside Japan. Sophisticated West Coast cuisine, fuelled by a cornucopia of regional seafood and a heaping basket of Fraser Valley produce, is also a specialty. If lunch on the run is more your style, pick up a gourmet pizza slice from Flying Wedge or a bulging burrito from Steamers – these Vancouver-grown, quality fast food-joints have branches throughout town.

Top dining streets, where you can throw a *kapamaki* in any direction and hit a good eatery, include Denman, Davie, Commercial

and Robson. Pick up free copies of *Eat Magazine* and *City Food* or head online to www .urbandiner.ca for listings and reviews.

Downtown
BUDGET

Templeton (Map pp64-5; ☎ 604-685-4612; 1087 Granville St; mains $6-12; ☉ 9am-11pm Mon-Wed, 9am-1am Thu-Sun) A funky and authentic chrome-and-vinyl diner with a twist, Templeton chefs up organic burgers, fair-trade coffee, vegetarian sausages and the best breakfast in town (served until 3pm). Sadly, the mini jukeboxes on the tables don't work, but you can console yourself with an ultra-thick Candy Bar Whirl milkshake.

MIDRANGE

Tropika (Map pp64-5; ☎ 604-737-6002; 1128 Robson St; mains $12-19; ☉ 11am-10pm) A sophisticated, contemporary fusion of the soul food cuisines of Indonesia, Thailand and Malaysia, this upstairs spot is ideally located for Robson St shoppers. The satay sticks ($1.20 each) are among the best in town, but the fish dishes are a specialty, all served in surprising house sauces that will have you licking your lips – check out the chili clams if you crave a taste bud-popping jolt.

Sanafir Restaurant & Lounge (Map pp64-5; ☎ 604-678-1049; 1026 Granville St; mains from $14; ☉ 5pm-midnight) Standing out like a beacon among Granville's grubby sex shops, Sanafir is a loungey, bedouin-themed eatery dripping with North African style. But it's not all about looks. The menu's small but perfectly formed dishes are designed for sharing and range from ahi tuna spring rolls to wine-braised short ribs and Indian-spiced scallops. Head to the decadent mezzanine level, where you can lay down and feed like a king.

Joe Fortes Seafood and Chop House (Map pp64-5; ☎ 604-669-1940; 777 Thurlow St; mains $14-34; ☉ 11am-11pm) Named after Vancouver's first official lifeguard, the chatty rooftop patio or the wood and brass grand room are excellent spots to enjoy a West Coast meat or seafood treat, ranging from slow-roasted prime rib to miso-glazed halibut. The hearty cob salad is recommended, while shellfish fans won't want to miss the oyster bar – these guys know how to shuck.

Nu (Map pp64-5; ☎ 604-646-4668; 1661 Granville St; mains $16-24; ☉ 11am-1am Mon-Fri, 10:30am-1am Sat, 10:30am-midnight Sun) A smashing talk-of-the-town eatery with an attractive waterfront location and a funky 1970s interior that feels like an old Cinzano Bianco advert, the experience here is all about sharing small plates with your best friends. The prices are such that you can afford to be adventurous and sample dishes such as duck confit with liquefied foie gras. The temporary tattoos in the washrooms give you something to do between courses.

TOP END

C Restaurant (Map pp64-5; ☎ 604-681-1164; 1600 Howe St; mains $18-46; ☻ 5:30-11pm) This pioneering West Coast seafood restaurant overlooking False Creek isn't cheap, but its revelatory approach to fish and shellfish is worth the extra dollars. The scallops wrapped in octopus bacon and served with foie gras is popular, while deceptively uncomplicated dishes of side stripe prawns and Queen Charlotte scallops are highly recommended. C is spearheading a local drive against farmed salmon and only uses superior-tasting wild sockeye.

West End
BUDGET

Hal Mai Jang Moi Jib (Map pp64-5; ☎ 604-642-0712; 1719 Robson St; mains $5-12; ☻ 10am-2am Mon-Thu & Sun, 8am-4am Fri & Sat) Part of the fascinating and fast-growing Korean colonization of the Stanley Park end of Robson St, this vibrant little nook is often packed with chattering students text messaging each other across the table. The good-value menu gives them something to talk about and includes favorites like ultra-filling noodle bowls and lip-smacking seafood pancakes.

Hamburger Mary's (Map pp64-5; ☎ 604-687-1293; 1202 Davie St; mains $7-12; ☻ 8am-3am Mon-Thu, 8am-4am Fri & Sat, 8am-2am Sun) A throwback to the days of checkered floors and chrome trim diners, the landmark, late-night-lovin' Mary's is everything a burger joint should be. But the menu is not your standard Big Mac fare; instead the prime beef patties are served with a kaleidoscope of original fillings and there's a heaping all-day breakfast that has plenty of locals hogging the patio.

MIDRANGE

Liliget Feast House (Map pp64-5; ☎ 604-681-7044; 1724 Davie St; mains $12-28; ☻ 5-10pm Wed-Sun) An unusual First Nations–themed culinary adventure, the subterranean Liliget dining room

is designed like a wooden northwest coastal longhouse, compete with pebble floors and cedar poles. The food is a rustic combination of oysters, elk, buffalo and caribou, all served traditionally and with a chewy serving of warm bannock bread.

Hapa Izakaya (Map pp64-5; ☎ 604-698-4272; 1479 Robson St; mains $15-22; ☻ 5:30pm-midnight Sun-Thu, 5:30pm-1am Fri & Sat) A midpriced reinvention of a Japanese tapas bar, this cozy black-on-black haunt has quickly become one of the city's most popular dine-outs. Combining delectable comfort food – check out the steaming hot pots – with Sapporo beer and highly welcoming service, you'll forget you're even in Vancouver until you stumble out onto the streets with a big smile on your face several hours later.

Lift Bar and Grill (Map pp64-5; ☎ 604-689-5438; 333 Menchions Mews; mains $17-23; ☻ 11:30am-midnight Mon-Fri, 11am-midnight Sat & Sun) Hanging over the seawall near Stanley Park, the swanky Lift serves unrivalled views of the verdant rain forest and mist-cloaked mountains from its wraparound windows. If you can pull yourself away from the vistas, dip into gourmet comfort dishes such as ahi tuna, bison strip loin and the ever-popular prosciutto-wrapped salmon.

Fish House in Stanley Park (Map p68; ☎ 604-681-7275; 8901 Stanley Park Dr; mains $18-30; ☻ 11:30am-4pm & 5-10pm Mon-Sat, 11am-4pm & 5-10pm Sun) Local fish lovers have been swimming upsteam to this legendary dine-out for decades, but it's never rested on its laurels or become a tourist trap for Stanley Park visitors. One of Vancouver's best spots to explore seasonal West Coast seafood at its best, specialties include cedar planked trout and sticky chili sablefish. The seafood-flavored Sunday brunch is highly recommended.

TOP END

Cin Cin Ristorante & Bar (Map pp64-5; ☎ 604-688-7338; 1154 Robson St; mains $20-48; ☻ 11:30am-11pm Mon-Fri, 5-11pm Sat & Sun) Tuscan ambience fused with West Coast sophistication means a host of homesick Hollywood movie stars keep coming back to this excellent restaurant. If they're not gorging on alder-smoked wild salmon pizza, they're salivating over local fish and game prepared in a simple yet always elegant manner. Reservations recommended, especially if you want to sit on the patio with the likes of Halle Berry and Robin Williams.

LOCAL VOICES, LOCAL FLAVORS

Visitors are spoilt for choice when they dine out in Vancouver, but where do some of the city's top chefs go when they fancy a good nosh? We asked three leading culinary exponents to comment on Vancouver's restaurant scene and reveal their favorite eating spots.

Andreas Wechselberger, Executive Chef, Cin Cin Ristorante & Bar (p91)
Vancouver is a great dining town because... 'Of the variety – there's so much great ethnic fare: terrific Thai, Chinese, Japanese, Malaysian etcetera. It's also still affordable. Unlike other cities, in Vancouver you can afford not only to go out to eat but also to get a babysitter and see a show.'
My favorite place to eat out is... 'Thai Café (☎ 604-299-4525; 4160 Hastings St; mains $8-16; ⓨ 11am-9:30pm Mon-Fri, 5-9:30pm Sat). It has the best Tom Yum Gai soup I've ever had.'

Andrea Carlson, Chef de Cuisine, Raincity Grill (below)
Vancouver is a great dining town because... 'Of our ethnic and culturally diverse restaurants, lots of different cuisines, and access to global products.'
My favorite place to eat out is... 'Salade de Fruits Café (☎ 604-714-5987; 1551 W 7th Ave; mains $5-13; ⓨ 10am-10pm Tue-Sat). It is excellent bistro food – really "hot," really simple; everything is well made. The food is great and it is always, always good.'

Frank Pabst, Executive Chef, Blue Water Café and Raw Bar (opposite)
Vancouver is a great dining town because... 'We have an enormous amount of very good ethnic restaurants. This diversity makes it very interesting for everyone who loves eating out. As chefs, we can learn so much in this city about different food cultures.'
My favorite place to eat out is... 'West Restaurant & Bar (☎ 604-738-8938; 2881 Granville St; mains $16-40; ⓨ 11:30am-11pm Mon-Fri, 5:30-11pm Sat & Sun). It has beautifully executed modern West Coast cuisine.'

Raincity Grill (Map pp64-5; ☎ 604-685-7337; 1193 Denman St; mains $24-30; ⓨ 11:30am-2:30pm & 5-10pm Mon-Fri, 10:30am-2:30pm & 5-10-pm Sat & Sun) A great showcase for fine West Coast cuisine, this convivial English Bay eatery was sourcing and serving unique BC ingredients long before the fashion for Fanny Bay oysters and Salt Spring Island lamb took hold. A fixture of the West End for more than a decade, it offers a bargain three-course $25 tasting menu between 5pm and 6pm, and one of the city's most formidable wine lists.

Yaletown
BUDGET
Elbow Room (Map pp64-5; ☎ 604-685-3628; 560 Davie St; mains $4-9; ⓨ 8am-4pm) A Vancouver breakfast legend, the campy Elbow Room's schtick is that it chefs up colorful abuse with its meals. Don't be put off; it's all meant in a friendly way, but make sure you give as good as you get. The menu highlights the mood – evidenced by 'The F-ing Kidding' burger, with two 8oz beef patties plus mushrooms

and bacon – and breakfast is served until closing.

MIDRANGE
Lucky Diner (Map pp64-5; ☎ 604-444-4855; 1269 Hamilton St; mains $10-18; ⓨ 11:30am-11pm Mon-Fri, 5:30-11pm Sat & Sun) It's an achievement to make a sparse, concrete warehouse feel cozy, but it must have something to do with the soothing qualities (and fresh-baked aromas) of the menu at this fab Yaletown eatery. The ideal place to head on one of those rainy Vancouver days, you'll feel instantly cheered by tummy-warming treats such as chunky stews, family-recipe meatloaf and pierogies served with German sausage.

Glowbal Grill & Satay Bar (Map pp64-5; ☎ 604-602-0835; 1079 Mainland St; mains $14-26; ⓨ 11:30am-midnight Mon-Fri, 10:30am-midnight Sat & Sun) Hip but unpretentious, this often clamorous restaurant has a comfortable, lounge-like feel and a menu of classy dishes fusing West Coast ingredients with Asian and Mediterranean flourishes. The grilled halibut, served with scampi butter, Dungeness crab and roasted tomato risotto, is hard to beat, but save room for some finger-licking satay stick chasers, especially the tequila lamb, served with lime mint glaze.

Elixir (Map pp64-5; ☎ 604-642-0557; 350 Davie St; mains $14-32; ⏰ 6:30am-2am Mon-Sat, 6:30am-midnight Sun) A fascinating fusion of French, Asian and West Coast influences makes this upscale Opus Hotel brasserie a favorite with visiting celebs. The breakfasts – especially the crepes – are a cut above standard fare, but it's worth saving your appetite for dinner, when star turns include vanilla poached lobster and pan-seared wild salmon. The wine list is impressive and there's an adjoining Parisienne bar that is comfort personified.

TOP END

Blue Water Café and Raw Bar (Map pp64-5; ☎ 604-688-8078; 1095 Hamilton St; mains $22-44; ⏰ 5pm-midnight) Vancouver's best oyster bar also serves some excellent sushi and an array of lovingly simple seafood dishes in a warm brick-and-beam dining room. If you feel like an adventure, head straight to the semicircular raw bar and watch the chef's whirling blades prepare delectable sushi and sashimi, served with the restaurant's signature soya–seaweed dipping sauce. Reservations recommended.

Gastown & Chinatown
BUDGET

Mouse and the Bean Café (Map pp66-7; ☎ 604-633-1781; 207 W Hastings St; mains $4-12; ⏰ noon-6pm Mon-Thu, noon-8pm Fri & Sat) Head downstairs under the Dominion Building and you'll find this smashing off-the-beaten path family-run Mexican joint. Everything – including the salsa and refried beans – is made in-house and the prices are eye-opening low, which probably explains why the floor is still unfinished concrete. There are plenty of vegetarian options among the bulging enchiladas and giant quesadillas, but the best way to order is to ask at the counter for some recommendations.

Phnom Penh (Map pp66-7; ☎ 604-682-5777; 244 E Georgia St; mains $5-10; ⏰ 10am-10pm) This bustling little spot combines the best in Cambodian and Vietnamese comfort food, including a hot-and-sour fish soup that would put a contented smile on anyone's face. Stay for a long lunch and explore the adventurous, taste-tripping menu but make sure you try the chicken wings – served with fried garlic,

green onions and lemon pepper sauce, they may be the best in the city.

MIDRANGE

Hon's Wun-Tun House (Map pp66-7; ☎ 604-688-0871; 268 E Keefer St; mains $6-18; ⏰ 11am-11pm Sun-Thu, 11am-midnight Sat & Sun) Vancouver's favorite Chinese restaurant minichain, Hon's flagship Chinatown branch is suffused with inviting cooking smells. Dishes range from satisfying dim sum to steaming wonton soup bowls, bobbing with juicy dumplings. Try the congee rice porridge: a fancy-free soul food dish that takes three hours to prepare and comes in seafood, chicken and beef varieties.

Wild Rice (Map pp66-7; ☎ 604-642-2882; 117 W Pender; mains $10-18; ⏰ 11:30am-midnight Mon-Thu, 11:30am-1am Fri, 5pm-midnight Sat & Sun) A loungey, minimalist reinvention of the traditional Chinese restaurant, Wild Rice fuses classic dishes with unexpected culinary influences from around the world. Wild boar with jasmine rice and plantain chips is particularly recommended, as is the comprehensive martini list. This is a popular late-night hangout on Friday and Saturday.

Chill Winston (Map pp66-7; ☎ 604-288-9575; 3 Alexander St; mains $12-20; ⏰ noon-1am Wed-Sat, 11am-midnight Sun) Golden hardwood floors and exposed brick walls do not alone make a great lounge restaurant, but this charming spot has moved beyond its trendy looks with a menu that encourages you to linger. House-cured smoked salmon, crispy crab cakes and Asian-sauced turkey suggest they're trying to be all things to all diners, which is exactly the approach: this is a place for a quick lunch, an after-work martini or a group hangout with buddies on the huge patio.

ourpick Irish Heather (Map pp66-7; ☎ 604-688-9779; 217 Carrall St; mains $14-16; ⏰ noon-midnight) Vancouver's best traditional pub, the Irish Heather is also the city's only real exponent of the European gastropub movement, where great draught beers (in this case Guinness and Harp) are offered alongside a menu of gourmet comfort food that would put higher-priced restaurants in the area to shame. That explains dishes such as bangers 'n' mash, here made with top-table pork sausages, a thyme Pinot Noir gravy and colcannon, and a mouth-watering potato and cabbage mash. If you have any room left over for dessert, the Belgian chocolate pâté is naughtily decadent, although just hanging around the brick courtyard out the back with a couple of beers is also a good way to wind down after a meal here.

SoMa & Commercial

BUDGET

Belgian Fries (Map pp66-7; ☎ 604-253-4220; 1885 Commercial Dr; mains $5-8; ⏰ 11am-10pm) The best fries in town are best accompanied by a Montréal-style smoked meat sandwich. For heart-attack-fans, the poutine is also highly regarded and you can suck down a deep-fried Mars Bar to push you right over the edge. The excellent beer selection includes satanic-labeled Quebec favorites and Storm, a rare but exquisite British Columbian brew.

Zanzibar Cafe (Map p69; ☎ 604-215-2008; 1851 Commercial Dr; mains $6-8; ⏰ 9:30am-8pm Mon-Thu, 9:30am-9pm Fri-Sun) Originally just a coffee shop, the quirky, red-walled Zanzibar now houses a clutch of tables where chatty diners can have their fill of authentic, good-value Moroccan dishes. The ultra-tender lamb with apricots is a winner but make sure you order some tea – despite the budget prices, it comes in a silver teapot.

MIDRANGE

Foundation (Map p69; ☎ 604-708-0881; 2301 Main St; mains $6-12; ⏰ 5pm-1am) One of SoMa's liveliest hangouts, this funky vegetarian (mostly vegan) restaurant is the kind of place where artsy students and chin-stroking young intellectuals like to be seen. Despite the clientele, it's not at all pretentious, and its mismatched Formica tables are often topped with unusual but tasty dishes such as braised tofu salad or mango and coconut pasta.

Habit Lounge (Map p69; ☎ 604-877-8582; 2610 Main St; mains $8-14; ⏰ 5pm-1:30am Mon-Sat, 5-11pm Sun) A smashing laid-back dining room with a welcoming ambience – who knew that orange vinyl benches and minimalist artwork could be so cozy – this is like an Ikea-esque update of the classic neighborhood bar. Encouraging shared plate experimentation, the menu includes savory treats such as duck ragout, halibut in curry sauce and crispy tofu, served with mushrooms and spinach (yes, there's plenty here for visiting vegetarians).

Nyala (☎ 604-876-9919; 4148 Main St; mains $10-16; ⏰ 5:30-11pm Tue-Sun) Served in traditional clay pots made by the owner, the signature dish at this colorful African eatery is *mafe*, a spicy Creole-style chicken and vegetable creation that features a warming fusion of tomato, okra, coriander and hot chili. If you're feeling more adventurous, sample the Ethiopian slow-cooked goat stew and drop by on Thursday when live music fills the room.

Havana (Map pp66-7; ☎ 604-253-9119; 1212 Commercial Dr; mains $11-20; ⏰ 11am-11pm Mon-Thu, 10am-midnight Fri, 9am-midnight Sat & Sun) The granddaddy of Commercial Dr, funky Havana combines a live theater and gallery with a roster of satisfying Afro-Cuban-Southern soul food dishes. Slow-roasted lamb curry and hearty paella are on offer but the simmered shellfish platter of clams, mussels, oysters and prawns is recommended. Don't forget to carve your name into the wall before you leave; it's a rite of passage.

Aurora Bistro (Map p69; ☎ 604-873-9944; 2420 Main St; mains $14-24; ⏰ 5:30-11pm Mon-Sat, 10am-2pm & 5:30-11pm Sun) In the culinary heart of the city's rising SoMa neighborhood, chef Jeff Van Geest takes the region's best seasonal ingredients and transforms them into instant favorites such as cornmeal-crusted Fanny Bay oysters and wild mushroom risotto (recommended). The BC wine selection is popular with local connoisseurs and there's a piquant array of local cheese featured on the dessert menu – including the excellent McLennan Blue Capri goat cheese.

Granville Island

BUDGET

Public Market Food Market (Map p69; 1689 Johnston St; mains $5-8; ⏰ 9am-7pm) As well as the Public Market's cornucopia of bakeries and deli stalls, the compact food court here is one of the city's best, combining an international array of quality fajitas, pierogies, pizzas, curries and fish and chips. Eat late or early to avoid the crowds, who cling to the tables like they've just been shipwrecked, or take your grub outside to catch the views and fend off the seagulls.

MIDRANGE

our pick Go Fish (Map p69; ☎ 604-730-5040; 1505 W 1st Ave; mains $8-13; ⏰ 11:30am-6:30pm Wed-Fri, noon-6:30pm Sat & Sun) Tucked along the pleasant seawall walk between Granville Island and Vanier Park, this unassuming little waterfront shack serves perhaps the best fish and chips in town, offering a choice of halibut, salmon or cod encased in crispy golden batter. But the treats don't stop there: the smashing fish tacos are highly recommended if you want a lighter meal, while the ever-changing daily specials – depending on the catch of the day brought in by the nearby fishing boats – often include praise-worthy scallop burgers or ahi tuna sandwiches. Favored by in-the-know locals, who often swarm around here during the half-hour before closing, all dishes are made to order and include house-chopped coleslaw. There's not much of a seating area – although perching on a stool here facing the waterfront and the shimmering glass towers of north False Creek is nice – so consider taking your grub to nearby Vanier Park for an alfresco dining experience.

Bridges Restaurant (Map p69; ☎ 604-687-4400; 1696 Duranleau St; mains $12-20; ⏰ noon-11pm) A casual 30-somethings bistro with views of the Burrard Bridge and the surrounding mountains, bright-yellow Bridges is hard to miss. In summer it offers one of the best patios in town from which to enjoy standard but well-executed classics such as chicken quesadillas, fish and chips and hearty thin-crust pizzas. Diners can also escape the chatter of the bistro and patio at the quieter, more upscale upstairs dining room, which serves a three-course fixed-price menu ($40).

Dockside Restaurant and Dockside Brewing Company (Map p69; ☎ 604-685-7070; 1253 Johnston St; mains $14-26; ⏰ 7am-10pm) A menu of wood-grilled steaks, mint-crusted lamb and grilled wild salmon are highlights in the main dining room here at the Granville Island Hotel (p89), but you can also kick back and enjoy a more casual (and less pricey) meal in the adjoining microbrew lounge. Both rooms have an intimate, wood-lined feel, with the shared patio becoming a noisy spot on summer evenings.

TOP END

Sandbar (Map p69; ☎ 604-669-9030; 1535 Johnston St; mains $18-35; ⏰ 11:30am-11pm Sun-Thu, 11:30am-midnight Fri & Sat) It's almost all about West Coast seafood at this high-ceilinged view restaurant under the Granville Bridge, in the same complex as the Arts Club Theatre. The oysters here rock and they're best sampled on the fireplace-warmed rooftop deck. The wine list is also something to write home about – around 1800 bottles are secreted in the cellar – but the urban professionals and beautiful people hanging around the bar on weekends seem more interested in cocktails. Reservations recommended.

Kitsilano

BUDGET

Capers Community Market (Map p70; ☎ 604-739-6676; 2285 W 4th Ave; mains $4-10; ⏰ 8am-10pm) A health-minded, mostly organic supermarket with a great café/takeout section, Capers is ideal for picking up picnic supplies. The quality salad bar and glutinous fruit smoothies are popular, but the hearty wraps ($4.50), especially the Masala Wrap, are recommended for those on the run. Additional branches include downtown's 1675 Robson St, the West Side's 3277 Cambie St and West Vancouver's 2496 Marine Dr.

Great Wok (Map p70; ☎ 604-739-7668; W 4th Ave; mains $5-10; ⏰ 11:30am-11pm Mon-Fri, 4:30pm-11pm Sat & Sun) Nothing special from the outside, this small, ambience-free eatery – check out those nasty pink tables – is a favorite among local die-hard Szechwan fans. Initially lured by the famed dry ginger beef and a menu of perfectly executed Chinese classics, they keep coming back for the swift service and the warm welcome from the stalwart staff.

MIDRANGE

Sophie's Cosmic Café (Map p70; ☎ 604-732-6810; 2095 West 4th Ave; mains $6-14; ⏰ 8am-9:30pm) A local legend for nearly 20 years, Sophie's is one of the best breakfast and weekend brunch spots in town. The memorabilia-lined diner ambience only adds to the taste of the great eggs Benedict, but if you're not here early, you may have a long wait for your hangover cure.

TOP FIVE SUNDAY MORNING-AFTER BRUNCH SPOTS

Your throat feels like sandpaper and your head is lolling about like a medicine ball on a toothpick. It's the morning after the night before and you're regretting those final eight pints of Granville Island Lager. But not to worry – the cure is out there, in the shape of a fortifying brunch. Roll out of bed and stagger to any one of these five great breakfast spots:

▪ Templeton (p90)

▪ Feenies (p96)

▪ Sophie's Cosmic Café (right)

▪ Elbow Room (p92)

▪ Hamburger Mary's (p91)

Consider coming back later in the day, when you might feel more inclined to sample the lovely key lime pie.

Naam (Map p70; ☎ 604-738-7151; 2724 W 4th Ave; mains $8-14; ⊙ 24hr) A legendary Kits vegetarian eatery that's been attracting herbivores and carnivores since the late 1960s, Naam is a highly welcoming restaurant that still has the feel of a hippy hangout. It's not unusual to have to wait for a table here at peak times, but it's worth it for the hearty stir-fries, Mexican platters and sesame-fried potatoes with miso gravy. Breakfast is worth the trek, there's regular live music during the week and there's a lovely patio for summertime scoffing

Rocky Mountain Flatbread Co. (Map p70; ☎ 604-730-0321; 1876 W 1st Ave; mains $14-20; ⊙ 11:30am-2pm & 5-10pm) For those whose lives have been a never-ending search for a healthy pizza, this friendly Kits eatery serves pies created with mostly organic ingredients and absolutely no additives, GMOs or trans-fatty acids. They still taste good, though, with varieties such as 'Rosemary Chicken' and the salmon-and-lobster 'Meet The Ocean' proving popular. Pasta and salads are also available, so don't feel you have to pig out on pizza.

Feenies (Map p70; ☎ 604-739-7115; 2563 W Broadway; mains $16-22; ⊙ 11:30am-2:30pm & 5:30-11:30pm Mon-Fri, 10am-2pm & 5:30-11:30pm Sat & Sun) Vancouver's favorite chef Rob Feenie (of Lumière fame) opened another winner with this contemporary West Coast diner that focuses on comfort food with a gourmet flair. The hamburgers and fries are worth the extra money, while the duck shepherd's pie, complete with truffle mashed potatoes, utterly transforms what was once a dish workers made from scraps. If you dare, ask to sink your teeth into 'Feenie's weenie,' a gourmet hot dog.

TOP END

Lumière (Map p70; ☎ 604-739-8185; 2551 W Broadway; prix-fixe $125-160; ⊙ 5:30-11pm Tue-Sun) One of the small band of city eateries that regularly wins the title of 'Vancouver's best restaurant,' swanky Lumière deploys deceptively unfussy preparations to create an array of French-inspired, Asian-brushed masterpieces. Diners are offered seasonal tasting menus (seafood, vegetarian or signature), which can feature anything from rhubarb and vanilla soup to sablefish marinated in sake and maple syrup. Sit back and enjoy. Reservations recommended.

West Side
MIDRANGE

Susuhi Aoki (Map p69; ☎ 604-731-5577; 1888 W Broadway; mains $8-14; ⊙ 11:30am-10pm Mon-Sat) It's hard to believe that such a tiny restaurant would have the kind of extensive menu usually found in places 10 times bigger, but Sushi Aoki is a fancy-free yet recommended nook that knows exactly how to do sushi well. Using only the freshest fish (it flies in what it can't source locally), it artfully crafts rolls such as the signature shrimp with mayonnaise and apricot sauce and the fab rainbow roll of salmon, clam, tuna and sea bass. Yum.

Bin 942 (Map p69; ☎ 604-734-9421; 1521 W Broadway; mains $15; ⊙ 5pm-2am) This tiny but exceedingly cozy lounge is a convivial late-night hangout for Vancouverites who fancy a few dishes of food and a bottle or two of wine with friends. Among the 'Tapatisers' are sashimi-style ahi tuna and Portobello mushroom cutlets, which pair perfectly with a select array of good beers – the Russell Brewing Cream Ale is best – and a compact but well-chosen wine list of Australian, Californian, European and BC tipples.

our pick **Tojo's** (Map p69; ☎ 604-872-8050; 1133 W Broadway; mains $16-26; ⊙ 5-10pm Mon-Sat) If you only have one sushi meal in Vancouver – quite a challenge in a city with around 300 such outlets – make sure it's at Tojo's. Expect to spend a few dollars more for the opportunity to sample an artful haiku of supreme seafood, prepared by the legendary, multiaward-winning Hidekazu Tojo. He's been sharpening his knives in Vancouver for 30 years and claims an encyclopedic mastery of 2000 recipes. Among his exquisite dishes are favorites such as lightly steamed monkfish, sautéed halibut cheeks and fried red tuna wrapped with seaweed and served with plum sauce. The sushi bar seats here are more sought after than a couple of front-row Stanley Cup tickets, so reserve as early as possible.

TOP END

Vij's (Map p69; ☎ 604-736-6664; 1480 W 11th Ave; mains $20-26; ⊙ 5:30-10pm) The high-water mark of contemporary East Indian cuisine, Vij's is all about fusing local ingredients, global cuisines and classic Indian dishes to produce an array of innovative new flavors. The unique and, judging by the line-ups, highly popular results range from wine-marinated 'lamb Popsicles' to halibut, mussels and crab in tomato–ginger curry. Reservations are not accepted here, but if you don't want to wait in line, there's now a takeout café next door.

DRINKING

For better or worse, Vancouver has replaced many of its low-key neighborhood bars with large brewpubs and cool lounges with bewildering martini lists. Wherever you end up drinking, check out some of BC's excellent craft beers, including ales and lagers from Nelson, Granville Island and Crannóg breweries.

Bars & Nightclubs

Backstage Lounge (Map p69; ☎ 604-687-1354; 1585 Johnston St; 11:30am-midnight Sun-Thu, 11:30am-2am Sat & Sun) Not cool enough to be a real lounge, this grungy but ever-lively Granville Island hangout serves up great patio views, enticing beer specials (Tuesday night is all about $2 draughts) and hopping local live bands. It's also a popular hangout for 'cougars' – those fun-loving Vancouver ladies who prowl the bars for younger men.

Bar None (Map pp64-5; ☎ 604-689-7000; 1222 Hamilton St; 9pm-2am Mon-Thu, 9pm-3am Fri & Sat) Yaletown's recently renovated hangout, Bar None is a smoky joint without the smoke. While it has the look of a beatnik underground bar, it's actually full of local hipsters discussing how much they made on the sale of their condos. There's a VIP cocktail lounge and funky live or turntable music every night.

Denman Street Freehouse (Map pp64-5; ☎ 604-801-6681; 1780 Davie St; 11am-2am Mon-Fri, 10am-2am Sat, 10am-midnight Sun) A compact but swanky reinvention of the neighborhood pub – think polished hardwood floors, modern furnishings and waitstaff all in black – the main draw here is the boutique selection of draught European beers, plus the fab patio views across English Bay. It's an ideal place to catch the sunset with a glass of Belgian cheery beer.

O'Douls (Map pp64-5; ☎ 604-661-1400; 1300 Robson St; noon-11pm) A good bar, excellent wine selection and live jazz every night attracts Vancouver's over-30s set to the Listel hotel's on-site watering hole. This is also the center of the action during the Vancouver International Jazz Festival (p85), when performers drop by to jam at the end of their regular gigs.

Shine (Map pp66-7; ☎ 604-408-4321; 364 Water St; cover from $4; 9pm-2am) With music from electro to funky house and hip-hop, subterranean Shine is divided into a noisy main room and an intimate cozy cave with a 40ft chill-out

sofa. The club's Saturday night 'Big Sexy Funk' (hip-hop and rock) is recommended, but Thursday's 1990s retro night appeals to all those ancient 25-year-old hipsters out there. Under-30s crowd.

Sonar (Map pp66-7; ☎ 604-683-6695; 66 Water St; cover from $6; 9pm-3am Wed-Sat) Top DJs from around the world sometimes spin their stuff at this club, but 'Playa's Club Saturday' is the main event for hip-hop, reggae and R&B fans. If you're serious about catching edgy DJs and experimental live club shows, check the schedule (www.sonar.bc.ca) and plan your visit accordingly. Under-30s crowd.

Lounges

Afterglow (Map pp64-5; ☎ 604-602-0835; 1082 Hamilton St) The city's most intimate lounge is tucked at the back of Glowbal Grill & Satay Bar (p92). Its sexy pink interior features giant silhouettes of naked women à la James Bond and its flirty cocktail list includes You Glow Girl and Pink Pussycat – perfect for washing down those finger-licking satay sticks. It's easy to relax so much here that, all of a sudden, it's the middle of the night and you've forgotten where your hotel is.

Alibi Room (Map pp66-7; ☎ 604-623-3383; 157 Alexander St; 5pm-midnight Mon-Thu, 4:30pm-2am Fri, 10am-2am Sat & Sun) It's all about great conversation at this edge-of-Gastown spot, where the design crowd and film industries congregate at long tables or hunker down in the low-ceilinged basement to bitch about work. A comfort food menu perfectly matches the drinks selection of fortifying martinis.

George (Map pp64-5; ☎ 604-628-5555; 1137 Hamilton St; 4pm-2am Mon-Sat) Yaletown's latest wheeze and Vancouver's new 'it' lounge, the moodily lit George attracts the see-and-be-seen crowd with its giant list of exotic cocktails – anyone for a Sazerac, featuring bourbon in an 'absinthe-washed glass'? Work your way down the list, sink further into your comfy chair and try to figure out what the giant glass thing above the bar is supposed to be.

Ginger 62 (Map pp64-5; ☎ 604-688-5494; 1219 Granville St; 8pm-1am Wed, Thu & Sun, 7pm-3am Fri & Sat) Like George, this was briefly the city's favorite lounge until those fickle fashionistas moved on. It's far more laid-back now but still busy on weekends when the Granville St clubbers stumble in for late-night refreshments. Many of them end up staying, lured by the calming decor and cutting-edge DJs.

Pubs

Bimini's Tap House (Map p70; ☎ 604-732-9232; 2010 W 4th Ave; ☿ 11am-1am Sun-Thu, 11am-2am Fri & Sat) A Kitsilano institution that's been recently refurbished, Bimini's is a trad-looking bar-restaurant where customers are just as happy sipping cocktails or knocking back a couple of beers. Drop by on Tuesday, when all draught domestic beer and hi-balls are $3 each, and consider busting your weekend hangover by returning to the scene of the crime for Sunday brunch.

Irish Heather (Map pp66-7; ☎ 604-688-9779; 217 Carrall St; ☿ noon-midnight) Vancouver's best traditional pub (U2 once dropped by for a St Patrick's Day drink), the Heather is an unpretentious labyrinth of bricklined nooks serving properly poured Guinness and great gourmet pub grub (p93). Warm up in winter with a restorative 'Hot Irish,' a concoction of whiskey, lemon, cloves, sugar and boiling water, or head straight for the hidden Shebeen Whisky House, a charming backroom bar with the largest (140-plus) whiskey selection around.

Limerick Junction (Map pp66-7; ☎ 778-896-8840; 315 Carrall St; ☿ noon-1am) The Heather's rougher younger brother, the recently opened Limerick Junction occupies an old pub that's seen plenty of raucous action over the years. While it's been scrubbed up for its latest incarnation, it still retains some of the edge that makes it worth coming here. Unlike the restaurant-style approach of most Vancouver pubs, this place is all about TV sports, dart contests and thumping live music.

Mill Marine (Map pp64-5; ☎ 604-687-6455; 1199 W Cordova St; ☿ 11am-11pm Sun-Wed, 11am-midnight Fri & Sat) The food is a little overpriced but the spectacular panoramic views of Stanley Park, the North Shore mountains and the seaplanes descending on Burrard Inlet more than makes up for it. There's a small but impressive selection of draught beers available – try the Whistler Export Lager – as well as specials on offer throughout the week. Arrive before 5pm on summer evenings or you'll have to wrestle someone for a table.

Steamworks Brewing Co (Map pp66-7; ☎ 604-689-2739; 375 Water St; 11:30am-midnight Sun-Wed; 11:30am-1am Thu-Sat) This multipurpose Gastown microbrewery is a sitting-room, pub and oyster bar all in one cavernous converted brick warehouse. The signature beer is Lions Gate Lager – a good summer tipple – and it has great views of the North Shore. A favorite place for the downtown after-work crowd, the library-style upstairs is perfect for sitting by the window or in one of the leather chairs by the fireplace.

Yaletown Brewing Company (Map pp64-5; ☎ 604-681-2739; 1111 Mainland St; ☿ 11:30am-midnight Sun-Wed, 11:30am-1am Thu, 11am-2pm Fri & Sat) As you walk in, there's a bricklined pub on the left and a giant dining room on the right; both serve pints of on-site-brewed beer, but the restaurant adds a menu of great comfort foods. In summer, the large patio is a sought-after perch from which to ogle the beautiful people of Yaletown as they strut past towards the chichi restaurants and lounges.

ENTERTAINMENT

Vancouver's full roster of entertainment options includes cool live music, cutting-edge theater and professional sports. Pick up the *Georgia Straight* and read the West Coast Life

---

✗ VANCOUVER'S BEST NIGHT OUT

For many Vancouverites the city's most authentic live music venue, the **Railway Club** (Map pp64-5; ☎ 604-681-1625; www.therailwayclub.com; 579 Dunsmuir St; shows $4-10) has been upstairs at the corner of Dunsmuir and Seymour Sts since the 1930s. It still feels like a well-kept secret, though – especially to those who 'discover the Rail' for the first time when they stumble in from some other bar late on a Saturday night. Combining a grungy Brit-pub feel with a determinedly eclectic roster of indie, folk, punk, new-wave, soul and everything in between, the clientele is a cheery mix of end-of-day office workers, turtle-necked musos and assignment-avoiding university students. They gather around the tiny stage to catch performances that have ranged from hundreds of obscure acts to some that ultimately became household names, including kd lang and the Tragically Hip. It's not just about the music here, though. While the club has steadily improved its selection of wines and spirits, the Rail will always be a favorite haunt for beer drinkers. West Coast drafts from Granville Island, Central City Brewing and Okanagan Spring feature heavily, and drafts are proffered in traditional dimpled glasses – perhaps the only real pints served in town.

section of the *Vancouver Sun* – both out on Thursday – to tap into what's happening.

Located in the information center, **Tickets Tonight** (☎ 604-684-2787; www.ticketstonight.ca) sells half-price tickets on the day of events; it also sells advance tickets on its website. In addition, tickets for many events are available from **Ticketmaster** (performing arts ☎ 604-280-3311, concerts 604-280-4444, sports 604-280-4400; www.ticketmaster.ca).

Live Music

If you can't catch local favorites such as Bif Naked, the New Pornographers or the Be Good Tanyas, you might still see the next best thing at the city's array of small music venues.

The **Commodore Ballroom** (Map pp64-5; ☎ 604-739-4550; www.commodoreballroom.com; 868 Granville St; shows $20-35) is Vancouver's favorite concert spot. Complete with a bouncy ballroom floor and a great mosh pit, it hosts non-stadium visiting bands and is also a showcase for the best in local talent. For a grungier crowd and a chance to see plenty of edgy regional talent, head to the **Media Club** (Map pp64-5; ☎ 604-608-2871; www.themediaclub.ca; 695 Cambie St; shows $5-20), staging an eclectic array of acts from indie to acoustic metal to rap.

Blues fans will likely prefer the **Yale** (Map pp64-5; ☎ 604-681-9253; www.theyale.ca; 1300 Granville St; shows $10-25), a blowsy, unpretentious joint with a large stage, a devoted clientele and a beer-sticky dance floor. Jazz aficionados will find themselves lured to the subterranean **Cellar Restaurant and Jazz Club** (Map p70; ☎ 604-738-1959; www.cellarjazz.com; 3611 W Broadway; shows $5-45), a serious muso venue where you're required to keep the noise down and respect the performances on the tiny corner stage.

Theater

Vancouver's live theater is spearheaded by the **Arts Club Theatre Company** (Map p69; ☎ 604-687-1644; www.artsclub.com; $28-60), which presents popular world classics and works by contemporary Canadian playwrights at both its **Granville Island Stage** (Map p69; 1585 Johnston St) and its **Stanley Theatre** (Map p69; 2750 Granville St) venues.

More mainstream and generally 'safer' in its selection, the main city-run theater is the **Vancouver Playhouse** (Map pp64-5; ☎ 604-873-3311; www.vancouverplayhouse.com; shows $38-50), which presents a six-play season from its large civic venue at the Queen Elizabeth Theatre complex.

Those looking for more-challenging performance will prefer the **Firehall Arts Centre** (Map pp66-7; ☎ 604-689-0926; www.firehallartscentre.ca; 280 E Cordova St; shows $10-30), an intimate fringe-style venue where 'difficult' dramas and performances are presented to an artsy crowd.

For a complete change of pace, the **Vancouver Theatre Sports League** (Map p69; ☎ 604-738-7013; www.vtsl.com; 1601 Johnston St; shows $10-16.50) performs comedy improv high jinks at its Granville Island base.

Cinemas

For multiplex fans, the new downtown **Paramount Vancouver** (Map pp64-5; ☎ 604-630-1407; www.cineplex.com; 900 Burrard St; admission $10.95) is a magnet for the latest blockbusters. Mixing its own blockbuster offerings with some of the more commercial films on the festival circuit, **Cinemark Tinseltown** (Map pp66-7; ☎ 604-806-0799; www.cinemark.com; 88 W Pender St; admission $10.50) is a downtown favorite.

Those of a more alternative movie bent can choose from the new **Vancity International Film Centre** (Map pp64-5; ☎ 604-683-3456; www.viff.org; 1181 Seymour St; admission $9.50), permanent headquarters of the Vancouver International

---

TOP TEN MOVIE CLUNKERS

While 'Hollywood North' has produced some great films over the years (*X-Men, Best in Show, Gods & Monsters* and so on), Vancouver's movie industry has also raised more than its fair share of turkeys. Head to your local video store and plan your trip with these forgettable flicks:

- *Slither*
- *Mr Magoo*
- *Lake Placid*
- *Ski School 2*
- *Reindeer Games*
- *Saving Silverman*
- *Neverending Story III*
- *Josie & the Pussycats*
- *Super Babies: Baby Geniuses 2*
- *Friday the 13th Part VIII: Jason Takes Manhattan*

See p30 for more on the local film industry – some of the stuff *is* good.

Film Festival (p86) and year-round venue for arthouse films, and **Pacific Cinémathéque** (Map pp64-5; ☎ 604-688-3456; www.cinematheque.bc.ca; 1131 Howe St; admission $8.50), an older cinema plying similar wares. Canada Place's **CN Imax Theatre** (Map pp64-5; ☎ 604-682-4629; www.imax.com/vancouver; 201-999 Canada Place; admission $11.50) screens worthy documentaries and the occasional rejigged *Matrix* or *Star Wars* movie.

On the West Side, **Fifth Avenue Cinemas** (Map p69; ☎ 604-734-7469; www.festivalcinemas.ca; 2110 Burrard St; admission $12) is a popular indie and foreign movie house, as is Kitsilano's long-established **Ridge Theatre** (Map p70; ☎ 604-738-6311; www.festivalcinemas; 3131 Arbutus St; admission $12).

Classical Music & Dance

Along with Vancouver's host of classical music festivals (p84), the city's **Vancouver Symphony Orchestra** (VSO; Map pp64-5; ☎ 604-876-3434; www.vancouversymphony.ca; Orpheum Theatre; shows $25-60) is a local favorite. Under avuncular maestro Bramwell Tovey, the VSO fuses complex and stirring recitals with crossover shows of movie music, opera and even Shakespearean sonnets.

For those who enjoy dance performance, the innovative **Scotiabank Dance Centre** (Map pp64-5; ☎ 604-606-6400; www.thedancecentre.ca; 677 Davie St; shows from $10) hosts entertaining and often challenging recitals by professional and student dancers. **Ballet British Columbia** (Map pp64-5; ☎ 604-732-5003; www.balletbc.com) is headquartered here and frequently performs when not on tour.

Sports

Raising the roof at GM Place the **Vancouver Canucks** (Map pp64-5; ☎ 604-899-4600; www.canucks.com; GM Place; tickets $32-$180; ☸ Oct-Apr) NHL hockey team is the city's leading sporting attraction. Aim to book your ticket way in advance – most games are sold to capacity – and expect local sports bars to fill up on game night with beer-fueled 'Go Canucks Go!' chanters.

If you're itching to see a hockey game but can't get your hands on Canucks tickets, the Western Hockey League's **Vancouver Giants** (Map pp62-3; ☎ 604-444-2687; www.vancouvergiants.com; Pacific Coliseum; tickets $16.50-21.25; ☸ Oct–mid-Mar) is an excellent alternative. Games are held at Pacific Coliseum in Hastings Park, and are often lively affairs, with enough brawls to please the crowds.

Vancouver's Canadian Football League (CFL) team, **BC Lions** (Map pp64-5; ☎ 604-589-7627; www.bclions.com; BC Place Stadium; tickets $24-64; ☸ Jun-Oct) games are played in downtown's cavernous BC Place Stadium. Tickets are usually easy to come by, so don't bother with the parasitic scalpers outside.

Soccer is a popular participatory sport here, but only a few thousand turn up for **Vancouver Whitecaps** (Map pp62-3; ☎ 604-669-9283; www.whitecapsfc.com; Swangard Stadium, Burnaby; tickets $14-24; ☸ May-Aug) games. That might change with the dual men's and women's teams aiming to move from their Burnaby base to a new purpose-built downtown stadium over the next few years. If they're still at Swangard when you arrive, dress warmly or plan to run around a lot – the venue is not well shielded from the cold.

In contrast, a sunny afternoon at Nat Bailey Stadium with the **Vancouver Canadians** (Map pp62-3; ☎ 604-872-5332; www.canadiansbaseball.com; Nat Bailey Stadium; tickets $7.50-20; ☸ Jun-Aug) is less about watching great baseball and more about cold beer in plastic cups, a fistful of übersalty pretzels and a great family atmosphere.

SHOPPING

Robson St is Vancouver's main shopping thoroughfare. The 140-shop **Pacific Centre** (Map pp64-5; ☎ 604-688-7235; main entrance cnr George & Howe Sts; ☸ 10am-7pm Mon, Tue & Sat, 10am-9pm Wed-Fri, 11am-6pm Sun) is just a credit card's throw away.

Souvenir shoppers can take care of business along Gastown's Water St, while hanging out on Granville Island is recommended if you want to watch artisans at work and weave around Public Market.

Slightly more adventurous shoppers should head to Yaletown for upscale boutiques or the Kitsilano and Commercial Dr areas, where galleries and artsy independent stores reign. Those craving artsy, one-of-a-kind clothing shops should make for SoMa.

Clothing

John Fluevog Shoes (Map pp64-5; ☎ 604-688-2828; 837 Granville St; ☸ 11am-7pm Mon-Wed & Sat, 11am-8pm Thu & Fri, noon-5pm Sun) While some of the footwear here looks like Doc Martens on acid and others could poke your eye out from 20 paces, Fluevog's funky shoes, sandals and thigh-hugging boots have been a homegrown fashion legend since 1970. It's tempting to try something on, but be aware that falling in love can happen in an instant.

Lululemon Athletica (Map pp64-5; ☎ 604-681-3118; 1148 Robson St; ⏰ 10am-7pm Mon-Wed, 10am-9pm Thu-Sat, 11am-7pm Sun) Another homegrown local store that's reached far beyond its original base (hence the Tokyo branches), Lululemon kick-started the fashion trend for yoga clothes. There are no statistics on how many customers actually practice yoga, but the widespread appeal of this laid-back, sporty clothing range is undisputed.

Motherland Clothing (Map p69; ☎ 604-876-3426; 2539 Main St; ⏰ 11am-6pm Mon-Wed & Sat, 11am-7pm Thu & Fri, noon-6pm Sun) Cute arthouse designer wear for bright young things, Motherland defines Main St's emergence as a fashion center. The clothes – quirky skirts, pants and Ts – are Canadian designed, in-house-made and well priced enough that even those on student loans can afford them.

Smoking Lily (Map p69; ☎ 604-873-5459; 3634 Main St; ⏰ 11am-5:30pm Thu-Sat, noon-5pm Sun & Mon) Art-student cool is the approach at this SoMa store, where skirts and halter tops are tastefully accented with prints of ants, skulls or squid, making their wearers appear interesting and complex. It's a fun spot to browse and the staff are friendly and chatty.

Markets

Chinatown Night Market (Map pp66-7; ☎ 604-682-8998; 100-200 Keefer St; ⏰ 6:30-11pm Fri-Sun mid-May–mid-Sep) Smaller and gentler than its raucous Richmond rival (see p109) this downtown evening street market still attracts plenty of visitors with its sensory combination of cheap toys, 'designer handbags' and pungent street food. In fact, the hawker cuisine is so tempting, it's best not to eat dinner before you come so you can sample as much as possible.

Granville Island Public Market (Map p69; ☎ 604-666-6477; Johnston St; ⏰ 9am-7pm) Colorful pyramids of fruit and veggies dominate at the city's leading covered market, but this is also a great spot for more eclectic purchases: take home some exotic loose tea, a bottle of Okanagan ice wine or some of Oyama Sausage Co's finest. A good spot for lunch, especially outside on the waterfront.

UBC Farm Market (Map pp62-3; ☎ 604-822-5092; 6182 South Campus Rd; ⏰ 9am-1pm Sat Jun-Sep) A tasty cornucopia of local farm produce hits the stalls here in summer. Seasonal highlights include lush apricots, peaches and blueberries, while artisan breads and cakes are usually available,

too. For other regional farm markets, check www.bcfarmersmarket.org.

Outdoor Gear

Mountain Equipment Co-op (Map p69; ☎ 604-872-7858; 130 W Broadway; ⏰ 10am-7pm Mon-Wed, 10am-9pm Thu & Fri, 9am-6pm Sat, 11am-5pm Sun) Outdoorsy visitors usually gravitate towards this gear store mecca, stuffed with clothing, kayaks, sleeping bags, clever camping gadgets and a respectable array of regional and international travel books. You'll have to be a member to buy, but that's easy to arrange and only costs $5.

Umbrella Shop (Map p69; ☎ 604-697-0919; Granville Island; 10am-6pm Mon-Sat) Sometimes (okay, often) the only outdoor gear you need in Vancouver is a good brolly to fend off the torrential rain. This family-run company has just the thing, with hundreds of bright and breezy designs that should put a smile on the face of any rain-soaked visitor.

GETTING THERE & AWAY
Air

The main BC hub for airlines from the rest of Canada, the US and destinations around the world, **Vancouver International Airport** (Map pp62-3; ☎ 604-207-7077; www.yvr.ca) is in Richmond, a 13km, 30-minute drive from downtown Vancouver. Regular domestic services include **Air Canada Jazz** (☎ 888-247-2262; www.aircanada.ca) flights from Victoria (from $108, 25 minutes) and **WestJet** (☎ 800-538-5696, 403-444-2552; www.westjet.com) flights from Calgary (from $99, 90 minutes). See Transport (p397) for general information on routes and airlines.

The **South Terminal** (Map pp62-3) is linked to the main airport by a free shuttle bus. It services smaller flights, floatplanes and helicopter routes to/from destinations mostly within BC. Regular arrivals here include **Baxter Aviation** (☎ 250-754-1066, 800-661-5599; www.baxterair.com) flights from Nanaimo, ($54, 20 minutes; six daily), **Pacific Coastal Airlines** (☎ 604-273-8666; www.pacific-coastal.com) services from Powell River (from $84, 30 minutes, four daily) and **Whistler Air** (☎ 603-932-6615, 888-806-2299; www.whistlerair.ca) flights from Whistler ($149, 30 minutes, two daily, May to September).

Several convenient floatplane services also fly directly to the Vancouver waterfront. These include frequent **Harbour Air Seaplanes** (☎ 604-274-1277, 800-665-0212; www.harbour-air.com) flights ($109, 35 minutes) and **West Coast Air** (☎ 604-606-6888, 800-347-2222; www.westcoastair.com)

planes ($119, 35 minutes) from Victoria's Inner Harbour.

Helijet (☎ 604-273-4688, 800-665-4354; www.helijet .com) helicopter services arrive on the waterfront, east of Canada Place, from Victoria (from $109, 35 minutes, four to 13 daily).

Boat

BC Ferries (☎ 888-223-3779, 250-386-3431; www.bcferries .com) services arrive at Tsawwassen, an hour from the city center, and Horseshoe Bay, 30 minutes from downtown in West Vancouver

Main services to Tsawwassen arrive from Vancouver Island's Swartz Bay (adult/child/ vehicle $10.30/5.15/34.20, 90 minutes) and Nanaimo's Duke Point (adult/child/vehicle $10.30/5.15/34.20, two hours). For services from the Southern Gulf Islands, see p194.

Services to Horseshoe Bay arrive from Nanaimo's Departure Bay (adult/child/vehicle $10.30/5.15/34.20, 90 minutes). Services also arrive here from Bowen Island (adult/ child/vehicle $6.80/3.40/21.45, 20 minutes) and from Langdale (adult/child/vehicle $9.15/4.60/32.65, 40 minutes), the only ferry route to and from the Sunshine Coast.

Bus

Vancouver's bus station is part of **Pacific Central Station** (Map pp64-5; 1150 Station St), the railway terminus near Science World. It's on the Sky-Train transit line (Main St Science World station).

Greyhound (☎ 800-661-8747; www.greyhound.ca) services arrive here from Whistler ($18.80, 2½ hours, eight daily), Kelowna ($61.50, six hours, seven daily), Hope ($20.45, two to three hours, nine daily) and Calgary ($133.90, 14 to 17 hours, four daily). For information on Greyhound routes from across the border see Transport (p399).

Pacific Coach Lines (☎ 250-385-4411, 800-661-1725; www.pacificcoach.com) services from downtown Victoria ($36, 3½ hours, up to 16 daily), also arrive here, via BC Ferries' Swartz Bay–Tsawwassen route.

Quick Coach Lines (☎ 604-940-4428, 800-665-2122; www.quickcoach.com) operates an express shuttle service between Seattle and Vancouver, departing from downtown Seattle (US$31.35, four hours, six daily) and the city's Sea-Tac International Airport (US$40.85, 4½ hours, seven daily).

Perimeter Tours (☎ 604-266-5386, 877-317-7788; www.perimeterbus.com) services arrive from

Whistler ($67, 2½ hours, seven to 11 daily) throughout the day. It will drop you off at downtown hotels if requested at time of booking.

Serving the Sunshine Coast, twice-daily **Malaspina Coach Lines** (☎ 604-886-7742, 877-227-8287; www.malaspinacoach.com) buses arrive from Gibsons ($24, two hours), Sechelt ($30, three hours) and Powell River ($51, five to six hours).

Car & Motorcycle

If you're coming from Washington state in the US, you'll be on the I-5 until you hit the border town of Blaine, then you'll be on Hwy 99 in Canada. It's about an hour's drive from here to downtown Vancouver. Hwy 99 continues through downtown, across Lions Gate Bridge to Horseshoe Bay, Squamish and Whistler.

If you're coming from the east, you'll probably be on the Trans-Canada Hwy (Hwy 1), which snakes through the city's eastern end, eventually meeting with Hastings St. If you want to go downtown, turn left onto Hastings and follow it into the city center, or continue on along the North Shore towards Whistler.

If you're coming from Horseshoe Bay, the Trans-Canada Hwy (Hwy 1) heads through West Vancouver and North Vancouver before going over the Second Narrows Bridge into Burnaby. If you're heading downtown, leave the highway at the Taylor Way exit in West Vancouver and follow it over Lions Gate Bridge towards the city center.

All the recognized car rental chains have Vancouver branches. Avis, Budget, Hertz, Lo-Cost and Thrifty also have airport branches.

Train

Trains arrive from across Canada and the US at Pacific Central Station. **VIA Rail** (☎ 888-842-7245; www.viarail.ca) services arrive from Kamloops North ($105, nine hours, three weekly), Jasper ($220, 17½ hours, three weekly) and Edmonton ($297, 24 hours, three weekly) among others.

The **Amtrak** (☎ 800-872-7245; www.amtrak.com) *Cascades* service arrives from Eugene (US$56, 13½ hours, two daily), Portland (US$42, eight hours, three daily) and Seattle (US$28, 3½ hours, five daily).

West Coast Express (☎ 604-683-7245; www.westcoast express.com) commuter trains arrive six times daily Monday to Friday at downtown's **Wa-**

terfront Station (601 W Cordova). Services arrive from Mission City ($10.25, 70 minutes), Pitt Meadows ($7.50, 45 minutes), Port Coquitlam ($6, 35 minutes) and Port Moody ($6, 35 minutes) among others.

GETTING AROUND
To/From the Airport

Taxis charge up to $35 for the 30-minute drive from the airport to downtown Vancouver.

Vancouver Airporter (☎ 604-946-8866, 800-668-3141; www.yvrairporter.com; adult/child one-way $13/6, round-trip $20/12; ☼ 5:30am-11:45pm, reduced in winter) buses drop off at 24 downtown hotels as well as Pacific Central Station. Reservations are not required – pay the driver or buy a ticket at the desk inside the airport.

Transit services are also available: take bus 424 from the airport, change at Airport Station and take the 98 B-Line express bus into the city (adult/child $3.25/2). The SkyTrain line is being extended to the airport from downtown and should be open by 2010.

Bicycle

Vancouver is a relatively good cycling city, with routes running across town. Cyclists can take their bikes for free on the SkyTrain, SeaBus and bike-rack fitted buses. Pick up a *Greater Vancouver Cycling Map & Guide* ($3.95) at convenience stores and bookshops for details on routes and resources. Touch base with the **Vancouver Area Cycling Coalition** (www.vacc.bc.ca) for additional tips.

Boat

Aquabus Ferries (Map pp64-5; ☎ 604-689-5858; www .aquabus.bc.ca; adult/child from $2.50/1.25; ☼ 6:40am-9pm) runs mini vessels (some big enough to carry bikes) between the foot of Hornby St and Granville Island. They service additional spots around False Creek, including Science World. If you're making multiple trips, consider an all-day pass ($11).

Aquabus' rival on these cutthroat waters is **False Creek Ferries** (Map pp64-5; ☎ 604-684-7781; www.granvilleislandferries.bc.ca; adult/child from $2.50/1.25; ☼ 7am-9pm), which operates a similar Granville Island service, this time from the Aquatic Centre, plus ports of call around False Creek. A day pass costs $12.

Car & Motorcycle

The city's evening rush-hour traffic can be a nightmare, with enormous lines of cars snaking along Georgia St waiting to cross Lions Gate Bridge. Try the alternative Second Narrows Bridge if you need to get across to the North Shore in a relative hurry. Other peak-time hot spots to avoid are the George Massey Tunnel and Hwy 1 to Surrey.

Parking is at a premium downtown: there are few free spots available on residential side streets (parking permits are often required) and traffic wardens are predictably predatory. Some streets have metered parking but pay-parking lots (from $4 per hour) are a better proposition – arrive before 9am at some for early bird discounts. Underground parking at either Pacific Centre or the Central Library will have you in the heart of the city.

Public Transportation

TransLink (☎ 604-953-3333; www.translink.bc.ca), the public transportation authority, oversees bus, SkyTrain commuter train and SeaBus boat services. Visit the website for a useful trip planning tool or pick up a copy of the *Getting Around* map ($1.95) from area convenience and bookstores.

A ticket bought on any bus, SkyTrain or SeaBus service is valid for up to 90 minutes of transfer travel across the entire network, depending on the zone you intend to travel in. There are three zones, which become progressively more expensive the further you intend to journey. One-zone tickets cost adult/child $2.25/1.50, two-zone tickets are adult/child $3.25/2 and three-zone tickets cost adult/child $4.50/3. An all-day, all-zone pass costs adult/child $8/6. If you're traveling after 6:30pm or on weekends or holidays, all fares are classed as one-zone trips.

BUS

Buses use on-board fare machines, so exact change (or more) is required. The network is extensive in the downtown area – especially along Granville St, Broadway, Hastings St, Main St and Burrard St. Many buses are wheelchair accessible.

B-Line express buses operate between Richmond, the airport and downtown Vancouver (98 B-Line) and between UBC and the Broadway and Commercial SkyTrain stations (99 B-Line). These buses have their own limited arrival and departure points and do not use regular bus stops.

TransLink also operates a 12-route night bus system that runs every 30 minutes from

1:30am and 4am across the Lower Mainland. The last bus leaves downtown Vancouver at 3am. Look for the night bus signs on designated bus stops.

SKYTRAIN

SkyTrain tickets must be purchased from station vending machines (change given for bills up to $20) prior to boarding. Spot checks from fare inspectors are frequent and they can issue an on-the-spot fine if you don't have the correct ticket. Avoid buying transfers from the 'scalpers' at some stations since they are usually expired or close to expiration (the transfers, not the scalpers).

The SkyTrain network consists of two routes. The 40-minute Expo Line takes passengers to and from downtown Vancouver and Surrey, via stops in Burnaby (for Swangard soccer stadium and Metrotown shopping centre) and New Westminster. The Millennium Line alights near shopping malls and suburban residential districts in Coquitlam and Burnaby.

Trains depart every two to eight minutes between 5am and 12:30am Monday to Friday (6am to 12:30am Saturday, 7am to 11:30pm Sunday). All SkyTrain services are wheelchair accessible.

SEABUS

This aquatic shuttle operates every 15 to 30 minutes throughout the day, taking 12 minutes to cross the Burrard Inlet between Waterfront Station and Lonsdale Quay. At Lonsdale there's a bus terminal servicing routes throughout North Vancouver and West Vancouver. SeaBus tickets must be purchased in advance from vending machines on either side of the route. Services depart from Waterfront Station between 6am and 12:45am Monday to Saturday (8am to 11:15pm Sunday). The vessels are wheelchair accessible and bike friendly.

Taxi

Flagging a cab on the main downtown streets shouldn't take too long, but it's easiest to get your hotel to call you one. Main operators include **Black Top** (☎ 604-731-1111) and **Vancouver Taxi** (☎ 604-871-1111), which has a fleet of wheelchair-accessible vehicles. For green travelers, **Yellow Cab** (☎ 604-681-1111) has some low-emission cars. Vancouver taxi meters start at $2.30 and add $1.25 per kilometer.

THE LOWER MAINLAND

While easy-access downtown Vancouver remains the main draw for those arriving in this part of the world, there's a supporting cast of Lower Mainland towns and cities that are well worth a day trip or two from the metropolis. Across the Burrard Inlet, in the shadow of the mountains that are part of the Vancouver scenery, North Vancouver and West Vancouver offer vibrant communities and outdoor activities. Head east of Vancouver to hit Burnaby, while south brings you to Richmond and then Delta. Transit will get you to most of the main places, but a car is recommended if you're planning to head further afield.

NORTH VANCOUVER

pop 134,000

Stretching west from Indian Arm to West Vancouver, 'North Van' is a predominantly residential area with some great views of the Vancouver skyline. Increased development has seen swathes of trees removed and housing climb further and further up the mountains here, with nature literally on the doorstep of many inhabitants. For information on what to do here, check out the visitors section of the municipal website (www.cnv.org) or pick up a copy of the *North Shore News*, the free local paper.

Sights & Activities

One of BC's most popular visitor attractions, the 140m-long cabled walkway of **Capilano Suspension Bridge & Park** (Map pp62-3; ☎ 604-985-7474; www.capbridge.com; 3735 Capilano Rd; adult/youth/child $26/15/8; 9am-5pm Nov-Mar, 9am-6:30pm Apr, 8:30am-8pm May-Aug, 9am-7pm Sep, 9am-6pm Oct) sways over the fast-running waters of tree-lined Capilano Canyon. It's an awesome sight for even the most jaded of travelers, especially when you get halfway across and realize your legs have turned to jelly. There are plenty of additional reasons to stick around for the afternoon, including totem poles, rain forest walks and a nifty network of cable bridges strung between some of the trees, providing a squirrel's-eye view of the natural world.

If you want to sway for free, **Lynn Canyon Park** (Map pp62-3; ☎ 604-984-3149; Park Rd; admission free; 7am-9pm May-Aug, 7am-7pm Sep-Apr), set in the heart of the temperate rain forest, has a no-cost, less-showy suspension bridge that's slightly smaller than Capilano's. There are also plenty of excellent hiking trails here and some good picnic spots. Find time to check out the park's **Ecology Centre** (Map pp62-3; ☎ 604-981-3103; www.dnv.org; 3663 Park Rd; ☺ 10am-5pm Apr-Sep, noon-4pm Sat & Sun Oct-May), where displays, films and slide shows illuminate the area's rich biodiversity. To get to the park, take the Lynn Valley Rd exit off Hwy 1, then turn right on Peters Rd, where you'll see signs pointing the way.

With unrivalled views over the shimmering metropolis, **Grouse Mountain** (Map pp62-3; ☎ 604-980-9311; www.grousemountain.com; 6400 Nancy Greene Way; adult/youth/child summer $33/19/12, winter $45/35/20; ☺ 9am-10pm) touts itself as the 'peak of Vancouver.' In summer, your Skyride ticket gives you mountain-top access to lumberjack shows, alpine hiking trails, a grizzly bear refuge and restaurants. You can also harden your calf muscles on the **Grouse Grind**, a steep 2.9km wilderness trek, which takes most people around 90 minutes. Grouse really comes into its own in winter, when it becomes a popular snowy playground for Vancouverites. They come for the two lifts, 25 ski and snowboard runs and outdoor ice-skating rink. To get here, head north over Lions Gate Bridge and veer right on Marine Dr, then turn left onto Capilano Rd.

An accessible nature escape from the city and a great spot to hug 500-year-old Douglas firs, the popular **Mt Seymour Provincial Park** (Map pp62-3; ☎ 604-986-2261; www.env.gov.bc.ca/bcparks; 1700 Mt Seymour Rd) is crisscrossed with hiking trails. Some areas are rugged, so backpackers should register at the park office, where trail maps are also available. Like Grouse, the park transforms in winter, when **Mt Seymour Resorts** (☎ 604-718-7771; www.mountseymour.com; adult/youth/child $36/29/19; ☺ 9:30am-10pm Mon-Fri, 8:30am-10pm Sat & Sun Jan-Mar) runs three lifts to take you skiing or snowboarding on its 21 runs. More family-oriented than Grouse, there's also a toboggan area ($6) and snow-tubing course ($14, two hours). To get to Seymour, take the Mt Seymour Parkway exit east, then turn north on Mt Seymour Rd. The resort operates a free winter shuttle bus from Lonsdale Quay.

A popular half-day excursion via a 12-minute SeaBus trip from downtown, the **Lonsdale Quay Market** (Map pp62-3; ☎ 604-985-6261; www.lonsdalequay.com; 123 Carrie Cates Court; ☺ 9:30am-6:30pm) offers a more touristy market than Granville Island. The product mix ranges from books

to salmon and the upper floors contain some clothing stores. There's a food court and some spectacular views of Vancouver's shimmering waterfront skyline.

Sleeping

Grouse Inn (Map pp62-3; ☎ 604-988-1701, 800-779-7888; www.grouseinn.com; 1633 Capilano Rd; s/d/ste from $99/109/145; ☻) Facilities abound at this popular modern motel favored by winter skiers and summer wilderness explorers. There's a playground, free movie channel and free continental breakfast. Family-friendly, the rooms have bright and breezy interiors – especially if you like busy, 1980s-style bedspreads – and come in a wide array of configurations, including Jacuzzi suites and larger rooms for groups.

Comfort Inn & Suites (Map pp62-3; ☎ 604-988-3181, 888-988-3181; www.vancouvercomfort.com; 1748 Capilano Rd; d/ste $129/169; ☻) The former Canyon Court Motel, this renovated sleepover has a chalet-like appearance and its rooms surround a quiet outdoor courtyard. The interiors have all been updated, with rooms now including business-hotel-style furnishings; some also have kitchenettes. Continental breakfast is included and there's an on-site laundry, as well as a pool, sauna and Jacuzzi to soak away those sore skiing muscles.

Lynn Canyon House B&B (Map pp62-3; ☎ 604-986-4741; 3333 Robinson Rd; www.vancouverinn.com; d $129-169; ☻) Looking like a compact Tudor manor, this place is right near the entrance to Lynn Canyon Park. Once you step inside it quickly takes the form of a charming English inn. It has the elegance of cherry wood furnishings, antique knickknacks and warm hospitality, and the modern conveniences of thick goose-down quilts and an outdoor pool. Rooms have views of the mountains or the garden.

Lonsdale Quay Hotel (Map pp62-3; ☎ 604-986-6111, 800-836-6111; www.lonsdalequayhotel.com; 123 Carrie Cates Ct; d/ste $149/189; ☻) With easy access to the mountains but also close to the SeaBus terminal for swift downtown trips, some of the rooms at this older boutique hotel have great views of the Vancouver skyline. Most interiors will be familiar to the business traveler crowd but some have been decorated with style, including two great family rooms with bunk beds and bath toys. Free high-speed internet access is included.

Inn Penzance (Map pp62-3; ☎ 604-681-2889, 888-546-3327; www.innpenzance.com; 1388 Terrace Ave; r/ste/cottage $160/195/185) Enveloped by an inviting

DETOUR: DEEP COVE

From Vancouver, take the Dollarton exit off Hwy 1 and go east – right if you just crossed the Second Narrows Bridge. Stop in Cates Park to enjoy the views of Belcarra Regional Park across the waters of Burrard Inlet, or follow the road as it turns left and becomes Deep Cove Rd.

The road will pass close to some ultra-rich homes before making a right turn, leading you down through the quaint hamlet of Deep Cove and the protected waters of…Deep Cove. It's a deeply relaxing part of the Lower Mainland where you can grab lunch or a yeast-free doughnut at **Honey's** (Map pp62-3; ☎ 604-929-4988; 4373 Gallant Ave; mains $4-8) before hitting the main attraction.

Deep Cove is an ideal spot for kayak virgins. The waters here are glassy calm and the setting, around North America's southernmost fjord, couldn't be more tranquil. **Deep Cove Canoe & Kayak Centre** (Map pp62-3; ☎ 604-929-2268; 2156 Banbury Rd) will tell you all you need to know on a three-hour intro course ($70) that's aimed at complete neophytes. For those with a little more experience, it also offers rentals (two/five hours $28/56) and some lovely guided tours of the region.

garden and incorporating some exotic interior design themes, this smashing little B&B offers an Asian-flavored lodge room, a secluded cottage and a large New Orleans suite (complete with three beds) that's ideal for groups. The small Caribbean Cottage, separated from the main house by a stream, includes its own fireplace and kitchenette, and is tranquility personified.

Eating

Tomahawk Restaurant (Map pp62-3; ☎ 604-988-2612; 1550 Philip Ave; mains $6-14; ⌚ 8am-9pm Sun-Thu, 8am-10pm Fri & Sat) A blast from Vancouver's past, the family-owned Tomahawk has been heaping diners' plates with comfort food since 1926. An excellent weekend breakfast spot – if this place doesn't kill your hangover, then nothing will – it's also great for lunch or dinner, when chicken potpies and organic meatloaf hit the menu.

Altitudes Bistro (Map pp62-3; ☎ 604-984-0661; Grouse Mt; mains $7-17; ⌚ 11:30am-10pm) The views here are almost as good as those from the adjacent observatory, and the atmosphere is decidedly more laid-back, with pub-style food in a casual ski lodge setting.

Brown's Restaurant & Bar (Map pp62-3; ☎ 604-929-5401; 1764 Lonsdale Ave; mains $12-18; ⌚ 11am-10pm Sun-Tue, 11am-11pm Wed-Fri, 11am-midnight Sun) This Yaletown-style lounge, located in the heart of the North Shore, has developed a strong local following since its recent opening. The bar features beer or cocktail specials throughout the week while the restaurant menu ranges from the hickory bacon burger (recommended) to such well-prepared mains as seared ahi tuna.

Gusto di Quattro (Map pp62-3; ☎ 604-924-4444; 1 Lonsdale Ave; mains $12-24; ⌚ 11:30am-2pm Mon-Fri, 5pm-10pm) A good-value, family-run gourmet Italian restaurant, Gusto di Quattro has a warm-hued dining room and service levels to match. All the pasta classics are here but more-adventurous diners might prefer the duck fusilli or tiger prawn linguini. The wine selection is good and some international tipples have started to infiltrate the mostly Italian selection in recent years.

Observatory (Map pp62-3; ☎ 604-998-4403; Grouse Mt; mains $35-40; ⌚ 5-10pm) Perched atop Grouse Mountain, the fine-dining Observatory serves up dishes of seared scallops and roasted beef tenderloin with some of the best views in BC – right down over the crenulated waterfront of Stanley Park and the shiny towers of Vancouver.

Getting There & Around

SeaBus vessels arrive at Lonsdale Quay from Vancouver's Waterfront Station ($3.50, 12 minutes) every 15 to 30 minutes throughout the day. There's a bus terminal at Lonsdale Quay; bus 236 runs from here to Capilano Suspension Bridge and Grouse Mountain.

The **Rocky Mountaineer Vacations** (☎ 604-606-8460, 888-687-7245; www.whistlermountaineer.com) *Whistler Mountaineer* train arrives in North Vancouver from Whistler (from $99, three hours, daily May to mid-October).

If you like cycling up hills, you can explore the area with a rental bike from the friendly folk at **Cove Bike Shop** (Map pp62-3; ☎ 604-929-2222, 877-929-2683; www.covebike.com; 1389 Main St; day rental from $35). For a less strenuous tour, **North Van Green Tours** (☎ 604-290-0145; www.northvan

greentours.com; adult/child $35/20) offers a four-hour guided trek of the area's natural treasures in an ecologically friendly biofuel van.

WEST VANCOUVER
pop 44,000

Claiming the highest per-capita income of any district in Canada, 'West Van' is a 20-minute bus ride from downtown through Stanley Park and across Lions Gate Bridge. It's not hard to believe the stats when you see some of the houses here, particularly those multilevel, multidecked West Coast mansions clinging to the cliffs over the oceanfront. Regarded among the veritable plebs in the rest of the region as snob central, West Vancouver is a stop-off point on your drive from downtown to Whistler or the Horseshoe Bay ferry terminal. For more information, visit the local council's website at www.westvancouver.ca.

Sights & Activities

Located 8km north of West Vancouver off Hwy 99, **Cypress Provincial Park** (Map pp62-3; ☎ 604-924-2200; www.env.gov.bc.ca/bcparks; Cypress Bowl Rd) has some great summertime hiking trails, including the fairly difficult Black Mountain Loop and the challenging Howe Sound Crest Trail. In winter, the park's **Cypress Mountain** (Map pp62-3; ☎ 604-926-5612; www.cypressmountain.com; adult/youth/child $46/39/20; ◷ 9am-4pm Dec, 9am-10pm Jan-Mar) ski area competes with Grouse for local outdoorsy types. If it's great slopes you're after, there's no competition: Cypress is the largest accessible mountain on the North Shore, has five lifts and a superior average snowfall. This helps explain why it has been chosen as the snowboarding and freestyle skiing venue for the 2010 Winter Olympics. A family-friendly area, Cypress also has snowshoeing trails and a snow-tubing course.

Some of the Lower Mainland's largest and oldest trees live within the 75-hectare **Lighthouse Park** (Map pp62-3; ☎ 604-925-7200; cnr Beacon Lane & Marine Dr), which includes a rare stand of original coastal forest including plenty of copper-trunked arbutus trees. About 13km of hiking trails wind through the park; the most popular leads to Point Atkinson Lighthouse with its views of the shimmering Burrard Inlet. To get here, turn west (left) on Marine Dr after crossing Lions Gate Bridge.

Head to the village marina near Horseshoe Bay and book a seat on a rigid-hulled inflatable with **Sewell's Sea Safari** (Map pp62-3; ☎ 604-921-3474; www.sewellsmarina.com; 6409 Bay St; adult/youth/child $64/59/34), for a two-hour, high-speed ride out to sea. With the spray in your face and the wind threatening to whip off your sunglasses, keep your eyes open for possible whale pod sightings. Barking seals and soaring eagles are a more likely proposition on most trips. If you don't have a car, you can get to the marina on bus 247 from downtown Vancouver.

Sleeping & Eating

Horseshoe Bay Motel (Map pp62-3; ☎ 604-921-7454, 877-717-3377; 6588 Royal Ave; s/d $99/119) This plain Jane, nothing-to-write-home-about motel is one of the only options available for a West Van sleepover. The 23 rooms are standard motel fare, but if you have an early-morning ferry to catch from nearby Horseshoe Bay, you'll be happy with even the minimum of home comforts.

Lighthouse Park B&B (Map pp62-3; ☎ 604-926-5959, 800-926-0262; www.lighthousepark.com; 4875 Water Lane; ste $165) Live like a West Van local at this elegant two-suite sleepover, with beautifully decorated Laura Ashley–influenced interiors and decadent flourishes such as thick bed linens, private entrances and a tranquil flower-strewn courtyard. Each suite has a fridge and DVD player, as well as a decanter of sherry for that essential alfresco evening tipple. It's within walking distance of Point Atkinson Lighthouse.

Vera's Burger Shack (Map pp62-3; ☎ 604-603-8372; Dundarave Pier; mains $5-7; ◷ 10am-9pm May-Sep) A local favorite, Vera's epic burgers are among Vancouver's best. Dare to try the double patty, double cheese and double onion special and see if you can still stand. Alternatively, there are toasted sandwiches, hot dogs and fries – complete with a frightening array of sauces and toppings.

Caspian (Map pp62-3; ☎ 604-921-1311; 1495 Marine Dr; mains $10-18; ◷ 11:30am-10pm) One of the Lower Mainland's only Iranian restaurants, Caspian is a hidden gem that attracts a knowing local crowd. Proving just how authentic the food is, there are always a few expat Iranians here, tucking into large platters of Barbary bread (with eggplant dip) and hearty, long-simmered stews. The fish, chicken and beef kabobs command the lion's share of the menu and are highly recommended.

Salmon House on the Hill (Map pp62-3; ☎ 604-926-3212; 2229 Folkestone Way; mains $24-30; ◷ 11:30am-2pm &

5-10pm) With Vancouver at your feet, it's tough to beat this place when it comes to views. But it's not just about looks here; this landmark West Van eatery has been cheffing up some of the Lower Mainland's best fish dishes for years. While the salmon is always worthwhile, there's also an ever-changing array of seasonal BC seafood treats – ask for recommendations before you order.

HORSESHOE BAY & BOWEN ISLAND

This small coastal community (population 1000) marks the end of the North Shore and the start of trips to Whistler via the Sea to Sky Hwy (Hwy 99) or Vancouver Island and the Sunshine Coast via the ferry terminal. Ferries also travel the 20-minute distance to Bowen Island from here. Both destinations enjoy great views across the bays to distant glaciated peaks. For Horseshoe Bay information, check www.horseshoebaybc.ca. Bowen Island has its own **visitor information center** (VIC; ☎ 604-947-9024; www.bowenisland.org; 432 Cardena Rd; ◷ 9:30am-4pm mid-May–mid-Oct, 11am-4pm Wed-Fri mid-Oct–mid-May).

Sights & Activities

Just west of Horseshoe Bay, **Whytecliff Park** (Map pp62-3; ☎ 604-925-7200; 7100 block Marine Dr) attracts scuba divers to its protected waters, hikers to its rocky trails and rock climbers to its granite cliffs. It's also a fun place for families and kids to visit, as there are plenty of picnic areas and views of the marine activity.

Hiking trails and picnic grounds are found all over Bowen, including the five-minute stroll from the old pioneer buildings to the tables at Snug Cove, and the 45-minute trek from the ferry dock to Killarney Lake, itself encircled by a 4km trail. Scenic kayaking tours are offered by **Bowen Island Sea Kayaking** (☎ 604-947-9266, 800-605-2925; www.bowenislandkayaking.com; rental 3hr/5hr/day $35/45/55, tours from $55). Its two-day Round Bowen tour ($250) is recommended, if you have time.

Sleeping & Eating

Lodge at the Old Dorm (Map pp62-3; ☎ 604-947-0947; www.lodgeattheolddorm.com; 460 Melmore Rd; r $90-140) A short stroll from the Bowen ferry dock, this elegant character B&B is dripping with art deco accents and arts and crafts flourishes but it's also a warm and convivial spot for a sleepover. The six rooms are bright and comfortable – the Lady 'Alexandra' with its

own private garden is recommended – and the continental buffet breakfast, served on a large island counter in the kitchen, is all about home-baked treats.

Doc Morgan's Inn (Map pp62-3; ☎ 604-947-0808; mains $8-22; ◷ 11:30am-11pm) Before your paddle at Bowen's, you can fuel up here, where the patios overlooking the park and the harbor make time seem irrelevant. Pub grub is the main focus of the menu – order the fish and chips and you won't be sorry – and there's a colorful sea salt air among the chatty locals who fill the place.

Boathouse (Map pp62-3; ☎ 604-921-8188; 6695 Nelson Ave; mains $10-20; ◷ 11am-10pm) Over on the mainland, Boathouse is a Horseshoe Bay dine-out landmark. Sitting prominently to the west of the ferry terminal with its big cedar-framed windows looking out over the water, it's a wonderful place for some West Coast seafood.

Getting There & Around

BC Ferries (☎ 888-223-3779, 250-386-3431; www.bcferries .com) services ply the short route between Horseshoe Bay and Bowen Island (adult/child/vehicle $6.80/3.40/21.45, 20 minutes, 16 daily).

The **Bowen Island Community Shuttle** (☎ 604-947-0229; adult/child $2.25/1.50) trundles locals and visitors around the island, while bike rentals are available from (where else) the **Bike Rentals Place** (☎ 604-999-7462; www.thebikerentalsplace.com; ferry dock; ◷ mid-May–mid-Sep).

BURNABY

pop 204,000

The city immediately east of Vancouver, Burnaby has the feel of a predominantly residential suburb. As well as its anonymous strip malls, it's also home to BC's largest shopping complex. In addition, there are a handful of attractions and parks that give the locals something other than shopping to occupy their time. To plan your visit, contact **Tourism Burnaby** (☎ 604-419-0377; www.toruismburnaby.com).

Sights & Activities

Sitting atop Burnaby Mountain, **Simon Fraser University** (Map pp62-3; ☎ 604-291-3111; www.sfu .com) was designed by noted Canadian architect Arthur Erickson. Although its striking concrete block appearance was initially controversial, the university has a unique campus and a captivating hilltop setting. Attractions here include the **Museum of Archaeology & Ethnology** (☎ 604-291-3325; 8888 University Dr; admission free;

10am-4pm Mon-Fri) and the **SFU Gallery** (☎ 604-291-4266; 8888 University Dr; admission free; 10am-5pm Tue-Fri, noon-5pm Sat). To get to campus follow Hastings St east or take a B-Line express bus from downtown Vancouver.

Offering a peaceful environment minus the hectic energy of downtown, **Deer Lake Park** (Map pp62–3) has paths that crisscross the meadows and woodlands, and circle the lake where fowl and other wildlife hang out. Also in the park, the smashing **Burnaby Village Museum** (Map pp62-3; ☎ 604-293-6515; 6501 Deer Lake Ave; adult/youth/child $8.25/6/5.25, carousel $1.40; 11am-4pm May-Aug) re-creates the atmosphere of a southwestern BC pioneer town. The replica village houses homes and businesses of the time and a wonderfully restored 1912 carousel, now retrofitted for wheelchair access. To get there, take the Sperling Ave exit off Hwy 1 and follow the museum signs.

An ever-expanding temple to commercialism, **Metropolis at Metrotown** (Map pp62-3; ☎ 604-438-4175; www.metropolisatmetrotown.com; 10am-9pm Mon-Fri, 9:30am-9pm Sat, 11am-6pm Sun) is the biggest shopping center around. Savvy shoppers usually arrive early in the morning to beat the crowds and get back home sometime the following week. You can give your credit cards a rest at the giant food court – Indian, Japanese and Chinese cuisines are the best here – or the multiplex theater. The mall is on the SkyTrain line from downtown Vancouver.

Sleeping & Eating

Kingsway Blvd, just west of Boundary Rd is Burnaby's main motel strip. There's a ubiquity of good-value Chinese restaurants here.

401 Motor Inn (Map pp62-3; ☎ 604-438-3451, 877-438-3451; www.401motorinn.com; 2950 Boundary Rd; s/d/tw $80/85/90;) Among the most popular of Burnaby's motels, this green-hued place has large rooms, predictable motel decor and some kitchenettes. There's a swimming pool, and continental breakfast is included in the room rates.

Pear Tree (Map pp62-3; ☎ 604-299-2772; 4120 E Hastings St; mains $22-32; 5-10pm Tue-Sun) For something a little different, head to the Pear Tree, where the surprisingly swanky contemporary look complements a menu of modernized, continental-influenced West Coast classics. Try the amazing lobster cappuccino.

RICHMOND
pop 173,000

The Lower Mainland's modern-day Chinatown, the city of Richmond combines Asian shopping malls and restaurants in a suburban setting. It's easy to access from downtown Vancouver – most of the action is centered on Richmond's No 3 Rd – and the city will be the host for the speed skating events at the 2010 Winter Olympics. Locals are divided on whether the giant Richmond Oval venue now under construction will turn out to be a white elephant. For information, drop into the **VIC** (Map pp62-3; ☎ 604-271-0077, 877-247-0777; www.tourismrichmond.com; North East Plaza; 9am-7pm May-Jun, Sep & Oct, 9am-8pm Jul-Aug, 10am-4pm Tue-Sat Sep-Apr)

Sights & Activities

Much bigger than downtown's Chinese night market, the 250-plus vendors at the **Richmond Night Market** (Map pp62-3; ☎ 604-244-8448;

DETOUR: BUNTZEN LAKE

A deeply relaxing natural gem that's been attracting savvy Lower Mainlanders for decades, **Buntzen Lake** (Map pp62-3; ☎ 604-469-9679) is a perfect example of how BC can strike the right balance between environmental stewardship and access for visitors. This huge, naturally occurring BC Hydro reservoir is surrounded on three sides by steep, tree-covered mountains and on its fourth side by a sun-kissed, gently curving beach, complete with picnic tables, old-growth trees and an ever-present gaggle of Canada geese. There's an array of well-marked hiking and mountain bike trails through the forest and if you don't bring your own canoe, there's a **rental store** (☎ 604-469-9928; Sunnyside Rd) near the park entrance.

If you're driving to Buntzen Lake from Vancouver, follow Hastings St (Hwy 7A) east through the city to Burnaby and Coquitlam, where it becomes Barnet Hwy. Take the Ioco exit and follow Ioco Rd to the left. Turn right on First Ave and continue to Sunnyside Rd. Turn right again and continue to the Buntzen Lake entrance. The journey should take less than 60 minutes. The lake can also be reached by transit; visit the TransLink website (www.translink.bc.ca) for route planning. It can get crowded here in summer, so arrive early if you want a picnic table.

www.richmondnightmarket.com; 12631 Vulcan Way; 7pm-midnight Fri & Sat, 7-11pm Sun, mid-May–Sep) will take you several hours to properly trawl. Don't eat before you come, so that you can sample the amazing variety of takeout – including Malaysian, Korean, Japanese and Chinese treats – while you peruse the Pokemon trading cards and kitsch-laden designer kitsch.

Known simply as the 'Buddhist Temple,' **Kuan Yin Temple** (Map pp62-3; 604-274-2822; 9160 Steveston Hwy; admission free; 9:30am-5pm) is one of Canada's finest traditional-style Chinese buildings. Modeled on the architecture of Beijing's Forbidden City, the complex's main structure is its sumptuous Gracious Hall, decorated with deep red and gold exterior walls and topped with a gently flaring roof of orange porcelain tiles. Don't miss the exquisite paintings and antiquities on display here and be sure to drop by the calm-inducing classical garden. Save room for a lip-smacking vegetarian lunch at the complex's cafeteria.

STEVESTON

In Richmond's southwest corner sits the old fishing village of Steveston. You can smell the salt in the air as you stroll along the waterfront boardwalk and check out the local catches on the backs of the boats – look out for halibut and sockeye salmon. It's a popular place for locals to come for an end-of-day sunset break and it's a hot spot of great fish and chips. To get here from Vancouver, take the 'Steveston Hwy' exit west off Hwy 99.

The colorful family-friendly, **Gulf of Georgia Cannery National Historic Site** (Map pp62-3; 604-664-9009; 12138 4th Ave; adult/child $7.15/3.45; 10am-5pm Thu-Mon May & Sep, 10am-5pm daily Jun-Aug) was a working fish processing plant until the 1970s, when it closed down and was slowly transformed into a fascinating museum. Most of the machinery is still in place and you can learn all about what a horrible job it was working the production line here.

It's worth the short walk from the waterfront to find the legendary local haunt of **Dave's Fish & Chips** (Map pp62-3; 604-271-7555; 3460 Moncton St; mains $6-8; 11am-8pm). With a simple brown wood and wobbly table interior that hasn't changed much in decades, Dave's puts all its effort into what goes on the plate. All the traditional dishes are here, but for something of a twist try the oysters and chips or the velvet-soft battered salmon and chips. It's great value.

At the fine-dining end of the fish restaurant trade, the long-established **Steveston Seafood House** (Map pp62-3; 604-271-5252; 3951 Moncton St; mains $20-26; 5:30-10pm) offers a bewildering array of excellent dishes for seafood connoisseurs. If you want to sample a selection of tastes, dive into the Captain Vancouver Platter, which includes king crab, scallops, halibut and prawns. Reservations are recommended.

Sleeping & Eating

Stone Hedge B&B (Map pp62-3; 604-274-1070; www.thestonehedge.com; 5511 Cathay Rd; s/d from $110/125;) A surprisingly peaceful location for this Richmond B&B, named after the privacy-enhancing 6.5ft stone wall that surrounds it. The best feature is the guest lounge – it opens directly onto a large, secluded swimming pool. The rooms are sumptuously decorated with reproduction antiques and landscape paintings and the owners are happy to help you plan your day out.

Fairmont Vancouver Airport (Map pp62-3; 604-207-5200, 800-441-1414; www.fairmont.com/vancouverairport; Vancouver International Airport; r from $210;) Accessed via a handy walkway next to the US departure hall, you can't stay any closer to the airport than this luxurious, amenity-laden hotel. A great option if you want to board a soul-destroying long-haul flight in a Zen-like state of calm, the rooms are elegantly furnished with high-end flourishes including remote-controlled drapes and marble-lined bathrooms.

Chiu Chow Garden (Map pp62-3; 604-270-8933; 8511 Alexandra Rd; mains $8-18; 11:30am-10pm) Cantonese specialties rule the roost here, with the chili pepper chicken served with deep-fried shredded broccoli well worth trying. Plenty of Chinese patrons make this a bustling lunchtime spot and prove that you're eating the real thing.

Kelong Singapore Cuisine (Map pp62-3; 604-821-9883; 130-4800 No 3 Rd; mains $8-18; 11am-10pm) Spicy Malaysian and Singapore approaches combine in this bright and breezy restaurant where vegetarians are also well served. If you're starving, tuck into the hearty beef *redang* or *sambal* chicken.

Getting There & Away

TransLink (604-953-3333; www.translink.bc.ca) 98B-Line express transit buses arrive in Richmond from downtown Vancouver (adult/child

---

DETOUR: CLOVERDALE FLEA MARKET

A decades-old Sunday shopping tradition, that draws thousands of keen-eyed, bargain-hunting Lower Mainland residents every Sunday, **Cloverdale Flea Market** (Map pp62-3; ☎ 604-856-1100; Cloverdale Fair Grounds; ⏰ 6am-4pm Sun) has gained a justifiable reputation as the best bazaar in the West, due to its winning combination of professional and amateur traders working hundreds of stalls. While it's a great place to pick up cheap consumer necessities such as batteries and branded razor blades, Cloverdale is also a good spot to browse for collectibles such as trading cards, comic books and antiques – it's not unusual to spot a collection of art deco teapots or some vintage Nike runners among the rummage boxes. Although much of the trading activity takes place outside, there are also several cavernous indoor halls for those frequent 'Wet Coast' days. While crafts are prominent at the indoor stalls, some of them also sell the best-value souvenirs in the region: savvy tourists have been known to leave with armfuls of maple leaf T-shirts for families and friends back home, with enough money left over for a heaping brunch on their way back to town. To get from Vancouver, head east on Hwy 1 over the Port Mann Bridge, exit right onto 176th St (Hwy 15), and continue south until you see the signs for the Cloverdale Fair Grounds and/or the market.

$3.25/2, 30 minutes) throughout the day. If traveling by car from the US, follow I-5 to the border, then Hwy 99 northbound. Driving from Vancouver, follow Hwy 99 southbound.

DELTA
pop 103,000

Home to some of the Lower Mainland's richest farmland, fertile Delta has mixed in some vineyards alongside its vegetable trade in recent years. Drop by the **VIC** (Map pp62-3; ☎ 604-946-4232; www.deltachamber.com; 6201 60th Ave; ⏰ 8:30am-5pm Jul & Aug, 8:30am-4:30pm Mon-Fri Sep-Jun) for tips and resources on the region.

North Delta's **Burns Bog** (www.burnsbog.org) is a natural haven housing the largest estuarine raised-peat bog on the west coast of the Americas. Habitat to 140 bird, 20 mammal and 126 plant species that have adapted to the wet and acidic conditions, access to the protected 3000-hectare site – that's 10 times larger than Vancouver's Stanley Park – is limited to the Delta Nature Reserve section. The enthusiastic **Burns Bog Conservation Society** (☎ 604-572-0373; www.burnsbog.org; adult/child $15/10; ⏰ tours noon every 3rd Sat) leads fascinating two-hour walking tours.

Tsawwassen

Serving as a gateway to Vancouver Island through its BC Ferries terminal, Tsawwassen (suh-wah-sen) claims to receive the most sunshine of any place in the Lower Mainland.

Long stretches of beach, excellent bird-watching and warm water for swimming at high tide make **Centennial Beach Park**, fronting

Boundary Bay, one of Greater Vancouver's best-kept secrets. Off Hwy 17, turn left on 56th St, and then left on 12th Ave to Boundary Bay Rd.

Ladner

A quaint pioneer-days town considered one of the aesthetic hidden gems of the Lower Mainland, Ladner's main attraction is the **Reifel Migratory Bird Sanctuary** (☎ 604-946-6980; www.reifelbirdsanctuary.com; 5191 Robertson Rd; adult/child $4/2; ⏰ 9am-4pm), which operates like a wetland nature stroll for ornithologists. A huge stopover for migrating birds – it's at its most cacophonous in the fall – the birds to watch out for are the Russian lesser snow goose, the yellow-breasted chat and the boreal owl. Off Hwy 17, turn right on Ladner Trunk Rd and follow it through Ladner to River Rd. Turn right on Westham Island Rd, go over the bridge and follow it to the sanctuary.

Tsawwassen and Ladner are both reached by taking Hwy 99 south through the George Massey tunnel, then exiting right to Hwy 17.

GOLDEN EARS PROVINCIAL PARK

You're engulfed by evergreens flanking the winding road before you pass the wooden sign with the mountain goat that says 'Golden Ears Provincial Park.' As you enter the **park** (☎ 604-795-6169; www.env.gov.bc.ca/bcparks), the strange sensation you get as urban growth disappears is serenity itself. At 55,900 hectares, Golden Ears is smaller than its northern neighbor, Garibaldi Provincial Park, but is still among BC's largest. It is named for Mt Blanshard's twin peaks, which sometimes glow in the sun like the ears of a golden retriever (honest, they do).

Pretty Alouette Lake is Golden Ears' centerpiece and a perfect spot for fishing, swimming, canoeing, windsurfing and waterskiing.

Hikers of all abilities should find something suitable in the 65km of trails. If time is short, the Spirea Nature Trail can take an hour for the whole information-plaque-lined route, or 20 minutes for the short loop. For a deeper appreciation of the park's wonders, the strenuous root-entangled Alouette Mountain Trail (10km, 1000m elevation change) is most rewarding in June when the meadows are green and Mt Robie Reid still has enough snow to make the view worthwhile.

Take Lougheed Hwy (Hwy 7) east through Maple Ridge and turn left on 232nd St. Turn right on Fern Cres just after Maple Ridge Park; tranquility sinks in 2km later.

FORT LANGLEY
pop 2600

Tiny Fort Langley's tree-lined streets and 19th-century storefronts make it as picturesque a village as you'll find in the Lower Mainland. It's the kind of place where you feel compelled to indulge in an ice-cream cone and explore the quirky stores and pioneer museums. The 4km Fort-to-Fort Trail is a leisurely walk that follows the Fraser River from the present location of the fort to the site of the original Fort Langley in Derby Reach Regional Park.

Fort Langley National Historic Site

During the early to mid-1800s, Fort Langley burned down and changed locations, yet still served as an important link between interior fur-trade posts and international markets. But gold fever and an influx of thousands of prospectors from California in the 1850s put the fear of an American takeover in James Douglas. On November 19, 1858, he stood in the Big House and read the proclamation creating the colony of British Columbia, giving Fort Langley a legitimate claim to the birthplace of BC.

Later that same year, paddle wheelers made it possible to travel further up the Fraser River, eliminating the fort's importance along the supply chain, and the place was eventually abandoned. In 1923 the federal government realized the historical importance of the **site**

(☎ 604-513-4777; 23433 Mavis Ave; adult/child $7.15/3.45; ⌚ 10am–5pm mid-Mar–Jun, 9am–8pm Jul & Aug, 10am–5pm Sep & Oct, 10am–4pm Tue-Sun Nov–mid-Mar) and preserved it as a museum. With costumed reenactors, re-created artisan workshops and a surprisingly entertaining movie presentation, this is an ideal place to bring the kids for an afternoon – they can even pan for gold, if they get bored with all the history.

Getting There & Away

A relatively easy and well-signposted 45-minute drive from Vancouver via Hwy 1, Fort Langley is a more challenging trek for **TransLink** (☎ 604-953-3333; www.translink.bc.ca) transit users. From the city, take the SkyTrain (adult/child $4.50/3) to Surrey Central Station before transferring to bus 320, 501 or 502 to Langley Center. From here, transfer to bus C62 which stops near the old fort.

MISSION
pop 35,000

Originally the home of the Stó:lo First Nations, the name Mission comes from a much later Catholic attempt to convert the people. The town sits on Lougheed Hwy and the **VIC** (☎ 604-826-6914; www.missionchamber.bc.ca; 34033 Lougheed Hwy) is east of town.

Now a celebrated historic site, **Xá:ytem** (*hay*tum) **Longhouse Interpretive Centre** (☎ 604-820-9725; www.xaytem.ca; 35087 Lougheed Hwy; adult/child $6/5; ⌚ 9am–4:30pm Mon-Sat) is on a stretch of land that was being cleared for housing when small tools were discovered. Further excavations produced artifacts as old as 9000 years. The center focuses on Stó:lo spirituality, archeology and history, and its centerpiece is the huge Hatzic Rock, thought to be three tribal leaders turned to stone.

It's not far from here to **Westminster Abbey** (☎ 604-826-8975; 33224 Dewdney Trunk Rd; admission free; ⌚ 1:30-4pm Mon-Fri, 2-4pm Sun), a stunning modernist church – complete with a 10-bell bell tower – that enjoys sweeping views of the Fraser Valley. The enormous stained glass windows are views in their own right and it's interesting to learn how the Benedictine monks have created a life of self-sufficiency. Set in 200 acres of verdant farmland, the grounds also include a seminary campus.

In complete contrast, the **Power House at Stave Falls** (☎ 604-462-1222; 31338 Dewdney Trunk Rd; adult/child $5/4; ⌚ 10am-6pm mid-May–mid-Oct) is a clever industrial interpretive center housed in a former 1912 BC hydro power plant. Mixing history, science and dozens of kid-friendly interactive games, there's a vivid movie presentation explaining what it was like to live and work here in the early 20th century. It's the old Generator Hall that impresses most, though, with its giant turbine and generator units cleaned and ready for action.

One early morning **Greyhound** (☎ 800-661-8747; www.greyhound.ca) bus arrives from Vancouver ($8.35. 80 mins) every day. **West Coast Express** (☎ 604-683-7245; www.westcoastexpress.com) trains arrive from Vancouver ($10.25, 70 minutes) six times per day, Monday to Friday. If you're driving from Vancouver, head east along Hwy 1 then take the Sumas exit in Abbotsford and continue north on Hwy 11.

Whistler & the Sunshine Coast

When you're strolling the streets of downtown Vancouver and catch a glimpse of the snow-capped mountains staring at you between the mirrored skyscrapers, it's a sharp reminder of the formidable outdoors that rests on the city's doorstep. But this spectacular ring of crags and coastline is not just for looks. It's a highly accessible natural backyard that's open for exploration and dripping with activities.

One of the most scenic coastal mountain drives in the world – now being seriously upgraded as the main road artery between the two 2010 Winter Olympics sites – is the winding Sea to Sky Hwy, which delivers spectacular views of Howe Sound and its mist-shrouded islands en route to Whistler. The world-famous ski resort is a hive of snow-based activity in winter, when it can be just as much fun hanging around with the beautiful people in the loungey bars as actually hitting the slopes. For those who prefer toasty temperatures, the resort in summer has grown to become a popular hiking and biking magnet.

Travelers who like to keep their tans topped up, should also make for the Sunshine Coast, which reputedly receives more rays than Hawaii. This 139km stretch of crenulated, mostly forested waterfront northwest of Vancouver is accessible via a 40-minute ferry ride from the outskirts of the city – many Vancouverites have little idea just how close they are to a region renowned for its diving, kayaking and string of quirky, rivaling communities.

HIGHLIGHTS

- Soaring over the peaks and valleys around **Pemberton** (p127) in a silent glider
- Tumbling down summertime bike trails or bustling wintertime ski slopes in **Whistler** (p121)
- Bumping around the roiling **Skookumchuck tidal rapids** (p132) on a water taxi
- Checking out the resurrected **Royal Hudson steam train** (see boxed text, p117) in Squamish
- Gearing-up in **Sechelt** (p131) for a dive, complete with friendly wolf eels, around a sunken warship reef

WHISTLER & THE SUNSHINE COAST

SEA TO SKY HIGHWAY

Defining a narrow ledge between the glassy waters of Howe Sound and the steep peaks of the Coast Mountains, the Sea to Sky Hwy (Hwy 99) snakes between Horseshoe Bay in West Vancouver and the cowboy country of Lillooet. While journey times are being cut by a massive Olympics-driven upgrade project, be aware that this scenery-hugging drive requires your full attention: the cliffs below the road are often very steep and a plunge over them is not recommended. There are several worthwhile stops along the way, especially for fans of outdoor activities, history buffs and those who just want to drink in the awe-inspiring landscapes. 'The Mountain' radio station (107.1FM in Squamish, 102.1FM in Whistler) provides useful traffic and road condition reports along the route.

SQUAMISH & AROUND
pop 15,730
Midway between Vancouver and Whistler, Squamish enjoys an incredible natural setting at the meeting of ocean, river and alpine forest. Until recently, it was exclusively the center of the area's logging industry and travelers drove straight through on their way to and from the chichi ski resort. Now it's a popular, ever-growing base for outdoor activities, especially in summer: the monolithic Stawamus

Chief on the edge of town regularly bristles with rock climbers, and the area is one of the best spots in Western Canada to watch bald eagles in flight.

Your first stop should be the swanky new visitor information center (VIC), named the **Squamish Adventure Centre** (☎ 604-815-4994, 866-333-2010; www.adventurecentre.ca; 38551 Loggers Lane; ⏰ 8am-8pm Jun-Sep, 9am-6pm Oct-May). It's a prominent wood-and-beam structure on the edge of town, complete with its own café, outdoor-gear store, mini movie theater and a plethora of helpful staff and useful flyers.

Sights

Located en route to Squamish at Britannia Beach – turn off when you see the humungous yellow truck – is the **BC Museum of Mining** (☎ 604-896-2233, 800-896-4044; www.bcmuseumofmining .org; adult/child $15/11.75; ⏰ 9am-4:30pm mid-May–mid-Oct, 9am-4:30pm Mon-Fri mid-Oct–mid-May). This National Historic Site was the British Empire's largest copper producer. Infamous in recent years as a giant pollution clean-up project, it's been saved and resurrected with an impressive restoration. Take an underground train tour into the dark mines, wander among refurbished buildings and pan for gold with the kids. Tours and panning from mid-May to mid-October only.

The **West Coast Railway Heritage Park** (☎ 604-898-9336; www.wcra.org; 39645 Government Rd; adult/child $10/8.50; ⏰ 10am-5pm) is the final resting place of the legendary *Royal Hudson* steam engine (see opposite). This smashing, volunteer-driven outdoor museum has around 90 railcars, including 10 working engines. Each one is painstakingly restored, and many are walk-through galleries of artifacts and exhibits – check out the opulent executive carriage. Diesel train trips are offered on weekends, and a main street of pioneer buildings was being added when we visited.

Just off the highway, 2km before Squamish, you'll hear the roar of the rushing water of **Shannon Falls Provincial Park** (☎ 604-986-9371; www .env.gov.bc.ca/bcparks) before you make it to the end of the short trail. British Columbia's third-highest waterfall (it's also six times higher than Niagara Falls), water cascades over a 335m drop here, making for some spectacular photo opportunities. A few picnic tables also make this a good stopping point for lunch. In winter when the falls freeze, ice climbers pick and pull their way to the top.

Stawamus Chief Provincial Park (www.env.gov.bc.ca /bcparks) is home to a 652m granite, flat-faced monster called 'The Chief'; this local landmark towers over the entrance to the Squamish Valley. A magnet for climbers – especially those enthralled with its challenging vertical walls – it has awesome views from the top. But you don't have to be geared up to enjoy it: there are (still challenging) hiking routes up the back so that anyone can enjoy the panorama. For information, guides or instruction, call **Squamish Rock Guides** (☎ 604-815-1750; www.squamishrockguides .com; guided climbs half-/full day from $175/230).

Just north of Squamish along Hwy 99, riverside Brackendale village is a fancy-free spot with a serious claim to fame. The winter destination of choice for thousands of salmon-scoffing bald eagles, it draws legions of binocular-clad visitors every day. The **Brackendale Art Gallery's** (☎ 604-898-3333; www.brackendale artgallery.com; 41950 Government Rd) eccentric Thor Froslev coordinates the January bird count from his funky wood-built complex. An art installation in itself, the complex is lined with paintings and photos inspired by the eagles, and has a café and live theatre that could be a Hobbit's banquet hall. Ask Thor about his new eagle aid station.

Activities

Renowned for the high winds whipped up where Howe Sound meets Squamish River – the Coast Salish named this place 'Mother of the Winds' – Squamish Spit is a popular windsurfing and kiteboarding destination. The season runs from May to October and the **Squamish Windsports Society** (☎ 604-892-2235; www.squamishwindsurfing.org; Squamish Spit, day pass $15) is your first point of contact for weather, water conditions and access to the Spit, which has change rooms, day storage and staffers with first aid skills.

Some of BC's best white-water rafting takes place on the Squamish River, where valleys, waterfalls and cliffs are par for the tumultuous course during the May to October season. **Sunwolf Outdoor Centre** (☎ 604-898-1537, 877-806-8046; www.sunwolf.net; 70002 Squamish Valley Rd; full-day package $139) offers full-day packages with lunch and a barbecue dinner and, along with frantic paddling, you can swim and cliff-jump. The center also has basic but cozy sleepover cabins (from $90).

The 100 or so trails around Squamish draw plenty of mountain biking enthusiasts. The

---

GETTING STEAMY IN SQUAMISH

Built in 1940 as one of Western Canada's last steam locomotives, the majestic **Royal Hudson** plied the Canadian Pacific Railway rails between Vancouver and Revelstoke (p249) for just 16 years before new-fangled diesel trains took over the tracks. Ignominiously slated for scrapping, she was rescued by a gaggle of rail enthusiasts and returned to Vancouver as a nonworking museum piece. Restoration was undertaken in the early 1970s and the old gal was returned to active service as a tourist train, running giddy visitors along the winding Sea to Sky route between North Vancouver and Squamish for 25 years.

Despite the train becoming an iconic BC tourist symbol, a slash-happy provincial government refused to support required repairs and, in 2002, the *Royal Hudson* was retired again, this time into the loving hands of Squamish's **West Coast Railway Heritage Park** (opposite), where she is carefully looked after by volunteer train fans. A major renovation was launched once the required $550,000 began trickling in. On our visit, smoke and steam began curling from the train's stack for the first time in more than five years. With plans to run the old train for special excursions, it looks like BC's *Royal Hudson* is back on track.

Cheekeye Fan trail near Brackendale has some easy forested rides, while downhill thrill seekers will prefer the Diamond Head/Power Smart area, where the trails have names like Dope Slope and Icy Hole of Death. Drop in to **Corsa Cycles** (☎ 604-892-3331; www.corsacycles .com; 1200 Hunter Pl; rental per day $35; ☷ 9:30am-6:30pm) for rentals, information and a handy trail guide.

Sleeping & Eating

Alice Lake Provincial Park (☎ 800-689-9025; www .discovercamping.ca; campsites $22) A large, family-friendly campground with more than 100 sites, this popular spot is 13km north of Squamish. There are two shower buildings with flush toilets, and accessible activities include swimming, hiking trails and ranger tours in July and August. Bike rentals are available and there's access to sandy beaches with picnic tables.

Squamish Inn on the Water (☎ 604-892-9240, 800-449-8614; www.innonthewater.com; dm/r from $27.50/60; ▣) This attractive lodge-style hotel, complete with hardwood floors and leather sofas, is a surprisingly short walk from downtown via a tunnel under the highway. The small to midsized dorms have lockers and large bathrooms, while the private rooms and suites are good for couples and small groups. There's a sun-swathed patio overlooking the water out back. Wireless internet access is $2 per hour.

Howe Sound Inn & Brewing Company (☎ 604-892-2603, 800-919-2537; www.howesound.com; 37801 Cleveland Ave; r $105) The 20 rooms are rustic and inviting and the duvets are thick enough to bounce off

at this comfortable sleepover. Guests have access to a sauna and outdoor climbing wall or can spend their time at the excellent brewpub downstairs. Try the Whitecap Ale for a summer tipple and tuck into a hearty menu of comfort food (mains $9 to $22), including thin-crust pizzas and the recommended yam fries.

Sunflower Bakery Café (☎ 604-892-2231; 38086 Cleveland Ave; mains $4-7; ☷ 8am-5:30pm Mon-Sat) A bright and breezy respite on a rainy day, this yellow-colored nook serves some great wraps and bagel sandwiches – the made-from-scratch quiches are recommended, too – plus an array of chunky cakes and bulging fruit pies that will have you committing to some heavy exercise.

Naked Lunch (☎ 604-892-5552; 1307 Pemberton Ave; mains $6-11; ☷ 8am-5pm Mon-Fri, 8am-4pm Sat) Adjacent to Save-On-Foods supermarket in Chieftain Mall, this popular spot is full of gossiping locals. When they've finished talking about Whistler house prices, they usually make for the panini sandwiches (the honey ham and salami is recommended) or tuck into a finger-licking halibut burger. The soups are great, too – especially the cream of mushroom.

Getting There & Away

Howe Sound Seaplanes (☎ 604-273-6864, 866-882-3252; www.howesoundseaplanes.com) arrive from Nanaimo ($99, 30 minutes, twice daily) behind the Squamish Adventure Centre. **Greyhound** (☎ 800-661-8747; www.greyhound.ca) buses arrive in Squamish from Vancouver ($8.35, 1½ hours, eight daily) and Whistler ($8.35, one hour, eight daily).

GARIBALDI PROVINCIAL PARK

A choice destination of BC outdoor enthusiasts for decades, 195,000-hectare **Garibaldi Provincial Park** (☎ 604-898-3678; www.env.gov.bc.ca/bcparks) is justly renowned for its hiking trails, which take in diverse fauna, snow-capped crags, abundant wildlife and some breathtaking wilderness vistas. You're not limited to exploring only in T-shirt weather; trails become marked cross-country ski routes in winter. Garibaldi has five main trail areas – directions to each are clearly marked by the blue-and-white signs off Hwy 99. Visitors must practice leave-no-trace hiking and camping and the use of mountain bikes is restricted to certain trails.

Diamond Head

The hiking and biking trail to Elfin Lakes (11km) is a beautiful and relatively easy day hike. For overnighters, the trail continues on to the extinct volcano of Opal Cone. There's a first-come, first-served overnight shelter once you reach Elfin, and backcountry camping ($5) is available at Red Heather, 5km from the parking lot. The parking lot is 16km east of Hwy 99.

Garibaldi Lake

The Garibaldi Lake trek (9km) is an outstanding crash course in 'Beautiful BC', combining scenic alpine meadows and breathtaking mountain vistas. The aqua hue of the undisturbed lake contrasts with the dark, jagged peak of Black Tusk rising behind it. Backcountry campsites ($5) are further up the trail at Taylor Meadows, on the lake's west shoreline

Cheakamus Lake

Among the park's most popular, the Cheakamus Lake hike (3km) is relatively easy, with minimal elevation. Also in this area and just outside the provincial park, the BC Forest Service's 3000-hectare **Whistler Interpretive Forest** offers a variety of summer activities, including hiking, mountain biking, kayaking and fishing. The trailhead is 8.5km from Hwy 99, opposite Function Junction at the south end of Whistler.

WHISTLER

pop 9775

The catch-all resort name for the pretty alpine village and the ski areas that have brought fame and wealth to the region – those giant lodges dotted around the edge of town don't come cheap – Whistler is one of the world's favorite winter destinations. While Vancouverites routinely complain that it's too expensive to come here, many still make the 123km drive for a weekend away in the snow. Increasingly the region is also becoming a summer destination, with zipliners, alpine hikers and mountain bikers replacing the skiers and snowboarders of winter. If you just want to soak up the ambience of the village, which has a theme park adherence to gabled roofs and timber-framed lodges, consider a fall trip, when shoulder season prices kick in at the hotels.

Hosting events for Vancouver's 2010 Winter Olympics (www.winter2010.com), Whistler is expanding its facilities and amenities to stage biathlon, bobsled, luge, alpine skiing and ski-jumping events. Don't be surprised to encounter construction while you're here.

ORIENTATION

Whistler is comprised of four neighborhoods: Whistler Creekside, Whistler Village, Village North and Upper Village. Approaching from

---

DETOUR: BRANDYWINE FALLS PROVINCIAL PARK

A popular day trip 9km south of Whistler, the highlight of the 143-hectare **Brandywine Falls Provincial Park** (☎ 604-986-9371; www.env.gov.bc.ca/bcparks) is the spectacular 70m waterfall, which drops suddenly out of the dense forest like a giant natural faucet. A short stroll among the trees leads to a platform overlooking the top of the falls, as well as offering surrounding vistas of Daisy Lake and the mountains of Garibaldi Provincial Park. Another 7km looped trail leads through dense forest and ancient lava beds to Cal-Cheak Suspension Bridge. For those who want to be at one with nature, there are 15 drive-in **campgrounds** (☎ 800-689-9025 www.discovercamping.ca; campsites $14) with picnic tables and pit toilets. Although the gate is closed in winter, you can still walk in for winter camping of the frosty variety.

ICE COLD IN BC

In a region where skiing and snowboarding are second nature, some locals have discovered new ways to challenge themselves in their own backyard. Igloo camping – where groups of snow-loving nutbars snowshoe into the backcountry for a day of construction and a night of fitful sleep – is an emerging winter phenomenon. It's essential to go with someone who knows how to build an igloo – the blocks need to be placed on a winding inward curve and the structure should not be too big – so you'll have to meet some snow-savvy locals or hire a winter camping guide from an outfit like **Canada West Mountain School** (☎ 604-878-7007, 888-892-2266; www.themountainschool.com; guides from $200). But the experience of building your own structure, enjoying a celebratory swig from a hip flask and crawling in through the U-bend entrance for a night under the crazy-paving ceiling is unforgettable. While our igloo adventure took place among the tranquil crags of Garibaldi Provincial Park (opposite), there are many other suitable spots around the province.

the south, you'll enter at Whistler Creekside, the original residential base. The other three areas, 4km north past Alta Lake, tend to blur into one large settlement.

From Hwy 99, turn right (east) onto Village Gate Blvd, which divides Whistler Village (at the base of Whistler Mountain) from Village North. At the end of the road, parking lots are on the other side of Blackcomb Way, which divides the other two areas from Upper Village (at the base of Blackcomb Mountain).

Whistler Village is the commercial center. With hotels and businesses winding around or on top of each other here – when space is at a premium, every square inch is of value – it's like negotiating a maze. Luckily, there are plenty of street signs and lots of people to ask for directions. Whether any of them actually live here is another matter, of course.

INFORMATION
Bookstores
Armchair Books (☎ 604-932-5557; 4205 Village Sq; 9am-9pm) Strong travel section.

Internet Access
Cyber Web (☎ 604-905-1280; 4340 Sundial Cres; per 10 mins $2.50; 9am-10:30pm May-Sep, 8am-10pm Oct-Apr)
Café de la Place (☎ 604-905-5645; 4314 Main St; per 10 mins $2.50; 8am-10pm May-Sep, 7am-10pm Oct-Apr)

Media
Two free weekly newspapers – the *Pique* and the *Whistler Question* – are available at stores and streetside boxes. Both provide good listings of events, with the *Question* more engaged in local news.

Medical Services
Whistler Health Care Centre (☎ 604-932-4911; 4380 Lorimer Rd; 8am-10pm)
Town Plaza Medical Clinic (☎ 604-905-7089; 4314 Main St; 9am-6pm)

Money
Custom House Currency Exchange (☎ 604-938-6658; 4227 Village Stroll; 9am-5pm May-Sep, 9am-6pm Oct-Apr)
Thomas Cook (☎ 604-938-0101; 4230 Gateway Dr; 9am-6pm Oct-Apr, 9am-5:30pm Mon & Tue, Thu-Sat May-Sep,) Inside the visitor center.

Post
Post office (☎ 604-932-5012; 106-4360 Lorimer Rd; 8am-5pm Mon-Fri, 8am-noon Sat).

Tourist Information
Whistler VIC (☎ 604-935-3357, 800-944-7857; www .tourismwhistler.com; 4230 Gateway Dr; 8am-6pm) Flyer-lined VIC with friendly staff.
Whistler Activity Centre (☎ 604-938-2769, 877-991-9988; 4010 Whistler Way; 9am-5pm) Activities bookings and recommendations.
Whistler 2010 Info Centre (☎ 877-408-2010; www .winter2010.com; 4365 Blackcomb Way; 11am-5pm) Information of Olympic proportions.

SIGHTS
The small but fascinating **Whistler Museum & Archives** (☎ 604-932-2019; www.whistlermuseum.com; 4329 Main St; adult/child $5/3; 10am-4pm Fri-Sun, 10am-8pm Thu Sep-Jun, 10am-4pm Fri-Mon, 10am-8pm Thu Jul-Aug) details the region's history and development, from its days as a pioneer outpost to its 1970s emergence as a ski resort. The diverse and eclectic exhibits include a rare collection of stuffed BC birds, an assortment of ski gear and

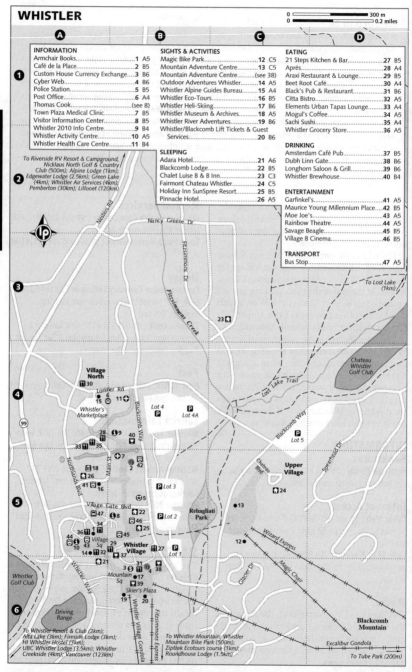

WHISTLER

0 ————— 300 m
0 ————— 0.2 miles

INFORMATION

Armchair Books.............................**1** A5	
Café de la Place...........................**2** B5	
Custom House Currency Exchange...**3** B6	
Cyber Web....................................**4** B6	
Police Station...............................**5** B5	
Post Office...................................**6** A4	
Thomas Cook..........................(see **8**)	
Town Plaza Medical Clinic.............**7** B5	
Visitor Information Center..............**8** B5	
Whistler 2010 Info Centre..............**9** B4	
Whistler Activity Centre...............**10** A5	
Whistler Health Care Centre.........**11** B4	

SIGHTS & ACTIVITIES

Magic Bike Park..........................**12** C5	
Mountain Adventure Centre.........**13** C5	
Mountain Adventure Centre....(see **38**)	
Outdoor Adventures Whistler.......**14** A5	
Whistler Alpine Guides Bureau.....**15** A4	
Whistler Eco-Tours......................**16** B5	
Whistler Heli-Skiing.....................**17** B6	
Whistler Museum & Archives........**18** A5	
Whistler River Adventures............**19** B6	
Whistler/Blackcomb Lift Tickets & Guest	
Services...................................**20** B6	

SLEEPING

Adara Hotel................................**21** A6	
Blackcomb Lodge........................**22** B5	
Chalet Luise B & B Inn.................**23** C3	
Fairmont Chateau Whistler...........**24** C5	
Holiday Inn SunSpree Resort........**25** B5	
Pinnacle Hotel............................**26** A5	

EATING

21 Steps Kitchen & Bar................**27** B5	
Aprés..**28** A4	
Araxi Restaurant & Lounge...........**29** B5	
Beet Root Café...........................**30** A4	
Black's Pub & Restaurant.............**31** B6	
Citta Bistro................................**32** B5	
Elements Urban Tapas Lounge......**33** A4	
Mogul's Coffee...........................**34** A4	
Sachi Sushi.................................**35** A5	
Whistler Grocery Store.................**36** A5	

DRINKING

Amsterdam Café Pub...................**37** B5	
Dubh Linn Gate..........................**38** B6	
Longhorn Saloon & Grill...............**39** B6	
Whistler Brewhouse.....................**40** B4	

ENTERTAINMENT

Garfinkel's.................................**41** A5	
Maurice Young Millennium Place...**42** B5	
Moe Joe's...................................**43** A5	
Rainbow Theatre.........................**44** A5	
Savage Beagle............................**45** B5	
Village 8 Cinema.........................**46** B5	

TRANSPORT

Bus Stop....................................**47** A5	

To Riverside RV Resort & Campground;
Nicklaus North Golf & Country
Club (500m); Alpine Lodge (1km);
Edgewater Lodge (2.5km); Green Lake
(4km); Whistler Air Services (4km);
Pemberton (30km); Lillooet (120km)

Nancy Greene Dr

To Lost Lake
(1km)

Chateau
Whistler
Golf Club

Lost Lake Trail

Village
North

Lorimer Rd

Whistler's
Marketplace

Lot 4

Lot 4A

Blackcomb Way

Lot 5

Spearhead Dr

Upper
Village

Lot 3

Chateau Blvd

Rebagliati
Park

Village Gate Blvd

Lot 2

Village
Sq

Whistler
Village

Lot 1

Mountain
Sq

Skier's Plaza

Driving
Range

Whistler
Golf Club

To Whistler Resort & Club (2km);
Alta Lake (3km); Fireside Lodge (3km);
HI Whistler Hostel (3km);
UBC Whistler Lodge (3.5km); Whistler
Creekside (4km); Vancouver (123km)

To Whistler Mountain; Whistler
Mountain Bike Park (500m);
Ziptrek Ecotours course (1km);
Roundhouse Lodge (1.5km)

Wizard Express

Glacier Dr

Magic Chair

Blackcomb
Mountain

Excalibur Gondola

To Tube Park (200m)

Whistler Village Gondola

Fitzsimmons Express

Fitzsimmons Creek

Nesters Rd

Fitzsimmons Dr

Northlands Blvd

Main St

Whistler Way

equipment through the ages and an archive of documents and artifacts relating to the six bids Whistler has made to host the Olympic Games. With the region now sharing in Vancouver's successful bid for the upcoming games, the museum is in a good position to record the 2010 event from scratch, which might explain why the trustees have been searching for larger premises in recent years. The museum offers summertime village **walking tours** (tours adult/child $11/8; ⓨ tours 7pm Fri & Sat Aug & Sep) that relate the colorful story of the area's growth.

ACTIVITIES

The increasing popularity of mountain biking and alpine hiking has allowed Whistler to become a happening summer destination – as well as these two pastimes, you can access just about any outdoor activity imaginable here. Head to the village's **Whistler Activity Centre** (☎ 604-938-2769, 877-991-9988; 4010 Whistler Way; ⓨ 9am-5pm) for useful advice and recommendations on both summer and winter activities.

Skiing & Snowboarding

Boasting more than 8100 skiable acres and at least 200 runs, the twin-mountain **Whistler-Blackcomb** (☎ 604-932-3434, 800-766-0449; www .whistlerblackcomb.com; 2-day lift ticket adult/youth/child $148/126/77) region has one of North America's largest ski areas and, so long as temperatures hold, Canada's longest winter season

(November through April on Blackcomb and November through June on Whistler). The snow-dusted crowds are usually at their height from December to March, when you'll be jostling for village space with visitors from around the globe. Thankfully, the 37 lifts allow skiers and snowboarders to spread out with relative ease, shifting nearly 60,000 people per hour at their height.

If you want to beat the crowds, buy an early-morning **Fresh Tracks ticket** (adult/child $15/11.30) in advance at Whistler Village Gondola Guest Relations and be at the gondola for a 7am start the next day. The price includes breakfast at the Roundhouse Lodge up top. Weekdays are recommended for this, since tickets sell out quickly on weekends. For a night-out twist, consider evening skiing or snowboarding on Blackcomb, available via the **Night Moves program** (tickets adult/child $15/10; ⓨ 5-9pm Thu-Sat).

The largest ski and snowboard equipment renter in town, **Mountain Adventure Centres** (www .whistlerblackcomb.com/rentals; 1-day ski or snowboard rental adult/child from $38/20; Whistler ☎ 604-905-2252; Blackcomb ☎ 604-938-7737) has several outlets in the area, including this one next to the Dubh Linn Gate pub. You can choose and reserve your favorite equipment online before you arrive. The centers also offer lessons for those unsteady on their snow feet.

To access the untouched powder of the backcountry, release your credit card and contact **TLH Heliskiing** (☎ 250-558-5379, 800-667-4854;

WORKIN' THE SLOPES

Working as a Whistler 'liftie' is considered a pretty sweet gig by those who can't get enough of the white stuff. And with BC struggling in recent years to keep pace with the surging demand for seasonal tourism workers, there's never been a better time to realize the dream.

For one of the hundreds of annually available jobs, ranging from lifties to restaurant servers, contact the **Whistler-Blackcomb Recruiting Department** (☎ 604-938-7366; www.whistlerblackcomb .com; 4896 Glacier Dr, Whistler BC, V0N 1B4, Canada) or call the **Job Line** (☎ 604-938-7367) for recorded listings of available vacancies. The **Whistler Employment Resource Centre** (☎ 604-932-5922, extension 23) also has information on regional openings.

Most jobs go to Canadian residents or people with Canadian work authorization, such as Australians and New Zealanders on working holiday visas. October to November and February to March are the peak recruiting times, and hourly wages range from $8 to $12. Benefits can include ski passes, restaurant discounts and free ski and snowboard lessons.

Once you get your job, finding cost-effective housing can be a major headache. You can check listings on the **Whistler Housing Authority** (www.whistlerhousing.ca), or consider staying in Squamish or Pemberton and making the commute. You can also download a copy of the *Whistler Survival Guide* (www.mywcss.org/survival_guide.htm), aimed at helping first-timers successfully move to the area.

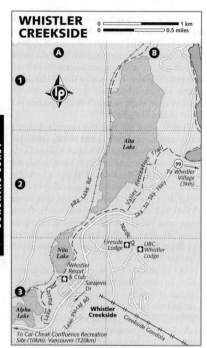

WHISTLER CREEKSIDE

To Cal-Cheak Confluence Recreation Site (10km); Vancouver (120km)

www.tlhheliskiing.com; trips from $2700), which offers spectacular two- to seven-day trips. For those with a lower credit limit, **Whistler Heli-Skiing** (☎ 604-932-4105, 888-435-4754; www.heliskiwhistler.com; 3-4241 Village Stroll; trips from $695) has lower-cost day trips.

Cross-Country Skiing & Snowshoeing

A five-minute walk from the village brings you to **Lost Lake** (adult/child $10/5; ☼ 8am-9pm Nov-Mar), a 32km network of tranquil cross-country ski trails characterized by scenic woodlands and lovely alpine vistas. Well maintained by the municipality, it's lit at night for those who want to slide around under the stars. There's a 'warming hut' offering rentals, lessons and maps, and the trails are suitable for both novices and experts.

Snowshoers are also well served in Whistler, where you can head out into the wilderness on your own or, if you're not sure of your bearings, rent a guide, who can take you though the forest and identify the trees and birds you'll see along the route. Or you can join a late-night group for an evening trek that concludes with a fondue meal.

Outdoor Adventures Whistler (☎ 604-932-0647; www.adventureswhistler.com; 4205 Village Sq; tours adult/child from $69/49) offers six snowshoeing tours, ranging from a two-hour morning trek ($69) to a three-hour fondue tour ($109). Prices include equipment. It also provides snowmobile tours (from $159), if you're looking for a different way to hit the powder.

Tubing

Whistler's family-friendly **Tube Park** (above Base II by parking lot 8; 1hr ticket adult/child/youth $15/10/12; ☼ 10am-8pm Sun-Wed, 10am-9pm Thu-Sat) has up to eight runs, a carpet-style lift and lanes up to 300m long. Scream your heart out as you relive the time when you were 10 years old, and nosh on hotdogs from the concession stand while you warm yourself at the welcome fire pits.

Mountain Biking

The excellent **Whistler Mountain Bike Park** (☎ 604-932-3434, 866-218-9690; www.whistlerbike.com; 1-day ticket adult/child/youth $45/23/39; ☼ 10am-5pm Sun-Fri mid-May–mid-Jun, 10am-5pm mid-Jun–mid-Aug, 10am-5pm Sep) has become a riders' paradise, with 1200m of vertical and 200km of lift-serviced trails on offer. There are plenty of high-energy jumps and ramps for thrill seekers, plus lots of fun, forested trails for the kind of people who like to be covered in mud. Popular routes include the A-line, Dirt Merchant and Freight Train – pick up a free trail map from the VIC. If you want to practice your skills before you hit the big trails, Blackcomb's **Magic Bike Park** (☎ 604-932-3434, 866-218-9690; www.whistlerbike.com; admission incl in Whistler Mountain Bike Park ticket; ☼ mid-Jun–Aug) offers introductory courses ($40 for three hours) for beginners. Bike rentals (half-/full-day $70/100) are available at both parks.

Hiking

With more than 40km of breathtaking alpine trails, most accessed via the Whistler Village Gondola, this region is ideal for those who like strolling among the meadows and mountain peaks humming their favorite *Sound of Music* tunes. Pick up a free trail map from the VIC. Among the best routes is the High Note Trail (8km), which traverses pristine alpine meadows stuffed with wildflowers and offers some stunning views of the blue-green waters of Cheakamus Lake below.

If you'd like company, **Whistler Alpine Guides Bureau** (☎ 604-938-9242; www.whistlerguides.com;

113-4350 Lorimer Rd; adult/child from $89/69) has a wide range of alpine and backcountry tours (ask about the popular Musical Bumps hike). It also provides excellent glacier hiking treks (from $99), and, for the more adventurous, you can rap jump (from $35), rock climb (from $95) or hit the Via Ferrata – a mountain obstacle course of cables, ladders and bridges (from $129).

Rafting

Dense forest, trickling waterfalls, glistening glaciers and a menagerie of local wildlife are some of the visuals you might catch as you lurch along the Elaho or Squamish Rivers on a multihour or all-day rafting trip. You'll have to work your passage as you paddle along the way but many of the operators provide meal stops on secluded beaches if you need to refuel. **Whistler River Adventures** (☎ 604-932-3532, 888-932-3532; www.whistlerriver.com; Whistler Village Gondola; ☒ mid-May–Aug) offers five rafting excursions, including the popular Green River paddle ($69), an adrenaline-rushing white-water rollercoaster.

Ziplining

While stepping out into thin air 70m above the forest floor may seem like madness (it feels like it as well, until you've done it a couple of times), ziplining is one of the best ways to encounter Whistler's natural beauty. Attached via a body harness to the cable you're about to slide down, you soon overcome your fear of flying solo and by the end of your time in the trees, you'll be turning mid-air somersaults. **Ziptrek Ecotours** (☎ 604-935-0001, 866-935-0001; www .ziptrek.com; per 5 lines adult/child $98/78; ☒ year-round) has a cool, 10-line course strung between Whistler and Blackcomb mountains, as well as **Treetrek** (adult/child $39/29), a gentle network of suspension bridges and walkways between the trees for those who prefer to keep their feet on something solid.

TOURS

The region offers plenty of touring action, including horseback riding, boat trips and 4x4 wilderness treks. Among the best operators, **Whistler Eco-Tours** (☎ 604-935-4900, 877-988-4900; www.whistlerecotours.com; 11-4308 Main St) runs a wide array of kayak, biking and hiking excursions, including paddles around Alta Lake and Green Lake ($79, 2½ hours), pedals around Whistler Valley ($60, two hours)

and hikes among the region's ancient cedars ($109, three hours).

For those who like to see their glaciers from above, **Whistler Air Services Ltd** (☎ 604-932-6615, 888-806-2299; www.whistlerair.ca; Green Lake; tours $119) flies a 30-minute floatplane tour over some of the region's most spectacular vistas.

FESTIVALS & EVENTS

Winter Pride Whistler (www.gaywhistler.com) Gay-friendly week of skiing, snowboarding and late-night partying, in early February.

TELUS World Ski & Snowboard Festival Clamorous 10-day fiesta of outdoor concerts and pro ski and snowboard competitions, held in mid-April.

Crankworx Freeride Mountain Bike Festival (www .crankworx.com) Nine-day adrenalin-filled showcase of stunts, speed events and world-leading mountain bikers peddling their stuff, in mid-July.

Cornucopia (www.whistlercornucopia.com) Bacchanalian celebration of fine wining and dining with tastings, seminars and parties in mid-November.

Whistler Film Festival (www.whistlerfilmfestival.com) Four days of Canadian and independent film screenings, events and parties, in late November.

First Night Alcohol-free New Year countdown on December 31, with street performers and live music.

SLEEPING

Hotel rates can double during winter months (especially in December and January), when booking ahead is highly recommended. Specials are available the rest of the year, especially in fall's shoulder season. Most hotels charge parking fees ($10 to $20 daily) and some charge resort fees ($12 to $25 daily). Contact **Central Reservations** (☎ 604-932-0606, 800-944-7853; www.whistler.com) for bookings.

Budget

HI-Whistler Hostel (☎ 604-932-5492; whistler@hihostels .ca; 5678 Alta Lake Rd; dm/r $30/68) Perched on the edge of Alta Lake, a 10-minute drive from the village, this secluded wood-lined hostel is ideal for those who don't have to make it back from a wild night out on the town. Bike storage and rental are available and there's a sauna to soothe your hiked-out muscles. The dorms are predictably institutional, but there are private rooms available if you don't want to listen to unfamiliar snoring. Book ahead.

UBC Whistler Lodge (☎ 604-822-5851; www.ubcwhis tlerlodge.com; 2124 Nordic Dr; dm summer/winter $32/21.25) It's 3km south of Whistler Village and the facilities are basic and quirky (the bunks are built into the walls and the rooms are separated by curtains), but the rates here are a bargain. The common area around the log fireplace is where you'll spend most of your time (movie rentals are available) or maybe you'll be more at home in the Jacuzzi. If you haven't brought your sleeping bag, you can rent linen. Book ahead.

Also recommended:

Riverside RV Resort & Campground (☎ 604-905-5533, 877-905-5533; www.whistlercamping.com; 8018 Mons Rd; tent sites summer/winter $35/25, cabins $165/205) Family-friendly campsite with forested tent areas, grocery store, café, and cozy cabins.

Fireside Lodge (☎ 604-932-4545; www.firesidelodge.org; 2117 Nordic Dr; dm/r $22/55) Small dorms and private rooms in a homey lodge-like setting 3km south of the village (on the bus route).

Midrange

our pick Alpine Lodge (☎ 604-932-5966; www.alpinelodge.com; 8135 Alpine Way; dm/tw/tr/ste $50/125/150/175) This smashing and highly recommended sleepover combines the rustic appeal of a wood-built lodge with the colorful interiors of an artsy boutique hotel. It's the kind of place that's hard to leave at the beginning of the day when the snow is falling heavily outside, but it's also the perfect end-of-day antidote to a tough day on the slopes. Interiors include the obligatory towering, rock-hewn fireplace and a cozy 'Great Room' where your free coffee-and-croissants breakfast is served at a large table overlooking the mountains. While the rooms – including some small dorms – are functional rather than palatial (most have private bathrooms and all have mountain views), the hospitality you'll encouter is superior. It also has a private purple-painted bus to ferry you to and from the lifts.

Whistler Resort & Club (☎ 604-932-5756, 877-932-5756; www.whistlerresortandclub.com; 2129 Lake Placid Rd; r/ste summer $75/130, winter $120/195) Capturing the appeal of 1970s Whistler with its yesteryear red-brick fireplaces, wood paneling and pull-down Murphy beds (selected rooms only), this is the place for you if you love brown carpets and brightly patterned duvet covers. It's a friendly spot, though, and it has a 10-person hot tub where you can hang out pretending to be Tom Jones.

Blackcomb Lodge (☎ 604-935-1177, 888-621-1117; www.blackcomblodge.com; 4220 Gateway Dr; r from $120; 🖳 🛇) Recently renovated to include loungey

new interiors, this centrally located boutique-style sleepover combines lofts and studios with kitchen facilities, and a selection of cheaper but very comfortable lodge rooms. A couple of minutes' walk from the Village Gondola, Araxi (p126), the hotel's on-site restaurant, is one of the best in town.

Chalet Luise B&B Inn (☎ 604-932-4187, 800-665-1998; www.chaletluise.com; 7461 Ambassador Cres; d summer/winter $125/150) A family-friendly, country-style inn with an old-school European feel, the rooms here are bright and breezy. If you get the munchies in the night, you can head down to the communal kitchenette. It's far better to wait until morning, though, when you'll be presented with a breakfast of fruit, bakery treats and a main course special (keep your fingers crossed for apple pancakes).

Pinnacle Hotel (☎ 604-938-3218, 888-999-8986; www.whistlerpinnacle.com; 4319 Main St; d summer/winter $139/199; 🖳) The kind of place any skier would want to come back to, rooms at the boutiquey Pinnacle have gas fireplaces, double Jacuzzi tubs and full kitchens. You can mix yourself a drink, slip into your robe and nip out onto your balcony to watch the winter world go by or choose from the many local bars and restaurants that are a short slide away. Includes wireless internet access and ski and snowboard storage lockers.

Holiday Inn SunSpree Resort (☎ 604-938-0878, 800-229-3188; www.whistlerhi.com; 4295 Blackcomb Way; r from $150; 🛇) It's hard to beat the location of this cut-above-average chain hotel; you're right in the heart of the restaurant and bar action and just a 10-minute walk from the Whistler Village Gondola. The rooms are generally well maintained, if not particularly imaginative, and the fireplaces and kitchenettes (some have full kitchens with laundry facilities) are welcome. There's also a small fitness center – complete with hot tub, of course.

Top End

Adara Hotel (☎ 604-905-4665, 866-502-3272; www.adarahotel.com; 4122 Village Green; r from $250; 🖳 🛇) Unlike all those small Whistler lodges now claiming to be boutique hotels, the sophisticated Adara is the real deal. Rooms are lined with swanky designer furnishings and have spa bathrooms and flat-screen TVs, while the front desk will loan you an iPod if you've left yours at home. Despite the cool aesthetics, the service is warm and relaxed. Wireless internet access is available.

Fairmont Chateau Whistler (☎ 604-938-8000, 800-441-1414; www.fairmont.com/whistler; 4599 Chateau Blvd; r summer/winter from $400/650; ⊠) Standing sentinel over the base of Blackcomb, this modern-day baronial castle fits its natural surroundings perfectly. The hallways, lobbies and 550 rooms are adorned in rich hues and tastefully furnished with classic West Coast elegance. Ask for a room with a mountain view and spend your time at the spa or the chichi après-ski lounge. Close enough to the lifts that you can enjoy ski-in/ski-out privileges.

EATING

Reflecting the growing sophistication (that is, wealth) of Whistler visitors in recent years, a full menu of chichi restaurants has emerged here, many of them satellites of some of Vancouver's top eateries. But not all is doom and gloom for those on a modest budget; there are still plenty of good midrange options.

Budget

Whistler Grocery Store (☎ 604-932-3628; 4211 Village Sq; ⊠ 9:30am-10pm Mon-Sat, 11am-7pm Sun) If your accommodation has kitchen facilities, you'll need a place to buy your pasta and veggies. Not much bigger than a large convenience store, this long-time Whistler shop has a surprising array of nosh, although the prices are not always great. Its location – in the heart of the village and next to the liquor store – is hard to beat.

Mogul's Coffee (☎ 604-932-4845; 203-4204 Village Sq; snacks $3-6; ⊠ 6:30am-5:30pm) If you're lucky enough to get a seat at this favored local hangout, don't give it up easily. It's a good spot to leaf through the newspaper and watch the hustle and bustle of alpine village life, at the same time as knocking back enough Java to get you back on the slopes.

our pick Beet Root Café (☎ 604-932-1163; 129-4340 Lorimer Rd; light mains $4-8; ⊠ 8am-5:30pm) It will likely be the comforting home-baked smells that draw you in the door at this cozy corner nook, but you'll stay for the killer muffins and perhaps the best cookies in town (ask when the next batch of apricot cookies will be ready, then consider changing your departure date accordingly). This friendly spot is not just about baked treats, though: the fresh fruit smoothies are popular, while lunch favorites include yam quesadillas and the recommended turkey, brie and cranberry sandwiches.

Midrange

Sachi Sushi (☎ 604-935-5649; 106-4359 Main St; mains $8-18; ⊠ 11:30am-10pm Tue-Fri, 5-10pm Sat-Mon) Whistler's best sushi spot, Sachi doesn't stop at California rolls. Serving everything from crispy popcorn shrimp to seafood salads and stomach-warming udon noodles (the tempura noodle bowl is best), this bright and breezy eatery is a relaxing après hang-out. Try a glass of hot sake on a cold winter day.

Black's Pub & Restaurant (☎ 604-932-6408; 4270 Mountain Sq; mains $8-18; ⊠ 9am-11pm) This convivial pub-restaurant is known for its hearty winter stews and heaping breakfasts, but the burgers and pizzas here are recommended, too. There are more than 100 beers and almost 50 whiskies available for booze fans: you can work your way through the selection on a patio that overlooks the ski slopes.

Citta Bistro (☎ 604-932-4177; 4217 Village Stroll; mains $8-22; ⊠ 10am-1am Mon-Fri, 9am-1am Sat & Sun) The hopping patio right on the edge of Village Square means there's no shortage of activity here. This place is always lively and serves up creative twists on comfort food classics – try the whiskey steak sandwich or the wild salmon club. The loungey, sometimes raucous, bar will keep you occupied until past midnight.

Elements Urban Tapas Lounge (☎ 604-932-5569; 4359 Main St; mains $12-18; ⊠ 8am-11pm) Despite the pretentious name, this buzzy little nook is laid-back and welcoming, with a menu that will warm you on the coldest winter days. An excellent spot for breakfast – the crab eggs Benedict is recommended – it also offers a day-long array of small plates and mains, ranging from smoked salmon tarts to beef tenderloin medallions. Good spot for a late-night Martini.

21 Steps Kitchen & Bar (☎ 604-966-2121; 4320 Sundial Cres; mains $14-22; ⊠ 5:30pm-1am Mon-Sat, 5:30pm-midnight Sun) With lots of small plates for nibblers (the fried goats cheese is a winner), the main dishes at this cozy upstairs spot have a high-end comfort food approach. Not a great place for vegetarians, steak, pork chops, and pasta feature heavily and the array of fish mains includes a yummy pesto-crusted halibut. Check out the great attic bar, one of Whistler's best lounges.

Top End

Après (☎ 604-935-0200; 103-4338 Main St; mains $18-35; ⊠ 6pm-midnight) An intimate, contemporary bistro, Après is worth searching out for its French-influenced West Coast cuisine. If you happen to be here in summer, take advantage of the bargain $33 three-course menu. At other times of the year, fish dishes such as house-smoked BC salmon and pan-roasted monkfish rule, along with a wine selection from boutique Pacific Northwest vineyards. If you like what you eat, you can learn to make it yourself: the restaurant offers cooking classes.

Araxi Restaurant & Lounge (☎ 604-932-4540; 4222 Village Sq; mains $30-45; ☺ 5-11pm) A leading contender for Whistler's best splurge restaurant, Araxi combines a sophisticated menu with courteous service that immediately puts you at ease. The main dishes are all about superb, mostly local West Coast ingredients, which can range from Queen Charlotte Islands cod to Cowichan Valley chicken. Save room for dessert: the cheese menu is small but perfectly formed and the Okanagan apple cheesecake will have you licking the pattern off your plate.

DRINKING

Amsterdam Café Pub (☎ 604-932-8334; Village Sq; ☺ 11am-1am) Attracting a younger, noisier crowd, this brick-lined party joint has a funky, neighborhood pub vibe and is perfectly located in the heart of the action – you can sit on the patio and heckle the cocktail set as they shuffle past. The beer ranges from the cheap but nasty Amsterdam Lager to Alexander Keith's Pale Ale, a recommended alternative. You can treat your hangover to a late breakfast the next day by coming in for a greasy fry-up.

Dubh Linn Gate (☎ 604-905-4047; 170-4320 Sundial Cres; ☺ 7am-11pm) A wee luck o' the Irish at the base of Whistler Mountain, this vibrant spot serves up live Celtic music nightly in winter. Staff know how to pour a Guinness and the heaping pub grub – including a Sunday carvery – hits the spot.

Longhorn Saloon & Grill (☎ 604-932-5999; 4290 Mountain Sq; ☺ 7am-11pm Sun-Thu, 7am-midnight Fri & Sat) Splayed out at the base of Whistler Mountain with a patio that threatens to take over the town, the Longhorn feels like it's been around ever since the first skier turned up. The service can be lackadaisical and the pub food is nothing to write home about, but it's hard to beat the atmosphere here on a hopping winter evening.

Whistler Brewhouse (☎ 604-905-2739; 4355 Blackcomb Way; ☺ 11:30am-midnight Sun-Thu, 11:30am-1pm Fri & Sat) This place creates its own beer on the premises and, like any artwork, the natural surroundings inspire the masterpieces, with names like 'Lifty Lager' and 'Twin Peaks Pale Ale'. It's an ideal pub if you want to hear yourself think – or if you just want to watch the game on one of the TVs. The food, including great fish and chips, is superior to standard pub fare.

ENTERTAINMENT

Pick up a copy of the *Pique* for local entertainment and events listings.

The nightclub of choice for many, **Garfinkel's** (☎ 604-932-2323; 1-4308 Main St) combines mainstream dance grooves with occasional live bands. Arrive early on weekends, when it's usually packed. The music is similar but it's a lot more intimate over at **Moe Joe's** (☎ 604-935-1152; 4155 Golfer's Approach), which always attracts the ski-bunny crowd. Those hovering around the 30-something mark will likely prefer **Savage Beagle** (☎ 604-938-3337; 4222 Village Sq). It's on two levels, so you can have a sit down if you exert yourself too much.

You can catch a flick at the **Rainbow Theatre** (☎ 604-932-2422; 4010 Whistler Way; adult/child $10/5), which offers discount rates for second-run movies. **Village 8 Cinema** (☎ 604-932-5833; Village Stroll; adult/child $11.50/7.50) is for first-run films.

For theater of the live variety, **Maurice Young Millennium Place** (☎ 604-935-8410; www.myplacewhistler.org; 4335 Blackcomb Way) hosts a wide array of plays and performances.

GETTING THERE & AWAY
Air
Whistler Air (☎ 603-932-6615, 888-806-2299; www.whistlerair.ca) floatplanes arrive at Green Lake from Vancouver ($149, 30 minutes, two daily, May to September).

Bus
Greyhound (☎ 800-661-8747; www.greyhound.ca) services arrive at Whistler Creek and Whistler Village from Vancouver ($18.80, 2½ hours, eight daily), Squamish ($8.35, 50 minutes, nine daily) and Pemberton ($4.25, 30 minutes, six daily).

Perimeter Tours (☎ 604-266-5386, 877-317-7788; www.perimeterbus.com) services arrive from Vancouver ($67, 2½ hours, seven to eleven daily) and Vancouver Airport ($67, three hours, seven to eleven daily) at hotals throughout Whistler.

Snowbus (☎ 604-685-7669, 866-7669-287; www .snowbus.ca) operates a November to April service to Whistler Village from Richmond ($31, three hours, two daily), Vancouver ($21, 2½ hours, two daily) and West Vancouver ($18, two hours, two daily).

Train

Rocky Mountaineer Vacations (☎ 604-606-8460, 888-687-7245; www.whistlermountaineer.com) operates the Whistler Mountaineer, a scenic, May to mid-October service from North Vancouver (from $99, three hours, daily). Price includes transportation to the North Vancouver station from Vancouver hotels and to Whistler Village from the Whistler station.

GETTING AROUND

Whistler's public transit system, **WAVE** (☎ 604-932-4020; www.busonline.ca; adult/child $1.50/1.25, 1-day pass $4.50) buses are equipped with ski and bike racks. As well as their regular schedules, they operate free shuttle services within Whistler Village, to and from Upper Village and Benchlands, and from the Village to Lost Lake. The Lost Lake service only operates in July and August.

Resort Cabs (☎ 604-938-1515; www.resortcabs.com) provides taxis, including some wheelchair-accessible vehicles.

NORTH OF WHISTLER

PEMBERTON & AROUND

More rustic and laid-back than Whistler – most of the people you'll meet are locals, despite the arrival of some lodge-style mega-homes in recent years – Pemberton (population 2520) is an outdoor playground just 20 minutes further along Hwy 99. Visitors here are generally adventurous, spending their time gliding or horseback riding in summer and snowmobiling in winter – unlike Whistler, summer is the high season here. To see what's on offer, drop by the **VIC** (☎ 604-894-6175; www.pemberton.net; ☽ 9am-5pm mid-May–Sep) on the main road into town.

Sights & Activities

Tracing the region's pioneer and agricultural roots – the local mascot is a smiling spud

called Potato Jack – the charming clutch of rescued wooden shacks that make up **Pemberton Museum & Archives** (☎ 604-894-5504; Prospect St; admission by donation; ☽ 10am-5pm Jun-Sep) is a little village from the past. You can wander among the homes, trying to imagine what it was like to sleep in a bed smaller than a coffee table, and ask the volunteers about the characters who lived here when the gold rush swept in. The gift shop stocks jams and handicrafts made by locals.

By far the best way to experience the tree-lined mountains of the Pemberton Valley is to jump into a two-person glider, get towed up into the sky and let the backseat pilot do all the hard work as you slide silently over the miniature landscape far below. The occasional bumps only add to the fun – if you tell the pilot you like roller coasters, he might also treat you to some heart-pumping loops, spins and stalls. **Pemberton Soaring Centre** (☎ 604-894-5776, 800-831-2611; www.permbertonsoaring.com; flights from $85; ☽ Apr-Oct) offers 15-minute taster trips for $85, while a truly spectacular 50-minute glide over the glaciers and snow-capped peaks costs $215.

As you'd expect from cowboy country, horseback riding is a popular pastime in this region. **Pemberton Stables** (☎ 604-894-6615; rides from $45) and **Adventures on Horseback** (☎ 604-894-6269; www.adventuresonhorseback.ca; rides from $60) offer trail rides and pack trips for horsey types. Bring your own chewing tobacco.

Situated 2km south of Pemberton along Hwy 99, 60m-high **Nairn Falls** (☎ 604-986-9371; www.env.gov.bc.ca/bcparks) collects, gurgles and sprays its way down the mountain like an aqua-ballet before continuing on as Green River. The trail to the falls (3km round trip) winds along the steep banks of the river. Another trail (4km round trip) leads to One Mile Lake, a popular spot for swimming and picnicking. The park has a 94-site **campground** (☎ 604-689-9025; 800-689-9025; www.discovercamping .ca; campsites $14, ☽ May-Oct).

Sleeping & Eating

C&N Backpackers (☎ 604-894-2442, 888-434-6060; www .cnnbackpackers.com; 1490 Harrow Rd; dm/r $25/80) There's nothing hip or funky about this large family home in a residential side street, but it's quiet and comfortable and has a welcoming host. Unlike most hostels, there are no bunks here, just five rooms housing one to five beds in each. Linen is provided and there's a mix of private and shared bathrooms. The lounge is equipped with cable TV and there's a communal kitchen adjoined by a small patio, plus laundry ($2) and equipment storage facilities (free).

Farmhouse B&B (☎ 604-894-6205, 888-394-6205; farmhouse@uniserve.com; 7611 Meadows Rd; s/d/tr from $75/85/95) Sleep in country comfort on 10 acres of pastoral bliss in this lovely 1928 farmhouse. You don't have to get up and do chores at 5am, but you can roll out of bed at your leisure and enjoy a fantastic full breakfast, then spend some time wandering around the surrounding meadows with Jade, the house cat. Look out for deer and check out the giant sunflower patch.

Pemberton Valley Lodge (☎ 604-894-2000, 877-894-2800; www.pembertonvalleylodge.com; 1490 Portage Rd; r/ste from $89/99; 🖳 🖳) Located just off Hwy 99, this smashing new midrange hotel looks like it was transplanted from Whistler. The lobby is all West Coast stone and wood and the comfortable, well-designed rooms each have kitchens and fireplaces – almost all have patios, too. There's an outdoor pool and hot tub area (heated in winter) and a free shuttle to the Whistler ski slopes.

our pick **Pony Espresso** (☎ 604-894-5700; 1392 Portage Rd; mains $8-14; ⏲ 8am-10pm) Moving from a shack to this larger pioneer-style wood building in 2006, this chatty local hang-out is the best place in town to tap into the neighborhood vibe. Pull up a chair, order a slab of quiche or a hearty sandwich and listen in on the local gossip. Better still, drop by on a Thursday night, when it's bursting to the gills (arrive by 6pm if you want to get in) with Pembertonians taking full advantage of the $14 beer-and-pizza special – the spinach, chorizo, mushroom and roast garlic pie is recommended. If you're just passing through, there's also a hopping on-site bakery serving chunky muffins and carrot cake for the road.

Getting There & Away

Greyhound (☎ 800-661-8747; www.greyhound.ca) services arrive in Pemberton from Vancouver ($23.25, 3½ hours, five daily), Squamish ($11, 2½ hours, five daily) and Whistler ($4.25, 40 minutes, six daily).

MEAGER CREEK HOT SPRINGS

The all-important bridge leading to this popular spot washed away during 2003 flooding and several levels of government have been

DETOUR: JOFFRE LAKES PROVINCIAL PARK

Located 32km east of town on Hwy 99, this **park** (www.env.gov.bc.ca/bcparks) has some great hiking to the first lake, or you can follow a more ambitious trail to the upper backcountry. Mountain peaks rise up from Lower Joffre Lake and tell their glacial tale through U-shaped valleys and cirques. The trail continues on to Joffre Lakes, where time, reflected in the lake's turquoise surface, seems to stand still. Along with fishing and wildlife watching, this is a popular spot for well-equipped mountaineers, who come for a host of area climbs.

shuffling their feet ever since about funding a replacement. At the time of research for this book, all were agreed that the bridge would be rebuilt but a time frame was not forthcoming. Once the link is back in place, visitors to this attraction 47km north of Pemberton can again dip into the Japanese-style bathing pools as well the area's many interpretive trails. Contact Pemberton's **Visitor Information Centre** (☎ 604-894-6175, www.pemberton.net) for the latest updates.

BIRKENHEAD LAKE PROVINCIAL PARK

Sharing its name with an ugly suburb in northern England, the rugged **Birkenhead Lake Provincial Park** (☎ 604-986-9371; www.env.gov .bc.ca/bcparks) could not be more different from its namesake. Located 55km from Pemberton, it's situated on mountain-fringed Birkenhead Lake, where casting for rainbow trout is a popular activity. The surrounding forest accommodates lots of trails and mountain-bike routes as well as being home to a cornucopia of wildlife – make sure you know what to do if you encounter bobcats and black bears unexpectedly. You might also spot deer, beaver and mountain goats, so have your camera at the ready. Suitable for paddling, the lake has a boat launch and is ideal for those seeking a tranquil jaunt around its shoreline. Keep an eye out for the stunning white-walled flank of Tenquille Ridge and the surrounding snow-capped peaks, which are often reflected in the lake's glassy surface. **Camping** (☎ 604-689-9025; 800-689-9025; www.discovercamping.ca; campsites $14) is available.

SUNSHINE COAST

Separated from the Lower Mainland by the formidable Coast Mountains, Vancouver-ites often have no idea where the Sunshine Coast actually is, and even less idea how easy it is to access. The psychological snub has turned the region somewhat in on itself: although stretching up the mainland 139km from Langdale to Lund, there's a palpable 'island feel' comprising quirky communities and opinionated, often eccentric locals. For visitors – you can get here via a 40-minute ferry from West Vancouver – it's a rewarding region of oceanfront scenery, colorful towns and activities that range from riverboat cruises to world-class scuba diving.

With Hwy 101 winding nearly the length of the coast – helped by an additional BC Ferries hop between Earls Cove and Saltery Bay – there's no excuse for not making it to communities like Gibsons, Sechelt and Powell River. But make sure you tell everyone you meet how much you enjoyed the last town you visited: there are strong rivalries here and few can resist a pop at the next town along the highway. For general information, visit the Sunshine Coast Tourism Partnership website (www.sunshinecoastcanada.com).

GIBSONS

pop 4350

A picturesque gateway to the Sunshine Coast, Gibsons' waterfront area (named Gibsons Landing) is a rainbow of painted wooden buildings perched over the pretty marina – check out the flower-covered floating garden adjoining one of the houseboats. Famous across Canada as the setting for *The Beachcombers*, a TV show filmed here in the 1970s that fiction-alized a town full of eccentrics, the place hasn't changed much since. Head up the incline from the water and you'll hit the shops on the main drag of Upper Gibsons and Hwy 101.

The **VIC** (☎ 604-886-2374, 866-222-3806; www.gibsonsbc.ca; 417 Marine Dr; ☽ 9am-5pm May-Sep) is in the heart of Gibson's Landing near the Bank of Montréal building.

Sights & Activities

A walk down **Gower Point Road** in Gibsons Landing will show you what this seaside village is all about. The cute shops and store-fronts blend nicely with the briny sea air. Be sure to also stroll along **Molly's Lane**, a back-street string of shops knocked together into an indoor market of local crafts and browsable trinkets. Watch out for Molly, the gargantuan fluffy cat that prowls the area looking for a stroke from gullible visitors.

Amble down the wooden jetty – looking for purple starfish under the water on your way – and you'll come across the sunny gallery of **Sa Boothroyd** (☎ 604-886-7072; www.saboothroyd.com; Government Wharf), an artist whose fun, af-fordable (from $4 to $800) paintings, fridge magnets, and tea cozies always raise a smile. If she's around, you can watch her at work. The region is home to a surprising plethora of artistic talent, so consider a guided cultural tour with **Artworks Tours & Workshops** (☎ 604-886-1200, www.artworkstours.ca; tours from $50).

The sheltered harbors and islands of Howe Sound make an idyllic setting for kayaking. Rental, lessons and tours are available from

WHISTLER & THE SUNSHINE COAST

DETOUR: GOLD BRIDGE

From Pemberton, follow the Upper Lillooet River Rd past acres of farmland along the Lillooet River. Cross the bridge and turn right on the Lillooet River Forest Service Rd, a gravel track that traverses the stark contrasts of clear-cut forests and forested hills. Keep your eyes open for deer and black bears as you follow the signs to Gold Bridge.

Keep right as you round the western end of Carpenter Lake and go through town to Bralorne. Head through Bralorne and follow the switchbacks to a real-life ghost town where the residents just up and left once mining in the area stopped.

Double back to Gold Bridge and stop in at the VIC. Follow the signs from here to Gun Lake for some excellent fishing, swimming and picnicking, and a visit to the extravagant **Tyax Mountain Lake Resort** (☎ 250-238-2221; www.tyax.com). Follow the well-maintained Lillooet Pioneer Rd No 40 east along the north shore of beautiful Carpenter Lake. There are some campgrounds along the road if you feel like stopping for the night. You'll pass by the Terzaghi Dam and through some jagged mountain and river valley scenery on the way to Lillooet.

the friendly folk at **Sunshine Kayaking** (☎ 604-886-9760; www.sunshinekayaking.com; Molly's Lane; rental 4hr/8hr $30/45, tours from $50; ☼ 9am-6pm Mon-Fri, 8am-6pm Sat & Sun). The guided sunset ($50) and full moon ($55) tours are always popular.

Local history buffs will enjoy the **Sunshine Coast Museum & Archives** (☎ 604-886-8232; 716 Winn Rd; admission by donation; ☼ 10:30am-4:30pm Tue-Sat), which houses an eclectic array of period costumes, First Nations baskets and nautical exhibits, including some *Beachcombers* memorabilia.

Sleeping & Eating

Ritz Inn (☎ 604-886-3343, 800-649-1138; www.ritzinn.com; 505 Gower Point Rd; r $72-92; 🐾) Set back by the marina, this conveniently located motel-style property is ideal if you want to be within walking distance of the Gibsons Landing attractions. The large, well-priced kitchenette rooms make it a good spot for families, and some rooms have balconies overlooking the water. It's not quite the Ritz, but rates do include continental breakfast.

Caprice B&B (☎ 604-886-4270, 866-886-4270; www.capricebb.com; 1111 Gower Point Rd; d $95-125; 🔳) Nestled among the arbutus trees, the adult-oriented Caprice is a large waterfront home (you can watch the cruise ships slip by) with three suites. While two rooms have handy kitchenettes, all three are comfortable and well maintained. Homemade baked treats are a feature of the breakfast menu and there's a small outdoor pool where you can enjoy the sun.

Soames Point B&B (☎ 604-886-8599, 877-604-2672; www.soamespointbb.com; 1000B Marine Dr; d $149) Set amid 1.5 acres of landscaped gardens, this immaculate and tranquil B&B has spectacular waterfront views. The large suite has a private entrance, vaulted ceilings and panoramic ocean views as well as its own deck – a great spot for breakfast. At the end of the day, you can head down to the water where another deck, complete with seats and a barbecue, is ideal for a sunset glass of wine.

Molly's Reach (☎ 604-886-9710; 647 School Rd; mains $7-12; ☼ 7am-9pm) Don't leave without hitting this legendary local hang-out (it's the bright yellow building on the waterfront, so there's no excuse for missing it). A great spot for a heaping greasy spoon breakfast – try the stomach-expanding 'Constable Constable' of two eggs, two sausages, two pancakes and two slices of bacon – it's also teeming with locals

at lunch and dinner. Snag a window seat so you can overlook the water.

Getting There & Around

BC Ferries (☎ 888-223-3779, 250-386-3431; www.bcferries.com) services arrive at Langdale, 6km northeast of Gibsons, from Horseshoe Bay (adult/child/vehicle $9.15/4.60/32.65, 40 minutes, eight daily). The **Sunshine Coast Transit System** (☎ 604-885-6899; www.busonline.ca; adult/child $2.25/1.75) runs services from Langdale into Gibsons, Roberts Creek and Sechelt.

Malaspina Coach Lines (☎ 604-886-7742; 877-227-8287; www.malaspinacoach.com) buses arrive twice daily in Gibsons from downtown Vancouver ($24, two hours) and Vancouver Airport ($38, three hours), via the Langdale ferry. Services also arrive in Gibsons from Powell River ($40, three to four hours) and Sechelt ($8, 30 minutes).

ROBERTS CREEK

pop 3100

Vietnam War draft dodgers who fled to Canada decided this place on the coast was as good as any to take up residence. Thirty years later, the area still retains a whiff of counter-culture ambience.

Roberts Creek Rd, off Hwy 101, leads to the center of town. Follow the road through the village to Roberts Creek Park and amble out to the spit. West of town, off Hwy 101, **Roberts Creek Provincial Park** (☎ 604-885-3714; www.env.gov.bc.ca/bcparks) is ideal for a beachfront picnic. Check the placards or visit www.robertscreek.com to see what's happening at the community hall.

Sleeping & Eating

our pick Up the Creek Backpackers (☎ 604-837-5943, 877-885-8100; www.upthecreek.ca; 1261 Roberts Creek Rd; dm/r $23/69; 🔳) The definition of a great hostel, this colorful, family-run spot has three small dorms, one private room and a predilection for green living (recycling is de rigueur and the $5 breakfast includes organic granola). There's a spacious kitchen if you want to chef up your own lentil casserole, and a warm, relaxed ambience in the conservatory and lounge (complete with its own fireplace and a raft of old travel books). Since the bus stop is just around the corner, you're encouraged to arrive here by transit; there are 10 loaner bikes to get you around once you've unpacked – browse the flyers hanging on little hooks by the kitchen to plan your day out. An internet-use computer is available (per 30 minutes $1).

Artists in Residence B&B (☎ 604-886-0041; www .artistsinresidencebb.com; 1881A Grandview Rd; d $99) A secluded, tree-shielded B&B with a rustic vibe, this good-value spot has hardwood floors, walls covered with artworks and a sculpture of a skateboarding chicken to greet you at the door. The one suite has two bedrooms – great for groups or families – and is lined with the owner's swirling glassworks. Discounts offered for stays of more than three nights.

Artist & the Quiltmaker B&B (☎ 604-741-0702, 866-570-0702; www.theartistandthequiltmaker.com; 3173 Mossy Rock Rd; d $99-150) Not every Roberts Creek B&B has an artist in residence, but you can see a definite creative flair at this large, three-room, Victorian-style property. Although stuffed with lace and antique flourishes, the interiors are never fussy – unlike most period B&Bs, it's not like staying with a maiden aunt. The large upstairs suite, complete with kitchenette, is popular with families but the lovely Renaissance Room is perfect for romantic couples.

Gumboot Restaurant (☎ 604-885-4216; 1041 Roberts Creek Rd; mains $7-14; ⊗ 8am-9pm) An ideal spot for a wholesome breakfast (the granola is recommended), the Gumboot comes into its own at dinner when curried pierogies and buffalo burgers hit the menu. Vegetarians are well catered for, too – the bulging 'Gumboot Garden' sandwich appears to contain every salad item known to man. There's regular live music and the walls are lined with a gallery of Sunshine Coast artworks.

Getting There & Away

Malaspina Coach Lines (☎ 604-886-7742, 877-227-8287; www.malaspinacoach.com) has twice-daily services that arrive from Vancouver ($27, 2½ hours), Gibsons ($5, 15 minutes), and Powell River ($37, three hours).

SECHELT

pop 8900

With water to the south and north and mountains rising steeply from its coastlines, Sechelt is the second-largest town on the Sunshine Coast. But while it has many useful amenities for those traveling through, it lacks the charm of Gibsons and is not as vibrant as the larger Powell River community.

The downtown area is centered on the intersection of Hwy 101 and Wharf Ave. From here, if you're coming from Roberts Creek,

turn right for Porpoise Bay or left for Half-moon Bay and Earls Cove. For information, drop into the **VIC** (☎ 604-885-1036, 877-885-1036; www.secheltvisitorinfo.com; 5790 Teredo St; ⊗ 9am-5pm May-Aug, 10am-4pm Mon-Fri, 10am-2pm Sat Sep-Apr).

Sights & Activities

Sechelt is a useful base for active travelers, with plenty of hiking, biking, kayaking and diving opportunities in the area. Ask at the VIC for information and pick up a copy of the *Sunshine Coast Recreation Map & Activity Guide* ($3), which highlights regional activities and operators.

With a good kayak launch and a sandy beach, **Porpoise Bay Provincial Park** (☎ 604-885-3714; www.env.gov.bc.ca/bcparks), 4km north of Sechelt, makes it popular with paddlers and cyclists. **Pedals & Paddles** (☎ 604-885-6440, 866-885-6440; www.pedalsandpaddles.com; Tillicum Bay Marina; 4hr rental from $30) organizes kayak rentals and tours of the inlet's wonderfully tranquil waters, while **On the Edge** (☎ 604-885-4888; www.ontheedgebiking .com; 5644 Cowrie St; rental per day $34) rents bikes and leads mountain bike treks.

For cold-water dive fans, **Porpoise Bay Charters** (☎ 604-885-5950, 800-665-3483; www.porpoisebay charters.com; 5718 Anchor Rd; dive trips from $100) offers single or multiday trips. Novices are taught how to dive right off the beach. The more advanced can encounter one of BC's leading dive regions, dripping with close-up sightings of huge wolf eels, enormous octopi and steely eyed blue sharks. There are spectacular underwater rock walls here plus *HMCS Chaudiere*, a 110m warship now serving as an artificial reef. While regional diving is year-round, the best visibility is from November to February.

Sleeping & Eating

Bayside Campground & RV Park (☎ 604-885-7444, 877-885-7444; www.baysidecampground.com; 6040 Sechelt Inlet Rd; campsites $20) Enjoying an ultrafriendly management team, this forested campsite features clean and well-maintained facilities, along with extras such as showers, picnic tables, a children's playground, and a small convenience store. It's within walking distance of a beach.

Upper Deck Guesthouse (☎ 604-885-5822; www .wuts.nu/upperdeck; 5653 Wharf St; dm/s/d $20/35/45; 🖳) It's easy to miss this upstairs hostel in the industrial-looking part of town but it's worth searching out. The huge sundeck (complete with a menagerie of plants and rusting Tonka toys) leads to a set of glass patio doors through which you'll find a kitchen and lounge as welcoming as your friend's apartment. All the rooms are small and there's a free-use internet computer.

Sechelt Inlet B&B (☎ 604-740-0776, 877-740-0776; www.secheltinletbandb.com; 5870 Skookumchuck Rd; d $109-129) Spectacular waterfront views are what entice guests to this lovely home but they come back for the three intimate, colorfully decorated suites. Hardwood floors are combined with immaculate contemporary decor – the purple-hued Maple Suite is our favorite – and all have access to a large shared deck. There's a hot tub overlooking the water and the breakfasts are smashing, especially the blueberry and lemon scones.

our pick Rockwater Secret Cove Resort (☎ 604-885-7038, 877-296-4593; www.rockwatersecretcoveresort.com; 5356 Ole's Cove Rd; r/ste/cabin/tent $149/179/189/325) It's worth continuing your drive along Hwy 101 for another 15 minutes past Sechelt to get to this resort, the latest incarnation of a vacation property that's stood here for decades. New owners have given the place a makeover, adding a West Coast designer flair to the main lodge rooms and transforming the cabins into romantic sleepovers. But it's the new tent suites on the adjoining cliff, accessed via a forested boardwalk, that make staying here exciting. About as far from camping as you can get, each canvas-walled cabin has a heated rock floor, Jacuzzi tub, gas fireplace, and a private deck overlooking the bay. The resort's restaurant (mains $16 to $28) is recommended, even if you're not staying here. With an ever-changing menu of fish and meat classics, each prepared with a fusion twist, it's an idyllic spot to watch the sunset.

Coracle Cove B&B (☎ 604-885-3790, 877-888-3790; www.coraclecove.com; 6055 Coracle Dr; d $169) The one suite at this tranquil waterfront property is almost at sea level, giving you immediate access to a truly special private deck overlooking the glistening brine – your breakfast (ask for the eggs Florentine) can be served here on request. The spacious suite has a private entrance (the driveway is quite steep, so be careful when you drive in) where you can book in-room spa services.

Old Boot (☎ 604-885-2727; 5330 Wharf St; mains $10-16; ☻ 11:30am-10pm Tue-Sun) Among the mostly ho-hum restaurants clustered around downtown Sechelt (keep in mind that most are closed on Monday), this charming Italian nook is a standout. It's lined with Dean Martin album covers, and the menu would likely keep Dino perfectly happy with its array of gourmet pizzas and well-prepared pasta dishes – the prawn linguini is a local favorite. You can watch busy Secheltians go about their business from the patio.

Getting There & Away

West Coast Air (☎ 604-606-6800, 800-347-2222; www.westcoastair.com) services arrive from Nanaimo ($59, 20 minutes, five daily) and from Vancouver Airport's South Terminal ($75, 30 minutes, three daily).

Malaspina Coach Lines (☎ 604-886-7742; 877-227-8287; www.malaspinacoach.com) has twice-daily services from Vancouver ($30, three hours), Gibsons ($8, 50 minutes) and Powell River ($34, three hours).

EGMONT & EARLS COVE

These communities of Egmont and Earls Cove at the top of the Lower Sunshine Coast are often overlooked, but are excellent access points for some nature-hugging Jervis Inlet trips to the rugged fjords of Princess Louisa Inlet and Chatterbox Falls.

You can take in both on a seven-hour cruise from Egmont on the *MV Malibu Express* with **Malibu Yacht Charters** (☎ 604-883-2003, 861-881-2003; www.malibuyachts.com; cruise $130; ☻ mid-Jun–mid-Sep) or, for a good hike to a natural wonder, the 4km trail in **Skookumchuck Narrows Provincial Park** (☎ 604-885-3714; www.env.gov.bc.ca/bcparks) leads to an inlet so narrow that water forced through during tides can cause 30km/h rapids. It's even more fun to hop aboard a steel-hulled water taxi operated by **High Tide Tours** (☎ 604-883-9220, 866-500-9220; www.hightidetours.com; Egmont Marina; trips $15) and take in the roiling, unpredictable waves first-hand. The boat crisscrosses the rapids like a dive-bomber and you can ask the driver all about the crazy kayakers who come here for white-knuckle paddling.

If you're not feeling queasy after your trip, the marina's **Backeddy Pub** (☎ 604-883-3614; Egmont Marina; mains $6-12) is a good spot for an 'Egmont burger' and a restorative beer. The nearby **West Coast Wilderness Lodge** (☎ 604-883-3667, 877-988-3838; www.wcwl.com; r/ste from $115/160) offers ideal accommodations for those who want to combine outdoor activities with rustic comforts and a good restaurant.

BC Ferries (☎ 888-223-3779, 250-386-3431; www.bcferries.com) services arrive in Earls Cove from Saltery Bay (adult/child/vehicle $9.15/4.60/32.65, 50 minutes, seven daily).

POWELL RIVER

pop 13,830

Situated 31km north of Saltery Bay ferry terminal, Powell River was built in 1910 to provide housing for the lumber mill workers, which explains why its older streets are named after trees. The steaming mill has dominated the waterfront here for decades but has been shrinking in recent years, allowing the town to look forward to a different future. Unlike other resource-dependent communities, the locals are embracing this new lease on life with energy and verve. Tangibly funkier than Sechelt, Powell River is well worth a sleepover and is a hot spot for outdoor activities.

The **VIC** (☎ 604-485-4701, 877-817-8669; www.discoverpowellriver.com; 111-4871 Joyce Ave; ☼ 9am-5:30pm) is replete with friendly advice and brochures, including free hiking and biking trail maps. The **Public Library** (☎ 604-485-4796; 4411 Michigan Ave; ☼ 10am-6pm Mon & Thu, 10am-8:30pm Tue, Wed & Fri, 10am-5pm Sat) has free internet access.

Sights & Activities

West of downtown, **Willingdon Beach City Park** has a sandy beach, children's playground and a fishing pier. It's an ideal spot for a picnic – you can walk off lunch with a stroll along the Beach Trail, punctuated by historic logging artifacts. The nearby **Powell River Museum** (☎ 604-485-2222; Marine Ave; adult/child $2/1; ☼ 9am-

---

DETOUR: PENDER HARBOUR

From Hwy 101, head east on Garden Bay Rd and follow its winding path through the woods and around Garden Bay Lake's north shore. Veer right onto Irvine's Landing Rd and watch for deer, eagles and the wonderfully jagged coast that can be seen through clearings in the trees. The road will take you to **Irvine's Landing**, the original settlement site in the Pender Harbour area, affectionately known as 'Venice of the North.' Stretch your legs along the beaches and rocky shore, checking tide pools for unbelievably colored sea critters. When you're ready, follow your path back to Hwy 101. If you're here in mid-September, visit the popular **Pender Harbour Jazz Festival** (☎ 877-883-2456; www.phjazz.ca).

5pm Jun-Aug, 10am-5pm Mon-Fri Sep-May) contains a replica of a shack once occupied by Billy Goat Smith, a hermit who lived here (with his goats) in the early 20th century.

Stroll uphill above the mill end of the town and you'll arrive at the lovely **Patricia Theatre** (☎ 604-483-9345; 5848 Ash St). This reminder of the golden age of cinema is reputedly Canada's longest-running movie house. Check out the art deco murals and ask nicely for an impromptu tour: if the staff are not too busy, you'll hear some colorful tales.

If the town's history piques your interest, take a guided **walking tour** (☎ 604-483-3901; guided tours $5; ☼ Wed 7pm, Sat 10am Jul & Aug) of the historic quarter. Or, if you want to zip around at your own pace, rent a scooter from **49cc Ride** (☎ 604-485-5576; 4690 Marine Ave; rental per hr $25).

Hikers should tackle all or part of the 180km **Sunshine Coast Trail** (www.sunshinecoast-trail.com) that wanders through forests and marine environments from Saltery Bay to Sarah Point. Or you can hit the water with a kayak from **Powell River Sea Kayak** (☎ 604-485-2144, 866-617-4444; www.bcseakayak.com; 10676 Crowther Rd; rental 3hr from $33). To access the area's ample scuba diving, **Alpha Dive Services** (☎ 604-485-6939; www.divepowellriver.com; 7013 Thunder Bay St; guides from $50 per day) rents gear and organizes guides and boat charters.

Sleeping

Harbour Guesthouse & Hostel (☎ 604-485-9803, 877-709-7700; www.powellriverhostel.com; 4454 Willingdon Ave; dm/r $24/55; ☐) In the heart of downtown (and close to a pub), this smashing little hostel has small dorms, a combined lounge and kitchen, and a DVD library for rainy-night movie watching. The best private room has a small balcony overlooking the waterfront and there's a free-access internet computer.

Oceanside Resort Motel (☎ 604-485-6608, 888-889-2435; www.oceansidepark.com; 8063 Hwy 101; cabins $55-105; ☐) This clutch of waterfront cabins a few minutes' drive south of Powell River on Hwy 101 is usually full of families with kids. They come for the playground, pedal boat hire and indoor swimming pool. But you don't have to have sprogs to stay here; the rustic cabins (the honeymoon suites are the best) are spick and span. There's an adjoining stretch of sand that's great for beachcombing.

Old Courthouse Inn (☎ 604-483-4000, 877-483-4777; www.oldcourthouseinn.ca; 6243 Walnut St; s/d from $59/69) In the heritage district, this beautifully restored hotel was once the town's courthouse and police station. Tell your friends you spent the night in jail, or in the judge's chambers or constable's office. In keeping with the historic theme, the rooms are nicely decorated with antique furnishings. There's also a good on-site restaurant if you don't want to go far for dinner.

Rodmay Heritage Hotel (☎ 604-483-7717; www .rodmayheritagehotel.com; 6251 Yew St; d/ste from $75/95) In the heart of the historic district, this cavernous old arts-and-crafts hotel is slowly returning to its former glory after years of neglect. Many of the rooms are a bit stark, although most have new furnishings, fittings, paintwork and hardwood floors. If you're into ghosts, ask about the four specters that occasionally show up.

Eating & Drinking

Local Loco's Music & Arts Café (☎ 604-485-5626; 4692 Willingdon Ave; mains $4-12; 🕙 10am-9pm Mon, Tue & Thu, 10am-midnight Wed & Fri, 11am-midnight Sat, 11am-9pm Sun) With its mismatched 1970s chairs and sofas, this place has the feel of someone's grungy basement. But while there's an undeniably laid-back vibe, the menu is stuffed with greatvalue comfort treats, including wraps, rice bowls and a near-legendary three-bean chili. A popular late-night hang-out, DJs drop by on the weekend to keep the place lively.

La Casita (☎ 604-485-7720; 4578 Marine Ave; mains $7-14; 🕙 11:30am-10pm Mon-Sat, 5-10pm Sun) This colorful and energetic Mexican restaurant has some delicious combo plates that nicely complement the bright blue-and-orange decor. The lip-smacking shrimp and scallop tacos are recommended and there's a wide array of options for visiting veggies – you'll be treated to a basket of handmade tortillas and houseblend salsa while making up your mind.

Shinglemill Pub & Bistro (☎ 604-483-3545; 6233 Powell Pl; mains $8-12; 🕙 11am-10pm) On Powell Lake north of town, this woodsy pub overlooking the water is a great place to end your day – arrive early for a patio table. A cut above usual pub grub, menu highlights include stuffed halibut and slow-braised barbecue ribs. There's also a more formal bistro for quieter dining and a free shuttle bus to get you safely to and from downtown.

Getting There & Around

Pacific Coastal Airlines (☎ 604-273-8666; www.pa cific-coastal.com) services arrive from Vancouver Airport's South Terminal (from $84, 30 min-

utes, four daily) and from Victoria ($146, 30 minutes, four daily).

BC Ferries (☎ 888-223-3779, 250-386-3431; www .bcferries.com) services arrive from Comox on Vancouver Island (adult/child/vehicle $8.65/4.35/29.50, 80 minutes, four daily).

Malaspina Coach Lines (☎ 604-886-7742; 877-227-8287; www.malaspinacoach.com) has twice-daily services from Vancouver ($51, five to six hours), Gibsons ($29, four hours) and Sechelt ($23, three hours).

BC Transit's **Powell River Regional Transit System** (☎ 604-485-4287; www.busonline.ca; adult/child $1.25/1) handles local bus services, including bus 14 to and from Lund.

LUND & BEYOND

At the northern end of Hwy 101, Lund (population 265) is a staging point for trips to Desolation Sound and tropical-like Savary Island. With its many sheltered bays, 8256-hectare **Desolation Sound Marine Provincial Park** (www.env .gov.bc.ca/bcparks) has plenty of boating, fishing, kayaking and swimming opportunities.

Savary Island, aka 'Hawaii of the North,' features white sandy beaches surrounded by turquoise and emerald water. It's in the rain shadow of the Coast Mountains, so it's very sunny here and the water is unusually warm.

To get to the island, call **Lund Water Taxi** (☎ 604-483-9749; www.lundwatertaxi.com; adult/child $8.50/4.25); it's a 30-minute trip. When you arrive, visit **Savary Island Bike Rental** (☎ 604-414-4079) to help you get around. There are no car ferries or paved roads, so it's very peaceful. For accommodations and a short rundown of the island's few services, visit www.savary.ca . Contact Lund's **Terracentric Coastal Adventures** (☎ 604-483-7900, 888-552-5558; www.terracentricadven tures.com) if you fancy a guided hike, kayak or boat tour around the region.

Sleeping & Eating

Lund Hotel (☎ 604-414-0474, 877-569-3999; www.lund hotel.com; 1436 Hwy 101; d/ste $120/195) An attractive wood-sided, pioneer property with a nautical feel, the century-old Lund Hotel combines romantic renovated suites overlooking the water with motel-style rooms towards the back of the property. Once you've finished playing the giant chess set out front, head to the bistro for some hearty fish and chips (the halibut is recommended) or a bowl of chunky seafood chowder, a house specialty.

Nancy's Bakery (☎ 604-483-4180; 1431 Hwy 101; mains $4-10; ☒ 8am-5:30pm) Across the street from the Lund Hotel, this bustling local hang-out has a pretty outdoor seating area and a great selection of house-cooked soups, pastas and pizzas. It's hard not to buy a rhubarb scone or gooey cinnamon bun for the road here.

Laughing Oyster (☎ 604-483-9775; 10052 Malaspina Rd; mains $12-26; ☒ 11:30am-9pm) The views are stunning enough to illicit laughs of disbelief, but the food prepared in this wooden restaurant is serious. Seafood and steaks are prominent on the menu. This is a great example of excellent West Coast dining in a spectacular setting.

Vancouver Island

While geography challenged tourists on the mainland regularly ask for directions to 'Victoria Island,' BC's wild, verdant and correctly named Vancouver Island has much more to offer than just its southern-tip provincial capital. Although a visit to Victoria shouldn't be missed by those who appreciate history-wrapped cities bubbling with sights and activities, it would be almost criminal not to use it as a base for spreading out and exploring what may be the most rewarding region in the province.

The largest island off the North American coast – it's 450km long and 100km wide – Vancouver Island is laced with colorful, often quirky towns, many founded on logging or fishing and featuring 'Port' in their name. Despite the general distaste among residents regarding the 'far-too-busy' mainland, there are plenty of parochial divides here, too.

The 'down-island' south, where the majority of people live, is carpeted with farmland, while the wild western side is populated by hippies who grew up, cast off their surfboards and opened tourism businesses. For nature fans, the north island remains a peaceful, undiscovered gem of tangled forest and deserted sandy bays that are among BC's most beautiful.

While much of the island has been a forgotten backwater left to its own devices for decades, recent years have seen developers popping up like forest mushrooms to snap up available land. Oil-rich Albertans are buying waterfront property for their vacation homes, while small towns such as Ucluelet and Sidney are selling off plots for hotels, resorts and condos like never before. With locals who have lived here for years in danger of being squeezed out, managing this development is now the island's defining issue.

HIGHLIGHTS

- Reliving 'olde England' on the streets of **Victoria** (opposite) and discovering a cool, contemporary dining scene at the same time
- Hiking through the forests and meadows of **Strathcona Provincial Park** (p187)
- Nibbling beach-grown seaweed on an unusual **Sooke** culinary tour (see boxed text, p158)
- Encountering the **Broken Group Islands** (p176) at sea level on a summertime kayak odyssey
- Trekking the dense forest and searching the bays for beach glass around **Cape Scott Provincial Park** (p191)

VICTORIA

pop 77,500

With a combined population, when you add in the surrounding suburbs, of 351,000, pretty Victoria – across the water on the southern tip of Vancouver Island – is British Columbia's historic capital. Visitors have traditionally flocked here to experience a theme park version of olde Englishness that's dripping with cream teas, immaculate gardens and faux Tudor buildings. But times are changing in a city that was once the dictionary definition of 'retirement community.'

Fueled by an increasingly younger demographic, a quiet revolution has seen tired old pubs, eateries and stores transformed into the kind of bohemian shops, quirky coffee bars and surprisingly innovative restaurants that would make any university city proud. It's worth a day of anyone's time to seek out these enclaves on foot, but it's also a smart move to use Victoria for some outdoor adventuring before heading up-island: the city has more cycle routes than any other in Canada, whales are just a short speedboat ride away from Inner Harbour and there are some excellent seafront walks combining historic waterfront buildings and windswept parklands crenulated with rugged cliffs.

ORIENTATION

Overlooked by the formidable landmarks of the Empress Hotel and the Parliament Buildings (the ultra-busy visitor information center, or VIC, is also here), Victoria's Inner Harbour is the city's beating waterfront heart, especially if you're a busker with a tourist-pleasing act. Wharf St radiates north from here towards the sky-blue Johnson St Bridge, but most walkers take the parallel inland route along Government St, where tacky tourist shops mingle with stores that are actually worth entering.

A parallel block east, Douglas St (Hwy 1, aka Trans-Canada Hwy) is the broad thoroughfare where the locals shop. One-way Fort St juts east from here towards the traditionally British Oak Bay area – transit buses trundle this way towards the University of Victoria. Blanshard St is the city's other main northern entrance/exit. It leads to the Patricia Bay Hwy (Hwy 17) and the Saanich Peninsula, site of the Swartz Bay ferry terminal.

Maps

Free downtown maps are piled high at the VIC. Available from convenience stores, the *Streetwise Map Book* ($5.95) has more than enough detail for most visitors – it also covers Sidney and Sooke – and includes discount coupons for several restaurants.

INFORMATION
Bookstores

Crown Publications Bookstore (☎ 250-386-4636; 521 Fort St; ☽ 9am-5:30pm Mon-Sat) Tomes on BC's history, cuisine and culture.
Munro's Books (☎ 250-382-2464; 1108 Government St; ☽ 9am-6pm Mon-Wed & Sat, 9am-9pm Thu & Fri, 9:30am-6pm Sun) Local favorite; great travel section.
Snowden's Bookstore (☎ 250-383-8131; 619 Johnson St; ☽ 10am-5pm Mon-Thu, 10am-6pm Fri & Sat, 10am-5:30pm Sun) Huge used books selection.

Internet Access

Greater Victoria Public Library (☎ 250-382-7241; 735 Broughton St; ☽ 9am-6pm Mon & Sat, 9am-9pm Tue-Thu, 1-5pm Sun) Free internet access.
James Bay Coffee & Books (☎ 250-386-4700; 143 Menzies St; per min 10c; ☽ 7:30am-10pm)
Stain Internet Café (☎ 250-382-3352; 609 Yates St; per hr $3.50; ☽ 10am-2am)

Media

The *Times Colonist* (www.timescolonist.com) is Victoria's slender daily broadsheet. The alternative (and free) weekly *Monday Magazine* (www.mondaymag.com) covers arts and entertainment. The regional arm of CBC public radio is at 90.5 FM, while the University of Victoria's CFUV (101.9 FM) provides the city's indie spin.

Medical Services

Downtown Medical Centre (☎ 250-380-2210; 622 Courtney St; ☽ 9am-6pm)
Royal Jubilee Hospital (☎ 250-370-8000; 1900 Fort St; ☽ 24hr)

Money

Many downtown businesses accept US dollars; major bank branches line Douglas St. You can change foreign dosh at branches of **Custom House Global Foreign Exchange** (Wharf St ☎ 250-389-6007; 815 Wharf St; ☽ 9:30am-6pm Mon-Sat, 11am-6pm Sun; Bay Centre ☎ 250-412-0336; 1150 Douglas St; ☽ 9:30am-6pm Mon-Sat, 11am-6pm Sun; Victoria International Airport ☎ 250-655-0385; 1640 Electra Blvd; ☽ 9:30am-6pm Mon-Sat, 11am-6pm Sun).

VANCOUVER ISLAND

VANCOUVER ISLAND

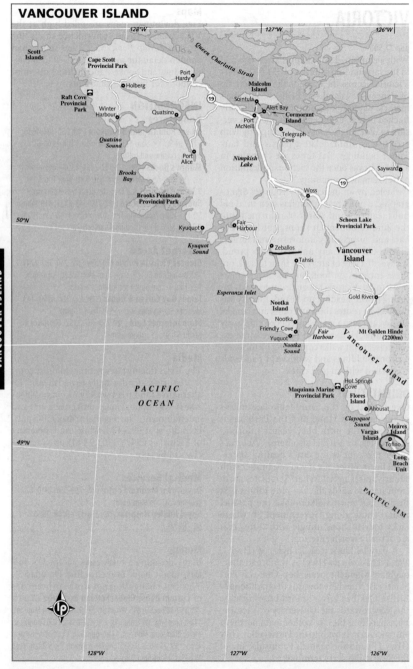

Scott Islands

Cape Scott Provincial Park

Raft Cove Provincial Park

Holberg

Winter Harbour

Quatsino

Quatsino Sound

Port Alice

Brooks Bay

Brooks Peninsula Provincial Park

Kyuquot

Kyuquot Sound

Brooks Bay

Port Hardy

Queen Charlotta Strait

Malcolm Island

Sointula

Port McNeill

Alert Bay

Cormorant Island

Telegraph Cove

Nimpkish Lake

Woss

Fair Harbour

Zeballos

Tahsis

Esperanza Inlet

Nootka Island

Nootka

Friendly Cove

Yuquot

Nootka Sound

Fair Harbour

Sayward

Schoen Lake Provincial Park

Vancouver Island

Gold River

Vancouver Island

Mt Golden Hinde (2200m)

Maquinna Marine Provincial Park

Hot Springs Cove

Flores Island

Ahousat

Clayoquot Sound

Vargas Island

Meares Island

Tofino

Long Beach Unit

PACIFIC OCEAN

PACIFIC RIM

50°N

49°N

128°W

127°W

126°W

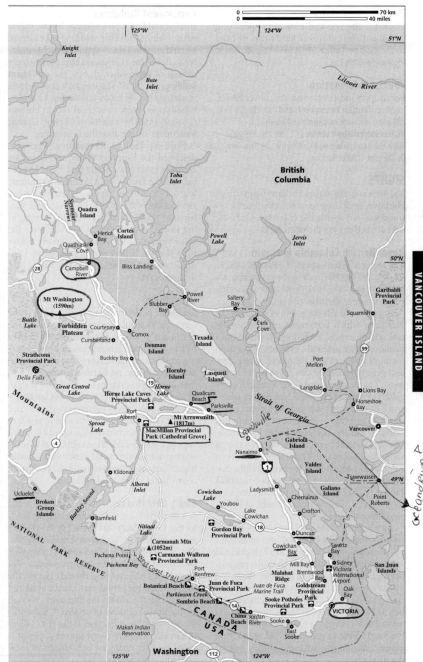

VANCOUVER ISLAND

Post

Look for the red-and-blue signs denoting postal outlets in stores around town, or head to the **main post office** (☎ 250-953-1352; 706 Yates St; ☺ 8am-5pm Mon-Fri).

Tourist Information

For tourism information on Vancouver Island, contact **Tourism Vancouver Island** (☎ 250-754-3500, 888-655-3843; www.vancouverisland.travel).

Visitor information center (VIC; ☎ 250-953-2033; www.tourismvictoria.com; 812 Wharf St; ☺ 9am-5pm) On the edge of Inner Harbour.

SIGHTS

Victoria's main sights radiate from Inner Harbour, including several tacky tourist 'attractions' not worth the entry fee. Only the best attractions are included here.

Royal British Columbia Museum

The region's best museum, the **Royal BC** (☎ 250-356-7226, 888-447-7977; www.royalbcmuseum.bc.ca; 675 Belleville St; adult/child $18/12; ☺ 9am-5pm) is the first stop for many Victoria visitors.

Fans of natural history should make for the 2nd floor which features some surprisingly realistic dioramas, including the museum's iconic woolly mammoth. Even better is a stroll through a re-created rain forest, where deer and grizzly bears eye you from between the trees. The evocative 3rd-floor human history gallery, covering the First Nations, is where you'll find ancient tools jostling for space with intricate carvings – check out the shamanist artifacts and the complete cedar longhouse. Finally, a stroll here among the re-created shops and houses of 'Old Town' provides a colorful introduction to the arrival of the Europeans. There's also a semi-independent **IMAX Theatre** (p152) on the ground floor, showing large-screen documentaries as well as Hollywood blockbusters.

As you make your way out, make sure you stop by **Thunderbird Park** (free), the museum's oft-photographed clutch of brightly painted totem poles, then duck into the adjacent pioneer buildings, including **Helmcken House** (free with museum entry or suggested donation $5; ☺ noon-4pm Jun-Sep). One of BC's oldest structures, this tidy 1852 doctor's residence is lined with the minutiae of everyday pioneer family life. Refreshingly little is roped off and wandering guides provide you with the stories behind the displays.

Parliament Buildings

If fairyland had a government house, this is what it would look like: wedding cake turrets, a grand entrance stairway and, at night, an exterior lit up like a Christmas tree. Surprisingly devoid of toy soldier guards, the **Parliament Buildings** (☎ 250-387-1400; www.leg.bc.ca; 501 Belleville St; admission free; ☺ 8:30am-5pm May-Sep, 8:30am-5pm Mon-Fri Oct-Apr) keep a watchful eye on the waterfront, aided by a statue of Captain George Vancouver sitting atop the main dome.

Built by Francis Rattenbury, who also designed the Empress Hotel, the elaborate complex is not just a pretty face. You can peek behind the facade on a colorful 30-minute **tour** (☎ 250-387-3046; tour free; ☺ 9am-4pm May-Sep, 9am-4pm Mon-Fri Oct-Apr) led by costumed Victorians; you'll learn the building's intriguing history and design quirks and view the sometimes-raucous debating chamber. Save time for lunch here at the Legislative Dining Room (p149), one of the city's best-kept dining secrets.

Chinatown

Small but perfectly formed, Fisgard St is the center of Victoria's compact Chinatown. One of Canada's oldest Asian districts, it's fronted by a towering red gate that looms over sprawling fruit and vegetable stores and the po-faced ancients meditating outside family-run restaurants. Twinkling neon signs add a dash of nighttime excitement, while **Fan Tan Alley** – a narrow passageway between Fisgard St and Pandora Ave – draws daytime explorers. Once the best spot in town to pick up your opium supplies, the slender thoroughfare is a miniwarren of traditional and trendy stores hawking cheap and cheerful trinkets, cool used records and funky mod fashions.

Emily Carr House

A short stroll south of Inner Harbour leads to the lovely **Emily Carr House** (☎ 250-383-5843; www.emilycarr.com; 207 Government St; admission by donation; ☺ 11am-4pm Jun-Aug, 11am-4pm Tue-Sat Sep-May), birthplace of BC's best-known painter. Restored to its original gingerbread exterior, the interior features period-furnished rooms and displays on the artist's life and work. As well as the limited number of original Carr works on display – the collection at the Art Gallery of Greater Victoria (opposite) is superior – there are ever-changing exhibitions of local contemporary works.

VANCOUVER ISLAND IN THREE DAYS

Start your odyssey with a hearty Victoria breakfast at **John's Place** (p149), then head north from the city on Trans-Canada Hwy 1 towards **Cowichan Bay** (see boxed text, p161), a quaint waterside community of painted wooden buildings perched on stilts over an ocean inlet. Drop into a couple of the region's many farms and wineries – especially **Merridale Estate Cidery** (see boxed text, p162) – before heading on to **Duncan** (p160), a once-remote logging outpost whose downtown is now a forest of intricately carved totem poles. If you're missing the big city, stay for a night in **Nanaimo** (p163), the island's other metropolis.

Hwy 1 becomes Hwy 19 after Nanaimo; on day two, continue along it and make for the family-friendly seaside towns of Parksville and Qualicum Beach, known jointly as **Oceanside** (p169), where leisurely beachcombing and finger-licking fish and chips are de rigueur. Take your time exploring some of the unexpected attractions in this region – including the **World Parrot Refuge** (p170) – then book into a B&B for the night. From Parksville, turn west on Hwy 4 towards the other coast, making sure you stop by **Cathedral Grove** (p172) en route to hug some ancient old-growth trees. Heading across the center of the island, you can stop at **Port Alberni** (p172) for a restorative pit stop or continue on to the **Pacific Rim National Park Reserve** (p174), heart of the breathtakingly wild west coast. Check in to your **Tofino** (p177) hotel, then hit the water. Even if you're not a surfer, the frothy, crashing waves, expansive sandy beaches and bracing sea air will restore your love for the natural world.

Beacon Hill Park

An easy walk south of downtown, this popular local hangout contains some surprisingly wild areas. Fringed by the Pacific on one side, it's a great spot to weather a wild storm – check out the windswept trees straining along the clifftops. Once the wind dies down and you can go exploring, you'll find one of the world's tallest totem poles, a traditional Victorian cricket pitch and a warren of landscaped gardens and ponds, complete with their own turtles. Ideal for a summer picnic, the park's landmarks include a marker for **Mile 0** of the Trans-Canada Hwy alongside a new **statue of Terry Fox**, the heroic one-legged runner whose attempted trek across Canada in 1981 gripped the nation.

Victoria Bug Zoo

The city's best attraction for kids, the **Bug Zoo** (☎ 250-384-2847; www.bugzoo.bc.ca; 631 Courtney St; adult/child $7/4.50; 🕓 9:30am-7pm mid-Jun–Aug, 10am-5pm Mon-Sat, 11am-5pm Sun Sep-May) houses creepy-crawlies such as glow-in-the-dark scorpions and ultra-industrious leaf-cutter ants. Informative 'bug guides' wander around explaining how the insects eat, mate and give birth. Those who can't restrain themselves can handle a few critters, including an alarmingly large 400-leg millipede. Hit the gift shop on your way out to pick up a souvenir tarantula for your favorite friend back home.

Craigdarroch Castle

Industrialist Robert Dunsmuir built the labyrinthine, 39-room **Craigdarroch Castle** (☎ 250-592-5323; www.thecastle.ca; 1050 Joan Cres; adult/child $11.50/3.50; 🕓 10am-5pm Sep–mid-Jun, 9am-7:30pm mid-Jun–Aug) with his enormous coal mining profits, but he died just a few months before its completion, leaving his mourning wife to take up residence alone. One of Victoria's postcard landmarks, the multiturreted property is an elegant, wood-lined stone mansion featuring delightful period architecture and antique-packed rooms. A climb up the castle tower's 87 steps (check out the stained glass windows en route) will reward visitors with views towards the snow-capped Olympic Mountains.

Art Gallery of Greater Victoria

East of downtown, just off Fort St, the city's main **art gallery** (☎ 250-384-4101; www.aggv.bc.ca; 1040 Moss St; adult/child $8/2; 🕓 10am-5pm Fri-Wed, 10am-9pm Thu) houses one of Canada's best Emily Carr collections, in a restored and extended heritage mansion. Carr's paintings, writings and photos are regularly rotated to keep the displays fresh but there's also an important collection of Asian artworks on permanent display. Regular temporary exhibitions color the seven gallery spaces and there's a hopping calendar of lectures and presentations if you want to rub shoulders with local arty types.

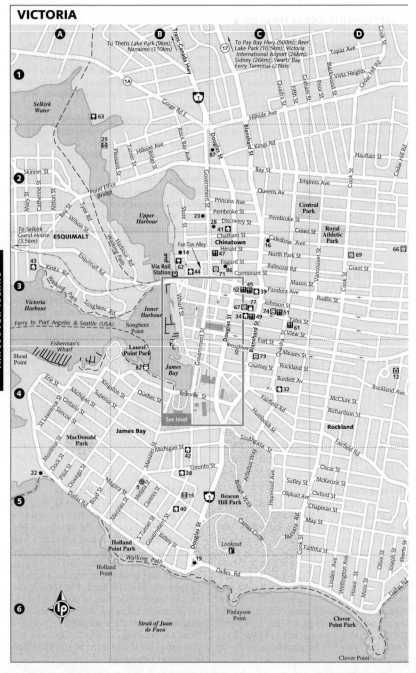

VICTORIA

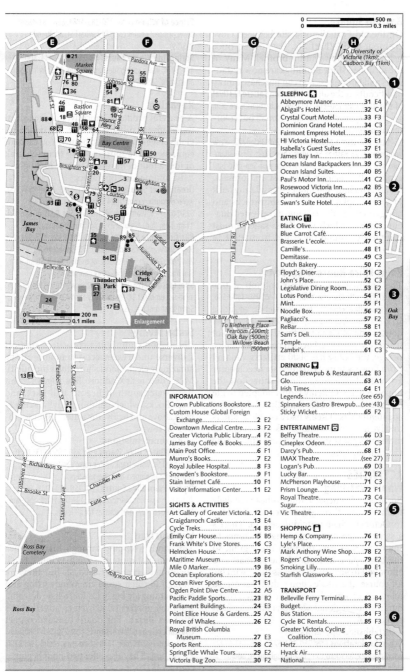

To University of
Victoria (1km);
Cadboro Bay (1km)

To Blethering Place
Tearoom (200m);
Oak Bay (500m);
Willows Beach
(500m)

Enlargement

INFORMATION

Crown Publications Bookstore...**1** E2	
Custom House Global Foreign	
Exchange.............................**2** F2	
Downtown Medical Centre........**3** F2	
Greater Victoria Public Library..**4** B5	
James Bay Coffee & Books.......**5** B5	
Main Post Office.....................**6** F1	
Munro's Books........................**7** E2	
Royal Jubilee Hospital..............**8** F3	
Snowden's Bookstore................**9** F1	
Stain Internet Café...................**10** E1	
Visitor Information Center........**11** E2	

SIGHTS & ACTIVITIES

Art Gallery of Greater Victoria..**12** D4	
Craigdarroch Castle...............**13** E4	
Cycle Treks...........................**14** B3	
Emily Carr House...................**15** B5	
Frank White's Dive Stores.......**16** C3	
Helmcken House....................**17** F3	
Maritime Museum..................**18** E1	
Mile 0 Marker.......................**19** B6	
Ocean Explorations................**20** E2	
Ocean River Sports................**21** E1	
Ogden Point Dive Centre........**22** A5	
Pacific Paddle Sports.............**23** B2	
Parliament Buildings..............**24** E3	
Point Ellice House & Gardens...**25** A2	
Prince of Whales....................**26** E2	
Royal British Columbia	
Museum..............................**27** E3	
Sports Rent...........................**28** C2	
SpringTide Whale Tours...........**29** E2	
Victoria Bug Zoo....................**30** F2	

SLEEPING

Abbeymore Manor..................**31** E4	
Abigail's Hotel.......................**32** C4	
Crystal Court Motel................**33** F3	
Dominion Grand Hotel............**34** C3	
Fairmont Empress Hotel...........**35** E3	
HI Victoria Hostel..................**36** E1	
Isabella's Guest Suites............**37** E1	
James Bay Inn........................**38** B5	
Ocean Island Backpackers Inn.**39** C3	
Ocean Island Suites................**40** B5	
Paul's Motor Inn....................**41** C2	
Rosewood Victoria Inn............**42** B5	
Spinnakers Guesthouses...........**43** A3	
Swan's Suite Hotel..................**44** B3	

EATING

Black Olive............................**45** C3	
Blue Carrot Café....................**46** E1	
Brasserie L'ecole....................**47** C3	
Camille's...............................**48** E1	
Demitasse..............................**49** C3	
Dutch Bakery........................**50** F2	
Floyd's Diner.........................**51** C3	
John's Place..........................**52** C3	
Legislative Dining Room.........**53** E2	
Lotus Pond...........................**54** F1	
Mint.....................................**55** F1	
Noodle Box...........................**56** F2	
Pagliacci's.............................**57** F2	
ReBar....................................**58** E1	
Sam's Deli.............................**59** E2	
Temple..................................**60** E2	
Zambri's................................**61** C3	

DRINKING

Canoe Brewpub & Restaurant.**62** B3	
Glo.......................................**63** A1	
Irish Times.............................**64** E1	
Legends..............................(see 65)	
Spinnakers Gastro Brewpub...(see 43)	
Sticky Wicket........................**65** F2	

ENTERTAINMENT

Belfry Theatre........................**66** D3	
Cineplex Odeon.....................**67** C3	
Darcy's Pub...........................**68** E1	
IMAX Theatre......................(see 27)	
Logan's Pub..........................**69** D3	
Lucky Bar..............................**70** E1	
McPherson Playhouse.............**71** C3	
Prism Lounge........................**72** F1	
Royal Theatre........................**73** C4	
Sugar....................................**74** C3	
Vic Theatre...........................**75** F2	

SHOPPING

Hemp & Company..................**76** E1	
Lyle's Place...........................**77** C3	
Mark Anthony Wine Shop.......**78** E2	
Rogers' Chocolates.................**79** E2	
Smoking Lilly........................**80** E1	
Starfish Glassworks.................**81** F1	

TRANSPORT

Belleville Ferry Terminal..........**82** B4	
Budget..................................**83** F3	
Bus Station............................**84** F3	
Cycle BC Rentals...................**85** F3	
Greater Victoria Cycling	
Coalition.............................**86** C3	
Hertz....................................**87** C2	
Hyack Air..............................**88** E1	
National................................**89** F3	

Bastion Square

On the old Fort Victoria site between Government and Wharf Sts, Bastion Sq once held a jail, gallows and a brothel. Many of the scrubbed stone buildings are now restaurants and boutiques. You can purchase quirky handicrafts at the all-day **Bastion Square Festival of the Arts** (☎ 250-413-3144; www.bastionsquare.com; 😊 Thu-Sun Apr, Wed-Sun May-Sep), a small but colorful summer market.

The **Maritime Museum** (☎ 250-385-4222; www .mmbc.bc.ca; 28 Bastion Sq; adult/child $8/3; 😊 9:30am-5pm mid-Jun–mid-Sep, 9:30am-4:30pm mid-Sep–mid-Jun) explores the region's salty past and present. Exhibits include 400 model ships dating back to 1810; displays on piracy, shipwrecks and navigation; and the *Tilikum*, a converted dugout canoe in which John Voss sailed almost completely around the world from 1901 to 1904.

Point Ellice House & Gardens

The colonial elite used to hobnob at this beautiful 1860s-era **mansion** (☎ 250-380-6506; www.pointellicehouse.ca; 2616 Pleasant St; adult/child $7/5; 😊 10am-4pm mid-May–mid-Sep), which now houses one of Canada's finest collections of trinkety Victoriana. Located near Point Ellice Bridge, the house has 5000 artifacts, ranging from flowery teapots to intricate needlepoint artworks. Fascinating photos show how the upper-echelon O'Reilly family adapted to life on the fringes of the far-flung British Empire – apparently Mrs O'Reilly had a couple of affairs to salve her homesickness. Ask staff about the mansion's ghost stories, and save time for the fragrant gardens.

ACTIVITIES
Whale-watching

Boatloads of raincoated tourists head out daily from Victoria throughout the lucrative May to October whale-watching season. There's a strict noncontact order when it comes to the orcas that pass through the region, so the boats park in front of the animals and allow you to gasp in wonder as they swim by. Of course, the whales don't always show, so many excursions also visit the favored rocky outcrops of regional sea lions and elephant seals.

Established operators:

Ocean Explorations (☎ 250-383-6722, 888-442-6722; www.oceanexplorations.com; 602 Broughton St; adult/ child $89/59)

Prince of Whales (☎ 250-383-4884, 888-383-4884; www.princeofwhales.com; 812 Wharf St; adult/child $85/69)

SpringTide Whale Tours (☎ 250-384-4444, 800-470-3474; www.springtidecharters.com; 1207 Wharf St; adult/child $89/59)

Kayaking

A peaceful paddle in Vancouver Island's calm waters gives a different perspective on the region's craggy, forest-lined beauty. You can rent equipment for a short- or long-term solo trek or join a tour of the area's watery highlights.

Recommended operators:

Ocean River Sports (☎ 250-381-4233, 800-909-4233; www.oceanriver.com; 1824 Store St; rental 2hr/24hr $25/50; 😊 9:30am-6pm Mon-Thu & Sat, 9:30am-8pm Fri, 11am-5pm Sun) Popular 2½-hour sunset tours ($59).

Pacific Paddle Sports (☎ 250-361-9365, 877-921-9365; www.pacificapaddle.com; 575 Pembroke St; rental 2hr/24hr $28/52; 😊 9:30am-6pm Mon-Sat & 10am-4pm Sun Apr-Oct) Good introductory courses.

Sports Rent (☎ 250-385-7368; www.sportsrentbc.com; 1950 Government St; rental 5hr/24hr $29/45; 😊 9am-5pm) Best rental rates.

Scuba Diving

The region's nutrient-rich waters support a diverse underwater ecosystem and can be amazingly clear. Good shore dives include 10 Mile Point near Cadboro Bay, Ogden Point Breakwater south of Beacon Hill Park, and Race Rocks, which combines idyllic scenery both above and below the water, 18km southwest of town.

Recommendations:

Frank Whites Dive Stores (☎ 250-385-4713; 1620 Blanshard St; www.frankwhites.com; 😊 9am-6pm) Courses for beginners and dive masters.

Ogden Point Dive Centre (☎ 250-380-9119, 888-701-1177; www.divevictoria.com; 199 Dallas Rd; 😊 9am-6pm) Guided dives and courses for all levels.

Windsurfing

The winds whipping through Juan de Fuca Strait are not quite as strong as those you'll encounter on the west coast, but they are enough to catch some air. Windsurfing and kiteboarding are big in Cadboro Bay, downhill from the university, as well as at Oak Bay's Willows Beach. For board rentals, contact **Coastal Cycle and Watersports** (☎ 250-391-1980; www .coastalwatersports.com; 1610 Island Hwy; rental 24hr $200; 😊 9am-5pm). They also offer two-hour beginner courses ($120).

CYCLING TOUR

Jump on your bike on the grassy lawn outside Inner Harbour's **Parliament Buildings** (**1**, p140), head west along Belleville St, then follow the curve of the waterfront around Laurel Point, Fisherman's Wharf and Shoal Point. When you reach the Ogden Point cruise ship terminal, you've hit Victoria's scenic **Dallas Road seaside route** (**2**). Continue cycling along this spectacular seawall course until you reach the **Terry Fox statue** (**3**, p141) and the marker denoting **Mile 0** (**4**, p141) of the Trans-Canada Hwy. Keep cycling along Dallas Rd, through the wild and windy seafront side of **Beacon Hill Park** (**5**, p141). After another kilometer or so, turn left onto tree-lined Cook St and cycle north – now's the time to stop for refresh-ment at a coffee shop, if required. Continue along leafy Cook St for almost 3km until you come to North Park St. Turn left, head over Blanshard St, and you're now on the edge of the city's colorful **Chinatown** (**6**, p140). From here, it's an easy cycle along Government St, to the lovely **Fairmont Empress Hotel** (**7**; see boxed text, p149).

SEA & CITY CYCLE

Start Parliament Buildings
Finish Fairmont Empress Hotel
Distance 9km
Duration Two hours

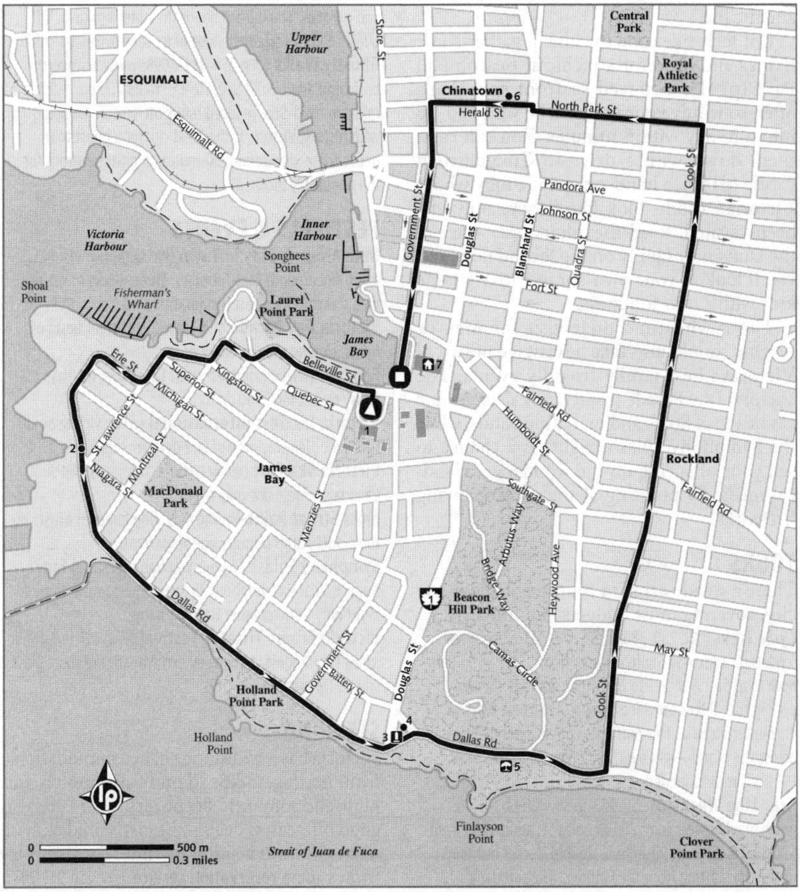

VANCOUVER ISLAND

VANCOUVER ISLAND

VICTORIA FOR CHILDREN

Victoria is dripping with activities and at-tractions for vacationing families. Ask at the visitor information centre (p140) for ideas, then hop on a nearby Harbour Ferry (right) for a fun trawl around the neighborhood on the water.

The city's main family-friendly attractions are within easy walking distance of the Inner Harbour and include the highly recommended Royal British Columbia Museum (p140) – complete with an evocative walk-though pio-neer town and an IMAX theater – and the creepy-crawly Victoria Bug Zoo (p141). If you have time, the Inner Harbour is also home to several whale-watching operations (p144) that can take you and your wide-eyed progeny up close and personal with some impressive aquatic life.

If it feels like time for lunch, gather some fixings and head for a picnic at Beacon Hill Park (p141), a rugged seafront spot that's often so windy your kids will be whipped-up into a frenzy within minutes. You can calm them down with a drive to Craigdarroch Castle (p141), a handsome stone folly whose Victorian rooms look like they've only just been vacated. Read the adults-only story of the Dunsmuir family on the second floor and you'll look at your own comparatively tame kids with a new fondness.

Those who time their visit for May or August should also take advantage of two of Victoria's best family-friendly events. The Victoria Day Parade (right) is a kaleidoscopic cavalcade of floats and marching bands, while the Symphony Splash (right) is a chance to sell your offspring on the wonders of classi-cal music by pointing at the accompanying fireworks.

TOURS

There's a wide array of tours available in the city, covering most budgets and interests.
Cycle Treks (☎ 250-386-2277, 877-733-6722; www .cycletreks.com; 450 Swift St; tours from $50; ☺ 9:30am-6pm Mon-Sat) A three- to four-hour seafront-themed cycling tour (bikes provided) is one of the best ways to encounter Victoria. This outfit also offers extended treks across the island – its Cowichan Valley Vineyards Tour ($139) is recommended.
Gray Line West (☎ 250-388-6539, 800-663-8390; www.graylinewest.com; 700 Douglas St; adult/child from $20.50/10.25) Runs 90-minute double-decker bus tours of the city starting from the Empress. The company's 13

additional tours include Butchart Gardens on the Saanich Peninsula (p157) and Craigdarroch Castle excursions.
Hyack Air (☎ 250-384-2499; www.hyackair.ca; 1234 Wharf St; tours $99) For a bird's-eye view of the city, this 30-minute floatplane tour is hard to beat – especially when it dive-bombs the water on landing.
Victoria Harbour Ferry (☎ 250-708-0201; www .victoriaharbourferry.com; adult/child $17/9; ☺ tours May-Sep) These tiny bathtub-like boats bounce across the water on tours of the busy Inner Harbour and storied Gorge Waterway. Services also include scheduled drop-off and pickup around the area (p154).

Walking Tours
Fairmont Empress Hotel (☎ 250-995-4688; www .walkabouts.ca; 721 Government St; tours $10; ☺ tours 10am May-Sep) Peek behind the curtains of Victoria's landmark hotel on this 65-minute stroll around the rooms and gardens. You'll learn about the hotel's colorful VIP guests and the grizzly demise of its controversial architect.
Ghostly Walks (☎ 250-384-6698; www.discoverthe past.com; adult/child $12/10; ☺ tours 7:30pm & 9:30pm mid-Jun–mid-Sep, reduced hours off-season) Dripping with history, Victoria is the ideal city for a ghost tour, hence these year-round, 90-minute nighttime strolls for the ghoulishly inclined.

FESTIVALS & EVENTS
Dine Around, Stay in Town (www.tourismvictoria .com/dinearound) Mid-February. Three weeks of cut-price meals at the city's best restaurants.
Victoria Day Parade Mid-May. Giant street fiesta of floats, clowns and marching bands.
Folkfest (www.icafolkfest.com) Late June. Ten days of folksy music, food and dance.
Victoria Jazzfest International (www.vicjazz.bc.ca) Late June. Ten-day orgy of jazz performance.
Victoria Ska Fest (www.victoriaskafest.ca) Mid-July. Canada's largest ska-only event.
Moss Street Paint-In Mid-July. One hundred artists ply their craft at this popular one-day event.
Symphony Splash (www.symphonysplash.ca) Early August. Victoria Symphony Orchestra performs for one night only from an Inner Harbour barge.
Victoria Fringe Theatre Festival (www.victoriafringe .com) Late August. Two-week extravaganza of short plays staged throughout the city.

SLEEPING

Victoria has a wide range of accommodations, from heritage B&Bs to midrange motels and high-end romantic sleepovers. There are also good off-season deals – the city's mild climate makes it worth visiting anytime. Tourism Vic-toria's **room reservation service** (☎ 250-953-2033,

800-663-3883; www.tourismvictoria.com) helps with bookings.

Budget

Ocean Island Backpackers Inn (☎ 250-385-1788, 888-888-4180; www.oceanisland.com; 791 Pandora Ave; dm/s/d $24/39/44; ☐) Part hostel, part budget hotel, this hopping heritage property is a maze of different-sized rooms. It's a great place to meet other travelers – there's a large communal kitchen and a licensed lounge where bands and DJs perform – and the front desk is a mine of information on local happenings. Clientele ranges from solo backpackers to traveling families. Wi-fi access (per two hours $1) available.

Selkirk Guest House (☎ 250-389-1213, 800-974-6638; www.selkirkguesthouse.com; 934 Selkirk Ave; dm/d/ste $25/90/125) Mostly a quiet, waterfront B&B with a clutch of comfortable, home-style rooms, this family-run heritage property across the Johnson St Bridge also has some good-value (women-only) dorm beds. A blue-painted 1909 character property, it's a 20-minute walk (or short bike ride) from downtown. Extras range from a hot tub to shared kitchen and laundry facilities.

HI Victoria Hostel (☎ 250-385-4511, 888-883-0099; www.hihostels.ca; 516 Yates St; dm/d $28/58) A converted brick warehouse in a good downtown location, this place is recommended for those who prefer quieter hostels. The decor is spartan and typically institutionalized, with gray walls and hospital-style corridors creating an efficient if faintly depressing ambience. There are two private rooms and several larger dorms, some with private bathrooms. The games room is a useful addition and every bed has a locker.

Midrange

Crystal Court Motel (☎ 250-384-0551; crystalcourt motel@shaw.ca; 701 Belleville St; r $95;) An older motel dwarfed by towering hotel neighbors, the Crystal Court offers good-value rooms near Inner Harbour. The location is the main draw, with the rooms offering a glimpse of the golden age of North American motels, right down to the shagpile carpets. Half the rooms have kitchens, so you can cook up your own cheese fondue and imagine it's 1976.

Dalton Hotel & Suites (☎ 250-384-4136, 800-663-6101; www.daltonhotel.ca; 759 Yates St; s/d $99/109) This formerly down-at-heel Victoria sleepover has new owners promising a new lease on life. A facelift has maintained the old gal's character with marble floors and chandeliers in the lobby, while giving its rooms a much-needed refurbishment. The standard rooms, many of them quite small, are respectable while not especially imaginative, but the pricier 'boutique rooms' have extra amenities such as fireplaces and air conditioners.

Paul's Motor Inn (☎ 250-382-9231, 866-333-7285; www.paulsmotorinn.com; 1900 Douglas St; r $109) Beneath an eye-opening shiny copper canopy that's now a Douglas St landmark, Paul's is a well-maintained 1970s-era motel that has a loyal band of repeat guests. Most rooms are spacious, with an anachronistic 1980s pastel decor, and there's a convivial 24-hour onsite restaurant serving comfort food. Avoid the main road traffic noises by requesting a courtyard room.

our pick **Ocean Island Suites** (☎ 250-385-1788, 888-888-4180; www.oisuites.com; 143 Government St; ste $120; ☐) This new venture from the guys who brought you Ocean Island Backpackers is a seriously good deal for groups of up to four ($15 extra per person after double occupancy). In this renovated heritage home in a quiet residential enclave a short walk from Inner Harbour, each suite has an individual international theme – request the Burma suite and you'll also get a claw-foot bathtub – along with hardwood floors, full kitchens and free wireless access. There's a shared laundry ($1.50 per load) in the basement plus a large deck and quiet garden for summertime chilling.

Rosewood Victoria Inn (☎ 250-384-6644, 866-986-2222; www.rosewoodvictoria.com; 595 Michigan St; d/ste $145/295) This bright and breezy guesthouse, minutes from Inner Harbour, is not shy with color: many of its 17 rooms have bold, flower-patterned themes. There's a wide array of room amenities, with fireplaces, balconies, Jacuzzi tubs and four-poster beds among the offerings, and the three-course breakfast is served in comfort in the property's lovely conservatory.

Abbeymore Manor (☎ 250-370-1470, 888-801-1811; www.abbeymoore.com; 1470 Rockland Ave; d/ste $149/229; ☐) A delightful 1912 mansion in the city's historic Rockland district, Abbeymore is not far from the downtown core. Behind its colonial facade hide antique-lined rooms, tastefully furnished with Victorian knick knacks, cozy rugs and the kind of beds you have to climb to get into. The property has wi-fi access.

James Bay Inn (☎ 250-384-7151, 800-836-2649; www
.jamesbayinn.bc.ca; 270 Government St; r $150) A few min-
utes' walk from the back of the Parliament
Buildings, this 19th-century charmer has a
loyal band of customers. They keep coming
back for the flower-strewn exteriors, wide
array of comfortable room configurations –
the kitchenettes and four-poster suites are
always popular – and the snug downstairs
pub and dining room.

Isabella's Guest Suites (☎ 250-595-3815; www
.isabellasbb.com; 537 Johnson St; ste $150) These two
immaculate, self-contained suites are a real
home away from home – especially if you're
used to high ceilings, hardwood floors and
quality reproduction furnishings. Each sunlit
suite has a full kitchen to call your own but
continental breakfast at the downstairs café is
included in the rates. Weekly lets are preferred
but nightly bookings are often available.

Top End

Spinnakers Guesthouses (☎ 250-384-2739, 877-838-
2739; www.spinnakers.com; 308 Catherine St; r/ste $179/249)
A short stumble away from its own excellent
brewpub (p151), this clutch of adult-oriented
guesthouses combines luxury details with
pampering home comforts. The Heritage
House is a restored 1884 family home with antiques, fireplaces and private patios. The larger
Garden Suites have a more contemporary feel
and a smattering of Asian design flourishes.
Gourmet continental breakfast included.

Swans Hotel (☎ 250-361-3310, 800-668-7926; www
.swanshotel.com; 506 Pandora Ave; ste $199-309) Once
a decaying brick warehouse, Swans has
been transformed into one of the city's best
sleepover discoveries. Its 29 large one- and
two-bedroom art-lined suites, some with two-
storey lofts, each have heritage-flavored wood-
beam ceilings coupled with modern skylights
and kitchens. Some also have balconies overlooking the nearby harbor. It's worth dining
onsite here: the downstairs bistro fuses Thai
and Pacific Northwest ingredients and the
brewpub produces some unique tipples.

Fairmont Empress Hotel (☎ 250-348-8111, 800-
257-7544; www.fairmont.com/empress; 721 Government St;
r from $249; 🖳 😊 🐾) Inner Harbour's grand
old lady, this ivy-covered, picture-postcard
edifice has been wowing tea-loving guests for
decades. Most rooms are elegant but conservative and some are downright small, but
the overall effect – including an oak-beamed
restaurant serving Raj-style curry and a high

tea sipped while overlooking the waterfront –
is classier than all of the city's other hotels
added together. Even if you don't stay, it's
worth strolling through to soak up the ambience of yesteryear Victoria.

Abigail's Hotel (☎ 250-388-5363, 800-561-6565;
www.abigailshotel.com; 906 McClure St; r $269-389; 🖳)
One of Victoria's most romantic sleepovers,
this sumptuous guesthouse is a short walk
from Inner Harbour. Behind its Tudoresque
facade, accommodations range from flowery standard rooms to antique-lined, gable-
ceilinged suites with canopy beds, marble
fireplaces and Jacuzzi tubs. Whatever your
price bracket, all guests enjoy perhaps the
city's best hotel breakfast: an inventive, three-
course extravaganza of regionally sourced
ingredients.

EATING

Once dominated by British-themed pub restaurants of dubious quality, Victoria's dining
scene has undergone a renaissance in recent
years. Old tourist trap eateries have been
taken over and transformed by adventurous
young chefs intent on discovering the region's
bounty of unique ingredients. For listings,
pick up *Eat Magazine* (free).

Budget

Floyd's Diner (☎ 250-381-5114; 866 Yates St; mains $3.50-
10; 😊 8am-5pm Mon-Fri, 9am-5pm Sat & Sun) A funky
eatery with an ultrafriendly vibe, Floyd's combines a sun-drenched patio, warming blood-
red interior and a menu of serious comfort
food – it's *the* spot to recover from a throbbing
hangover. Along with the all-day breakfast
menu (try the 'Elton,' a heaping bowl of fruit,
yogurt and honey), there are some bulging
burgers and sandwiches and a great lunch
deal: a $5.50 bottomless bowl of soup.

our pick Dutch Bakery (☎ 250-385-1012; 718 Fort St;
mains $4-7; 😊 7:30am-5:30pm Mon-Sat) If diners had
been invented by little old ladies with purple
hair, this is what they'd look like. This charming downtown institution has been packing
them in for 50 years with its Formica counter-
tops, chatty ambience and simple, old-school
meals. Rub shoulders with the regulars and
they'll recommend a beef pie with potato salad
followed by a fruit pie chaser. After your meal,
try to leave without buying from the Alad-
din's cave of handmade candies at the front –
where else can you pick up marzipan teeth
on your travels?

Sam's Deli (☎ 250-382-8424; 805 Government St; mains $5-8; ⏰ 7:30am-7pm Mon-Fri, 8am-7pm Sat, 9am-6pm Sun) It's not just its proximity to Inner Harbour that makes this fuel-up spot ever popular – it also makes darn good sandwiches, although you'll have to have a particularly large mouth to chomp down on some of them. Its signature sarnies feature roast beef or pastrami but the bulging vegetarian sandwich is also popular. A good takeout spot.

Blue Carrot Café (☎ 250-381-8722; 18B Bastion Sq; mains $6-9; ⏰ 8:30am-5pm Mon-Sat) An ideal hangout in the shadows of Bastion Sq, this wood-floored family-run nook serves local favorite Salt Spring Island coffee along with a host of chunky, mostly organic cakes and muffins. It's also a good lunch spot – regulars enjoy the ever-changing roster of made-from-scratch soups (carrot and ginger is frequently requested), and the hearty burgers are as far from fast food as it gets.

Midrange

ourpick Legislative Dining Room (☎ 250-387-3959; Room 606, Parliament Buildings; mains $6-16; ⏰ 9am-3pm Mon-Thu, 9am-2pm Fri) One of Victoria's best-kept dining secrets, the city's handsome waterfront Parliament Buildings has its own restaurant where MPs and VIPs can drop in for sustenance. Far from being a simple pit stop between debates, the subterranean eatery is a delightful, silver-service restaurant showcasing the best in regional ingredients. Happily, the subsidized menu has some of the best prices in town and it's also open to anyone who happens to be passing by – you have to leave your government-issued photo ID at the building's security desk, pick up your pass and follow the signs along the marble corridors of power. Once seated, you can select from a menu of delights that range from warm shrimp quesadilla to smoked tofu salads, mouth-melting steaks and an array of fresh fish specials. Save room for dessert – the pastries and puddings are exquisite. Since this place is used to dealing with spoiled politicians, the service is excellent, but make sure you have enough cash on you: credit cards are not accepted.

Demitasse (☎ 250-386-4442; 1320 Blanshard St; mains $7-11; ⏰ 7am-4pm Mon-Fri, 9am-2pm Sat & Sun) This art school–style hangout is where local grunge geeks come to sup endless cups of coffee and compare their latest Value Village purchases. It's very laid-back, with high ceilings and old wooden tables. The food is chunky, fresh and satisfying but never gets much further than great soups, wraps and sandwiches – simple, satisfying food done well: check out the banana bread French toast breakfast.

John's Place (☎ 250-389-0711; 723 Pandora Ave; mains $7-16; ⏰ 7am-9pm Mon-Thu, 7am-10pm Fri, 8am-10pm Sat, 8am-9pm Sun) Victoria's favorite brunch spot – hence the weekend lineups – John's is

TEA FOR YOU

Outside England (of about 100 years ago), Victoria is one of the world's most evocative locations to indulge in a spot of afternoon tiffin. More than a bunch of old biddies, pinkies cocked, jabbering about 'the youth of today' between minute sips of Earl Grey, it's an event for everyone, involving pastries, finger sandwiches, fruit…and tea.

The prim and proper **Fairmont Empress Hotel** (☎ 250-389-2727; www.fairmont.com/empress; 721 Government St; afternoon tea $54.95) is the tea lovers' favorite, where mouthwatering scones, fresh Devonshire cream and decadent pastries are all on the menu. Reserve at least a week ahead during the busy season, and make sure you're properly attired – those wearing ripped jeans are relegated to their own room as if they've done something very naughty, and those wearing shorts are likely to be shot and mounted alongside the wildlife trophies in the colonial Bengal Room.

Luckily, the hoity Empress doesn't hold a monopoly on Victoria tea quaffing. Other choices:

- **Blethering Place** (☎ 250-598-1413; 2250 Oak Bay Ave; afternoon tea $16.95) The name means 'voluble, senseless talking' but don't act like a blethering idiot at this traditional tearoom.

- **Point Ellice House & Gardens** (☎ 250-380-6506; 2616 Pleasant St; afternoon tea $16.95) Tea and fresh-baked scones are served in the fragrant gardens. If you have a monocle, this is the time to wear it.

- **Gatsby Mansion** (☎ 250-663-7557; 309 Belleville St; afternoon tea $21.95) Great views of Inner Harbour to accompany your genteel sipping.

VANCOUVER ISLAND

worth the wait to get in. It has a wood-floored, high-ceilinged heritage room lined with funky memorabilia, and the menu is a cut above usual diner fare. Heaping Belgian waffles are served with homemade cream cheese, and those who come for dinner can choose from a medley of international comfort food, from calamari to pierogies.

Noodle Box (☎ 250-384-1314; 818 Douglas St; mains $8-12; 🕑 11am-9pm Mon-Thu, 11am-10pm Fri & Sat, noon-7pm Sun) Southeast Asian cuisine with a strong Malaysian influence is the approach at this buzzing business that started out as a street vendor. A great place for takeout – served in those funky boxes – it's also a chatty eat-in spot. Popular stir-fries include Thai-style chow mein, and the Cambodian jungle curry is recommended for those who like their meals with a spicy kick.

Lotus Pond (☎ 250-380-9293; 617 Johnson St; mains $8-16; 🕑 11am-3pm & 5-9pm Tue-Sun) Behind the unassuming, almost shabby exterior of this downtown Chinese restaurant is an extensive, all-vegan menu of delights created using Buddhist principles. Even meat eaters have been known to swoon here, as they tuck into surprisingly tasty spring rolls, dim sum and pot stickers. Combo meals are the best option, as they offer an array of different flavors.

Mint (☎ 250-386-6468; 1414 Douglas St; mains $8-16; 🕑 5:30pm-2am) This loungey late-night hangout is popular with bar staff winding down after their shifts. But they don't just come to bitch about their nontipping customers; Mint offers an eclectic, finger-licking menu of Nepalese, Tibetan and fusion delicacies that runs from spicy lamb cooked with apricots to almond-and-cashew pesto fettuccine. There's an equally diverse line up of regular DJ performances.

ReBar (☎ 250-360-2401; 50 Bastion Sq; mains $9-14; 🕑 8:30am-9pm Mon-Wed, 8:30am-10pm Thu-Sat, 8:30am-3:30pm Sun) A relaxing and contemporary Victoria dining favorite, ReBar fuses colorful interiors with a natty, mostly vegetarian menu. Carnivores will be just as happy to eat here, though, with hearty savory dishes such as shitake-tofu pot stickers and an array of dense fruit smoothies. Weekend brunch is popular and heavily patronized by hung-over University of Victoria (UVic) students moaning quietly from every corner.

Temple (☎ 250-383-2313; 525 Fort St; mains $14-22; 🕑 11:30am-10pm Mon-Fri, 5-10pm Sat & Sun) A soothingly trendy interior might indicate style over substance at this compact downtown restaurant but the opposite turns out to be the case. With a focus on Pacific Northwest cuisine, the menu is a taste-tripper's dream, with seafood particularly well represented: sample the Quadra Island mussels and you won't be disappointed. A Belgian beer focus at the bar means that you can try pairing food with an array of unusual ales.

Pagliacci's (☎ 250-386-1662; 1011 Broad St; mains $16-22; 🕑 11:30am-10pm) A popular local hangout for decades, 'Pag's' is a small restaurant with a big heart. You're almost guaranteed to make a couple of new friends here since you'll be sitting elbow-to-elbow with the diners at the next table, but it's worth it for a menu of dishes such as Mae West Veal Medallions and Hot Transvestite Sautéed Chicken, each served with salad, vegetables and perfect pasta. Save room for dessert: a frightening array of delectable cheesecakes.

Black Olive (☎ 250-384-6060; 739 Pandora Ave; mains $16-24; 🕑 11am-11pm) This sophisticated but convivial downtown restaurant fuses a foundation of Mediterranean dishes with West Coast and international flourishes, offering meals that range from tiger prawn linguine to olive-topped wild salmon. While the starched white tablecloths suggest formality, the staff are bend-over-backwards friendly.

Top End

Camille's (☎ 250-381-3433; 45 Bastion Sq; mains $18-26; 🕑 5:30-10pm Tue-Sat) One of the grandes dames of Victoria fine dining, adventurous Camille's still challenges the city's new young chefs. Its charming subterranean dining room offers a lively, ever-changing menu reflecting whatever the chef can source locally: if wild strawberries are in season, they'll appear in soups and savory dishes as well as desserts. With a great wine menu, this spot invites adventurous foodies.

Brasserie L'Ecole (☎ 250-475-6260; 1715 Government St; mains $19-28; 🕑 5:30-11pm Tue-Sun) Incongruously abutting Chinatown, this superb bistro offers country-style French cuisine in a warm, casual atmosphere. Locally sourced produce is de rigueur, so the menu constantly changes to reflect seasonal highlights such as heirloom tomatoes, delicate figs and foraged salmonberries. A local favorite is lamb shank, served with mustard-creamed root vegetables and braised chard.

Zambri's (☎ 250-360-1171; 911 Yates St; mains $20-25; 🕑 11:30am-3pm & 5-9pm Tue-Sat) While this

---

TOP FIVE CHILL-OUT BREAKFAST SPOTS

▪ John's Place (p149) – Bright and chatty, with killer Belgian waffles.

▪ ReBar (opposite) – Cozy, subterranean and veggie friendly.

▪ Floyd's Diner (p148) – Low-cost, all-day breakfast joint with quirky, themed menu.

▪ Demitasse (p149) – Wholesome student hang-out with finger-licking banana bread French toast.

▪ Dutch Bakery (p148) – Light breakfast specials and a chocolate and candy counter on the way out.

---

eponymous downtown restaurant is run by a second-generation Italian chef, its menu is far beyond traditional trattoria fare. Deceptively unassuming from the outside, the ever-changing dishes might range from a hearty squash soup with butter-fried sage to a mouth-melting sablefish, served with rapini-poached eggs. Diners in the know drop by on Saturday, when a creative five-course tasting menu hits the blackboard.

DRINKING

Victoria is the drinking capital of BC, with a frothy array of great watering holes for those who like to wind down with a pint or three at the end of a hard day on the tourist trail. After extensive first-hand research, we recommend the following.

Spinnakers Gastro Brewpub (☎ 250-386-2739; 308 Catherine St; ⏰ 11am-10:30pm) A pioneer of the North American craft brewing renaissance, Spinnakers is a local legend that lives up to its billing. Its wood-floored, waterfront pub setting is ideal, and its selection of own-brewed tipples is second to none. Fans of lighter beers enjoy the Honey Blonde Ale, while those with darker palates quaff the Nut Brown Ale. Save room to eat: the menu of seasonal dishes – many designed for pairing with specific beers – is far superior to most pubs.

Irish Times (☎ 250-383-7775; 1200 Government St; ⏰ 11am-1am) Residing in a handsome old bank building, this lively Celtic bar is a cut above standard Irish pubs. The interior is a pleasing fusion of high ceilings and dark wood finishes and the draft selection is a cornucopia of popular favorites from Ireland, France, Belgium and the UK. The menu has some gourmet flourishes (the shareable seafood tower is recommended) and there's live Irish music every night.

Sticky Wicket (☎ 250-383-7137; 919 Douglas St; ⏰ 11am-11pm Sun-Thu, 11am-midnight Fri & Sat) This cavernous complex is the place to head if you want a noisy night out with the locals. The Wicket's main bar serves popular (if slightly pricey) Irish beers, while its menu serves up heaping plates of pub grub, ranging from burgers all the way to chicken strips. Live sports are pumped through the TVs and there's a poolroom upstairs. The highlight bar is Big Bad John's, a tiny hillbilly nook with tree stump tables and a carpet of peanut shells.

Glo (☎ 250-385-5643; 2940 Jutland Rd; ⏰ 11am-11pm Sun-Thu, 11am-1am Fri & Sat) Victoria's best mod lounge bar, Glo has waterfront views, cozy oversized booths and a warming red-hued ambience. A great spot for nighttime cocktails, this is where the city's beautiful young people come to ogle each other. The food is also worth an ogle: the flatbread pizzas are great and the dessert menu covers all the bases. DJs spin a few tracks on weekends.

Canoe Brewpub & Restaurant (☎ 250-361-1940; 450 Swift St; ⏰ 11:30am-midnight Sun-Thu, 11:30am-1am Fri & Sat) This huge brick-lined warehouse is surprisingly intimate, though on sunny days you'll want to sit on the patio. Canoe's own-brewed beers – that's the stuff in the giant copper tanks – include the popular Beaver Brown Ale, but adventurous quaffers should sample the maltier Red Canoe Lager or the Siren's Song Pale Ale, a great summer beer.

ENTERTAINMENT

Check listings in *Monday Magazine* or visit www.livevictoria.com for local happenings.

Live Music

Logan's Pub (☎ 250-350-2711; www.loganspub.com; 1821 Cook St; cover free-$15) A short stroll from downtown, this old-school sports pub looks like nothing special from the outside, but its roster of shows is the heart and soul of the local indie scene. Friday and Saturday are your best bet for performances but other nights are frequently also booked – check the pub's online calendar before you arrive.

Darcy's Pub (☎ 250-380-1322; www.darcyspub.ca; 1127 Wharf St; cover free) Eschewing the DJ route, this laid-back pub offers free live acts every night, ranging from weekend cover bands to a Monday night open-mike session. In between, it's singer-songwriters with weepy love songs to get off their chests. While few of the acts are likely to set the world on fire, they provide a relaxing accompaniment to the pub's convivial atmosphere.

Lucky Bar (☎ 250-382-5825; www.luckybar.ca; 1127 Wharf St; cover free-$10) A Victoria night out institution, Lucky Bar offers an eclectic array of live music from ska and indie to electroclash. Bands perform at least twice a week, while the remaining evenings are filled by club nights that range from Wednesday's mod fest to Saturday's dance mix night.

Nightclubs

A long-standing, popular club that's only open a few days a week, **Sugar** (☎ 250-920-9950; 858 Yates St; cover free-$22; ☾ Thu-Sat) offers mainstream house and Top 40 DJ sounds (under a giant disco ball) plus regular live events. Conveniently located under the Sticky Wicket pub, **Legends** (☎ 250-383-7137; www.legendsnightclub.com; 919 Douglas St; cover free-$15) is another mainstream hangout known for its Saturday Top 40, hip-hop and R&B night. Friday is also popular and there are additional live acts throughout the month. The city's raucous gay and lesbian hangout, **Prism Lounge** (☎ 250-388-0505; www.prism lounge.com; 642 Johnson St; cover free-$10) hosts nightly events, including drag fests, karaoke evenings and bear rendezvous. The Friday and Saturday night dance parties are its main attraction.

Theatre

McPherson Playhouse (☎ 250-386-6121; www.rmts .bc.ca; 3 Centennial Sq) and **Royal Theatre** (☎ 250-386-6121; www.rmts.bc.ca; 805 Broughton St) are Victoria's twin center stages. Both offer mainstream theater productions, but the latter is also home of the **Victoria Symphony** (☎ 250-385-6515; www.victoriasymphony.bc.ca) and **Pacific Opera Victoria** (☎ 250-382-1641; www.pov.bc.ca). The excellent **Belfry Theatre** (☎ 250-385-6815; www.belfry.bc.ca; 1291 Gladstone Ave) is a showcase for contemporary, especially Canadian, plays and is one of the country's most respected independent theatre companies. It's housed in a converted 1890s Baptist church.

Cinemas

Victoria's best arthouse cinemas are the **Vic Theatre** (☎ 250-383-1998; 808 Douglas St; adult/child $8.50/5), which screens lesser-known first-run movies, and UVic's **Cinecenta** (☎ 250-721-8365; www.cinecenta.com; University of Victoria; adult/child $6.25/4.75), where old classics and curiosities rub shoulders on a nightly changing schedule. The city's main first-run cinema is **Cineplex Odeon** (☎ 250-383-0513; 780 Yates St; tickets $8.25). The Royal BC Museum's (p140) **IMAX Theatre** (☎ 250-953-4629; www.imaxvictoria.com; adult/child $10.50/8.25; ☾ 8am-10pm) shows larger-than-life documentaries and reformatted Hollywood blockbusters.

SHOPPING

While Government St remains the best place in Victoria to pick up souvenirs, the back alleys of Chinatown and the Johnson St stretch between Store and Government Sts are hotbeds of explorable independent retailing.

Smoking Lilly (☎ 250-382-5459; 569 Johnson St; ☾ 11am-5:30pm Thu-Sat, noon-5pm Sun & Mon) Only a couple of people can fit in this tiny boutique at any given time – try something on and you'll be behind a curtain in the middle of the shop – but it's worth the squeeze to check out eclectic garments and accessories displaying an art school chic. Tops with insect prints and skirts displaying the periodic table are hot items, but there are also lots of cute handbags, socks and brooches to tempt your credit card.

Hemp & Company (☎ 250-383-4367; 547 Johnson St; ☾ 10am-8pm Mon-Sat, 11am-6pm Sun) Not your standard West Coast hippy-dippy hemp shop; the top-selling item here is an Oxford shirt that any self-respecting banker could wear to work. About as mainstream as a hemp boutique could be, the approach is to attract non-hempsters with classic clothing lines, hemp soaps and cool vegan shoes.

Mark Anthony Wine Shop (☎ 250-384-9994; 1007 Government St; ☾ 10am-9pm) Reflecting BC's wine-producing provenance, this swanky store showcases the tipples of Mission Hill, one of the Okanagan's most celebrated producers. A mini theater walks you through the process, a tasting bar serves those who like to try before buying and an impressive selection of vintages is offered for sale.

Rogers' Chocolates (☎ 250-727-6851; 913 Government St; ☾ 9am-7pm Sun-Wed, 9am-9pm Thu-Sat) This lovely old-fashioned emporium serves the best ice cream bars in town but repeat visitors are usually working their chocolaty way through the menu of glutinous Victoria Creams, one of which is usually enough to substitute for lunch. Flavors range from peppermint to chocolate nut.

Lyle's Place (☎ 250-382-8422; 770 Yates St; ☑ 10am-6pm Mon-Thu, 10am-9pm Fri, 10am-6pm Sat, noon-5pm Sun) The city's best new and used record store, Lyle's is the perfect place to hang out with like-minded music fans on a rainy afternoon. Ask staff about the local music scene and they'll point you in the direction of Victoria's best live venues – you can also buy tickets for local concerts here.

Starfish Glassworks (☎ 250-388-7827; 630 Yates St; ☑ 10am-6pm Mon-Sat, noon-6pm Sun) The perfect place to pick up that glass ray-gun you've always wanted, Starfish is a gallery of colorful glass artworks ranging in price from a few dollars right up to remortgage-the-house level. If you time your visit right (afternoon is usually best), you can also watch the mesmerizing glass-blowers at work.

GETTING THERE & AWAY
Air
Victoria International Airport (☎ 250-953-7500; www.victoriaairport.com) is 26km north of the city via Hwy 17. Regular **Air Canada Jazz** (☎ 514-393-3333, 888-247-2262; www.aircanada.com) flights arrive from Vancouver (from $108, 25 minutes, 16 daily) and **WestJet** (☎ 800-538-5696; www.westjet.com) flights arrive from Calgary (from $150, 90 minutes, three daily).

Frequent floatplane services arriving at Inner Harbour include **Harbour Air Seaplanes** (☎ 800-665-0212, 604-274-1277; www.harbour-air.com) flights from downtown Vancouver ($109, 35 minutes) and downtown Nanaimo ($59, 20 minutes). **West Coast Air** (☎ 800-347-2222, 604-606-6888; www.westcoastair.com) services arrive from Vancouver ($119, 35 minutes) and from Whistler ($249, one hour). **Kenmore Air** (☎ 866-435-9524, 425-486-1257; www.kenmoreair.com) floatplanes arrive from Seattle ($149, one hour).

Helijet (☎ 800-665-4354, 604-273-4688; www.helijet.com) helicopter services arrive in Inner Harbour from Vancouver (from $109, 35 minutes, four to 13 daily).

Boat
Year-round **BC Ferries** (☎ 888-223-3779, 250-386-3431; www.bcferries.com) services arrive at Swartz Bay, 27km north of Victoria via Hwy 17, from Tsawwassen on the mainland (adult/child/vehicle $10.30/5.15/34.20, 90 minutes). Services also arrive from the Southern Gulf Islands (p194). See p401 for more details on ferry travel.

Black Ball Transport (☎ 250-386-2202; www.northolympic.com/coho) runs its *MV Coho* service from Port Angeles (passenger/vehicle US$11/$23, 90 minutes, up to four daily) into Inner Harbour. The **Victoria Clipper** (☎ 250-382-8100, 800-888-2535; www.victoriaclipper.com) passenger-only service also arrives here from Seattle (US$66, three hours, up to three daily). **Victoria Express** (☎ 250-361-9144; www.victoriaexpress.com) runs passenger-only services into Inner Harbour from Port Angeles (US$12.50, one hour, up to four daily) and the Sun Juan Islands (US$35, three hours, daily).

Bus
Out-of-town services arrive at the main **bus station** (700 Douglas St). These include **Greyhound** (☎ 800-661-8747; www.greyhound.ca) routes from Nanaimo ($18.75, 2½ hours, six daily), Campbell River ($46, six hours, four daily) and Port Alberni ($77, 9½ hours, daily).

Pacific Coach Lines (☎ 250-385-4411, 800-661-1725; www.pacificcoach.com) services arrive from downtown Vancouver ($36, 3½ hours) and Vancouver International Airport ($41.50, four hours) up to 16 times per day. **Tofino Bus** (p180) services arrive from Tofino ($53.50, 5½ hours) and Ucluelet ($50, five hours, two daily).

Car & Motorcycle
The Swartz Bay ferry terminal is a 27km, well-signposted drive away via Hwy 17. Local car rental agencies:

Budget (☎ 260-953-5300, 800-668-9833; www.budgetvictoria.com; 757 Douglas St)
Hertz (☎ 250-385-4440, 800-654-3131; www.hertz.ca; 2634 Douglas St)
National (☎ 250-386-1213; www.nationalvictoria.com; 767 Douglas St)

Train
The **VIA Rail** (☎ 888-842-7245; www.viarail.ca) *Malahat* service arrives in downtown Victoria from Courtenay ($48, 4½ hours, daily), with stops in Nanaimo, Parksville and Chemainus, among others.

GETTING AROUND
To/From the Airport
AKAL Airport Shuttle (☎ 250-386-2525, 877-386-2525; www.victoriaairporter.com; one way $15) provides a 30-minute door-to-door service between the airport and area hotels and motels plus the University of Victoria. It operates throughout the day, coordinating with flight schedules.

A downtown-bound taxi costs around $45, while transit bus 70 ($2.75, 35 minutes, three to five daily) also runs to the city.

Bicycle

The **Greater Victoria Cycling Coalition** (☎ 250-480-5155; www.gvcc.bc.ca; 12 Centennial Sq) is a good place to start for maps, resources and information.

Bike rental joints:

Cycle BC Rentals (☎ 250-380-2453, 866-380-2453; www.cyclebc.ca; 747 Douglas St; bike rental hr/day $6/19; 🕑 9am-5pm Nov-Feb, 9am-7pm Mar-Oct) Motorcycles and scooters also available.

Sports Rent (☎ 250-385-7368; www.sportsrentbc.com; 1950 Government St; bike rental 2hr/day $12/25; 🕑 9am-5pm) Additional rentals, from kayaks to roller-blades, also available

Boat

Victoria Harbour Ferry (☎ 250-708-0201; www.victoriaharbourferry.com; fares from $4) covers Inner Harbour, Ocean Pointe Resort, Songhees Point (for Spinnakers Brewpub), Fisherman's Wharf and other stops along the Gorge Waterway with its armada of tiny boats.

Public Transport

Victoria Regional Transit (☎ 250-382-6161; www.bctransit.com; 1-/2-zone $2/2.75) buses cover a wide area – two-zone travel takes you into the suburbs to places such as Colwood and Sidney, with some routes served by double-deckers. Good-value day passes ($6) aren't sold on buses but are widely available from convenience and grocery stores.

Taxi

Two-seater, human-powered **Kabuki Kabs** (☎ 250-385-4243; per min $1) are fun, if only to hear the 'driver' spin a yarn.

Traditional taxi services:

Blue Bird Cabs (☎ 250-384-1155, 800-665-7055)
Empress Taxi (☎ 250-381-2222, 800-808-6881)

SOUTHERN VANCOUVER ISLAND

A short drive from Victoria's busy streets, Southern Vancouver Island delivers a cornucopia of quirky little towns, an array of cycling and hiking routes and some rocky, waterfront landscapes teeming with dense forests – check out the copper-colored arbutus trees and gnarly Garry oaks. The wildlife here is abundant and impressive and you're likely to spot bald eagles swooping overhead, sea otters cavorting on the beaches or perhaps the occasional orca sliding quietly by just off the coast.

SIDNEY

pop 11,860

Seafront Sidney, at the northern end of Saanich Peninsula, is a recommended relaxing afternoon excursion from Victoria – especially if you love books: the town has possibly more bookstores per capita than any other in BC. Wandering the tidy streets, ducking into a coffee shop and checking out a waterfront restaurant are popular pastimes here. For those of a more active disposition, there's an offshore provincial park and an access point for the Lochside Regional Trail (see boxed text, p159), where you can cycle to and from Victoria.

The **VIC** (☎ 250-656-3260; www.sidney.ca; 2295 Ocean Ave; 🕑 10am-2pm & 4-7pm Jun-Sep) is on the west side of town.

Sights & Activities

The biggest of Sidney's bookshops, **Tanners** (☎ 250-656-2345; 2436 Beacon Ave; 🕑 8am-10pm) has an extensive travel guide selection, lots of magazines and a back room of maps and regional-interest books. In contrast, **Beacon Books** (☎ 250-655-5283; 2372 Beacon Ave; 🕑 10am-5:30pm Mon-Sat, noon-4pm Sun) has a vast array of used titles – especially mystery novels – all guarded by a portly but affectionate cat.

A floating barge amid the bobbing boats of the marina, the **Marine Ecology Centre** (☎ 250-655-1555; www.mareco.org; 9835 Seaport Pl; adult/child $4/3; 🕑 noon-5pm) feels like a community museum for the sea. Illuminating the salty wildlife found just off the coast here, visitors can check out a host of water-based local critters, guide a remote-controlled submarine and dip their hands in some educational touch tanks.

You can get even closer to nature at **Sidney Spit**. Accessed via a 15-minute **ferry ride** (☎ 250-655-4995; www.alpinemarineadventurecenter.ca; adult/child $11.75/9.75; 🕑 10am-5pm Jul & Aug, 10am-3pm Mon-Fri, 10am-5pm Sat & Sun May, Jun & Sep), this sandy island is ideal for swimming, sunbathing, beach-combing and bird-watching. Bring a picnic and make a day of it.

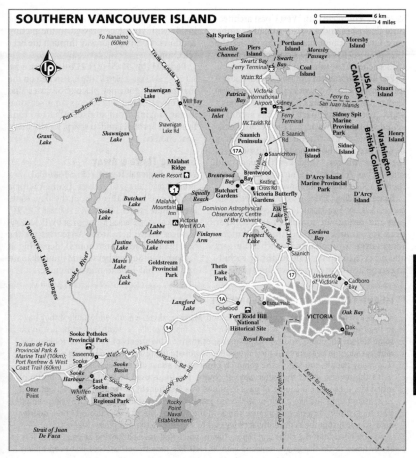

SOUTHERN VANCOUVER ISLAND

For those who want to try sea kayaking but are a little bit wary of setting out for the first time, **Sea Quest Adventures** (☎ 250-655-9256, 888-656-7599; www.seaquestadventures.com; 2537 Beacon Ave; ⏲ 7am-11pm Mar-Nov) offers kayaking **lessons** (4hr lesson $85; ⏲ May-Aug) tailored to accommodate all levels, as well as whale-watching treks.

Sleeping & Eating

McDonald (☎ 250-654-4000; tent site $13.85) Formerly a provincial park and now part of the Gulf Islands National Park Reserve (see boxed text, p194), this place, near the Swartz Bay ferry terminal offers camping with basic, well-maintained facilities and fine white sand as your mattress.

Sidney Spit (☎ 250-654-4000; tent site $13.85) Enjoying a 2km stretch of beach this rustic, walk-in site is ideal for those campers who don't mind pit toilets and cold water taps. Idyllic but basic.

Sidney Waterfront Inn & Spa (☎ 250-656-1131, 888-656-1131; www.hotelsidney.com; 9775 First St; d $130-150, ste $195-275) Well located in the center of all the Sidney action, this place has an array of different rooms – some face the water and others look back across the town – but most have pastel interiors and amenities ranging from kitchenettes to flat-screen TVs.

Miraloma on the Cove (☎ 250-656-6622, 877-956-6622; www.miraloma.ca; 2326 Harbour Rd; ste $169-475) Old Shoal Harbour Inn has been transformed into Miraloma, a swanky but intimate waterfront sleepover, complete with West Coast architectural flourishes and a warm, romantic ambience. Once a vacation home for dignitaries, the 1925 property has 22 large, designer suites, each with kitchenettes, tubs and heated floors.

Pier Bistro Restaurant (☎ 250-655-4995; 2550 Beacon Ave; mains $9-12; ☺ 8:30am-5pm Mon, 8:30am-8:30pm Tue-Sun) Almost hanging off the end of Sidney's short pier, this compact spot has stunning island-fringed views across the ocean. Luckily, the food is just as good, with a wide array of well-prepared home-style fish dishes – try the oyster burger – plus hearty salads and sandwiches. After 4pm (Thursday to Sunday), there's a $5 cod 'n' chips special.

Beacon Landing (☎ 250-656-6690; 2537 Beacon Ave; mains $12-24; ☺ 9pm-11pm) This large, inviting pub and restaurant complex has a popular deck for summertime quaffing. Its menu ranges from bar food classics such as burgers and pizzas to heaping seafood dishes, including some hearty stuffed prawns and plates of Fanny Bay oysters. If it's raining, you can sit inside with your face pressed to the picture windows, working your way through the beer selection.

Dock 503 (☎ 250-656-0828; 2320 Harbour Rd; mains $21-30; ☺ 11:30am-2:30pm & 5-10pm) Perched on the marina, this gourmet place showcases fine Vancouver Island ingredients on a seasonal menu ranging from smoked albacore tuna from Salt Spring Island to sharp, locally made goat cheese.

Getting There & Away

Victoria Regional Transit (☎ 250-382-6161; www .bctransit.com) bus 70 arrives from Victoria ($2.75, one hour) throughout the day. **Washington State Ferries** (☎ 206-464-6400, 888-808-7977; www.wsdot.wa.gov/ferries; passenger/car US$15.60/52.40) services arrive here from Anacortes via the San Juan Islands (three hours), departing at 7:45am mid-September to mid-June, 8:15am and 2pm mid-June to mid-September.

ISLAND TIME, ISLAND TALK, ISLAND LIFE

Time is a nebulous concept on Vancouver Island. Many residents feel uncomfortable if they have to head to the mainland and will only go there as a matter of life or death, or maybe just to do some serious shopping. You can sometimes spot them on the streets of Vancouver, looking like rabbits caught in headlights as they struggle to negotiate the rush of two oncoming pedestrians. 'Too many people, too fast' is the common observation about life east of Nanaimo.

It's the reverse effect the other way, of course. For those used to the hustle and bustle of urban life, it can take a couple of days to adjust to a less frenetic pace. But once you get used to it, 'island time' fits like a pair of well-worn jeans. Those accustomed to big-city living should start their trip in Victoria to minimize shock to the system. The city operates on 'three-quarter time' so you'll soon be sufficiently acclimatized to experience the rest of the island.

As you head from the cities and bigger towns, you'll find yourself looking at your watch less, as set times to do things are replaced with 'It feels like time to eat' or 'Let's just keep hiking' or 'I've fished enough; let's sit on the deck and have some beers.' The passing of the day (or week) hardly seems to matter, especially on the surf-happy west coast, where an hour on the beach can easily stretch to a day, and in the rugged north where the dominant forests inspire a different, more natural pace of life. These areas are tangibly less stressful; nobody's in a rush, everyone's got time to stop and talk and moving around is based on a 'We'll get there when we get there' approach.

Once you feel like you could get used to island time, take it up a notch and learn 'island talk.' Call it 'the Island' instead of 'Vancouver Island.' 'Up-island' is north and 'down-island' is south, relative to your position – if you're in Victoria, Ladysmith is up-island but if you're in Parksville, Ladysmith is down-island.

For the most part, you can drop 'Port' from town names and 'Island' from island names – Port Hardy becomes 'Hardy' and Gabriola Island is 'Gabriola.' Port Alice and Port Alberni are exceptions; for whatever reason, they keep the 'Port.'

Practice before you go. Tuck away your watch and when someone asks where you're going, say: 'Over to the Island. The ferry lands in Nanaimo and from there it's up-island to McNeill, with maybe a stop at Denman and Hornby.'

Now you're ready for 'island life.'

SAANICH PENINSULA

Southern Vancouver Island's transportation hub – home of the main airport and ferry terminal – this peninsula north of Victoria has more to offer than just a way to get from here to there. The **Saanich Peninsula VIC** (☎ 250-656-0525; 10382 Patricia Bay Hwy; ☼ 8:30am-5:30pm Jun-Sep) can offer some suggestions.

Butchart Gardens

Robert Butchart spotted limestone deposits and chose this site in 1904 for his cement factory; meanwhile, his wife Jennie planted sweet peas and a single rose at the nearby residence, despite knowing little about gardening. More than a century later, the cement operation is gone but the elaborately coiffured **Butchart Gardens** (☎ 250-652-5256, 866-652-4422; www.butchartgardens.com; 800 Benvenuto Ave; adult/youth/child $23/11.50/2.50; ☼ 9am-10:30pm mid-Jun–Aug, shorter hrs at other times) is one of BC's top visitor attractions.

Offering an explosion of colors and textures, the immaculate grounds are divided into separate gardens – the tranquil Japanese Garden is a favorite – where there's always something in bloom. Summer is crowded here but daily afternoon and evening music performances and Saturday night fireworks (July and August) make it all worthwhile. December visitors are treated to thousands of fairy lights draped among wintering plants.

Victoria Butterfly Gardens

On the way to Butchart Gardens, this family-friendly collection of **tropical aviaries** (☎ 250-652-3822, 877-722-0272; www.butterflygardens.com; 1461 Benvenuto Ave; adult/child $10/5.50; ☼ 9:30am-4:30pm Mar-mid-May, Sep & Oct, 9am-5:30pm mid-May–Aug) offers a kaleidoscope of 35 different butterfly species – that's a minimum of 2400 butterflies – in a free-flying environment. As well as having the thrill of watching them flutter around, visitors can learn about the creatures' life cycles, as well as eyeballing other exotic birds, fish and plants – look out for Spike, a naughty Puna Ibis bird that likes to accost visitors.

Centre of the Universe

Perched on Observatory Hill, the grandly named, family-friendly **Centre of the Universe** (☎ 250-363-8262; 5071 W Saanich Rd; adult/child $9/5; ☼ 1-4:30pm Tue-Thu Sep-Apr, 10am-6pm Tue-Thu, 10am-11pm Fri & Sat May-Aug) is a government-run facility housing the Plaskett Telescope (in use since

1918), several hands-on exhibits and a mini-planetarium. Starry-eyed visitors can drop by for a Star Party on Friday or Saturday evening (May to October), when the astronomers chill out, show off their equipment and tackle themes from asteroids to extraterrestrials.

Getting There & Away

Victoria Regional Transit (☎ 250-382-6161; www.bctransit.com) bus 75 arrives from Victoria at Butchart Gardens ($2.75, 50 minutes) and at points around the area. **Gray Line West** (☎ 250-388-6539, 800-663-8390; www.graylinewest.com) runs three-hour excursions (adult/youth/child $47.50/36/14.75) from the city that include a narrated Saanich Peninsula tour and entry to Butchart Gardens.

BC Ferries (☎ 888-223-3779, 250-386-3471; www.bcferries.com) has a 25-minute marine shortcut over Saanich Inlet from Mill Bay (passenger/vehicle $5.25/13.05, eight to nine daily) arriving at Brentwood Bay, near Butchart Gardens.

MALAHAT

North of Victoria on Island Hwy, this mountainous area makes for a scenic day trip. **Goldstream Provincial Park** (☎ 259-474-1336; www.env.gov.bc.ca/bcparks), 16km from downtown, is stuffed with moss-covered old trees, a moist carpet of plant life and has a forested **campground** (☎ 604-689-9025, 800-689-9025; www.discovercamping.ca; campsite $22). It's known for its chum salmon spawning season (late October to December). The park is crisscrossed with hiking trails – some wheelchair accessible – and its **visitor center** (☎ 250-478-9414; ☼ 9am-4:30pm) houses interesting exhibits and occasional lectures on the region's human and natural history.

Sleeping & Eating

Victoria West KOA (☎ 250-478-3332; victoriakoa@shaw.ca; 230 Trans-Canada Hwy 1; campsite/cabin $37/90; ☐ ☎) There are plenty of campsites in this rustic, tree-lined, family-friendly campground 26km northwest of Victoria. But for those who've had enough of sleeping under canvas, there's also a clutch of basic log cabins. The staff can arrange local activities, including fishing, whale-watching and bungee jumping, and there's wireless internet throughout the site.

Aerie Resort (☎ 250-743-7115, 800-518-1933; www.aerie.bc.ca; 600 Ebedora Lane; ste $395-550; ☒ ☎) While the peak-season rates quoted here make this seem like a pricey sleepover, the Aerie is consistently voted one of Canada's top resorts.

VANCOUVER ISLAND

SEAWEED LADY

Trudging across the muddy beach at Whiffen Spit in a pair of oversized gumboots may not seem like everyone's idea of fun, but when you're in the company of Sooke's very own Seaweed Lady – aka Diane Bernard – it becomes a revelatory experience. Bernard leads small groups up to the water's edge, across ribbons of slippery seaweed, then launches into an animated explanation on the health and culinary properties of the 250 varieties growing in the unkempt ocean garden around her. You'll learn about a raft of natural cosmetics and you'll be able to sample, straight from the water, some strangely textured foods that you probably wouldn't normally put in your mouth – the sea lettuce is surprisingly tasty, though. Once you've had your fill, you can watch the seals lounging on nearby rocks or keep your eyes peeled for otters, mink and eagles. The Seaweed Lady's seasonal **tours** (☎ 250-642-5328, 877-713-7464; www.outercoastseaweeds.com; $35; ☉ May-Sep) run for two hours and rates include a pair of loaned gumboots.

And for those who like deals, rates are seriously reduced off-season. Whatever the price, you'll luxuriate in one of three stylish, hilltop villas with 29 Mediterranean-themed suites. Dining is a major treat here: the resort has partnered with local farmers to combine regional ingredients with French and Pacific Northwest influences. Ask about the culinary tours where you forage with experts for your dinner.

Malahat Mountain Inn (☎ 250-478-1979, 800-913-1944; 265 Trans-Canada Hwy 1; mains $8-20; ☉ 7am-8pm) The sign says 'fine dining,' there's a neon martini glass in the window and a flourish of purple napkins on the tables. But the menu isn't as outrageous as the decor. The food is casual and tasty, and there are good vegetarian options to go with the steaks and burgers. If it's fine, head to the patio and watch the sunset.

SOOKE

pop 10,120

Rounding the southern tip of Vancouver Island towards Sooke, the roads are suddenly lined with unkempt bushes, and the houses – many of them artisan workshops or rustic B&Bs – are glimpsed only in the shadows of the forest. But while it may not seem enticing, the area has plenty of somewhat hidden attractions. For more information, visit the **Sooke Region Visitor Centre** (☎ 250-642-6351, 866-888-4748; www.sooketourism.bc.ca; 2070 Philips Rd; ☉ 9am-5pm).

Sights & Activities

One of the island's renowned swimming spots, **Sooke Potholes Provincial Park** (www.env .gov.bc.ca/bcparks) is a 5km drive from Hwy 14 (turnoff is east of town). A series of rock pools and potholes carved into the river base during the last ice age, it's also popular for sunbathing, picnicking and tube floating.

Sharing the same building as the visitor center, **Sooke Region Museum** (☎ 250-642-6351, 866-888-4748; www.sookeregionmuseum.com; 2070 Philips Rd; admission free; ☉ 9am-5pm) houses forestry artifacts and illuminates the area's tough pioneer days. Check out Moss Cottage in the museum grounds: built in 1869, it's the oldest house west of Victoria and is now 'home' to Aunt Tilly, who'll tell you all about raising two children here in 1902.

For hikers, **East Sooke Regional Park** has outstanding trails. With waves crashing against bluffs and a canopy of towering Douglas fir trees, it offers short strolls to the beach as well as the tough 10km Coast Trail.

If more activity is required, **Rush Adventures** (☎ 250-642-2159; www.rush-adventures.com; 5449 Sooke Rd; rental hr/day $25/48, tours from $55) rents equipment and arranges tours for kayakers. Sooke is also the end of the line for the Galloping Goose cycling trail (opposite); consider a bike rental from **Sooke Cycle** (☎ 250-642-3123; www .sookebikes.com; 6707 West Coast Rd; rental hr/day $5/20; ☉ 9am-6pm Tue-Fri, 9am-5pm Sat & Sun).

Sleeping & Eating

Sooke Potholes Campground (☎ 250-383-4627; www .sookepotholes.ca; campsite $20; ☉ mid-May–mid-Sep) is at the north end of the provincial park, with a spectacular riverside location, nestled among Douglas fir trees. There are no showers or electrical hook-ups but there are cold-water taps and pit toilets. Book ahead in summer – this campground is very popular.

Wildflower B&B (☎ 250-642-1331, 877-642-1331; www.wildflowerhouse.com; 7067 Briarwood Pl; r from $75) is a good midrange option among the 60 or so

Sooke-area guesthouses. A spacious, older but well-maintained property, it has two sleepover options (the rooms are comfortable but a little austere), a large family room for guest use and a deck overlooking a rhododendron garden.

our pick Sooke Harbour House (☎ 250-642-3421, 800-889-9688; www.sookeharbourhouse.com; 1528 Whiffen Spit Rd; ste $375-450) You can save a lot of money booking here off-season but it's still worth splurging for a summertime stay. One of the most eclectic and inventive hotels you're likely to come across, it's like staying in an art installation. Each of the 28 rooms is different, with acres of carved wood, paintings and sculptures lining its interiors. But it's not all quirky aesthetics; staying here is also about serious pampering. Some rooms have fireplaces and steam showers and nearly all have ocean views – if yours doesn't, step into the sea-themed elevator. Rates include a gourmet breakfast and picnic lunch, but save room for dinner – the dining room's highly creative menu is a feast of local delights, ranging from adventurous seafood and meat dishes to the kind of vegetarian selection that could tempt a carnivore.

Mom's Cafe (☎ 250-642-3314; 2036 Shields Rd; mains $6-13; ☸ 8am-10pm) A warm and welcoming throwback to the days of the classic café, this home-style eatery has been a local hangout since 1963. Nothing much has changed, from the blue vinyl banquettes to the Formica tabletops and old-school jukebox (playing Elvis tunes on our visit). The grilled-cheese sandwiches and chunky soups are recommended, but save room for dessert: there's some serious pie action on the menu.

JUAN DE FUCA PROVINCIAL PARK

While the West Coast Trail (p176) is still BC's favorite long-distance hike, the 47km **Juan de Fuca Marine Trail** (www.juandefucamarinetrail.com) in

Juan de Fuca Provincial Park (☎ 250-474-1336; www.env.gov.bc.ca/bcparks) is increasing in popularity. Unlike the West Coast Trail, the Juan de Fuca does not require hiking reservations and it has four trailhead access points so you can tramp for a day without having to go all the way. From east to west, these points are China Beach, Sombrio Beach, Parkinson Creek and Botanical Beach.

The trail has several backcountry campgrounds – four beach and two forest – and you can pay your camping fee ($5) at each trailhead. It usually takes four days to complete the full route, with the most difficult stretch between Bear Beach and China Beach. Slippery tree roots, mud and changeable weather can make other sections unpredictable at any time.

West Coast Trail Express (p177) minibuses run between Victoria, the trailheads and Port Renfrew (from $27, once daily in each direction). Booking is essential.

China Beach Campground (☎ 604-689-9025, 800-689-9025; www.discovercamping.ca; campsite $14) is a popular campground with trail hikers. It has pit toilets and cold-water taps but no showers, and is family-friendly. China Beach Campground also has vehicle-accessible sites. There is a waterfall at the western end of the beach. Book ahead.

PORT RENFREW
pop 190

At the southern node of the West Coast Trail and the northern node of the Juan de Fuca Marine Trail, the tiny fishing village of Port Renfrew busts from its sleepy shell between May and September when the hikers turn up to tackle (or recuperate from) their treks. For regional information, drop by the **VIC** (www.portrenfrew.com; ☸ 10am-6pm May-Sep) on your left as you arrive in town.

GALLOPING GOOSE

Starting north of Sooke, the Galloping Goose Trail – named for a noisy 1920s gas railcar that ran between here and Victoria – is a 55km bike and walking path on abandoned railway beds. If you're not wiped out by the end of your ride from Victoria, you can cycle another 29km up the Saanich Peninsula to Sidney on the Lochside Regional Trail. It's long been said that some of the best scenery is seen from the window of a train, and that's true here. This route goes a step further by getting cyclists off the highways and into some usually unseen backcountry. Getting on and off the trails is easy since bus lines along both routes are equipped with bike racks. You can download free maps and guides for both routes from **Capital Regional District Parks** (☎ 250-478-3344; www.crd.bc.ca/parks).

Hikers enjoy the 2.7km **Botanical Loop**, connecting lovely Botanical Beach and Botany Bay, known for their amazing tide pools and sandy beaches. Allow about 90 minutes, and go at low tide. The nearby **Mill Bay Trail** accesses a small pebble-and-shell beach and is an easy walk.

Sleeping & Eating

Trailhead Resort (☎ 250-647-5468; www.trailhead-resort .com; 17268 Parkinson Rd; ste/cabin $95/250) There's an array of comfortable, well-maintained modern rooms here – the lodge suites all have kitchens and large decks and can sleep up to four, while the large, newly built cabins have two bedrooms with three beds in each. An ideal place to wind down after a long hike, the grounds are tranquil and the facilities include hot tubs and barbecues. Discounts off-season.

Botanical Getaway Guesthouse (☎ 250-647-5483, 888-528-0080; www.botanicalgetaway.com; 6528 Cerantes Rd; d $150) A home-style B&B with three comfortable bedrooms. Guests share a kitchen, large satellite TV room and claw-foot tub bathroom. There's also a laundry room and a veranda with its own barbecue – perfect for cooking up locally caught fish.

Lighthouse Pub & Restaurant (☎ 250-647-5505; Parkinson Rd; mains $8-12; 11am-10pm) This large, red-roofed family-run pub and dining room combo serves heaping comfort food platters of burgers, pasta and seafood. Grab a couple of beers and rub shoulders with the locals on the patio.

Coastal Kitchen Cafe (☎ 250-647-5545; 17245 Parkinson Rd; mains $8-14; 5am-8pm) Almost out of place in Renfrew, this quality café serves fresh salads and sandwiches, plus burgers and pizzas. The seafood is the star attraction, though – especially the Dungeness crab and chips. Hikers, either replenishing or fueling up, are often outside at the picnic tables.

COWICHAN VALLEY

A 60km Hwy 1 drive northwest of Victoria, the verdant Cowichan Valley is ripe for discovery, especially if you're a foodie; there are lots of farms and wineries here that welcome visitors. Once dominated by forestry – most of the towns were built on the logging industry – the area is also home to the Cowichan First Nations. A good area for multiday cy-

cling treks, its highlight is Cowichan Bay. For regional information, contact **Tourism Cowichan** (☎ 250-746-1099, 888-303-3337; www.visit .cowichan.net).

DUCHAN
pop 4900

Originally an isolated railroad outpost of the logging industry – VIA Rail's *Malahat* service still stops here – latter-day Duncan has the region's main amenities and a collection of more than 80 totem poles dotted around town. Some of them decades old, these poles are maintained by local First Nations artisans.

The **VIC** (☎ 250-746-4636, 888-303-3337; www .duncancc.bc.ca; 381 Hwy 1; 9am-5pm mid-Apr–mid-Oct) offers free, 45-minute guided **pole tours** (☎ 250-715-1700; 10am-2pm Mon-Sat May & Jun, 10am-3pm Jul & Aug) and can direct you to the 28,000kg **World's Largest Hockey Stick**, which looks ready to fall off the front of the community center at any moment.

Sights & Activities

A grassy park of totems and artisan workshops, the fascinating **Quw'utsun' Cultural & Conference Centre** (☎ 250-746-8119, 877-746-8119; www .quwutsun.ca; 200 Cowichan Way; adult/youth/child $13/11/2; 9am-5pm May-Sep, 10am-4pm Oct-Apr) immerses visitors in Cowichan First Nations culture. Try your hand at carving or beading, learn about the importance of salmon and consider buying a chunky Cowichan Bay sweater. The **River Walk Café** (☎ 250-746-4370; mains $9-20; 11am-4pm Mon-Sat) here has a traditional menu – meals are served with mouthwatering bread and salmon butter.

To understand what happened when the Europeans arrived, check out the **BC Forest Discovery Centre** (☎ 250-715-1113, 866-715-1113; www .discoveryforest.com; 2892 Drinkwater Rd; adult/child $11/6; 10am-4pm mid-Apr–mid-May & Sep, 10am-5pm mid-May–Aug). A 3km drive north of Duncan, it's a hands-on clutch of logging machinery, vintage trucks, pioneer buildings and a full-size, working steam engine that trundles visitors around the 40-hectare grounds.

You don't have to be a bird fan to head over to **Pacific Northwest Raptors** (☎ 250-746-0372; www .pnwraptors.com; 1877 Herd Rd; adult/child $9/5; 11am-4:30pm Apr-Oct), an eye-opening educational facility housing dozens of eagles, falcons, hawks and owls. The dedicated staff here are highly knowledgeable about their charges but make sure you time your visit for the 30-minute daily display (1:30pm), where four species show you just what flying is all about.

COWICHAN LAKE & AROUND

West of Duncan on Hwy 18, Cowichan Lake's curving waterfront is home to several communities. Not to be confused with the name of the lake, the town of **Lake Cowichan** (population 2900) maintains a **VIC** (☎ 250-749-3244; www.lake cowichan.ca; 125C South Shore Rd; ☺ 9am-5pm Tue-Sat, 10am-2pm Sun & Mon), behind which lies **Kaatza Station Museum** (☎ 250-749-6142; admission $2; ☺ 9am-4pm Mar–mid-Dec). An impressive museum for such a small town, it has realistic walk-through displays of pioneer life.

Sleeping & Eating

Lakeview Park Campsite (☎ 250-749-3350; www.town .lakecowichan.bc.ca/camping.shtml; 885 Lakeview Park Rd; campsite $20) A good base for a sleepover in the region, Lakeview, on the lake's southern shore, has showers, toilets and free firewood.

South Shore Motel (☎ 250-749-6482, 888-749-6482; www.cowichanlakemotel.com; 266 South Shore Rd; s/d $45/65) For those who prefer a bed, South Shore offers standard but comfortable rooms (some with kitchenettes) and excellent service from its friendly owners.

Greendale Riverside Cabins (☎ 250-749-6570; www .greendalecabins.ca; 8012 Greendale Rd; d $110-130) For those who like a little more independence, this place has five large, well-decorated and extremely homely cabins – especially Blue Heron House – where you can kick back in comfort. Facilities include kitchens, covered porches and fireplaces.

Shaker Mill (☎ 250-749-6350; 72 Cowichan Lake Rd; mains $8-11; ☺ 8am-8pm) Once you've found somewhere to stay, head over to this restaurant to feed your face. This family-oriented

fixture serves up home-style specials and has a couple of patios where you can watch over the town.

CARMANAH WALBRAN PROVINCIAL PARK

Ranking high among the mythical figures of BC's backcountry, Randy Stoltmann stumbled on the giant trees of the Carmanah Valley on a 1988 hiking trip. Learning they were slated to be logged, he argued for their preservation, and his determined efforts led to the creation of the **Carmanah Walbran Provincial Park** (☎ 250-474-1336; www.env.gov.bc.ca/bcparks) in 1990.

Although one of BC's newest parks, the area is home to some of Vancouver Island's oldest residents – moss-covered, old-growth spruce trees and some giant 1000-year-old cedars. Canada's tallest tree, the 95m Carmanah spruce, also calls the park home. The whole place feels ancient and mythical, almost forgotten. Carmanah can only be reached via active logging roads – pick up a map at an area VIC and bring a spare tire.

For those without a map: follow South Shore Rd from Lake Cowichan to Nitinat Main Rd and bear left. Then follow Nitinat Main to Nitinat Junction and turn left onto South Main. Continue to the Caycus River Bridge and, just south of the bridge, turn right and follow Rosander Main (blue-and-white BC Parks signs reassuringly point the way) for 29km to the park. From Port Alberni follow Bamfield Rd to South Main, bear left and follow the directions above.

Despite the park's remote location, the trails are well maintained and easy to follow. Once you're there, it's a half-hour walk down the valley into the tallest trees. Campgrounds with tent pads, tables and water are provided at the trailhead, and dedicated campgrounds

VANCOUVER ISLAND

DETOUR: COWICHAN BAY

Heading north up-island along Hwy 1 (follow the signs for the 'Sea-Side Route') brings you to the pretty village of **Cowichan Bay** (www.cowichanbay.com), a clutch of brightly painted clapboard buildings that perch on stilts over the ocean inlet. Dripping with artisan workshops, funky eateries and local characters, highlights here include the samples and bakery treats at the shared premises of **Hilary's Cheese Company** (☎ 250-748-5992; 1725 Cowichan Bay Rd; ☺ 8am-6pm Wed-Sat, 8am-5pm Sun) and **Grain Bread** (☎ 250-746-7664; 1725 Cowichan Bay Rd; ☺ 8am-6pm Wed-Sat, 8am-5pm Sun). It's a good spot to create your own picnic of goat camembert and chewy German pretzels, before sitting on the dock to drink in the scenery. Also duck into the **Maritime Centre** (☎ 250-746-4955; www.classicboats.org; 1761 Cowichan Bay Rd; admission by donation; ☺ 9am-dusk), where you can chat with artist Herb Rice about Coast Salish culture, traditional carving and boat building.

and food stashes are found up the trail. The closest phone and gas station are on the Didtidaht Reserve at Nitinat Lake.

CHEMAINUS
pop 4500

When the sawmill, the lifeblood of the town, shut down in 1983, tiny Chemainus responded with what has become a model for BC towns faced with disappearing resource jobs. Rather than submit to the town's slow death, town officials commissioned a large outdoor mural depicting local history. People took notice, 37 more murals and 12 additional sculptures were ordered, and a tourist industry was born, giving Chemainus the well-earned nickname of 'The Little Town That Did.'

Chemainus is a popular stop on VIA Rail's *Malahat* route. Town information is available at the **VIC** (☎ 250-246-3944; www.chemainus.bc.ca; 9796 Willow St; ☿ 9am-5:30pm May-Oct, 9am-5pm Mon-Fri & 10am-4pm Sat Nov-Apr).

Sights & Activities

Walking the streets of Chemainus on a mural-spotting trek is a popular visitor pastime, and there are plenty of artsy boutiques and ice-cream parlors if you want to take a breather. For the really lazy, **Chemainus Tours** (☎ 250-246-5055; www.chemainustours.com; adult/child $10/5) offers 30-minute ambles around town in horse-drawn carriages and kid-friendly trolleys pulled by a 'steam train.'

For such a small town, **Chemainus Theatre** (☎ 250-246-9820, 800-565-7738; www.ctheatre.bc.ca; 9737 Chemainus Rd; tickets $25-31) is a surprisingly large and sophisticated facility. It stages professional productions – mostly classics and musicals from the past 100 years – and its

handsome building has helped make it a major visitor draw.

Sleeping & Eating

Bird Song Cottage (☎ 250-246-9910, 866-246-9910; www .birdsongcottage.com; 9909 Maple St; s/d/tw $95/115/125) Not only are the rooms in this Victorian gingerbread home luxuriously romantic, the service is top rate. The inventive, home-baked breakfasts look almost too good to eat, while the three rooms are a symphony of deep beds, flowery decor and elegant furnishings. If you like privacy, the Nightingale room has its own entrance to a secluded garden.

Chemainus Festival Inn (☎ 250-246-4181, 877-246-4181; www.festivalinn.ca; 9573 Chemainus Rd; r $139-219; ☒) Developed in partnership with the theater, this new 75-room hotel indicates big plans for increased tourism. With staid business hotel interiors, the rooms are bizarrely named after Shakespearean characters but lack the quirky appeal of local B&Bs. Despite the slightly boring approach, facilities include fridges and (in some rooms) kitchens.

Twisted Sisters Tea Room (☎ 250-246-1541; 9885 Maple St; mains $5-12; ☿ 11am-11pm; ☐) Despite the name, the twin sisters who run this joint are friendly and welcoming. Their menu features light meals, vegetarian options and finger-licking desserts, and there are dozens of tea varieties to choose from. It's best to drop by on Friday or Saturday night, when the locals arrive for live music or movies on the big screen.

LADYSMITH
pop 7300

Steep-streeted Ladysmith stretches languidly along a park-lined harborfront but was once a buzzing center of the island's coal and forestry

---

EAT, DRINK & BE MERRIDALE

South Cowichan has lots of artisan farms and little boutique wineries tucked along shady, tree-lined lanes. Ask at area VICs for maps and guides to these spots, then consider heading to one that's a little different. **Merridale Estate Cidery** (☎ 250-743-4293, 800-998-9908; www.merridalecider .com; 1230 Merridale Rd, Cobble Hill; ☿ 10:30am-4:30pm) is an inviting, rustic-chic complex where apples from the surrounding orchards are used to produce an array of lip-smacking tipples. Visitors can take a free self-guided tour of the facilities, then head to the tasting room for free samples of up to six ciders, ranging from traditional to champagne-style and velvety winter varieties. The on-site bistro, overlooking the orchards, is also worth a visit: it has great brick-oven-baked pizzas and uses cider as a flavoring in dishes such as candy-smoked salmon.

If you're a true foodie, you should time your visit for the three-day **Cowichan Wine & Culinary Festival** (☎ 888-303-3337; www.wines.cowichan.net) in late September, when Merridale joins other regional producers to showcase their wares in a series of tasty events.

DETOUR: FOLLOW THE YELLOW POINT ROAD

From Hwy 1, head east on Yellow Point Rd north of Ladysmith. You'll wind in and out of valleys and through farmland and forest on your way to the coast, where the road turns left and heads north at **Yellow Point Lodge** (☎ 250-245-7422; www.yellowpointlodge.com; 3700 Yellow Point Rd; s/d $112/185). The log lodge and cabins in this adults-only inclusive resort look out over the rocky point onto the Strait of Georgia. Activities include kayaking, tennis, swimming, and mountain biking.

Continue north along Yellow Point Rd and turn right on Decourcy Dr until you get to the **Barton & Leier Gallery** (☎ 250-722-7140; 3140 Decourcy Dr; admission free; 11am-5pm Thu-Sun mid-Mar–mid-Sep), a quirky menagerie of artworks created from garage sale finds that will keep you occupied for an hour or more – especially when you hit the tangly garden that's teeming with whimsical installations and decorative follies.

Jump back in the car and retrace your drive back to Yellow Point Rd; head north again to the magnificent **Crow & Gate** (☎ 250-722-3731; 2313 Yellow Point Rd; mains $8-12). Set back in the countryside, this is arguably the most authentic British-style pub west of the Atlantic. The low-sloped roof and white walls with dark trim on the outside complement the well-used wooden furniture and brickwork inside. Pints of Guinness, poured the proper way, and beef-and-kidney pie enjoyed in the impeccable back garden are the perfect way to spend any afternoon.

Follow the Yellow Point Rd north through the town of Cedar – stopping for a dip in the river if you like – and drive on to Nanaimo.

---

industries. The solid Victorian buildings that still line First Ave are evidence of just how important this town once was. These old banks and trading houses are now occupied by shops and coffee bars.

Plan your visit at the **VIC** (☎ 250-245-2112, 877-245-2112; www.ladysmithcofc.com; 132C Roberts St; 9am-4pm Mon-Fri Sep-May, 9am-4pm Mon-Sat Jun, 9am-4pm daily Jul & Aug).

Nearby is **Black Nugget Museum** (☎ 250-245-4846; 12 Gatacre St; 9am- 3:30pm Jul & Aug) – a treasure-trove of memorabilia in the former Jones Hotel. Down the hill, **Transfer Beach Park** attracts swimmers and picnickers and has summertime live music in its amphitheatre.

Hit the water here with the help of **Sealegs Kayaking** (☎ 250-245-4096, 877-529-2522; www.sealegs kayaking.com; rental hr/day $15.50/48, tours from $39; May-Sep), which offers rentals and a popular monthly full-moon tour.

NANAIMO & AROUND

The island's other metropolis, Nanaimo is the standard city stopover for those moving up or down the east coast. But with its own ferry service from the mainland, it's also a drop-off point for travelers taking a shortcut from Vancouver. A short marine hop from Gabriola – the most northerly of the Southern Gulf Islands (p192) – the region is a useful hub for exploring further afield.

NANAIMO
pop 79,600

Sneered at for decades by the tea-quaffing residents of Vancouver Island's other metropolis, Nanaimo has never had the same pulling power as Victoria. But the once-grungy 'Harbour City,' which has its own mainland BC Ferries service and is a good hub for those traveling up-island, has grown in charm in recent years. Independent stores, restaurants and coffee shops have reinvigorated the downtown core, while annual events such as the World Championship Bathtub Race (see boxed text, p166) attract out-of-towners.

Orientation

The city center lies behind the attractive inner harbor, with most shops located on Commercial St and Terminal Ave. Old City Quarter, a small section up the hill from downtown and bordered by Fitzwilliam, Selby and Wesley Sts, has recently been spruced up to reflect some pioneer history charm.

Nicol St, the southern extension of Terminal Ave, leads south to the Trans-Canada Hwy 1 and the BC Ferries Duke Point terminal. Heading north, Terminal Ave forks: the right fork becomes Stewart Ave (Hwy 1), leading to the BC Ferries Departure Bay terminal; the left fork becomes Hwy 19A (Island Hwy), heading up-island.

VANCOUVER ISLAND

NANAIMO

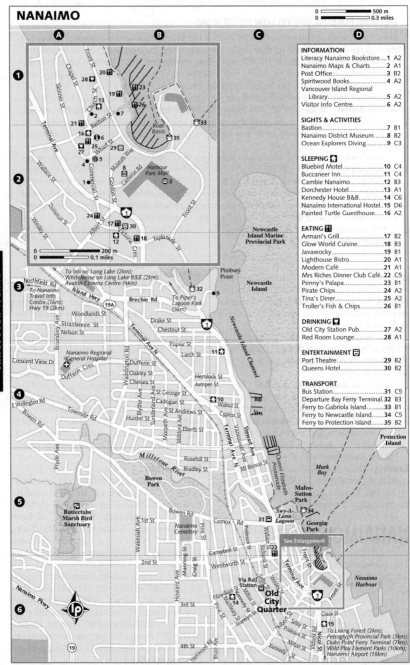

0 — 500 m
0 — 0.3 miles

INFORMATION
Literacy Nanaimo Bookstore....**1** A2
Nanaimo Maps & Charts..........**2** A1
Post Office..................................**3** B2
Spiritwood Books......................**4** A2
Vancouver Island Regional
  Library....................................**5** A2
Visitor Info Centre....................**6** A2

SIGHTS & ACTIVITIES
Bastion......................................**7** B1
Nanaimo District Museum........**8** B2
Ocean Explorers Diving............**9** C3

SLEEPING
Bluebird Motel........................**10** C4
Buccaneer Inn.........................**11** C4
Cambie Nanaimo....................**12** B3
Dorchester Hotel.....................**13** A1
Kennedy House B&B...............**14** C6
Nanaimo International Hostel..**15** D6
Painted Turtle Guesthouse.....**16** A2

EATING
Armani's Grill.........................**17** B2
Glow World Cuisine................**18** B3
Javawocky..............................**19** B1
Lighthouse Bistro....................**20** A1
Modern Café...........................**21** A1
Mrs Riches Dinner Club Café..**22** C5
Penny's Palapa.......................**23** B1
Pirate Chips............................**24** A2
Tina's Diner............................**25** A2
Troller's Fish & Chips.............**26** B1

DRINKING
Old City Station Pub...............**27** A2
Red Room Lounge...................**28** A1

ENTERTAINMENT
Port Theatre...........................**29** B2
Queens Hotel..........................**30** B2

TRANSPORT
Bus Station.............................**31** C5
Departure Bay Ferry Terminal.**32** B3
Ferry to Gabriola Island.........**33** B1
Ferry to Newcastle Island.......**34** C5
Ferry to Protection Island.......**35** B2

VANCOUVER ISLAND

Newcastle
Island Marine
Provincial Park

Newcastle
Island

Pimbury
Point

Protection
Island

Mark
Bay

Mafeo-
Sutton
Park

Swy-A-
Lana
Lagoon

Georgia
Park

Nanaimo
Harbour

See Enlargement

To Inn on Long Lake (2km);
Whitehouse on Long Lake B&B (2km);
Avalon Cinema Centre (4km)

To Nanaimo
Travel Info
Centre (1km);
Hwy 19 (2km)

To Piper's
Lagoon Park
(3km)

Northfield Rd

Island Hwy

Brechin Rd

Woodlands Rd

Strathmore St

Nelson St

Crescent View Dr

Nanaimo Regional
General Hospital

Dufferin St

Dufferin Cres

Oakley St

Chelsea St

St George St

Cadogan St

St Andrews St

Hunter St

Eberts St

Rosehill St

Bradley St

Bowen
Park

Bowen Rd

Comox Rd

Nanaimo
Cemetery

Wakesiah Ave

1st St

2nd St

Nanaimo Pkwy

Butteртubs
Marsh Bird
Sanctuary

Millstone River

Campbell St

Wentworth St

Via Rail
Station

Old
City
Quarter

3rd St

4th St

Drake St

Chestnut St

Poplar St

Larch St

Hemlock St

Juniper St

Walnut St

Cypress St

Queen Elizabeth Promenade

Terminal Ave N

Mt Benson St

Stewart Ave

Wallace St

Richards St

Terminal Ave

Front St

Crace St

To Living Forest (2km);
Petroglyph Provincial Park (3km);
Duke Point Ferry Terminal (7km);
Wild Play Element Parks (10km);
Nanaimo Airport (18km)

Chapel St

Front St

Skinner St

Terminal Ave

Wallace St

Dunsmuir St

Wesley St

Bastion St

Commercial St

Museum Way

Cameron Rd

Cordova St

Albert St

Victoria Cres

Esplanade St

Front St

Boat
Basin

Harbour
Park Mall

0 — 200 m
0 — 0.1 miles

Information

BOOKSTORES

Literacy Nanaimo Bookstore (☎ 250-754-8988;
19 Commercial St; 9am-5pm Mon-Sat) Profits go to
helping people learn to read.

Nanaimo Maps & Charts (☎ 250-754-2513; 8 Church
St; 9am-5pm Mon-Fri, 10am-4pm Sat) Good for
regional travel guides, books and maps.

Spiritwood Books (☎ 250-753-2789; 99 Commercial
St; 9am-5pm Mon-Sat) New Age and metaphysical
tomes.

INTERNET ACCESS

Literacy Nanaimo Bookstore (☎ 250-754-8988; 19
Commercial St; per hr $1; 9am-5pm Mon-Sat)

Vancouver Island Regional Library (☎ 250-753-
1154; 90 Commercial St; per 30 mins $1; 10am-8pm
Mon-Fri, 10am-5pm Sat, noon-4pm Sun)

MEDICAL SERVICES

Nanaimo Regional General Hospital (☎ 250-754-
2121; 1200 Dufferin Cres) Northwest of downtown.

POST

Post office (☎ 250-267-1177; Harbour Park Mall;
8:30am-5pm Mon-Fri)

TOURIST INFORMATION

Nanaimo Travel Info Centre (☎ 250-756-0106, 800-
663-7337; www.tourismnanaimo.com; 2290 Bowen Rd;
8am-7pm May-Aug, 9am-5pm Mon-Fri, 10am-4pm
Sat & Sun Sep-Apr) Poorly located away from downtown.
The staff are nevertheless extremely helpful.

VIC (☎ 250-754-8141; www.nanaimodowntown.com;
150 Commercial St; 8:30am-4:30pm Mon-Fri, 11am-
3pm Sat) Superior location but the staff seem disinterested.

Sights & Activities

With bungee jumping now passé, **Wild Play
Element Parks** (☎ 250-716-7874, 888-668-7874; www
.wildplayparks.com; 35 Nanaimo River Rd; adult/youth/child
$39/29/19; 10am-5:30pm mid-Jun–Aug, 11am-5pm
Fri-Mon Sep-Nov), a former jump site, has reinvented itself with five obstacle courses strung
between the trees – once you're harnessed,
you can hit ziplines, rope bridges, tunnels
and Tarzan swings, each aimed at different
skill and strength levels. The 45m bungee
jump is still there if you feel like ending on
a high.

In a city filled with parks, the windswept,
waterfront treat **Piper's Lagoon Park** (3600 Place Rd)
is a winner. It's a great spot for an afternoon
picnic; you can check out the birds hanging
around the lagoon, take a short hike through

the gnarly Garry oak forest, sit on a beached
log and watch the cruise ships slip by or give
the climbing wall your best shot. Then take
some time out to head over to Shack Island.
It's home to a straggle of storied old fish-
ermen's sheds that are kept as unserviced
cottages for those traveling with their own
sleeping bags.

Offering picnicking, cycling, hiking and
beaches, **Newcastle Island Marine Provincial Park**
(☎ 250-754-7893; www.env.gov.bc.ca/bcparks) is one
of Nanaimo's favorite parks. Walks or hikes
range from 1km strolls to the 7.5km perimeter trek. Get here via a 10-minute **ferry** (return
adult/child $7/6; 11am-4pm Apr, 10am-7pm May-Jun &
Sep, 10am-9pm Jul & Aug). A serviced **campground**
(www.newcastleisland.ca; campsite $14; Apr-Oct) is
available.

Overlooking downtown, the colorful
Nanaimo District Museum (☎ 250-753-1821; www
.nanaimomuseum.ca; 100 Cameron Rd; adult/youth/child
$2/1.75/0.75; 10am-4pm mid-May–Aug) explores
the growth of the city, from its First Nations
heritage to its Hudson's Bay Company days.
There are regular temporary exhibitions to
keep the lineup fresh.

Built by the Hudson's Bay Company in
1853, the landmark fortified **Bastion** (☎ 250-
753-1821; cnr Front & Bastion Sts; adult/youth/child
$2/1.75/0.75; 10am-5pm mid-May–Aug, 10am-5pm
Tue-Sat Sep-May) tower only fired occasional
cannons to simmer down regional ruckuses.
A brief but charming ceremony sees one of
the canons fired for tourists at noon each
day – the polystyrene 'cannonball' is surprisingly loud.

South of Nanaimo on Hwy 1, **Petroglyph
Provincial Park** (☎ 250-474-1336; www.env.gov.bc.ca
/bcparks) is seldom visited, despite some neat old
First Nations sandstone carvings that depict
everything from mystical wolflike creatures to
fish and human figures. Sadly, the petroglyphs
are fading fast and most are barely visible, but
kids like making rubbings from the re-created
castings.

For scuba fans, Nanaimo and its nearby
islands offer some great dives. Sunk to order
in 1997, the HMCS *Saskatchewan* is BC's most
popular dive site. It was joined in 2001 by the
134m *Cape Breton*, the world's second-largest diver-prepared reef. For information on
regional sites, and for guides, lessons or equipment, contact **Ocean Explorers Diving** (☎ 250-
753-2055, 800-233-4145; www.oceanexplorersdiving.com;
1690 Stewart Ave).

VANCOUVER ISLAND

Sleeping

Nanaimo is not overly endowed with great sleepover options; book your accommodation ahead of time in summer. South of town, Nicol St is lined with basic, plain but clean motels.

BUDGET

Nanaimo International Hostel (☎ 250-753-1188; www .nanaimohostel.com; 65 Nicol St; dm/r $20/45; 💻) The views are amazing from the backyard of John and Moni Murray's home on the hill, and it may well be where you'll spend most of your time. The hostel is a quick five-minute walk from downtown. It's great for families and features an airy outdoor shower, barbecue facilities and a fun mural created by past guests.

our pick Painted Turtle Guesthouse (☎ 250-753-4432, 866-309-4432; www.paintedturtle.ca; 121 Bastion St; dm $24, r $45-70; 💻) An excellent addition to Nanaimo's sleepover options, this exemplary budget property in the heart of downtown combines four-bedded dorms with family and private rooms. Interiors are decorated with hardwood floors and an Ikea-esque élan and facilities range from a large and welcoming kitchen to a laundry room and en suite showers. You can book a wide range of activities through the front desk – or just stay in the lounge and strum the communal guitar for your entire stay.

BATHTIME

Launched in 1967 to help celebrate Nanaimo's centennial, the grandly named **International World Championship Bathtub Race** (☎ 250-753-7223; www.bathtubbing.com), held in the third week of July, has grown to become the city's signature summer event. Now a four-day marine-themed extravaganza that includes a street fair, colorful parade and a giant fireworks display, the main draw remains the big race in which hundreds of salty sea dogs jump into customized bathtub-sized crafts and head out over a grueling 58km course around Entrance Island and Winchelsea Island before finishing – if they make it – at Departure Bay. Speedboat engines and helmets are de rigueur for the 90-minute sprint, with thousands of spectators lining the bay for the spectacular finish.

Additional recommendations:

Cambie Nanaimo (☎ 250-754-5323, 877-754-5323; www.cambiehostels.com/nanaimo; 63 Victoria Cres; dm/r $23.50/50) Nanaimo's party hostel, the Cambie has no kitchen – breakfast is included in the price.

Living Forest Oceanside RV & Campground (☎ 250-755-1755; www.campingbc.com; 6 Maki Rd; campsite $10) With 193 sites; closest campground to town.

MIDRANGE

Bluebird Motel (☎ 250-753-4151, 877-764-3831; www.thebluebirdinn.com; 995 N Terminal Ave; s/d/tw from $59/69/74) This family-friendly bright-blue throwback motel – two stories high, hundreds of feet long, outdoor walkways – covers all the basics: free coffee, clean rooms with 1970s-style furnishings and some kitchenettes ($6 extra) for those who like to make their own grub. It's 2km north of downtown.

Buccaneer Inn (☎ 250-753-1246, 877-282-6337; www .buccaneerinn.com; 1577 Stewart Ave; s/d/ste $70/79/150) Handy for the Departure Bay ferry terminal, this family-run motel has an immaculate white paint job that probably needs to be redone every few months. The spick-and-span rooms have a cozy, nautical theme and most have kitchenettes. If you can stretch to the spacious top-end suites, they come with fireplaces, full kitchens and flat-screen TVs. The friendly owners have plenty of good suggestions for how to explore the region.

Kennedy House B&B (☎ 250-754-3389; kennedy house@shaw.ca; 305 Kennedy St; r $85-125) One of the only Nanaimo B&Bs within walking distance of downtown, this restored 1913 heritage mansion has two lovely rooms, combining antique and contemporary chintzy flourishes. It's elegant, quiet and adult oriented, and the owners serve a smashing cooked breakfast.

Dorchester Hotel (☎ 250-754-6835, 800-661-2449; www.dorchesternanaimo.com; 70 Church St; r/ste $109/119) Downtown Nanaimo's signature hotel, this Best Western affiliate has a great location overlooking the harbor. It's been refurbished in recent years but the hallways running at odd angles couldn't be changed, nor could its historic character: it still has its Victorian moldings and sitting rooms on the southwest corners of each floor. Disappointingly, the rooms have standard business hotel–style interiors.

Whitehouse on Long Lake B&B (☎ 250-758-5010, 877-956-1185; www.nanaimobandb.com; 231 Ferntree Pl; r/ste $109/129; 💻) As the name would suggest, Whitehouse is on Long Lake, north of

VANCOUVER ISLAND

Nanaimo via Hwy 19A. Huge south-facing windows overlook the water (boat rentals available) and bring the sun into the three rooms. The romantic interiors are elegant and comfortable but the surprisingly good-value Presidential Suite is recommended: it's self-contained, has a large kitchen and includes a private balcony.

TOP END

Inn on Long Lake (☎ 250-758-1144, 800-565-1144; www
.innonlonglake.com; 4700 N Island Hwy; r/ste $159/219;
🖳 🐾) A 10-minute drive north of the Departure Bay ferry terminal, this retreat-style, lakeside hotel is a good spot to rest if you've been roughing it around the island. The large rooms, each with balcony, have plenty of amenities and some have kitchenettes, while the hotel also has a sauna, fitness center and some rental canoes so you can hit the lake.

Eating

BUDGET

Pirate Chips (☎ 250-753-2447; 1 Commercial St; mains $4-
7.50; 🕚 11:30am-10pm Mon-Wed, 11:30am-midnight Thu,
11:30am-3am Fri & Sat, noon-9pm Sun) Locals originally came here for the best fries in town but they keep coming back for the funky ambience – the quirky pirate-themed decor makes it a great late-night hangout after some beers. You'd have to be fairly drunk to down a large order of poutine (french fries topped with cheese and gravy) or a deep-fried chocolate bar but it's hard to beat the fries served with toppings such as curry or garlic.

Tina's Diner (☎ 250-753-5333; 187 Commercial St;
mains $6-10; 🕚 8am-3pm Wed-Fri, 8am-2pm Sat, 9am-2pm
Sun & Mon) Still known by its former name (Flo's) by many locals, this popular 1950s-style spot is the best place in town for breakfast. The massive menu runs from eggs Benedict to breakfast wraps, and there are plenty of burgers, sandwiches and salads for those who don't make it here until lunchtime. There are some special live music events, when dinner and singer-songwriters share the menu.

MIDRANGE

Mrs Riches Dinner Club Café (☎ 250-753-8311; 199
Fraser St; mains $7-11; 🕚 11:30am-8pm Sun-Fri) Like stepping into a comic book about a carnival, Mrs Riches is a family-oriented place lined with an eclectic array of memorabilia (life-sized stuffed toys and car fenders are the norm here) but the food is not just for looks.

The heaping burger platters are second to none (tackle the Mountain Burger, if you're starving) but the pasta dishes and old-school milkshakes are great, too.

Penny's Palapa (☎ 250-753-2150; 10 Wharf St H
Dock; mains $7-12; 🕚 11am-9pm mid-Apr–Oct) This tiny, flower-decked floating hut and patio in the harbor is a lovely spot for a meal among the jostling boats. An inventive, well-priced menu of Mexican delights includes seasonal seafood specials – the signature halibut tacos are recommended – and some good vegetarian options.

Troller's Fish & Chips (☎ 250-741-7994; 104 Front
St; mains $8-13; 🕚 11am-10pm) Nothing beats the ambience of Troller's when it comes to grubbing on some fish and chips. This shack on the docks at the boat basin always cooks the fresh catch of the day, selecting its prawns and salmon straight from the boats in the harbor. It's also a good spot to watch the maritime world float by.

Armani's Grill (☎ 250-754-5551; 22 Victoria Cres; mains
$8-14; 🕚 11:30am-10pm) They're not just burgers, they're works of art. Armani's uses ground sirloin, not chuck, and makes each patty by hand after you order. There's 3oz of Jack Daniels in the Jack Burger and the Mushroom Burger has enough mushrooms to tap a small farm's entire crop.

Modern Café (☎ 250-754-5022; 221 Commercial St;
mains $9-19; 🕚 9am-11pm) This reinvented old coffee shop has cool loungey interiors combining exposed brick and comfy booths or, if it's sunny, a sun-warmed outdoor patio. The menu runs from the kind of wraps, burgers and sandwiches that are a cut above standard diner fare and there are some small-plate options for those who just want to snack.

Glow World Cuisine (☎ 250-741-8858; 7 Victoria Rd;
mains $16-24; 🕚 11:30am-10pm Tue-Sat, 11am-10pm Sun) Occupying a handsome old brick fire hall building, the dark tones and mood lighting at Glow create a mysterious and secluded atmosphere. The adventurous menu combines traditional meat and seafood dishes with international influences (especially Asian) and local ingredients. Drop by for the Sunday brunch, a $21 smorgasbord of Western and Asian breakfast treats.

TOP END

Lighthouse Bistro (☎ 250-754-3212; 50 Anchor Way;
mains $18-26; 🕚 5pm-10pm) This popular white-linen bistro is located on the waterfront and

features a selection of conventional but well-prepared favorites, ranging from blackened halibut to veal scallopine and wild mushroom ravioli. The wine list has an excellent BC selection. The pub upstairs has lower prices and a more casual atmosphere, but there's an excellent view of the harbor from either floor as well as a great patio to catch the sunset.

Drinking

Javawocky (☎ 250-753-1688; 90 Front St; snacks $2-5; ✹ 8am-5pm Mon-Fri, 9am-5pm Sat & Sun) It's a Nanaimo tradition to get a coffee here and sit outside to watch the ships roll in and out of the harbor. A great place to rub shoulders with the locals, this is also your big chance to try a Nanaimo bar, the ultrarich brownie treat made from thick layers of custard and chocolate.

Dinghy Dock Floating Pub (☎ 250-753-2373; 8 Pirates Lane) The name is no lie; this popular pub and restaurant combo floats offshore from Protection Island. See Nanaimo from the outside (especially pretty at night), rub shoulders with some salty locals and knock back a few malty brews. The menu doesn't stretch far beyond standard pub fare but there's live music on weekends. To access the pub, take a 10-minute **ferry** (☎ 250-753-8244; return $4; ✹ 11am-midnight mid-May–Sep, 11am-11pm Oct–mid-May) from the harbor.

Red Room Lounge (☎ 250-753-5181; 75 Front St) A smoking nighttime hangout (with no smoking) for Nanaimo's beautiful people, the Red Room has dark, rich interiors and an epic cocktail menu. Live music or DJs perform Tuesday to Saturday on the tiny stage.

Old City Station Pub (☎ 250-716-0030; 150 Skinner St) A convivial recent addition to Nanaimo's nightlife options (it used to be Press Room nightclub), this pub has plenty of finger-licking food options available. The equally healthy beer selection includes a significant proportion of Canadian tipples, including Alexander Keith's and Granville Island brews.

Entertainment

Nanaimo's best live music and dance spot, the **Queen's Hotel** (☎ 250-754-6751; www.thequeens .ca; 34 Victoria Cres) hosts an eclectic roster of live performances and club nights throughout the week, ranging from indie to jazz and country. In contrast, the **Port Theatre** (☎ 250-754-8550; www .porttheatre.nisa.com; 125 Front St) presents local and touring fine-arts performances. Movie houses include the 10-screen **Avalon Cinema Centre** (☎ 250-390-5021; Woodgrove Centre, 6631 N Island Hwy).

Getting There & Away

AIR

Nanaimo Airport (☎ 250-245-2147; www.nanaimo -airport.com) is 18km south of town via Trans-Canada Hwy 1. **Air Canada** (☎ 888-247-2262; www .aircanada.ca) services from Vancouver (from $89, 22 minutes) arrive several times daily.

Baxter Aviation (☎ 250-754-1066, 800-661-5599; www.baxterair.com) floatplanes arrive in Nanaimo harbor several times daily from downtown Vancouver ($59, 25 minutes) and Vancouver International Airport South Terminal ($54, 20 minutes). **Harbour Air Seaplanes** (☎ 604-274-1277, 800-665-0212; www.harbour-air.com) operates similar services from downtown Vancouver ($59, 25 minutes) and the South Terminal ($49, 20 minutes).

BOAT

BC Ferries (☎ 888-223-3779, 250-386-3431; www.bcfer ries.com) services from Tsawwassen (passenger/vehicle $10.80/$37.80, two hours) arrive at Duke Point, 14km south of Nanaimo via Trans-Canada Hwy 1. Services from West Vancouver's Horseshoe Bay (passenger/vehicle $10.80/$37.80, 90 minutes) arrive at Departure Bay, 3km north of Nanaimo via Trans-Canada Hwy 1. Reservations are recommended in summer.

BUS

Greyhound (☎ 800-661-8747; www.greyhound.ca) services arrive in Nanaimo from Victoria ($18.75, 2½ hours, six daily), Campbell River ($23.90, three hours, four daily), Port Alberni ($13.05, 90 minutes, four daily) and Tofino ($30.20, four hours, daily). **Tofino Bus** (☎ 866-986-3466, 250-725-2871; www.tofinobus.com) services arrive from Tofino and Ucluelet ($35, 3½ hours) and from Port Alberni ($20, 1½ hours).

TRAIN

The daily **VIA Rail** (☎ 888-842-7245; www.viarail.ca) *Malahat* service arrives from Victoria ($25, 2½ hours), Parksville ($15, 35 minutes) and Courtenay ($25, 2 hours), among others.

Getting Around

Downtown Nanaimo is easily accessed on foot, but after that the city spreads out and vehicular transport or strong bike legs are required. Taxis are expensive here.

Nanaimo Regional Transit (☎ 250-390-4531; www
.rdn.bc.ca; s/day pass $2.25/5.75) buses stop along
Gordon St, west of Harbour Park Mall. Bus 2
goes to the Departure Bay ferry terminal. No
city buses run to Duke Point.

Nanaimo Seaporter (☎ 250-753-2118; from Departure
Bay/Duke Point $8/16) provides door-to-door serv-
ice to downtown from both ferry terminals.
For cabs, call **AC Taxi** (☎ 250-753-1231).

GABRIOLA ISLAND
pop 3500
The most northerly of the Southern Gulf Islands, Gabriola makes a fun day trip from
Nanaimo. Dozens of artists live here, but it's
also known for its tranquility, scenery and recreation. The **VIC** (☎ 250-247-9332, 888-284-9332; www
.gabriolaisland.org; 575 North Rd; ☯ 9am-5pm Jul & Aug) is
on your second left after you leave the ferry.

Sights & Activities
Gabriola Sands Provincial Park (☎ 250-474-1336;
www.env.gov.bc.ca/bcparks) includes shaded Taylor Bay Beach and sandy Pilot Bay Beach,
separated by a grassy field and picnic area.
It's also home to Malaspina Galleries, a series of eroded sandstone shelves known for
their wavy patterns and spooky caves. On
the island's southeast end, **Drumbeg Provincial
Park** (☎ 250-474-1336; www.env.gov.bc.ca/bcparks) offers good swimming, while Brickyard Beach
features tide pools and clam digging.

Many Gabriola artists open their studios
to the public. Find out who, what, where and
when from the VIC. For a crash course on
more than 150 painters, potters, and jewelers,
head to **Gabriola Artworks** (☎ 250-247-7412; www
.gabriolaartworks.com; 575 North Rd; ☯ 9am-5pm Tue-Fri,
10am-5pm Sat, 11am-4pm Sun & Mon) which stages an
ever-changing roster of creativity – drop by on
Thursday evening in summer, when there's a
new exhibition every week.

Sleeping & Eating
Hummingbird Lodge B&B (☎ 250-247-0933, 877-551-
9383; www.hummingbirdlodgebb.com; 1597 Starbuck Lane;
d $119-129) The definition of the word 'retreat,'
this rustic wood-lined lodge is the perfect
place to get away from it all. Each of the three
airy, gabled-ceilinged rooms tempt you to stay
more than one night, especially with their
large decks, shared outdoor hot tub and seven
acres of surrounding woodland.

Surf Lodge (☎ 250-247-9231; www.surflodge.com;
885 Berry Point Rd; r/cabin $90/145) A family-friendly
clutch of oceanfront cabins and a large lodge
building, you can almost taste the tranquility as you stroll the grounds here. The lodge
rooms are comfortable but fairly basic – like
sleeping in a wooden cave – while the cabins
are a good deal for small groups. You'll spend
most of your time in the communal areas –
the Great Hall, with its towering rock fireplace
and adjoining small bar, is especially cool.

Suzy's Restaurant & Deli Bakery (☎ 250-247-2010;
560 North Rd; mains $4-12; ☯ 8am-5pm) You'll find lots
of gossiping islanders hanging out at this busy
but casual bistro-style eatery. Menu staples
include seafood, sandwiches and pizza, or
you can just pick up some piquant cheese
and chewy artisan bread and create your own
picnic.

Getting There & Away
BC Ferries (☎ 888-223-3779, 250-386-4331; www.bcferries
.com) services arrive from Nanaimo (passenger/
vehicle $6.30/15.95, 20 minutes, 16 daily).

CENTRAL VANCOUVER ISLAND

Vancouver Island's attractive midriff includes
some great recreation and visual pleasures, be
it on the storm-tossed west coast, the serene
and sandy east coast, or in the mountainous,
forest-covered areas in between. A popular,
low-key hangout for mainlanders, the region
has plenty of accommodations options.

OCEANSIDE & AROUND
Comprising the quaint and family-friendly
seaside towns of Parksville (population 11,700)
and Qualicum Beach (population 8800) along
with the area around Coombs, **Oceanside**
(☎ 250-248-6300, 888-799-3222; www.oceansidetourism
.com) is located on the island's eastern stretch
above Nanaimo. Protected by the Beaufort
Mountain Range, the climate and water temperature here are among BC's balmiest.

For regional information, drop by either of
the two main **VIC**s (Parksville ☎ 250-248-3613; www
.chamber.parksville.bc.ca; 1275 E Island Hwy; ☯ 9am-6pm Mon-
Sat; Qualicum Beach ☎ 250-752-9532, 866-887-7106; www
.qualicum.bc.ca; 2711 W Island Hwy; ☯ 9am-4pm Mon-Sat).

Parksville's handy **Walk-in Clinic** (☎ 250-
248-5757; 154 Memorial Ave; ☯ 9am-5pm Mon-Fri) and
After-Hours Clinic (☎ 250-248-7200; ☯ 5-9pm Mon-Fri;
9am-9pm Sat) occupy the same building.

SAY CHEESE

Pungent evidence of Vancouver Island's rediscovered love for its own agricultural bounty can be found at **Little Qualicum Cheeseworks** (☎ 250-954-3931; www.cheeseworks.ca; admission free; ☷ 9am-4pm Mon-Sat mid-May–Sep, 10am-3pm Mon-Sat Oct–mid-May), a small working farm that has developed into a family-friendly visitor attraction. It's worth spending a couple of hours here, ducking into the cowsheds and watching the cheese makers (both bovine and human) at work. Young kids will particularly enjoy the roaming pigs, goats and chickens and the rabbit enclosure is noisy with plaintive cries from children who want to take one home. Parents should head straight for the on-site shop where samples of the farm's curdy treats are provided – this is a great place to pick up some picnic supplies. The creamy, slightly mushroomy brie is a bestseller but the Qualicum Spice is recommended: it's flavored with onions, garlic and sweet red pepper.

Sights & Activities

With a mission to rescue exotic birds from captivity and nurse them back to physical and mental health, the excellent educational facility **World Parrot Refuge** (☎ 250-248-5194; www.worldparrot refuge.org; 2116 Alberni Hwy, Coombs; adult/child $12/8; ☷ 10am-4pm) preaches the mantra that parrots are not pets. Pick up your earplugs at reception and stroll among the enclosures, each alive with recovering (and very noisy) birds. Like a particularly scary movie, there are hundreds of kids toys hanging from the ceilings for them to play with. Don't be surprised when some of the birds say hello as you walk past.

A clutch of transplanted old wooden homes at **Craig Heritage Park** (☎ 250-248-6966; 1245 E Island Hwy, Parksville; adult/child $4/2; ☷ 10am-4pm mid-May–Sep, 10am-4pm Wed Oct–mid-May) comprises one of the island's best museums. The re-created hamlet includes a church, fire hall (plus 1950s fire truck) and a schoolhouse full of tiny desks. Chat to the elderly volunteers on duty; they're stuffed with stories about the horse snowshoes and cougar fat soap on display.

It's a 45-minute drive from Parksville (take Hwy 19 towards Courtenay, then exit 75 and proceed for 12km on the gravel road to the park entrance) to get to **Horne Lake Caves Provincial Park** (☎ 250-248-7829; www.env.gov.bc.ca/bcparks, www.hornelake.com; tours adult/child from $17/15; ☷ 10am-5pm Jul & Aug, off-season by arrangement) but it's worth it for some of BC's best spelunking treats. Two caves are open to the public for self-exploring, or you can take a guided tour of Riverbend Cave. Activities include interpretive tours for novices and four-hour rock climbing treks ($99) for the adventurous.

Spreading the word on BC's unique wildlife, **North Island Wildlife Recovery Centre** (☎ 250-248-8534; 1240 Leffler Rd, Errington; adult/child $3/2; ☷ 9am-5pm mid-Mar–Oct) is a short drive from Parksville. This fascinating 'museum of nature' has an excellent walk-through display on west coast animals and their habitats. Dedicated to treating sick or injured animals brought to its doors, the facility also has active rehabilitation programs for eagles and black bears.

A landmark shopping stop that attracts the summer crowds, **Coombs Old Country Market** (☎ 250-248-6472; www.oldcountrymarket.com; 2326 Alberni Hwy, Coombs ☷ 9am-6pm) is a rustic complex of galleries, boutiques and trinket emporiums centered around a large food store stuffed with bakery and produce treats. Most visitors spend time pointing their cameras at the sky here: in summer, a herd of goats lives on the roof of the main building.

Located at the south end of Parksville via Hwy 19A, the 5km sandy beach of **Rathtrevor Beach Provincial Park** (☎ 250-474-1336; www.env.gov .bc.ca/bcparks) is an ideal spot for family-friendly exploring. At low tide, the ocean recedes almost a kilometer, revealing a salty array of sand dollars and starfish.

Additional sights and activities:

Butterfly World & Gardens (☎ 250-248-7026; www .nature-world.com; 1080 Winchester Rd, Coombs; adult/ child $8.75/3.75; ☷ 10am-5pm) A walk-through tropical paradise of birds and butterflies.

Oceanside Kayaks (☎ 250-951-3512; www.oceanside kayaks.ca; Qualicum Beach; rental hr/day $18/56) Tranquil ocean kayaking from Qualicum Beach, with a special course for first-timers ($60).

Paradise Adventure Fun Park (☎ 250-248-6612; www.paradisefunpark.net; 375 W Island Hwy, Parksville; adult/child $6.25/4.25; ☷ 9am-9pm Jul & Aug, shorter hrs spring & fall) The best of many miniature golf attractions.

Sleeping

Riverbend Resort & Campground (☎ 250-248-3134, 800-701-3033; www.riverbendresort.bc.ca; 1-924 E Island

Hwy, Parksville; campsite/cabin/yurt $20/129/129; ☐) This ultra-welcoming campground has some cozy wooden cabins and secluded tree-shaded campsites, many of them along the riverbank. But the main sleepover attractions are the circular yurt tents. Fitted with baths, kitchens, double beds and flat-screen TVs, they're way more comfortable than a regular night under canvas. The rest of the campground has showers, laundry and a playground and is popular with young families.

ourpick Free Spirit Sphere (☎ 250-757-9445; www .freespiritspheres.com; 420 Horne Lake Rd, Qualicum Beach; cabin $100) For anyone who's ever dreamt of sleeping in a Christmas bauble, Vancouver Island craftsman Tom Chudleigh has developed a nature-hugging cabin with a difference. Suspended by a web of cables high in the trees, his beautifully crafted 3m-diameter wood and fiberglass sphere enables guests to cocoon themselves in the forest canopy. Reached via a spiral wooden staircase, the sphere is compact and cozy inside – it's like sleeping in a small boat cabin – and has a couple of beds, lots of storage cupboards, a microwave oven and a water cooler. Try not to get caught short in the night, though: the sphere's private bathroom facilities are on the ground in a nearby house.

Blue Willow Guest House (☎ 250-752-9052; www .bluewillowguesthouse.ca; 524 Quatna Rd, Qualicum Beach; s/d/ste $105/115/125) An immaculate cottage property with the ambience of a Victorian manor house, this lovely B&B has a book-lined lounge, exposed beams and a fragrant country garden. The two rooms and one large, self-contained suite are lined with antiques and knick knacks and are extremely homely. The attention to detail carries over to the breakfast: served in the conservatory, it includes homebaked treats and a gourmet main course.

Maclure House Inn (☎ 250-248-3470; www.maclure house.com; 1051 Resort Dr, Parksville; d $130-200) Pamper yourself like a decadent colonial in this 1920s oceanfront Tudor-style house set amid perfectly manicured gardens. The rooms are flowery and romantic – check out the blue Kipling room, where the famed English author slept in 1928 – and the fine-dining restaurant combines Pacific Northwest and French influences.

Casa Grande Inn (☎ 250-752-4400, 888-720-2272; www.casagrandeinn.com; 3080 W Island Hwy, Qualicum Beach; r $130-165; ⚡) Despite the exotic name, the rooms here are standard motel fare, although each comes with a fridge and a balcony and some have kitchenettes. One room is wheelchair accessible and there's an on-site guest laundry. The main draw is the location overlooking Qualicum Beach and across the street from pubs and restaurants.

Tigh-Na-Mara Resort (☎ 250-248-2072, 800-663-7373; www.tigh-na-mara.com; 1155 Resort Dr, Parksville; r from $149; ⚡) Set amid forests yet close to the beach, this resort has become an Oceanside favorite in recent years. Rooms of all types – lodge rooms, cottages and condos – are available and they are just as rustic-chic luxurious on the inside as they look on the outside. For additional pampering, the Cedar Room restaurant is superb and the spa is one of BC's biggest.

Additional options:

Ocean Crest Motel (☎ 250-752-5518; www.motel oceancrest.com; 3292 W Island Hwy, Qualicum Beach; r $89-99) Classic motel with spick-and-span facilities and good rates.

Rathtrevor Beach Provincial Park (☎ 604-689-9025, 800-689-9025; www.discovercamping.ca; campsite $22) Tucked in the trees 3km south of Parksville, this popular campground has showers, flush toilets and 5km of hiking trails.

Eating & Drinking

Westhill Restaurant (☎ 250-752-7148; 1015 McLean Rd, Qualicum Beach; mains $4-8; ⏱ 4:30-8pm Thu-Sat) Behind the facade of this anonymous-looking house beats the heart of one of the region's best dining treats. Home-cooked Malaysian food never tasted better, despite the bizarre decor of Formica tables and wall-mounted coats of arms. Ask for recommendations and you'll be treated to dishes of steaming wonton soup, piquant curry and green tea ice cream. Yum.

Lefty's (Parksville ☎ 250-954-3886; 101-280 E Island Hwy; Qualicum Beach ☎ 250-752-7530; 710 Memorial Ave; mains $8-14; ⏱ 8am-8pm Sun-Thu, 8am-9pm Fri & Sat) You'll find little else but good-quality, fun casual dining at these laid-back eateries that started out vegetarian but have allowed meat to creep onto the menu. Funky colors emphasize the 'fresh' ideals they seek in their 'Left Coast' dishes. Drop by for breakfast – the pancakes and fruit syrup are great.

Fish Tales Café (☎ 250-752-6053; 3336 W Island Hwy, Qualicum Beach; mains $9-16; ⏱ 5-10pm) Fish and chips are the centerpiece but it's worth exploring seafood dishes of the non-deep-fried variety at this Qualicum dine-out favorite: the two-person platter of scallops, shrimp, smoked salmon and mussels is highly recommended. It has the kind of faux Tudor decor more commonly found in an olde English teashop, and the garden here is the perfect dining spot on a balmy evening.

Shady Rest (☎ 752-9111; 3109 W Island Hwy, Qualicum Beach; ☉ 8am-10pm) A casual neighborhood pub perched over the beach, the Shady Rest is popular with both locals and visitors. Drop by for some fortifying pub grub and a couple of beers or head into the slightly more upmarket restaurant, where fish, steak, and pasta dishes vie for menu attention. An ideal spot for a leisurely weekend brunch.

Getting There & Away

Greyhound (☎ 800-661-8747; www.greyhound.ca) buses arrive in Parksville from Victoria ($24.95, 3½ hours, five daily), Nanaimo ($5.80, 40 minutes, eight daily), Tofino ($24.95, 3½ hours, daily), Campbell River ($17.90, two hours, four daily) and Port Hardy ($59.30, six hours, daily). The same buses also serve Qualicum Beach – times and rates similar.

The **VIA Rail** (☎ 888-842-7245; www.viarail.ca) *Malahat* service arrives at Parksville from Victoria ($31, three hours, daily), Nanaimo ($15, 35 minutes) and Courtenay ($17, one hour, daily), among others. The same trains also serve Qualicum Beach – times and rates are similar.

PORT ALBERNI
pop 18,690

Living off the fat of fishing and forestry for decades, Alberni was initially slow to grasp the importance of tourism once those traditional employers began to decline. But with excellent wilderness access and some fascinating First Nations heritage, the waterfront town has now come to life as a visitor destination. For information, contact the **Alberni Valley VIC** (☎ 250-724-6535; www.avcoc.com; 2533 Redford St; ☉ 8am-6pm mid-May–Aug, 9am-5pm Mon-Fri, 10am-2pm Sat & Sun Sep–mid-May).

Sights & Activities

Between Parksville and Port Alberni, **Cathedral Grove** (☎ 250-248-9460) is the mystical highlight of MacMillan Provincial Park. Unfortunately the mysticism is hard to appreciate in summer, when tourists jam the limited parking stalls, causing an ongoing visitor manage-ment problem. It's hard to blame the tourists, though: they come to trip along the easy trails in this dense canopy of vegetation, glimpsing some of BC's oldest trees, including 800-year-old Douglas firs that are more than 3m in diameter.

The cultural heart of Alberni's reinvented waterfront, the **Maritime Discovery Centre** (☎ 250-723-6161; www.alberniheritage.com; Industrial Rd; admission by donation; ☉ 10am-5pm mid-Jun–Aug) hosts displays on the region's salty heritage. Visitors can peer into the harbor depths through an underwater camera and check out a 1950s lifeboat. There's also a gallery where local artists interpret the maritime past.

There's an eclectic but impressive array of exhibits in the little **Alberni Valley Museum** (☎ 250-723-2181; www.alberniheritage.com; 4255 Wallace St; admission by donation; ☉ 10am-5pm Mon-Sat), which does a good job of combining the region's First Nations and pioneer heritage – including the history of the Chinese who came here in the 19th century. The section on the West Coast Trail shows how the route was once a life-saving trail for shipwreck victims.

With **Choo Kwa Ventures** (☎ 250-724-4006, 866-294-8687; www.chookwa.com; 4500 Victoria Quay; tours adult/child from $35/17), you can dip into the area's deep First Nations past on an authentic three-hour canoe trip down the Somass River. You can help paddle if you want or just sit back and listen to the ancient stories and songs from the local Hupacasath people. If you're lucky, you might spot a bear on the riverbank. The company offers longer cruises for those with time to spare.

Lady Rose Marine Services (☎ 250-723-8313, 800-663-7192; www.ladyrosemarine.com; 5425 Argyle St; return $35-60; ☉ departs 8am Tue, Thu & Sat) day trips down Alberni Inlet on the 100-passenger *MV Lady Rose* or 200-passenger *MV Frances Barkley* have been popular here for years. The boats stop en route to deliver mail and supplies, with a 60- to 90-minute layover before returning. The trip is an enjoyable, scenic day excursion, plus a practical means of returning from the West Coast Trail's north end at Bamfield.

A one-stop shop for active types, **Batstar Adventure Tours** (☎ 250-724-2098, 877-449-2098; www.batstar.com; 4785 Beaver Creek Rd; ☉ 7am-10pm Mon-Sat, 9am-8pm Sun; ☐) is a combined internet café/restaurant/tour operator, arranging everything from guided bike trips into the wilderness to multiday kayak odysseys around the

---

DETOUR: FALLING FOR DELLA

At 440m tall, Della Falls is among the highest in Canada, and getting there can be a tall task in itself. Though set deep within Strathcona Provincial Park, the 'easiest' way to reach Della is from Port Alberni.

Take Hwy 4 13km west of town to Great Central Lake Rd. You'll then need to cross 35km Great Central Lake; before you begin to don your swim gear, plan on seven to 12 hours in a canoe or consider taking a water-taxi shuttle (see below) to the trailhead. It's then a 16km, five- to eight-hour, 510m-elevation-gain scramble through the woods and up steep slopes to the falls. Set aside a minimum of two days for the trip (four if you're canoeing) but once you're there – 'Whooooo boy!' prepare to be amazed.

Ark Resort (☎ 250-723-2657; www.arkresort.com; 11000 Great Central Lake Rd, Port Alberni; campsite/r $23/85) offers a water-taxi service ($100) to the trailhead. The resort also rents boats, canoes and camping gear for Della-bound trekkers.

Broken Group Islands. If time is an issue, take the four-hour kayak harbor tour ($59) or 20km streams-and-forest bike ride along an old train route ($89).

Sleeping & Eating

Fat Salmon Backpackers (☎ 250-723-6924; www.fatsalmonbackpackers.com; 3250 Third Ave; dm $20; ⏳ Apr-Sep; 🖳) Funky, eccentric and full of character, this colorful backpacker joint is driven by its energetic, ultrawelcoming owners, along with Lilly the house dog. The four to eight-bed dorms, with names like 'Knickerbocker' and 'Mullet Room,' feature beds inventively crafted from drainpipes and aluminum ladders. There are lots of books to read, free hot drinks and a kitchen bristling with utensils.

Arrowvale Riverside Campground & Cottages (☎ 250-723-7948; www.arrowvalecottages.com; 5955 Hector Rd; campsite/cottage $22/150) Situated on the Somass River, 6km west of Port Alberni, the Arrowvale has showers, swimming, a playground, laundry and great fruit pies in its on-site café. For those who've had enough of camping, there are also two deluxe riverview cottages with fireplaces, Jacuzzi tubs and timber-trussed ceilings.

Hummingbird B&B (☎ 250-720-2111, 888-720-2114; hummingbirdguesthouse.com; 5769 River Rd; ste $125-160) With three huge suites and a large deck (complete with hot tub), relaxing is easy at this modern B&B property. There's a shared kitchen on each of the two floors but there's a substantial cooked breakfast provided that should keep you from having to cook until supper. Each suite has satellite TV, one has its own sauna and there's a games room with full-sized pool table. A family-friendly option, the largest suite fits up to six.

Blue Door Café (☎ 250-723-8811; 5415 Argyle St; mains $5-9; ⏳ 6:30am-8:30pm) This nookish hole in the wall draws an early-morning crowd of Albernians who've made this place their home away from home. While stomach-stuffing burgers and sandwiches are made up for lunch, breakfast is the highlight. Don't bother asking for muesli here: this place is all about giant pancakes, steak 'n' eggs and coffee that would wake a sleeping grizzly.

Clam Bucket (☎ 250-723-1315; 4479 Victoria Quay; mains $8-14; ⏳ 11:30am-9pm) Renowned for its seafood – try any of the surf 'n' turf – Clam Bucket also makes bulging sandwiches and gourmet burgers. Funky oranges and blues provide a casual atmosphere indoors, or head to the patio with its calming view of the inlet.

Getting There & Away

Greyhound (☎ 800-661-8747; www.greyhound.ca) bus services arrive here from Victoria ($30.20, five hours, four daily), Nanaimo ($13.05, 1½ hours, four daily), Tofino ($18.75, two hours, daily) and Parksville ($5.80, one hour, four daily).

BAMFIELD

pop 245

Named after settler William Eddy Banfield in 1861 – the name change is thought to be the result of a map-maker's error – waterfront Bamfield was a vital lumber port and whaling station for many years. Today, it's a quaint and attractive harbor village lining both sides of the forested Bamfield Inlet. Linked only by boat, Bamfield East is your entry point after the 100km drive from Port Alberni, and boardwalked Bamfield West is where you'll

VANCOUVER ISLAND

alight from the *MV Lady Rose* or *MV Frances Barkley*. For regional information, drop by the **visitor information booth** (☎ 250-728-3006; www.bamfieldchamber.com; Centennial Park; ⏰ 9am-6pm Jul & Aug).

Sights & Activities

Bamfield is the northern gateway for the **West Coast Trail** (p176) but there are other trails in the area. Ask at the visitor information booth for information on Brady's Beach Trail, a short trek from West Bamfield, and the Pachena Bay stroll, where you can combine beachcombing and sunbathing. **Broken Island Adventures** (☎ 250-728-3500, 888-728-6200; www.brokenislandadventures.com) specializes in kayaking, scuba diving and marine wildlife tours in Barkley Sound.

Sleeping & Eating

Pachena Bay Campground (☎ 250-728-1287; www.huuayaht.com; campsite $20; ⏰ Apr-Jun) This First Nations–run place, 3km east on Port Alberni Rd, enjoys a splendid forested setting just a few meters from the beach. It has a wheelchair-accessible washhouse with hot showers and flush toilets.

Marie's Bed & Breakfast (☎ 250-728-3091; www3.telus.net/marie; 468 Pachena Rd; s/d $50/80) This rustic wooden house up on the hill offers a home-style sleepover. A longtime artist and local resident, Marie is a welcoming host and a font of regional knowledge. Each room has a fridge and microwave and bikes are available for those who want to hit the nearby trails.

Bamfield Trails Hotel (☎ 250-728-3231, 877-728-3474; www.hawkeyemarinegroup.com; 22 Frigate Rd; dm/r/ste $39/119/179) A recently upgraded former motel near the dock at Bamfield East, overlooking the inlet, this place is popular with West Coast Trail hikers and Pacific Ocean salmon fishers. Its rooms range from a 10-bed bunkhouse to those with kitchenettes to large suites.

Hawk's Nest Pub (mains $7-12; ⏰ 11am-11pm) Adjacent to the Bamfield Trails Hotel, this is where Bamfield relaxes – or gets ripped.

Getting There & Away

Lady Rose Marine Services (☎ 800-663-7192, 250-723-8313; www.ladyrosemarine.com) boats arrive from Port Alberni ($28, 5½ hours, year-round) and Sechart in the Broken Group Islands ($28, 2½ hours, mid-June to mid-September).

The **West Coast Trail Express** (☎ 888-999-2288, 250-477-8700; www.trailbus.com; ⏰ May-Sep) buses in

hikers from Port Alberni ($43, three hours), Victoria ($64, six hours) and Nanaimo ($64, four hours).

PACIFIC RIM NATIONAL PARK RESERVE

With mist-shrouded rain forests and tremendous Pacific Ocean waves, the spectacular **Pacific Rim National Park Reserve** (☎ 250-726-7721; www.pc.gc.ca/pacificrim; park fee adult/child $6.90/3.45) is justifiably one of BC's most popular outdoor destinations. The 50,000-hectare park includes three units: the northern section is Long Beach, between Tofino and Ucluelet; the Broken Group Islands in Barkley Sound is the central section; and the well-used West Coast Trail is the southern section.

For casual visits to the popular Long Beach Unit, you won't need anything beyond the map in this book and an informational stop at the **Pacific Rim Visitor Centre** (☎ 250-726-4600; www.pacificrimvisitor.ca; 2791 Pacific Rim Hwy; ⏰ 9am-5pm mid-Mar–Jun & Sep, 9am-7pm Jul & Aug, 10am-4pm Thu-Sun Oct–mid-Mar).

For detailed information on camping options and activities in the park, visit the Parks Canada website (www.pc.gc.ca/pacificrim). For hiking ideas, pick up a copy of *Pacific Rim Trails* ($5), available at stores around the region.

Long Beach Unit

Easily accessible by car along the Pacific Rim Hwy, Long Beach Unit attracts the most park visitors. Wide sandy beaches, untamed surf, lots of beachcombing nooks and old-growth rain forest are some of the reasons for the summer tourist congestion.

Drop by the exhibits covering local cultural and natural history at the **Wickaninnish Interpretive Centre** (⏰ 9am-6pm mid-Mar–mid-Oct). Named for a chief of the local Nuu-chah-nulth tribe, it also loans all-terrain wheelchairs to visitors. Then try one or more of the following trails, ranging from 100m to 5km. Keep an eye out for bald eagles, banana slugs, purple starfish and the occasional whale sliding by offshore. The usual safety precautions apply on these routes: tread carefully over slippery rocks and tree roots and never turn your back on the surf when you're in the water or on the water's edge.

Easy to moderate trails:

Shorepine Bog (800m; easy & wheelchair accessible) Loops around a moss-layered bog.

Long Beach (easy) Great scenery along the sandy shore.

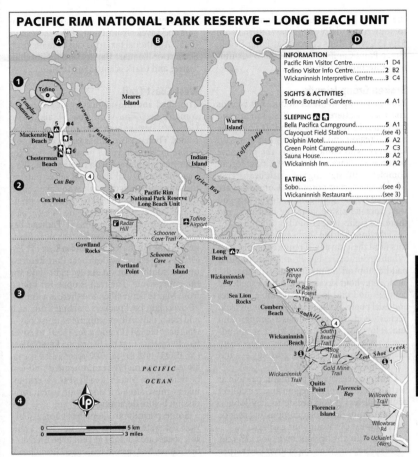

PACIFIC RIM NATIONAL PARK RESERVE – LONG BEACH UNIT

INFORMATION
Pacific Rim Visitor Centre....................1 D4
Tofino Visitor Info Centre....................2 B2
Wickaninnish Interpretive Centre.......3 C4

SIGHTS & ACTIVITIES
Tofino Botanical Gardens...................4 A1

SLEEPING
Bella Pacifica Campground.................5 A1
Clayoquot Field Station...................(see 4)
Dolphin Motel....................................6 A2
Green Point Campground..................7 C3
Sauna House.....................................8 A2
Wickaninnish Inn..............................9 A2

EATING
Sobo..(see 4)
Wickaninnish Restaurant.................(see 3)

VANCOUVER ISLAND

Rainforest Trail (1km; moderate) Two interpretive loops through old-growth forest.

Schooner Trail (1km; moderate) Through old- and second-growth forests, with beach access.

Spruce Fringe Trail (1.5km; moderate) Loop trail featuring hardy Sitka spruce.

South Beach (800m; easy to moderate) Through forest to a pebble beach.

Wickaninnish Trail (2.5km; easy to moderate) Shoreline and forest trail.

SLEEPING & EATING

Green Point Campground (250-689-9025, 877-737-3783; www.pccamping.ca; campsite $20.80; mid-Mar–mid-Oct) Midway between Ucluelet and Tofino on the Pacific Rim Hwy, this is the only Long Beach Unit campground and it's very popular in summer. Its 105 campsites are located on a forested terrace and have trail access to Long Beach. The faucets are cold but the toilets are flush. Book ahead in summer.

Wickaninnish Restaurant (250-726-7706; mains $10-22; lunch & dinner) Located in the Wickaninnish Interpretive Centre, this is a great spot to enjoy superb dining on fresh and delicious local seafood while overlooking the crashing surf of Long Beach – an especially spectacular view on stormy days. It's also a good place to for a cup of coffee and a dessert while you're passing through.

GETTING THERE & AWAY

The **Tofino Bus** (866-986-3466, 250-725-2871; www.tofinobus.com) 'Beach Bus' service run between the Tofino VIC and Ucluelet lighthouse up to four times daily (one way/return from $10/15), with stops en route at Long Beach, Green Point Campground and the Wickaninnish Interpretive Centre

Broken Group Islands

Broken Group includes about 300 islands and rocks scattered across 80 sq km around the entrance to Barkley Sound. It's a serene natural region and is especially popular with kayakers, who come to enjoy the awesome water-level views of the coastal rain forest, complete with sightings of black bears, gray whales and harbor porpoises. Compasses are required for navigating here – if you lose your way, your next stop could be Hawaii – and there are eight campgrounds available.

Lady Rose Marine Services boats take visitors (and their kayaks, if required) to Sechart Whaling Station Lodge. From there, popular paddle stop-off points include Gibraltar Island, a one-hour kayak away. It has a sheltered campground and lots of explorable beaches and tidal pools. Willis Island (90 minutes from Sechart) is also popular. It has a campground and, at low tide, you can walk to the surrounding islands. Benson Island (four hours from Sechart) has a campground, grazing deer and a blowhole.

Camping fees are $9 per night, payable at Sechart. Staff patrol the region and can collect additional fees if you decide to stay longer. Campgrounds have solar composting toilets, but you must carry out your garbage.

If you didn't bring your own, you can rent kayaks at Sechart Whaling Station Lodge (per day $35 to $50). **Broken Island Adventures** (☎ 250-728-3500, 888-728-6200; www.brokenislandadventures.com) also rents kayaks and runs popular three-hour powerboat tours (adult/child $72/26). Other operators include **Wildheart Adventures** (☎ 250-722-3683, 877-722-3683; www.kayakbc.com), which runs four-day camping and kayaking tours ($775), and **Batstar Adventure Tours** (☎ 250-724-2098, 877-449-2098; www.batstar.com), which leads small groups on all-inclusive trips (six/seven days $1149/1389) from Port Alberni.

GETTING THERE & AWAY

Lady Rose Marine Services (☎ 800-663-7192, 250-723-8313; www.ladyrosemarine.com) boats run to Sechart from Ucluelet ($30, three hours, mid-June to mid-September) and Bamfield ($28, 2½ hours, mid-June to mid-September). The company also operates a water taxi for passengers and kayaks from Toquart Bay to Sechart ($35). Additional taxi trips can be made from Sechart or Toquart Bay to Dodd, Gibraltar, Turret and Clark islands ($40 to $45).

West Coast Trail

The third and most southerly park section contains the 77km West Coast Trail, one of Canada's best-known and toughest hiking routes. There are two things you need to know before tackling it: you'll break your back (or your butt); and once won't be enough. It's a magnificent natural stage that never puts on the same show twice; people who have done it five or more times still aren't through with it.

The route runs between the West Coast Trail information centers at **Pachena Bay** (☎ 250-728-3234; ◷ 9am-5pm May-Sep), near Bamfield on the north end, and **Gordon River** (☎ 250-647-5434; ◷ 9am-5pm May-Sep), near Port Renfrew on the south. Plan on six to eight days for the entire route. The trail is open for hiking from May to September and there is a limit of 26 overnight backpackers starting from each end each day. All overnighters must pay a trail user fee ($110) and a fee ($30) to cover two ferry crossings on the route. **Reservations** (☎ 250-387-1642, 800-663-6000; nonrefundable reservation fee $25) are highly recommended and can be made from March 1 each year. Overnight hikers must attend a one-hour orientation session before departing.

Some permits are kept back for a daily wait-list system: five of each day's 26 available spaces are set aside at 1pm to be used on a first-come, first-served basis at each trailhead. If you win this lottery you can begin hiking that day, but keep in mind that hikers might wait three days to get a permit this way.

Hikers must be able to manage rough terrain, rock-face ladders, stream crossings and adverse weather conditions. Pack reliable gear and break in your boots before you start. On the trail, be prepared to carry – and read – tide tables; treat or boil all water; and cook on a lightweight camping stove. Filling, nutritious and low-odor foods are ideal. Hikers can camp at any of the designated sites along the route, most of which have solar-composting outhouses. Theoretically, supplies are unattainable on the trail, though soda, beer and food are sometimes available at the Nitinat Narrows Ferry and the store just south of the Carmanah lighthouse.

Some people do a day hike or hike half the trail from Pachena Bay, considered the easier end of the route. Overnight hikers who only hike this end of the trail can leave from Nitinat Lake. Day hikers are allowed on the trail from each end, but need a free day-use permit available from the registration centers. Permits are not issued to children aged six and under.

GETTING THERE & AWAY

West Coast Trail Express (☎ 250-477-8700, 888-999-2288; www.trailbus.com; ☺ May-Sep) runs a daily shuttle to Pachena Bay from Victoria ($64, six hours), Nanaimo ($64, four hours) and Port Alberni ($43, 2½ hours). It also runs a service to Gordon River from Victoria ($43, 2½ hours), Bamfield ($59, 3½ hours) and Pachena Bay ($49, three hours).

TOFINO & AROUND

pop 1850

The tourist-friendly heart of BC's wild and wonderful Pacific Coast, Tofino has exploded in recent years from a sleepy, eco-friendly backwater perched between the rain forest and the ocean to a resort town bursting with summer visitors. The transition has not been trouble free. In 2006 the town had to temporarily shut down its water system, when demand outstripped supply – an indication of the serious growing pains encountered in becoming one of the region's favorite outdoor destinations. It's not surprising that the visitors keep coming, though: packed with activities and blessed with stunning beaches, Tofino sits on Clayoquot (clay-kwot) Sound, where forested mounds rise from the rolling waves.

Information

The **VIC** (☎ 250-725-3414; www.tourismtofino.com; 1426 Pacific Rim Hwy; ☺ 10am-6pm May-Sep) is 6km south of town and has detailed information on area accommodations. Staff can help with the hot surf spots or recommend some good hikes. If pressed, they'll even point you towards the **post office** (☎ 250-267-1177; 161 First St).

Sights

Among the most popular day trips from Tofino, **Hot Springs Cove** is the central attraction of **Maquinna Marine Provincial Park** (☎ 250-474-1336; www.env.gov.bc.ca/bcparks), 37km north of town. Sojourners travel here by Zodiac boat or seaplane, watching for whales and other sea critters en route. From the boat landing, 2km of boardwalks lead to a series of restorative natural hot pools.

Visible through the mist from the Tofino waterfront, **Meares Island** is home to the **Big Tree Trail**, a 400m-boardwalk through old-growth forest that includes a stunning 1500-year-old red cedar. The island was the site of the key 1984 Clayoquot Sound antilogging protest that kicked off the region's modern environmental movement.

Situated on remote Flores Island, mystical **Ahousat** is home to the spectacular **Wild Side Heritage Trail**, a moderately difficult path that traverses 10km of forests, beaches and headlands between Ahousat and Cow Bay. There's a natural warm spring on the island and it's also home to a First Nations band. It's a popular destination for kayakers but although camping is allowed, there are no facilities provided.

Activities

Surfing is the town's most popular activity but there are plenty of opportunities for kayaking, whale-watching and hiking for those who want to mix it up a little.

Tofino is also the starting point for tours of Clayoquot Sound.

VANCOUVER ISLAND

THE PERFECT STORM

From mid-October through March (the absolute best times are January and February), Tofino has a front-row seat for perhaps the most spectacular storms on the North American West Coast. The wide beaches are deserted, the sky is a dramatic rumbling collage of dark cloud and the surf is pounding to a foam-licked frenzy. While many local resorts – especially the Wickaninnish Inn (p180) – have created cozy storm-watching packages for winter visitors, you can also check out the natural drama on your own. The best DIY spots are the clifftop Wild Pacific Trail, the trails above South Beach, Ucluelet lighthouse and the Wickaninnish Interpretive Centre (p174). Make sure you have your raingear on and be aware that the seafront can be dangerous during storm season: avoid clambering over rocks and never turn your back on the waves.

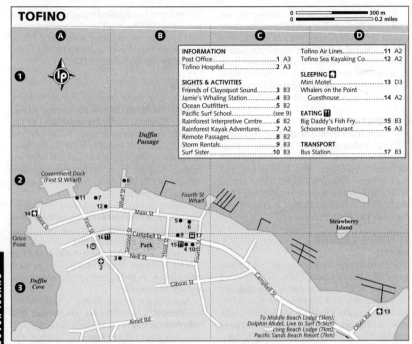

TOFINO

INFORMATION
Post Office.....................................1 A3
Tofino Hospital.............................2 A3

SIGHTS & ACTIVITIES
Friends of Clayoquot Sound..........3 B3
Jamie's Whaling Station................4 B3
Ocean Outfitters...........................5 B2
Pacific Surf School.....................(see 9)
Rainforest Interpretive Centre......6 B2
Rainforest Kayak Adventures........7 A2
Remote Passages..........................8 B2
Storm Rentals...............................9 B3
Surf Sister..................................10 B3

Tofino Air Lines...........................11 A2
Tofino Sea Kayaking Co..........12 A2

SLEEPING
Mini Motel..................................13 D3
Whalers on the Point
  Guesthouse...........................14 A2

EATING
Big Daddy's Fish Fry...................15 B3
Schooner Resturant....................16 A3

TRANSPORT
Bus Station..................................17 B3

SURFING

Live to Surf (☎ 250-725-4464; www.livetosurf.com; 1180 Pacific Rim Hwy; board rental 24hr $25) Tofino's first surf shop also supplies skates and skimboards.

Pacific Surf School (☎ 250-725-2155, 888-777-9961; www.pacificsurfschool.com; 440 Campbell St; board rental 4 hr/24hr $15/20) Rentals, camps and lessons for beginners.

Storm Rentals (☎ 250-725-3344; www.stormsurf shop.com; 444 Campbell St; board rental 4hr/8hr/24hr $15/20/25) Popular and established, with student discounts.

Surf Sister (☎ 250-725-4456, 877-724-7873; www .surfsister.com; 625 Campbell St) All-female surf school offers introductory lessons (from $65) to boys and girls but no dudes are allowed in multiple-day courses (from $195).

KAYAKING

Rainforest Kayak Adventures (☎ 250-725-3117, 877-422-9453; www.rainforestkayak.com; 316 Main St; courses from $660) Specializes in four- to six-day guided tours and courses for beginners and intermediates.

Tla-ook Cultural Adventures (☎ 250-725-2656, 877-942-2663; www.tlaook.com; 2hr/4hr/6hr $44/64/140) Learn about First Nations culture while paddling an authentic dugout canoe.

Tofino Sea Kayaking (☎ 250-725-3330, 800-863-4664; www.tofino-kayaking.com; 320 Main St; 2hr/4hr/6hr $54/68/90) Guided paddles around the region, including a popular four-hour Meares Island trip.

WHALE-WATCHING

Jamie's Whaling Station (☎ 250-725-3919, 800-667-9913; www.jamies.com; 606 Campbell St; tours adult/child $79/50) One-stop shop for whale-, bear- and sea lion-spotting tours.

Ocean Outfitters (☎ 250-725-2866, 877-906-2326; www.oceanoutfitters.bc.ca; 421 Main St; tours adult/child $79/49) Popular whale-watching tours, with bears and hot springs treks also offered.

Remote Passages (☎ 250-725-3330, 800-666-9833; www.remotepassages.com; Wharf St; tours adult/child $69/55) Three-hour whale-watching and seven-hour hot springs tours.

TOURS

Clayoquot Connections Tours (☎ 250-725-3919; tours from $25) Good-value tours on an old open-deck lifeboat, including sunset, fishing and Meares Island treks. Book through **Jamie's Whaling Station** (☎ 250-725-3919, 800-667-9913; www.jamies.com; 606 Campbell St).

VANCOUVER ISLAND'S GREEN COAST

A major center for environmental activism, Tofino is home to the **Friends of Clayoquot Sound** (☎ 250-725-4218; www.focs.ca; 331 Neill St), a grassroots organization working to defend rain forests and marine ecosystems throughout the region. Efforts to curb indiscriminate logging haven't been in vain: a decade after massive protests in Clayoquot, major forestry companies' logging rates in the area have dropped almost 80%. The group also concerns itself with salmon farming and operations practices in regards to sewage, antibiotics use and other impacts on Clayoquot's fragile ecosystem. For more information, write to Box 489, Tofino, BC, V0R 2Z0.

The **Raincoast Interpretive Centre** (☎ 250-725-2560; www.tofinores.com; 451 Main St; ☺ noon-5pm Wed-Sun mid-May–Sep) is a project of the Raincoast Education Society, part of a growing international network exploring sustainable forest management. Visit the center to learn about Clayoquot Sound and its ecosystems. There are many interactive displays and resources – and lots of knowledgeable staff – that can make your visit to the region an eye-opening education. Admission and programs are free but donations are appreciated – you can also support the work here by buying a couple of the excellent trail guides.

Visitors can see what coastal temperate rain forests are all about at the strictly conservation-minded **Tofino Botanical Gardens** (☎ 250-725-1220; www.tofinobotanicalgardens.com; 1084 Pacific Rim Hwy; 3-day admission adult/youth/child $10/6/free; ☺ 9am-dusk), which explores the region's flora and fauna through a network of paths and boardwalks. With a frog pond, forest walk, native plants and an ongoing program of workshops and field trips, there's a $1 entry discount for car-free arrivals. There's also excellent dorm-style accommodation in the new Field Station building (below).

Tofino Air Lines (☎ 250-725-4454, 866-486-3247; www.tofinoair.ca; tours 3/6 people $369/534) Chartered 20-minute scenic tours over beautiful Clayoquot Sound.

Walk the Wild Side (☎ 250-670-9586, 888-670-9586; adult/child $75/25) Guided hikes of Ahousat.

Sleeping

BUDGET

Whalers on the Point Guesthouse (☎ 250-725-3443; www.tofinohostel.com; 81 West St; dm/r $27/75-130) Built as a hostel in 1999, this HI affiliate is the Cadillac of backpacker joints. Close to the center of town but with a secluded waterfront location, it's a showcase of rustic West Coast wood and stone architecture – the dining room overlooking the water is a great place to watch the natural world drift by. The dorms are small and facilities include a library, barbecue patio, games room and a free wet sauna.

Bella Pacifica Campground (☎ 250-725-3400; www.bellapacifica.com; Mackenzie Beach Rd; campsite $32-45; ☺ mid-Feb–mid-Nov) Peak-season reservations are essential at this very popular, family-friendly campground on Mackenzie Beach, 3km south of Tofino via the Pacific Rim Hwy. There's an array of different oceanside or forested tent pitches and facilities include flush toilets, pay showers ($1) and a campground office that sells ice and firewood.

Clayoquot Field Station (☎ 250-725-1220; www.tofinobotanicalgardens.com; 1084 Pacific Rim Hwy; dm/d $32/120; 🖳) In the grounds of the botanical gardens (room rates include entry), this immaculate and attractive wood-built educational center has a selection of four-bedded dorm rooms, a large stainless steel kitchen and an on-site laundry. There's also a tranquil private room overlooking the forest. A great sleepover for nature lovers, there's a natural history library and regular speakers and events. Wheelchair accessible.

MIDRANGE

Mini Motel (☎ 250-725-3441; www.tofinoinletcottages.com; 350 Olsen Rd; d $90-175) A five-unit clutch of A-frame buildings on a quiet stretch of waterfront overlooking Meares Island, these old-school vacation cottages are like sleeping in a wood-lined boat cabin. The interiors are a little faded but all is neat, tidy and well-maintained. The decks are a great spot to watch the sunset.

Dolphin Motel (☎ 250-725-3377; www.dolphinmotel.ca; 1190 Pacific Rim Hwy; r $95-139) A single-level, old-school motel with a family-friendly ambience, the Blue Dolphin's rooms include fridges that double as bedside tables. A short walk from Chesterman Beach, the property has a barbecue area with picnic tables and a couple of self-catering units with full kitchens.

Sauna House (☎ 250-725-2113; saunahouse@alberni.net; 1286 Lynn Rd; r/cabin $110/130; 🖳) On a tree-lined street of secluded B&Bs across from Chesterman Beach, this rustic nook includes a gabled loft above the main property and a small, self-contained cabin out back. The tranquil, wood-lined cabin is recommended: it has a small kitchenette, a sunny deck that's great for breakfast (included in rates) and its own compact sauna – the perfect place to end a strenuous day of hiking.

InnChanter (☎ 250-670-1149; www.innchanter .com; per person $120) A handsome heritage vessel moored near Hot Springs Cove (access via water taxi or floatplane), the InnChanter has been restored and refitted to include five wood-lined sleeping cabins. There's no surly captain here – instead this makes for a memorable stay. Rates include breakfast, dinner and use of canoes.

Middle Beach Lodge (☎ 250-725-2900, 866-725-2900; www.middlebeach.com; Mackenzie Beach, Pacific Rim Hwy; r/cabin from $135/250) The forested grounds on this beach site south of town are more reminiscent of a lodge than a resort, giving a greater feeling of seclusion. Room types range from the adults-only 'At-the-Beach' to the family-oriented 'At-the-Headlands.' Interiors are West Coast rustic chic, with plenty of wood floors, nature-hugging balconies and high, gabled ceilings.

TOP END

ourpick **Pacific Sands Beach Resort** (☎ 250-725-3322, 800-565-23224; www.pacificsands.com; 1421 Pacific Rim Hwy; r/villa from $220/450) Jostling for attention with the other chichi resorts hanging around the coast here like a string of expensive pearls, family-owned Pacific Sands wins our attention for its 22 stunning waterfront villas. Adding to its conventional lodge buildings, these dramatic timber-framed houses open directly onto the beach and include washing machines, large kitchens, stone fireplaces, slate and wood floors and ocean-view bedrooms with soaker tubs and private decks. But it's not just about looks: the villas were built on raised concrete pillars to preserve rain forest root systems and have an 'earth-source' energy-efficient heating and cooling system with low greenhouse gas emissions.

Long Beach Lodge (☎ 250-725-2442, 877-844-7873; www.longbeachlodgeresort.com; 1441 Pacific Rim Hwy; r/ste/ cottage $279/369/459) A beachfront resort with tons of West Coast charm, this elegant property overlooks a dramatic sandy bay. The lower-level rooms, all with tasteful interiors and

high-end wood-accented furnishings, have individual access to the grass-fringed beach – the best way to wake up in the morning is to poke your head out the window for a blast of salty sea air. The soothing upstairs bar and restaurant enjoys panoramic seascape views.

Wickaninnish Inn (☎ 250-725-3100, 800-333-4604; www.wickinn.com; Chesterman Beach; r/ste from $440/560) They've cornered the market in luxury winter storm-watching packages but 'the Wick' is worth a stay anytime of year. Embodying nature with recycled old-growth furniture, natural stone tiles and the atmosphere of a place grown rather than constructed, the sumptuous guest rooms have push-button gas fireplaces, two-person hot tubs and private balconies.

Eating

Big Daddy's Fish Fry (☎ 250-725-4415; 411 Campbell St; mains $5.50-15; ⏰ 11am-10pm) An excellent spot to hook some freshly prepared seafood, this friendly shack serves a great, spicy clam chowder. It's hard to beat the wild salmon and fries but more adventurous seafood scoffers should sample the prawns, oysters and creamy local scallops.

ourpick **Sobo** (☎ 250-725-2341; 1084 Pacific Rim Hwy; mains $6-10; ⏰ 11am-9pm) Now on the grounds of the Botanical Gardens, this legendary purple dining truck eatery serves the best (and best value) home-cooked food in town. Locally renowned chefs Lisa and Aaron prepare and serve gourmet salads, hearty soups and polenta fries. But it's the fish treats that draw the regulars: the sizzling shrimp cakes are mouthwatering and the fish tacos are a staple of every diet within a 5km radius. Save room for a giant, gooey chocolate-chip cookie.

Schooner Restaurant (☎ 250-725-3444; 331 Campbell St; mains $22-29; ⏰ 9am-10pm) A local favorite, this attractive, white-tablecloth eatery has uncovered many new ways to prepare the region's seafood bounty. The halibut stuffed with crab, shrimp, brie, and pine nuts is popular but the Mates Plate of Clayoquot Sound treats including grilled oysters, garlic prawns and charbroiled salmon has been a staple here for 35 years.

Getting There & Around

Tofino Airport (☎ 250-725-2006) is south of town via the Pacific Rim Hwy. **Orca Airways** (☎ 604-270-6722, 888-359-6722; www.flyorcaair.com) flights arrive from Vancouver International Airport's

South Terminal ($159, 55 minutes, one to three daily). **Sound Flight** (☎ 424-254-8063, 866-921-3474; www.soundflight.net) services also arrive from Seattle (US$290, three hours, daily, mid-June to mid-September).

Greyhound (☎ 800-661-8747; www.greyhound.ca) buses arrive from Port Alberni ($18.75, two hours, daily), Nanaimo ($30.20, four hours, daily) and Victoria ($54.50, seven hours, daily).

Tofino Bus (☎ 250-725-2871, 866-986-3466; www.tofinobus.com) is the local bus company that keeps expanding. It runs a 'Tofino Transit' bus between the town's CIBC bank and the information center at Cox Bay ($2). It also runs a 'Beach Bus' between Tofino and Ucluelet (one way/return $13/20). In addition, it operates an 'Express Service' from Vancouver ($35 plus ferry, seven hours), Victoria ($53.50, 5½ hours), Nanaimo ($35, four hours) and Port Alberni ($20, 2½ hours). The route runs daily year-round and twice daily from mid-March to mid-November.

UCLUELET
pop 1900

Unfairly regarded by next-door Tofino as its less-charming sibling, Ucluelet (yew-klew-let) shares the same scenery and the same activities, and is generally cheaper and more accessible. But that's not to say that 'Ukee' is sleepy. In fact, the town has expanded in recent years to cope with visitor demand, successfully avoiding some of the growing pains experienced by Tofino. For information, head to the tiny **VIC** (☎ 250-726-4641; www.uclueletinfo.com; 277 Main St; ☼ 9am-5pm) near the government wharf.

Sights & Activities

The recommended 8.5km **Wild Pacific Trail** (www.wildpacifictrail.com) runs through rain forest and along the unkempt coastline, with views of the Broken Group Islands and Barkley Sound. Seabirds and whales are abundant here and it's a good spot for watching storms. Alternatively, the tide pools, seashells and kelp beds at **Big Beach** make it a great spot to potter around for a few hours.

If you're feeling active, **Subtidal Adventures** (☎ 250-726-7336, 877-444-1134; www.subtidaladventures.com; 1950 Peninsula Rd; tours adult/child from $40/50) has boat tours covering whales, sunsets, and bears, although not necessarily at the same time. For paddle fans, **Majestic Ocean Kayaking** (☎ 250-726-

2868, 800-726-2868; www.oceankayaking.com; 1167 Helen Rd; tours from $60) leads watery treks around the harbor or into the Barkley Sound wilderness.

You can learn to surf with **Inner Rhythm Surf Camp** (☎ 250-726-2211, 877-393-7873; www.innerrhythm.net; 1685 Peninsula Rd; 3hr lesson $79) or rent a bike from **Ukee Bikes & Kites** (☎ 250-726-2453; 1599 Imperial Lane; rental 1hr/24hr $5/25). For an alternative beach activity, you can buy a kite here.

Sleeping & Eating

Surf Junction Campground (☎ 250-726-7214, 877-922-6722; www.surfjunction.com; 2650 Pacific Rim Hwy; campsite $25; ☼ mid-Jan–mid-Oct) This small, private campground has an array of forest and more open sites but each is equipped with a picnic table and fire ring. Flush toilets, a hot tub and a basic convenience store are available; for those traveling light, you can rent tents, camping gear and surfboards.

C&N Backpackers (☎ 250-726-7725, 888-434-6060; www.cnnbackpackers.com; 2081 Peninsula Rd; dm/r $25/65) You'll have to take your shoes off to enter this calming 'resort hostel' – they're very protective of the hardwood floors. The dorms are mostly small, but private rooms are available, and there's a spacious kitchen. The highlight is the landscaped garden overlooking the inlet, complete with hammocks and a rope swing.

Surf's Inn (☎ 250-726-4426; www.surfsinn.ca; 1874 Peninsula Rd; dm/cabin $24/200) While this bright-blue, well-maintained adapted family home contains some cozy dorm rooms and is high on the friendly approach, it's the two-bedroom self-contained cabin out back that attracts many. Sleeping up to seven, it has a full kitchen and its own deck and barbecue.

Canadian Princess Resort (☎ 250-598-3366, 800-663-7090; www.canadianprincess.com; 1943 Peninsula Rd; r $79-229; ☼ Apr-Sep) You can choose from tiny but cool staterooms on an old steam ship moored in Ucluelet Harbour (this is also the site of the resort's restaurant and bar) or much larger and more traditional hotel rooms in the lodge. Be cool and stay on the boat.

Ukee Dogs (☎ 250-726-2103; 1576 Imperial Lane; mains $4-6; ☼ 9am-5pm Mon-Sat) With a focus on homebaked treats and comfort foods, this bright and breezy eatery serves hotdogs of the gourmet variety, plus made-from-scratch soups and focaccia bread pizzas– the smoked garlic sausage pie is recommended. Also, any joint that puts that many sprinkles on its cakes deserves high praise.

VANCOUVER ISLAND

Matterson House Restaurant (☎ 250-726-6600; 1682 Peninsula Rd; mains $6-16; 8am-9pm) This charming farmhouse-turned-restaurant features a refined rustic atmosphere with lace curtains and homebaked goods. Breakfasts include build-your-own omelettes.

Getting There & Away

Greyhound (☎ 800-661-8747; www.greyhound.ca) buses arrive from Port Alberni ($13.90, 1½ hours, daily), Nanaimo ($24.95, 3½ hours, daily) and Victoria ($46, 6½ hours, daily).

Tofino Bus (☎ 866-986-3466, 250-725-2871; www .tofinobus.com) 'Beach Bus' services arrive from Tofino ($13, 45 minutes; two to four daily). The company also operates an 'Express Service' from Vancouver ($35 plus ferry, 6½ hours), Victoria ($53.50, five hours), Nanaimo ($35, 3½ hours) and Port Alberni ($20, two hours). This route runs daily year-round and twice daily from mid-March to mid-November.

DENMAN & HORNBY ISLANDS

Both **Denman** (www.denmanisland.com) and **Hornby** (www.hornbyisland.com) combine laid-back attitudes with an artistic flare and a wealth of outdoor activities. Denman has three provincial parks: **Fillongley** (☎ 250-474-1336; www.env .gov.bc.ca/bcparks), with easy hiking and beachcombing; **Boyle Point** (www.env.gov.bc.ca/bcparks), with a beautiful walk to the lighthouse; and **Sandy Island** (☎ 250-474-1336; www.env.gov.bc.ca/ bcparks), only accessible by water from north Denman.

Among Hornby's provincial parks, **Tribune Bay** features a long sandy beach with safe swimming, while **Helliwell** offers notable hiking. **Ford's Cove**, on Hornby's south coast, offers the chance for divers to swim with six-gill sharks.

For kayaking rentals contact **Denman Hornby Canoes & Kayaks** (☎ 250-335-0079; 4005 East Rd, Denman Island; rental 3hr/6hr $35/50) or **Hornby Ocean Kayaks** (☎ 250-335-2726; hikayak@telus.net; rental 3hr/6hr $35/50) – they also offer guided tours, including a sunset trip ($50, 2½ hours).

Sleeping & Eating

DENMAN ISLAND

Fillongley Provincial Park (☎ 604-689-9025, 800-689-9025; www.discovercamping.ca; campsite $20) Situated on the east coast of the island, this basic oceanfront campground has only 10 campsites but they fill up quickly in summer – booking ahead is advised. Facilities include toilets,

cold water, picnic tables and fire pits. There are several easy trails around the park and the beach is a beachcombing haven of driftwood.

Denman Island Guest House & International Hostel (☎ 250-335-2688; 3806 Denman Rd; dm/r $20/45) Conveniently located up the hill and on the left from the ferry landing, this 1912 farmhouse is a combination hostel/B&B. The tree-lined property has an on-site bistro and guests can rent bikes to tour the area then jump in the hot tub after a long day's peddling.

Ships Point Inn (☎ 250-335-1004, 877-742-1004; www.shipspointinn.com; 7584 Ships Point Rd; d $135-175) A pampering waterfront sleepover perched on the edge of Fanny Bay, the six rooms and common areas in this lovely home are tastefully decorated – the romantic Bay View room has a Parisian feel and impressive sea to sky vistas. An innovative four-course breakfast will get you out of bed.

Denman Island Bakery & Pizzeria (☎ 250-335-1310; Denman Rd; mains $7-11; 9am-9pm Mon-Sat) This little café in the village is the local hangout. Nosh on some pizza or talk to some of the local artists over a cuppa and a muffin. Friday night is Greek Night but don't smash your plate until you're told.

HORNBY ISLAND

Hilltop Magic B&B (☎ 250-335-1524; www.hilltop magic.com; 8535 Keith Wagner Way; ste $95) A smashing forest-hidden B&B property with a single, immaculate suite, the twist here is that the owners are master magicians who are likely to wow you with a few illusions. The large suite includes hardwood floors, a gabled ceiling, a private deck and a claw-foot tub bathroom.

Sea Breeze Lodge (☎ 250-335-2321, 888-516-2321; www.seabreezelodge.com; adult/youth/child $150/90/70) This 12-acre family-friendly retreat, with cottages overlooking the ocean, has the feel of a Spanish villa with a Pacific Rim twist. You can swim, kayak and fish here and the rates – which include three daily meals – are reduced for under-17s.

Wheelhouse Restaurant (☎ 250-335-0136; mains $7-14; 11am-9pm) Near the ferry, this casual spot's boardwalk patio is at ground level, among gardens and hanging baskets. Summer evenings feature a barbecue buffet specializing in fresh local fare, while the main menu focuses on comfort soups, sandwiches and burgers.

Getting There & Away

BC Ferries (☎ 888-223-3779, 250-386-3431; www.bcferries .com) services arrive on Denman from Buckley Bay (adult/child/vehicle $6.05/3.20/14.65, 10 minutes, hourly from 7am to 11pm). Hornby Island is accessed via ferry from Denman (adult/child/vehicle $5.75/2.90/13.85, 10 minutes, hourly from 7:45am to 6:35pm).

COMOX VALLEY

Comprising waterfront Comox, charming Courtenay and tiny but unmissable Cumberland, the Comox Valley is a temperate region of rolling mountains, alpine meadows and quirky communities founded on the logging industry. A good base for outdoor adventures, it includes the Mt Washington ski resort area.

For regional information, drop by the **VIC** (☎ 250-334-3234, 888-357-4471; www.comox-valley-tour ism.ca; 2040 Cliffe Ave, Comox; ☽ 9am-5pm mid-May–Aug, 9am-5pm Mon-Sat Sep–mid-May).

Sights & Activities

Mt Washington Alpine Resort (☎ 250-338-1386, 888-231-1499; www.mountwashington.ca; lift ticket adult/child winter $46/25, summer $28/18) is Vancouver Island's skiing mecca. With 50 ski runs, a snowshoeing park (adult/child $16/11) and cross-country trails (adult/child $19/10), it's a popular winter spot. The resort's summer activities include horseback riding, fly-fishing and the increasingly popular mountain biking (http://bike .mountwashington.ca). Hiking routes include the Paradise Meadows Loop Trail (2km), starting at the Nordic ski area parking lot.

Courtenay & District Museum (☎ 250-334-0686; www.courtenaymuseum.ca; 207 Fourth St; admission by donation; ☽ 10am-5pm Mon-Sat, noon-4pm Sun mid-May–Aug, 10am-5pm Mon-Sat Sep–mid-May) is known for its life-sized replica of an elasmosaur, a prehistoric marine reptile first discovered in the area. You can hunt for your own fossils along the banks of the Puntledge River on a museum **fossil tour** (tours adult/child $20/12.50; ☽ Apr-Sep).

Check out some flying dinosaurs over at **Comox Air Force Museum** (☎ 250-339-8162; www .comoxairforcemuseum.ca; 19 Wing Comox; admission by donation; ☽ 10am-4pm). Jam-packed with exhibits from Canada's aviation history, it's an excellent find for enthusiasts and casual fans of air history.

Outdoorsy types should make for **Miracle Beach Provincial Park** (☎ 250-755-2483; www.env.gov .bc.ca/bcparks), home to some excellent hiking trails and tranquil sandy beaches. For watery fun, contact Courtenay's **Pacific Pro Dive & Surf** (☎ 250-338-6829, 877-800-3483; www.scubashark.ca; 2270 Cliffe Ave). It offers tours, lessons and equipment rentals to traveling surf and scuba fans

Sleeping

our pick **Riding Fool Hostel** (☎ 250-336-8250, 888-313-3665; www.ridingfool.com; 2705 Dunsmuir St, Cumberland; dm/r $20/45; ⌨) Symbolizing the funky reclamation of Cumberland's pioneering clapboard main street – it looks like a bright-painted reinvention of Dodge – this is one of Vancouver Island's best hostels. The restored heritage building has immaculate wooden interiors – much of it recycled – large but spacious dorms, a massive kitchen and lounge area and the kind of private rooms often found in hotels. Free wireless access is included and there's a barbecue on the porch, a great evening hangout spot. The staff here are adept at recommending local activities and there's an on-site bike rental shop (rental half-/full day $25/40).

Shantz House Hostel (☎ 250-703-2060, 866-603-2060; www.shantzhostel.com; 520 Fifth St, Courtenay; dm/r $20/51.75; ⌨) This quiet and perfectly maintained heritage house is a hostel that feels like a family home. Well located in downtown Courtenay, its two dorms are small and its private rooms are ideal for families. There's a full kitchen, free laundry and a cozy, gas-fired common room, plus a patio with barbecue. Free wireless access is included and the host is an expert in local outdoor pursuits.

Cumberland Gardens B&B (☎ 250-336-2867; www .cumberland-gardens.ca; 3303 First St, Cumberland; s/d $50/75) The roses and raspberries in the lovely garden will sway your attention but the two basement suites, each with their own entrance, are also worth a look. The chatty host has lots of local stories and he'll tailor your breakfast to whatever takes your fancy. The suites share a bathroom and kitchen.

Fraser House B&B (☎ 250-339-3588, 877-339-3588; www.fraserhouse.com; 204 Rodello St, Comox; s/d $60/75) Like staying in a favorite aunt's home, this close-to-downtown Comox B&B has a family-friendly feel. The ground-level accommodation has a separate entry, two spick-and-span bedrooms and a large lounge with fireplace. Breakfasts range from toast to eggs Benedict and everything in between.

Anco Motel (☎ 250-334-2451, 877-393-2200; www .ancomotelbc.com; 1885 Cliff Ave, Courtenay; s/d $65/75; 🐾) With 66 rooms (request one in the new wing), the Anco is a cut above the average. Interiors have a standard 1980s look but the level of maintenance and cleanliness is high and non-standard facilities include an outdoor pool, some kitchenettes and rooms with wheelchair access. Accommodation in the new wing has air-conditioning and high-speed internet access.

Eating

Orbitz Gourmet Pizza (☎ 250-338-7970; 492 Fitzgerald St, Courtenay; slice/pie $3.70/21.95; ☼ 11:30am-10pm Mon-Sat) Not only the best pizza in town – the 'Saturn Return' spinach and artichoke is recommended – Orbitz is also a cool hangout. There's a wide selection of vegetarian and meat toppings, and you can add organic chocolate bars and fair-trade coffee to your order.

Tarbells Coffee Bar (☎ 250-336-8863; 2705 Dunsmuir St, Cumberland; mains $4-7; ☼ 8am-5pm) The funksters' hangout, this is the best place in Cumberland to meet the young locals who are driving the town's regeneration. Find a corner nook and choose from focaccia sarnies, fresh wraps and lots of hearty juices. In summer, this is a hopping Sunday brunch spot.

Atlas Café (☎ 250-338-9838; 250 Sixth St, Courtenay; mains $12-18; ☼ 8:30am-3pm Mon, 8:30am-10pm Tue-Sat, 8:30am-9pm Sun) Courtenay's best splurge meal, Atlas has an intimate, loungey feel (try a Purple Haze at the martini bar) yet remains warm and welcoming. The menu fuses Asian, Mexican and Mediterranean dishes – including gourmet fish tacos and peanut stir-fry – with some impressive vegetarian options.

Martine's Bistro (☎ 250-339-1199; 1754 Beaufort Ave, Comox; mains $14-25; ☼ 11:30am-10pm) There's tons of fresh seafood – try the Cajun seared tuna – and a plethora of great international and BC wines at this charming and relaxed Comox bistro. It has a large patio for summertime dining and there are regular wine-tasting dinners and live music nights.

Getting There & Around

Central Mountain Air (☎ 250-877-5000, 888-865-8585; www.flycma.com) flights arrive at **Comox Valley Airport** (☎ 250-897-3123; www.comoxairport.com) from Vancouver International Airport ($160, 40 minutes, four daily). **WestJet** (☎ 800-538-5696; www.westjet.com) services arrive from Calgary ($160, 1½ hours, two daily).

Greyhound (☎ 800-661-8747; www.greyhound .ca) buses arrive in Courtenay from Victo-

ria ($38.70, four to five hours, four daily), Campbell River ($5.80, 45 minutes, four daily) and Nanaimo ($17.90, two hours, four daily). There are no stops in Comox or Cumberland.

The **VIA Rail** (☎ 888-842-7245; www.viarail.ca) *Malahat* service arrives in Courtenay from Victoria ($48, 4½ hours, daily) and Nanaimo ($25, two hours, daily), among others.

BC Ferries (☎ 888-223-3779, 250-386-3431; www .bcferries.com) services arrive at Comox's Little River terminal from the mainland's Powell River (adult/child/vehicle $8.65/4.35/29.50, 80 minutes, two to four daily).

The **Comox Valley Transit System** (☎ 250-339-5453; www.busonline.ca; adult/child $1.50/1.25) operates buses between Comox, Courtenay and Cumberland.

CAMPBELL RIVER

pop 30,810

Regarded by many as the end of civilization on the island (try telling that to someone from the north end), Campbell River is a logging and salmon fishing town that's reinvented itself as an access point for wilderness tourism. It's the main departure point for Strathcona Provincial Park (p187) and has all the amenities that those in rustic outlying regions lack. Check out the driftwood carvings around the town and stroll the pier for some great views of the forested islands. For regional information, drop by the **VIC** (☎ 250-287-4636, 866-830-1113; www.campbellriver.travel; 1235 Shoppers Row; ☼ 9am-7pm).

Sights & Activities

The excellent **Museum at Campbell River** (☎ 250-287-3103; www.crmuseum.ca; 470 Island Hwy; adult/child $6/4; ☼ 10am-5pm Mon-Sat, noon-5pm Sun mid-May–Sep, noon-5pm Tue-Sun Oct–mid-May) features a good collection of First Nations masks, an 1890 pioneer cabin and video footage of the world's largest-ever artificial, non-nuclear blast, which destroyed Ripple Rock – a submerged mountain in Seymour Narrows north of Campbell River that caused more than 100 shipwrecks before it was blown apart in 1958.

Campbell River lives up to its 'Salmon Capital of the World' billing with fishing a popular pastime. You can wet a line off the downtown **Discovery Pier** – rod rentals are available (rental per day $6) on this busy jetty or you can just stroll along with the crowds and see what everyone else has caught. Fish and chips are also available here, served in giant cones of newspaper.

Dive further into the region's watery past at the nearby **Maritime Heritage Centre** (☎ 250-286-3161; www.bcp45.org; admission free; 🕑 9am-5pm Mon-Fri), which is dominated by the *BCP 45*, a lovingly-restored 1927 fishing vessel that plied the waters here for decades.

The artificial reef provided by *HMCS Columbia*, sunk near Campbell River, is a major draw for scuba diving. Contact **Beaver Aquatics Limited** (☎ 250-287-7652; 760 Island Hwy; 🕑 9:30am-5pm Mon-Fri. 10am-5pm Sat) for gear and lessons.

Sleeping & Eating

Thunderbird RV Park (☎ 250-286-3344; www.thunderbirdrvpark.com; 2660 Spit Rd; campsite $15) Bereft of trees, this campground looks a bit barren, but it's within walking distance of shops and supermarkets (as well as the ocean and a fascinating First Nations burial ground). The facilities are superior, with laundry, heated bathrooms, flush toilets, hot showers, and wheelchair access.

Rustic Motel (☎ 250-286-6295, 800-567-2007; www.rusticmotel.com; 2140 N Island Hwy; s/d $100/110; 😷) North of downtown, this place sits quietly in the trees by the river. The rooms are clean but a little spartan – the three-room suites and cabins are a good option for groups – but the facilities available include a sauna, Jacuzzi and barbecues. Rates include continental breakfast.

our pick Dolphins Resort (☎ 250-287-3066, 800-891-0287; www.dolphinsresort.com; 4125 Discovery Dr; cabin $150-175) A beautifully maintained nest of pretty cedar cabins spilling down to the water's edge among the trees, this lovely miniresort is dripping with charm. The cabins have a cozy, rustic feel and each has a full kitchen and a porch (barbecue rentals are $10 extra). Most also have outdoor hot tubs. The flower-strewn, landscaped grounds are immaculate and there's a secluded beach area with its own fire pit for evening hangouts. Good fish-and-stay packages are available.

Heron's Landing (☎ 250-923-2848, 888-923-2849; www.heronslandinghotel.com; 492 S Island Hwy; r/ste $155/175; 🖳) This place was formerly one of those old Bavarian pensions that still dot the BC landscape; its new owners have done a good job of updating the property. Most rooms have been fitted with fresh furnishings, bathrooms, and kitchen appliances, while new extras include free wireless access and laundry

($1). Consider the bargain loft room: it's massive and sleeps up to four.

Painter's Lodge Resort (☎ 250-286-1102, 800-663-7090; www.painterslodge.com; 1625 MacDonald Rd; r/ste from $189/275, cabin 245-255; 😷 🖳) More than just a place to stay, this handsome waterfront confection on Discovery Passage is a pampering treat for anyone passing through the region. The spacious rooms are bright and cheery and some have lofts that are perfect for small groups. The resort offers lots of fishing and adventure packages and has a first-class restaurant.

Lookout Seafood Bar & Grill (☎ 250-286-6812; 921 Island Hwy; mains $7-12; 🕑 8:30am-10pm) In business since 1929, this waterfront diner-like spot has better-than-diner food. Oysters, halibut burgers and fish and chips are on the menu and historical photos of Campbell River are on the walls.

Getting There & Around

Campbell River Airport (☎ 250-923-5012; www.crairport.ca) is 20 minutes from downtown. **Pacific Coastal Airlines** (☎ 604-273-8666; www.pacific-coastal.com) services arrive from Vancouver International Airport ($140, 45 minutes, six daily).

Greyhound (☎ 800-661-8747; www.greyhound.ca) buses arrive from Port Hardy, ($38.70, three hours, daily), Nanaimo ($23.90, three hours, four daily) and Victoria ($46, five to six hours, four daily).

Campbell River Transit (☎ 250-287-7433; www.bctransit.com; adult/child $1.75/1.50) operates local buses.

QUADRA & CORTES ISLANDS

Quadra is a quick hop from Campbell River; Cortes is a bit more remote. Together they're the 'Discovery Islands,' either for their location in the Discovery Passage, or the fact they offer condensed versions of the area's natural splendors, with much to discover.

Quadra's **visitor information booth** (www.quadraisland.ca; 🕑 9am-4pm Jun-Sep) is in the parking lot of the Quadra Credit Union, a short uphill walk from the ferry dock. For Cortes information, visit www.cortesisland.com, and for planning a trip around the Discovery Islands, check out www.discoveryislands.ca.

Sights & Activities

Replace the evergreens with palm trees, and Quadra's **Rebecca Spit Provincial Park** (☎ 250-474-1336; www.env.gov.bc.ca/bcparks) could be a

Caribbean postcard. The sandy beaches and clear waters offer excellent swimming and boating access. On Cortes, **Manson's Landing Marine Provincial Park** (☎ 250-474-1336; www.env .gov.bc.ca/bcparks) boasts abundant shorebirds and shellfish, and **Smelt Bay Provincial Park** (☎ 250-474-1336; www.env.gov.bc.ca/bcparks) is ideal for watching the sunset. Nearby **Mittlenatch Island Nature Park** is called the 'Galapagos of Georgia Strait' for its natural diversity.

Near the ferry dock, **Abyssal Diving Charters & Lodge** (☎ 250-285-2420, 800-499-2297; www.abyssal.com) is the island's leading scuba-diving excursion operator. **Coastal Spirits Sea Kayak Tours** (☎ 250-285-2895, 888-427-5557; www.kayakbritishcolumbia.com; tours from $105) offers half-, full-day and sunset tours. For those who don't want to paddle, **Quadra Island Tours** (☎ 250-285-3627; www.quadra islandtours.com; tours adult/child from $29/18) provides boat, bike, and hiking treks.

Sleeping

Smelt Bay (☎ 604-689-9025, 800-689-9025; www.discover camping.ca; campsite $14) Located on Cortes Island this remote campground is 20km from the ferry dock via a paved road. Facilities are predictably rustic, with pit toilets and cold water taps providing the main luxuries.

Gorge Harbour Marina Resort (☎ 250-935-6433; campsite $14.50) Doubling as an RV park, this family-friendly campground has plenty of useful facilities including showers, laundromat, a shop and a restaurant that's open from May to September. Boat and scooter rentals are available for active travelers.

Tsa-Kwa-Luten Lodge (☎ 250-285-2042; 800-665-7745; www.capemudgeresort.bc.ca; 1 Lighthouse Rd, Quadra Island; r/cabins $65/119) Approached via a winding tree-lined road, this First Nations–owned resort on Quadra's southern tip features native art in its wood-accented rooms. Set in 1100 acres of lush green forest with stunning views of Discovery Passage, it's intended as a real retreat, so there are no TVs.

Cortes Island Motel (☎ 250-935-6363, 888-935-6363; www.cortesislandmotel.com; Seaford Rd, Cortes Island; r $79-99) Set amid the tall trees at Manson's Landing, this is a good-value spot. The rooms are a bit basic, with small bathrooms, linoleum-floored kitchens and standard furnishings, but it's one of only a handful of accommodations on the island.

Heriot Bay Inn (☎ 250-285-3322, 888-605-4545; www.heriotbayinn.com; Heriot Bay, Quadra Island; r/cabin/ ste $99/199/249) This beautiful white-painted pioneer-style inn is near the ferry to Cortes. A country-farmhouse look is prominent in the rooms and the cabins are pure rustic and fancy-free. There's a good, on-site restaurant (mains $18-27) that's worth a splurge, and you can book activities ranging from bear watching to sea kayaking.

Whiskey Point Resort (☎ 250-285-2201, 800-622-5311; www.whiskeypoint.com; 725 Quathiaski Rd, Quadra Island; s/d/ste $119/119/149; 🐾 💻) A good-value midrange option overlooking the ferry dock, the rooms at this family-oriented motel-style sleepover all have small kitchens and free wireless access. There's an outdoor hot tub and pool and several packages available; the rates drop massively off-season.

Eating

Amped on Nutrition (☎ 250-285-3142; 658 Harper Rd, Quadra Island; mains $4-8; ⏲ 9am-7pm) Everything is vegan and organic at this sunny spot, where the friendly staff point you towards the hearty soups, bean burgers and heaping salad dishes. Stand your ground and go for the excellent tahini spread sandwich stuffed with sprouts and veggies and follow it with a chunky dessert.

Lovin' Oven II (☎ 250-285-2262; 648 Harper Rd, Quadra Island; mains $4-9; ⏲ 8am-8pm May-Sep, 8am-8pm Tue-Sat Oct-Apr) Home to the best pizza on Quadra (OK, so there's not much competition), the Lovin' also extends to fresh-baked bread and cakes. It's a popular hangout for locals, who drop by for coffee and a gossip.

Old Floathouse Restaurant (☎ 250-935-6631; Hunt Rd, Cortes Island; mains $7-14; ⏲ 11:30am-9pm May-Sep) With a great location overlooking Gorge Harbour Marina and specializing in seafood and West Coast dining, this convivial restaurant has been a regional favorite for years. If it's a sunny day, dine on the patio among the towering trees.

Getting There & Around

BC Ferries (☎ 888-223-3779, 250-386-3431; www.bc ferries.com) services arrive from Campbell River at Quadra's Quathiaski Cove dock (adult/ child/vehicle $5.75/2.90/14.10, 10 minutes, 16 to 18 daily). On the other side of Quadra, ferries leave from Heriot Bay for Whaletown on Cortes Island (adult/child/vehicle $6.80/3.40/17.25, 45 minutes, six daily).

Both Quadra and Cortes are fairly large, so it's something of a challenge to get around without a car: check if your accommodation offers ferry pick-up, **Island Cycle** (☎ 250-285-3627;

Heriot Bay, Quadra Island; rental per day $25) has bike rentals.

STRATHCONA PROVINCIAL PARK

Vancouver Island's largest park, 250,000-hectare **Strathcona Provincial Park** (☎ 250-337-2400; www.env.gov.bc.ca/bcparks) is BC's oldest protected area. Campbell River is the main access point, and Hwy 28 between Campbell River and Gold River cuts across the park's Buttle Lake district. Its Forbidden Plateau area is reached via Courtenay, as is the Mt Washington alpine resort. The park is centered around Mt Golden Hinde (2200m), the island's highest point.

Activities

Strathcona is a hiker's park. In the Forbidden Plateau area, notable trails include the **Paradise Meadows Loop** (2.2km), an easy walk through wildflower meadows; the summit of **Mount Albert Edward** (6.5km); and **Mount Becher** (5km), with great views of the Comox Valley, the Strait of Georgia, and the Coast Mountain Range. The 9km, unmaintained **Comox Glacier Trail** sounds like quite an adventure – and it is – but it's not advised unless you're an advanced hiker.

In the Buttle Lake area, easy walks include **Lady Falls** (900m) and the trail along **Karst Creek** (2km), which winds past sinkholes, disappearing streams and beautiful waterfalls.

Sleeping & Eating

Buttle Lake Campground (☎ 604-689-9025, 800-689-9025; www.discovercamping.ca; campsite $14) This place offers both first-come-first-served and reservable sites. The swimming area and the nearby playground make it a good choice for families.

Ralph River Campground (☎ 604-689-9025, 800-689-9025; www.discovercamping.ca; campsite $14) Located 26km south of the Hwy 28 junction, this campground has non-reservable first-come-first-served sites. Backcountry sites ($5) are available throughout the park.

Strathcona Park Lodge (☎ 250-286-3122; www .strathcona.bc.ca; r/cabins from $50/169) Begun in 1959 as an outdoor education center, Strathcona, on Hwy 28, still takes teaching as its mission. In keeping with its low-impact proximity to nature, there are no telephones or TVs in the rooms, which range from college-style bedrooms to timber-framed cottages. The lodge's array of outdoor programs include

kayaking, ziplining and rock climbing adventures (half-/full day adult $35/63 child $25/44) plus classes in land and marine activities. The casual Whale Room is where wholesome buffet meals (breakfast/lunch/dinner $9.50/9.50/19) are served, and the HiBracer Lounge & Bar is where you'll head for an end-of-day beer. Outside visitors are welcome at these facilities.

GOLD RIVER

pop 1360

The gateway to Nootka Sound, this small burg is a relative newcomer to Vancouver Island. Built in the 1960s for workers in the now-defunct pulp mill, it's a hidden-gem base for sports fishing and hiking excursions.

Gold River is at the end of Hwy 28, 89km west of Campbell River. The **VIC** (☎ 250-283-2418; www.goldriver.ca; 🕑 9am-6pm Jul-Sep) is at the corner of Hwy 28 and Scout Lake Rd.

Sights & Activities

Nootka Sound Service (☎ 250-283-2325; www.mvuchuck.com) uses the *Uchuck III*, a converted WWII minesweeper, to deliver supplies to settlements up-island. It offers a Nootka Sound day trip to Friendly Cove for visitors (adult/child $60/25). The more adventurous can take an overnight trip to Zeballos (single/return $215/335) or further up the coast to Kyuquot (single/return/$260/395). Overnight accommodation and one meal is included, and this is a great way to see some otherwise inaccessible scenery.

Ask at the VIC about organized and self-guided caving tours to the 450m of passages and 16 known entrances of **Upana Caves**, north of town on the gravel road toward Tahsis. If you fancy a fish, **Nootka Sound Fishing Charters** (☎ 250-338-7679, 877-283-7194; www.nootkasoundfish .com) will assist.

Sleeping & Eating

Ridgeview Motor Inn (☎ 250-283-2277, 800-989-3393; www.ridgeview-inn.com; 395 Donner Court; r $79-99) This hilltop motel-style property has impressive views of the inlet. It has surprisingly upmarket rooms, some with gas fires and microwaves. There's a fish cleaning station and barbecues available so you can scoff your catch of the day. The attached Ridge Pub & Dining Room (☎ 250-283-2600, mains $8 to $14) has better-than-average pub food and excellent seafood.

NORTH VANCOUVER ISLAND

Although covering nearly half the island, the wild and rugged northern region only accounts for 5% of its population. That math leads some to argue there's 'nothing up there worth seeing' – how wrong they are. Old-growth rain forests, little-changed pioneer communities and rustic beaches raw with natural beauty: North Island is a rare wilderness treat that's more accessible than almost any other in the world – although your own transport of the 4x4 variety is required for more remote areas. The people are different here, too: while Vancouver Islanders often distinguish themselves by virtue of their 'island mentality,' those in the north have a hardy, independent streak that marks them out from anyone south of Campbell River. For information, contact **Vancouver Island North Visitors Association** (☎ 250-949-9094, 800-903-6660; www.vinva.bc.ca).

SAYWARD & WOSS

The winding, tree-lined 200km stretch of Hwy 19 between Campbell River and Port McNeill has plenty to see. Keep your eyes open for black bears feasting on roadside berries and stop at the lookout for **Seymour Narrows** and **Ripple Rock**, but keep in mind that only Sayward (population 407) and Woss (population 380) have services. The **Sayward information center** (☎ 250-282-3821; www.sayward.com; ☺ noon-6pm Tue-Sun), at Sayward Junction, has a front desker who can recommend area sleeps, eats, and activities.

If you're staying in the area, Sayward's **Fisherboy Park** (☎ 250-282-3204, 866-357-0598; www.fisherboypark.com; 714 Sayward Rd; campsite/s/d $12/49/55) is a short drive from the information center. It's a well-maintained, family-friendly campground with an additional small motel building and some private cabins. Campers have access to a laundromat, showers, and flush toilets and there's also a liquor store.

Woss' **Rugged Mountain Motel** (☎ 250-281-2280; r $55) is a popular sleepover for those biking around the region. The rooms are basic motel-style and there's an adjoining pub and general store.

If it's mealtime when you arrive in Sayward, don't miss the legendary **Cable Cookhouse** (☎ 250-282-3433; 1741 Sayward Rd; mains $7-14; ☺ 8am-9pm), an old café building cocooned in 2700m of steel logging cables. The interior includes 1950s frescoes of regional industrial scenes and the menu features packed sandwiches, surprisingly good salads and smashing fruit pies. The salmon melt sandwich is recommended, and pick up a brick-sized cinnamon bun for the road.

TELEGRAPH COVE

In 1911 it was a lonely telegraph station 190km north of Campbell River, but today Telegraph Cove is a charming boardwalk resort with dozens of buildings standing on stilts above the marina and a picture-perfect pioneer feel. The road into the resort was recently paved for the first time, bringing controversial new housing and hotel developments.

Sights & Activities

The fascinating **Whale Interpretive Centre** (☎ 250-928-3129, 250-928-3117; www.killerwhalecentre.org; admission suggested donation $2; ☺ May-Sep) is stuffed with hands-on artifacts plus the artfully displayed skeletons of wildlife including cougars, sea otters and a giant fin whale hanging overhead.

Hundreds of orcas migrate through Johnstone Strait every year, making Telegraph Cove among the island's best spots to take a marine wildlife boat trek. **Stubbs Island Whale-watching** (☎ 250-928-3185, 800-665-3066; www.stubbs-island.com; tours $69-79; ☺ May-Sep) will get you up close, if the beasts are around, and you might also spot some humpbacks, minkes, dolphins and sea lions.

For a grizzly bear alternative, **Tide Rip Tours** (☎ 250-928-3092, 888-643-9319; www.tiderip.com; tours adult/child from $233/149; ☺ May–mid-Oct) leads full-day trips to local beaches and Knight Inlet. You stay on the boat, so you don't have to get too close. Paddle fans can rent kayaks or take tours via **North Island Kayaks** (☎ 250-949-7707, 877-949-7707; info@kayakbc.ca; rental hr/day from $10/55, tours from $49; ☺ May-Sep).

Sleeping & Eating

Telegraph Cove Resorts (☎ 250-928-3131, 800-200-4665; www.telegraphcoveresort.com; campsite/cabin from $21/99) For years the only sleepover option, this place provides forested tent spaces, a clutch of heritage buildings, and a string of cabins on stilts overlooking the marina. The popular cabins, all without TVs and telephones, are rustic and cozy and all have kitchens. All are good-value for groups, especially cabin six, which has three bedrooms and sleeps up to nine.

Dockside 29 (☎ 250-928-3163, 877-835-2683; www .telegraphcove.ca; d $135, family r $155; ◻) lacks the charm of the old resort but has the ambience and facilities of a good-quality motel. All rooms have kitchenettes with hardwood floors, satellite TVs, waterfront views and free wireless internet access. Family rooms and laundry facilities are available and upper-level rooms have vaulted ceilings.

Killer Whale Café (☎ 250-928-3155; mains $14-18; ⏲ 10am-9pm May-Sep) The cove's best eatery – the seafood linguini of salmon, mussels and prawns is recommended. The adjoining Old Saltery Pub is an atmospheric, wood-lined nook with a central fireplace and Killer Whale Pale Ale.

PORT MCNEILL
pop 2930

Tumbling down the hill almost into Broughton Strait, Port McNeill began as a 1920s logging camp. Today's it's the second-largest North Island community, and while forestry remains its number one concern, it's also a good stop for travelers: there are restaurants and supermarkets and easy access points for wilderness activities. The log cabin **VIC** (☎ 250-956-3131; www.portmcneill.net; 351 Shelley Cres; ⏲ 9am-5pm Mon-Fri May-Sep) can help plan your time here. Its adjoining **museum** (☎ 250-956-9898; ⏲ 10am-5pm Jul-Sep, 1-3pm Sat & Sun Oct-Jun) is bristling with pioneer and logging industry artifacts.

A short walk away, you can check out the ugliest thing you'll ever see. Like an old giant's wart, the **world's largest burl**, removed from a 260ft spruce, sits somewhat unloved in a parking lot. Ask about the region's other great burls on a wilderness guided hike with **North Island Daytrippers** (☎ 250-956-2411, 800-956-2411; www.islanddaytrippers.com). Guide Dave Trebett has lived in the area for 25 years and customizes treks for all fitness and ability levels.

More a top-quality motel than a resort, the hilltop **Black Bear Resort** (☎ 250-956-4900, 866-956-4900; www.blackbearresort.net; 1812 Campbell Way; d/tw/ste $135/155/155; ◻) overlooks the town and is across the street from shops and restaurants. Its standard rooms are small but clean and include microwaves and fridges; full-kitchen units are also available. Rates include a large continental breakfast buffet (with make-your-

own waffles), a free-access computer in the lobby and on-site spa treatments.

For heaping plates of Mexican nosh, plus eye-popping decor that includes orange walls, green tablecloths and the kind of dollar-store ornaments that would make a connoisseur of kitsch blush, **Bo-Banees** (☎ 250-956-2739; 1705 Campbell Way; mains $6-9; ⏲ 8am-10pm) serves burritos, burgers and Lucky Lager, the logger's favorite tipple.

Getting There & Away

Greyhound (☎ 800-661-8747; www.greyhound.ca) buses arrive from Port Hardy ($5.80, 30 minutes, daily), Campbell River ($30.20, 2½ hours, daily) and Nanaimo ($59.30, six hours, daily).

BC Ferries (☎ 888-223-3779, 250-386-3431; www.bc ferries.com) services arrive from Alert Bay and Sointula (adult/child/vehicle $6.80/3.40/17.25, times and schedule vary). Check the schedule carefully: the first and last sailings visit all three locations, then alternate round trips between each island and Port McNeill.

ALERT BAY & SOINTULA

The village of Alert Bay (population 600) on Cormorant Island has an aura both mythical and ancient. Its First Nations community and traditions are prevalent, but its blend with an old fishing settlement makes the place a fascinating day trip. Malcolm Island and the town of Sointula (population 800) is a one-time socialist commune founded in 1901 by Finns, for whom the town's name meant 'harmony.' Drop by the **VIC** (☎ 250-974-5024; www.alertbay.ca; 116 Fir St; ⏲ 9am-4:30pm Mon-Fri).

The excellent **U'Mista Cultural Centre** (☎ 250-974-5403; www.umista.ca; adult/child $5/1; ⏲ 9am-5pm daily Jun-Aug, 9am-5pm Mon-Fri Sep-May) immaculately presents its impressive collection of Kwakwaka'wakw masks and other potlatch items originally confiscated by the federal government. Singing, dancing and barbecues are often held in a scaled-down big house here, while modern-day totem pole carvers usually work out front. At 53m, the world's tallest totem pole was carved in the 1960s and is appropriately placed on the front lawn of the enormous **Big House** which hosts traditional dances in July and August.

Amazing tranquility is the highlight of the lovely, mossy walk among giant cedars at **Alert Bay Ecological Park** (also known as Gator Gardens); an excellent interpretive guide is available at the information center. While Sointula

VANCOUVER ISLAND

is not as tourist oriented as Alert Bay, it does have some great hiking.

Seasmoke Whale Watching (☎ 250-974-5225, 800-668-6722; www.seaorca.com; tours adult/child $89/75) offers a five-hour whale-watching sailing experience aboard its classic yacht, including afternoon tea.

PORT HARDY
pop 4600

Settled by early-18th-century Europeans, this small town at the northern end of the island – 'Where the highway ends and the adventure begins,' according to its tourism slogan – is best known as a gear-up spot for Cape Scott. It's also the arrival/departure point for BC Ferries Inside Passage trips.

The **VIC** (☎ 250-949-7622; www.ph-chamber.bc.ca; 7250 Market St; ☻ 8:30am-6pm Mon-Fri, 9am-5pm Sat & Sun mid-May–Sep, 9am-5pm Mon-Fri Oct–mid-May) also operates the small **museum** (☎ 250-949-8143; 7110 Market St; ☻ 10am-3:30pm Tue-Sat May-Oct), where you can learn about the 8000 years of First Nations history before the Europeans arrived.

Sights & Activities

The weather is often foggy and wet but this area has lots of activities for those hardy enough.

Sea Legend Charters (☎ 250-949-6541, 800-246-0093; www.sealegend.com) offers hiking, diving and whale-watching adventures, while **Vancouver Island Nature Exploration** (☎ 250-902-2662; www.nature-exploration.com; guided tours adult/child from $70/50) can help spelunkers access the wealth of area caves, including sites such as Eternal Fountain and Disappearing River.

For dive fans, **Catala Charters** (☎ 250-949-7560, 800-515-5511; www.catalacharters.net; dive trips from $125) options include trips to Browning Passage. Dripping with octopus, wolf eels and corals, it's one of BC's top cold-water dive sites.

For those who like a paddle, **Odyssey Kayaking** (☎ 250-902-0565, 888-792-3366; www.odysseykayaking.com; tours from $99) can take you on guided tours around Malei Island, Bear Cove, and Alder Bay.

It would be odd if you didn't see deer or elk on the drive up and it's not uncommon to spot black bears or cougars within town limits. But **Great Bear Nature Tours** (☎ 250-949-9496, 888-221-8212; www.greatbeartours.com; tours from $700) can boat you in for a comfortable overnight stay (one to seven days) at its charming floating lodge. Trips are offered from mid-May to

mid-October and prices include transport, accommodations, meals, and guided wildlife viewing.

Sleeping & Eating

C&N Backpackers (☎ 250-949-3030, 888-434-6060; www.cnnbackpackers.com; 8470 Main St; dm/r $25/65) From the outside, it looks like a light industrial unit where you might assemble circuit boards, but the interior of this hostel is completely different, with a hardwood floor lobby, large kitchen and comfortable lounge area. There's a deficiency of windows, however, and the dorm rooms are bare and institutional – how about some color on the walls, guys?

Quarterdeck Inn (☎ 250-902-0455, 877-902-0459; www.quarterdeckresort.net; 6555 Hardy Bay Rd; s/d $105/135) A suite gives you a lot more room (plus a fireplace and Jacuzzi tub) and is worth the extra dollars here, especially if you've been roughing it on the road for a few days. The upper-floor waterfront rooms have excellent views once the clouds burn off, and the on-site IV's Quarterdeck Pub & Dining Room (☎ 250-949-6922, mains $8 to $14) serves traditional bar grub and comfort food and a halibut burger that can't be beat.

Glen Lyon Inn (☎ 250-949-7115, 877-949-7115; www.glenlyoninn.com; 6435 Hardy Bay Rd; s/d/tw $115/125/135) This newly renovated hotel has large rooms with balconies and a decidedly aqua color scheme. Most rooms have fridges and microwaves and some have kitchenettes and heart-shaped Jacuzzi baths. There's an exercise room and laundry facilities and, for ferry catchers, this sleepover is close to the terminal.

Getting There & Around

Pacific Coastal Airlines (☎ 604-273-8666; www.pacific-coastal.com) flights arrive in Port Hardy from Vancouver ($227, one hour, two daily).

Greyhound (☎ 800-661-8747; www.greyhound.ca) buses arrive from Port McNeil, ($5.80, 45 minutes, daily), Campbell River ($38.70, 3½ hours, daily) and Nanaimo ($61.50, seven hours, daily).

BC Ferries (☎ 888-223-3779, 250-386-3431; www.bcferries.com) services arrive from Prince Rupert (adult/child/vehicle $110/56/263, 17 hours, schedules vary) via the Inside Passage route. The company also operates a summer-only Discovery Coast Passage route (adult/child/vehicle from $120/60/241), which serves Bella Coola and at times McLoughlin Bay,

Shearwater, Klemtu and Ocean Falls. Reservations are required.

North Island Transportation (☎ 250-949-6300; nit@island.net; $7) runs a shuttle to/from the ferry terminal via area hotels.

CAPE SCOTT PROVINCIAL PARK & AROUND

It's a 70km gravel road drive from Port Hardy to **Cape Scott Provincial Park** (www.env.gov .bc.ca/bcparks) but it's worth the stones pinging off your paintwork for the chance to access untamed nature in all its glory.

Take the well-maintained, relatively easy 2.5km hiking trail to **San Josef Bay** and you'll stroll from the shady confines of the rain forest right onto one of the best beaches in BC; a breathtaking, windswept expanse of roiling waves, tree-lined crags and the kind of caves that could easily harbor ancient smugglers. You can camp ($5) right here on the beach or just admire the passing ospreys before plunging back into the forest.

With several wooded trails here to tempt you – most are aimed at well-prepared hikers with plenty of gumption – the forest offers moss-covered yew trees, old-growth cedars that are centuries old and a soft carpet of sun-dappled ferns covering every square inch.

Among the giant slugs, you'll also spot historic plaques showing that the area was once settled by Scandinavian pioneers who arrived here from Europe on a promise from the government of a main road link from down-island. Now mostly reclaimed by the forest, the crumbling shacks of these settlers, most of whom eventually left when the road failed to materialize, can still be seen.

One of the area's shortest trails (2km) in adjoining **Raft Cove Provincial Park** (www.env.gov .bc.ca/bcparks) brings you to the crescent beach and beautiful lagoons of **Raft Cove**. You're likely to have the entire 1.3km beach to yourself, although the locals also like to access it for surfing.

Hiking further in the region is not for the uninitiated or unprepared. For information on the area's routes – and progress reports on the development of the **North Island Trail** – visit www.northernvancouverislandtrailssociety .com. For a guided hike in the region, contact **North Island Day Trippers** (☎ 250-956-2411, 800-956-2411; www.islanddaytrippers.com).

On the gravel road out from Cape Scott, make sure you turn off and walk up the signposted trail to **Ronning's Garden**. One of the later Scandinavian settlers, Bernt Ronning lived here until the 1960s, working as a trapper and fisherman, while growing a vast outdoor museum of trees and plants from seeds imported from around the world. His incongruous garden was reclaimed by the forest after Ronning died, but hard-working locals Ron and Julia Moe stripped back the bushes and re-established it in the 1980s. Best known for its towering pair of male and female monkey-puzzle trees (the female was looking sickly on our visit), the garden is a lovely menagerie of nonindigenous plant life. If Ron is around when you arrive, he'll regale you with colorful stories about Ronning's life and he might even hand you a monkey-puzzle seed as a souvenir of your visit.

VANCOUVER ISLAND

Southern Gulf Islands

Once a refuge for US draft dodgers, solitude-seeking eccentrics and hippie Canadians who smoked up and dropped out, the Southern Gulf Islands – including Salt Spring, Galiano, Mayne, Saturna and the North and South Penders – is now a favored and relatively accessible retreat for regional city dwellers. They come for the all-enveloping tranquility associated with this Edenesque clutch of forested rocks, many bristling with gnarly Garry oak trees and colored with flower-strewn meadows. Even the ferry trips to get here are the visual equivalent of a soothing back rub.

Once visitors have restored their equilibrium with a few hours of unhurried beachcombing and a couple of golden sunsets, most discover there's way more to do here than simply breathe deeply and relax. With a high proportion of practicing artists among the islands' cumulative population of 20,000, this is an ideal spot to meet creative types in their workshops and even get handy with a paintbrush or pottery wheel yourself. The locals are also an outdoorsy bunch, so there are lots of activities to partake in, including biking, hiking, kayaking and scuba diving. Surprisingly, the islands also house some good restaurants, often half-hidden around the region like buried beach glass.

Gulf Islanders are usually friendly to visitors, but the islands themselves are not the laid-back utopia they once were. Local politics can quickly become hotter than a sun-baked beach here, usually over the issue of development. While the region was populated with rustic shacks until just a few years ago, slick, glass-sided millionaire holiday homes have colonized many waterfront locations, leading to a tricky balancing act between old-school residents and new-era islanders. It's hoped that the recent creation of the Gulf Islands National Park Reserve (see the boxed text, p194) will help keep the region's magic intact.

HIGHLIGHTS

- Scoffing organic apples at the **Saturday Market** (p195) on Salt Spring Island
- Tootling around the **North and South Penders** (p198) to visit the artists in their creative spaces
- Watching the whales, without even getting on a boat, from the shores of **East Point Regional Park** (p200) on Saturna
- Kayaking around **Mayne Island's** (p201) crenulated coastline
- Catching up on juicy local gossip at the **Hummingbird Pub** (p204) on Galiano

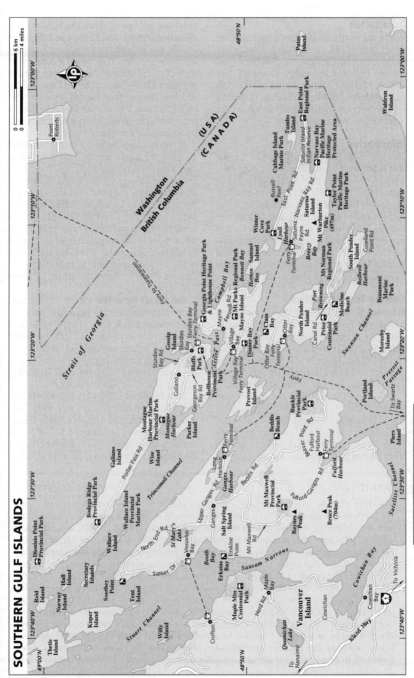

SOUTHERN GULF ISLANDS

Orientation

While the entire Gulf Islands region comprises around 200, mostly uninhabited, rocks in the Strait of Georgia, the Southern Gulf section includes the easily accessible Salt Spring, Mayne, Galiano, Saturna and North and South Pender Islands. Each is reached by regular ferry or floatplane services from the mainland or Vancouver Island.

Information

Dip into local gossip with a copy of the **Gulf Islands Driftwood** (www.gulfislands.net) newspaper, available on ferries or at local Visitor Information Centres (VICs). The free, bi-monthly newspaper **Island Tides** (www.islandtides.com) is also recommended for its news and 'What's on' listings. For a wealth of general information and extensive local listings, visit www.gulfislandsguide.com. For holiday home lets, **Island Vacation Rentals** (☎ 877-662-3414; www.gulfislandvacationrentals.com) is a good place to start.

Getting There & Around

BC Ferries (☎ 888-223-3779, 250-386-3431; www.bcferries.com) serves the main Southern Gulf Islands. There are direct routes from Vancouver Island's Swartz Bay terminal to Salt Spring and North Pender. From North Pender, you can connect to Mayne, Galiano or Salt Spring. From Mayne, you can connect to Saturna.

If you want to travel to the region from the mainland, there is a direct service from the Tsawwassen terminal, near Vancouver, to Galiano, which then connects to North Pender. There are also direct weekend services from Tsawwassen to both Mayne (Sunday only) and Salt Spring (Friday to Sunday). For more frequent services to these and the other islands, you will need to travel from Tsawwassen to Swartz Bay, then board a connecting ferry. If you're using this method, you need to request a 'throughfare ticket' at Tsawwassen, which is cheaper than buying separate tickets for the two legs of your journey. Vehicle reservations are required on some routes and recommended on others.

If you're planning some extensive island hopping, the hassle-free SailPass (four/seven days $164/194) is recommended. It includes round-trip passage for two adults (under-12s are included for free) and a vehicle on each of the mainland to Vancouver Island routes as well as unlimited travel on Gulf Islands and Sunshine Coast sailings. Travel must be on consecutive days and passes must be booked in advance. A popular seven-day circle tour is the Tsawwassen–Gulf Islands–Victoria–Comox–Powell River–Sunshine Coast–Vancouver odyssey.

Gulf Islands Water Taxi (☎ 250-537-2510; www.saltspring.com/watertaxi) runs passenger-only ferries between Salt Spring, North Pender and Saturna (one-way/return $15/25, two daily September to June, one daily July and August) and between Salt Spring, Galiano and Mayne (one-way/return $15/25, two daily September to June, one daily July and August).

Seair Seaplanes (☎ 604-273-8900, 800-447-3247; www.seairseaplanes.com) services run from Vancouver International Airport's South Terminal to Salt Spring (adult/child $77/38.50, 20 minutes, three daily), North Pender ($82/42, 20 minutes, three daily), Saturna ($82/42,

---

PARK IT

More than 200 years after Captain George Vancouver placed this region under British protection, the Southern Gulf Islands received a more environmentally meaningful protected status in 2003 with the creation of the **Gulf Islands National Park Reserve** (☎ 250-654-4000; www.pc.gc.ca/pn-np/bc/gulf). Canada's 40th (and one of its smallest) national parks, it was established to protect the fragile Mediterranean-like ecosystem of a 35-sq-km tapestry of reefs, islets and coastal island stretches. A vulnerable region bordered by increasing development and crisscrossed by transit routes, the area has been a traditional haven for uncounted species of flora and fauna. Plant life given a new lease on life by the creation of the park include the gnarly Garry oak, copper-trunked arbutus, indigo-blue camas lily and the rare phantom orchid. With its protected 25m intertidal zone (Parks Canada also manages an additional 175m area from each shore), the new park also helps to protect California sea lions, orca pods and one of the world's largest octopus species. The park will be in a state of transition for some time as land slowly changes hands, but the federal–provincial plan has been well received by residents who don't want the beauty that drew them here to be overrun with unchecked development.

20 minutes, three daily), Mayne ($82/42, 20 minutes, two daily) and Galiano ($82/42, 20 minutes, two daily).

Harbour Air (☎ 800-665-0212, 604-274-1277; www .harbour-air.com) floatplanes run from downtown Vancouver to Salt Spring and South Pender ($74, 30 to 40 minutes, two to three daily). The company operates a similar service from Vancouver International Airport's South Terminal ($69, 30 to 40 minutes, one to three daily).

It helps to have a vehicle or a bike on the islands, but it's not crucial. Lodgings exist within walking distance of ferry terminals and some places offer free pick-ups. Taxis operate on every island except Saturna.

SALT SPRING ISLAND
pop 10,500
The largest and most populous of the Southern Gulf Islands – it also has Bruce Peak, the area's highest crag – Salt Spring is dotted with orchards, organic farms and art studios. Originally settled by the Salish First Nations, it's an ideal spot for visitors who want to experience the region's rustic charms without sacrificing too many home comforts. Salt Spring is also where many millionaire developers have had their wicked way: there's a string of upscale homes on the drive from the Long Harbour ferry dock.

Orientation
Ganges village is the heart of Salt Spring, and Fulford-Ganges Rd, Long Harbour Rd and Vesuvius Bay Rd are the main routes to its three BC Ferries terminals. Unless you have your own boat or arrive by plane, you'll hit the island at Fulford Harbour (via Swartz Bay) on the south; Long Harbour (via Tsawwassen or another Gulf Island) on the east; or Vesuvius Bay (via Vancouver Island's Crofton) on the west. Beaver Point Rd, near Fulford Harbour, leads to Ruckle Provincial Park on Salt Spring's southeast reach, while North End Rd winds past St Mary Lake toward the island's northern tip.

Information
Ganges has banks, and ATMs can be found at island pubs and stores.
Fulford Harbour post office (☎ 250-653-4313; 101 Morningside Rd; ◷ 8:45am-5pm Mon & Tue, Thu & Fri, 8:45am-12:15pm Wed & Sat)
Ganges post office (☎ 250-537-2321; 109 Purvis Lane; ◷ 8:30am-5:30pm Mon-Fri, 8:30am-noon Sat)

Salt Spring Books (☎ 250-537-2812; 104 McPhillips Rd, Ganges; per min $0.10; ◷ 9am-5pm) Check your email courtesy of the friendly folks here.
Visitor Info Centre (☎ 250-537-5252, 866-216-2936; www.saltspringtoday.com; 121 Lower Ganges Rd, Ganges; ◷ 11am-3pm) The volunteers here are keen to help with maps and resources.

Sights
Harborfront **Ganges** (population 700) is Salt Spring's vibrant focal point. Not just a sleepy village by the sea, it has a creative and artistic vibe, without the hurry-up of larger tourist centers.

This approach is exemplified at the smashing **Saturday Market** (☎ 250-537-4448; www.saltspring market.com; Centennial Park, Ganges; ◷ 8:30am-3pm Sat Apr-Oct), where you'll spend most of your time locked in an internal battle over whether to buy lip-smacking organic fruit (dozens of apple varieties are grown on the island, as well as melons, pears and figs) or hearty home-baked cakes and cookies. Have 'em both and you'll be happy. Then try some piquant products from Salt Spring Island Cheese Company and dip into the wealth of locally made arts and crafts on offer at many stalls.

You can locate and visit many of these artisans in their workshops by downloading a free, 42-studio self-guided tour map from **Salt Spring Island Studio Tour** (☎ 250-537-9476; www .saltspringstudiotour.com). The VIC (above) also has copies. Keep your culture vibe alive with a visit to **ArtSpring** (☎ 250-537-2102; www.artspring.ca; 100 Jackson Ave), a theater with a busy calendar of performances. The village's annual **Fibre Festival** (www.fibrefestival.com; ◷ mid-Jul) also showcases artworks, many of them wearable, created from natural yarns and fabrics. Events include gallery walks and a fashion show.

PARKS & BEACHES
A southeastern Salt Spring gem, **Ruckle Provincial Park** (☎ 250-539-2115; www.env.gov.bc.ca/bcparks) features ragged seashores, arbutus forests and verdant, sun-kissed farmlands. In 1872, Henry Ruckle settled on what is now one of the oldest still-active family farms in British Columbia – it still has some original pioneer buildings and visitors can wander among them. The Ruckles donated most of their land to the government and it now makes up the park's forested hiking trails and 7km of cove-ridden shoreline, complete with tidal pools. There are trails here for all skill levels, with Yeo Point

making an ideal picnic pit stop. Nonreservable **camping** ($14) is available.

South of Ganges, via Cranberry and Mt Maxwell Rds, **Mt Maxwell Provincial Park** (☎ 250-539-2115; www.env.gov.bc.ca/bcparks) offers accessible and quite captivating vistas. The dirt road is steep, so a 4WD is recommended if you're driving. The 588m Baynes Peak climbs far above sea level here, making the Strait of Georgia seem like a bathtub dotted with tiny, green islands. It's a great spot to watch a panoramic sunset.

Popular Salt Spring beaches include **Southey Point** at the island's north end and **Beddis Beach** on the east side, noted for good swimming and sunbathing. Head to **Erskine Bay** or **Vesuvius Bay** for some vivid sunsets. Most beaches are popular with beachcombers and you should keep your eyes peeled for marine wildlife.

Activities

The steep, winding roads here present more of a challenge than a deterrent for cyclists. Pick up a *Heritage of Salt Spring Island* ($8.50) map, showing bike routes, camping sites, parks and historic spots. Proceeds are used to build and maintain local bike trails. Bike rentals (per two hours/day $15/30) are available from **Salt Spring Kayaking** (☎ 250-653-4222; www.saltspringkayaking.com; 2923 Fulford-Ganges Rd, Fulford Wharf; rentals 2hr/day from $30/50).

Paddlers can partake of a range of enjoyable kayak tours – sunset trips are recommended –

with **Island Escapades** (☎ 250-537-2553, 888-529-2567; www.islandescapades.com; 163 Fulford-Ganges Rd, Ganges; tours from $40, rentals 2hr/day from $25/55) or Salt Spring Kayaking (tours from $38). Both offer additional multi-day camping expeditions.

If you prefer to let others do the work, take the enjoyable four-hour maritime meander from Ganges aboard the handsome **L'Orenda sailboat** (☎ 250-538-0084; www.haynes.ca/sail; Ganges Harbour; $49), or let your horse take the strain with a guided trot around Mt Maxwell with **Salt Spring Guided Rides** (☎ 250-537-5761; 121 Wright Rd; per hr $40).

Sleeping

The VIC (p195) has a wealth of accommodation information and there's also a good online listing at www.saltspringtoday.com.

Ganges Campground (☎ 250-537-12109; www.gangescampground.com; 150 Leisure Lane; campsite $20) Located in an open meadow near the harbor and within easy walking distance of the village, you'll soon get to know your neighbors here – especially in summer, when their tent will be a couple of feet away from yours. Popular with families, there are showers and flush toilets and a farm stand selling treats – the smoked salmon pâté is excellent.

our pick Salt Spring Forest Retreat (☎ 250-537-4149; www.saltspringforestretreat.com; 640 Cusheon Lake Rd; d $70-90; ⌨) Located 5km south of Ganges, the island's former hostel has been transformed into a good-value woodland lodge with two bright, spacious bedrooms occu-

---

WHAT'S IN A NAME?

The body of water encompassing the Southern Gulf Islands can be called a strait, channel, passage, sound, archipelago or even canal, but one of the last things it can technically be called is a 'gulf.' In 1792, when Captain George Vancouver was making his way through the area, he made the brief notation 'gulf' before continuing on his way to fame and greatness. Apparently, his brilliance was not questioned and the name 'Gulf Islands' stuck.

In a less erroneous fashion, the original settlers of Salt Spring (the Salish First Nations) named the island after the saltwater springs on its north end; the town of Ganges takes its name from *HMS Ganges,* a 19th-century British Royal Navy ship; Saturna Island was named after the Spanish ship *Saturina;* and Spanish explorer Dionisio Galiano illustrated his vanity by naming that island after himself.

HMS Plumper has perhaps the most claims to Gulf Island namesakes. Dispatched in 1858 to fact-check a few 'cartographical discrepancies,' residents coined the name Plumper Pass for the waters between Mayne and Galiano. Captain Richard Mayne, wanting to give credit where credit was due, renamed the passage 'Active Pass' after the *USS Active,* the first steamship to navigate the waters. But vanity got the better of him also: he named Mayne Island after himself, Pender Island after his second in command and the waterway between Saturna and Pender became the 'new' Plumper Pass.

pying the spots where sweaty backpacker's socks once hung. But it's much more fun to stay in the alternative accommodations that nestle among the trees here. A bright red and exceptionally cozy gypsy caravan, complete with an antique coal stove (it's just for looks: you'll have to use the electric heater to warm up) attracts romantic bohemians. But it's the two hexagonal tree houses that sparks the child-like imaginations of many. Nestled among cedar branches, each is fully insulated and has wicker furnishings, comfy beds and opening windows – the larger one is aimed at families and has its own porch and Winnie the Pooh kids bedding. Close to the beach, bike rentals are available (per day $15) and wireless internet access covers much of the property.

Lakeside Gardens (☎ 250-537-5773; www.saltspring .com/lakesidegardens; 1450 North End Rd; campsite/cabana/ cottage $25/70/125; ◯ Apr-Oct) An old-school wooded retreat where the pristine natural surroundings are the main attraction, this tranquil, family-friendly clutch of cottages and cabanas is ideal for some low-impact fishing, swimming and boating activities. Overlooking the lawn, the simple cottages have fireplaces and a shared hot tub, while the rustic, shack-like beachfront cabanas are great value. Even cheaper are the sprinkling of campsites, which share hot showers with the cabanas.

Seabreeze Inne (☎ 250-537-4145; 800-434-4112; www.seabreezeinne.com; 101 Bittancourt Rd, Ganges; r $105-165; ▢) With many island accommodations moving upscale (with accompanying price increases) in recent years, it's good to know that the family-run Seabreeze is still good value. A short downhill walk to the village, this is a friendly, motel-style sleepover with plenty of added extras. The rooms are spacious and well maintained – some have kitchenettes, sea views and Jacuzzi tubs – and facilities include barbecues, a heated gazebo and an outdoor hot tub. Free wireless internet access is included.

Salt Spring Vineyards (☎ 250-653-9463; www .saltspringvineyards.com; 151 Lee Rd; d $140) Located 6km north of the Fulford ferry terminal, this charming boutique vineyard (is there nothing they can't grow on Salt Spring?) offers a couple of intimate B&B rooms, each with hardwood floors and rustic-chic furnishings. Both have great bathrooms: the Vineyard Room has a Jacuzzi, the Winery Room has

a deluxe bathtub and rain-soak shower and they share an outdoor hot tub. Once you've dried off, stroll over to the winery and try its fruity Pinot Gris.

Madrona Valley Farm (☎ 250-537-1989; www .madronavalleyfarm.com; 171 Chu-An Dr; r/cottage $150/175) Stay at this lovely Victorian B&B 6km from Ganges and you'll learn all about the challenges and pleasures of organic farming: the 2.4 hectares produce fruit, vegetables, herbs and free-range eggs, much of which will appear on your table for breakfast. The rooms (all cleaned with ecologically sound products) combine antique flourishes with high ceilings and views of the farm and surrounding ocean. The farm's secluded, self-catering cottage is ideal for groups or families.

Eating & Drinking

There's a full menu of cozy cafés and increasingly chic bistros in Ganges, with pockets of pubs and diners secreted around the island.

Tree House Café (☎ 250-537-5379; 106 Purvis Lane; mains $5-11; ◯ 8am-dusk May-Sep, 8am-3pm Oct-Apr) This hip outdoor café in the heart of Ganges' action is the kind of place where a hobbit would feel at home. Enjoy a sandwich, espresso or pint on the terrace under the plum tree on a sunny afternoon, or come on a summer evening, when live music is a regular feature.

Barb's Buns (☎ 250-537-4491; 121 McPhillips Ave; mains $6-9; ◯ 7am-5pm Mon, 7am-10pm Tue-Sat, 10am-2pm Sun) Good wholesome treats are the menu mainstays here, with heaping pizza slices, hearty soups and bulging sandwiches drawing the lunch crowd, many of them grateful vegetarians. Others repeatedly fail to resist the mid-afternoon lure of cookies, cakes and, of course, Barb's lovely buns. Organic coffee is de rigueur here.

Oystercatcher Seafood Bar & Grill (☎ 250-537-5041; 100 Manson Rd; mains $8-16; ◯ 10am-dusk) The waterfront views from the two patios here are smashing but the dining at this casual, local favorite is what it's all about. Fresh, regionally caught seafood is the specialty, with delectable oysters and wild salmon particularly popular. It also serves lamb and steak dishes (and beer) for those who are not fish fans.

Restaurant House Piccolo (☎ 250-537-1844; 108 Hereford Ave; mains $20-28; ◯ 5-11pm) Fusing Scandinavian influences with locally sourced ingredients, this elegant, white-tablecloth eatery is well worth the extra bucks. With an intimate, heritage dining room (plus a tiny patio), dishes range from exquisite duck, beef and lamb mains (they eat vegetarians here, too) to the highly recommended seafood meals – if scallops are on the menu, snap 'em up. It also has one of the best wine lists on Salt Spring. Reservations recommended.

Moby's Marine Pub (☎ 250-537-5559; 124 Upper Ganges Rd; ☾ 11am-11pm) Located on the rocky shore, Moby's is up there among Salt Spring's most popular eateries, mainly due to its lively atmosphere, excellent harbor views and good, honest food. The menu features the usual pub grub with seafood cameos. On Sunday, come for brunch in the morning or live jazz in the evening.

Like most islands, Salt Spring is a neighborhood pub kind of place. **Fulford Inn** (☎ 250-653-4432; 2661 Fulford-Ganges Rd; mains $8-14; ☾ 11am-12:30am) on the south end and **Vesuvius Inn Pub** (☎ 250-537-2312; 805 Vesuvius Bay Rd; mains $8-12; ☾ noon-10pm) on the west coast are warm and welcoming spots to rub shoulders with the locals and have your fill of beer and greasy comfort food.

Getting There & Around

BC Ferries (p194) has three terminals on Salt Spring, each serving different destinations. Direct services arrive into Long Harbour from North Pender (adult/child/vehicle $3.95/2/8.10, 40 minutes, one to four daily), into Fulford Harbour from Swartz Bay ($7.05/3.55/23, 35 minutes, eight daily), and into Vesuvius from Vancouver Island's Crofton ($7.05/3.55/23, 20 minutes, 14 daily). See p194 for additional route information.

Gulf Island's Water Taxis (p194) arrives in Ganges from North Pender, Saturna, Galiano and Mayne (one-way/return $15/25, one to two daily).

Seair Seaplanes (p194) arrives in Ganges Harbour from Vancouver International Airport's South Terminal (adult/child $77/38.50, 20 minutes, three daily). **Kenmore Air Seaplanes** (☎ 800-543-9595, 425-486-1257; www.kenmoreair.com) also arrives here from Seattle (US$165, 1½ hours, daily).

If you don't have your own car, **Ganges Faerie** (☎ 250-537-6758; www.gangesfaerie.com) shuttles between the three ferry terminals and the Ganges, Ruckle Park and Fernwood areas ($7.50 to $13), with pick-ups and drop-offs anywhere along the route. **Silver Shadow Taxi** (☎ 250-537-3030) provides cab service.

NORTH & SOUTH PENDER ISLANDS
pop 2200

Originally linked by a sandy isthmus, the North and South Penders are the geographical center of the Gulf and San Juan Islands. But unlike Salt Spring, the Penders are a less obvious vacation destination, traditionally focusing more on their own residents than holidaymakers. This, of course, makes them even more attractive to those looking for a true retreat. With pioneer farms, old-time orchards and almost 40 coves and beaches – along with the now-obligatory millionaire vacation homes – the Penders are a good spot for bikers, hikers and drivers.

Orientation

The ferry terminal is at North Pender's Otter Bay, where most of the islands' residents live – the two landmasses are now joined only by a one-lane road bridge. With no dedicated town center, North Pender's Driftwood Centre shopping plaza is where most people flock for services and gossip, with additional smaller business centers at Port Washington, Hope Bay and several small marinas.

Information

At the **Driftwood Centre** (4605 Bedwell Harbour Rd, North Pender) you'll find a **post office** (☎ 800-267-1177; ☾ 8:30am-4pm Mon-Fri, 8:30am-noon Sat) and an **Auto Centre** (☎ 250-629-3005; ☾ 8:30am-5pm Mon-Sat), with a gas pump, launderette and ATM.

Visitor Info Centre (☎ 250-629-6541, 866-468-7924; www.penderislandchamber.com; 2332 Otter Bay Rd, North Pender; ☾ 9am-5pm Jul & Aug, 9am-5pm Thu-Sun May & Jun) If the VIC isn't open when you arrive, scan the information board listing local lodgings and other businesses.

Sights & Activities

It's worth checking out the sandy expanses at **Medicine Beach** and **Clam Bay** on North Pender and **Gowlland Point** on the east coast of South Pender. Near the canal between the two islands, **Mortimer Spit** is rarely crowded but offers one of the best beaches around.

Just over the bridge to South Pender is **Mt Norman Regional Park**; the hike up its namesake peak (255m) rewards you with grand views of the San Juan and Gulf Islands. The trail can be accessed via Ainslie Point Rd (1km hike) or Canal Rd (2.5km hike). Get out your binoculars to spot smiling Salt Spring Islanders waving at you from their restaurant patios.

Dozens of artists call Pender home. Download a free map of galleries and studios and check out the artists before you arrive via **Pender Creatives** (www.pendercreatives.com).

You can hit the water with a paddle (and hopefully a boat) with the friendly folk at **Kayak Pender Island** (☎ 250-629-6939, 877-683-1746; www.kayakpenderisland.com; 2319 MacKinnon Rd, North Pender; tour adult/child from $39/25), while **Sound Passage Adventures** (☎ 250-629-3920, 877-629-3930; www .soundpassageadventures.com; Port Browning Marina, North Pender) customizes a range of regional eco-tours and scuba-diving trips.

Sleeping

Prior Centennial Park (☎ 604-689-9025, 800-689-9025; www.discovercamping.ca; campsite $14; ☺ mid-May–mid-Oct) Located 6km southeast of the ferry terminal, this former provincial park (it's now part of the Gulf Islands National Park Reserve) is a good base from which to explore North Pender. Nestled among alder and cedar trees, it's within walking distance of two beaches and is popular with kayakers. The fairly basic facilities include a cold water pump, pit toilets and picnic tables.

Inn on Pender Island (☎ 250-629-3353, 800-550-1572; www.innonpender.com; 4709 Canal Rd, North Pender; s/d/cabin $79/89/149) A compact lodge motel situated on 2.8 hectares of wooded land, this spot attracts cyclists and wandering deer in almost equal numbers. While the deer come for the wildflower shoots, the vacationers stop here for the good-value, well-appointed motel rooms or the cool log cabins, complete with their own fireplaces, kitchens and private hot tubs – there are even two-person swings on each deck.

Beauty Rest By The Sea (☎ 250-629-3855; www.pen derisle.com; 1301 MacKinnon Rd, North Pender; d $140-150) There are three private-entrance suites in this large, wooden family home overlooking the water – there are also seated lookout points around the property where you can watch for passing orcas. Our favorite room is the blue-hued Nautica overlooking Port Washington, lined with maritime prints. Extras include a reading room and windowed breakfast nook and there's a private beach for guests.

Arcadia-by-the-Sea (☎ 250-629-3221, 877-470-8439; www.arcadiabythesea.com; 1329 MacKinnon Rd, North Pender; d $175; ☺ May-Sep; ☒) Less than 1km from the ferry terminal, this adults-only sleepover could stand in as a backdrop for *The Great Gatsby*. The three self-contained cottages are bright and pastel-colored – Rose Cottage is

a favorite – and each includes a full kitchen and the kind of relaxing deck you'll want to spend a lot of time on. Not content to end its facilities at the ubiquitous hot tub, the Arcadia also has a tennis court and a heated outdoor pool.

OUR PICK Poet's Cove Resort & Spa (☎ 250-629-2100, 888-512-7638; www.poetscove.com; 9801 Spalding Rd, Bedwell Harbour, South Pender; lodge from $289; ☒) What it lacks in quantity, South Pender makes up for in quality at this luxurious west coast resort. Lodge rooms feature arts and crafts flourishes and patios overlook the water – the perfect spot to sip a glass of wine and check your stock prices. If you've made a killing, transfer to a cottage or villa, complete with fireplaces, home theater systems and huge bathrooms. There's an elegant on-site restaurant (p200) that combines Pacific Northwest classics with international influences, and you can work off your dinner in the swimming pool. There's also an activity center for booking eco-tours, fishing excursions and kayak treks. But if you really want to make your credit card sweat, book a full menu of treatments at the spa, complete with its own eucalyptus steam cave.

Eating

Pender Island Bakery Café (☎ 250-629-6453; Driftwood Centre, 1105 Stanley Point Dr, North Pender; mains $4-8; ☺ 8am-5pm Mon-Sat, 9am-5pm Sun) The locals' coffeehouse of choice, this chatty nook has moved beyond the truck-stop caffeine of most neighborhood hangouts. For a start, the coffee is organic, as are many of the bakery treats, including some giant cinnamon buns that might have you wrestling an islander for the last one. While ciabatta sandwiches are readily available, the gourmet pizzas are the highlight – try the Gulf Islander (smoked oysters, anchovies, spinach and three cheeses).

Memories at the Inn (☎ 250-629-3353; Inn on Pender Island, 4709 Canal Rd, North Pender; mains $8-14; ☺ 5:30-8:30pm May-Sep, 5:30-8pm Wed-Sun Oct-Apr) Specializing in pizzas, this family-friendly neighborhood restaurant also successfully creates seafood dishes like wild spring salmon or crab cakes. Vegetarian options are available and, while the dining room is small, there are additional tables out on the patio for those who prefer alfresco dining.

Islanders Restaurant (☎ 250-629-3929; 1325 MacKinnon Rd, North Pender; mains $17-30; ☺ 5-9pm Wed-Mon) Everything about this place is local: the art on the walls, the music from the speakers, and the ingredients on the menu – except for the baked arctic char and wild arctic musk ox. Try the excellent salmon filet stuffed with cream cheese and baby shrimp and you'll need to schedule a long hike for the next morning. Reservations recommended.

Aurora (☎ 250-629-2100; 9801 Spalding Rd, Bedwell Harbour, South Pender; mains $17-30; ☼ 7:30am-9:30pm) Regional and seasonal are the keywords on the ever-changing menu at the islands' most sophisticated restaurant. Allow yourself to be tempted by a Salt Spring goat cheese tart starter but save room for main dishes like the local seafood medley of crab, scallops and mussels. Dinner reservations are recommended, but if you can't get in head to the resort's casual lounge bar.

Getting There & Around

Direct and non-direct BC Ferries (p194) services arrive at Otter Bay from Galiano (adult/child/vehicle $3.95/2/8.10, 45 minutes to one hour, two to four daily), Mayne ($3.95/2/8.10, 20 to 25 minutes, four to five daily), Salt Spring ($3.95/2/8.10, 40 minutes, one to two daily), Saturna ($3.95/2/8.10, 50 minutes to 1¼ hours, one to three daily) and Swartz Bay ($7.35/3.70/25.35, one to two hours, four to six daily). See p194 for additional route information.

Gulf Island Water Taxis (p194) arrives at Otter Bay from Salt Spring and Saturna (one-way/return $15/25, one to two daily).

Seair Seaplanes (p194) arrives at North Pender's Port Washington from Vancouver International Airport's South Terminal (adult/child $82/41, 20 minutes, three daily).

Having a car isn't crucial since several lodgings are close to the ferry. If you don't have wheels, and your host can't pick you up, catch a **Pender Island Taxi** (☎ 250-629-3555).

SATURNA ISLAND
pop 350

Small, remote and undeniably tranquil, Saturna is a stunning natural retreat, where gently rolling farmlands sit side by side with towering arbutus trees. Almost half the island is now part of the Gulf Islands National Park Reserve (see the boxed text, p194) and the only crowds you're likely to come across are the wild goats that have called the munchable landmass home for more than a century. If you've had enough of civilization and want to be at one with nature, this is the place to be.

Orientation & Information

Download a visitor map from the **Saturna Island Tourism Association** (www.saturnatourism.com). The site also lists local restaurant and accommodations options. The **post office** (☎ 800-267-1177; 101 Narvaez Bay Rd; ☼ 9am-3pm Tue-Sat) is in the General Store. Get some cash before you come – there are no ATMs on Saturna. The ferry docks at Lyall Harbour on the west of the island.

Sights & Activities

Winter Cove Park, on Saturna's northern side, has a white, sandy beach with access to fishing, boating and swimming. The hiking trail that wanders between forest and coastline here is especially lovely in spring, when wildflowers are in bloom. At the top of **Mount Warburton Pike** (497m) you'll find soaring eagles, and smashing views across the islands.

You can partake of tastings and tours at **Saturna Island Winery** (☎ 250-539-5139, 877-918-3388; www.saturnavineyards.com; 8 Quarry Rd; ☼ 11:30am-4:30pm), which has a beautiful post-and-beam main building and an on-site **bistro** (☼ May-Oct) that's popular for lunch.

Whales migrating through the region typically travel between the Gulf and San Juan Islands. Since Saturna is the easternmost of the Gulf Islands, some of the best whale-watching – without getting on a boat – can be seen from the shores of **East Point Regional Park**.

Near the ferry, **Saturna Sea Kayaking** (☎ 250-539-5553; www.saturnaseakayaking.com; 121 Boot Cove Rd; rentals 4hr/8hr $35/50, tours $50-100) offers tours and rentals, along with good advice on paddling the region.

Saturna hasn't been left off the 'places where artists live' list; the tourism association's website (www.saturnatourism.com) catalogues those who welcome visitors.

Sleeping & Eating

There are no Saturna campgrounds and island eateries typically close by 8pm.

East Point Resort (☎ 250-539-2975, 877-762-2073; www.eastpointresort.com; 723 Tumbo Channel Rd; cabin $150) Six individual cabins sit on 16 hectares of forested land (there are lots of hiking trails) at this rustic east coast sleepover. The private sandy beaches and water-facing patios are ideal for watching passing birdlife and migrating whales. All cabins have full kitchens. There's a seven-day minimum stay in summer.

Saturna Lodge (☎ 250-539-2254, 888-539-8800; www.saturna.ca; 130 Payne Rd; d $130-195; 🖳) Unpretentious charm is the common theme at this lovely seven-room sleepover. The country furnishings contrast the coastal setting, but the result is relaxing harmony. Rates include breakfast, but nonguests can also stop in for dinner in the restaurant (mains $24), where regional delicacies like Opal Valley lamb and Queen Charlotte Islands halibut (highly recommended) are offered. Wireless internet access is included. There's a minimum two-night stay in summer.

Pick up picnic goodies at the **General Store** (☎ 250-539-2936; 101 Narvaez Bay Rd; snacks $3-8; 🕑 9am-6pm Mon-Sat, 9:30am-5pm Sun) or drop by for Crab Night, a local favorite, at the adjoining café. Overlooking Plumper Sound, the **Lighthouse Pub** (☎ 250-539-5725; 102 East Point Rd; mains $8-12) is a chatty spot for beer and bar grub.

Getting There & Around

Direct and nondirect BC Ferries (p194) services arrive at Lyall Harbour from Galiano (adult/child/vehicle $3.95/2/8.10, one to two hours, one to two daily), Mayne ($3.95/2/8.10, 35 minutes to 1¼ hours, one to two daily) and Swartz Bay ($7.35/3.70/25.35, one to two hours, two to four daily). See p194 for additional route information.

Gulf Island Water Taxis (p194) arrives from Salt Spring and North Pender (one-way/return $15/25, one to two daily).

Seair Seaplanes (p194) arrives at Lyall Harbour from Vancouver International Airport's South Terminal (adult/child $82/41, 20 minutes, three daily).

You don't absolutely require a car on Saturna, since some lodgings are near the ferry terminal, but there are no taxis or shuttle services to get you around.

MAYNE ISLAND
pop 900

Perhaps the most historic Gulf Island, Mayne was once an important stopover for Gold Rush miners on their way to the mainland. While its time as a main commercial hub has passed, there are several heritage sites to check out, including a pioneer-era church and an agricultural hall. Others might prefer to visit an artist's studio – like its neighbors, Mayne is home to a colorful clutch of writers, musicians and painters.

Orientation & Information

Historic Miners Bay is the island's main hub. Visit the website of the **Chamber of Commerce** (www.mayneislandchamber.ca) for accommodations and restaurant listings, as well as a downloadable *Discover Mayne Island* map. It's a good idea to check the ferry's brochure racks on your way over and it's worth noting that Mayne has no ATMs.

Library (☎ 250-539-2597; 🕑 11am-3pm Wed, Fri & Sat) In Miners Bay, offers free internet access.

Miners Bay Books (☎ 250-539-3112; 400 Fernhill Rd) Next door to the library, it carries a good selection of tomes.

Post office (472 Village Bay Rd, Miners Bay; 🕑 9am-6pm Mon-Fri, 9am-noon Sat)

Sights & Activities

Drop by the wooden agricultural hall in Miners Bay, where the lively **Farmers' Market** (🕑 Sat Jul-Sep) brings out the best in local produce and crafts. The nearby **Plumper Pass Lock-up** (☎ 250-539-5286; 🕑 11am-3pm Fri-Mon late Jun-early Sep) is a tiny museum that served as a 19th-century jailhouse.

Your *Discover Mayne Island* map will highlight many of the most visit-worthy galleries and artisan studios on the island. Among these is the **Mayne Island Glass Foundry** (☎ 250-539-2002; www.mayneislandglass.com; 🕑 10am-5pm Jun-Sep, reduced hours off-season), where recycled glass is used to create a kaleidoscope of jewelry and ornaments – keep an eye out for those cool green slugs.

The south shore's **Dinner Bay Park** has a lovely sandy beach, as well as a **Japanese Garden**. Built by locals to commemorate early-20th-century Japanese residents, it's immaculately landscaped and is lit up with fairy lights at Christmas.

At the island's north end, **Georgina Point Heritage Park** is home to a lighthouse that was established in 1885 and staffed until 1997. The lighthouse and the keeper's house are still there and it's an invigorating place to be when the waves are pounding the shore. There's a small beach here with lots of explorable tidal pools.

For paddlers and cyclists, **Mayne Island Canoe & Kayak Rentals** (☎ 250-539-2667; www.maynekayak .com; 411 Fernhill Rd; kayak rentals 2hr/8hr from $25/45, bike rentals 4hr/8hr $18/25) and **Blue Vista Resort & Kayaking** (☎ 250-539-2463, 877-535-2424; 536 Arbutus Dr; kayak rentals 2hr/4hr from $25/45, bike rentals 4hr/8hr $18/25) rent boats and bikes.

Sleeping & Eating

Mayne Island Eco-Camping (☎ 250-539-2667; www
.mayneisland.com/camp; 359 Maple Dr, Miners Bay; campsite per person $12) Combining oceanfront and
forested sites, this eco-friendly campground
includes an outdoor 'tree shower' where you
can bare it all among the branches. Many
campers arrive here via kayak at the adjacent
pebbly beach (they also welcome traveling
kayakers who just want to drop in for a
shower). Rentals are also available for those
inspired to hit the waves.

Cobworks (☎ 250-386-7790; www.cobworks.com; 640
Horton Bay Rd; cottage $80) If Bilbo Baggins had a
summer cottage, this is what it would look
like. Made from sand, clay and straw, with a
grass-covered roof and cave-like, irregular interiors, Mayne's pioneering cob house (a show
home for a cheap-as-chips building method) is
a self-contained holiday let with a difference.
Make sure you book far in advance – there are
lots of hobbits ahead of you in line.

Mayne Inn (☎ 250-539-3122; www.mayneinn.com;
494 Arbutus Dr; d $99-119) This waterfront hotel
on Bennett Bay has eight bright, spacious
rooms with outstanding east-facing views.
There's a sand volleyball court outside and
funky, owner-created pottery caricatures in
the lobby. The restaurant and bar downstairs
serve up the usual family dining fare but the
huge deck outside has one of the calmest views
on the island.

Tinkerers' B&B (☎ 250-539-2280; www.bbcanada
.com/133.html; 417 Sunset Pl; d $90-115) In Miners
Bay, this charming house overlooking Active
Pass has rooms of various configurations in a
calming garden setting. Language and knife-
sharpening tutorials are offered, or you can
take the 'I'm on vacation' route and laze in the
hammock. The upstairs rooms share a shower,
but they've got the best views.

Oceanwood Country Inn (☎ 250-539-5074, 866-539-
5074; www.oceanwood.com; 630 Dinner Bay Rd; d $179-349)
Hidden behind tall trees and nestled against
the rocky coast sits this unassumingly plush
inn. All rooms are spacious and the views of
Navy Channel are incredible. Rates include
breakfast and afternoon tea in the downstairs
restaurant, which is also open to nonguests for
dinner. The menu is an ever-changing four-
course affair ($55) focused on regional meat,
seafood and produce.

Sunny Mayne Bakery Café (☎ 250-539-2323; Village
Bay Rd; mains $4-10; ♡ 7am-5pm Mon-Sat, 8am-5pm Sun)
This bright and welcoming café is open for
breakfast at 7am (8am on Sunday) and offers
bakery treats, hearty soups, daily-special sandwiches and some great herb crust pizzas. If
it's sunny, sit outside and watch the world go
by or wait for it to come to you: the informal
'Old Geezers Club' meets here every morning
to disperse the local gossip.

Getting There & Around

Direct BC Ferries (p194) services arrive at
Village Bay from Galiano (adult/child/vehicle
$3.95/2/8.10, 25 minutes, three to five daily),
North Pender ($3.95/2/8.10, 25 minutes, three
daily) and Saturna ($3.95/2/8.10, 35 minutes,
two to three daily). Indirect services arrive
from Salt Spring ($3.95/2/8.10, 45 to 85 min-
utes, two daily), Swartz Bay ($7.35/3.70/25.35,
35 minutes to 1¼ hours, six daily) and Tsawwassen ($11.25/5.65/41.50, 1½ hours, one
to two daily). See p194 for additional route
information.

Gulf Island Water Taxis (p194) arrives
from Salt Spring and Galiano (one-way/re-
turn $15/25, one to two daily).

Seair Seaplanes (p194) arrives at Miners
Bay from Vancouver International Airport's
South Terminal (adult/child $82/41, 20 min-
utes, two daily).

Many accommodations offer guest bikes
but if you're not the pedaling type, contact
MIDAS Taxi Company (☎ 250-539-3132).

GALIANO ISLAND

pop 1070

Once you're past the busy ferry terminal,
slender Galiano assumes a quiet, unhurried
approach. In fact, the ferry end – Galiano's
commercial hub – is markedly different to the
rest of the island, which becomes ever more
tranquil and thickly forested as you continue
your drive. Supporting the widest ecological
diversity of the Southern Gulf Islands, the
ribbonlike landmass offers a bounty of activities for marine enthusiasts and landlubbers
alike.

Information

Galiano Chamber of Commerce (☎ 250-539-2233; www
.galianoisland.com) has a **Visitor Info Booth** (☎ 250-
539-2507; 2590 Sturdies Rd; ♡ Jul & Aug) on your right-
hand side as you leave the ferry. Its website is
a font of accommodations, activity and eatery
listings and has several maps. There are no
banks here but there's an ATM at Galiano
Garage near the ferry.

Galiano Island Books (☎ 250-539-3340; 76 Madrona Dr; 🕑 9:30am-5pm, reduced hrs in winter) Has a good travel section.

Post office (23 Madrona Rd; 🕑 9am-4:30pm Mon-Fri, 9am-2pm Sat)

Sights

The sheltered peninsula of **Montague Harbour Marine Provincial Park** (☎ 250-539-2115; www.env.gov.bc.ca/bcparks) offers awe-inspiring sunrises as well as lush sunset vistas. A trail leads through the ecological hodgepodge of white shell beaches, open meadows, towering forests and a cliff carved by glacial movements.

Bluffs Park boasts great views of Active Pass, along with 5km of hiking trails. Known for its abundant and colorful birdlife, **Bodega Ridge Provincial Park** (☎ 250-539-2115; www.env.gov.bc.ca/bcparks) contains some sheer drop-off viewpoints. Tiny **Bellhouse Provincial Park** (☎ 250-539-2115; www.env.gov.bc.ca/bcparks), the island's easternmost point, looks over Active Pass and the incoming and outgoing ferries.

Activities

Galiano's sandstone cliffs are best appreciated from offshore; the protected waters of Trincomali Channel and the chaotic waters of Active Pass satisfy paddlers of all skill levels. **Gulf Island Kayaking** (☎ 250-539-2442, 888-539-2930; www.seakayak.ca; Montague Marina; rental 3hr/day $28/48, tours from $40) will help with rentals and specializes in multi-day tours. It also rents canoes.

For dive fans, Alcala Point with its friendly wolf eels, Baines Bay with its anemone walls, and the sunken Point Grey tugboat – plus the ever-present possibility of meeting a giant Pacific octopus – make Galiano a popular spot for those with their own scuba gear.

You can explore the island at your own pace with a bike from **Galiano Bicycle** (☎ 250-539-9906; 36 Burrill Rd; rental 4hr/day $23/28), or if you want company consider a customized guided tour with Bodega Ridge (right). To take in the island's vistas by moped, head to Montague Harbour and rent from **Galiano Adventures** (☎ 250-539-3443, 877-303-3546; www.galianoadventures.com; 300 Sticks Allison Rd; rental 3hr/day $18/79). It can also rent you a boat (per hour from $36) if you want to explore the region from the water.

Sleeping

Montague Harbour Marine Provincial Park (☎ 604-689-9025, 800-689-9025; www.discovercamping.ca; campsite $17) With 25 drive-in and 15 walk-in sites, this

LIGHTS, CAMERA, SLEEP

Galiano provides an unusual retreat for traveling cinephiles with its **Gulf Islands Film & TV School** (☎ 250-539-5729, 800-813-9993; www.giftsfilms.com; packages from $345). Billing itself as a 'film boot camp' it's mainly aimed at teaching teenagers the art of filmmaking through various courses. It has programs for adults, as well, and every student leaves with a complete, original video. Accommodations are of the shared, hostel variety and sessions are organized by age group and movie genre. Rates range from $345 for a weekend workshop and include tuition, room and board.

is a popular campground with outdoor types, many of whom are kayaking or biking their way around the island. Facilities are basic (there are no showers but there are pit toilets and cold water taps) and there's a fascinating 'floating nature house' offering eco-educational programs throughout the summer.

Bodega Ridge Lodge & Cabins (☎ 250-539-2677; www.bodegaridge.com; 120 Manastee Rd; d $125-150; 🖳) It's hard to imagine a more peaceful retreat than this north island nest of cabins, in a wooded area of arbutus trees and rolling grass hills. The seven fully equipped, two-story log homes (each with three bedrooms) are furnished in rustic country fashion, as are the two B&B rooms in the lodge. Wireless internet access is included and bike rentals are also offered.

Island Time B&B (☎ 250-539-3506, 877-588-3506; www.islandtimebc.com; 952 Sticks Allison Rd; d $165-195) It's enough that this place enjoys a spectacular wooded setting right on the water, but hospitality and comfort are taken up a notch when you wander down to enjoy an English breakfast made by real English people (the owners hail from the Old Country). The east-facing wall is seemingly constructed from glass, so you may spend the bulk of your time glued to the windows watching the surf.

Galiano Oceanfront Inn & Spa (☎ 250-539-3388, 877-530-3939; www.galianoinn.com; 134 Madrona Dr; r $249-299; 🖳) This Sturdies Bay villa houses 10 elegant, Tuscan-style rooms, each with a fireplace and romantic ocean terrace. The ambience is sophisticated and soothing and the amenities include a spa where you can choose outdoor treatments in the flower garden. The fine-dining restaurant (mains $18 to

$30) – the smoked duck ravioli is a winner – has some great BC wines. Wireless internet included.

Eating & Drinking

Daystar Market Café (☎ 250-539-2505; 96 Georgeson Bay Rd; mains $4-8; ❧ 10am-5pm Mon-Wed, 9am-6pm Fri, 10am-6pm Sat, 9:30am-5pm Sun) Where the locals hang out, this funky little spot is an ideal mid-morning pit stop (gotta love those chunky cranberry muffins). The hearty salads and thick sandwiches are likely to entice you back for lunch and the organic juices and fruit smoothies will bring you back the next day. Why not just move in?

Max & Moritz Spicy Island Food House (☎ 250-539-5888; 322 Clanton Rd; mains $4-8; ❧ 8am-7pm Apr-Sep) Cornering the market in Indonesian and German combo menus, this busy vending van at the ferry terminal is hard to beat for comfort food. The service is fast and friendly but it's worth getting in the ferry line early to tuck into an array of curried dishes and scaschliktasche – grilled meat and vegetables in a pita.

La Berengerie (☎ 250-539-5392; 2806 Montague Rd; mains $12-24; ❧ 5-11pm) Tucked along a winding, tree-lined drive in a shack that looks like it has seen better days, La Berengerie is a culinary adventure. Overseen by Huguette Benger, a quiet, twinkly eyed middle-aged chef who moved here from Avignon more than 20 years ago, her daily-changing menu fuses rustic French bistro approaches with whatever is available locally. Sit outside on the patio, where there's an open fireplace.

Hummingbird Pub (☎ 250-539-5472; 47 Sturdies Bay Rd; mains $8-12; ❧ 11am-midnight Sun-Thu, 11am-1am Fri & Sat) Where locals and visitors sup together, the Hummingbird's huge log columns and chatty outdoor deck lend this pub a comfortable, down-to-earth feel. The menu is full of the usual bar classics and the pub runs a May to September shuttle to and from Montague Harbour, so feel free to drink as much as you like.

Getting There & Around

Direct BC Ferries (p194) services arrive at Sturdies Bay from Mayne (adult/child/vehicle $3.95/2/8.10, 30 minutes, three to four daily), Swartz Bay ($7.35/3.70/25.35, 70 minutes, two to three daily) and Tsawwassen ($11.25/5.65/41.50, one hour, two daily). Indirect services arrive from North Pender ($3.95/2/8.10, 45 to 55 minutes, two to four daily), Salt Spring ($3.95/2/8.10, one to two hours, one to two daily) and Saturna ($3.95/2/8.10, one to two hours, one to two daily). See p194 for additional route information.

Gulf Island Water Taxis (p194) arrives from Salt Spring and Mayne (one-way/return $15/25, one to two daily).

Seair Seaplanes (p194) arrives at Montague Harbour from Vancouver International Airport's South Terminal (adult/child $82/41, 20 minutes, two daily).

Go Galiano Island Shuttle (☎ 250-539-0202; www .gogaliano.com) provides a bus service for the Saturday ferries from Vancouver (from $3.50, July to September only). Reserve in advance. The rest of the time, it runs a taxi service – book before you arrive.

Fraser-Thompson Region

While the stereotypical view of BC is one of tranquil rain forests, glassy lakes and verdant, tree-covered mountains, the Fraser-Thompson region is where the clichés begin to crumble.

East of the Lower Mainland on Hwy 7, the expansive, mountain-fringed Fraser Valley is parted by a mighty river that sustains lush meadows, low-lying woodlands and the giant farms that feed the West Coast. While the coiffured agricultural plots, spreading across the valley floor like huge patchwork blankets, indicate that human endeavors have tamed nature here, a glimpse at the looming mountains suggests otherwise.

Once the farms shrink away, the Fraser Canyon takes over. It's an uncompromising area of jagged peaks and fierce rivers where nature is barely kept at bay by a series of small towns. While the valley's Harrison Hot Springs may be one of BC's most tranquil villages, it's only a couple of hours from the canyon town of Lytton, where the Fraser and Thompson Rivers collide. For outdoor fans who like a challenge, this is destination central for calf-hardening hikes, backcountry camping, and white-water rafting that would raise anyone's heart rate.

Continuing east to the Thompson Valley, the scenery becomes even wilder, as the climate begins to dry out, livestock ranches take over and the mountains become dusty and stubbled with scrub. Welcome to the start of cowboy country; a region of pioneer towns that have been here since the gold rush and that now attract visitors with their rugged charms and frontier land panoramas. While the city of Kamloops is a major draw here, this area is a great base for natural pursuits. The hikes are spectacular and, since this is high country, the skiing – especially at Sun Peaks – is second-to-none.

HIGHLIGHTS

- White-water rafting around **Lytton** (p212) where the Fraser and Thompson Rivers clash

- Sliding around the village at **Sun Peaks Resort** (see the boxed text, p217) during the annual Icewine Festival

- Taking the warming waters of **Harrison Hot Springs** (p209) at the public pool or the spa hotel

- Trundling along the rails from **Kamloops** (p213) on a handsome old steam train

- Biking the exhilarating Poland Lake Trail at **EC Manning Provincial Park** (p211) and acquiring several layers of mud in the process

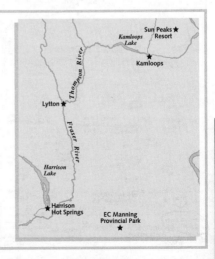

THE FRASER CANYON & THOMPSON VALLEY

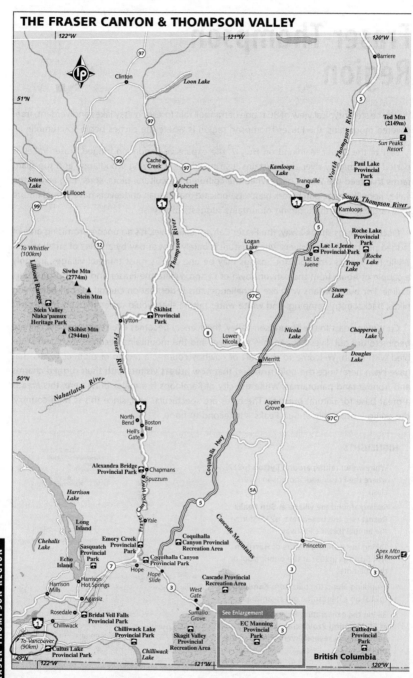

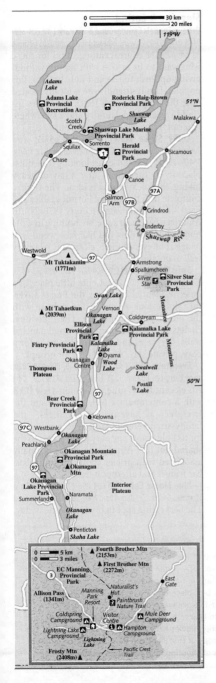

FRASER CANYON

When pioneering explorer Simon Fraser paddled up the river here in 1808 – generously lending his name to the canyon, valley and waterway in the process – he would have seen an area rich in forests and meadows leading to a natural wonder that rivals the Grand Canyon. Between the Lower Mainland and the town of Hope, the Fraser Valley is all about farmland, but beyond Hope lies the extremely rugged Fraser Canyon, where gold rush pioneers battled through on their way to search for glittering riches. It's a shame they didn't stop to take in the sights. The small towns, roiling rivers and accessible wilderness here make for some great stopovers on your way through – since the gold rush is over, you have no excuse for not sticking around, and it's also a highly recommended weekend trip from Vancouver for those who've had enough of city life. For information on traveling in the canyon area, contact **Explore Gold Country** (☎ 877-453-9467; www.exploregoldcountry.com).

HOPE

pop 6600

Theories abound on how this old Hudson's Bay Company fort got its name, but Vancouverites will say once you head past here you're literally 'beyond Hope.' Apart from retelling this tired old gag, the main reason to visit the former pioneer settlement – 'Gateway to Holidayland' as the perimeter sign says – is to access the verdant natural wonderland that rings the town, looming on the edges as if it's ready to reclaim the area at any moment. The Fraser and Coquihalla Rivers join at Hope and the town is tucked between the Cascade and Coastal Mountain ranges.

Hwys 1, 3, 5 and 7 converge east of Hope making it the standard pit stop on the way to or from the interior. You'll also see legions of bleary-eyed Greyhound bus travelers wandering the streets waiting for their connections and not really knowing where they are. Tell them they're on Vancouver Island.

Information

Blue Moose Café (p208) You can check email here (per 20 minutes $1).

Fraser Canyon Hospital (☎ 604-689-5656; 1275 7th Ave)

Post office (☎ 800-267-1177; 777 Fraser Ave;
☽ 8:30am-5pm Mon-Fri)
Visitor Info Centre (VIC; ☎ 604-869-2021, 866-4673-
842; www.hope.ca; 919 Water Ave; ☽ 9am-5pm) Offers a
backpack full of suggestions for local outdoor activities and
produces a free guide for day-trippers.

Sights & Activities

Most visitors amble over to **Memorial Park** in
the town center with its **Friendship Garden**, built
by local Japanese-Canadians, and **chainsaw
carvings** created by Hope artist Pete Ryan.
Built in 1861, the nearby Anglican **Christ
Church** (☎ 604-869-5402; 681 Fraser Ave) is one of
the oldest BC churches still used for regular
services.

Don't miss out on the formidable **Othello-
Quintette Tunnels** in **Coquihalla Canyon Provincial
Park** (☎ 604-795-6169; www.env.gov.bc.ca/bcparks; ☽ Apr-
Oct), which reveal awesome canyon views and
eyebrow-raising engineering prowess. Cut by
hand for the Kettle Valley Railway (see p238)
between 1911 and 1919, they are now the trailhead for a popular hiking route.

If your trekking muscles crave more, **Hope
Mountain School** (☎ 604-869-1274; www.hopemountain
.org; treks from $99) offers guided hikes with themes
like birding, alpine flowers and fall foliage.
You can also raft (from $99) and kayak (from
$85) the Fraser River with them. **Fraser River
Raft Expeditions** (☎ 604-863-2355, 800-363-7238; www
.fraserraft.com; trips from $120) will also get you out
on the water, with heart-pumping one- to
six-day trips throughout the region. For an
alternative, bird's-eye take on the area, the
Vancouver Soaring Association (☎ 604-869-7211;
www.vsa.ca; flight $120) offers exhilarating 20- to
30-minute introductory glider flights from
its Hope Airport base.

If you're here in late July, consider dropping
by the hopping **Hope Music Fest** (☎ 604-869-2021;
www.hopemusicfest.com) at venues around town.

Sleeping & Eating

Othello Tunnels Campground & RV Park (☎ 604-869-
9448, 877-869-0543; www.othellotunnels.com; 67851 Othello
Rd; campsite $20) A great campground for those
who want to be at one with nature without
giving up flush toilets and hot showers, this
popular, family-friendly site is ideally located
near the famed tunnels (left). Amenities include a small shop, laundry and a lake where
you can try to catch rainbow trout.

Lucky Strike Motel (☎ 604-869-5715; www
.luckystrikemotel.com; 504 Old Hope Princeton Way; s/d/tw
$64/74/89; ☻) For those just looking for a quiet
place to lay their head after a day of heavy
hiking, the Lucky Strike is ideal. The rooms,
complete with the kind of Formica tables and
fuzzy sofas found in almost every 1970s North
American basement suite, are nothing to write
home about, unless you like fake wood wall
panels, but everything is clean and relatively
well maintained.

Swiss Chalets Motel (☎ 604-869-9020, 800-663-4673;
456 Hwy 1; cabins $105; ☻) A cute little place in a
quiet residential area near the Fraser River,
this alpine-look sleepover fits right in with
the mountainous backdrop. The individual
chalets with dark brown trim, wood paneled
walls, fireplaces and kitchenettes make for a
cozy, private stay. A good deal for groups.

Evergreen B&B (☎ 604-869-9918, 800-810-7829;
www.evergreen-bb.com; 1208 Ryder St; s/d $119/129; ☻)
An elegant three-suite, mountain-view B&B
with a contemporary feel, the rooms at the
Evergreen all have private entrances – the
family-sized Serenity Suite is recommended
for its bold colors and easy patio access to the
shared hot tub. Among the extras normally
associated with pricier spots are bathrobes,
bar fridges and afternoon tea.

Blue Moose Café (☎ 604-896-0729; 322 Wallace
St; mains $4-10; ☽ 8am-10pm Mon-Sat, 9am-10pm Sun)
The best eating spot in town anytime of day,

HOPE & PROSPERITY

The obvious star of carnage-heavy *First Blood*, first of the *Rambo* movies, was Sylvester Stallone,
but a nod for best supporting actor should go to Hope. In the fall of 1981 a crew of Hollywood
set designers arrived with tools and American flags in hand to create buildings and false fronts
to convert Hope into the small-town American birthplace of John Rambo. Fortunately, the old
'Welcome to Hope' sign at the southern entrance to town was retained and is seen in the movie's
opening scenes. Canyons, rivers, even the Othello-Quintette Tunnels played a significant role, and
the natural beauty of the area got real ugly. Other movies have been filmed in Hope since, but
this movie has such a cult-like following that a copy of *First Blood* can be viewed in the museum,
and the VIC has directions for self-guided tours of shooting, pun intended, locations.

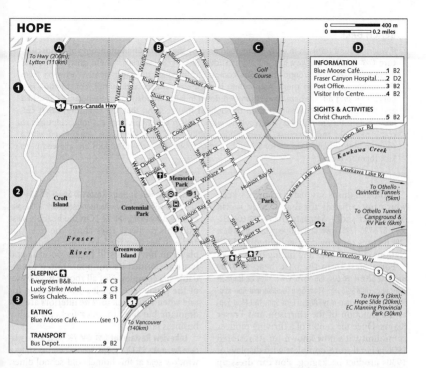

HOPE

| | 0 | 400 m |
| 0 | | 0.2 miles |

INFORMATION
Blue Moose Café...............**1** B2
Fraser Canyon Hospital.....**2** D2
Post Office........................**3** B2
Visitor Info Centre............**4** B2

SIGHTS & ACTIVITIES
Christ Church....................**5** B2

To Hwy (200m);
Lytton (110km)

Trans-Canada Hwy

Golf Course

Kawkawa Creek

Kawkawa Lake Rd

Kawkawa Lake Rd

Union Bar Rd

To Othello
Quintette Tunnels
(5km)

To Othello Tunnels
Campground &
RV Park (6km)

Croft
Island

Centennial
Park

Memorial
Park

Park

Fraser
River

Greenwood
Island

Old Hope Princeton Way

To Hwy 5 (3km);
Hope Slide (20km);
EC Manning Provincial
Park (30km)

SLEEPING
Evergreen B&B..................**6** C3
Lucky Strike Motel............**7** C3
Swiss Chalets....................**8** B1

EATING
Blue Moose Café.............(see **1**)

TRANSPORT
Bus Depot........................**9** B2

Flood Hope Rd

To Vancouver
(140km)

the funky, art-lined Blue Moose is a chatty local hangout that's ideal for a mid-afternoon cake and cappuccino. For something more substantial, the well-stuffed panini sandwiches – the veggie-friendly Greek variety is best – and the house-prepared soups and nacho-plates are worthwhile. Live music is scheduled about once a month, usually on weekends.

Getting There & Away

Greyhound Canada (☎ 800-661-8747; www.greyhound .ca) bus services arrive in Hope from Vancouver ($20.45, 2½ hours, nine daily), Chilliwack ($8.35, 35 minutes, eight daily), Kamloops ($33.35, 2½ hours, five daily) and Kelowna ($38.70, three hours, four daily).

HARRISON HOT SPRINGS & AROUND
pop 1600

Fanning around the southern end of a 60km-long lake, Harrison has been a resort destination for Vancouverites for more than a century. But the Victorian-era locals didn't just come here to amble along the sandy crescent beach and stare at the rugged mountain-locked water; they came for the hot springs, already revered for centuries by local Coast Salish people. Drop into the **Visitor Info Centre** (☎ 604-796-5581; www.harrison.ca; 499 Hot Springs Rd; ⊙ 9am-5pm May-Oct) on your way into town for more about the region.

Sights & Activities

The hot springs are a five-minute walk west of the lake but aren't open to the public. Their waters are pumped into the **Public Hot Pool** (☎ 604-796-2244; cnr Lillooet Ave & Eagle St; adult/child $9/7; ⊙ 9am-9pm), where you can cavort in tropical comfort.

The lake has been steadily growing in popularity for all manner of watery activities. If you fancy boating (per hour from $135) or Sea-Dooing (per hour $80), **Harrison Water Sports** (☎ 604-796-3513; www.harrisonwatersports.com; ⊙ 10am-6pm) at the marina will take care of you with its rentals and charters. You can also whiz around the area on a mountain bike (per hour $6) or 49cc scooter (per hour from $28.10) from **Harrison Scooter Rentals** (☎ 604-796-8955; www.ganobles.ca; 439 Lillooet Ave; ⊙ 10am-4pm Thu-Mon).

FRASER-THOMPSON REGION

BEACH BALL

If you're around Harrison in early September, drop by the **World Championships of Sandsculpture** (☎ 604-796-5581; www.harrisand.org; adult/child $8/5; 🕑 8:30am–dusk), where gritty teams and master soloists from around the globe compete to produce the most creative artworks from the grains surrounding them. Astounding in their size, artistry and humor, construction is a nerve-wracking affair where sand is tamped down in large wooden forms then carved, brushed and shaped – fingers remain crossed throughout the weekend that the sculptures don't collapse before they're finished. The resulting works, which can range from abstract sculptures to comic dioramas and, of course, several huge, multiturreted fairy-tale castles, are sprayed with a solution and displayed on the beach until mid-October, when the local kids are allowed in to kick them to pieces.

Although this is Sasquatch country – keep your camera handy for that *Weekly World News* cover shot – **Sasquatch Tours** (☎ 604-991-0613, 877-796-1221; www.sasquatchtours.com; treks from $29) focuses on providing enlightening First Nations cultural boat and hiking treks.

For a blast from the past, head to **Kilby Historic Site** (☎ 604-796-9576; www.kilby.ca; Harrison Mills; adult/child $8/6; 🕑 11am-5pm Thu-Mon mid-Apr–mid-May, 11am-5pm mid-May–Aug, 11am-5pm Thu-Mon Sep) at the junction of the Harrison and Fraser Rivers. Once the center of a thriving pioneer community, it's now known for its restored 1906 general store, complete with displays of 1930s product packaging. You can dress up in period costume, feed the farm animals and wander around the buildings.

Sleeping & Eating

Bungalow Motel (☎ 604-796-3536; www.bungalowmotel.com; 511 Lillooet Ave; cabins $75-100; 🐕) The 12 individual cabins here, most with kitchenettes and small fridges, are bigger than they look from the outside. VCRs are available for those rainy days and there's a heated outdoor pool if the sun kicks in. Popular with families, there are picnic tables and barbecue facilities around the grounds. The on-site ice cream and coffee bar is handy.

Harrison Beach Hotel (☎ 604-796-1111, 866-338-8111; www.harrisonbeachhotel.com; 160 Esplanade Ave; r/ste from $150; 🐕 🐕) There's a swish, contemporary feel to this bright new boutique property that makes it a breath of fresh air when compared to many regional hotels and motels. Large picture windows are much in evidence in the 42 rooms and suites, even those that have the cheaper mountainside views. If you're traveling in a group or staying longer, the spacious kitchen suites are recommended.

Harrison Hot Springs Resort & Spa (☎ 604-796-2244, 800-663-2266; www.harrisonresort.com; 100 Esplanade Ave; d from $175; 🐕 🐕) On the beach's west side, this property rises above the tree tops and watches over the lake. Once the only big player in town, it's still hugely popular and has transformed its hot pools into a formidable spa complex. Not all rooms have views of the glassy lake, but it's worth asking for one when you check in. The interiors are not dramatic but have the slick feel of a quality business hotel.

Lakeview Restaurant (☎ 604-796-9888; 2150 Esplanade Ave; mains $5-12; 🕑 8am-8pm) Try and snag a window seat at this homely old-school diner, then tuck into some smashing fish and chips. It's been a local fixture for more than 50 years – some regulars look like they've been here since opening day – and the menu hasn't changed much, but at least they're now experts at cooking schnitzels and ham steaks. Order takeout and hit the beach for an alfresco lunch.

Getting There & Away

Driving from Vancouver, head east on Hwy 1 then take exit 135 to Agassiz. Follow Hwy 9 through Agassiz to Harrison. The journey should take around 90 minutes.

EC MANNING PROVINCIAL PARK

East of Hope on Hwy 3 in the heart of the Cascade Mountains, this is the ideal **park** (☎ 604-795-6169; www.env.gov.bc.ca/bcparks) to encounter the region's magnificent dark forests, rushing rivers and craggy peaks. It's a year-round affair, with visitors flocking in for both summer treks and winter alpine adventures. A model of diversity, the 71,000-hectare park includes easy access interpretive trails (some with wheelchair access) where you'll encounter up to 200 bird and 60 mammal species. Manning also marks the end of the 4240km Mexico to Canada **Pacific Crest Trail**.

The **Visitor Info Centre** (☎ 250-840-8836; ⊙ 8:30am-4:30pm Jun-Oct, 8:30am-4pm Mon-Fri Oct-May) has detailed hiking descriptions and a 3D relief model of the park. If you're headed out on a hike, fill your bottle with mountain water at the faucet near the resort's parking lot.

Activities

Manning is dripping with activities, including canoeing, fishing, biking, skiing, horseback riding and almost 200km of often strenuous hikes. Drop by the VIC for details or stay at the resort (right) to combine comfort and outdoorsy camaraderie.

Visitors looking for a gentle **hike** through the wilderness should consider the 9km (two to three hours) Lightning Lake Loop, which meanders around four lakes. In contrast, the Dry Ridge Trail (3km) crosses from arid interior to alpine climate and is excellent for wildflowers and natural vistas. The more challenging Heather Trail (21km) is usually an overnight hike. It takes in premier alpine scenery and lovely lupine meadows – make sure you bring the bug spray.

Bike fans will have a blast here, since there are dozens of great trails. If you don't have your wheels with you, you can rent at the resort (right; from $11.35 per hour). Among the popular trails are Little Muddy (5km), South Gibson (3.5km) and the more challenging Poland Lake Trail (16km).

If you're here in winter, there are 140 acres of **ski** and **snowboard** terrain at Manning, with four lifts and 25 marked trails accessed via the resort (day pass adult/youth/child $41/35/29). You can also **snowshoe** and **cross-country ski** in the area. Manning Park winter specialists **Sigge's** (☎ 604-731-8818; www.sigges.com) rents equipment and offers a host of cross-country ski treks in the region – it also teaches novices how to do it on a fun day-out excursion (adult/child from $99/109).

Sleeping

For **camping** (☎ 604-689-9025, 800-689-9025; www.discovercamping.ca; campsite summer/winter $22/17), the park has four summer drive-in campgrounds and two areas set aside for winter campers. In summer, head to Coldspring, Hampton, Mule Deer or Lightning Lake; in winter you'll have to head to Lightning Lake or Lone Duck. Book ahead in summer. There are also 10 wilderness campgrounds throughout the park ($5 per night).

Manning Park Resort (☎ 250-840-8822, 800-330-3321; www.manningpark.com; r/ste/cabin $164/184/229) The resort dominates the area, hosting many of the activities for visitors who prefer not to encounter the park alone. Its lodge rooms and cabins are the park's only indoor accommodations. All have a comfortable, rustic charm with many enjoying mountain views. As well as hosting the ski slopes, the resort is bursting with additional year-round activities.

Getting There & Away

Direct **Greyhound Canada** (☎ 800-661-8747; www.greyhound.ca) bus services arrive at Manning Park Resort from Vancouver ($37.85, three to four hours, three daily), Hope ($13, 50 minutes, one daily) and Chilliwack ($21.05, 1½ hours, two daily).

HOPE TO LYTTON

North of Hope, Hwy 1 takes a field trip through the handsome steep-sided scenery and glacial creations of the monumental Fraser Canyon. Make use of the many roadside pullouts to stop and enjoy the view. It's traditional to honk your horn while passing through the **Seven Canyon Tunnels** that were blasted through the mountains between Yale and Boston Bar.

Founded by – big surprise – the Hudson's Bay Company, **Yale** (population 17) marked the furthest point paddle wheelers could go during the gold rush, making it allegedly the largest city north of San Francisco at the time. Check out the **Pioneer Cemetery** and **Yale Museum** (☎ 604-863-2324; 31187 Douglas St; adult/child $4.50/2.50; ⊙ 10am-5pm May-Oct) for a glimpse of this colorful past.

North of Yale on Hwy 1, you'll hit **Alexandra Bridge Provincial Park** (☎ 604-795-9169; www.env.gov.bc.ca/bcparks). The 1861 bridge can be admired – especially for its graffiti – as it still spans the Fraser, although traffic now uses the 1926 replacement.

Tourists often pass this way en masse to get to **Hell's Gate Airtram** (☎ 604-867-9277; www.hellsgateairtram.com; adult/child $15/9; ⊙ 10am-4pm mid-Apr–mid-May, 9:30am-5:30pm mid-May–Aug, 10am-4pm Sep–mid-Oct). The tram is neither scary nor exhilarating, and if you can't justify the cost, it is possible to walk down a steep 1km switchback to the bridge – trains can arrive here without warning, so be careful.

LYTTON

pop 350

A pretty pioneer town nestled among pine forests where the rushing Thompson River meets the silt-laden Fraser – creating a system of 18 major rapids with names like Devil's Gorge and Witch's Cauldron – Lytton has justifiable claim to be the rafting capital of BC. It also serves as the gateway to the spectacular Stein Valley. The helpful staff at the **Visitor Info Centre** (☎ 250-455-2523; www.lytton.ca; 400 Fraser St; ⏰ 10am-4pm May, Jun & Sep, 9am-5pm Jul & Aug, 11am-2pm Oct-May) offers heaps of history and activity information.

Sights & Activities

Spiritual home of the Nlaka'pamux (nuh-la-ka-pa-mux) nation, the ecologically diverse **Stein Valley Nlaka'pamux Heritage Park** (www.gov .bc.ca/bcparks) starts near Lytton. One of BC's top spots for experienced multiday wilderness backpacking, its climates range from dry heat in the lower Stein Valley to snow on the summit of Skihist Mountain. One of the park's most popular treks is the Stein Trail, which includes First Nations pictographs and Asking Rock, a promontory where some Nlaka'pamux still pray for safe passage through the valley.

Lytton-based **Kumsheen Rafting Resort** (☎ 250-455-2296, 800-663-6667; www.kumsheen.com; adult/youth from $115/89), 6km east of town, offers both motorized and paddleboats – either way, you'll get soaked. It also organizes bike, kayak and rock-climbing tours, as well as accommodations in a string of funky tent-cabins ($89). You can wet your pants with plenty of other rafting companies in the area, including **Fraser River Raft Expeditions** (☎ 604-863-2355, 800-363-7238; www.fraserraft.com; trips from $120) in Hope and **Hyak Wilderness Adventures** (☎ 604-734-8622, 800-663-7238; www.hyak.com; $99).

Sleeping & Eating

Skihist Provincial Park (☎ 604-689-9025, 800-689-9025; www.discovercamping.ca; campsite $17) Campers should head here, 6km east of town on Hwy 1. Among its basic facilities are cold water taps and flush toilets.

Totem Motel (☎ 250-455-2321; www.totemmotel lytton.com; 320 Fraser St; s/d $60/65; ❄) If you'd prefer a bed for the night, this hotel has 12 cute red and white cottages sitting on a cliff above the Fraser and three motel-style rooms in a 1912 lodge. All rooms are spick and span

and the owners have done their best to retain the pioneer look.

Acacia Leaf Café (☎ 250-455-2626; 437 Main St; mains $7-10; ⏰ 8am-9pm Mon-Sat) For some hearty sustenance, drop by the Acacia Leaf where the warm welcome is combined with pizza, espressos and a menu full of soups and sandwiches.

Getting There & Away

Greyhound Canada (☎ 800-661-8747; www.greyhound .ca) bus services arrive in Lytton from Vancouver ($38.70, 4½ hours, three daily), Hope ($21.05, 1½ hours, two daily) and Chilliwack ($28.05, two hours, two daily).

LILLOOET

pop 2760

The 64km stretch of Hwy 12 between Lytton and Lillooet (lil-*oo*-ett) winds through the steep rocky canyons and flat river valleys of prospector country. Lillooet's semi-arid microclimate sees some of the hottest temperatures in Canada, resulting in a landscape akin to northern New Mexico.

Pick up the informative area *Visitor's Guide* at the **Visitor Info Centre** (☎ 250-256-4308; www .lillooetbc.com; 790 Main St; ⏰ 9am-7pm Jul & Aug, 10am-4pm Tue-Sat May, Jun, Sep & Oct), which is inside a converted church that also serves as the **museum**. The **public library** (☎ 250-256-7944; 930 Main St; ⏰ 11am-7pm Tue-Thu, 11am-7pm Fri & Sat) has free internet access.

You can don your Stetson and mosey around the region with a horseback trek organized by **Red Rock Trail Rides** (☎ 250-256-4495; www.redrocktrailrides.net; Red Rock Ranch; half-day $100). Latter-day cowboys might prefer to mount a two-wheeled steed on a bike tour with **Gravity Fed Adventures** (☎ 250-238-0170; half-day $150). In contrast, **Fraser River Jet Boat Adventures** (☎ 250-256-4180, 877-748-2628; www.rivboat.com; adult/child from $55/45) shows why paddling is for suckers – take one of its adrenalin-rushing tours for some wild (and wildlife) action.

The VIC has sleepover suggestions or consider amenity-packed **Cayoosh Creek Campground** (☎ 250-256-4180, 877-748-2628; www .cayooshcampground.com; campsite $23), centrally located **4 Pines Motel** (☎ 250-256-4247, 800-753-2576; www.4pinesmotel.com; s/d $50/75; ❄) or the new downtown **Goldpanner Hotel** (☎ 250-256-2335, 888-256-0228; www.goldpannerhotel.com; s/d $65/75; ❄), complete with business hotel-style rooms and an on-site restaurant.

THOMPSON VALLEY

Converging on the city of Kamloops, the tumbling North Thompson and South Thompson Rivers together forge the mighty Thompson River, a rich and richly historic waterway that was the lifeblood of this region long before the settlers arrived – the valley is steeped in untold centuries of Shuswap ('shoe-swap') First Nations culture and folklore. These days, it's an area where ranches and outdoor pursuits mingle together, radiating from Kamloops, the area's de facto capital city. East of Kamloops, just north of the Okanagan Valley, is the Shuswap, an area known for lake-based house boating. West of the city, the Thompson River passes through rolling green hills to Ashcroft, Cache Creek and Logan Lake. And due north, Sun Peaks is one of BC's leading winter resort towns. For regional visitor information contact **Thompson Okanagan Tourism Association** (☎ 250-860-5999, 800-567-2275; www.totabc.com).

KAMLOOPS

pop 87,750

Sitting pretty at the confluence of the North and South Thompson Rivers, Kamloops has historically been the region's key transport and trading hub. The Shuswap First Nations ('Kamloops' translates as 'meeting of rivers') used the waterways for transportation and salmon fishing before the fur traders arrived in 1811 to barter for pelts. In 1885 the Canadian Pacific Railway rolled in, enhancing the area's crossroads status. The road network came next: the Trans-Canada Hwy (Hwy 1) cuts east to west through town, the Yellowhead Hwy (Hwy 5) heads north to Jasper and the Coquihalla Hwy (Hwy 5) heads southwest to Vancouver. Now the area's main service center, Kamloops is a worthwhile stop for its hills-and-lakes scenery and relatively vibrant downtown.

Orientation

The Thompson River is separated by train tracks from the downtown area. The principal shopping street is Victoria St. Hwy 1 runs through the hills above the center. You can reach the north shore of town via the Overlander Bridge (called Blue Bridge by locals) or the Red Bridge at the north end of downtown.

Information

Merlin Books (☎ 250-374-9553; 448 Victoria St; 8:30am-7pm Mon-Sat, noon-5pm Sun) Independent bookstore with regional books and maps.

Post office (☎ 250-374-2444; 217 Seymour St; 8:30am-5pm Mon-Fri)

Public library (☎ 250-372-5145; 465 Victoria St; 10am-5pm Mon, Fri & Sat, 10am-9pm Tue-Thu year-round, noon-4pm Sun Oct-Apr) Free-use internet terminals.

Royal Inland Hospital (☎ 250-374-5111; 311 Columbia St; 24hr)

Visitor Info Centre (☎ 250-372-8000, 800-662-1994; www.tourismkamloops.com; 1290 W Trans-Canada Hwy, exit 368; 8am-6pm mid-May–Aug, 9am-6pm Mon-Fri Sep–mid-May)

Sights & Activities

The three-story **Kamloops Museum** (☎ 250-828-3576; www.kamloops.ca/museum; 207 Seymour St; admission by donation; 9am-4:30pm Tue-Sat) explores the area's rich history, from the early Shuswap era to the passing gold prospectors and the arrival of the railroad. A video library includes the history of mapmaker and river namesake David Thompson.

Culture vultures should also take in **Kamloops Art Gallery** (☎ 250-377-2400; www.kag.bc.ca; 465 Victoria St; adult/child $3/2; 10am-5pm Mon-Wed, Fri & Sat, 10am-9pm Thu, noon-4pm Sun) where a focus on contemporary regional works is housed in a modern, industrial-style building. There's a busy roster of temporary exhibitions, so check ahead if you're into the likes of performance art or computer-generated installations.

If you've had enough of all that serious stuff, consider a fun (and educational, of course) tour of **Kamloops Brewery** (☎ 250-851-2543; www.kbbeer.com; 965 McGill Pl; tours Jun-Aug), BC's second-largest independent microbrewer. You'll be walked through the processes before sampling some top tipples – the hearty Black Bear Ale is recommended.

They likely won't let you drive an engine if you've been drinking, so it's best to just sit back and enjoy one of the steam train rides at the smashing **Kamloops Heritage Railway** (☎ 250-374-2141; www.kamrail.com; 510 Lorne St). A popular attraction for years, its **Spirit of Kamloops** (adult/child $14/9.50; Fri-Mon Jun-Sep) trek takes you on an 11km round-trip, complete with stops and stories covering the region's history. If you have more time, the day-long **Armstrong Explorer** (adult/child $149/99; irregular Sat May-Oct) trundles through tunnels, around horseshoe

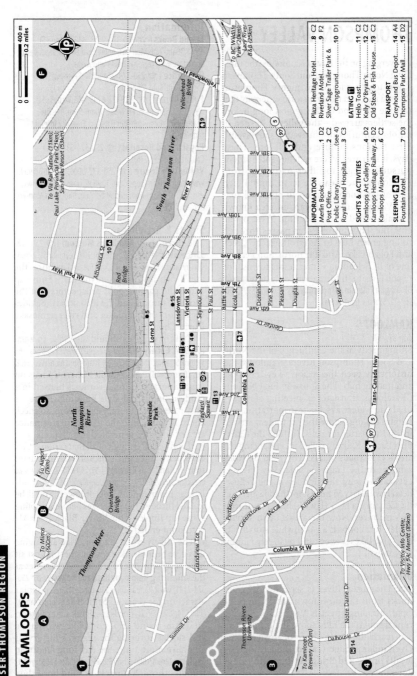

FRASER-THOMPSON REGION

KAMLOOPS

INFORMATION
Merlin Books.................................1 D2
Post Office....................................2 C2
Public Library...........................(see 4)
Royal Inland Hospital...................3 C3

SIGHTS & ACTIVITIES
Kamloops Art Gallery....................4 D2
Kamloops Heritage Railway.....5 D2
Kamloops Museum.......................6 C2

SLEEPING
Fountain Motel.............................7 D3
Plaza Heritage Hotel....................8 C2
Riverland Motel.............................9 F2
Silver Sage Trailer Park &
    Campground..........................10 D1

EATING
Hello Toast...................................11 C2
Kelly O'Bryan's............................12 C2
Old Steak & Fish House..............13 C2

TRANSPORT
Greyhound Bus Depot..............14 A4
Thompson Park Mall..................15 D2

turns and past forested mountain vistas for a lunch in Armstrong before returning to Kamloops.

If you haven't seen many indigenous animals on your BC trip, head to the **British Columbia Wildlife Park** (☎ 250-573-3242; www.kamloopswildlife.org; adult/youth/child $10/9/7; ⓨ 9am-6pm Jun-Sep, 9am-4:30pm Oct-May) to cross them off your list. A conservation-minded facility, it's populated by snakes, grizzlies and timber wolves. Check out the fascinating Wildlife Rehabilitation program.

Hikers and beach fans should also head to **Paul Lake Provincial Park** (☎ 250-578-7376; www.env.gov.bc.ca/bcparks), 5km north of Kamloops on Hwy 5, then 19km on Pinantan Rd. Mountain bikers favor the 20km trip around the lake, while fisher types try for rainbow trout. This is a protected habitat for coyote, bald eagles and mule deer, so keep your eyes peeled.

Sleeping

Scores of chain motels lurk amid the Columbia St strip malls, west of downtown. The usual characterless chains populate more central locations.

Silver Sage Trailer Park & Campground (☎ 250-828-2077, 877-828-2077; www.silversage.kamloops.com; 771 Athabasca St E; campsite $20-25) You can see across the river to downtown – just a five-minute walk away – from this grassy, tree-lined site. The facilities include flush toilets, coin laundry, hot showers and picnic tables, and there's a small beach on the river that's ideal for swimming.

Fountain Motel (☎ 250-374-4451, 888-253-1569; www.fountain.kamloops.com; 506 Columbia St; s/d from $56/62; 🔊) Losing its HI Hostel in 2005, this Kamloops sleepover is now the best deal in town for noncampers. Cheap 1980s furnishings and old-school wood paneling abound, but kitchenettes are available if you want to save money on eating out. Well located in the center of the action, the hospital is across the street if you fall over in the shower.

Riverland Motel (☎ 250-374-1530, 800-663-1530; www.riverlandmotel.kamloops.com; 1530 River St; s/d $95/110; 🔊 🔊) With Thompson River and mountain views, this pleasant sleepover features bright, good-sized rooms, plus an indoor pool and hot tub. Most rooms have kitchenettes and some have Jacuzzi tubs. It's a nice stroll to the center but there's a restaurant next door if you don't want to walk too far, plus a barbecue

terrace out back if you prefer to cook your own steaks.

Lazy River B&B (☎ 250-573-3444, 877-552-3377; www.lazyriverbnb.com; 1701 Old Ferry Rd; d $95-165; 🔊) It's a 25km drive east of Kamloops on Hwy 1, but it's worth it to find this magnificent, meadow-surrounded, post-and-beam inn. Stuffed with artworks, it has three rustic chic rooms full of custom-made wooden furniture. Guests can partake of a library, fitness room and a deep sense of tranquility.

Plaza Heritage Hotel (☎ 250-377-8075, 877-977-5292; www.plazaheritagehotel.com; 405 Victoria St; s/d $109/129; 🔊) Built in 1927 to the soaring height of six stories, the Plaza has traditionally been *the* place to stay in Kamloops. It's still in good shape, with plenty of character – the rooms boast period furnishings and each is decorated differently, many with eye-poppingly loud wallpaper. Good sunset views of the river from the high floors.

Eating & Drinking

Not exactly a culinary capital, still you won't go hungry in Kamloops. There are numerous restaurants and café pit stops around Victoria St.

Hello Toast (☎ 250-372-9322; 428 Victoria St; mains $5-10; ⓨ 8am-5pm Mon-Sat) For a well-priced breakkie in warm, convivial surroundings, head to this tiny café, combining traditional sausage 'n' egg plates with organic, veggie-friendly options – the rib-sticking oatmeal is guaranteed to put hairs on your chest. The fair trade coffee is a nice touch.

Minos (☎ 250-376-2010; 262 Tranquille Rd; mains $18-26; ⓨ noon-10pm Mon-Sat, 5-10pm Sun) The owner's name is George and, fittingly, Greek can be heard wafting over the tops of the booths at this fine Greek restaurant. Everything is as it should be: from the warm welcome to the buttery-soft, marinated lamb chops. A five-minute drive across the river from downtown – take the Overlander Bridge.

Old Steak & Fish House (☎ 250-374-3227; 172 Battle St; mains $18-30; ⓨ 5-11pm) Occupying a charming old heritage house, this romantic spot is a great place to bring your Kamloops date. If you're not sure about popping the question, wait until after you've eaten: the excellent steaks and seafood dishes, many with a Mexican influence, may take your mind off the whole thing. If you decide to go ahead, there's an impressive wine selection to toast your engagement.

Kelly O'Bryans (☎ 250-828-1559; 244 Victoria St; mains $9-24; ❂ 11am-midnight Mon-Sat, 11am-10pm Sun) Bringing the heart of Ireland to downtown Kamloops, this merry Celtic spot serves the usual combination of Irish tipples – whisky, Guinness, 'Strawberry Mockaritas' etc – and makes its male employees wear kilts, which they no doubt thoroughly enjoy. Large menu of pub grub classics.

Getting There & Away

Seven km northwest of town, **Kamloops Airport** (☎ 250-376-3613; www.kamloopsairport.com) receives Air Canada Jazz services from Vancouver (from $119, 55 minutes, five daily) and Calgary (from $129, 30 minutes, one daily). In addition, Central Mountain Air services arrive from Prince George ($240, 55 minutes, one daily), and Horizon Air services arrive from Seattle (from US$149, 1¼ hours, one daily, December to April only).

Greyhound Canada (☎ 250-374-1212, 800-661-8747; www.greyhound.ca; 725 Notre Dame Dr) is southwest of the downtown area off Columbia St W. Services arrive from Vancouver ($57, five hours, seven daily), Hope ($35.85, 2½ hours, three daily), Chilliwack ($41.20, three hours, seven daily), Kelowna ($30.55, three to four hours, five daily) and Calgary ($89.30, nine to 11 hours, four daily).

VIA Rail (☎ 888-842-7245; www.viarail.ca) train services arrive at Kamloops North Station – 11km from town – from Vancouver ($79, 8½ hours, Sunday, Tuesday and Friday) and Jasper ($104, 7½ hours, Monday, Thursday and Saturday).

Getting Around

Airporter (☎ 250-314-4803) buses deliver passengers from the airport to all local hotels ($12). **Kamloops Transit Service** (☎ 250-376-1216; www.bus online.ca) operates public buses to areas around the region (adult/child $2/1.50), including the airport. The main stop, where you can catch almost any bus, is Thompson Park Mall, at Lansdowne St and 6th Ave. For taxis, call **Yellow Cabs** (☎ 250-374-3333, 877-870-0003).

AROUND KAMLOOPS
Cache Creek

Heading west on Hwys 1 and 97, you'll hit Cache Creek (population 1135), a tiny town prospectors rushed through on their way to find Cariboo gold. The story goes that the miners would hide their gold or cache in a nearby creek. Locals insist that there are still unclaimed stashes buried deep in the creek bed. If you want to hear local boosterism at its most fervent, tune to 105.9 FM. For more information on visiting this quirky spot, check www.cachecreekvillage.com.

Ashcroft

Just south of Cache Creek is Ashcroft (population 1835), a charming, little cattle-ranching community surrounded by sagebrush and tumbleweeds. When the railroad rolled through in the 1880s, Ashcroft was already a small farming community settled by gold prospectors, who realized early that they weren't going to find any gold. From here, avoid the road through **Logan Lake** unless you want to see open-pit copper mining at its most frightening and dramatic. For more information on the community, visit www.village .ashcroft.bc.ca.

Sun Peaks Resort

Favored over Whistler by many for its down-to-earth, family-friendly appeal, **Sun Peaks Resort** (☎ 250-578-5474, 800-807-3257; www.sunpeaks resort.com) is 53km northeast of Kamloops via Hwy 1.

While it's now a year-round recreation spot, it rarely looks more picturesque than in winter, when snow blankets the gable-roofed village of restaurants, shops and lodges. The three mountains here boast 121 runs, 12 lifts, a snowboard park and 881m of vertical rise. Legendary Olympian Nancy Greene is the resort's director of skiing and she's often out on the slopes passing on her wisdom to youngsters hitting the snow (usually literally) for the first time. In fact, since almost 70% of the runs at Sun Peaks are novice or intermediate, you're more likely to come across skiers who are just out to have fun rather than show off. Snowshoeing, dog sledding and Nordic skiing are also popular, and winter **lift rates** (adult/youth/child $60/51/33) are well priced. You can rent equipment, guides and tours from Guest Services in the **Valley Day Lodge** (☎ 250-578-5422).

In summer, Sun Peaks is popular with alpine hikers and mountain bikers, with canoeing and horseback riding not far behind. You can pick up maps and information from Guest Services to plan your own activities or hire equipment and guides from them. Popular hiking trails include the challenging Tod Lake Trek, while the growing Mountain Bike Park

---

CHEERS!

There are plenty of good reasons to visit the **Sun Peaks Icewine Festival** (☎ 250-861-6654; www .thewinefestivals.com; ⊗ mid-Jan): accessible educational seminars, lip-smacking dinner events, cozy alpine lodge ambience and the chance to sample Canada's signature dessert wine, made only from grapes frozen on the vine. But it's the Saturday evening **Progressive Tasting** (admission $50; ⊗ 6-9pm) that has become the big draw every year. Twenty wineries set up their stalls and offer more than 100 wines at locations throughout the twinkling, Christmas-card village – while increasingly tipsy visitors slip and slide their way between them in an attempt to keep their glasses as full as possible. The next morning is usually a late one for many, but a couple of hours on the slopes can do wonders to dispel any hangover.

---

is ever-popular. For an exhilarating, mud-splattering all-terrain vehicle (ATV) drive, contact **Thompson Valley Tours** (☎ 250-851-8687; www.thompsonvalleytours.com; 4hr tour $149). In summer, Sun Peaks' **lift rates** (adult/youth/child $14/13/11) are a bargain.

Skiers on a budget like to stay at **Sun Peaks International Ski Hostel** (☎ 250-578-0057; www .sunpeakshostel.com; 1140 Sun Peaks Rd; dm $20-25; 🖳), which is right in the ski village by the lifts. **Sun Peaks Lodge** (☎ 250-578-7878, 800-333-9112; www .sunpeakslodge.com; 3180 Creekside Way; d/ste $119/159) attracts visitors on a midrange budget.

Those not driving to Sun Peaks usually fly into Kamloops and take the **Sun Star shuttle** (☎ 250-377-8481; www.sunstarshuttle.com). Reserve in advance (one way/return $35.85/71.70).

MERRITT
pop 7560

Nestled in the pretty Nicola Valley 115km north of Hope, Merritt offers the only services along the Coquihalla Hwy (Hwy 5) between Hope and Kamloops.

Motels sprang up with the building of the highway, and that's pretty much all the action Merritt sees today – car traffic. Until mid-July, that is, when the toe stompin' **Mountainfest** (☎ 250-525-3330; www.mountainfest.com) two-steps into town. This four-day country music hoedown attracts up to 150,000 hootin' and hollerin' cowboy-hatted dudes who camp on the festival grounds. The rest of the year you can put your foot on the spirit of the event by following the downtown **Walk of Stars**, a collection of bronze plaques bearing the cemented handprints of festival legends like Johnny Cash, Merle Haggard and the Dixie Chicks.

From Merritt, Hwy 97C heads east to Kelowna (p234) and the Okanagan Valley (p220) or northwest to the Cariboo (p309). Before continuing on, stop by the **Visitor Info Centre** (☎ 250-378-0349; www.tourismmerritt.com; 2250 Voght St; ⊗ 9am-7pm mid-May–Aug, 9am-5pm Mon-Fri Sep–mid-May) for extensive regional information and resources. It's also a good idea to check road conditions here before heading south or north.

Standing out from the plethora of standard motels, the copper-domed 1908 **Coldwater Hotel** (☎ 250-378-2821; www.coldwaterhotel.com; 1901 Voght St; r from $40) occupies a stunning corner plot and has a great bar that's popular with local and visiting cowboys. The rooms are basic but the burgers ($6) are great.

Greyhound Canada (☎ 800-661-8747; www.grey hound.ca) bus services arrive in Merritt from Vancouver ($38.70, four hours, nine daily), Kamloops ($15.80, one hour, five daily) and Jasper ($75, 7½ hours, two daily).

THE SHUSWAP

Distant snowcapped crags and miles of pristine, cove-ridden waterways that are home to a menagerie of bird and marine life: the area around the Shuswap lakes is green with wooded hills and farms that invite visitors to stop and catch their breath. Although the main town of **Salmon Arm** is little more than a functional stop, the grazing cattle and lush, cultivated land make a pleasant change of scenery no matter which direction you're coming from. Many provincial parks dot the area offering an abundance of water-related activities. Accommodations are tight in summer – if you're coming in July and August, reserve ahead.

Shuswap Lake squiggles about a series of valleys, looking like a mutant spider. The top right arm of the lake is Seymour Arm, and below it is Anstey Arm. At the bottom left is Salmon Arm (also the name of the town). The top left of the lake thickens into Little Shuswap Lake. Salmon Arm, on Trans-Canada Hwy 1,

SALUTE TO THE SOCKEYE

Sockeye salmon are some of the most hardcore travelers around. These wily fish travel from the Adams River to the Pacific Ocean and back again in what is one of nature's most miraculous and complete cycles of life. It all starts on the shallow riverbed in Roderick Haig-Brown Provincial Park, a massive breeding ground for sockeye salmon. Since glaciers carved out river valleys, pairs of male and female sockeye have fought starvation, currents and grueling rapids to return from the ocean to the place of their birth. In early fall, the lower Adams River hosts a frenzy of spawning salmon.

Each spawning female lays about 4000 eggs; many of which are unsuccessfully fertilized or munched on by rainbow trout and other predators. The ones that do survive spend the winter tucked into the gravel on the riverbed, waiting out frost and weather while slowly growing in the soft, jelly-like casing of the eggshell. In spring the eggs hatch and tiny salmon fry – measuring about 2.5cm in length – emerge and float downriver to spend their first year in Shuswap Lake. Though the calm lake water keeps the fry safe from the rushing currents of the river, only one out of four fry eludes the hungry jaws of predators. Survivors of that ordeal grow in the lake, becoming smolt. These hardy fish, up to 10cm long, then begin the long journey to the mouth of the Fraser River, which they follow all the way to the Pacific Ocean. Once in the salty water, the salmon grow up to 3kg, needing size and agility to escape more ravenous predators like killer whales, seal and commercial fishing nets. Once they've reached maturity, about four years after their birth, a biological signal as sharp as intuition takes hold and the salmon know it's time to make the great journey back home.

Of every 4000 eggs produced at Roderick Haig-Brown Provincial Park, only two fish survive long enough to make the long, grueling journey home to spawn. When the internal alarm rings, the sleek, silvery ocean sockeye stop eating as they reach the Fraser's freshwater mouth. From here on, for the next 21 days, the fish rely on body fat and protein to energize their 29km-a-day swim over rocks and raging rapids.

Scraped, beaten and torn, the fish slowly turn a bright crimson red, a color they'll carry like cloaks until they reach the spawning grounds. There, the red heads turn a deep green, the male's snout elongates and his teeth get sharper, ready to fend off intruders as he and the female, now heavy with eggs, search for a place to nest. But good real estate on the shallow riverbed is hard to come by, and the pairs of fish fight like crazed parents to find a sheltered spot. The female digs her nest by furiously flopping her tail while simultaneously laying eggs. The male quickly swims by, dropping a shower of milt to fertilize the eggs. The female then covers the nest with gravel. Upon completion of this exhausting ordeal of procreation, the hardy couple quietly dies, leaving their eggs to follow this incredible journey.

Though the salmon spawn annually, every four years a mass migration occurs (the next one is 2010) that far overshadows the intermittent-year spawns. In these years, up to four million sockeye return home. The best time for viewing is in October – check with the Salmon Arm **Visitor Info Centre** (☎ 250-832-2230, 877-725-6667; www.shuswap.bc.ca; 200 Trans-Canada Hwy 1 SW; ☺ 9am-7pm mid-May–Aug, 9am-5pm Mon-Fri Sep–mid-Aug) for the best times each year. For the latest information, visit the website of the **Adams River Salmon Society** (www.salmonsociety.com).

is the main service center, although nearby Sicamous proclaims itself the 'houseboat capital of Canada.' On the north shore of the lake, are two excellent provincial parks, more camping and accommodations.

Salmon Arm houses the area's main **Visitor Info Centre** (☎ 250-832-2230, 877-725-6667; www.shuswap.bc.ca; 200 Trans-Canada Hwy 1 SW; ☺ 9am-7pm mid-May–Aug, 9am-5pm Mon-Fri Sep–mid-Aug).

Greyhound Canada (☎ 800-661-8747; www.greyhound.ca) services arrive from Vancouver ($68,

seven to 9½ hours, five daily), Merritt ($33.35, three to four hours, four daily) and Kamloops ($21.05, 1½ hours, four daily).

Roderick Haig-Brown Provincial Park

Located on the north shore of Shuswap Lake, this **park** (☎ 250-851-3000; www.env.gov.bc.ca/bcparks) takes its name from Roderick Haig-Brown (1908–76), a BC naturalist and angler who devoted much of his life to conserving sockeye salmon. The 1059-hectare park protects either side of the Adams River, from the northwest side of Shuswap Lake to Adams Lake. If you're here in October, you'll see the bright red sockeye running upriver to spawn (see the boxed text, opposite). Interpretive displays here tell all about this great event. You can hike in the park but camping is not permitted.

Activities

WHITE-WATER RAFTING

Popular on the Adams River – it's mostly a Class 3 river, so it'll get your adrenaline pumping but won't send you into cardiac arrest – you can get kitted-out and taken aboard for a jaunt with **Adams River Rafting** (☎ 250-955-2447, 888-440-7238; www.adamsriverrafting.com; 3843 Squilax-Anglemont Hwy, Scotch Creek; 2hr adult/youth $58/46; May–mid-Sep).

HOUSEBOATING

This is a fun way to explore the Shuswap – especially in summer, when the lake looks like a village of floating houses. Most houseboats are totally self-contained, with kitchens and running water. Some even come with hot tubs and waterslides. Most rent by the week, can sleep about 10 people and cost from $2000. Fuel is extra, and you have to bring your own food. If you're up for it, pick up a list of rentals from the Salmon Arm **VIC** (☎ 250-832-2230, 877-725-6667; www.shuswap.bc.ca; 200 Trans-Canada Hwy 1 SW).

Sleeping & Eating

Motels line the Trans-Canada Hwy on both sides of Salmon Arm. It's not hard to find a truck-stop diner or cozy coffee hole nearby.

For campers, **Herald Provincial Park** (☎ 604-689-9025, 800-689-9025; www.discovercamping.ca; campsite $22), 25 minutes northwest of Salmon Arm, sits on the homestead of one of Shuswap's first farmers. It features sandy beaches, waterfalls and 119 reservable sites. To get there, turn off the Trans-Canada Hwy 1 onto Sunnybrae Rd. You can't reserve at **Shuswap Lake Marine Provincial Park** (☎ 250-955-0861; www.env.gov.bc.ca/bcparks; campsite $22), on the north shore at Scotch Creek, but it has 49 lovely wooded sites on the lake.

HI-Shuswap Lake Hostel (☎ 250-675-2977, 888-675-2977; www.hihostels.ca; 229 Trans-Canada Hwy 1; dm/d $21/46;) This hostel is about 10km east of Chase and 45km west of Salmon Arm on Hwy 1. Get your head around the rustic charm and this hostel can make a good hub for exploring the area. Plus, if you've ever wanted to explore the rear of a train, here's your chance: the dorm-style beds are in three old cabooses.

Quaaout Resort (☎ 250-679-3090, 800-663-4303; www.quaaout.com; r $120-180;) This beautiful resort on Little Shuswap Lake, 8km east of Chase on Trans-Canada Hwy 1, was built by the Little Shuswap Band, part of the Shuswap First Nations. The entrance area and dining room resemble a *kekuli*, or winter house, which is usually buried in the ground. First Nations art decorates the hotel, and the kitchen serves up gourmet meals based on traditional cooking methods. Even if you are not staying here, it is a good place for lunch.

Shuswap Farm and Craft Market (☎ 250-832-6990; Piccadilly Place Mall, 1151 10 Ave SW; 8am-12:30pm Tue & Fri Apr-Oct) Sample the fruits of the many orchards, yummy home-baked treats and unique artisan offerings here at Salmon Arm. The Mall is south of Hwy 1 and just west of the town center. Many of the farms also have their own well-marked produce stands.

For classic European-influenced baked goods and hearty soups, try **Penkert's Bakery** (☎ 250-832-4010; 420 4th St NE, Salmon Arm; mains $4-6; 9am-5pm Mon-Fri).

Okanagan Valley

The only thing sprouting faster than grapes in the beautiful Okanagan Valley is people. Lured by some of Canada's mildest weather (the average high never gets below freezing, although in January it comes close), a beautiful setting among lakes and hills and a rich culture that includes plenty of excellent galleries and restaurants, this region in south-central British Columbia is one of Canada's fastest growing.

Residents and visitors alike enjoy the results of bounteous harvests. Long famous for their succulence, local peaches and apples are now being outshined by grapes of almost every variety. More than 70 wineries can be found along the length of the 200km valley. Many are producing world-class wines that have the Okanagan Valley being mentioned in the same breath as the Napa Valley. Besides giving the hillsides sinuous green striations amid the orchards, the vineyards and wineries offer tastings and tours, with many running their own exquisite restaurants.

Touring is easy as Hwy 97 runs south to north, linking almost every city. Right on the US border, Osoyoos is the modest start to the valley. North, roadside stands punctuate vineyards through cute towns like Oliver. Relaxed Penticton rims the southern shore of 97km-long Okanagan Lake. Near the center of the valley, Kelowna is the hub, with a vibrant culture, nightlife and good beaches. In the north, Vernon is a good base for outdoor pursuits.

Throughout the valley, you'll find beaches, hiking trails, golf courses and other opportunities to give more than just your palate a workout. In the surrounding hills are several excellent ski resorts.

HIGHLIGHTS

- Finding your own favorite dozen or two wines at the nearly 80 **wineries** (p228)
- Enjoying nature both unadorned *and* fermented on the drive to **Naramata** (p233)
- Soaking up art and more in **Kelowna's Cultural District** (p236)
- Perfecting your beach-bum act in **Penticton** (p225)
- Hiking the newly rebuilt bridges of the **Kettle Valley Rail Trail** (p238) near Kelowna

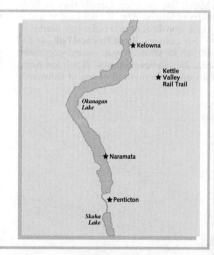

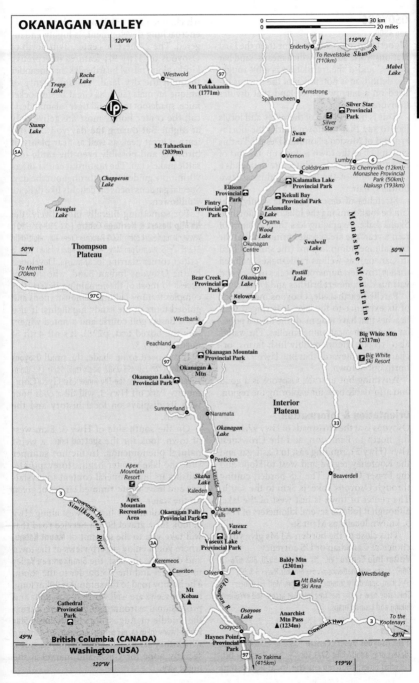

OKANAGAN VALLEY

0 ____ 30 km
0 ____ 20 miles

120°W · 119°W

Enderby
To Revelstoke (110km)
Shuswap R.
Mabel Lake
Westwold
97
Mt Tuktakamin (1771m)
Spallumcheen
Armstrong
Roche Lake
Trapp Lake
Silver Star Provincial Park
Silver Star
Swan Lake
Stump Lake
Mt Tahaetkun (2039m)
Vernon
Lumby
6
5A
Coldstream
To Cherryville (12km); Monashee Provincial Park (50km); Nakusp (193km)
Chapperon Lake
Kalamalka Lake Provincial Park
Ellison Provincial Park
Kekuli Bay Provincial Park
Douglas Lake
Fintry Provincial Park
Kalamalka Lake
Oyama
Wood Lake
Swalwell Lake
50°N
Thompson Plateau
Okanagan Centre
Monashee Mountains
50°N
To Merritt (70km)
Bear Creek Provincial Park
97
Okanagan Lake
Postill Lake
97C
Kelowna
Big White Mtn (2317m)
Westbank
Big White Ski Resort
Peachland
Okanagan Mountain Provincial Park
97
Okanagan Mtn
Okanagan Lake Provincial Park
Interior Plateau
Summerland
Naramata
33
Okanagan Lake
Penticton
Beaverdell
Apex Mountain Resort
Skaha Lake
Lakeside Rd
3
Kaleden
Crowsnest Hwy
Apex Mountain Recreation Area
Okanagan Falls Provincial Park
Okanagan Falls
Simikameen River
Vaseux Lake
Vaseux Lake Provincial Park
3A
Baldy Mtn (2301m)
Westbridge
Keremeos
Cawston
Oliver
Mt Baldy Ski Area
Okanagan R.
Cathedral Provincial Park
Mt Kobau (1234m)
Osoyoos Lake
Anarchist Mtn Pass (1234m)
Crowsnest Hwy
3
To the Kootenays
British Columbia (CANADA)
Washington (USA)
Osoyoos
Haynes Point Provincial Park
97
To Yakima (415km)
49°N
120°W · 119°W

OSOYOOS

pop 4800

Modest Osoyoos takes its name from the First Nations word 'soyoos,' which means 'sand bar across,' and if the translation is a bit rough, the definition is not: much of the town is indeed on a narrow spit of land that divides Osoyoos Lake.

This is the arid end of the valley and locals like to say that the town marks the northern end of Mexico's Sonoran Desert. To this end, much of the town is done up in a sort of faux tile-and-stucco architecture that lends a certain south-of-the-border (in this case two borders) flair.

Stretches of desert (Canada's only one) can be found among the hills, 50km north to Skaha Lake. Averaging less than 200mm of rain a year, the area creates prime habitat for the calliope hummingbird (the smallest bird in Canada), as well as rattlesnakes, painted turtles, coyotes, numerous species of mice and various cacti, desert brushes and grasses.

Parched earth aside, Osoyoos owes much of its existence to the lake. It is ringed with beaches that have long made the town a popular place with vacationing families. The waters also irrigate the incredibly lush farms, orchards and vineyards that line Hwy 97 going north out of town.

Anything but upscale, Osoyoos is a good and affordable base for exploring the region.

Orientation & Information

Osoyoos is at the crossroads of Hwy 97, heading north to Penticton, and the Crowsnest Hwy (Hwy 3), running east to Castlegar and the Kootenay region and west to Hope and the Fraser Canyon. The US border, cutting through Osoyoos Lake, is 5km to the south. The center of town is just west of the lake, although it follows several kilometers of Hwy 3, known locally as Main St.

This close to the border, ATMs give you a choice of Canadian or US currency.

Visitor Info Centre (VIC; ☎ 250-495-5070, 888-676-9667; www.destinationosoyoos.com; cnr Hwys 3 & 97; ☼ 9am-5pm daily summer, 9am-5pm Mon-Fri winter) This large new center has free internet access and excellent hiking and touring maps.

Sights

The **Osoyoos Desert Centre** (☎ 250-495-2470; www .desert.org; adult/child $7/3.50; ☼ 9am-7pm Apr-Oct, call other times) focuses on the local ecosystem which, due to its small size and persistently encroaching development, is highly endangered. The 27-hectare center, 3km north of Osoyoos off Hwy 97, features interpretive kiosks along raised boardwalks that meander through the dry land. Though plenty of unique animals (such as Great Basin pocket mice, spadefoot toads and tiger salamanders) call the center home, most are active only at night. But during the day you can still learn a great deal, as well as hear plenty of birdsong and possibly even the rattle of a rattlesnake's tail. The nonprofit center offers 90-minute guided tours throughout the day. Special gardens focus on delights like delicate wildflowers.

For something literally more lively, the **Nk'Mip Desert & Heritage Centre** (☎ 250-495-7901; www.nkmipdesert.com; 1000 Rancher Creek Rd; adult/child $12/8; ☼ 9:30am-7pm May-Sep, until 4pm winter) has a 'critter corner' starring local fauna. Developed by the Osoyoos Indian Band, who control access to most of the remaining desert, this complex features cultural demonstrations and guided tours of the sandy highlights. It also has a desert golf course and a noted winery (see the boxed text, p228). It's off 45th St north of Hwy 3.

If you need some shade, the small **Osoyoos Museum** (☎ 250-495-2582; adult/child $3/1; ☼ 10am-3:30pm Jun-Sep, 2-5pm Tue-Thu winter), in Gyro Community Park off Hwy 3, will fill a cool hour with its displays on local history and the orchards.

On the south side of Hwy 3, 8km west of town, look for the **spotted lake**, a weird natural phenomenon. In the hot summer sun, the lake's water begins to evaporate, causing its high mineral content to crystallize and leave white-rimmed circles of green on the water.

Three kilometers further west along Hwy 3, look for a gravel Forest Service road that will take you to the summit of **Mount Kobau**, where you'll enjoy superb views of the town and desert to the east, the **Similkameen Valley** to the west and the US border to the south. The bumpy road to the summit is 20km long, but the views are well worth it. Amateur and professional astronomers flock here during the middle of August for the **Mt Kobau Star Party** (www.mksp.ca; per person per night $20), during which they set up telescopes, enjoy lectures, secretly hope for UFOs and marvel at the night sky.

Activities

The climate makes **Osoyoos Lake** among the warmest lakes in the country, and every summer thousands of people lounge on the sandy beaches and splash around in the water. Most of the motels can hook you up with paddleboat and other water-sport rentals. **Okanagan Kayak Centre** (☎ 250-485-8880; www.okanagankayak centre.com; 10 Wren Pl; per hr from $20) offers rentals, lessons and tours.

In winter, take the rough Camp McKinney Rd from Hwy 97 east to the **Mt Baldy Ski Area** (☎ 866-754-2253; www.skibaldy.com; 1-day lift ticket adult/ child $40/24). This small resort has cross-country trails and downhill runs with a vertical drop of 420m. It has chairlifts and T-bar lifts. It's 46km from Osoyoos; check the website for details on bus service.

Sleeping

There are more than a dozen modest motels lining the shores of the lake. Many cluster around Hwy 3 and there's another clump on the southwest shore near the border. Chains can be found at the junction. Quality varies among the older properties, so it's good to compare. Rates plummet in winter.

Haynes Point Provincial Park (☎ 250-494-0321, 800-689-9025; www.discovercamping.ca; campsites $22; ⊙ Apr–mid-Oct) This is the most sought-after campground. In fact, you're not likely to get one of the 41 sites until next year unless you reserved early. The park has beaches, nature trails and more. It's 2km south of the center off Hwy 97.

Nk'Mip Campground & RV Resort (☎ 250-495-7279; www.campingosoyoos.com; campsites $22-27) Part of the Nk'Mip empire, there are over 300 sites at this year-round resort, off 45th St north of Hwy 3. The long list of services includes cable hook-ups so those with RVs can feel like they never left home.

Avalon Inn (☎ 250-495-6334, 800-264-5999; www .avaloninn.com; 9106 Main St; r from $80; ☒ ▣) Away from the lake, this 24-unit motel has very large and modern rooms, which all have broadband. Right in the center of town, there are several restaurants within easy walking distance.

THE BOUNTIFUL VALLEY

The region's fertile soil and heavy irrigation, combined with the relatively warm climate (summers tend to be hot and dry), have made the Okanagan Canada's top fruit-growing area. Its 100 sq km of orchards represent 85% of the nation's total.

During April and May, fragrant blossoms coat the valley in color. In late summer and autumn, the orchards drip with delicious fresh fruit. Stands dotting the roads sell the best and cheapest produce in Canada.

Reveling in the region's produce through visits to farms, orchards and wineries is major activity throughout the valley. The drive north along Hwy 97 from Osoyoos passes an almost endless succession of orchards, farms and fruit stands. You'll have plenty of time to smell the apples, peaches and, yes, even the roses. More than 50% of the farms are organic. Rather than single out certain producers, its best to just wander at will, comparing the bounty along the way.

Even as wineries proliferate, fruit and vegetable growers have held on by switching to higher-value crops. Mass-market apples may be a commodity but there's still money in organically grown heirloom varieties.

If you wish to tie your trip to a specific fruit, the approximate harvest times are as follows (but confirm with the VICs if it's vital you arrive at, say, peak cherry season):

- strawberries – mid-June to early July
- raspberries – early July to mid-July
- cherries – mid-June to mid-August
- apricots – mid-July to mid-August
- peaches – mid-July to mid-September
- pears – mid-August to late September
- apples – early September to late October
- grapes – early September to late October

DETOUR: CATHEDRAL PROVINCIAL PARK

Rock hounds and others who thrill to weird things mineral, will enjoy **Cathedral Provincial Park** (☎ 250-494-6500), more than 33,000 hectares of mountain wilderness characterized by unusual basalt and quartz rock formations. The park offers excellent backcountry camping and hiking around wildflower meadows and turquoise lakes. To reach the park, go 30km west of Osoyoos on Hwy 3 to Ashnola River Rd and then another 21km.

Three steep trails lead to the park's core area around Quiniscoe Lake and the gorgeous **Cathedral Lakes Lodge** (☎ 250-492-1606, 888-255-4453; www.cathedral-lakes-lodge.com; 2 nights from $375). It's all a Bavarian fantasy with a central lodge and cabins. Hearty meals are included in the price and there is transport available.

Sun Beach Motel (☎ 250-495-7766, 866-395-7766; sunbeachmotel@otv.cabelan.net; 7303 Main St; r $75-150; ❸) This basic place on the south shore of the lake has open walkways where you can sit in the shade and enjoy the view. The 22 rooms have the sort of interior that you would expect from cinder blocks.

Poplars Motel (☎ 250-495-6035; 6404 Cottonwood Dr; r from $100; ❸ ❹) The 34 units here are in a two-story block right on the beach. Families enjoy the simple playground, shady sands, use of a heated pool and kitchen facilities in every room.

Sandy Beach Motel (☎ 250-495-6931, 866-495-6931; www.sandybeachmotel.com; 6706 Ponderosa Dr; r $100-200; ❸) Go for an adventure with the free rowboats at this beachside place just north of Hwy 3. Bungalows and a two-story block surround a grassy common area with barbecues. Many of the 25 units have views.

Eating & Drinking

Osoyoos Gelato (☎ 250-495-5425; 9150 Main St; treats from $2; ❂ 10am-10pm summer) The perfect respite on a hot day, there are always at least 24 house-made flavors.

Lady on the Lake (☎ 250-495-3274; 7603 Spartan Ave; meals $7-20; ❂ noon-late) At the east end of the center, this large, modern pub has good views of the lake. There are plenty of beer and wine choices along with big burgers.

Diamond (☎ 250-495-6223; 8903 Main St; meals $15-25; ❂ 5-9pm) It's a timeless '60s supper club setting at this steak and seafood house that swaddles diners in commodious booths. Needless to say, the beef is grilled to perfection and the menu has a Greek accent which means you can order tzatziki and moussaka.

Wildfire Grill (☎ 250-495-2215; 8526 Main St; meals $15-25; ❂ 11am-10pm Mon-Fri, 9am-11pm Sat & Sun) A breath of style on the otherwise stolid Main St, Wildfire serves up a range of global cuisine from its open kitchen. Asian food mixes with popular fare like pasta and BC seafood. Tables on the patio and courtyard are always in demand. At night, throngs sample local wine in the Lizard Lounge.

Getting There & Away

Greyhound (☎ 250-495-7252), at the visitor info centre on the corner of Hwys 3 and 97, runs to Vancouver ($68, eight hours, twice daily) and Kelowna ($23, 2½ hours, once daily).

OSOYOOS TO PENTICTON

With its hot, dry weather, the Osoyoos region produces the earliest and most varied fruit and vegetable crops in Canada. The 20km drive along Hwy 97 from Osoyoos to Oliver alone is worth the trip. The oodles of ripe hanging fruit are matched by the oodles of fruit stands selling the same. Look for – often organic – cherries, apricots, peaches, apples and other fruit. Many places offer samples and will let you pick your own. These days diversions can include lavender farms and the many wineries.

North of Oliver to Penticton, the orchards and vineyards abate a little and the scene is dominated by mountains, rock formations and forests.

Oliver

pop 4300

The small town of Oliver is right in the midst of the Okanagan's bounty.

The **Visitor Information Centre** (☎ 250-498-6321; 36250 93rd St; ❂ 9am-5pm daily May-Sep, 9am-5pm Mon-Fri Oct-Apr) is in the old train station near the center of town. There are numerous galleries to check but the real star is **Toasted Oak** (☎ 250-498-4867; 34881 97th St; meals $10-25; ❂ 11am-9pm), a renowned place for sampling local wine. At any given time there are at least 250 BC wines on offer in this former firehouse. Bare brick walls make a classy backdrop to relaxed dining and drinking areas. Menus focus on locally sourced items from salads and sandwiches to elaborate mains.

Vaseux Wildlife Centre

Just south of Okanagan Falls (below), watch for the small sign for **Vaseux Wildlife Centre** (☎ 250-494-6500; admission free; ⏲ dawn-dusk) at the north end of Vaseux Lake off Hwy 97. From the 300m boardwalk you'll see lots of birds, and you might catch a glimpse of bighorn sheep, mountain goats or some of the 14 species of bats. You can also hike to the Bighorn National Wildlife Area and the Vaseux Lake National Migratory Bird Sanctuary, with more than 160 bird species.

You can **camp** (sites $14) at one of the 12 simple lakeside sites along Hwy 97, popular for bass fishing, swimming and canoeing in summer. In winter, people head to the lake for skating and ice fishing.

Okanagan Falls

This small town at the south end of Skaha Lake is mostly a place where you have to choose your course. The main road, Hwy 97, heads north along the west side of the lake. However, you can also follow a series of smaller but paved roads that wander the hills and vineyards on the east side of the lake bringing you out in Penticton.

PENTICTON

pop 33,100

Not as frenetic as Kelowna, Penticton combines the idle pleasures of a beach resort with its own edgy vibe. Long a final stop in life for Canadian retirees (which added a certain spin to its Salish-derived name Pen-Tak-Tin, meaning 'place to stay forever'), the town today is growing fast, along with the rest of the valley.

Condos are appearing all over and the long-sleepy center is developing a bit of a buzz, especially along 'colorful' Front St. Making certain that things stay amped, there is a multitude of annual festivals, most during the summer months when, as boosters are quick to note, the sun shines at least 10 hours a day.

From its central location, Penticton is a good choice for a base as you can alternate

between lakeside fun and explorations of the region's bounty.

History

Penticton became an official town in 1892, while several nearby mine claims were being developed. But agriculture soon became the main industry. Local peaches were sold all over Canada and exported to points beyond. After WWII, summer tourism gradually supplanted tree fruit until high-value vineyards became the rage. Today the city is ringed by orchards and vineyards and is attracting large numbers of people looking for a second home.

Orientation

Penticton, the southernmost of the three Okanagan sister cities, sits directly between Okanagan Lake and Skaha Lake, which are connected by the Okanagan River Channel.

The core downtown area extends for about 10 blocks southward from Okanagan Lake along Main St. It has a full range of shops, banks and services. Go further, however, and you'll encounter strip malls, sprawl and big-box this and franchise that.

At the southern end of town, you'll find the 1.5km-long Skaha Beach, with sand, trees and picnic areas.

Information

BOOKSTORES

Book Shop (☎ 250-492-6661; 242 Main St) Huge collection of used books.

Okanagan Books (☎ 250-493-1941; 233 Main St) Good selection of regional books and maps.

INTERNET ACCESS

Several of the cafés listed on p232, as well as the VIC (p226), have internet access.

Penticton Library (☎ 250-492-0024; 785 Main St; access free; ⏲ 9:30am-5pm Mon-Sat, to 9pm Tue & Thu, 1-5pm Sun winter)

LAUNDRY

Laundry Basket (☎ 250-493-7899; 976 Eckhardt Ave W; ⏲ 8am-5pm)

MEDICAL SERVICES

Penticton Regional Hospital (☎ 250-492-4000; 550 Carmi Ave; ⏲ 24hr)

POST

Shopper's Drug Mart (☎ 250-492-8000; Penticton Plaza Mall, 1301 Main St; ⏲ 9am-6pm Mon-Sat)

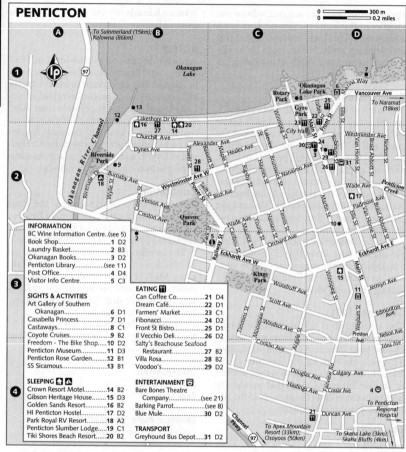

PENTICTON

0 ――――― 300 m
0 ――――― 0.2 miles

TOURIST INFORMATION

BC Wine Information Centre (☎ 250-493-4055; www.bcwineinfo.ca; 553 Railway St, at Hwy 97 & Eckhardt Ave W; ⏰ 9am-8pm May-Sep, 10am-6pm Oct-Apr) With the VIC; voluminous information, tastings and sales. See the boxed text, p228, for details on tasting your way through the region.

Visitor Information Centre (☎ 250-493-4055, 800-663-5052; 553 Railway St, at Hwy 97 & Eckhardt Ave W; ⏰ 9am-8pm May-Sep, 10am-6pm Oct-Apr) One of BC's best, with free internet access.

Sights

SS Sicamous (☎ 250-492-0403; 1099 Lakeshore Dr W; adult/child $5/1; ⏰ 9am-9pm May-Oct, 10am-4pm Mon-Fri Nov-Apr) is a classic stern-wheeler that hauled passengers and freight on Okanagan Lake

from 1914 to 1936. Now both restored and beached, it has been joined by the equally old *SS Naramata*, a tugboat.

If the *Sicamous* gets you in the mood for a boat ride, the **Casabella Princess** (☎ 250-492-4090; www.casabellaprincess.com; adult/child $15/8; ⏰ 2pm Sat & Sun May-Oct) offers one-hour, open-air lake tours on a faux stern-wheeler. There are multiple daily sailings at summer's peak.

If you want to take some time out to smell the roses, you can stroll around the **Penticton Rose Garden** (admission free), beside the *SS Sicamous*. The waterfront **Art Gallery of Southern Okanagan** (☎ 250-493-2928; 199 Marina Way; admission $2; ⏰ 10am-5pm Tue-Sat) displays an engaging collection of regional, provincial and national artists. Watch for special exhibits.

The **Penticton Museum** (☎ 250-490-2451; 785 Main St; admission by donation; ⌚ 10am-5pm Tue-Sat) is an excellent small-town museum with well-done, delightfully eclectic displays, including the de rigueur natural history exhibit with stuffed animals and birds. Showing a tad more spunk than many of these places, it has a fun display on a typical Penticton living room from the 1960s. Speaking of spunk, check out the history of the Peach Festival and its contestants.

Activities

Kids of all ages will find mini-golf and other classic holiday pursuits at the west end of **Okanagan Beach**. Okanagan Beach boasts about 1300m of sand, with average summer water temperatures of about 22°C. If things are jammed, there are often quieter shores at **Skaha Beach**, south of the center.

The paved **Okanagan River Channel Biking & Jogging Path** follows the channel from lake to lake. It's great for running, walking, cycling or in-line skating.

WATER SPORTS

Both Okanagan and Skaha Lakes enjoy some of the best sailboarding, boating and paddling in the Okanagan Valley. **Castaways** (☎ 250-490-2033; Penticton Lakeside Resort, 21 Lakeshore Dr; kayaks per hr $19) rents just about anything that floats. A full day's rental of a ski boat is $480.

Coyote Cruises (☎ 250-492-2115; 215 Riverside Dr; rental & shuttle $11; ⌚ 10am-4:30pm Jun-Aug) rents inner tubes that you can float on all the way down the Okanagan River Channel to Skaha Lake. After a languid two hours, the company transports you back to the start.

MOUNTAIN BIKING

Long dry days and rolling hills add up to great conditions for mountain biking. Get to popular rides by heading east out of town, toward Naramata (p233). Follow signs to the city dump and Campbell's Mountain, where you'll find a single-track and dual-slalom course, both of which aren't too technical. Once you get there, the riding is mostly on the right side, but once you pass the cattle guard, it opens up and you can ride anywhere.

In summer, the fast quad **chairlift** (adult/child $10/5) at **Apex Mountain Resort** zips riders and their bikes to the top of the mountain (p234). You can explore the backcountry or simply get a rush from following a trail down again.

Rent bikes and pick up a wealth of information at **Freedom – The Bike Shop** (☎ 250-493-0686; 533 Main St; bikes per day $35).

ROCK CLIMBING

Drawn by the dry weather and compact gneiss rock, climbers from all over the world come to the **Skaha Bluffs** to enjoy a seven-month climbing season on more than 400 bolted routes across the 120 cliffs. The rock is compact but has plenty of holes making the climbing excellent for experienced and novice climbers.

You'll need a car to get to the Bluffs, which are about 3km south of town off Valleyview Rd. However, late in 2006 the longtime access route and parking area was permanently closed by the private owners. Check with the VIC (opposite) or the local climbing group, **Skaha.org** (www.skaha.org), to find out the new access route and any associated fees.

Skaha Rock Adventures (☎ 250-493-1765; www .skaharockclimbing.com; 2-day courses from $265) offers advanced technical instruction and introductory courses for anyone venturing into a harness for the first time.

Festivals & Events

Penticton festivals large and small happen almost nonstop throughout the summer. The most important are listed below.

June

Elvis Festival (www.pentictonelvisfestival.com) Dozens of dueling Elvis impersonators could be your idea of heaven or hell at this festival with a name that says it all. Real die-hards may enjoy the afternoon of open-mike sing-alongs open to everyone.

July

Beach Blanket Film Festival (www.beachblanketfilm fest.ca) Bring a lawn chair or blanket and kick back to watch the movie screen, which is set up on Skaha Lake.

August

Ironman Triathlon (☎ 250-490-8787; www.ironman .ca) Almost 2000 athletes swim 3.9km, cycle 180km and then, just for the heck of it, run a full marathon (42km). You, however, can sit in the shade, watch the action and sip wine.

Peach Festival (☎ 800-663-5052; www.peachfest.com) The city's premier event is basically a weeklong party that has taken place since 1948. The festivities include sports activities, novelty events, street music and dance, nightly entertainment and a major parade that's held on Saturday. Peach queen competition is fierce.

OKANAGAN VALLEY WINERIES

With the number of wineries on track to soon blow past a hundred, the Okanagan Valley and the noble grape are clearly in the midst of a major romance. Long a producer of low-end table wine, the valley began moving to more expensive and exclusive varieties of wine in the 1980s. The abundance of sunshine, fertile soil and cool winters has produced many wines of note. Kelowna and the region north are known for their whites like Pinot Grigio. South, near Penticton and Oliver, reds are the stars, especially ever-popular merlots; while the sweet elixir known as ice wine (it's made from grapes frozen on the vine) is not to be missed.

That the wineries are all on or close to Hwy 97 means that tasters and tourists alike barely have a chance to get their car up to speed before another vast vineyard swings into view. Most offer tours and all offer sales (in fact many of the best wines are only sold at the wineries) but a growing number are also adding top-end restaurants that offer fine views and tasty regional fare to complement what's in the glass.

FESTIVALS

In 1979, the first Okanagan Wine Festival was held. Over the years, this celebration of valley wine grew in popularity to where it lasted more than a week and was a virtual nonstop orgy of banquets, special tastings, parties and more. Lots of people came, so many in fact that now there are festivals throughout the year.

Okanagan wineries certainly know how to put on a party. Expect vintners to premiere special vintages, hold tastings of rare wines, host special tasting dinners and more. You can check up on the seasonal happenings at the valley's very good **festival website** (www.thewinefestivals.com).

The festivals (fall is the major one):

- Fall – early October
- Spring – early May
- Winter – mid-January
- Summer – mid-August

INFORMATION

Two good sources of information on Okanagan Valley wines are the **BC Wine Information Centre** (☎ 250-493-4055; 553 Railway St, at Hwy 97 & Eckhardt Ave W; ☷ 9am-8pm May-Sep, 10am-6pm Oct-Apr) in Penticton and the **Wine Museum** (☎ 250-868-0441; admission free; ☷ 10am-6pm Mon-Sat, 11am-5pm Sun) in Kelowna. At each of these places, you can get guidance if you are looking for wineries specializing in certain types of wines. VICs are also good resources. And don't hesitate to follow your own instincts – if you enjoy a valley wine, go find the winery.

It's also worth looking for guidebooks by John Schreiner, the dean of BC wine writers. His *John Schreiner's Okanagan Wine Tour Guide* is up-to-date, authoritative and voluminous in its coverage.

TOURS

There are several companies that let you do the sipping while they do the driving. See the companies listed under Naramata (p234) and Kelowna (p238) for details.

VISITING THE WINERIES

At all the wineries open for visitors, you can expect to taste wine, but the quality of the experience varies widely. Some establishments are simple, with just a couple of wines on offer. Others are grander affairs with dozens of vintages ready for your attention. Some tasting rooms seem more like glorified sales areas, others have magnificent views of the vines, valley and lakes. Some charge for tastings, while at others they remain free. More and more wineries are adding

Okanagan Valley Wineries (continued p230)

OKANAGAN VALLEY WINERIES

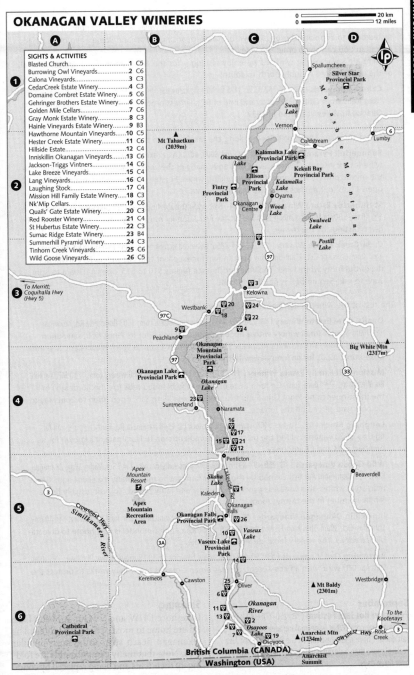

0 ——————— 20 km
0 ——————— 12 miles

SIGHTS & ACTIVITIES
Blasted Church.....................................1	C5
Burrowing Owl Vineyards...................2	C6
Calona Vineyards.................................3	C3
CedarCreek Estate Winery.................4	C3
Domaine Combret Estate Winery......5	C6
Gehringer Brothers Estate Winery.....6	C6
Golden Mile Cellars.............................7	C6
Gray Monk Estate Winery...................8	C3
Hainle Vineyards Estate Winery.........9	B3
Hawthorne Mountain Vineyards.......10	C5
Hester Creek Estate Winery..............11	C6
Hillside Estate...................................12	C4
Inniskillin Okanagan Vineyards........13	C6
Jackson-Triggs Vintners....................14	C6
Lake Breeze Vineyards......................15	C4
Lang Vineyards..................................16	C4
Laughing Stock..................................17	C4
Mission Hill Family Estate Winery....18	C3
Nk'Mip Cellars...................................19	C6
Quails' Gate Estate Winery..............20	C3
Red Rooster Winery...........................21	C4
St Hubertus Estate Winery...............22	C3
Sumac Ridge Estate Winery.............23	B4
Summerhill Pyramid Winery.............24	C3
Tinhorn Creek Vineyards..................25	C6
Wild Goose Vineyards.......................26	C5

Okanagan Valley Wineries (continued from p228)

restaurants to supplant the usual bowl of palate-cleansing bread and some have plans to add rooms so you can sleep amid the vines.

Here are some of the wineries we enjoy visiting – for the wine, views, food, welcome or all of the above (listed roughly north to south).

■ **Calona Vineyards** (☎ 250-762-3332; 1125 Richter St, Kelowna; ⊙ 9am-6pm summer, 10am-5pm winter) Near Kelowna's Cultural District, and one of BC's largest producers, Calona was the first in the Okanagan Valley; it started in 1932.

The next three are south of Kelowna along the lake's eastern shore.

■ **Summerhill Pyramid Winery** (☎ 250-764-8000; 4870 Chute Lake Rd) One of the most popular wineries for visitors. Owner Steve Cipes ages many of the wines in a huge pyramid. Celebrate the mystic powers with one of their sparkling wines. Forster's Sunset Bistro (mains $10 to $20, open 11am to 9pm) has a view to match its name.

■ **St Hubertus Estate Winery** (☎ 250-764-7888; www.st-hubertus.bc.ca; 5225 Lakeshore Rd, Kelowna; ⊙ 10am-5:30pm May-Oct, noon-5pm Tue-Sat Nov-Apr) A family-run winery where you are likely to be given tastings by the owner.

■ **CedarCreek Estate Winery** (☎ 250-764-8866; www.cedarcreek.bc.ca; 5445 Lakeshore Rd, Kelowna; ⊙ 10am-6pm Apr-Oct, 11am-5pm Nov-Mar) Known for excellent tours as well as its Ehrenfelser, a delightful fruity white wine. The Vineyard Terrace (mains $10 to $15, open 11:30am to 3pm June to mid-September) is good for lunch.

The rest of the wineries can be reached via Hwy 97.

■ **Quails' Gate Estate Winery** (☎ 250-769-4451; www.quailsgate.com; 3303 Boucherie Rd, Kelowna; ⊙ 10am-5pm) A small winery with a huge reputation; known for its Pinot Noir, sauvignon blanc and more. The restaurant (meals $15 to $25, open 11am to 9pm) is excellent. See the boxed text, p232, for an interview with the owner.

■ **Mission Hill Family Estate Winery** (☎ 250-768-7611; www.missionhillwinery.com; 1730 Mission Hill Rd, Westbank; ⊙ 10am-5pm) Go for a taste of one of the blended reds (try the Bordeaux) or the thirst-quenching Pinot Gris. Simple lunches (mains $8 to $15, open noon to 2pm May to October) are served on the terrace.

■ **Laughing Stock** (☎ 250-493-8466; www.laughingstock.ca; 1548 Naramata Rd, Penticton; ⊙ call for hr) One of 20 wineries along the pretty road from Penticton to Naramata. It's known for its blended reds and Chardonnay.

■ **Wild Goose Vineyards** (☎ 250-497-8919; www.wildgoosewinery.com; 2145 Sun Valley Way, Okanagan Falls; ⊙ 10am-5pm Apr-Oct) Owned by the Kruger family who make many excellent light German-style whites, this winery is especially friendly *and* fairly priced. You can usually find a family member in the tasting room.

■ **Inniskillin Okanagan Vineyards** (☎ 250-498-6663; www.inniskillin.com; Rd 11 W, Oliver; ⊙ 10am-5pm May-Oct, 10am-3pm Mon-Fri Nov-Apr) BC's first producer of Zinfandel is also home to delectable ice wines. The winery looks deceptively humble.

■ **Burrowing Owl Vineyards** (☎ 250-498-0620; www.bovwine.ca; 100 Burrowing Owl Pl, Oliver; ⊙ 10am-5pm Apr-Oct) Wine with an eco-accent. Besides organic grapes the winery works to protect the

September

Penticton Hot Jazz Festival (☎ 250-770-3494; www .pentasticjazz.com) What wine-making area worth its salt doesn't have a jazz festival? At the Penticton Hot Jazz Festival more than a dozen bands perform at five venues over three days.

Sleeping

Lakeshore Dr W and S Main St/Skaha Lake Rd are home to most of the local motels. The Okanagan Beach strip is the most popular area. Note that many campgrounds are folding up their tents and being replaced by condo habitat of its namesake bird and other threatened species. Enjoy the Syrah at one of the Sonora Room restaurant's (mains $10 to $20, open 11am to 3pm April to October) balcony tables.

■ **Nk'Mip Cellars** (☎ 250-495-2985; www.nkmipcellars.com; 1400 Rancher Creek Rd, Osoyoos; ☼ 9am-5pm May-Oct, 10am-4pm Nov-Apr) The first winery in North America owned by a First Nations band, the main building boasts a pueblo style. The restaurant (mains $10 to $15, open 11am to 3pm June to September) is a good place to enjoy their excellent Pinot Blanc.

Aside from the favorites we list above, there are many, many more wineries you can visit. The following list we recommend (north to south) isn't exhaustive, so you'll have to find a few you can call your own.

Okanagan Centre

■ **Gray Monk Estate Winery** (☎ 250-766-3168; 1055 Camp Rd) Try the Pinot Gris.

Peachland

■ **Hainle Vineyards Estate Winery** (☎ 250-767-2525; 5355 Trepanier Bench Rd) Dry Rieslings.

Summerland

■ **Sumac Ridge Estate Winery** (☎ 250-494-0451; 17403 Hwy 97) Sparkling wines.

Penticton to Naramata

More than 20 wineries line this good detour:

■ **Lake Breeze Vineyards** (☎ 250-496-5659; 930 Sammet Rd)

■ **Lang Vineyards** (☎ 250-496-5987; 2493 Gammon Rd)

■ **Hillside Estate** (☎ 250-493-6274; 1350 Naramata Rd)

■ **Red Rooster Winery** (☎ 250-496-4041; 910 De Beck Rd)

Okanagan Falls

■ **Blasted Church** (☎ 250-497-1125; 378 Parsons Rd) Fine views from the Lakeside Rd alternative to Hwy 97.

■ **Hawthorne Mountain Vineyards** (☎ 250-497-8267; Green Lake Rd) Ice wine.

Oliver

■ **Jackson-Triggs Vintners** (☎ 250-498-4981; 38619 Hwy 97) One of BC's best-known.

■ **Tinhorn Creek Vineyards** (☎ 250-498-3743; 32830 Tinhorn Creek Rd) A festival of merlot.

■ **Gehringer Brothers Estate Winery** (☎ 250-498-3537; Rd No 8) Good range of whites.

■ **Hester Creek Estate Winery** (☎ 250-498-4435; 13163 326th Ave) Noted Pinot Blanc.

■ **Domaine Combret Estate Winery** (☎ 250-498-6966; 32057 Rd No 13) Tasty light whites.

■ **Golden Mile Cellars** (☎ 250-498-8330; 13140 316A Ave) A wide range of top-end wines.

developments; several are along Skaha Lake. The VIC has a long list of B&Bs. Expect off-season discounts.

HI Penticton Hostel (☎ 250-492-3992; www.hi hostels.ca; 464 Ellis St; dm $18-24, r from $40; ⚇ 🖥) This hostel is near the center in a worn old house

the hostel says has 'character.' Rooms have one to six beds. The hostel arranges all sorts of activities, including wine tours.

Park Royal RV Resort (☎ 250-492-7051; 240 Riverside Dr; car/RV sites from $35) Right near the busy end of Okanagan Beach, the 40 sites here are set among shady lawns. That's not a bear you hear growling hungrily at night, it's a condo developer.

Golden Sands Resort (☎ 250-492-4210, 877-389-6888; www.goldensandspenticton.com; 1028 Lakeshore Dr W; r $80-250; 🔀 🗩) Another of the Okanagan Beach vacation-apartment–style motels, the 47 units have one to three bedrooms each. The beige decor will hide a week's worth of sand. Enjoy barbecues by the pool.

Penticton Slumber Lodge (☎ 250-492-4008, 800-663-2831; www.slumberlodge.com; 274 Lakeshore Dr W; r from $100; 🔀 🗩) Right across from the beach, the 44 units here are large, some have multiple bedrooms and all have kitchen facilities. It's a modern and tidy place.

Gibson Heritage House (☎ 250-492-2705; www.ibsonbb.com; 112 Eckhardt Ave W; r $100-150; 🔀) Close to the center, this 1906 colonial revival B&B offers four rooms, each named after local pioneers. Each has its own bathroom. Breakfast is of the lavish English variety.

Crown Resort Motel (☎ 250-492-4092, 866-447-9610; www.crownmotel.ca; 950 Lakeshore Dr W; r $100-180; 🔀 🗩) A mix of 30 older and newer units, although all have updated decor. Each has a patio or balcony from which you can see the lake – albeit over the parking courtyard. In peak months, there's an ice cream café.

Tiki Shores Beach Resort (☎ 250-492-8769, 866-492-8769; www.tikishores.com; 914 Lakeshore Dr W; condos from $130-300; 🔀 🗩) This lively resort has 40 condo-style units with separate bedrooms and kitchens. Throw your own toga party in one of the 'Roman theme units,' which offer bathtime bacchanalia in their whirlpool tubs.

Eating & Drinking

Penticton definitely has its share of good eats. Stroll around Main and Front Sts and you will find numerous choices. The **Farmers' Market** (☎ 250-770-3276; 🕙 8am-noon Sat May-Oct) has large numbers of local organic producers, based at Gyro Park in the 100 block of Main St.

BUDGET

Il Vecchio Deli (☎ 250-492-7610; 317 Robinson St; sandwiches $4; ☎ 10am-4pm Mon-Sat) Save your money, skip the trip to Florence and enjoy this aromatically spot-on deli where locals take as many deep breaths as possible while enjoying excellent sandwiches and other treats. Note: it's about the size of a ball of fresh mozzarella.

Can Coffee Co (☎ 250-493-3044; The Cannery, 1475 Fairview Rd at Duncan Ave; meals $6; 🕙 7am-8pm; 🖳) Housed in a quirky old cannery, this high-ceilinged café has lots of space for lounging while enjoying good coffees, breakfasts and sandwiches. There's wi-fi and a nice porch.

Fibonacci (☎ 250-770-1913; 219 Main St; meals from $7; 🕙 8am-8pm Mon-Sat) Middle Eastern fast food mixes with coffee in this attractive café and coffeehouse downtown. Patrons can enjoy free wi-fi inside or at one of the many sidewalk tables.

MIDRANGE

Voodoo's (☎ 250-770-8867; 67 E Nanaimo Ave; meals $8-20; 🕙 5pm-late) Small tapas-style plates are the thing at this dark and stylish place where black will never go out of fashion. The menu reflects

---

LOCAL VOICES: TONY STEWART

Quails' Gate Estate Winery (see the boxed text, p228) is one of the Okanagan Valley's top producers. First planted as an orchard in 1873, the land was switched over to grapes beginning in 1961. Today an original log cabin is flanked by a stunning restaurant and sales complex, which have great views of Okanagan Lake from the west bank.

Tony Stewart is the latest member of the family to preside over the land. As proprietor of the winery, he has seen – and enjoyed – many of the recent changes to the region. 'Wines have saved a lot of the land from development,' he says, noting the growing subdivisions that even now are hovering around his vineyards.

'There's government protection for the land and growing grapes is a high enough value use of the land that it keeps some of the old orchard people from just selling out to developers.'

'Wineries in general have been good for employment. We use a lot of skilled and better paid people. When I was a kid I remember you hired fruit-pickers outside bars in Kelowna.'

But pressures to get as much revenue from the land and the wineries are relentless: 'We aim to get people to do more than have a quick sip and leave. We want them to stay for three or four hours by taking a tour, doing some free sampling and then enjoying a meal. Our next big project will be to add boutique rooms.'

THE MONSTER WITH A HAPPY FACE

Soon after you reach the Okanagan Valley, you may wonder: 'What the heck is that odd, sinuous creature I keep seeing all over?' Assuming you're not referring to something on your own person then you probably mean the Ogopogo, the local answer to Loch Ness and its monster. A subject of many myths – some have locals in the misty past tossing hapless critters into the lake as offerings – the creature is generally depicted as a sort of giant snake- or worm-like aberration. However, in a uniquely Canadian twist, the Ogopogo is depicted as a cheery fellow, kind of an ambassador to children and wine-slurping adults alike. Look for him on signs, in business names and in statue form in almost every major valley park.

the inventiveness of the kitchen. Expect to be surprised. Enjoy any of a myriad of cocktails at the long bar. On many nights there's live blues or other music.

Dream Café (☎ 250-490-9012; 67 Front St; meals $10-20; ☺ 8am-late Tue-Sun; ☐) Funky is defined by this fun-filled place that hums from breakfast right through dinner. Many mains are served 'gypsy' style, which means you get to choose from several brightly spiced dishes like gumbo or tandoori chicken. The outdoor patio is a treat. On many nights there's live acoustic guitar by noted performers.

Front St Bistro (☎ 250-770-1949; 151 Front St; meals $10-25; ☺ 11am-11pm) Once you arrive you may not leave. Two patios are heated or misted as conditions demand and there's a long list of local wines, microbrews and cocktails. The menu is an eclectic mix of salads, soups and everything from roasts to seafood to fondue. Work it off by dancing the night away to classic Top 40.

TOP END

Salty's Beachouse Seafood Restaurant (☎ 250-493-5001; 1000 Lakeshore Dr W; mains $12-25; ☺ 5-10pm Apr-Oct) *The* open-air seafood joint at the fun end of Okanagan Beach. If it swims it's liable to be deep-fried here and served with chips and a cold beer. Make that several cold beers.

Villa Rosa (☎ 250-490-9595; 795 Westminster Ave W; meals $12-25; ☺ 11:30am-2pm & 5-9pm Tue-Sun) Northern Italian food is celebrated at this always popular restaurant which combines a certain formality with a laid-back vacationer haven. Outside there are a few tables on a vine-shaded patio; this is a major score in summer. The Okanagan Beach motels are just a short walk away.

Entertainment

Many dinner places and pubs also feature live entertainment many nights (see opposite).

Bare Bones Theatre Company (☎ 250-492-2202; The Cannery, 1475 Fairview Rd at Duncan Ave; tickets from $10) Sharing space in the old cannery with Can Coffee Co, this well-regarded theater stages everything from comedy to serious drama.

Blue Mule (☎ 250-493-1819; 218 Martin St; cover varies; ☺ 8pm-late Sat & Sun) Dancers groove to DJs spinning Top 40 hits here.

Getting There & Around

Penticton Regional Airport (YYF; 250-492-6042; www .cyyf.org) is served by Air Canada Jazz, which has daily flights to Vancouver.

Greyhound (☎ 250-493-4101; 307 Ellis St) offers services within the Okanagan Valley as well as operating routes to Vancouver ($62, 7½ hours, one daily) and Kamloops ($39, 4½ hours).

The lake-to-lake shuttle bus of **Penticton Transit** (☎ 250-492-5602; www.busonline.ca; ☺ Mon-Sat) runs hourly along both waterfronts ($1.75, day pass $4) from 9am to 7pm.

NARAMATA

On all but the busiest summer weekends, you can escape many of the valley's mobs by taking the road 18km north from Penticton along the east shore of Okanagan Lake. The route is lined with wineries as well as farms producing the kinds of crops you won't find at Safeway – think organic lavender and the like. There are lots of places to hike, picnic, bird-watch or do whatever else occurs to you in beautiful and often secluded surroundings.

The historic town itself is small and boasts a few galleries and cafés. The small selection of accommodations ranges from the budget **BC Motel** (☎ 250-496-5482; 365 Robinson; r $65-85) with its 10 basic units near town to the swank **Naramata Heritage Inn & Spa** (☎ 250-496-6808, 866-617-1188; www.naramatainn.com; 3625 1st St; r $150-500; ☒ ☐). The latter was built in 1908 by a fruit-growing millionaire. Recently restored, the rooms are lavishly furnished with period pieces; bathrooms feature claw-foot tubs. Sample local wines and savor local cuisine in the fine dining room, which has a patio. Soothe your senses at the in-house spa.

If you'd rather make the trip to Naramata without the distraction of driving, or you just want to pillage a few wineries, **Top Cat Tours** (☎ 250-493-7385; www.topcattours.com; tours from $70; ☷ May-Oct) runs five-hour trips from Penticton that visit several wineries and include lunch.

APEX MOUNTAIN RESORT

Skiers and snowboarders of all abilities head to **Apex Mountain Resort** (☎ 877-777-2739, conditions 250-487-4848; www.apexresort.com; lift tickets adult/child $53/32), 33km west of Penticton off Green Mountain Rd and one of Canada's best small ski resorts. It features over 65 downhill runs, but the mountain is known for its plethora of double-black-diamond and technical runs (the drop is over 600m). The crowds are smaller than at nearby Big White Mountain (p241). Close to the village, which has hostel and lodge accommodations (see the website), you'll find 30km of cross-country trails.

Apex is also a popular summer spot, when the downhill trails open up to horseback riders, hikers and mountain bikers.

SUMMERLAND

pop 11,400

A small lakeside resort town 18km north of Penticton on Hwy 97, Summerland features some fine 19th-century heritage buildings on the hillside above the lake.

Kettle Valley Steam Railway (☎ 877-494-8424; www.kettlevalleyrail.org; 18404 Bathville Rd; adult/child $18/11; ☷ trains 10:30am & 1:30pm Sat, Sun & holidays mid-May–mid-Oct) features old steam locomotives and open-air cars. Orchard views abound along the 16km route. Some trains – and passengers – enjoy attacks by histrionic 'robbers.' From Hwy 97 take Prairie Valley Rd west out of town to Doherty Ave, then Bathville Rd.

For great views of Okanagan Lake head up to **Giant's Head Mountain**, an extinct volcano south of the downtown area. You can follow trails to the 845m peak.

Summerland Ornamental Gardens (☎ 250-494-6385; admission free; ☷ 8am-dusk), 7km south of Summerland on Hwy 97, was designed for the study of fruit trees, their growth, diseases and production. You can take self-guided tours among the lush gardens.

PEACHLAND

pop 5300

This small lakeside town 25km south of Kelowna on the west bank of Okanagan Lake lives up to its evocative name: let your spirits ripen, and you'll feel all warm, fuzzy and juicy strolling the compact downtown which is right on the lake. Parks alternate with marinas and cafés.

KELOWNA

pop 110,000

Kelowna's boosters try to describe the town as 'undiscovered.' Hah! Maybe for a few folks living just east of Mongolia this is the case but otherwise the hub city of the Okanagan Valley is very much on many people's map. Visitors who haven't been by in a few years will be amazed at the ever-lengthening urbanized stretch of tree-lined Hwy 97 north of the city. In the center, where the skyline was once defined by fruit trees, there's now a proliferation of high-rise condos. Think Vancouver's West End in the heartland.

But if Kelowna is nobody's secret, that's only because its charms are so apparent. Its long lakefront boasts many of the town's 65 parks, many with beaches. The downtown is vibrant and boasts excellent places to eat, drink and partake of the thriving local cultural scene.

The surrounding hills are home to orchards, subdivisions, vineyards, golf courses and more. With attractions and activities like superb hiking in all directions, Kelowna makes a good valley base for exploration. Summer days are usually dry and hot, the nights pleasantly cool. Winters are snowy but dry, making nearby Big White a big attraction for skiers and snowboarders.

The town's population has more than doubled in the last 30 years, partly due to its thriving economy and moderate weather, and traffic at times can be a mood-breaker. But as you tipple a few examples of the local liquid produce, you probably won't care at all.

History

Kelowna, an Interior Salish word meaning 'grizzly bear,' owes its settlement to a number of missionaries who arrived in 1858, hoping to convert the First Nations. One of the priests, Father Charles Pandosy, a sort of Canadian Johnny Appleseed, established a mission in 1859 and planted the area's first apple trees

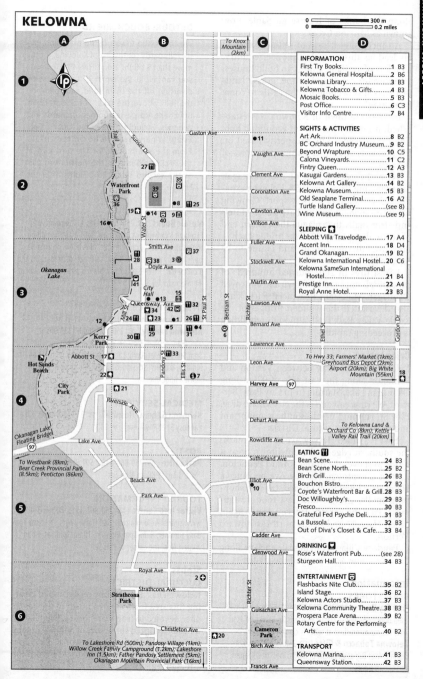

KELOWNA

0 — 300 m
0 — 0.2 miles

along the banks of L'Anse au Sable, now known as Mission Creek.

An increasing trickle of settlers followed his lead, as this was ideal pioneer country, with lots of available timber to build houses, a freshwater creek and prime, grassy lands that were just begging for the cattle to come munching.

In 1892 the town of Kelowna was established; it quickly became an economic hub. The next decades saw prosperity based on the orchards and other natural resources of the area.

With the completion of the Okanagan Lake Floating Bridge in 1958, Kelowna experienced yet another growth spurt. Growing pains are evident in the barrage of motels and strip malls that plague the eastern end of town along Hwy 97. The bridge itself is now woefully inadequate and is due to be replaced in 2008.

Forest fires in 2003 burned hundreds of expensive homes south of town and destroyed Okanagan Mountain Provincial Park. They also devastated the wooden bridges of the Kettle Valley Rail Trail, although rebuilding is proceeding rapidly.

Orientation

Kelowna sits midway between Vernon and Penticton along the east side of 97km-long Okanagan Lake. Starting from City Park, Bernard Ave runs east and is the city's main drag. Ellis St, running north–south, is important and parallels the Cultural District.

Hwy 97, called Harvey Ave in town, marks the southern edge of the downtown area; it heads west over the bridge toward Penticton. East of downtown, Harvey Ave becomes a 10km strip lined with service stations, shopping malls, motels and fast-food restaurants. Past the sprawl, Harvey Ave is again called Hwy 97 and heads northeast toward Vernon.

Pandosy Village is an upscale enclave along the lake, some 3km south of the center.

Information

BOOKSTORES

First Try Books (☎ 250-763-5364; 426B Bernard Ave) Used bookstore whose classic motto is 'In literature as in love, we are astonished at what is chosen by others.'

Kelowna Tobacco & Gifts (☎ 250-762-2266; 521 Bernard Ave) Big assortment of magazines, newspapers and Cuban cigars.

> ### DETOUR: BOUCHERIE RD
>
> Westbank, the town of strip malls and garish billboards southwest of Kelowna, is little more than a blight along Hwy 97. However, you can avoid the worst of the excess by diverting off the main road and following the hills above the lake. For about 12km, Boucherie Rd passes homes, orchards and wineries, including the noted Quails' Gate Estate Winery (see the boxed text, p232). From the south, look for the turn east at the McDonald's; from the north, turn east at the second set of stop lights after the bridge.

Mosaic Books (☎ 250-763-4418; 411 Bernard Ave) Excellent independent bookstore. Sells maps (including topographic ones), travel guides, plus books on First Nations history and culture. Good selection of magazines and a coffee bar. There is a bargain branch almost next door at 441 Bernard Ave.

INTERNET ACCESS

Many downtown cafés have wi-fi access.

Kelowna Library (☎ 250-762-2800; 1380 Ellis St; 🕑 10am-5:30pm Mon, Fri & Sat, 10am-9pm Tue-Thu, 1-5pm Sun Oct-Mar) Online access is free with registration. The building is cleverly designed to look like an open book – albeit a huge one.

MEDICAL SERVICES

Kelowna General Hospital (☎ 250-862-4000; 2268 Pandosy St at Royal Ave; 🕑 24hr)

POST

Post office (☎ 250-868-8480; 591 Bernard Ave; 🕑 8:30am-5:30pm Mon-Sat)

TOURIST INFORMATION

Visitor Info Centre (☎ 250-861-1515, 800-663-4345; www.tourismkelowna.com; 544 Harvey Ave; 🕑 8am-7pm daily summer, 8am-5pm Mon-Fri, 10am-3pm Sat & Sun winter) Near the corner of Ellis St.

Sights

CULTURAL DISTRICT

Kelowna has done an impressive job of creating this area from an area north of the center once devoted to fruit warehouses. Even better, it hasn't adopted some sort of Soho-wannabe name like CuDi, FruWa or worse. Pick up a walking tour map in the district or from the VIC (above).

The **Kelowna Art Gallery** (☎ 250-979-0888; www
.kelownaartgallery.com; 1315 Water St; admission free;
☻ 10am-5pm Tue-Sat, 10am-9pm Thu, 1-5pm Sun) features the work of the vibrant local arts community. The light, airy gallery has regular
special exhibits.

Nearby are two more worthwhile art gal-
leries. **Art Ark** (☎ 250-862-5080; 1295 Cannery Lane;
☻ 10am-5pm, later in summer) shows and sells a
wide range of works (paintings, sculpture,
photography, mixed media and so on) by
western Canadian artists. Next door, the tiny
Turtle Island Gallery (☎ 250-717-8235) sells and
displays pottery, carvings, paintings and more
by First Nations artists.

Located in the old Laurel Orchards packing
house, the **BC Orchard Industry Museum** (☎ 250-
763-0433; 1304 Ellis St; admission by donation; ☻ 10am-5pm
Mon-Sat) recounts the conversion of the Okanagan Valley from ranch land to orchards. The
exhibits have great appeal and show just about
everything you can do with fruit. Note the
displays of beautiful old packing crate labels
such as the mouthwatering art for Earl's Court
brand apples.

In the same building is the **Wine Museum**
(☎ 250-868-0441; admission free; ☻ 10am-6pm Mon-
Sat, 11am-5pm Sun). The knowledgeable staff
can recommend tours, steer you to the best
wineries for tastings and help you fill your
trunk with examples of the myriad local wines
on sale. See the boxed text, p228, for more
information.

A part of the civic center complex, the
Kelowna Museum (☎ 250-763-2417; 470 Queensway
Ave; admission by donation; ☻ 10am-5pm Tue-Sat) has
everything from the bones of early valley
inhabitants to displays on the roots of local
agriculture. Special exhibits may draw you in
on a nonrainy day.

Behind the museum, **Kasugai Gardens** (admission free; ☻ 9am-6pm) are good for a lovely
peaceful stroll around the beautifully manicured grounds. Named for Kelowna's sister
city in Japan, the gardens do the relationship
proud.

CITY PARK & PROMENADE
City Park & Promenade, the central downtown
park, is a lovely spot to while away a few
hours. Pick up the guide to the many sculptures at the VIC (opposite). Plunge into the
water at frolicsome **Hot Sands Beach**, read under
one of the many shade trees or just marvel at
the flower gardens blooming with tulips and

enjoy the soothing views across **Okanagan Lake**.
Given the bucolic setting and the warm lake
water (just slightly cooler than the summer
air), it's no wonder would-be fruit pickers are
sitting around picking only guitars.

From Bernard Ave, the lakeside promenade
extends north past the marina, Grand Okanagan hotel and condominiums to **Waterfront
Park**, where trails wander through the islets.
Island Stage looks out over a serene lagoon.

You'll find several **beaches** south of Okanagan Lake Floating Bridge along Lakeshore
Rd. Gyro Beach, at the south end of Richter
St and Pandosy Village, attracts crowds on
weekends.

The 10.5-sq-km **Okanagan Mountain Provin-
cial Park** (☎ 250-494-6500; www.elp.gov.bc.ca/bcparks),
south of Kelowna at the end of Lakeshore
Rd, was 95% burned by the 2003 fires. The
park is now closed to vehicles but BC Parks
is restoring trails which give you a close-up
look at nature's recovery and an unobstructed
view of the lake. See Tours, p238, for other
options.

About 8.5km northwest of Kelowna, **Bear
Creek Provincial Park** (☎ 250-494-6500; www.elp.gov
.bc.ca/bcparks) offers opportunities for hiking as
well as windsurfing, fishing, swimming and
wilderness camping. From Kelowna, cross
the floating bridge and go right (north) on
Westside Rd.

FATHER PANDOSY SETTLEMENT
The **Father Pandosy Settlement** (admission free;
☻ 8am-dusk Mar-Oct) is Kelowna's major historical site. Granted it only dates to 1859, but
this is where the good father enthusiastically
planted his seed (among other places) and
built a mission. The church, school, barn, one
house and a few sheds from what was the first
white settlement in the Okanagan have been
restored. The site is small, well away from
the center of town and rather serene. To get
there, go south along Lakeshore Rd, then east
on Casorso Rd to Benvoulin Rd.

Activities
The weather makes Kelowna a great spot for
outdoorsy stuff, whether on the lake or in the
surrounding hills.

HIKING & MOUNTAIN BIKING
You'll find great hiking and mountain-bike
riding all around town. The 17km **Mission
Creek Greenway** is a meandering, wooded path

following the creek along the south edge of town. The western half is a wide and easy expanse, but to the east the route becomes sinuous as it climbs into the hills.

Knox Mountain, which sits at the northern end of the city, is another good place to hike or ride. Along with bobcats and snakes, the 235-hectare park has well-maintained trails and rewards with excellent views from the top.

The famous **Kettle Valley Rail Trail** is making a remarkable comeback from the fire destruction of 2003. This abandoned old railway line, which in one 24km stretch affords fantastic views of the Myra Canyon, is a highly popular trail. However 12 of 18 historic wooden trestles that spanned the gorges and valleys were destroyed by the fires. Many feared the route would be a memory, but a combination of public will and the fact that it's a lot easier to build bridges for people instead of trains means that all of the spans should be replaced by the end of 2007 – follow progress with the **Myra Canyon Trestle Restoration Society** (www.myratrestles.com). The overall 174km network of trails follow the old railway as far south as Penticton and beyond.

To reach the trail, follow Harvey Ave (Hwy 97) east to Gordon Dr. Turn south and then east on KLO Rd and follow it all the way to the end of McCulloch Rd. About 2km after the pavement ends, you'll come to a clearing where power lines cross the road. Turn south on the Myra Forest Service Rd and follow it for 8km to the parking lot. You'll see the trailhead along with current news about conditions. See Tours, right, for a guided tour option.

SPAS
Most upscale hotels and resorts now offer spas for folks who want their cares rubbed and scrubbed away. **Beyond Wrapture** (☎ 250-448-8899; www.beyondwrapture.com; 1965 Richter St; treatments from $85) has a range of offerings including some with a local twist: massages and wraps using antioxidant-rich grape seeds and skins, wine and local honey.

WATER SPORTS
You can rent speedboats (starting at $60 per hour), arrange fishing trips and cruises or rent windsurfing gear at **Kelowna Marina** (☎ 250-861-8001) at the lake end of Queensway Ave. Windsurfers take to the water from the old seaplane terminal, near the corner of Water St and Cawston Ave.

Kelowna for Children
At the foot of Bernard Ave in City Park, the old ferry boat **Fintry Queen** (☎ 250-763-2780; ☼ May-Oct) is docked in the lake. Kids love the old-boat atmosphere and the 90-minute cruises offer good views from the lake. The boat was undergoing significant restoration during 2006, so check to see if it has again set sail.

Kelowna Land & Orchard Co (☎ 250-763-1091; 3002 Dunster Rd; orchard tours adult/child $6/free; ☼ 10am-4pm May-Oct, tour times vary seasonally) is the largest of the many local orchards open for tours. You can ride wagons, buy fruit and baked goods and guzzle fresh-pressed apple juice. Many will want to stroke the llamas.

Tours
Monashee Adventure Tours (☎ 250-762-9253, 888-762-9253; www.monasheeadventuretours.com) offers scores of biking and hiking tours of the valley, parks, Kettle Valley Rail Trail and buckets of wineries. Tours are accompanied by entertaining local guides. Prices, which average $100, include a bike, lunch and shuttle to the route.

Selah Outdoor Explorations (☎ 250-762-4968, 866-695-2972; half-day tours from $35) runs ecological tours by canoe to see the 2003 fire's destruction and nature's recovery along the shore of Okanagan Mountain Provincial Park.

WINERY TOURS
Numerous Kelowna companies offer tours to many of the region's wineries. There are myriad programs that last from a few hours to a full day, with various eating options as well. Tour prices usually include pick-up at hotels and motels.

Club Wine Tours (☎ 250-762-9951, 866-386-9463; www.clubwinetours.com; 3-8 hr tours $49-125)

Okanagan Wine Country Tours (☎ 250-868-9463, 866-689-9463; www.okwinetours.com; tours $65-130) Also offers custom tours and longer ones lasting several days.

Wildflower Trails and Wine Tours (☎ 250-979-1211, 866-979-1211; www.wildflowersandwine.com; tours $59-139) Offers tours with hikes through the scenic hills, garden tours and the usual plethora of winery options.

Festivals & Events
Kelowna's festivals span the year, in summer they overlap. See p228 for details on the many wine festivals.

In July hundreds of boat owners celebrate boat ownership in the **Kelowna Regatta**

(☎ 250-860-0529; www.kelownaregatta.com), while September's **International Dragon Boat Festival** (☎ 250-868-1136) sees teams race spectacular Chinese boats on the lake, followed by drinking wine.

Sleeping

As in the rest of the Okanagan Valley, accommodations here can be difficult to find in summer if you haven't booked. Other times look for bargains. The VIC (p236) has lists of dozens of B&Bs in the area.

BUDGET

There are few camping options close to town; most are west of the lake toward unbucolic Westbank.

Bear Creek Provincial Park (☎ 250-494-0321; www .discovercamping.ca; campsite $22) This park has 122 shady sites on the west side of the lake 9km north of the bridge off Westlake Rd. There's a 400m-long beach.

Willow Creek Family Campground (☎ 250-762-6302; www.willowcreekcampground.ca; 3316 Lakeshore Rd; campsite/RV site from $29/32; 🖳) Close to Pandosy Village and a beach, this 81-site facility has a laundry and wireless internet access.

Kelowna International Hostel (☎ 250-763-6024; www.kelowna-hostel.bc.ca; 2343 Pandosy St; dm/d from $15/40; 🖳) Keg parties are among the highlights at this simple hostel located in an old house about 12 blocks from downtown. Live the backpacker cliché with the available bongo drums. There's free transport to/from the bus station.

Kelowna SameSun International Hostel (☎ 250-763-9814, 877-562-2783; www.samesun.com; 245 Harvey Ave; dm/r $24/50; 🗙 🖳) Near the center and the lake, this purpose-built 130-bed hostel is downright spiffy. Activities include barbecues year-round and delights like 'party boat trips' in the summer. The hostel offers free pickup at the bus depot as well as shuttles to the SameSun Big White and Silver Star ski resort hostels (see p241).

MIDRANGE

Motels abound downtown, along Hwy 97 and at Pandosy Village.

Abbott Villa Travelodge (☎ 250-763-7771, 800-578-7878; www.travelodge.com; 1627 Abbott St; r from $80; 🗙 🖳 🐾) Right downtown and across from City Park, this 52-room motel is good value and has free wi-fi in the strictly standard-issue rooms, a nice outdoor pool and a hot tub.

Royal Anne Hotel (☎ 250-763-2277, 888-811-3400; www.royalannehotel.com; 348 Bernard Ave; r $80-130; 🗙 🖳) Stay right in the heart of Kelowna at this unassuming motel. Most of the 64 rooms have minute balconies and high-speed internet access. Standard rooms have two queen-size beds while deluxe rooms have king-size beds and sitting areas. Decor throughout is more standard than deluxe.

Accent Inn (☎ 250-862-8888, 800-663-0298; www .accentinns.com; 1140 Harvey Ave; r from $100; 🗙 🖳 🐾) This is the pick of the litter at this motel-lined corner of Hwy 97. The 102 units in three-story blocks have nice touches like hanging baskets of flowers and high-speed internet. For once the wall-unit air-con units don't rattle like a snoring Ogopogo.

Lakeshore Inn (☎ 250-763-4717, 877-657-5253; www.lakeshoreinn.com; 3756 Lakeshore Rd; r from $120; 🗙 🖳 🐾) On a bucolic stretch of lake just south of Pandosy Village and a beach, this 46-room property is well maintained and features a pool right on the waterfront. Rooms – half with views – have microwaves, fridges and toasters.

Prestige Inn (☎ 250-860-7900, 877-737-8443; www .prestigeinn.com; 1675 Abbott St; r from $150; 🗙 🖳 🐾) This 66-room place has a great location across from City Park. It's all very understated yet with some trappings of luxury like four-poster beds and an indoor pool. Rooms have high-speed internet and fridges.

TOP END

New luxury hotels will soon join the condos north of downtown.

Hotel Eldorado (☎ 250-763-7500, 866-608-7500; www .eldoradokelowna.com; 500 Cook Rd; r $165-380; 🗙 🖳 🐾) This historic lakeshore hotel has undergone a transformation that has seen its 19 heritage rooms raised to antique-filled luxury status. In addition, a new low-key wing has 30 more rooms, most with tiny balconies and water views. The older rooms are the pick here, but opulent touches can be found throughout the property.

Grand Okanagan (☎ 250-763-4500, 800-465-4651; www.grandokanagan.com; 1310 Water St; r from $170; 🗙 🖳 🐾) The sprawling Grand anchors the upscale developments north of the Cultural District. This lakefront property boasts artwork in the common areas, a spa, a splendid pool area and much more, all attended to by an attentive staff. The best picks of the 320 rooms have balconies, lake views and bedside Jacuzzis. There's a small casino for the financially unwise.

Eating & Drinking

Kelowna boasts many restaurants that take full advantage of the local bounty of food-stuffs. Needless to say, you can get a good glass of wine with your meal.

The **Farmers' Market** (☎ 250-878-5029; cnr Spring-field Rd & Dilworth Dr; ♡ 8am-1pm Wed & Sat Apr-Oct) has over 150 vendors, including many with pre-pared foods. Local artisans also display their wares. It's off Hwy 97.

BUDGET & MIDRANGE

Bean Scene (☎ 250-763-1814; 274 Bernard Ave; coffee $2; ♡ 6:30am-10pm) has a great bulletin board to check up on local happenings while you munch on a muffin amid the buzz. A quieter location, **Bean Scene North** (☎ 250-763-4022; 1289 Ellis St; ♡ 6am-6pm) offers caffeinated respite in the Cultural District.

Out of Diva's Closet & Cafe (☎ 250-860-3090; 1623 Pandosy St; snacks $3; ♡ 9am-6pm Mon-Sat; ▯) Quirky and funky are some of the more mainstream adjectives for this combo wi-fi café, coffee and tea bar, juice joint and used clothing bazaar.

Grateful Fed Psyche Deli (☎ 250-862-8621; 509 Bernard Ave; meals from $7; ♡ 7am-9pm Mon-Sat, later in summer) Only someone thicker than one of this deli's sandwiches wouldn't guess that this place has a rock and roll theme. There's full bar service and sidewalk tables.

Sturgeon Hall (☎ 250-860-3055; 1481 Water St; meals $7-15; ♡ 11am-midnight Mon-Sat) Fanatical fans of hockey's Kelowna Rockets feast on favorites like jumbo burgers while quaffing brews at the bar or outside at sidewalk tables. Others ponder the pizza and sports-spewing TVs dotting the walls.

Doc Willoughby's (☎ 250-868-8288; 353 Bernard Ave; meals $8-12; ♡ 11:30am-2am) Right downtown, this classic pub boasts numerous tables and a vaulted interior much lined with wood. The menu is as comfortable as padded booths: nachos, burgers, sandwiches and weekend brunch. This is the place to find brews from Cannery Brewing in Penticton.

Coyote's Waterfront Bar & Grill (☎ 250-860-1226; Grand Okanagan, 1352 Water St; meals from $15; ♡ 11am-11pm) There are great lake views from this upstairs Southwestern steak joint in the wa-terfront resort. Rose's, the adjoining bar, hops in summer.

TOP FIVE THINGS TO PUT IN YOUR MOUTH

- A Peachland peach (p234)
- An organic apple (p224) from an Oliver fruit stand
- A sip of Burrowing Owl Vineyards' Syrah (see the boxed text, p228)
- The surprising sweet explosion of In-niskillin Okanagan Vineyards ice wine (see the boxed text, p228)
- A Bean to Brew blueberry muffin (p243) in Vernon

TOP END

Bouchons Bistro (☎ 250-763-6595; 1180 Sunset Dr; meals from $20; ♡ 5-10pm) A local fave in the heart of condoland, this upscale café brings a bit of French fun to Kelowna. Gallic standards are faithfully rendered using local produce – is it us or does the cassoulet here beat the cassoulet there?

our pick **Birch Grill** (☎ 250-860-3103; 526 Bernard Ave; meals from $20; ♡ 11:30am-2pm Mon-Fri, 5-10pm Wed-Sat) Personality almost trumps the menu at chef Jeff Jefferson's storefront joint. But that's not bad as both are bigger than life. The open kitchen is almost as large as the smallish dining room which allows easy viewing of the action. Look for boldly flavored meat and seafood dishes. As you'd expect, local wines and produce star.

La Bussola (☎ 250-763-3110; 1451 Ellis St; meals from $25; ♡ 5-10pm Mon-Sat) A recent move has put this local favorite close to the Cultural District. Since 1974 Franco and Lauretta Coccaro have worked to perfect their Italian supper house. The menu spans the boot, from pesto to red sauce, veal to seafood. Dine on the flower-bedecked sidewalk tables or in the smart dining room.

Fresco (☎ 250-868-8805; www.frescorestaurant.net; 1560 Water St; meals from $40; ♡ 5-10pm Tue-Sat) The Okana-gan Valley's finest restaurant is also one of BC's best. Noted chef Rod Butters (definitely no relation to the winsome *South Park* character) celebrates the produce of the region in this exquisite location in a restored brick storefront. The menu changes constantly – a surprise find at the farmers' market can appear that night – but always features intensely flavored yet sim-ple prepared dishes. Book ahead.

Entertainment

CLUBS

Downtown Kelowna boasts several clubs. There are usually one or two fairly grungy ones in the grungy 200 block of Leon St – names change frequently.

Flashbacks Nite Club (☎ 250-861-3039; 1268 Ellis St; cover varies; ☽ 8pm-late Wed-Sun) In a former cigar factory, this is the big mainstream venue for live music. It often attracts major touring Canadian bands like Sloan.

PERFORMANCE & ART

Rotary Centre for the Performing Arts (☎ 250-717-5304, tickets 250-763-1849; 421 Cawston Ave) This impressive facility anchors the Cultural District and has galleries, a theater, a café, craft workshops and more. This place for live music from groups such as Chamber Music Kelowna (☎ 250-764-7179).

our pick **Kelowna Actors Studio** (☎ 250-862-2867; www.kelownaactorsstudio.com; 1379 Ellis St; tickets from $57) Enjoy works as diverse as *Hello Dolly* and *The Diary of Anne Frank* while chowing down on upscale fare at this dinner theater with serious ambitions.

Kelowna Community Theatre (☎ 250-762-2471; 1375 Water St) is a venue for music and theater. The **Sunshine Theatre Company** (☎ 250-763-4025; www.sunshinetheatre.org) stages a range of productions at both Rotary Centre for the Performing Arts and Kelowna Actors Studio.

Free summer concerts, featuring everything from rock to classical music, take place in downtown's Kerry Park on Friday and Saturday nights and on Island Stage Wednesday nights.

SPORTS

Kelowna Rockets (☎ 250-860-7825; www.kelownarockets .com; tickets from $18) is the much-beloved local WHL hockey team. It plays in the flashy 6000-seat **Prospera Place Arena** (☎ 250-979-0888; cnr Water St & Cawston Ave).

Getting There & Away

Kelowna airport (YLW; ☎ 250-765-5125; www.kelowna airport.com) is a surprisingly busy place and has a very good wine shop. Discount carrier Westjet serves Vancouver, Victoria, Edmonton, Calgary and Toronto. Air Canada Jazz serves Vancouver and Calgary. Horizon Air provides international service and has connections to Seattle. The airport is a long 20km north on Hwy 97 from Kelowna.

The **Greyhound bus depot** (☎ 250-860-3835; 2366 Leckie Rd) is north of the downtown area, off Hwy 97. Daily buses travel to other points in the Okanagan Valley such as Osoyoos ($23, 2½ hours, one daily), as well as Kamloops ($28, three hours, three daily), Vancouver ($62, six hours, six daily) and Calgary ($87, 10 hours, one daily). The station contains a restaurant and coin lockers. To get there, take city bus 10 from **Queensway station** (Queensway Ave btwn Pandosy & Ellis Sts). It runs every half-hour, roughly, from 6:30am to 9:45pm. Better, use the depot phone to request a pick-up from your accommodations.

Getting Around

TO/FROM THE AIRPORT

There are two buses connecting with the airport: **Kelowna Airporter Shuttle** (☎ 250-765-0182), costing $10 to $15 one-way per person, and **Vernon Airporter** (☎ 250-542-7574), about $20 per person. A one-way taxi fare is about $30.

BUS

For timetables, pick up a copy of *Kelowna Regional Rider's Guide* from the VIC (p236), or try **Kelowna Regional Transit Systems** (☎ 250-860-8121; www.busonline.ca). There are three zones for bus travel, and the one-way fare in the central zone is $1.75. A day pass for all three zones costs $5. All the downtown buses pass through, one daily. The station contains a restaurant and coin lockers. To get there, take city bus 10 from **Queensway station** (Queensway Ave btwn Pandosy & Ellis Sts).

CAR & TAXI

Major car rental companies at Kelowna airport include Budget, Enterprise, Hertz and National.

Taxi companies include:
Checkmate Cabs (☎ 250-861-1111, 250-861-4445)
Kelowna Cabs (☎ 250-762-4444, 250-762-2222)

BIG WHITE SKI RESORT

Known for its near-perfect powder, **Big White Ski Resort** (☎ 250-765-8888, 800-663-2772, snow report 250-765-7669; www.bigwhite.com; 1-day lift pass adult/child $65/33), 55km east of Kelowna off Hwy 33, is one of BC's best and most popular ski resorts. The highest ski resort in the province, it features 1200 hectares of runs, which are covered in the noted deep dry powder for excellent downhill and backcountry skiing, and deep gullies that make for superb snowboarding. The drop is 777m. There is also night skiing.

Because of Big White's distance from Kelowna, most people stay up here. The resort includes numerous restaurants, bars, hotels and hostels. Contact **central reservations** (☎ 800-663-2772; www.bigwhite.com; r $100-900) for full details and pricing. With ski runs right outside the door, 42-room **Chateau Big White** (r from $175; 🖳) is a popular boutique hotel.

SameSun Ski Resort Hostel (☎ 250-765-7050, 877-562-2783; www.samesun.com; Alpine Centre; dm from $24; 🖳) has direct ski access to the runs. Rooms have four to eight beds and there's a hot tub. There are daily shuttles to/from the Kelowna SameSun International Hostel (p239).

VERNON

pop 36,300

Winters start to get pretty cold as you head north to Vernon. This precludes much grape-growing, although there are lots of orchards and truck farms. The compact city lies in a scenic valley encircled by three lakes: the Okanagan, Kalamalka and Swan.

The entire area is pleasant and there are some interesting farms to visit. The compact downtown boasts dozens of murals, part of an ongoing project to celebrate Vernon's history, culture and people.

History

Once the hub of the Okanagan Valley, Vernon used to be a major crossroads town that connected the valley with the rest of the interior. Voyageurs first used its strategic location, followed by an onslaught of gold prospectors streaming up the valley to the Cariboo district. Later, cattle were brought in, and in 1891 the railway arrived. But it was in 1908, with the introduction of large-scale irrigation, that the town took on an importance that was more than transitory. Soon the area was covered in orchards and farms.

Orientation

Surrounded by rolling hills, downtown Vernon is a good respite along Hwy 97. Main St, also called 30th Ave, rarely bustles. At 25th Ave, Hwy 6, which leads southeast to Nelson and Nakusp, meets Hwy 97, which runs north–south, becoming 32nd St in Vernon and bisecting the city. On 32nd St, north of 30th Ave, you'll find a commercial strip with service stations, motels and fast-food outlets.

All the downtown sights are within easy walking distance of each other.

Information

BOOKSTORES

Bookland (☎ 250-545-1885; 3400 30th Ave) Topographical maps, travel guides and books on activities in the Okanagan Valley and BC. Excellent selection of local works, magazines and newspapers.

INTERNET ACCESS

Vernon Public Library (☎ 250-542-7610; 3001 32nd Ave; 🕑 10am-5:30pm Mon & Thu-Sat, 10am- 4pm Tue & Wed) Free access; next to the Vernon Museum.

MEDICAL SERVICES

Vernon Jubilee Hospital (☎ 250-545-2211; 2101 32nd St; 🕑 24hr)

POST

Main post office (☎ 250-545-8239; 3101 32nd Ave, at 31st St)

TOURIST INFORMATION

Visitor Info Centre North of town (☎ 250-542-1415; 6326 Hwy 97 N; 🕑 8:30am-6pm May-Oct) Near the southeastern shore of Swan Lake & 701 Hwy 97 S, about 5km north of town; South of town (☎ 250-545-3016, 800-665-0795; www.vernontourism.com; 701 Hwy 97 S; 🕑 8:30am-6pm May-Oct, 10am-4pm Nov-Apr) This is the main office covering the south approach, about 2km south of the center.

Sights & Activities

Vernon has almost 30 **murals** that have been painted by local artists with help from school kids and other volunteers. These are not your usual faded-flag-with-a-poorly-drawn-national-icon murals either. Rather, these are building-sized works of art. Pick up a copy of the 'Heritage Murals' guide at the VIC (above).

You can do a complete tour on foot in under 90 minutes. A **trompe l'oeil scene** (3306 30th Ave) looks through the building wall to see orchard workers busily packing fruit. **The World Wars** (3202 32nd St) is a moving study of war and its effects. Note the text of the telegram carrying the news that families dread in wartime. **Multiculturalism** (3101 32nd St) turns a humdrum building into a thing of beauty. The newest one celebrates Canada's World Cup **cross-country skiing team** (cnr 32nd St & 32nd Ave).

Polson Park, off 25th Ave next to 32nd St, bursts with spring and summer flowers. If it's hot outside, this is a good, cool rest spot, thanks to the shade and trickling Vernon Creek. It has many Asian design touches.

Behind Polson Park is a **skateboard park** and the **Okanagan Science Centre** (☎ 250-545-3644; 2704 Hwy 6; adult/child $7/4; ☼ 10am-5pm Mon-Fri, 11am-5pm Sat) where science buffs and little kids can ponder evolution and more.

The **Vernon Museum** (☎ 250-542-3142; 3009 32nd Ave at 31st St; admission free; ☼ 10am-5pm Tue-Sat) has the usual collection of stuff that once moldered in attics, then got declared junk and now sits behind glass with a label. If only the settlers knew…

The dedicated staff at the **Vernon Art Gallery** (☎ 250-545-3173; 3228 31st Ave; admission by donation; ☼ 10am-5pm Mon-Fri, 11am-4pm Sat) will happily apprise you of the local art scene.

The **Allan Brooks Nature Centre** (☎ 250-260-4227; adult/child $4/3; ☼ 10am-5pm Tue-Sun May–mid-Oct) is named for the famous local wildlife painter. It features interactive displays on the North Okanagan's diverse ecosystems. To get there, follow 34th St until it becomes Mission Rd. Follow that for about 2km, then turn left onto Allan Brooks Rd. Follow the signs to the center. See real nature on the numerous walks in the area.

Davison Orchards (☎ 250-549-3266; 3111 Davison Rd; ☼ daylight hr May-Oct) is one of many orchards in the surrounding area, however Davidson is more attraction than farm. Kids love the tractor rides, homemade ice cream, fresh apple juice, pettable farm critters and, dare we say it, fudge.

Right next to Davison Orchards, **Planet Bee** (☎ 250-542-8088; 5011 Bella Vista Rd; admission free; ☼ daylight hr May-Oct) is a working honey farm where you can learn all the sweet secrets of the nectar and see a working hive up close. (Those males you see really are just a bunch of drones.)

Sleeping

Vernon has some decent, if not brand-new, motels in the center. Many chains can be found among the strip malls north of town on Hwy 97. The VIC (opposite) has lists of B&Bs, many set among local farms.

Ellison Provincial Park (☎ 800-689-9025, information only 250-494-6500; www.discovercamping.ca; campsite $17; ☼ Apr-Oct), 16km southwest of Vernon on Okanagan Landing Rd, is a great place (see p245). The 71 campsites fill up early, so reserve.

Beaver Lake Mountain Resort (☎ 250-762-2225; www.beaverlakeresort.com; 6350 Beaver Lake Rd; campsite from $19, cabins $50-140) Set high in the hills east of Hwy 97 about midway between Vernon and Kelowna, this postcard-perfect lakeside resort has a range of rustic and more luxurious cabins that sleep up to six people. Canoe, star-gaze, swim, fish, enjoy the hearty chow or just ponder the lake.

Swan Lake RV Park (☎ 250-545-2300; www.swanlakecampground.com; 7255 Old Kamloops Rd; campsite from $25) On the west side of Swan Lake, 5km north of Vernon, this 73-site campground has nicely landscaped grounds. Other choices are nearby.

Polson Park Motel (☎ 250-549-2231, 800-480-2231; 3201 24th Ave; r $45-100; ☒ ☎) Right at the southern entrance to downtown, the Polson Park is not fancy. But it does let you walk everywhere and you can cool off in the vintage pool. The 28 units have fridges.

Schell Motel (☎ 250-545-1351, 888-772-4355; 2810 35th St; r $65-130; ☒ ☎) Another example of the concrete-block designer's art (check out the groovy balcony dividers), the Schell has a pretty pool area with hot tub. Located downtown at 30th Ave, the 323 rooms are good-sized. Guests can use a barbecue.

Richmond House B&B (☎ 250-549-1767, 866-267-4419; www.richmondhousebandb.com; 4008 Pleasant Valley Rd; r $75-90; ☒) This large, white Victorian house dates from 1894. The three rooms are cozy and have the kind of decor favored by Laura Ashley's aunt. Breakfasts are good but best is the hot tub – a prefect après-ski refuge.

Tiki Village Motel (☎ 250-503-5566, 800-661-8454; www.tikivillagevernon.com; 2408 34th St; r $80-100; ☒ ☎) An older 1960s-style motel that makes the most of cement blocks and lush plantings to exude a vague Polynesian theme. The 30 units are pretty standard, but brightly colored.

Eating

Like the rest of the valley, Vernon has some fine places to eat.

Bean Scene (☎ 250-558-1817; 2923 30th Ave; coffee $2; ☼ 7am-5pm Mon-Sat) The hub of what's happening in town, this café has sidewalk tables and a buzz that transcends the caffeine.

Bean to Brew (☎ 250-260-7787; 3202 31st Ave; meals from $5; ☼ 6am-10pm Mon-Fri, 8am-4pm Sat & Sun; ☐) The outdoor area here is heated when it's cold and there's wi-fi. Try the amazing blueberry muffins, made with local berries. There are also soups and sandwiches.

Tita's Italian Bistro (☎ 250-545-1950; 3002 41st St; meals from $10; ⏱ 5-9pm Tue-Sat) This local institution has been run by the same family for over 40 years. The emphasis is on freshly made Italian pasta classics. It's an easy walk from the chain-motel gulch north of town.

our pick DiVino's Ristorante Italiano (☎ 250-549-3463; 3224 30th Ave; meals $12-20; ⏱ 5-9pm Tue-Sat) Popular DiVino's is a compact and cute little spot right in the center. Under the gaze of shelf-mounted statuary, you can enjoy creative dishes like mesclun salad, addictive focaccia fritters and much more. You should probably just order the amazing Penne Prawnferno, which is a garlic and spice explosion.

Phoenix Steakhouse (☎ 250-260-1189; 3117 30th Ave; mains $12-25; ⏱ 11:30am-late Tue-Sat) The steaks here don't emerge from the vault of this old 1914 bank, but they could. They're mighty darn tender and are joined on the menu by pasta, seafood and other popular items. It's all very stylish here – straight-laced bankers would run away in terror – although the wise ones would have a martini first.

The evening **Vernon Farmers' Market** (☎ 250-546-6267; 2200 58th Ave; ⏱ 4-8pm Fri) adds some much-needed class to the Wal-Mart parking lot. There's also a **morning market** (cnr Hwy 97 & 43rd Ave; ⏱ 8am-noon Mon &Thu).

More good picnic fare can be found at **Simply Delicious** (☎ 250-542-7500; 3419 31st Ave; ⏱ 9am-5:30pm), with a good selection of organic food. Across the lot, **Nature's Fare** (☎ 250-260-1117; 30th Ave; ⏱ 9am-6pm Mon-Sat) has local produce plus prepared foods like organic soups.

Drinking

Sir Winston's Pub (☎ 250-549-3485; 2705 32nd St; meals $8-14; ⏱ noon-late) A big, rollicking pub right in the center of town. It has a good range of beer choices and a large patio. Food items include pizza and fish and chips.

Each of the local lakes boasts a great waterfront pub. The best outdoor patio in town is on Kalamalka Lake at **Alexander's Beach Pub** (☎ 250-545-3131; 12408 Kalamalka Rd; ⏱ 11am-late summer), right beside the beach. **Blue Heron Waterfront Pub** (☎ 250-542-5550; 7673 Okanagan Landing Rd; ⏱ 11am-late Apr-Oct) has sweeping views of Okanagan Lake. Both are places to hang and mingle on lazy summer days.

Getting There & Around

The **Greyhound bus depot** (☎ 250-545-0527; 3102 30th St at 31st Ave) has service to Kelowna ($13, one hour, seven daily), as well as Kamloops ($21, two hours, two daily), Vancouver ($68, 7½ hours, three daily) and Calgary ($75, nine hours, one daily).

Buses of the **Vernon Regional Transit System** (☎ 250-545-7221) leave downtown from the bus stop at 31st St and 30th Ave ($2). For Kalamalka Lake, catch bus 1 or 6; for Okanagan Lake, bus 7. A day pass costs $4; service is infrequent.

For a cab, call **Vernon Taxi** (☎ 250-545-3337).

AROUND VERNON

The **O'Keefe Historic Ranch** (☎ 250-542-7868; www.okeeferanch.bc.ca; adult/child $10/8; ⏱ 9am-5pm May, Jun, Sep & Oct, 9am-8pm Jul & Aug), 12km north of Vernon on Hwy 97, is just what the name implies. Home to the O'Keefe family from 1867 to 1977, it still has an original log cabin, a general store, old farm machines and St Ann's, probably the oldest Roman Catholic church in the province. Before orchards – and later grapes – covered the valley, ranching as portrayed here was the way of life for most.

On Hwy 97A, 23km north of Vernon, you'll come across **Armstrong** (population 4500), known mostly for its cheese and excellent **farmers' market** (☎ 250-546-1986; ⏱ 8am-12:30pm Sat May-Oct). It's the valley's oldest market, running since 1973, and is held downtown at the IPE Grounds.

Thirteen kilometers further north, **Enderby** (population 3100) is on the banks of the Shuswap River. Rock climbers scale the vertical rocks at Enderby Cliffs, north of town. The Enderby **Visitor Info Centre** (☎ 250-838-6727, 877-213-6509; www.enderby.com/chamber; 706 Railway St) has climbing information.

East of Vernon on Hwy 6, farms and forests line the road to **Lumby** (population 1800) and **Cherryville** (population 1000), about 20km and 48km from Vernon, respectively. Outdoor opportunities abound, and the many lakes draw lots of anglers.

From Cherryville, you can drive northeast on Sugar Lake Rd to the backcountry wonderland of remote **Monashee Provincial Park**. This is a great place to absorb nature amid old-growth cedars, spruce and hemlocks. There's backcountry camping around several remote lakes.

Hwy 6 heads east over a scenic road to Needles, where you can catch the ferry to the Kootenays and the road to Nakusp (p254).

Kalamalka Lake

This 8.9-sq-km park lies on the eastern side of warm, shallow Kalamalka Lake (simply called 'Kal' by the locals), south of Vernon. The park offers great swimming at Jade and Kalamalka Beaches, as well as good fishing and public picnic areas. A network of mountain-biking and hiking trails takes you to places such as cougar-free **Cougar Canyon**, where the rock climbing is excellent. To get to Kalamalka Lake from downtown Vernon, follow Hwy 6 east to the Polson Place Mall, then turn right on Kalamalka Lake Rd and proceed to Kal Beach.

Ellison

A 15-minute drive takes you to this beautiful park on Okanagan Lake, 16km southwest from Vernon on Okanagan Landing Rd. Ellison includes campsites (see p243), more hiking and biking trails and the only freshwater marine park in western Canada. Scuba divers can plunge into the warm water to explore a sunken wreck. You can rent scuba gear and kayaks in Vernon at **Innerspace Dive & Kayak** (☎ 250-549-2040; 3103 32nd St). Ellison is also known for its world-class rock climbing. To get to Ellison from downtown, go west on 25th Ave, which soon becomes Okanagan Landing Rd. Follow that and look for signs to the park.

SILVER STAR

Renowned for its deep, dry powder, **Silver Star** (☎ 250-542-0224, 800-663-4431, snow report 250-542-1745; www.silverstar.com; 1-day lift ticket adult/child $65/33) has 112 runs, 10% of which are double black diamond, across 1240 hectares. The vertical drop is 760m and there are 12 lifts. Snowboarders enjoy a half-pipe and a terrain park. Many marvel at the resort's high standard of grooming.

The ski season usually lasts from late October to early April. At the end of June – the official start of the summer season – the chairlifts begin operating again, and ski runs become excellent hiking and mountain-biking trails. Stunning views let you see all the way west to the Coast Mountains.

Contact Silver Star for a range of accommodations options within the resort. Most let you ski right out your front door. **SameSun Budget Lodge** (☎ 250-545-8933, 877-562-2783; www.samesun .com; 9898 Pinnacles Rd; dm/d $24/60; ⌨) is an upscale hostel of the usual SameSun quality. The common area is huge and the kitchen cozy. Reserve well in advance in winter. **Silver Creek Hotel** (☎ 250-549-5191, 800-610-0805; www.silverstar clubresort.com; r $150-300) has 69 fairly luxurious condo-style units in a modern complex. Enjoy the resort views from the rooftop hot tubs.

To get to Silver Star, take 48th Ave off Hwy 97. The resort is 20km northeast of Vernon.

The Kootenays

Taking their name from the Ktunaxa, a First Nations people David Thompson encountered on his exploration, the Kootenays have come to have a new meaning: mountains. Lots of mountains. If you like snow-covered peaks, then you'll find plenty in the region's four major ranges: the Selkirks and Monashees in the west and the Rockies and Purcells in the east.

Transportation here has always been problematic and even today you'll find isolated towns that feel far removed from life elsewhere in BC. Glacier-fed lakes divide many of the ranges and there are numerous ferries linking important roads – something many don't expect this far from the coast.

Fed by mineral mania in the late 1800s, a slew of towns grew up on gold and silver speculation. Today places such as Fernie and Revelstoke have preserved their heritage and make for highly atmospheric places to pause in your travels. For a compelling mix of offbeat charm, modern vibe and natural beauty, however, head straight to Nelson, one of BC's most appealing cities.

All that rugged terrain also means that whether you want to plunge down a hill on skis, a board or a bike, your opportunities are almost limitless. On the water, the rivers boil with white water, while the remote lakes invite exploring kayakers.

You may find that 'explore' should replace 'mountains' in the list of Kootenays definitions. Or better yet, go define your own.

HIGHLIGHTS

- Getting sucked into the groove in **Nelson** (p258)
- Skiing until it hurts in the fabulous powder above **Revelstoke** (p248)
- Looking for ghosts in the slumbering former boomtown of **New Denver** (p256)
- Surviving the white water of the Kicking Horse River in **Golden** (p273)
- Tackling the hills winter or summer that surround cute little **Fernie** (p266)

WEST KOOTENAYS

If you're heading east from the bustling Okanagan Valley, you may be in for a bit of a shock: things get very quiet, very quiet indeed, as you enter the West Kootenays.

Hemmed in by water – the western boundary is 230km-long Arrow Lake, while 145km-long Kootenay Lake defines the eastern border – this hilly, forested region feels like a world apart from the rest of BC. In fact, you may just find that you like this world, given the serenity you'll find in places like the Slocan Valley.

Little towns such as New Denver and Kaslo definitely march to the beat of different – and somnolent – drummers. In fact, even the region's premier town, the absolutely fabulous Nelson, marches to its own beat – albeit a more vibrant one. If you're crossing on the Trans-Canada Hwy, take a break in Revelstoke, which hums with diversions and activities year-round. Then consider heading south, where the pace is set by the slow-moving ferries (see boxed text, p255) that provide vital links across the lakes.

Meanwhile, gaze upwards at the misty Selkirk and Purcell Mountains. Several free ferries across lakes and rivers connect highways throughout the region (see boxed text, p255).

History

Stern-wheeler transportation on the long lakes in the late 1800s and early 1900s connected the area to the US via rivers and lakes.

THE KOOTENAYS

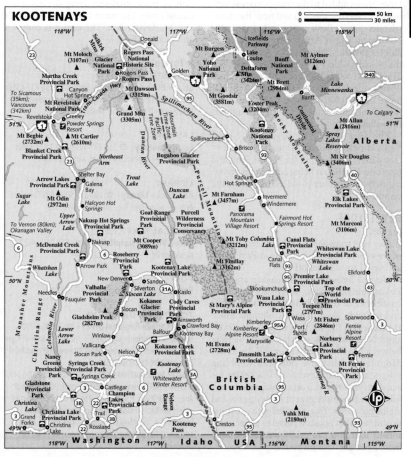

KOOTENAYS

TOP FIVE PLACES TO TAKE IN THE WATERS

- The kayak-friendly crags of the **Kaslo shore** (p257)
- The view from the **Kootenay Lake Ferry** (see boxed text, p255)
- Most **Nelson bars** (p263), which serve Nelson Brewing Co's fermented waters
- One of the ubiquitous **Revelstoke** (p251) motel hot tubs after a day on the slopes
- The natural hot springs at **Whiteswan Lake Provincial Park** (p272)

Later, trains added to the transportation network by carrying goods to and from the stern-wheeler ports. Busy ports included pretty Nakusp on Upper Arrow Lake and Kaslo on Kootenay Lake, where today you can visit the world's oldest surviving stern-wheeler. The Slocan Valley boomed with silver mines during the late 1800s, and during WWII more than 20,000 Japanese Canadians were forced into internment camps throughout the valley.

The area around Castlegar and Grand Forks is rich in Russian Doukhobor history (see p264). Throughout the region, land and forest exploitation is being replaced by enjoyment. Ski resorts are proliferating across the remote peaks.

REVELSTOKE

pop 8000

It may be a transport hub, but there's plenty of reasons to stop your travels in Revelstoke and yell 'I want to get off.'

Nestled between the Monashee and Selkirk mountain ranges, Revelstoke sits at the confluence of the rushing Illecillewaet River and the wide, slow-moving Columbia River. It perches on the western edge of Mt Revelstoke National Park, which is about halfway between the Okanagan Valley and the Rocky Mountains. All those hills and tumbling waters mean that Revelstoke is a centre for activities year-round. You can ski, snowboard, hike, bike or simply gaze at snowy peaks and alpine meadows. This, coupled with a historic downtown that boasts a passel of attractions, means that you can easily wait some time before you get back on your trip.

History

Originally known to First Nations people as 'Big Eddy,' for the respite it offered canoe travelers, Revelstoke was later named for Edward Charles Baring (aka Lord Revelstoke), the British financier who came through with a much-needed cash advance that saved the Canadian Pacific Railway (CPR) from total bankruptcy. The coming of the the railway in the 1880s, along with the opening of the Trans-Canada Hwy in 1962, contributed to Revelstoke becoming a viable transportation hub.

Orientation

Revelstoke is south of the Trans-Canada Hwy. Victoria Rd runs parallel to the very busy railway tracks that run along the northeast end of town. The main streets include 1st St and Mackenzie Ave. The center is compact and easily walked.

Information

BOOKSTORES

Grizzly Book & Serendipity Shop (☎ 250-837-6185; 208 Mackenzie Ave) Offers magazines, a wide selection of New Age stuff and regional books.

LAUNDRY

Family Laundry (☎ 250-837-3938; 409 1st St; loads from $4; ⏱ 8am-8pm Mon-Sat, 8am-5pm Sun)

LIBRARY

Revelstoke Library (☎ 250-837-5095; 605 Campbell Ave; ⏱ noon-8pm Tue, 10am-5pm Wed-Sat)

MEDICAL SERVICES

Queen Victoria Hospital (☎ 250-837-2131; 6622 Newlands Rd; ⏱ doctor on call 24hr)

POST

Post office (☎ 250-837-3228; 313 3rd St)

TOURIST INFORMATION

Parks Canada Regional Office (☎ 250-837-7500; revglacier.reception@pc.gc.ca; 301 3rd St; ⏱ 8am-4:30pm Mon-Fri) Offers information about Mt Revelstoke National Park and Glacier National Park.

Visitor Information Center (VIC; ☎ 250-837-5345, 800-487-1493; www.seerevelstoke.com; 206 Campbell Ave; ⏱ 8:30am-4:30pm Mon-Fri; 10 mins $1) Internet access available. From May to September, a second, larger VIC at 110 Mackenzie Ave is open from 8:30am to 8pm; it has parking and internet access ($1 for ten minutes).

THE KOOTENAYS

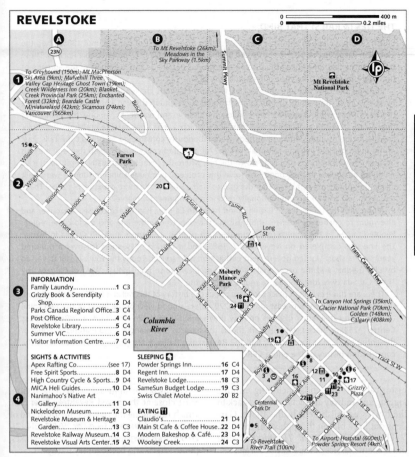

REVELSTOKE

0 — 400 m
0 — 0.2 miles

To Mt Revelstoke (26km);
Meadows in the
Sky Parkway (1.5km)

To Greyhound (150m); Mt MacPherson
Ski Area (9km); Mulvehill Three
Valley Gap Heritage Ghost Town (19km);
Creek Wilderness Inn (20km); Blanket
Creek Provincial Park (25km); Enchanted
Forest (32km); Beardale Castle
Miniatureland (42km); Sicamous (74km);
Vancouver (565km)

Mt Revelstoke
National Park

Farwel
Park

Moberly
Manor
Park

Columbia
River

Long
St

To Canyon Hot Springs (35km);
Glacier National Park (70km);
Golden (148km);
Calgary (408km)

Grizzly
Plaza

Centennial
Park Dr

To Revelstoke
River Trail (100m)

To Airport; Hospital (600m);
Powder Springs Resort (4km)

INFORMATION	
Family Laundry	1 C3
Grizzly Book & Serendipity Shop	2 D4
Parks Canada Regional Office	3 C4
Post Office	4 C4
Revelstoke Library	5 D4
Summer VIC	6 D4
Visitor Information Centre	7 C4

SIGHTS & ACTIVITIES	
Apex Rafting Co	(see 17)
Free Spirit Sports	8 D4
High Country Cycle & Sports	9 D4
MICA Heli Guides	10 D4
Nanimahoo's Native Art Gallery	11 D4
Nickelodeon Museum	12 D4
Revelstoke Museum & Heritage Garden	13 C4
Revelstoke Railway Museum	14 C3
Revelstoke Visual Arts Center	15 A2

SLEEPING	
Powder Springs Inn	16 C4
Regent Inn	17 D4
Revelstoke Lodge	18 C3
SameSun Budget Lodge	19 C3
Swiss Chalet Motel	20 B2

EATING	
Claudio's	21 D4
Main St Cafe & Coffee House	22 D4
Modern Bakeshop & Café	23 D4
Woolsey Creek	24 C3

Sights

Grizzly Plaza, between Mackenzie and Orton Aves, is a pedestrian square and the centre of downtown, where free live music performances – some achingly sincere if not good – take place in the evening throughout July and August. Life-sized bronze grizzly bears flank the plaza. Throughout downtown, look for historical plaques on the many restored buildings.

Don't miss the great **Revelstoke Railway Museum** (☎ 250-837-6060; www.railwaymuseum.com; adult/child $6/3; ☉ 9am-8pm summer, 9am-5pm Mon-Fri winter), which houses restored steam locomotives, including one of the largest steam engines ever used on CPR lines. Photographs and artifacts document the construction of the CPR, pay tribute to its hardy workers

and relate the railway's original financial woes. Volunteer railway engineers are often on hand to offer yarns about the heyday of rail travel. You'll be forgiven if you get a bit wistful pondering the noble past of railway dining – there's not a paper plate in sight. See the boxed text, p117, for details of the Royal Hudson locomotive that used to pass through Revelstoke. The museum bookstore carries a huge selection of books about the building of the CPR, which was instrumental – if not essential – in linking Canada (see boxed text, p250).

The **Revelstoke Museum & Heritage Garden** (☎ 250-837-3067; 315 1st St; adult/child $4/2; ☉ 9am-5pm Mon-Sat, 1-4pm Sun May-Sep, 1-4pm Mon-Fri Oct-Apr) holds a permanent collection of furniture and

---

THE TIES (& RAILS) THAT BIND

British Columbia had an almost separate existence from the rest of Canada until 1885, when the Canadian Pacific Railway (CPR) completed its line over the previously impenetrable Rockies. These tracks for the first time linked the disparate territories of Canada and were part of the agreement that had brought BC into the confederation in 1871.

Running the rails through the Rockies was an enormous challenge that was accomplished by the work of thousands of immigrant laborers who endured harsh conditions to complete the dangerous work. Hundreds were killed by disease and accidents. Among the challenges they faced were the avalanches of Rogers Pass, which swept away people and trains like toys. Eventually long tunnels and snow sheds were laboriously constructed to protect the rails. East of the town of Field in Yoho National Park (p278), the gradients were so steep that any braking problem caused trains to run away down the hill, where they would eventually fly off the tracks, plunging all aboard to their doom. To solve this problem, two huge spiraling tunnels were built inside the granite mountains so that the grades were reduced to a more manageable 2.2%. These remain in use and are an internationally recognized engineering marvel.

Along with the trains, the CPR built grand hotels in Calgary, Banff, Lake Louise, Vancouver and elsewhere to encourage tourists and business travelers to ride the line and explore the region. People jumped at the chance to experience such rugged wilderness and still sip tea in luxury. The line was completed on November 7, 1885, and it carried passengers for over a hundred years until a short-sighted government cutback on rail services. Today the route is still traversed by CPR freights and the occasional *Rocky Mountaineer* cruise train (p404). West of Calgary, the Trans-Canada Hwy runs parallel to much of the route.

There are three excellent places to learn about the history of this rail line in BC: a **lookout** from the Trans-Canada Hwy 8km east of Field (p279) offers a good view of the lower of the two spiral tunnels, with explanatory displays on how they work; the museum area inside the **Rogers Pass Centre** (p254) in Glacier National Park shows the hazards of avalanches and features a model of the entire route over the Rockies; and the **Revelstoke Railway Museum** (p249) documents the construction history of the entire CPR.

---

historical odds and ends, including mining, logging and railway artifacts that date back to the town's establishment in the 1880s. Gardens out back bloom through summer.

Thrill to *The Titfield Thunderbolt* and other silent classics at the **Nickelodeon Museum** (☎ 250-837-5250; 111 1st St; adult/child $10/5; ☀ 11am-7pm May-Oct), which demonstrates the intricate workings of old Victrolas, player pianos and movie projectors.

Nanimahoo's Native Art Gallery (☎ 250-837-0831; 107 1st St; ☀ 11am-7pm) has a stunning collection of native art from more than 40 artists. The carvings are extraordinary. The **Revelstoke Visual Arts Centre** (☎ 250-814-0261; 320 Wilson St) has frequent exhibits by local artists.

Activities

Sandwiched in between the vast but relatively lesser-known Selkirk and Monashee mountain ranges, Revelstoke draws serious snow buffs looking for untracked powder and no crowds. When the snow melts, white-water rafting is the thing.

Hiking opportunities abound in the region. Start close at the paved **Revelstoke River Trail**, which runs along the rivers at the south end of town. **Arrow Adventure Tours** (☎ 250-837-6014, 877-277-6965; www.arrowadventuretours.com) organizes hikes, photo safaris and backcountry transport.

SKIING & SNOWBOARDING

Whether you ski, board or just like to romp around in the snow, Revelstoke's long, snowy winter season and experienced tour operators give you plenty of options.

For downhill skiing, head to **Powder Springs Resort** (☎ 250-837-5151, 877-991-4455; www.catpowder.com/indexsprings.html; 1-day lift tickets adult/child $30/free). This small ski hill on Mt Mackenzie, just 4km southeast of Revelstoke, lacks the pizzazz of bigger resorts, but its heavy snowfall (up to 12m), access to backcountry slopes, and small crowds make it a spectacular spot. However, many more people may soon be enjoying the view, as plans are afoot to pour $1 billion into the hills, creating more than 100 ski runs, resort hotels and condos, condo, condos.

Heli-skiing is all the rage, especially among folks who think Hummers aren't just afford-able but also good ideas. Helicopters take you high into the alpine to ski or snowboard steep slopes, deep powder and even glaciers. **Mica Heli Guides** (☎ 877-837-6191; www.micaheli.com; 122 Mackenzie Ave) runs three-day tours starting at $4800.

Though sometimes called the poor man's heli-skiing, snowcat skiing isn't exactly cheap. Snowcats are large, heated tractors that easily navigate ice and snow, allowing you to reach some pretty pristine alpine conditions. **CAT Powder Skiing** (☎ 250-837-5151, 800-991-4455; www.catpowder.com) offers packages, including ac-commodations and meals at Powder Springs Inn (p252). Prices average about $500 to $600 a day.

For **cross-country skiing**, head to the Mt MacPherson Ski Area, 7km south of town on Hwy 23. You'll pay under $10 to use the 22km of groomed trails here.

Free Spirit Sports (☎ 250-837-9453; 203 1st St W) rents a wide variety of winter gear including essential avalanche equipment.

WATER SPORTS

Apex Rafting Co (☎ 250-837-6376, 888-232-6666; www.apexrafting.com; 112 1st St E; adult/child $80/65) runs mellow, two-hour guided trips on the Ill-ecillewaet River in spring and summer. The trips are perfect for first-time rafters, kids or anyone wanting to just kick back and enjoy the scenery.

Navigate the rivers with a kayak from **Natural Escapes Kayaking** (☎ 250-837-2679; www.naturalescapes.ca). Rentals start at $25 for two hours and you can arrange tours of the re-gion's waterways.

MOUNTAIN BIKING

Once the snow melts, ski runs become excellent mountain-biking trails. Pick up a copy of the *Biking Trail Map* from the VIC or **High Country Cycle & Sports** (☎ 250-814-0090; 118 Mackenzie Ave), where you can also rent bikes (from $15 for two hours).

Sleeping

There are lots of motels vying for attention out on the Trans-Canada Hwy, but you're much better off staying in town, where you can sample things on foot.

BUDGET

Blanket Creek Provincial Park (☎ 800-689-9025; www.discovercamping.ca; campsite $14) This park, 25km south of Revelstoke along Hwy 23, includes 63 campsites, with flush toilets and running water. There's a playground, and a waterfall nearby.

SameSun Budget Lodge (☎ 250-837-4050, 877-562-2783; www.samesun.ca; 400 2nd St W; dm/d $24/60; ☐) In a nicely restored but somewhat labyrinthine

---

AVALANCHE!

As you marvel at all the snowy peaks, take a second to realize that you are in the pumping heart of avalanche country, where heavy slides of falling snow have enough power and weight to crush an entire city. An avalanche – the name is derived from the French verb 'avaler' (to swallow) – occurs when a slab of snow separates from more stable snow or ground cover. This most often happens when there's a dramatic shift in temperature or when there's a heavy snowfall or, for that matter, heavy snowmelt.

Watching a distant avalanche is perhaps one of the most spectacular sights in nature. Up close, an avalanche can be the most thunderous and frightening exertion of power you'll ever encounter – and you want to be well out of the way. Avalanches kill more people in BC each year than any other natural phenomenon. The deaths of seven heli-skiers and seven students near Revelstoke in 2003 garnered international headlines. More typical were the deaths of two skiers near Nakusp in 2006.

In Revelstoke, the Canadian Avalanche Centre is operated by the **Canadian Avalanche Association** (CAA; ☎ 250-837-2435, 24hr info 800-667-1105; www.avalanche.ca). It analyzes avalanche trends, weather patterns and avalanche accidents. The worst month is March, although avalanches occur year-round.

If you're planning on doing any trips in the backcountry, you'll want to contact the CAA first to check conditions. Whether you're backcountry ski-touring or simply hiking in the alpine region, you'll want to rent a homing beacon; most outdoor shops can supply one.

OH FUDGE!

West of Revelstoke on the Trans-Canada Hwy to Sicamous, kids shriek and parents flinch as one after another schlocky roadside attraction comes into view. Some prime examples include **Three Valley Gap Heritage Ghost Town** (☎ 250-837-2109; www.3valley.com), 19km west of Revelstoke; the **Enchanted Forest** (☎ 250-837-9477), 32km west of Revelstoke; and **Beardale Castle Mini-atureland** (☎ 250-836-2268), 42km west of Revelstoke.

The first combines historical buildings, a stage show and a motel in a large, frilly complex; the second involves numerous fairies and other figures, including a crafty pirate, scattered around a forest of old cedar trees; the third displays handcrafted tiny towns and teensy trains. If you're in the mood to buy trinkets or hunks of, yes, fudge, you'll get your fill at any of these places. Opening dates match the summer travel season.

---

building, this 80-bed, 15-room hostel attracts an international crowd. Many ponder foreign affairs in the outdoor hot tub.

Canyon Hot Springs Resort (☎ 250-837-2420; www .canyonhotsprings.com; campsite from $30; ☒) The principal allure of this place, 35km east of Revelstoke, is right in the name. Soak your cares away before retiring to one of the 200 campsites or 16 cabins (from $105).

MIDRANGE

Revelstoke Lodge (☎ 250-837-2181, 888-559-1979; www .revelstokelodge.com; 601 1st St W; r $55-120; ☒ ▢ ☒) Featuring views of passing trains and a location just a short walk to the town's best restaurant (right), this 42-room pink-hued motel overcomes its inherent flaws, such as an all-encompassing parking area and stark cinder-block construction. The small rooms have wi-fi.

Powder Springs Inn (☎ 250-837-5151, 800-991-4455; www.catpowder.com; 200 3rd St W; r $60-80; ☒ ▢) This place is part of the empire that includes the ski resort and the snowcat skiing operation. In fact, guests get free ski passes. The whole 55-room place is pretty basic, but most guests are too pooped to care after a day of hard fun. The bar gets lively with those not too pooped to pop.

Swiss Chalet Motel (☎ 250-837-4650, 888-272-4538; www.swisschaletmotel.com; 1101 Victoria Rd; r from $70; ☒ ▢) Walk to town from this cozy motel while trains rumble past. The 22 rooms have wi-fi, fridges and extra-soft beds.

Regent Inn (☎ 250-837-2107, 888-245-5523; www .regentinn.com; 112 1st St E; r $110-150; ☒ ▢) The poshest place in the center is popular with groups. The 50 modern rooms belie the historic roots of the building. There's a good restaurant and a popular lounge. Many bob the night away in the outdoor hot tub.

TOP END

Mulvehill Creek Wilderness Inn (☎ 250-837-8649, 877-837-8649; www.mulvehillcreek.com; 4200 Mulvehill Creek Rd; r $110-225; ☒) The lights and pool heater are powered by a river turbine at this eco-lodge, which boasts stunning views of Upper Arrow Lake. Borrow a canoe, savor the buffet breakfast, doze in the library or hit one of the myriad trails. All eight rooms can be called 'mountain posh.'

Eating

Modern Bakeshop & Café (☎ 250-837-6886; 212 Mackenzie Ave; meals from $5; ☒ 7am-5pm Mon-Sat; ▢) Try a blueberry–lemon Danish or a *croque-monsieur* (grilled ham and cheese sandwich) for a taste of Europe at this cute art moderne café. Sandwiches come on artisan bread and there's free wi-fi.

Main St Café & Coffee House (☎ 250-837-6888; 317 Mackenzie Ave; meals from $5; ☒ 8am-5pm; ▢) In a beautifully restored gingerbread house, this sunny café has a popular outside terrace and an internet kiosk inside. There are omelettes for breakfast and lots of sandwiches for lunch.

Grizzly Sports Bar & Grill (☎ 250-814-1002; 314 1st St W; meals $8-10; ☒ noon-late) 'Who stole the puck?' might be just one of the phrases on your lips at this classic sports bar with good pub grub. Mt Begbie microbrewed beers are on tap.

Claudio's (☎ 250-837-6743; 206 Mackenzie Ave; meals $8-20; ☒ 11am-11pm) Classic Italian fare and pizzas are served to ravenous hordes at this old-fashioned but oh-so-popular storefront. Tables outside are in demand in summer. Many opt for takeout and the comfort of their rooms.

our pick Woolsey Creek (☎ 250-837-5500; 604 2nd St W; meals $10-20; ☒ 8am-10pm) The region's best restaurant, now housed in an old German restaurant, is run by two women who came for a visit from Québec and never left. The stuffed animal heads are long gone, but in their place is an eclectic and changing menu that ranges from jambalaya to seafood to pasta. The vast patio is shielded by sunflowers in season. The bar often gets packed with buddies and stays open late.

Getting There & Away

Greyhound (☎ 250-837-5874; 1899 Fraser Dr) is west of town, just off the Trans-Canada Hwy. It has storage lockers. Buses go east to Calgary ($55, six hours, four daily) via Banff, west to Vancouver ($83, nine to 10 hours, four daily) via Kamloops or Kelowna.

MOUNT REVELSTOKE NATIONAL PARK

Known for their jagged peaks, the compact Selkirks are an espresso shot of rugged terrain and steep valleys. This compact (260 sq km) national park has it all. Just northeast of Revelstoke in the Clachnacudainn Range, the park comes alive with blankets of wildflowers in summer.

From the 2223m summit of Mt Revelstoke, the views of the mountains and the Columbia River valley are excellent. To get to the summit, take the 26km **Meadows in the Sky Parkway**, 1.5km east of Revelstoke off the Trans-Canada Hwy. Open when enough snow melts (usually not until July, although officially it is June to September), the paved road winds through lush cedar forests and alpine meadows and

THE KOOTENAYS

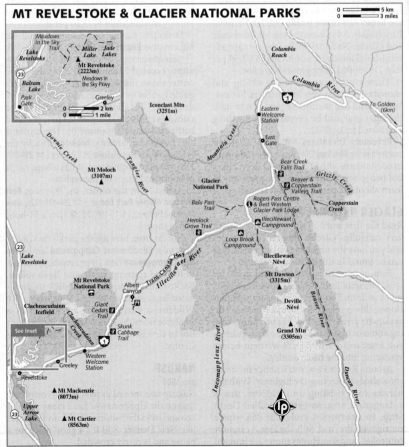

MT REVELSTOKE & GLACIER NATIONAL PARKS

ends at Balsam Lake, within 2km of the peak. From here walk to the top or take the shuttle, which runs from 10am to 4pm daily.

Umbrella-sized leaves are just some of the highlights of the **Skunk Cabbage Trail**, 28km east of Revelstoke on Hwy 1. Meanwhile, a 1.2km boardwalk along the Illecillewaet River gives an up-close view of the eponymous skunk cabbage, the marshes and myriad birds. Another 4km east, the **Giant Cedars Boardwalk** winds a 500m course around a grove of enormous old-growth cedars.

There are several good hiking trails from the summit. You can camp only in designated backcountry campgrounds, and you must have a $10 Wilderness Pass camping permit (in addition to your park pass), which, along with lots of useful information, is available from **Parks Canada** in Revelstoke (p248) or from the **Rogers Pass Centre** inside Glacier National Park (right). Admission to both Mt Revelstoke and Glacier National Parks (the two are administered jointly) is adult/child $7/3.50 per day. Developed campgrounds are few.

There's good cross-country skiing and snowshoeing in the very long winters, but avalanches and bad weather require you to have the right gear and be prepared for anything (see boxed text, p251).

Revelstoke Edventures (☎ 250-837-4235; www.revedventures.ca; hikes from $30) runs tours of the park in conjunction with Okanagan College. Hikes last two to seven hours and are a great way to learn about the park's flora and fauna.

GLACIER NATIONAL PARK

Read the first word in the name of this park very carefully. 'Glacier.' Repeat it 430 times and you have the number of icy expanses that can be found in this 1350-sq-km park.

Fans of rain and snow will revel in the almost precipitation. Annual snowfall can be as much as 23m. Because of the sheer mountain slopes, this is one of the world's most active avalanche areas. For this reason, skiing, caving and mountaineering are closely regulated; you must register with park wardens before venturing into the backcountry.

Around Rogers Pass, you'll notice the many snow sheds protecting the highway. With the narrow road twisting up to 1330m, this is a dangerous area, sometimes called Death Strip; an unexpected avalanche can wipe a car right off the road. Still, the area is carefully controlled, and sometimes snows are brought tumbling down with artillery before they fall by themselves. Call for a daily **avalanche report** (☎ 250-837-6867) in season.

In summer the road is clear of snow, though you can encounter rains even on the sunniest of days. Whether you travel by car, bus, trail or bicycle (more power to you), Rogers will likely rank as one of the most beautiful mountain passes you'll ever have the pleasure of traversing. Be sure to pause at the **Hemlock Grove Trail**, 54km west of Revelstoke, where a 400m boardwalk winds through an ancient hemlock rain forest.

At the east side of the park is the dividing line between Pacific Standard and Mountain Standard time zones, which means that if it's noon in the park, it's 1pm just outside the east gate. Admission to this and Mt Revelstoke National Park (the two are administered jointly) is adult/child $7/3.50 per day.

Definitely plan to spend some time at the informative **Rogers Pass Centre** (☎ 250-814-5233; 8am-7pm summer, 9am-5pm spring & fall, 9am-7pm winter). Located 72km east of Revelstoke, the center shows films on the park and organizes guided walks in summer. Also check out the dramatic CPR dioramas documenting the railway's efforts to conquer the pass (in most battles it's snow 1, railway 0). The center is also home to a fantastic **bookstore** run by the Friends of Mt Revelstoke & Glacier (☎ 250-837-2010; www.friendsrevglacier.com). It has a huge range of books and maps on the region.

Across from the center, the 50-room **Best Western Glacier Park Lodge** (☎ 250-837-2126; www.glacierparklodge.ca; r $115-150;) has a 24-hour coffee shop.

Not far from here are the park's two campgrounds: **Illecillewaet Campground** and **Loop Brook Campground** (both $19 per campsite; Jul-Sep). Both have running water and flush toilets. Backcountry campers must stick to designated backcountry sites and must have a $10 Wilderness Pass camping permit, which is available from the Parks Canada regional office in Revelstoke (p248) or the Rogers Pass Centre.

NAKUSP

pop 1800

Nakusp was moved as part of dam construction on the Upper Arrow Lake many decades ago and lacks the historical feel found at places like New Denver. Still it's a good place for a pause and is rarely crowded.

Nakusp, a First Nations word meaning 'sheltered bay,' was a major steamship port during the Slocan mining boom in the 1890s. Steamships carried ore up to the CPR tracks in Revelstoke. When the boom subsided and new highways took business away from the stern-wheelers, the economy shifted to forestry. The last great stern-wheeler to ply the lake's waters was the SS *Minto*, which was retired in 1954 (it was then given a Viking funeral and torched).

The lakes were forever changed by the dams built as part of the Columbia River energy and flood control projects in the 1950s and 1960s. The level of Upper Lake was raised and several small towns were flooded in the process. This is why even today you see little of the shoreline development you might expect. Hwy 23 between Nakusp and Revelstoke is rather desolate, and Nakusp, which had to be relocated to higher ground, feels like a planned community. For details on the Hwy 23 **Upper Arrow Lake ferry**, see below. While riding the ferry you might enjoy reading the panels trying to explain the rather tortured and ongoing efforts to restore the ecological balance of the lake (eg that stuff dumping out the back of the ferry is fertilizer…).

This section of the province is overlooked by most travelers. Good camping and hiking areas, pleasant travel roads and nearby hot springs make Nakusp a relaxed place to spend a couple of days. If you're in the area on a Wednesday night in summer, stop by Recreation Park on the east side of town and listen to some **free live music** in the park bandstand.

Southwest of Nakusp, Hwy 6 splits, heading southwest to Fauquier past Arrow Park, the official dividing line between Upper and Lower Arrow Lakes, and to the Needles ferry from Fauquier to Needles (see below). Once on the other side, you'll climb over the 1189m-high Monashee Pass en route to Vernon (p242) in the Okanagan Valley. You'll pass a few small provincial parks along this route.

Information

Nakusp VIC (☎ 250-265-4234, 800-909-8819; www.nakusp hotsprings.com; 92 W 6th Ave; ❥ 9am-5pm Jun-Sep) has good hiking information for the area. Next door, the **Nakusp Museum** (adult/child $3/2; ❥ 9am-5pm Jun-Sep) shows what the area looked like before the floods.

Sights & Activities

Local springs get a diverse crowd of families, aging hippies, backpackers and others who want to soak up the hot water vibe.

Nakusp Hot Springs (☎ 250-265-4528; www.nakusp hotsprings.com; adult/child $11/free; ❥ 9:30am-10pm), 12km northeast of Nakusp off Hwy 23, are newly reopened after installation of a water filtration system. Though the squeaky-clean pools tend to ruin some of the natural vibe, the gorgeous scenery reminds you that you are steping deep into nature. Instead of driving you might want to make the beautiful 8km hike on the Kuskanax Interpretive Trail from Nakusp; the VIC has a detailed brochure with the route. There are cramped sites for camping ($15), and simple chalets (from $60).

THE KOOTENAYS

KOOTENAY FERRIES

The long Kootenay and Upper and Lower Arrow Lakes necessitate some ferry travel. All ferries (www.th.gov.bc.ca/marine/ferry_schedules.htm) are free. On busy summer weekends you may have to wait in a long line for a sailing or two before you get passage.

Upper Arrow Lake Ferry (☎ 250-837-8418) runs year-round between Galena Bay (49km south of Revelstoke) and Shelter Bay (49km north of Nakusp) on Hwy 23. The trip takes 20 minutes and runs from 6am to 11pm every hour on the hour from Shelter Bay and every hour on the half-hour between 6:30am and 11:30pm from Galena Bay.

Needles Ferry (☎ 250-837-8418) crosses Lower Arrow Lake between Fauquier (57km south of Nakusp) and Needles (135km east of Vernon) on Hwy 6; the trip takes five minutes. The ferry runs every day, leaving from Fauquier every 30 minutes on the hour and the half-hour from 5am to 10pm. From Needles it runs on the quarter and three-quarter hour between 5:15am and 9:45pm. After hours the ferry travels on demand only.

Kootenay Lake Ferry (☎ 250-229-4215) sails between Balfour on the west arm of Kootenay Lake (34km northeast of Nelson) and Kootenay Bay. Its 45-minute crossing makes it the world's longest free car ferry. In summer the ferry leaves Balfour every 50 minutes between 6:30am and 9:40pm, and from Kootenay Lake from 7:10am to 10:20pm. In winter the sailings are less frequent.

THE KOOTENAYS

Thirty-two kilometers north of Nakusp on Hwy 23, **Halcyon Hot Springs** (☎ 250-265-3554; www .halcyon-hotsprings.com; adult/child $12/8; ❀ 8am-10pm) caters to every budget, with accommodations that range from campsites ($20) and camping cabins ($80 for two people) to luxurious chalets ($180). You don't need to stay here to enjoy the hot springs, which sit high on a nearly personality-free ledge above Upper Arrow Lake.

Anyone wishing to soak for free should ask around about two nearby natural hot springs: **St Leon's**, a favorite with locals for its seclusion and kidney-shaped pools, and **Halfway**, 24km north on Hwy 23. Getting to both undeveloped springs requires driving on logging roads, and a little hiking. Ask at the VIC for specific directions, as these spots are, after all, secluded.

Sleeping & Eating

Nakusp and Halcyon hot springs also offer accommodations.

Village of Nakusp Campsite (☎ 250-265-4019; cnr 8th Ave & 4th St; campsite from $16; ❀ Apr-Oct) Facilities here include flush toilets, showers and 38 wooded sites.

Hot Springs Guesthouse (☎ 250-265-3069; www .enjoynakusp.com; 1950 Hwy 23 N; dm $25m, r from $50) This fun and friendly place has a superb location on the lake across from Hot Springs Rd. Enjoy the quiet on one of the many hammocks or borrow a kayak and go for a paddle. Rooms now include a tree house.

Kuskanax Lodge (☎ 250-265-3618, 800-663-0100; 515 Broadway; r $60-90; ❀) Sports fans in the sports bar here may straddle the ivy covering the walls for Wrigley Field – well, maybe drunken sports fans might. The 49 rooms are basic motel through and through.

Leland Hotel (☎ 250-265-4221; 96 4th Ave SW; meals $6-12; ❀ noon-11pm) Join the old codgers at the bar or take in the lake views outside this 1892 veteran.

Picardo Restaurant (☎ 250-265-3331; 401 Broadway St; meals from $7; ❀ 8am-9pm) has a flamboyant menu to match its colorful exterior. Tex-Mex standards mingle with Canadian favorites for a selection straight outta Nafta.

NEW DENVER

pop 550

A sleepy gem of a near-ghost town, New Denver has an almost clichéd spot on Slocan Lake. It didn't suffer the indignity of having to move up a hill when a dam was put in, so it still feels rooted to its past. Prowl the tree-lined streets and you might start hearing the theme from the *Andy Griffith Show* – albeit with each verse ending with 'Eh?'

A major boomtown in the heyday of the Silvery Slocan Mines and originally named Eldorado, New Denver grew quickly with seemingly endless potential, enough (it was felt) to rival the also-booming town of Colorado. This optimism shrank as the boom subsided, and New Denver is now just a twinkle in its namesake's eye. But greatness is a subjective thing; New Denver's quiet, progressive and artistic community lives surrounded by gorgeous mountain peaks on the shoulder of beautiful Slocan Lake. Ask anyone who lives here and they'll tell you it doesn't get better than this. Nearby Silverton (population 220) also boomed but went bust, and this pretty spot is scarcely more than a ghost town now.

Sights

The **Silvery Slocan Museum** (☎ 250-358-2201; www .newdenver.ca; 202 6th Ave; ❀ 9am-5pm Jun-Sep) is also home to the very helpful VIC. Housed in the 1897 Bank of Montreal, it features well-done displays from the booming mining days, a tiny vault and an untouched tin ceiling.

During WWII, 22,000 Japanese Canadians in Vancouver were rounded up and shipped to remote places in the BC interior for reasons of 'security.' The **Nikkei Internment Memorial Centre** (☎ 250-358-7288; www.newdenver.ca/nikkei; 306 Josephine St, New Denver; adult/child $6/4; ❀ 9:30am-5pm May-Sep) sits on the site of one of 10 former internment camps in the Slocan Valley. The center includes a beautiful Japanese garden. Three of the old huts remain, two furnished to show how people lived. Note the efforts to try to make the walls a little warmer. A few internees still live in the area.

Sleeping & Eating

New Denver Municipal Campground (☎ 250-358-2316; waterfront campsite from $15) Camping with plenty of amenities can be had at this 44-site place near the marina at the bottom of 3rd Ave.

Villa Dome Quixote (☎ 250-358-7242; www .domequixote.con; 602 6th Ave; r from $48) Who can resist a place with such a name? It's a Buckminster Fuller fantasy of domed buildings. Corners are few in the 15 rooms, which have a certain minimalist flair. Revel in all things round as you bubble away in the hot tub.

Valhalla Inn (☎ 250-358-2228; www.valhallainn.biz; 509 Slocan Ave; r from $55) More conventional than Villa Dome Quixote, the Valhalla Inn is a lively pub, a restaurant and 28 good-sized rooms.

Apple Tree (☎ 250-358-2691; 210 6th Ave; meals $6; ☼ 7am-4pm Mon-Sat) A good place for breakfast or lunch, Apple Tree attracts friendly locals who lounge in the back garden reading old issues of the *Economist*.

Panini Bistro & Delicatessen (☎ 250-358-2830; 306 6th Ave; meals $6; ☼ 9am-4pm Tue-Sun) This place has big breakfasts and tasty namesake panini.

Getting There & Away

New Denver is 47km southeast of Nakusp, along a gas station–free stretch of Hwy 6.

VALHALLA PROVINCIAL PARK

Already large at almost 50,000 hectares, Valhalla (and all its bucolic glory) is one of BC's underappreciated treasures and you'll find few others enjoying its expanse in the lovely Slocan Valley.

Southwest of New Denver and across Slocan Lake, the park encompasses most of the Valhalla Range of the Selkirk Mountains. The range takes its name from the Norse mythological palace for slain warriors. Ochre rock paintings along the shoreline are believed to represent the dreams and visions of ancient Arrow Lakes First Nations, who treasured the natural sanctuary. There are many trails through the park; try to get a map at the New Denver VIC (housed in the Silvery Slocan Museum).

You can drive 30km south along Hwy 6 from New Denver and marvel at the jaw-dropping vistas of the Valhallas' sharp, snow-covered peaks. Or you can enjoy even better views by packing your backpack for a day hike or overnight trip. Slocan Lake serves as the park's eastern boundary; its other sides butt up against more rugged peaks and dense forest. You can only access the main areas of the park by boat or commercial water taxi. In New Denver, **Valla Venture** (☎ 250-358-7775) offers water-taxi services (from $25) to the Nemo Creek trailhead, a good point of departure for day hikes. You can also get access to the nine beach **campgrounds** in the park – all have fire rings, picnic tables and outhouses.

Valhalla was protected as parkland in 1983, mostly due to the intense efforts of the **Valhalla Wilderness Society** (☎ 250-358-2333; www.vws.org;

307 6th St; ☼ call for hrs), an advocacy group that formed in the 1970s to save the Valhalla Range from logging. Since then the now-thriving group has also successfully campaigned to protect the Khutzeymateen Grizzly Sanctuary near Prince Rupert, and the nearby White Grizzly Wilderness. A current focus is the commercialization of BC's parks (p57). When open, the society's office is a great place to learn more about current issues and to get excellent park topographic maps and helpful trail information.

NEW DENVER TO KASLO

Sandon (☎ 250-358-7920; ☼ 10am-6pm May-Oct), a ghost town off Hwy 31A, 12km east of New Denver, features historic buildings restored to reflect the chaotic days in the 1890s when the silver mines boomed and the population was 5000.

Near Sandon you can get one of the best views of the Slocan Valley from the **Idaho Lookout**, a 2244m-high viewpoint above the ghost town. A rough logging road leads up to a parking lot. From there an easy 1.5km (one-way) hike takes you to this awesome vista. In July and August spare your poor car from navigating the bumpy road and take the shuttle from Sandon. Ask at the museum for information. For less of a hike, try the **K&S Railway Historic Trail**, which also starts in Sandon. The 5km trail dallies along, passing interpretive signs, old mine shafts and remnants of the railway. You'll also get good views of the surrounding mountains.

The entire 47km route traverses some gorgeous mountain scenery, replete with spurting springs and babbling brooks.

KASLO

pop 1100

Tree-lined streets, restored Victorian buildings and access to outdoor fun make Kaslo a highly recommended stop for travelers. Downtown on Front St is both busy and picturesque. It has a good view of Kootenay Lake and a nice mix of shops, cafés and attractions.

Unlike what happened in surrounding towns in the Slocan Valley, it was timber, not silver, that lured the first European settlers to Kaslo. In 1895 the Kaslo & Slocan Railroad, backed by the US-based Great Northern Railroad, brought Kaslo out of isolation by linking it with the silver mines in the Slocan Valley. With the building of hotels, bars and brothels, the population boomed along with the mines.

Once the mining slowed, Kaslo became a thriving fruit-growing community noted especially for its cherries, some of which were said to be the size of plums.

The **VIC** (☎ 250-353-2525; www.klhs.bc.ca; 324 Front St; ☿ 9am-5pm mid-May–mid-Oct) has good information on hiking and mountain-biking trails in the area, as well as the diverse range of accommodations.

Sights & Activities

Right outside the VIC, the 1898 **SS Moyie** (adult/child $5/2; ☿ 9am-5pm mid-May–mid-Oct) has been restored after much community agitation to prevent it suffering the fate of other riverboats. For 59 years the boat provided a vital link south to Nelson. Now a national historic site, the SS *Moyie* is moored permanently on the downtown lakeside and has a good museum that covers its active years.

The **Kootenay Star Museum** (☎ 250-353-2115; 402 Front St; admission by donation; ☿ 9am-6pm) is like a garage sale of old artifacts from the mines. It has a tiny café with home-baked items. The beautifully restored **Langham Cultural Centre** (☎ 250-353-2662; 477 A Ave; ☿ 1-4pm Thu-Sun) features displays by local artists in two galleries and live music performances in the 75-seat theater.

Kaslo Kayaking (☎ 250-353-9649; 331 Front St; rental per day from $45) rents kayaks, offers tours and gives lessons on paddle-perfect Kootenay Lake.

Sleeping & Eating

The Kaslo VIC has a book bulging with B&B and rental accommodations. Front St is lined with delis, juice bars, cafés and pubs.

Mirror Lake Campground (☎ 250-353-7102; www.mirrorlake.kaslobc.com; campsite $18, cabins from $50; ☿ Apr-Oct) This campground has 100 shady sites, nine cabins, a store, lake access and more. It's 5km south of Kaslo on Hwy 31.

Kaslo Municipal Campground (☎ 250-353-2311; Vimy Park; campsite $19; ☿ May-Sep) The 25 barebones sites are close to Front St.

Kootenay Lake Hostel (☎ 250-353-2551; www.kaslohostel.com; 232 B Ave; dm/d $20/50; ▣) This attractive European-style hostel has a big common kitchen, deck, sauna and vegetable garden. You can rent kayaks, canoes and bikes.

Kaslo Motel (☎ 250-353-7603; www.kaslomotel.com; 330 D Ave; r from $60; ▨) The 17 rooms at this

---

> ### AHOY! IT'S BEDTIME!
>
> Why look at the lake from your room when you can float on the lake in your room? **Kaslo Shipyard Co** (☎ 250-353-2686; www.netidea.com/shipyard) has four custom-designed lake boats for overnight cruising. Boats have full galleys and come with everything you need for a water-borne holiday on Kootenay Lake, including linens, utensils and the always handy shovel and axe. There's little to compare to lounging in a deck chair in your own secluded cove on a moonlit night. Rates start at $250 for one-night trips. The boats sleep four to eight.

central place are in a mix of cottages and a two-story block. Not all units have air-con but some have kitchens.

Kaslo Bay Resort (☎ 250-353-7777, 888-300-2225; www.kaslobay.com; 551 Rainbow Dr; r from $70; ▨) Just around Kaslo Bay from the center, the 12 units at this modest but spick-and-span motel all have full kitchens. Bring your boat; mooring at the marina is free for guests!

KASLO TO NELSON

The 70km drive to Nelson hugs the lake for most of the way. It's all very scenic. **Ainsworth Hot Springs** is a cute little old town with a spa resort. At Balfour, Hwy 31 ends at the Kootenay Lake Ferry (see boxed text, p255), but the road continues on as Hwy 3A 34km to Nelson.

NELSON

pop 9800

'Keep Nelson Weird' is a bumper sticker you'll spot around Nelson, a bromide many locals are doing their best to uphold. Case in point: when a law was passed banning dogs from the center (a misguided effort to put some of the street folks on a leash as it were), residents responded by taking signs with the universal 'no' symbol over a dog and changing the critter's species to pigs, moose and so on.

Couple this free spirit with one of Canada's best-preserved towns and a hillside setting on the West Arm of Kootenay Lake and you have one of the most appealing cities east of Vancouver. The vibrant cultural mix is fueled by students at the renowned Kootenay School of the Arts, the Selkirk School of Music and a school of Chinese medicine.

Downtown – dogs or no dogs – is a compact hub of cafés, bars and shops. Down at the water, paths, beaches and parks line the shore. So pull up a seat outside and enjoy the vibe. You won't be barking up the wrong tree.

History

Nelson was born in the late 1800s, when two down-on-their-luck brothers from Washington sat bemoaning their bad fortune on top of Toad Mountain, just southwest of what is now Nelson. While the brothers rested, some of their party found the copper-silver deposit that later became the Silver King Mine. A town began to build up around the ore-rich mine, and its mass production prompted two transcontinental railways to serve Nelson in order to carry the goods away to smelters. When this proved too costly, the mining company built its own smelter, which only lasted as long as the ore. The smelter buildings were destroyed in a massive fire in 1911, and like most mined-out towns, Nelson turned to its forests.

In 1977 Nelson was chosen for the government's project on heritage conservation. Today it boasts more than 350 carefully preserved and restored late-19th- to early-20th-century buildings.

Orientation

Nelson sits on the west arm of Kootenay Lake. Traveling from the north, Hwy 3A becomes a series of streets before heading west to Castlegar. Hwy 6 skirts the west side of down-

THE KOOTENAYS

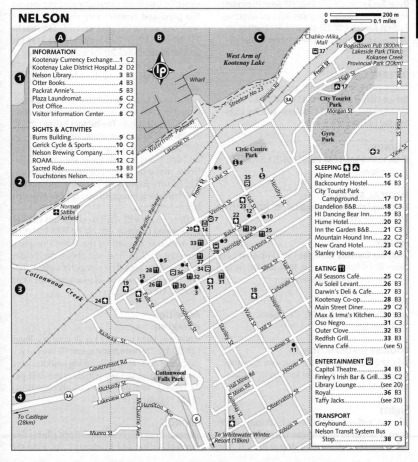

NELSON

0 ——— 200 m
0 ——— 0.1 miles

INFORMATION
Kootenay Currency Exchange....1 C2
Kootenay Lake District Hospital..2 D2
Nelson Library...........................3 B3
Otter Books.............................4 B3
Packrat Annie's.........................5 B3
Plaza Laundromat......................6 C2
Post Office...............................7 C2
Visitor Information Center..........8 C2

SIGHTS & ACTIVITIES
Burns Building..........................9 C3
Gerick Cycle & Sports..............10 C2
Nelson Brewing Company.........11 C4
ROAM....................................12 C2
Sacred Ride...........................13 B3
Touchstones Nelson................14 B2

SLEEPING
Alpine Motel...........................15 C4
Backcountry Hostel.................16 B3
City Tourist Park
 Campground.........................17 D1
Dandelion B&B.......................18 C3
HI Dancing Bear Inn................19 B3
Hume Hotel.............................20 B2
Inn the Garden B&B................21 C3
Mountain Hound Inn...............22 C2
New Grand Hotel.....................23 C2
Stanley House.........................24 A3

EATING
All Seasons Café......................25 C2
Au Soleil Levant.......................26 B3
Darwin's Deli & Cafe................27 B3
Kootenay Co-op.......................28 B3
Main Street Diner.....................29 C2
Max & Irma's Kitchen...............30 B3
Oso Negro...............................31 C3
Outer Clove.............................32 B3
Redfish Grill............................33 B3
Vienna Café.........................(see 5)

ENTERTAINMENT
Capitol Theatre.......................34 B3
Finley's Irish Bar & Grill............35 C2
Library Lounge....................(see 20)
Royal.....................................36 B3
Taffy Jacks........................(see 20)

TRANSPORT
Greyhound.............................37 D1
Nelson Transit System Bus
 Stop....................................38 C3

West Arm of Kootenay Lake

Chahko-Mika Mall
To Bogustown Pub (800m);
Lakeside Park (1km);
Kokanee Creek
Provincial Park (20km)

Wharf

Streetcar No 23

Simpson Rd

City Tourist Park
Morgan St

Gyro Park

Civic Centre Park

Waterfront Pathway

Lakeside Dr

Norman Stibbs Airfield

Canadian Pacific Railway

Cottonwood Creek

Railway St

Government Rd

Cottonwood Falls Park

McHardy St

Lakeview Cres

Hamilton Ave

McQuarrie Ave

Munro St

To Castlegar (28km)

To Whitewater Winter Resort (18km)

Front St
Lake St
Vernon St
Hall St
Hendryx St
Baker St
Herridge Lane
Victoria St
Silica St
Hall St
Carbonate St
Josephine St
Ward St
Mill St
Latimer St
Kootenay St
Falls St
Stanley St
Hall Mines Rd
Mines Rd
Hoover St
Observatory St
Robson St
Front St
High St
Pine St
View St

town, and goes to Castlegar or south to the small lumber town of Salmo before connecting with Hwy 3 and heading to Creston and the East Kootenays.

Baker St is the main drag and has many shops and restaurants. (And who couldn't love a town with a corner of Josephine and Baker?)

Information

For a good sense of the local scene, pick up a copy of the *Daily News*. You'll find events listings posted at the Kootenay Co-Op (see p262) at 295 Baker St. And tune into the community-run radio station, CJLY 93.5FM, which features a lot of work by local bands.

BOOKSTORES

Otter Books (☎ 250-352-7525; 398 Baker St) Excellent selection of local books, topographic maps and magazines.
Packrat Annie's (☎ 250-354-4722; 411 Kootenay St) Good array of used books and the delightful Vienna Café (p262).

INTERNET ACCESS

Many cafés have internet access.
Nelson Library (☎ 250-352-6333; 602 Stanley St; ☝ 1-8pm Mon, Wed & Fri, 10am-6pm Tue & Thu, 11am-6pm Sat) Free internet access.

LAUNDRY

Plaza Laundromat (☎ 250-352-6077; 616 Front St; ☝ 8am-6pm)

MEDICAL SERVICES

Kootenay Lake District Hospital (☎ 250-352-3111; 3 View St; ☝ 24hr)

MONEY

Kootenay Currency Exchange (☎ 250-354-1441; 715 Vernon St; ☝ 9am-5pm Mon-Fri, 10am-3pm Sat) Typical for Nelson, this is also an art gallery.

POST

Post office (☎ 250-352-3538; 514 Vernon St; ☝ 8:30am-5pm)

TOURIST INFORMATION

VIC (☎ 250-352-3433, 877-663-5706; www.discovernelson.com; 225 Hall St; ☝ 8:30am-6pm May-Oct, 8:30am-5pm Mon-Fri Nov-Apr)

Sights

Almost a third of Nelson's buildings have been restored to their Victorian architectural splendor. It's well worth a stop at the VIC for the excellent companion brochures detailing self-guided tours of the area's architectural heritage by foot and car.

You can easily cover all 26 buildings on the walking tour in a couple of hours. Highlights include the 1899 **Burns Building** (560 Baker St), which has a carved cow head over the door courtesy of its cattle-baron builder. And note that you'll be passing by some of the town's most refreshing cafés and bars…

Lakeside Park by the iconic Nelson Bridge boats a profusion of posies, shade trees and picnic tables. It backs a popular beach. Watch swimmers debate whether to swim to the other side. This area is a good destination for walkers from the center, who can follow the **Waterfront Pathway**, which runs all along the shore (it's western extremity past the airport has good and remote river vistas). You can walk one way to the park and ride **Streetcar No 23** (adult/child $3/2; ☝ 11am-5pm daily Jun-Sep, 11am-5pm Sat & Sun May & Sep–mid-Oct) the other way. One of the town's originals, it follows a 2km track from Lakeside Park to the wharf at the foot of Hall St.

Nelson's baronial old city hall (1902) reopened in 2006 after an enormous renovation transformed it into **Touchstones Nelson** (☎ 250-352-9813; 502 Vernon St; adult/child $10/4; ☝ 11am-7pm Wed-Sat, noon-4pm Sun), a museum of local history and art. Every month there are new exhibitions, many of which celebrate local artists. The history displays are engaging and interactive, banishing images of musty piles of poorly labeled old junk.

Beer lovers will want to check out the **Nelson Brewing Company** (☎ 250-352-3582; 512 Latimer St), which is housed in the town's original brewery. Call to find out about the Friday tours and tastings. The company's many top-notch brews are served all over town; the Wild Honey Ale is a treat.

Activities

KAYAKING

Kootenay Lake is prime kayak country. **Roam** (☎ 250-354-2056; www.roamshop.com; 579 Baker St) is a gear store dedicated to kayaking and canoeing locally. Rental kayaks (single from $60 per 24 hours), and the shop can arrange tours of the region.

HIKING

The two-hour climb to Pulpit Rock affords fine views of Nelson and Kootenay Lake. Find the trailhead on your right at the west end of Johnstone Rd (on the north bank across the bridge). Excellent hikes abound at **Kokanee Creek Provincial Park**, 20km northeast of town off Hwy 3A. Stop in at the park's **visitor center** (☎ 250-825-4212) for information on specific hikes, including the Canyon Trail, which winds through lush forest to views of waterfalls spilling off Kokanee Glacier. Eight trails begin right at the visitor center. **Kokanee Glacier Provincial Park** (☎ 250-825-3500 for trail conditions) covers 32,000 hectares and boasts dozens of lakes. Its 85km of hiking trails are some of the area's most superb. The two-hour hike to Kokanee Lake is wonderful and can be continued to the glacier.

MOUNTAIN BIKING

Most of this area's mountain-biking trails wind up from Kootenay Lake along steep and rather challenging hills, followed by wicked downhills. Trail names like 'Boneyard' and 'Fat Chance' are not misnomers, but there are some intermediate trails for those wishing to finish in one piece. Check with the excellent local bike shops for more details. **Gerick Cycle & Sports** (☎ 250-354-4622, 877-437-4251; www.gericks.com; 702 Baker St; rental per day from $40) rents road and mountain bikes. **Sacred Ride** (☎ 250-362-5688; www.sacredride.ca; 213B Baker St; rental per day $35-55) is also a good choice. Both shops sell *Your Ticket to Ride*, an extensive trail map, for $10.

SKIING & SNOWBOARDING

Known for its heavy powdery snowfall, which averages 1050cm per year, **Whitewater Winter Resort** (☎ 250-354-4944, 800-666-9420, snow report 250-352-7669; www.skiwhitewater.com; 1-day lift tickets adult/child $46/28) features good skiing and boarding. Unlike more-commercial places, Whitewater maintains its small-town charm. Whitewater has only two double chairs and a rope tow, but they can take you to an elevation of 2040m (the drop is 396m), where you can enjoy great powdery snow on 20 marked runs. Several snowcat operators can take you to virgin territory from $400 for the day. There are 11 groomed Nordic trails. The resort is 18km south of Nelson off Hwy 6.

You can rent equipment at the resort or at Roam (see opposite) as well as the mountain-biking shops in Nelson.

Tours

Nestled on its hillside, Nelson is best viewed from the lake. And the views aren't just limited to the town either. Much of the surrounding region is still undeveloped, so you can see some rugged forest right from the water.

As you can tell from the name, **Sail With Us** (☎ 250-359-7772; Balfour) offers submarine tours of the… No, of course not – these tours are aboard a 10m sailboat. Lake tours for two start from $110 for two hours. Its located 30km east of Nelson in Balfour, near the Kootenay Lake Ferry (which also offers great views).

Sleeping

By all means stay in the heart of Nelson so you can fully enjoy the city's beat. The VIC has a free phone for calling local accommodations. Ask for lists of B&Bs and rental homes.

BUDGET

City Tourist Park (☎ 250-352-7618; campnels@telus.net; 90 High St; sites from $17; ☽ May-Oct) Just a five-minute walk from Baker St, this small campground is right in an urban park and has 35 shady sites.

HI Dancing Bear Inn (☎ 250-352-7573, 877-352-7573; www.dancingbearinn.com; 171 Baker St; dm/r from $18/50; ☐) This Lexus of hostels is beautifully renovated and has 14 quiet and immaculate rooms. The comfortable living room makes a great place to read a book or find out about local happenings.

Backcountry Hostel (☎ 250-352-2151; www.thebackcountryhostel.com; 198 Baker St; dm/r from $20/60; ☐) Located above a popular bar, this hostel is busy, unadorned and has a constant stream of international guests drawn by Nelson's mellow yet goofy rep.

Kokanee Creek Provincial Park (☎ 800-689-9025; www.discovercamping.ca; campsite $22; ☽ May-Sep) Situated 20km northeast of Nelson off Hwy 3A, this park contains 132 wooded sites with toilets and showers. It has its own visitor center and offers daily interpretive programs. Redfish, set among old hemlocks, is the quieter of the two campgrounds here.

MIDRANGE

Dandelion B&B (☎ 250-505-5466; www.bbcanada.com/thedandelion; 519 Carbonate St; r $60-85; ☽ May-Sep) One of several cute and simple B&Bs sprouting up like, well, weeds near downtown, the Dandelion has two comfy rooms furnished in bright, contemporary hues. There's a patio and a view of the water from this restored old bungalow.

New Grand Hotel (☎ 250-352-7211, 888-722-2258; www.newgrandhotel.ca; 616 Vernon St; r $60-85; ✖) There's a vague Spanish/Old Hollywood feel here thanks to the mustard stucco and wrought iron accenting the exterior. The 30 rooms have rich mission-style furniture and restored hardwood floors. At times there is hostel-style accommodations available from $20 per person.

Mountain Hound Inn (☎ 250-352-6490, 866-452-6490; 621 Baker St; r $70-90; ✖ 🖥) This former flophouse has been nicely renovated into a midrange motel upstairs off Baker St. The 20 rooms feature flat-screen TVs, wi-fi and a relaxed industrial edge. Located in back, rooms 121 and 122 have lake views.

Alpine Motel (☎ 250-352-5501, 888-356-2233; www .alpine-motel.com; 1120 Hall Mines Rd; r $75-150; ✖ 🖥) The grounds at this Swiss-style place are lovely and you can view the cool waters of the lake from the warm waters of the hot tub. The 30 rooms are a good size and have wi-fi. The motel is near Observatory St, just up the hill south of the center.

Hume Hotel (☎ 250-352-5331, 877-568-0888; www .humehotel.com; 422 Vernon St; r $80-115; 🖥) This 1898 classic hotel is slowly being renovated back to its former glory. Hallways are now lined with an array of vintage Nelson photos. The 43 rooms vary greatly in quality. Avoid those overlooking the kitchen exhaust stack and opt for the huge corner rooms with stunning views of the hills and lake. The breakfast is bounteous and the hotel is home to several nightspots, including the Library Lounge and Taffy Jack's (opposite).

Inn the Garden B&B (☎ 250-352-3226, 800-596-2337; www.innthegarden.com; 408 Victoria St; r $90-200; ✖) Right downtown, this B&B offers five posh guest rooms in a wicker-laden Victorian home. As the name implies, the place is surrounded by posies and other lovely plantings.

Stanley House (☎ 250-352-377; www.stanleyhousebb .com; 420 Railway at Baker St; r $110-160; ✖) Right at the south end of the centre, this was the 1908 home of a railway boss, who could ponder the workings of his employees in the yards below. The three rooms are all richly furnished in period furniture and there's a fine porch.

Eating

Nelson has a great range of eating options. Baker St and its precincts are lined with cool cafés, restaurants and pubs. Note that on weeknights, even in summer, Nelson betrays its small-town roots and starts putting away the sidewalks by 9pm.

Nelson's **outdoor market** (cnr Josephine & Baker Sts; 🕑 9:30am-3pm Wed Jul-Sep) is a community event with all sorts of organic growers and craft makers offering their goods for sale.

Part community centre, part market, the **Kootenay Co-op** (☎ 250-354-4077; 295 Baker St; 🕑 8am-7pm Mon-Sat) has local produce and foodstuffs and good prepared foods in its bakery.

BUDGET

Oso Negro (☎ 250-532-7761; 604 Ward St; coffee from $1.50; 🕑 7am-5pm; 🖥) This local favorite (with a the corner location) roasts its own coffee. The café is bright and open, and outside there are tables in a garden with gurgling water features.

Au Soleil Levant (☎ 250-352-2030; 281 Herridge Lane; snacks from $2; 🕑 9am-7pm Tue-Sat) This tiny European-style back-alley bakery makes an exquisite range of French baked goods and baguette sandwiches.

Vienna Café (☎ 250-354-4722; 411 Kootenay St; dishes from $6; 🕑 9am-5pm) Part of Packrat Annie's bookstore (p260), this place has a tie-dyed vibe and a long menu of healthy foods, many both organic and vegetarian. Enjoy the rich coffee at one of the many sidewalk tables.

Darwin's Deli & Cafe (☎ 250-352-2120; 460 Baker St; meals from $6; 🕑 7:30am-10pm; 🖥) A classic deli with good sandwiches, internet access and a few tables outside.

MIDRANGE

Redfish Grill (☎ 250-352-3456; 491 Baker St; meals $5-20; 🕑 8am-10pm) Redfish serves excellent cuisine throughout the day. The $5 breakfast special groans with eggs, bacon and more. By lunchtime things are more stylish, with a mix of sandwiches and salads. At night there's tapas-style small plates and a range of global cuisine made with local produce. And there are sidewalk tables.

Outer Clove (☎ 250-354-1667; 536 Stanley St; meals $8-18; 🕑 5-9pm Mon-Sat) Dishes at this funky joint are redolent with the namesake garlic. Burgers are spiked with cloves, while the pasta emits fragrant joy. Vegetarian choices abound – and for once they are not your bland ho-hum pap. Try to snare one of the tables on the sidewalk.

Main Street Diner (☎ 250-354-4848; 616 Baker St; meals $8-20; 🕑 11am-10pm) This classic diner has a dash of panache and is always busy. People queue for the covered sidewalk tables. The menu runs through the classics with color and flair. The burgers are tasty, the steaks tender.

Max & Irma's Kitchen (☎ 250-352-2332; 515A Kootenay St; meals $10-17; ☺ noon-9pm Mon-Sat) The creative sandwiches here are best enjoyed on the sunny patio. At dinner there are Mediterranean dishes and excellent pizza.

TOP END

our pick **All Seasons Café** (☎ 250-352-0101; www .allseasonscafé.com; 620 Herridge Lane; meals $20-40; ☺ 5-10pm Mon-Sat) Sitting out on the magical patio here, with little lights twinkling in the big tree above, you may not even care about the food, but you should. This is one of BC's best restaurants, with a casual and eclectic menu that changes with the seasons. Dishes are boldly seasoned and prepared using BC produce with global influences. There's also a great, reasonable wine list.

Entertainment

Nelson has some good venues; many have live entertainment and also serve bar food such as burgers and nachos. Be sure to order one of the fine Nelson Brewing Co ales.

PUBS

Royal (☎ 250-352-1269; 330 Baker St; ☺ 11am-2am) A huge rollicking bar right on Baker St. There are tables out front and many more in the high-ceilinged space that sees many bands.

Library Lounge (☎ 250-352-5331; Hume Hotel, 422 Vernon St; ☺ 11am-late) This refined space in a renovated hotel has some good sidewalk tables where you can ponder the passing parade. Inside it's all very dark wood and leaded glass, with live jazz some nights.

Finley's Irish Bar & Grill (☎ 250-352-5121; 705 Vernon St; ☺ noon-late) The only thing Irish about this place is the name. It's a big, modern pub with a back deck that has sweeping lake views. Inside, there's live rock many nights, backed up by the beat of pool cues.

Bogustown Neighbourhood Pub (☎ 250-354-1313; 712 Nelson Ave; ☺ noon-late) Featuring a fun, relaxed atmosphere, pub food, pool tables and a good patio, this bar has eschewed pretension for decades.

CLUBS

Taffy Jack's (☎ 250-352-5331; Hume Hotel, 422 Vernon St; ☺ 11am-late) Top-40 music dancing plus live acts such as faux Neil Diamonds. Cover charges vary.

THEATER

Capitol Theatre (☎ 250-352-6363; 421 Victoria St) This restored 1927 theater has offbeat films, performance art and live drama.

Getting There & Around

The closest airport with commercial service to Nelson is in Castlegar. **Queen City Shuttle** (☎ 250-352-9829; www.kootenayshuttle.com; adult/child one way $22/11; 1hr) serves the Castlegar Airport.

Greyhound (☎ 250-352-3939; Chahko-Mika Mall, 1112A Lakeside Dr) has services to Calgary ($94, 11 to 13 hours, two daily) via various south Kootenays cities and Vancouver ($105, 12 to 13 hours, one daily) via Kelowna ($55, 5½ hours, two daily).

The main stop for **Nelson Transit System Buses** (☎ 250-352-8228; www.busonline.ca) is on the corner of Ward and Baker Sts. Bus 2 serves Chahko-Mika Mall and Lakeside Park. Bus 10 serves the North Shore and runs to the Kootenay Lake ferry in summer.

CASTLEGAR

pop 7900

You're bound to pass through Castlegar (or at most pause), a sprawling town known primarily as a highway junction (Hwys 3 and 3A merge here), it sits at the confluence of the Kootenay and Columbia Rivers. It's a vital hub, even if it is not a vital stop.

Head to the north end of Columbia Ave to see the strip of stores known as downtown Castlegar. In the southern part of town, you'll find the **VIC** (☎ 250-365-6313; www.castlegar.com; 1995 6th Ave at 20th St; ☺ 9am-5pm Jun-Aug, 9am-5pm Mon-Fri Sep-May). Its motto: 'Optimism is in the air

---

DETOUR: KOOTENAY LAKE

If you're traveling south from Nelson, rather than travel through Castlegar, you can follow Kootenay Lake the entire way. From Nelson head east on Hwy 3A to the Kootenay Lake ferry in Balfour (see boxed text, p255). The lake views will keep you on deck the entire journey. At minute Kootenay Bay (it's really just a ferry dock) Hwy 3A continues south 78km to Creston (p266). It's a quiet road, and except for a few villages, it'll just be you and the sweeping lake views.

for the continued growth and prosperity of Castlegar.'

History

Local history is spiced up by the Doukhobors, members of a Russian Christian pacifist sect who followed their leader, Peter Verigin, west from Saskatchewan between 1908 and 1913. The Doukhobors, small groups of peaceful, communal-living people, rejected the teachings of the Russian Orthodox Church during the 18th century. They refused ritual worship, believing instead that god's spirit lived within each individual and that it was up to individuals, not an outside god, to have peaceful and harmonious lives. Needless to say, this sort of self-reliance was rejected by the church, which, in the best spirit of goodwill to all men, exiled the Doukhobors to cold, barren corners of Russia in the hope that the group would fizzle out. But the Doukhobors thrived, and by 1899, 7500 members immigrated to Canada, first to Saskatchewan and then to Castlegar and nearby Grand Forks.

By the 1930s the local population had reached 5000. Most were farmers and in the years since, the community has mostly integrated with local life.

Sights & Activities

The reconstructed **Doukhobor Historical Village** (☎ 250-365-6622; Hwy3A; adult/child $6/3; ☺ 9am-5pm May-Sep) has a couple of buildings, a statue of Tolstoy and a small museum. Frequent weaving demonstrations give you a real feel for the passive life these good folk led. It's across from the airport.

A better bet for sampling the Doukhobor legacy is **Zuckerberg Island Heritage Park** (☎ 250-365-6440; admission by donation; ☺ dawn-dusk). The island was the home of Alexander Feodorovitch Zuckerberg, a Russian teacher brought in to educate Doukhobor children (those who could spell his name got to advance a grade). Today the park contains a suspension bridge, trails and restored buildings, including the former chapel house.

The **Castlegar Museum** (☎ 250-365-6440; 400 13th Ave; admission by donation; ☺ 9am-5pm Mon-Sat) is housed in the grand old CPR train station. Dam-building and farming dominate the exhibits.

South of town, the Columbia River Valley is postcard perfect. Beautiful in all seasons, it comes alive with golden colors when the leaves change in the fall. North of town, however, you'll see a huge pulp mill that's poster perfect for Greenpeace. Over on the Kootenay River, **Keenleyside Dam** is a major source of hydroelectric power.

Sleeping

Syringa Creek Provincial Park (☎ 800-689-9025; www .discovercamping.ca; campsite $17; ☺ Apr-Oct) Old-growth Douglas fir and open grasslands highlight this park, which sits on Lower Arrow Lake, 17km northwest of Castlegar off Broadwater Rd, on the north side of the Columbia River. It offers 63 campsites, a long beach, swimming and good hiking.

Cozy Pines Motel (☎ 250-365-5613; www.cozypines .com; 2118 Crestview Cres; r $55-80; ☒) Although you really should head east to Nelson, should you stay the night, this motel, west of town on Hwy 3, has 18 rooms with kitchens and free broadband internet. It's a tidy place under a brilliant blue roof.

Getting There & Away

Castlegar Airport (YCG; ☎ 250-365-5151) is on Hwy 3A southeast of town. It is the major airport for the region. Air Canada Jazz has daily flights to Vancouver and Calgary. Major rental car firms have offices in the airport terminal. Nelson is 41km northeast of Castlegar.

ROSSLAND

pop 3800

Like a pearl amid the rolling hills of the Southern Monashee Mountains, Rossland is one of Canada's best places for mountain biking. A long history of mining has left the hills crisscrossed with old trails and abandoned rail lines, all of which are perfect for riding.

At 1023m, this high-elevation town sits in the eroded crater of an ancient mineral-rich volcano. The area was first encountered by Europeans in 1865, when builders of the historic Dewdney Trail passed by and simply marveled at the reddish mineral stains on nearby Red Mountain. Prospectors didn't come sniffing around for another 25 years. It wasn't until 1890 that a guy named Joe Moris decided to do more than marvel and finally tapped into the incredibly rich gold deposits that induced Rossland's birth. After old Joe's discovery, the town built up quickly. Sourdough Alley (today's Columbia Ave) became the province's wildest and roughest main thoroughfare, and by 1895, 7000 residents and hundreds of prostitutes could take their pick of 42 saloons. By 1929 most of the claims were mined out, and the boom shrank to a whisper, but in less than 45 years Rossland had produced $165 million worth of gold.

As well as biking, skiing has long been a favorite activity, and the Red Mountain Resort boasts some of the best technical trails in the world. Canadian Olympic gold medalists Kerrin Lee-Gartner and Nancy Greene hail from Rossland.

Information

VIC (☎ 250-362-7722, 888-448-7444; www.rossland .com; ☼ 9am-5pm mid-May–mid-Sep) Located in the museum building, at the junction of Hwy 22 and Hwy 3B. Ask about local walking tours.

Sights & Activities

The **Rossland Museum** (☎ 250-362-7722; adult/child $9/6; ☼ 9am-5pm mid-May–mid-Sep, mine tours 9:30am-3:30pm) does a good job of capturing local history. It's on the site of the former Black Bear Mine; 45-minute tours of the mine give you a good idea of what miners had to endure in blasting through the hard rock underfoot. It also has a section devoted to local skiing triumphs. It's beside the VIC.

Mountain biking is a big deal and you can't go wrong on trails with names like Overdrive (a 1.5km drop), the Flume (tight trail flanked by slabs of rock) and the Dewdney Trail (75km of easy riding past lakes). Free-riding is all the rage, as the ridgelines are easily accessed and there are lots of rocky paths for plunging downhill. Download maps and trail descriptions at www.rossland.com/Seedo/trails.html or pick up a copy of *Trails of the Rossland Range* ($8).

As you'd expect, local bike shops are the places to start. **Revolution Cycles** (☎ 250-362-5688; www.revolutioncycles.ca; 2044 Columbia Ave; rental per day from $30) has a wide range of rentals, maps, advice and much more.

Good in summer for riding, **Red Mountain Ski Resort** (☎ 250-362-7384, 800-663-0105, snow report 250-362-5500; www.redresort.com; 1-day lift pass adult/child $48/25) really shines in winter. Red, as it's called, includes the 1590m-high Red Mountain and 2040m-high Granite Mountain, for a total of 485 hectares of powdery terrain. Geared mostly toward intermediate and advanced skiers and snowboarders, the area is known for its steep, tree-filled runs (83 at last count). There are six lifts and a drop

of 880m. It's only 5km north of downtown on Hwy 3B.

You can rent gear at the resort, and its website has links to various transport options for reaching Red from other parts of BC and the US.

Across the highway from Red Mountain, **Black Jack Cross Country Area** (☎ 250-362-9465; www .skiblackjack.ca; day pass adult/child $9/5) is a ski club open to all, with 25km of groomed skating and classic trails.

Sleeping & Eating

The ski resort has detailed listings of the many places to stay near the slopes. The rates listed here cover the peak season, which in Rossland means winter; unlike much of BC, summer here is low season. Columbia Ave is home to several pubs and cafés.

Mountain Shadow Hostel (☎ 250-362-7160, 877-562-2783; www.mshostel.com; 2125 Columbia Ave; dm from $20; ▣) Right near the center of town, this hostel has 38 beds in tidy and colorful rooms.

Ram's Head Inn (☎ 250-363-9577, 877-267-4323; www.ramshead.bc.ca; r $90-170; ▣) The 12 large guest rooms have fridges and wi-fi. A large common room with vaulted ceilings and a hefty stone fireplace, an outdoor hot tub and a games room make this a real oasis among the deep forest. It's 3km west of Rossland on Red Mountain Rd, off Hwy 3B at the base of the ski resort. (There are more choices here as well.)

Flying Steamshovel (☎ 250-362-7323; 2003 2nd Ave; r $90-110; ▣ ▣) A popular pub (☼ 11am-late) and restaurant with a great deck and free wi-fi for one and all, it also has three rather idiosyncratic rooms with narrow windows and Jacuzzi baths.

AROUND ROSSLAND

West of Rossland, **Christina Lake** is a beautiful place to stay for a day or two, especially if you're camping at **Gladstone Provincial Park**. The **Texas Creek Campground** (☎ 800-689-9025; www .discovercamping.ca; campsite $14; ☼ Jun-Oct) is 10km east of Christina Lake off Hwy 3 and can be tricky to find, so keep a good eye out for the signs for East Lake Dr and then follow it for one kilometer to the campground. The 63 sites are large, private and shaded by the heavy forest.

Further west you'll hit the pretty border town of **Grand Forks**, known for its borscht and relatively abundant sunshine. The town was a byproduct of the Phoenix Mine, once the biggest copper-producing smelter in BC. Some of the Doukhobors (p264) who settled in Castlegar came here, and their influence still lends character and hearty food to the town.

Going east from Rossland you pass through one of the most industrialized parts of BC. Those smokestacks on the skyline belong to the industrial town of **Trail** (population 7900), where even the hospital has a big smokestack. The good-sized town has traded a potentially scenic spot on the Columbia River for an economy based on a vast smelting plant.

CRESTON
pop 5100

Apples abound in Creston, an unflashy agricultural center in a region dotted with orchards that thrive in the fertile ground and mild weather. Other thriving crops include asparagus, peaches and canola. Lapin cherries (large, juicy and dark red) are supplanting apples as the cash crop of choice.

Creston comes after the Crowsnest Hwy 3 climbs the 1774m Kootenay Pass east of Trail. The US is close by and Creston is only 11km from the border. It's a gateway to the Kootenays from Washington and Idaho. The **VIC** (☎ 250-428-4342; www.crestonbc.com/chamber; 711 Canyon St; ⊙ 9am-5pm summer, 8:30am-4:30pm Mon-Fri winter) can help you sort out your direction.

The interesting **Creston & District Museum** (☎ 250-428-9262; 219 Devon St; adult/child $3/1; ⊙ 10am-3:30pm mid-May–mid-Sep) is a thick-walled idiosyncratic stone structure with animal heads (fake) embedded into the walls. It includes a restored trappers cabin.

Fans of bland lager will want to take the hour-long tour through the **Columbia Brewery** (☎ 250-428-9344; 1220 Erickson St; admission free; ⊙ tours 9:30am-2pm Mon-Fri mid-May–mid-Oct, daily Jul & Aug), where BC's popular Kokanee beer is brewed and bottled. It's just south of the center.

Bird-lovers flock to **Creston Valley Wildlife Management Area** (☎ 250-402-6900; www.crestonwildlife.ca; admission free; ⊙ dawn-dusk), 11km west of Creston along Hwy 3. Some 7000 hectares of marshy wetlands sit on protected provincial land. More than 100,000 migrating birds use the area to nest and breed each year. Look for black terns, white-fronted geese and blue herons. You can walk along a 1km boardwalk to a watchtower. An interpretive center is open for varying hours from April to mid-October.

Many people blow right through Creston, stopping only for some fruit or fudge.

However, should you stop, **Little Joe's Campground** (☎ 250-428-2954; 4020 Hwy 3; campsite $19-23), about 5km east of town, has shady sites surrounded by old cedar trees. For fun, try squeezing something in the fruit stand.

In the middle of Creston's modest center, **Downtowner Motor Inn** (☎ 250-428-2238, 800-665-9904; downtown@kootenay.com; 1218 Canyon St; r $47-70; 🗙 🖵) has 23 simple but comfortable rooms, with wi-fi. However, what with the ready availability of Kokanee beer and nearby bowling and curling, you may not come home.

Finding someplace to actually enjoy food made with the valley's bounty is harder than you might expect. Ask a local in the know where to, say, get a good apple pie and you may get a blank stare. Your best bet is to take matters into your own hands at the profusion of **fruit stands** and orchard markets east of town on Hwy 3. If you crave protein, **Famous Fritz** (☎ 250-402-9050; 1238 Northwest Blvd/Hwy 3; treats from $3; ⊙ 9am-5pm Tue-Sat) is a great deli that features a winsome weenie logo that proclaims 'Nice to meat you!' It's west of the center.

EAST KOOTENAYS

Skiing, snowboarding, hiking and mountain biking are the industries of choice in the East Kootenays, a hilly region buttressed by the Purcell Mountains in the west and the Rocky Mountains in the east. Golden, in the north, sits between Glacier and Yoho National Parks, while Cranbrook, in the south, is a major highway crossroad. Most attractive is the old railway town of Fernie, in the east, where ski slopes overlook the beautiful old town.

The region teems with creeks and lakes that are perfect for fly-fishing. The 16km-long Columbia Lake, at Canal Flats, is the source of the mighty Columbia River, which winds around BC, Washington and Oregon for 1953km before spilling into the Pacific Ocean.

FERNIE
pop 5200

A sort of undiscovered Nelson, Fernie has a compact downtown that has been beautifully preserved. Better yet, the entire town has a vibrancy that radiates off the yellow brick buildings. It's a great place to spend a couple of hours strolling.

The town's history was tied to mining, but when the mines closed many years ago the town went to sleep. Which is just as well, as nobody was awake to tear things down in the name of progress, a fate that befell many another BC town.

You can still find plenty of old miners about town more than happy to share harrowing tales of life underground. But these days you're more likely to find folks ready to share harrowing tales of their exploits on the slopes of the Fernie Alpine Resort. In the non-ski season, Fernie seems to be half full of people lounging around while keeping one eye cocked for the first sign of snow.

Happily, constant winter storms travel over the Rockies and dump vast amounts of snow on the area, making it a powdery paradise for skiers and snowboarders. In summer the run-off means great rafting on local rivers, while the hills buzz with mountain bikers.

Orientation & Information

Downtown Fernie lies southeast of Hwy 3. Galleries, cheap variety stores, cafés, bakeries and outdoor shops can all be found along 2nd Ave (aka Victoria Ave). The historic center is bounded by 3rd and 7th Sts and 4th and 1st Aves.

Fernie District Hospital (☎ 250-423-4453; 1501 5th Ave; ⏰ 24hr)

Fernie Heritage Library (☎ 250-423-4458; 492 3rd Ave; ⏰ 11am-8pm Tue-Fri, noon-5pm Sat, also Sun Nov-Mar) In the 1907 Post Office & Customs House. Free internet access.

Polar Peek Books (☎ 250-423-3736; 592 2nd Ave) An eclectic mix of books with a good section of local interest. Great recommendations.

JUMP FORWARD, FALL BACK

The East Kootenays lie in the Mountain Time Zone, like Alberta and Idaho. The West Kootenays and the rest of BC fall in the Pacific Time Zone. If you're heading west on the Trans-Canada Hwy (Hwy 1) from Golden, the time changes at the east gate to Glacier National Park. Or, as you travel west on the Crowsnest Hwy (Hwy 3), the time changes between Cranbrook and Creston. Mountain Time is one hour ahead of Pacific Time. For example, when it's noon in Golden and Cranbrook, it's 11am in Glacier National Park and Creston.

VIC (☎ 250-423-6868; www.ferniechamber.com; 102 Commerce Rd; ⏰ 9am-7pm summer, 9am-5pm Mon-Fri winter) East of town off Hwy 3, just past the Elk River crossing. Good displays about the area.

Sights

Fernie experienced a devastating fire in 1908, which resulted in a brick-and-stone building code. Thus, today you'll see many fine **early-20th-century buildings**, many of which were built out of local yellow brick, giving the town an appearance unique to the East Kootenays. Get a copy of *Heritage Walking Tour*, a superb booklet produced by the **Fernie & District Historical Society** (☎ 250-423-7016; 362 2nd Ave; admission by donation; ⏰ 9:30am-5pm). This small museum has big displays on the area's skiing history. Check out the hand-built skis from the 1920s.

Located in the old CPR train station, the **Arts Station** (☎ 250-423-4842; 601 1st Ave) has a small theatre, galleries and studios for some of the many local artists. Opening hours depend upon what's on.

FERNIE ALPINE RESORT

A five-minute drive from downtown Fernie, this fast-growing resort, which dreams of rivaling Whistler, gets a whopping 875cm of snow per year on average. The **Fernie Alpine Resort** (☎ 250-423-4655, 877-333-2339, snow conditions 250-423-3555; www.skifernie.com; 1-day pass adult/child from $69/22) boasts 107 runs, five bowls and almost endless dumps of powder. Thirty percent of the runs are rated expert. Condos and developments are sprouting like mushrooms after a storm, so expect this resort to only get more high-profile.

To get to the resort from town, follow Hwy 3 west and turn right onto Ski Hill Rd. Most hotels run shuttles daily. You can rent equipment for about $25 per day at the resort or at the sporting gear stores listed under Activities in this section. Also recommended are **Guides Hut** (☎ 250-423-3650; www.theguideshut.com; 671 2nd Ave), which has extensive winter sales and rentals. If you are planning any backcountry skiing, this is the place to get the scoop on conditions, rent avalanche kits, buy topographic maps and find out about organized tours.

Activities

Although much of the focus in winter is on the ski resort, there are hundreds of kilometers of cross-country trails in and around Fernie. Ask at the ski shops or the VIC.

THE KOOTENAYS

MOUNTAIN BIKING

From easy jaunts in Mt Fernie Provincial Park (3km from town) to wild rides up and down in the hills in and around the ski resort (which runs lifts in summer), Fernie has lots for riders. Many come just to tackle the legendary epic Al Matador, which drops over 900m before finishing in the terrific Three Kings Trail.

Two bike stores have lots of advice and rent bikes from $35 a day: **Fernie Sports** (☎ 250-423-3611; 1191 7th Ave) and **Ski & Bike Base** (☎ 250-423-6464; 432 2nd Ave). Get a copy of *Fernie Trail Guide* at the shops or the VIC. **Fernie Fat-Tire Adventures** (☎ 888-423-7849; www.ferniefattire.com) organizes all manner of adventures for people at all skill levels.

WHITE-WATER RAFTING

The Elk River is a classic white-water river, with three Class IV rapids and 11 more class IIIs. It passes through beautiful country and you can often see large wildlife such as bears. Two Fernie outfits, **Canyon Raft Company** (☎ 250-423-7226, 888-423-7226; www.canyonraft.com) and **Mountain High River Adventures** (☎ 250-423-5008, 877-423-4555; www.raftfernie.com), offer day trips for about $100 and half-day floats for $50. In spring you may be able to get a trip to the wilder Bull River.

HIKING

Great hiking trails radiate in all directions from Fernie. The excellent and challenging **Three Sisters hike** winds through forests and wildflower-covered meadows, along limestone cliffs and scree slopes. The 2744m summit offers incredible 360-degree views of the Elk Valley, Fisher Peak and surrounding lakes. From the VIC, take Dickens Rd to Hartley Lake Rd and follow it to the lake. Turn left onto the dirt track and hike 3km to the trailhead. Allow at least four hours each way. Another hike affording spectacular views, the **Hosmer Mountain Trail**, is also off Hartley Lake Rd (there is a parking area and a well-marked trailhead). This moderate hike takes about 2½ hours one way.

Mountain Pursuits (☎ 866-423-6739; www.mountain pursuits.com) offers guided hikes and backpacking trips for one or more days. Explore the beautiful hills and flat canyon land around Fernie with **Fernie Nature Tours** (☎ 250-423-4306; www.fernienature.com). There's wildlife viewing in summer and snowshoeing in winter.

FISHING

Stretches of the Elk River offer superb fly-fishing. **Fernie Wilderness Adventures** (☎ 877-423-6704; www .fernieadventures.com) offers everything from fully guided outings (from $550) to ice fishing (brrrr, $175).

Sleeping

Fernie's high season is the winter. **Fernie Central Reservation**s (☎ 800-622-5007; www.ferniecentralreser vations.com) can book you a room in town or at the ski resort.

Mt Fernie Provincial Park (☎ 800-689-9025; www .discovercamping.ca; campsite $14) Only 3km from town, leafy Mt Fernie Provincial Park features 40 sites, flush toilets, waterfalls, a self-guided interpretive trail and access to mountain-bike trails.

HI Raging Elk Hostel (☎ 250-423-6811; www.raging elk.com; 892 6th Ave; dm from $20; 🖥) The rooms are stark but that just means you'll not be lured away from the pool table, sauna or nearby center of Fernie.

Snow Valley Motel & RV Park (☎ 250-423-4421, 877-696-7669; www.snowvalleymotel.com; 1041 7th Ave; r $60-180; 🌊) The 21 rooms here are large and include fridges and microwaves. Outside, there's a shady campground as well as a barbecue area. It's close to the centre.

Cedar Lodge (☎ 250-423-4622, 800-977-2977; www .cedarlodge.bc.ca; 1101 7th Ave; r $65-100; 🌊 🖥 💺) Right on the main drag, this unassuming place has a small indoor pool and relatively small prices on the 47 simple rooms.

Park Place Lodge (☎ 250-423-6871, 888-381-7275; www.parkplacelodge.com; 742 Hwy 3; r $85-200; 🌊 🖥 💺) There's a small pool inside; the 64 comfortable rooms have balconies, fridges, microwaves and high-speed internet. It's close to the center.

Best Western Fernie Mountain Lodge (☎ 250-423-5500, 800-937-8376; www.bestwesternfernie.com; 1622 7th Ave; r from $100-200; 🌊 🖥 💺) The 95 rooms are mostly standard high-end motel but after a long day of activities that may be just what you want. The building surrounds a heated indoor pool.

Eating & Drinking

Fernie has a good assortment of joints in and around the old center. On summer Sunday mornings, the **Mountain Market** is held in Rotary Park at 7th St and Hwy 3. It's a fun and eclectic mix of artists, bakers, farmers, musicians and more.

THE KOOTENAYS

> **DETOUR: FERNIE'S COTTONWOODS**
>
> BC's greatest stand of old cottonwoods is only 12km west of Fernie. Look for Morrisey Rd and turn south off Hwy 3. Cross a bridge and look for a trailhead just on the far side. It's only a 20-minute walk around the loop and you'll be in the midst of 400-year-old trees that are 10m in diameter. Amazingly, they were only discovered in 2003.

Mug Shots Bistro (☎ 250-423-8018; 591 3rd Ave; coffee $2; ☯ 7am-6pm; 🖳) Always hopping, there are coffees, baked goods, sandwiches and 10 internet terminals. You can lounge on sofas or toil at tables.

Blue Toque Diner (☎ 250-423-4637; 500 Hwy 3; meals $8; ☯ 8:30am-3:30pm) This places is part of the Arts Station (p267). The long menu features lots of seasonal and organic vegetarian specials. The morning pancakes and omelettes are a hit, as are the lunch sandwiches. You can have a coffee out on the old station platform.

Rip 'n' Richards Eatery (☎ 250-423-3002; 301 Hwy 3; meals $8-20; ☯ 11am-11pm) Enjoy the views of the Elk River and surrounding peaks from the deck here. But save some attention for the long menu of good burgers, steaks, fish and pizza.

Brickhouse (☎ 250-423-0009; 401 2nd Ave; meals $8-25; ☯ 5pm-2am Mon-Sat) This upscale old pub serves steaks, burgers and other carnivore-friendly fare. The long wooden bar complements the bare brick walls and there's a long list of pricey and fancy drinks. On some nights, there's a groovy lounge in the basement.

Royal Hotel (☎ 250-423-7750; 501 1st St; ☯ noon-late) The old corner bar in this 1909 hotel has live music many nights and pours the full range of the tasty local beers from the Fernie Brewing Company.

Getting There & Away

Fernie Airport Express (☎ 250-423-4023; 888-823-4023; www.mountainperks.ca) makes at least one run daily to/from Calgary airport (adult/child $65/40; 4½ hours).

Greyhound (Park Place Lodge, 742 Hwy 3) runs buses west to Vancouver ($133, 11½ hours, one daily) via Cranbrook and Nelson ($55, six hours, two daily) and east to Calgary ($55, 5½ to seven hours, two daily).

CRANBROOK

pop 19,800

Many a family holiday has foundered in the traffic-clogged streets of Cranbrook. 'The Strip,' a 2km slice of Hwy 3 called Cranbrook St as it runs through town, is dominated by fast-food chains, auto-parts stores, malls and roadside motels.

The downtown is diminutive, and unless you need a cheap motel your best bet is to check out the city's one great museum and then literally head for the hills that ring the valley in snow-capped splendor. The base of the Steeples Range of the Rocky Mountains is to the east.

The **VIC** (☎ 250-426-5914, 800-222-6174; www.cranbrookchamber.com; 2279 Cranbrook St N; ☯ 9am-5pm Jun-Aug, 9am-5pm Mon-Fri Sep-May) has the usual array of great info. There's a summer-only **information center** (☯ 9am-5pm Mon-Fri Jun-Aug) at the south end of town on Hwy 3.

Sights

The magnificent **Canadian Museum of Rail Travel** (☎ 250-489-3918; www.traindeluxe.com; adult/child $15/7.50; ☯ 10am-6pm summer, 10am-5pm Tue-Sat winter) is reason enough to stop in Cranbrook. The museum and its dozens of railcars stretch along Hwys 3 and 95 near the center at Baker St. It features much of the classic, luxurious 1929 edition of the *Trans-Canada Limited*, a legendary train operated by Canadian Pacific Railway from Montreal to Vancouver. The cars, along with those from other Canadian lines, are undergoing painstaking restoration.

Some 14km north of town (off into those hills!), **Fort Steele Heritage Town** (☎ 250-426-7342; www.fortsteele.bc.ca; adult/child $12.50/2.75 summer, less other times; ☯ 9:30am-6pm Jul & Aug, 9:30am-5pm Apr-Jun & Oct, 10am-4pm Nov-Mar) takes historical preservation to histrionic extremes. It's named for the diplomatic North West Mounted Police (later to become the RCMP) superintendent Samuel Steele, who worked to ease tensions between gold seekers and the Ktunaxa First Nations during the East Kootenay gold rushes in the late 1800s. Once a boomtown, then a ghost town, today it has more than 60 restored buildings, many populated by characters in historical garb. Unlike most tourist traps, it is well done and always a fave with kids.

Sam Steele Days, a four-day pioneer themed party, is a hit every third weekend in June in Cranbrook.

THE TRUTH ABOUT TROUT

For all the babble about trout fishing in BC (eager and polite fish that all but jump from water to fisher to fry pan), the story is far more complex than you'd imagine. In many cases that 'wild' fish that ends up on your hook is the result of a vast fish-stocking campaign.

What few people realize is that the provincial government's **Ministry of Water, Land and Air Protection** (www.env.gov.bc.ca/fw/fish/hatch-stock/stocking-pgrm.htmls) plays a major role in keeping the fish count up. Anglers catch an estimated nine million freshwater fish every year. To keep up with demand, more than 1100 BC lakes and streams are augmented with 12 million fish born and raised in metal containers in fish hatcheries throughout the province. Five major hatcheries produce inland fishes, including steelhead trout, anadromous cutthroat, brook char, land-locked kokanee salmon, rainbow trout and westslope cutthroat.

The process of stocking the rivers is complex. Biologists consider a school of variables regarding weather, food supply, other fish counts and more. Transport is on pick-ups and special trucks that bounce down tracks to remote spots province-wide.

The **Kootenay Trout Hatchery** (☎ 250-429-3214; admission free; ☼ 8am-4pm), 32km southeast of Cranbrook along the Bull River, raises about three million rainbow, brook and cutthroat trout a year. Here you'll see how the fertilized eggs are captured and raised from fry to fish until they're able to return to local rivers and lakes. You may even get the chance to feed a few. To get there from Cranbrook, take Hwy 3 east and turn north onto the Fort Steele–Wardner Rd. Look for signs.

Sleeping & Eating

The Strip (Hwys 3 and 95) is littered from end to end with motels; most of the chains are here and finding a room should not be a problem.

Jimsmith Lake Provincial Park (☎ 250-422-4200; campsite $14) About 5km east of Cranbrook on Hwy 3/95, this park has 29 good, shady sites and beach access, although there are only pit toilets and no showers.

Hospitality Courtyard Inn (☎ 250-489-4124, 888-489-4124; www.hospitalitycourtyardinn.com; 1209 Cranbrook St N; r $55-65; ✷ ▣) Baskets of flowers front a grassy courtyard at this inn that's a good break from the chain gang. All rooms have wi-fi.

Kootenay Roasting Company (☎ 250-489-0488; 821 Baker St; coffee $2; ☼ 7am-6pm) Before or after the train museum, enjoy a good coffee at this place, where the heady scents confirm that the coffee is roasted here. Seats outside overlook the tiny downtown.

Getting There & Around

Cranbrook Airport (YXC; ☎ 250-426-7913) has services to Vancouver and Calgary on Air Canada Jazz. It's just north of town on Hwy 95A. The **Greyhound station** (☎ 250-489-3331; 1229 Cranbrook St N) is in the midst of the strip.

KIMBERLEY

pop 6700

Before 1973 Kimberley looked like what it is – a small mountain mining town. Since then the center – called the Platzl – has been revamped to resemble a Bavarian alpine village. Kimberley's mascot, Happy Hans, lives in a huge cuckoo clock on the Platzl. Every hour on the hour, people will stand in awed anticipation waiting for Hans to pop out of his oddly squat home and yodel.

If it seems like Kimberley is pushing the Bavarian schtick a bit hard you'd be right. All of the town's fire hydrants have been hand-painted to look like little people wearing lederhosen. And while day-trippers trek about the Platzl in search of fudge, many more folks are heading to the hills above town where yet another major ski resort is taking shape.

History

The discovery of rich minerals here in 1891 prompted the birth of the North Star Mine. The following year, on the other side of Mark Creek, another claim staked out what would grow to become the largest lead and zinc mine in the world, the Sullivan Mine. Mark Creek Crossing was renamed Kimberley in 1896, after the successful South African diamond mine. In 1909 Cominco took over operations, drawing more than 162 million tons of ore out of the Sullivan, though the metal isn't worth as much as diamonds. The mine's closure was anticipated years in advance and the town, with help from Cominco, has been busily diversifying into tourism.

At 1113m, Kimberley can claim to be the highest city in Canada (at 1397m, Banff in

Alberta is higher, but it's technically a town, not a city).

Information

The **VIC** (☎ 250-427-3666; www.kimberleychamber.ca; 270 Kimberley Ave; ☼ 9am-9pm Jun-Aug, 10am-5pm Mon-Fri Sep-May) sits in the large parking area behind the Platzl.

Sights & Activities

Take a 13km ride on the **Sullivan Mine & Railway Historical Society** (☎ 250-427-7365; 350 Ross St; ☼ noon-5:30pm mid-May–mid-Sep) train as it chugs through the steep-walled Mark Creek Valley toward some sweeping mountain vistas. The trip ends at the base of the chairlift for the Kimberley Alpine Resort, from where you can ride to the top for more great views (combined train and lift tickets adult/child $21/12). The station is about 1km north of the Platzl off Gerry Sorensen Way.

The highlight of the **Kimberley Heritage Museum** (☎ 250-427-7510; 115 Spokane St; admission free; ☼ 9am-4:30pm Mon-Sat summer, 1-4pm Mon-Fri winter) is the hapless Brutus, the stuffed remains of a grizzly bear bagged by a local 12-year-old. It's beside the library at the east end of the Platzl.

The 12-acre **Cominco Gardens**, beside the hospital above Kimberley, are full of roses, tulips and gnomes. If you're walking from town, take the stairway and trail at the west end of Howard St. It takes about 15 minutes.

The extensive network of trails (100km worth) of the **Kimberley Nature Park** wind around Kimberley. You can cross-country ski or walk along the well-marked trails while observing the active wildlife. Get a copy of *Kimberley Nature Park Trail Guide* ($3) at the VIC.

Just west of town, in the nearby community of Marysville, take the short walk to see the **Marysville Waterfalls**. Park at the Mark Creek bridge where Hwy 95A becomes 304 St and follow the boardwalk along the creek. The walk takes about 10 minutes.

KIMBERLEY ALPINE RESORT

Condos are more common than moguls at the **Kimberley Alpine Resort** (☎ 250-427-4881, 877-754-5462; www.skikimberley.com; 1-day lift pass adult/child $53/17), as speculators bet that lots of people will want to own a piece of the mountain – at least one they can time share. The resort boasts 729 hectares of skiable terrain, mild weather

and 68 runs. There are eight lifts and 45% of the runs are intermediate. The highlight is the 8200m Main Run, which has a 609m drop and is fully lit for night skiing.

Festivals & Events

Kimberley hosts numerous events through the year. Most are designed to keep the lederhosen warm while the tour buses idle. The main event is September's **International Folk Festival**, which features lots of colorful dancing and other less likely activities such as kung fu demonstrations and rib cook-offs.

Sleeping & Eating

Most of Kimberley's accommodations are condos at the ski resort, which runs a central **reservations service** (☎ 877-754-5462; www.skikimberley.com). Expect to pay $100 to $200 a night depending on season. Various no-name motels lurk around the outskirts of town.

Kimberley SameSun Budget Lodge (☎ 250-427-7191, 877-562-2783; www.samesun.com; 275 Spokane St; dm/r from $24/60) Right in the middle of the Platzl, this lodge makes the most of its location above a bar. It's a fun place where you can revive yourself over a pancake breakfast. It's also one of the few places to stay near the Platzl.

Bean Tree Cafe (☎ 250-427-7889; 295 Spokane; meals $4-8; ☼ 8am-8pm) Grab a good coffee and a snack here, at the east end of the Platzl. The menu has many sandwiches and salads, and on many Friday nights local musicians jam.

Mozart House (☎ 250-427-7671; 130 Spokane St; meals $9-20; ☼ 11am-9pm) Tuck into a German fantasy of wursts, schnitzels and cabbage rolls. It's all tasty and the bar has a good wine list.

Getting There & Away

Greyhound (☎ 250-427-3722; 1625 Warren Ave), 3km east of Kimberley, has pricey buses to Cranbrook ($9, 30 minutes, two daily).

KIMBERLEY TO RADIUM HOT SPRINGS

Hwy 95A heads northeast out of Kimberley and connects up with Hwy 93/95. Just south of the junction on Hwy 95 is **Wasa Lake Provincial Park** (☎ 250-422-3003; campsite $17), home to the warmest lake in the Kootenays. The popular campground contains 104 sites, 55 of which can be reserved, and offers good lake access, interpretive programs and flush toilets. The park protects an increasingly rare chunk of BC's grassland, most of which has been turned into golf courses or farmland. A 2.7km

THE KOOTENAYS

interpretive trail highlights the continent's most northern stand of ponderosa pines.

After Wasa, Hwy 93/95 continues north along the scenic Kootenay River. At minute **Skookumchuck**, 18km north of Wasa, the Lussier and Skookumchuck Rivers join the Kootenay.

Almost 5km south of Canal Flats look for Whiteswan Forestry Rd, a gravel road that travels east 25km to **Whiteswan Lake Provincial Park**, a remote 1994-hectare park that is home to both Whiteswan and Alces Lakes. This is a great destination for those wanting to escape the touristy valley and really immerse themselves in nature. The park's highlight, **Lussier Hot Springs**, is near the west entrance, some 17km from the turn off Hwy 93/95. Unlike many of the region's hot springs which look like they'd be at home in a Holiday Inn, the waters here flow through natural rock and sand pools. A well-marked trailhead leads you down to the springs, which, despite their remoteness, can get downright crowded in summer.

The park's five campgrounds have 114 rustic sites ($14). All have pit toilets and are not reservable. Trails also lead to several more alpine places good for backcountry camping.

Fairmont Hot Springs Resort

Once you know that the waters have been filtered to remove any trace of mineral odor, you know you're not going to have a natural experience. Condos surround the vast pool, which could be the centerpiece of a bland planned community…like this one. There's little reason to pause here.

Windermere Valley

This narrow valley between the Purcell and Rocky Mountains has long been a well-used transportation route, first for the Ktunaxa and Kinbasket First Nations people. Pioneer David Thompson began his exploration of the Columbia River here in 1807. The towns of **Windermere** and **Invermere** are home to the new grasslands taking over the valley floors: golf courses. They are also good places for supplies if you are planning any backcountry adventures.

Panorama Mountain Village Resort

Once a low-key haunt of locals only a generation beyond using barrel staves, **Panorama Mountain Village Resort** (☎ 250-342-6941, 800-663-2929; www.panoramaresort.com; 1-day lift pass adult/child $63/27) is now a full-on, big-ticket ski resort run by Intrawest and meant to rival those in Whistler. Boasting a 1220m drop, the resort has more than 120 trails, the longest of which is 5.5km. A gondola shuttles people between the upper to lower villages, with the now-ubiquitous condos. Add in a golf course, summer lift service for mountain bikers and you have the future of outdoor activities in much of the province. The resort is at the end of an 18km drive up a winding road from Invermere.

RADIUM HOT SPRINGS

pop 900

There you sit, stalled out in the middle of this small mountain town, your car surrounded by Rocky Mountain bighorn sheep. Could there be a better welcome to this, the gateway to all four Rocky Mountains national parks (Kootenay, Banff, Jasper and Yoho)?

Of course, most visitors don't get up close and personal with a sheep here, but your odds of seeing one wandering across the road are good, and the pull of the critters' namesake Rockies palpable. Radium Hot Springs is named for the famed hot springs, which are just inside the southwest corner of **Kootenay National Park** (p281). Its name came after a government test conducted in 1914 showed small levels of radioactivity in the springs.

DETOUR: TOP OF THE WORLD

If Whiteswan Lake isn't far enough off the beaten path, you can follow Whiteswan Forestry Rd for another 25 gravelly kilometers to remote **Top of the World Provincial Park**. When the road ends, it's an easy 6km hike or mountain-bike ride to Fish Lake, so named for its thick population of Dolly Varden and cutthroat trout. You can camp at one of the backcountry sites at Fish Lake or stay in the large rustic cabin often used by anglers ($15 per person). Much of the park lives up to its name: the average elevation is 2200m. In precolonial times, First Nations people came from as far away as Montana and Alberta to obtain chert, a grey, translucent, obsidian-like rock that was mined and traded for use as worked into tools and weapons.

For most people, Radium is a way station on their way into the parks. Many will be amused at the incongruous blending of Alpine schtick and frontier cliché found in local businesses.

The **Kootenay National Park & Radium Hot Springs VIC** (☎ 250-347-9331, 800-347-9704; www.radiumhotsprings.com; 7556 Main St E/Hwy 93/95; ⏰ 9am-7pm May-Sep, 9am-5pm Oct-Apr) includes Parks Canada information for the nearby parks.

Sleeping & Eating

Radium Hot Springs contains more than 30 motels, most of which are close to the highways. Book ahead for peak summer season. The best camping is in the park.

Misty River Lodge B&B (☎ 250-347-9912; www.mistyriverlodge.bc.ca; 5036 Hwy 93; r $50-100) Right outside the park gate, this four-room B&B has owners who are enthusiastic about the parks and ready to share their knowledge with guests. Rooms vary in size – the one that sleeps five is a great deal for larger parties.

Park Inn (☎ 250-347-9582, 800-858-115; www.parkinn.bc.ca; 4873 Stanley St; r $70-160; ⏰ 🛇) Hanging baskets of flowers add color to this older 54-room motel. Amenities include an indoor pool, hot tub, sauna and barbecues. Units are large and many have kitchens.

Rocky Mountain Springs Lodge & Restaurant (☎ 250-347-9548, 877-457-1117; www.milliondollarview.com; 5067 Madsen Rd; r $69-99; ⏰ restaurant 5:30-9pm; 🛇) The web address says it all for this 10-room place, which includes a large breakfast in the rates. The views from the patio of the excellent Hungarian restaurant (think warming goulash) are what you'd expect. Rooms have microwaves and fridges.

Getting There & Away

Greyhound (☎ 250-347-9726; Radium Esso, 7507 Main St W) has a service along Hwy 95 to Golden ($19, 1¼ hours, one daily) and Cranbrook Hwy 95 to Golden ($25, 2½ hours, one daily). There's also a service through Kootenay National Park to Banff ($24, two hours, one daily)

GOLDEN

pop 4400

Sandwiched between the Purcell and Rocky Mountains and surrounded by six national parks, this is the first town of any size you encounter if you're coming west from Field (p279), Banff (p283) and Alberta on the Trans-Canada Hwy. Those blowing through may only notice the usual strip of franchises that lines the highway, but turn off into the town itself and you'll find a tidy and attractive little place that makes a good base for enjoying the area's white-water rafting. Sitting near the confluence of the Columbia and Kicking Horse Rivers, Golden has white water in abundance.

History

Before prospectors came rolling into the area in search of gold, the town was referred to as the 'Cache' because it was little more than a storage spot for supplies. It was later renamed Golden City (the 'City' was later dropped) to compete with Silver City, a nearby, momentary boomtown where someone had planted decoy deposits of silver ore.

Information

The center of town lies 2km south of the highway; many businesses are along 10th Ave.

A huge new **VIC** (☎ 250-344-7711; ⏰ 9am-6pm) is 1km east on the Trans-Canada Hwy from the Hwy 95 turn-off into Golden. Impressive as the building looks, however, it's all a bit of a ruse. When we were there it was easier to find information on Abbotsford than Golden. Queries brought an explanation from one of the unfailingly polite staffers: rates to display information at the new VIC are prohibitive for most local businesses. Until things get sorted out, the best source for local information is the **Golden Chamber of Commerce** (☎ 250-344-7125, 800-622-4653; www.goldenchamber.bc.ca; 500 10th Ave North; ⏰ 9am-5pm daily Jul & Aug, 9am-5pm Mon-Fri Sep-Jun), which has information on just about everything local.

Sights

Golden's compact center is not far from the Trans-Canada Hwy. The obvious highlight is the **Kicking Horse Pedestrian Bridge**, a covered bridge in the grand tradition which was erected in 2001. Using almost 100,000 board feet of mostly local lumber, the bridge spans the turbulent – and picturesque – waters of the Kicking Horse River.

Activities
WHITE-WATER RAFTING

Golden is the center for white-water rafting trips on the turbulent and chilly Kicking Horse River. Powerful Class 3 and 4 rapids and breathtaking scenery along the sheer walls of the Kicking Horse Valley make this rafting experience one of North America's best. The fainter of heart can take a mellow but equally scenic float trip on the upper river. Many operators run the river in the busy summer season, sometimes creating jams.

Full-day trips on the river average about $90; half-day trips are about $65. Local operators include **Glacier Raft Company** (☎ 250-344-6521; www.glacierraft.com; 612 7th Ave) and **Wet 'n' Wild** (☎ 250-344-6546, 800-668-9119; www.wetnwild.bc.ca).

MOUNTAIN BIKING

For easy riding in town, you can bike along the trails following the Kicking Horse River or head across the Columbia River to the West Bench, where you can tool around on 40km worth of trails. Hardcore types pedal the steep trails up Mt 7 and then scream down a really, really long technical single track. Summer lifts at Kicking Horse Mountain Resort access some of Canada's longest descents.

Summit Cycle & Ski (☎ 250-344-6600; 1007 11th Ave S; bike rental per day from $35) has knowledgeable staff that can help plan trips. The website for the **Golden Cycling Club** (www.goldencyclingclub.com) has maps and other info.

KICKING HORSE MOUNTAIN RESORT

Sprawling across Whitetooth Mountain, **Kicking Horse Mountain Resort** (☎ 250-439-5400, 866-754-5425; www.kickinghorseresort.com; 1-day lift pass adult/child from $45/21) has a gondola and three lifts. A challenging 60% of its 106 runs are rated advanced or expert. With 1260 vertical meters and a relatively snow-heavy, wind-free position between the Rockies and the Purcells, the resort is a future contender in the race for ski-resort tourist dollars and overall condo count. Kicking Horse Resort is 14km from Golden on Kicking Horse Trail.

Sleeping

There are scores of chain motels along the Trans-Canada Hwy.

Sander Lake Campground (☎ 250-344-6517; www.rockies.net/~bsander; campsite from $15, cabins $75) Located 12km southwest of Golden off Hwy 95, this campground has a sweet location amid trees and hills. There are 27 sites and three log cabins.

Packers Place (☎ 250-344-5941; packerinn@cablerocket.com; 429 9th Ave; r $40-50; 🖳) A bustling bar and restaurant near the pedestrian bridge and with tables overlooking the river, Packers has a predictable menu of burgers and the like. Rooms are simple, their best feature being that you can stumble upstairs after listening to frequent live rock.

Mary's Motel (☎ 250-344-7111, 866-234-6279; www.marysmotel.com; 603 8th Ave N; r $80-120; 🐾 🖳) In town right along the river, Mary's has 81 rooms spread across several buildings. Opt for one with a balcony or patio, leave the windows open and let the river's roar lull you to sleep. There are other choices nearby.

Alpine Meadows Lodge (☎ 250-344-5863, 888-700-4477; www.alpinemeadowslodge.com; r $90-130; 🐾 🖳) Located at the end of a 7km road off Hwy 1, this family-run chalet has sweeping views of the valley from its hillside perch. The 10 rooms all have Jacuzzi tubs and there's a high-ceilinged lounge with a huge fireplace.

Eating

Eleven22 (☎ 250-344-2443; 1122 10th Ave S/Hwy 95; meals $12-25; 🕑 5-11pm Tue-Sat) Local art adorns the walls at this sleek little gem set in a pretty residential neighborhood near the center. The menu combines European, American and Asian influences – you can watch things come together in the open kitchen. The lounge area is inviting and there are tables outside in a pretty garden.

WOLF IN THE FOLD

Wolves, the great pack hunters of the wild, are in constant danger in BC and throughout Canada. Seen more as pest than treasure, there are regular culls in an effort to protect cattle and even to help preserve other endangered species. Near Golden, two people are passionate about changing the wolf's fate. Casey and Shelley Black have created the **Northern Lights Wolf Centre** (☎ 250-344-7698; www.northernlightswildlife.com; adult/child $10/6; 🕑 9am-9pm Jul & Aug, 10am-6pm Sep-May), a refuge in the wild for wolves born into captivity. Visitors can expect to meet a resident wolf or two and learn about their complex and humanlike family structure. More than anything, the goal of the centre is to educate as many people as possible and motivate them to join the Blacks and others in working to protect BC's wolves.

Kicking Horse Grill (☎ 250-344-2330; 1105 9th St S; meals $20-30; ⏲ 5-9pm) At first glance the log cabin motif may scream 'steak!' but one look at the menu and you'll see that the creative kitchen draws inspiration globally. Dishes change depending on the season. It's all eclectic and fun – try for a table outside under the huge tree. (And yes, it does have steaks.)

Getting There & Away

Greyhound (☎ 250-344-2917; www.greyhound.ca; Husky Travel Centre, 1050 Trans-Canada Hwy) offers frequent bus services from Golden along the Trans-Canada highway to Vancouver ($105, 11 to 13 hours, four daily) and Calgary ($45, four hours, four daily) via Banff ($24, two hours, four daily).

THE KOOTENAYS

The Rockies

For dramatic untamed wilderness that's accessible to the casual visitor, few places equal the Canadian Rockies. Soaring peaks are crowned by glaciers glistening in the sun. Alpine lakes glow with radiant greens and blues depending on the time of day. Waterfalls blast stark rock faces, while white water thunders through canyons and valleys. The green carpet of forests is interrupted by mountain meadows that burst with color from summer flowers.

These are the kind of scenes you'd expect in a vast jigsaw puzzle, except here you get to enjoy every piece. And you're not alone either. Bear, mountain goats, beaver, elk, raptors and hundreds more species carve out livings here.

It's truly magnificent and you'll immediately see why Alberta's Banff and Jasper National Parks and British Columbia's Kootenay and Yoho National Parks, together with Mt Robson and Mt Assiniboine Provincial Parks, comprise the Canadian Rocky Mountain Parks Unesco World Heritage area, one of the largest protected areas in the world.

And while the passive are amazed, the active are enthralled. Skiing, snowboarding, mountain biking, climbing, hiking, canoeing and more await, many in some of the most fabled spots on earth. But what seals the deal for the Rockies is the towns. Banff boats every pleasure one could find in a big city and then some. Jasper is everyone's idea of a mountain village.

So hop on the bus, get in your car, saddle up on your bike and come enjoy and delight in one of the planet's best places.

HIGHLIGHTS

- Taking the plunge in **Radium** (p282), **Miette** (p305) or **Banff Hot Springs** (p288)
- Escaping the masses – and life – in the trails of **Yoho National Park** (p278)
- Spotting your first bear along the **Icefields Parkway** (p296)
- Choosing your adventure in **Jasper National Park** (p298)
- Leaving the **Lake Louise** (p294) crowds behind for the stunning backcountry

INFORMATION

On entering Banff and Jasper National Parks, you'll be given the excellent *Mountain Guide*. As well as outlining policies for the parks, the guide is full of information including what to do if you encounter a cougar (don't run, don't act like prey, find a rock to nail the sucker). There's lots more information available at the various park visitor information centers (VICs). Booklets outlining the myriad hikes and other activities, as well as backcountry guides, are highly useful.

Parks Canada offers links to all of the country's national parks from its website (www .parkscanada.ca). For more information, call or write to the parks:

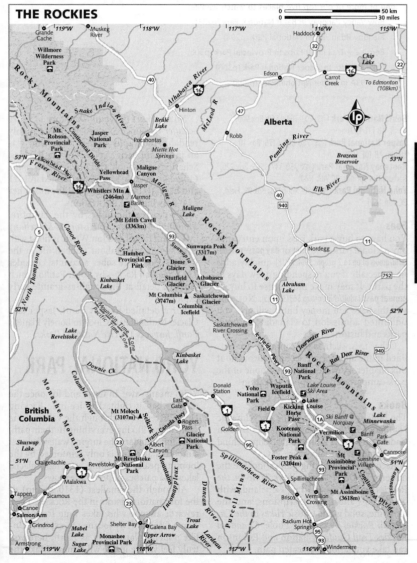

THE ROCKIES

TOP FIVE PLACES TO SEE WILDLIFE

Like most people, you're probably looking out for big game in the Canadian Rockies – black and grizzly bear, moose, bighorn sheep and elk – but keep your eyes and ears open and your senses in tune to the murmurings of nature. There's wildlife moving all around you, whether you can see it or not. Small animals such as pikas, marten, marmots and squirrel skitter by, while almost 300 species of birds nest, hunt, mate, sing and squawk in the parks. It's hard to say where you'll definitely spot critters, so your best bet is to stay watchful. Sometimes the best thing to do is just stand still for a while and see what pops up. However, if you want to narrow the odds, try one or more of our top five places to watch wildlife:

- Bow Valley Parkway in Banff National Park (p283)
- Maligne Rd in Jasper National Park (p298)
- Berg Lake Trail in Mt Robson Provincial Park (p306)
- Lake Annette in Jasper National Park (p300)
- Hwy 93A in Jasper National Park (p298)

Banff National Park (☎ 403-762-1550; Box 900, Banff, AB T1L 1K2)

Jasper National Park (☎ 780-852-6176; Box 10, Jasper, AB T0E 1E0)

Kootenay National Park (☎ 250-347-9505; Box 220, Radium Hot Springs, BC V0A 1M0)

Yoho National Park (☎ 250-343-6783; Box 99, Field, BC V0A 1G0)

Fees

You have to buy a park pass upon entry into any national park. The cost of **day passes** (adult/child/group of up to 7 people $9/4.50/18) quickly adds up, especially if you're spending a few days in the parks. It may make more sense to buy an **annual pass** (adult/child/group $63/32/125). Not only will this save you money but it will give you unlimited admission to Canada's national parks and historic sites.

Other fees, such as for camping, are outlined in the appropriate sections throughout this chapter. However, note that none of the park campgrounds accepts reservations.

Books

The bible for the region is the encyclopedic *Handbook of the Canadian Rockies* by Ben Gadd. You'll find a well-thumbed copy behind the counter at virtually every VIC.

Recommended hiking guides include the discerning *Don't Waste Your Time in the Rockies* by Kathy and Craig Copeland, with good maps and trail descriptions, and the longtime, solid guide *Classic Hikes in the Canadian Rockies* by Graeme Poole. *Canadian Rockies Trail Guide* by Patton and Robinson can take you far off the beaten path.

No Ordinary Woman: the Story of Mary Schaffer by Janice Sanford Beck is a highly readable biography of a woman who was an important early explorer of the Rockies. Schaffer's own book, *Old Indian Trails of the Canadian Rockies*, was first published in 1911 and has now been released with some of her own drawings and illustrations.

For passing the hours by the campfire, *Mountain Madness: An Historical Miscellany* by Edward Cavell and Jon Whyte is filled with entertaining yarns about oddball life in the Rockies. For more sober accounts, consider *The Canadian Rockies* by Roger Patillo, which looks in detail at the tough-as-granite early explorers.

For a detailed look at Banff, Jasper and Glacier National Parks, look to Lonely Planet's *Banff, Jasper & Glacier National Parks*.

YOHO NATIONAL PARK

Yoho means 'awe' in Cree, and for once the namers had it right. The ice-blue Kicking Horse River plows through the valley of the same name. Taking everything in their path, including boulders, the surging waters help set a mood of awe that is only reinforced by the looming peaks, pounding waterfalls, glacial lakes and patches of pretty meadows.

Although the smallest (1310 sq km) of the four national parks in the Rockies, Yoho rewards anyone who takes time from their Trans-Canada Hwy journey to explore. Unlike popular places such as Banff, here you truly feel you're in the wilderness. Make the

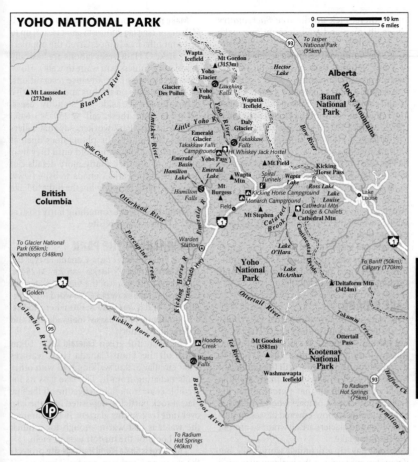

effort to see Lake O'Hara and some of the sights further a field and you'll find your own word for awe.

FIELD

The village of Field, which lies in the middle of the park along the Kicking Horse River, is a must-stop as you pass on the Trans-Canada Hwy. Sitting astride the river, it's a quaint yet unfussy place. Many of its buildings date from the early days of the railways, when it was the Canadian Pacific Railway (CPR) headquarters for exploration and, later, for strategic planning when engineers were trying to solve the problem of moving trains over the Kicking Horse Pass. Check out the **'Dollhouse'** (2nd St E), a cute little 1927 house that was once a Royal

Canadian Mounted Police (RCMP) jail and later – fittingly enough – a liquor store.

Field has a growing number of inviting B&Bs and cafés. It is the last town in BC as you head east along the Trans-Canada Hwy from Golden (see p273) and is a good place to stock up on supplies if you're heading out into the backcountry.

At the **Yoho National Park Visitor Centre** (☎ 250-343-6783; ☒ 9am-4pm Sep-Apr, 9am-5pm May & Jun, 9am-7pm Jul & Aug), Alberta Tourism staff a desk in summer for those heading east. If you're heading west into BC, you'll have to wait until you reach the rather dubious VIC in Golden (p273) for gathering much information. The Yoho center also contains an interesting display on the Burgess Shale. While

THE ROCKIES

you're there, pick up the free *Backcountry Guide;* its map and trail descriptions make it an excellent overview for exploring the park. The nonprofit support group Friends of Yoho National Park has a useful website (www.friendsofyoho.com).

Ask at the visitor center for a list of Field's 20 and counting B&Bs. Take in the river valley and railway views from the **Kicking Horse Lodge** (☎ 250-343-6303, 800-659-4944; www.kickinghorselodge .net; 100 Centre St; r $120-150), a three-story motel with 14 inviting rooms. Across the street, **Truffle Pigs Cafe** (☎ 250-343-6462; 318 Stephen Ave; meals $6-20; ☒ 8am-8:30pm Tue-Sun) is reason enough to stop in Field. Part gourmet grocery, part bistro, it has a constantly changing menu of creative dishes on offer from the tiny open kitchen where the chef prefers using regional organic produce.

Greyhound buses stop at the visitor center on their trips west to Golden ($13, 1½ hours, three daily) and beyond and east to Banff ($18, one hour, three daily).

LAKE O'HARA

If it weren't for crowd control everybody would be tramping around Lake O'Hara making its many exalted pleasures all but moot. But this mountain gem more than lives up to its reputation and is well worth the significant hassle involved in a visit. Its many walking trails encapsulate all that's great about the Canadian Rockies. Compact wooded hillsides, alpine meadows, snow-covered passes, mountain vistas and glaciers are all wrapped around the stunning lake.

A basic day trip is definitely worthwhile, but if you stay overnight in the backcountry you'll be able to access many more trails, some quite difficult, all quite spectacular. Take the Alpine Circuit Trail (12km) for a bit of everything.

To reach the lake, you can take the **shuttle bus** (adult/child $15/7.50; ☒ mid-Jun–early Oct) from the Lake O'Hara parking lot, 15km east of Field on the Trans-Canada Hwy. This is prime grizzly bear habitat and a major wildlife corridor. In an effort to alleviate human pressure on the trails and wildlife, park officials have come up with a quota system that governs bus access to the lake and limits permits for the popular backcountry campgrounds. You can freely walk the 13km from the parking area, but no bikes are allowed. The area around Lake O'Hara usually remains snow-covered or very muddy until mid-July.

Make reservations for the **bus trip** (☎ 250-343-6433) or for **camping** (backcountry permit adult $8) up to three months in advance. Given the popularity of Lake O'Hara, reservations are basically mandatory (unless you want to walk). However, if you don't have advance reservations, six day-use seats on the bus and three to five campsites are set aside for 'standby' users. To try to snare these, call ☎ 250-343-6433 the day before. Park workers say that callers should call right as the phone lines open at 8am and should stay on hold until they hear one way or another. Many more details can be found at the Parks Canada website (www .pc.gc.ca/yoho) by following the links to Lake O'Hara.

Should you desire something fairly posh at Lake O'Hara, see opposite.

ELSEWHERE IN THE PARK

East of Field on the Trans-Canada Hwy is the **Takakkaw Falls road** (☒ late Jun–early Oct). At 254m, Takakkaw Falls is one of the highest waterfalls in Canada. Takakkaw is a Cree word for 'magnificent,' and it certainly is. From here, **Iceline**, a 20km hiking loop, passes many glaciers and spectacular scenery.

The beautiful green **Emerald Lake**, 10km north off the Trans-Canada Hwy, features a flat circular 5.2km walking trail with other trails radiating from it. The lake gets its incredible color from light reflecting off the fine glacial rock particles, deposited into the lake over time by grinding glaciers. In late summer the water is just warm enough for a quick swim. Look for the turnoff west of Field.

The **Burgess Shale World Heritage site** protects the stunning Cambrian-age fossil beds on Mt Stephen and Mt Field. These 515-million-year-old fossils preserve the remains of marine creatures that were some of the earliest forms of life on earth. (The Royal Tyrrell Museum in Drumheller, Alberta, contains a major display on these finds.) You can only get to the fossil beds by guided hikes, which are led by naturalists from the **Burgess Shale Geoscience Foundation** (www.burgess-shale.bc.ca). The 10-hour hike to **Burgess Shale** in **Walcott Quarry** (adult/child $70/27; ☒ Jun-Sep 15) covers 20km, and guides discuss how fossils for water-born creatures came to be high in the mountains. Try your luck exploring trilobites on the strenuous and steep six-hour, 6km climb to **Mount Stephen** and the **fossil beds** (adult/child $25/15; ☒ Jun-Sep 21). You need to be in good shape for either, and you must make **reservations** (☎ 800-343-3006; burgshal@rockies.net) well ahead of time.

The famous **spiral tunnels** – the engineering feat that enabled CPR trains to navigate the challenging Kicking Horse Pass (see boxed text p250) – lie 8km east of Field along the Trans-Canada Hwy. When the railway was completed, it demanded that trains climb the steep 4.5% grade, the steepest railway pass in North America. Many accidents occurred when the trains lost control either hauling themselves up or down the tricky pass. In 1909 the spiral tunnels were carved into the mountain, bringing the grade to a more reasonable 2.2%. If you time it right, you can see trains twisting in on themselves as they wind through the spirals.

Near the south gate of the park, you can reach pretty **Wapta Falls** via a 2.4km trail. The easy walk takes about 45 minutes each way.

SLEEPING

Yoho National Park has four campgrounds, however, Hoodoo is closed until further notice; the three campgrounds within Yoho all close October to April. The small town of Field contains several B&Bs and a lodge; ask for details at the park visitor center.

Monarch Campground (campsite $16) Right at the turnoff to Yoho Valley Rd, this quiet campground offers 46 basic sites. No fires are allowed here.

Takakkaw Falls Campground (campsite $16) Located 13km along the gravel Yoho Valley Rd, this place has 35 walk-in (200m) campsites for tents only. The absence of cars around the campsites makes this the most appealing of the Yoho trio.

HI Whiskey Jack Hostel (☎ 403-670-7580, 866-762-4122; www.hihostels.ca; dm from $20; ☼ Jul-Sep) This isolated hostel offers 27 dorm-style beds in a chalet-style building. It's 15km off the Trans-Canada Hwy on Yoho Valley Rd, just before the Takakkaw Falls Campground and close to the falls itself.

Kicking Horse Campground (campsite $24) This is the only campground that has showers, making its 92 sites the most popular. Interpretive programs run on summer nights. To get there, drive 3.2km east of Field on the Trans-Canada Hwy, then proceed 1km along the Yoho Valley Rd.

Lake O'Hara Lodge (☎ 250-343-6418; www.lakeohara.com; r per person from $100) Something of an environmental legend, this lodge dates back

---

---

80 years and offers the only place to stay at breathtaking Lake O'Hara beyond wilderness campsites. All wastewater is treated for recycling, and conservation is the watchword. Rooms are in the main lodge and cabins are hidden in the trees. Rates include all meals and activities, and transport from the parking area is on the lodge's biodiesel bus.

KOOTENAY NATIONAL PARK

A shortage of cash is responsible for the creation of Kootenay National Park. In the 1920s the BC government – at great expense – set out to build what became Hwy 93 from Radium Hot Springs across the Rockies towards Banff. Money soon ran out and the feds stepped in with a solution: in return for money, BC would give the federal government land comprising roughly 8km on either side of the road. It seems everybody got a good deal. Some amazing and diverse scenery that includes glaciers and deep canyons was saved from possible future logging and the first road across the Rockies was completed.

Today there are three popular campgrounds and some trails leading off Hwy 93, which runs for 94km in the park. Its main attraction is Radium Hot Springs, near the

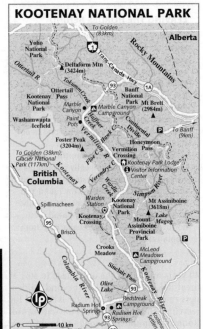

KOOTENAY NATIONAL PARK

southern entrance. Otherwise it's pure wilderness, 13% of which is recovering from fires in 2003. Kootenay experiences a more moderate climate than the other Rocky Mountain parks and, in the southern regions especially, summers can be hot and dry. It's the only national park in Canada to contain both glaciers and cactuses.

INFORMATION

Kootenay National Park is on Mountain Time, one hour ahead of most of BC (see boxed text, p267).

Kootenay National Park & Radium Hot Springs Visitor Centre (☎ 250-347-9331, 800-347-9704; www.radiumhotsprings.com; 7556 Main St E/Hwy 93/95; 9am-7pm May-Sep, 9am-5pm Oct-Apr) Includes Parks Canada information about the park.

Kootenay Park Lodge Visitors Centre (9am-7pm Jul-Aug, 10am-5pm mid-May–Jun & Sep) At Vermilion Crossing, 63km north from Radium Hot Springs.

SIGHTS

The park boundary between Banff and Kootenay National Parks marks the **Continental Divide**, which runs through Yellowhead, Kicking

Horse, Vermilion and Crowsnest Passes. At the Divide, rivers flow either west to the Pacific or east to the Atlantic. The short interpretive **Fireweed Trail** loops through the surrounding forest. Panels explain how nature is recovering from a 1968 fire here.

Many sights such as **Marble Canyon** were closed after the 2003 fire. Check to see when these conditions will change.

Some 2km further south on the main road is the short, easy trail through forest to ochre pools known as the **Paint Pots**. For years first the Kootenay people and then European settlers collected this orange- and red-colored earth. They'd shape it into patties, dry it, grind it, then mix it with fish or animal oil to make paint. Today you can walk past the muddy red pools and read panels describing both the mining history of this rusty earth and its past importance to First Nations people.

Learn how the park's appearance has changed over time at the **Kootenay Valley Viewpoint**, where good new panels trace the park's geologic past. Of course, with this view you may have a hard time looking down. Just 3km south, Olive Lake makes a perfect picnic or rest stop. A lakeside interpretive trail describes some of the visitors who've come before you.

Radium Hot Springs (☎ 250-347-9485; adult/child $7/6; 9am-11pm mid-May–early Oct, noon-9pm other times), 3km north of the town of Radium Hot Springs, is always popular. Even though they are the largest hot springs pools in Canada, the pools, which are quite modern, can get very busy in summer. Come early or late for a more intimate experience. The facilities include showers and lockers. The water comes from the ground at 44°C, enters the first pool at 39°C and hits the final one at 29°C.

SLEEPING

Radium Hot Springs has scores of motels at all price ranges.

Marble Canyon Campground (campsite $19; Jul & Aug) Inside the park, 88km north from Radium Hot Springs and about 8km from the park's east gate, this campground offers flush toilets but no showers with its 61 sites.

McLeod Meadows Campground (campsite $19; mid-May–Aug) With similar facilities to Marble Canyon, this place features 98 pretty, wooded sites along the Kootenay River. Some are secluded, others are on the water.

Redstreak Campground (campsite from $24) Near the park's west gate, Redstreak contains 242 sites (154 sites and 88 partial- and full-hookup sites for RVs). It's a busy place with lots of roadways and offers full services, including flush toilets, showers and nightly interpretive programs. Ask for a list of the park's backcountry campsites at the visitor information centers.

Kootenay Park Lodge (☎ 403-762-9196; www .kootenayparklodge.com; r $100-145; ☯ mid-May–Sep) The 10 cabins here date from the 1930s. This is the choice if you want an old-time woodsy holiday. The beds are snug and you can plop down on your porch and just let nature roll right over you.

AROUND KOOTENAY NATIONAL PARK
Mount Assiniboine Provincial Park

Often called the Matterhorn of Canada, the craggy summits of Mt Assiniboine (3618m), look down onto this 39-sq-km provincial park that's nestled between Kootenay and Banff National Parks. It's a magnet for experienced rock climbers and mountaineers. The park also attracts lots of backcountry hikers and those who just want to sniff the alpine wildflowers.

This park takes its eyebrow-raising name from the Assiniboine (ass-*in*-a-boyne) First Nations, who are also referred to as 'Stoney' for the way they cook some foods – by putting hot stones in pots of water to warm them up. The park's main focus is Lake Magog, which is reachable only by hiking in summer or skiing in winter. A **campground** (campsite $5) here is one of several rustic camping areas in the park.

Also at the lake, **Mount Assiniboine Lodge** (☎ 403-678-2883; www.canadianrockies.net/assiniboine/; r per person from $120) has accommodations for 30 guests each night in a combination of rooms and cabins. Originally built by the Canadian Pacific Railway in 1928, the main lodge is comfortable and well known for its tasty meals (which are included in room rates) Some simple lakeside **Naiset cabins** ($15 per person) may also be reserved through the lodge. Note that the BC government would like to have luxury accommodations built in the park, see boxed text, p39.

The main trail to the lodge begins at Sunshine Village Ski Resort (p290) in Banff National Park; allow a good eight hours to make this 27km trek to Lake Magog.

BANFF NATIONAL PARK

The peaks of Banff National Park tower in all directions from wherever you are in this, the most popular of Canada's parks. The view is stunning, to say the least, and the delights that lie within – hiking, skiing, backcountry exploring, camping, luxuriating and more – keep the crowds coming year after year. But if places like the town of Banff or Lake Louise frequently seem overrun, with only minimal effort you can escape into the kind of natural beauty promised by the gorgeous peaks. Meadows, canyons, white water and rock faces compete for your attention.

Banff National Park was established in 1885. It's named for two CPR financiers who hailed from Banffshire in Scotland, and was Canada's first national park. The original inspiration was the thermal sulfur springs at what has become the Cave and Basin National Historic Site in Banff town. The park covers an area of 6641 sq km and contains 25 mountains of 3000m or more in height.

BANFF
pop 7400

When you see those shots of vast Arctic herds of caribou clawing their way along, you'll know what it can feel like to be in the middle of Banff in summer. Quite simply, the hordes descend daily to the tune of more than five million visitors a year. When you're pushing your way up Banff Ave, it's easy to forget about those gorgeous peaks ringing town.

Still, Banff is a necessary hub to the park. It has several worthwhile attractions – including the iconic hot springs – as well as the best range of accommodations, eating, drinking and more. But you'll be forgiven if you cast a jaundiced eye at the hordes who can't seem to do anything but clog the entrances to mundane chain stores.

The best strategies for dealing with Banff are to either avoid the peak summer season entirely or, if you are there in August, escape the town during the day and set off into the wilderness. It is there, trust us.

History

Created because of the CPR company's dream to build a health spa town in the middle of the park, Banff was destined to draw tour-

THE ROCKIES

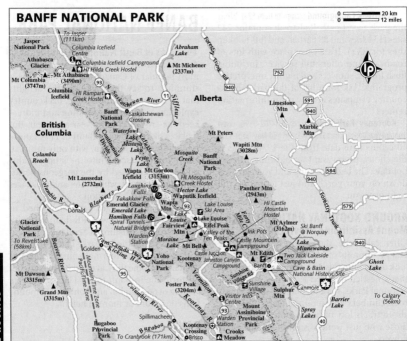

BANFF NATIONAL PARK

ists from its beginnings in the 1880s. The growth happened quickly. Wealthy, well-traveled Victorian adventurers flowed into the park on the CPR trains, ready to relax in the rejuvenating hot springs or hire one of the many outfitters to take them up the mountains. In 1912 the decision to allow cars in Banff opened up the area to auto travelers. Soon, people other than the affluent wanted to check out the scene, and the town began pushing its boundaries. The south side of the river, with the Banff Springs Hotel, catered to the wealthy crowd. The north side of the river, however, resembled more of a prairie town, with small lots zoned in a grid system. This class-distinctive boundary is still evident today.

Banff continues to face conflicts over its growth. Many people complain that the town site is too crowded and argue that it should build more hotels and streets to accommodate all the shopping-bag-laden tourists. Others decry this idea as only adding to the sprawl that has already claimed so much of the valley. Meanwhile, small buildings in the center are giving way to flashy enclosed low-rise malls

filled with the likes of Gap, Burger King and Starbucks.

Orientation

Banff Ave, the main street, runs north–south through the whole length of town, then heads northeast to meet the Trans-Canada Hwy.

South of town past the Bow River Bridge, Mountain Ave leads south to Sulphur Mountain, while Spray Ave leads east to the Banff Springs Hotel, the town's most famous landmark. To the west, Cave Ave goes to the Cave and Basin National Historic Site, which contains the first hot springs found in the area.

Information

BOOKSTORES

Banff Book & Art Den (☎ 403-762-3919; 94 Banff Ave; ☑ 9am-9pm summer, 9am-7pm winter) Lovely store with a good selection; a wall full of books on the area's mountains, history and outdoor activities.

EMERGENCY

Police, medical and fire emergencies (☎ 911) Use both in town and in the backcountry.

INTERNET ACCESS

Many cafés and motels have wi-fi.

CyberWeb (☎ 403-762-9226; 215 Banff Ave; per hr $6; ☯ 9am-9pm) In the Sundance Mall; has laptop connections.

Underground Station (☎ 403-760-8776; 211 Banff Ave; per hr $6; ☯ 9am-midnight) In the Park Ave Mall.

LAUNDRY

Cascade Coin Laundry (☎ 403-762-3444; 317 Banff Ave; per load from $5; ☯ 8am-10pm) Situated on the concourse level of Cascade Plaza; has a good public posting board.

LIBRARY

Banff Public Library (☎ 403-762-2661; 101 Bear St; ☯ 10am-8pm Mon-Thu, 10-6pm Fri, 11am-6pm Sat, 1-5pm Sun Oct-Apr) Internet access for email $1 per 30 minutes; free surfing; reserve in advance. Good place for a literary respite.

MEDICAL SERVICES

Mineral Springs Hospital (☎ 403-762-2222; 301 Lynx St; ☯ 24hr) Treats 15,000 emergency patients each year.

MONEY

Calforex (☎ 403-762-4478; 117 Banff Ave; ☯ 10am-7pm) In the Clock Tower Village Mall.

POST

Main post office (☎ 403-762-2586; 204 Buffalo St; ☯ 9am-5:30pm Mon-Sat)

TOURIST INFORMATION

Parks Canada (☎ 403-762-1550; www.parkscanada .ca/banff) and **Banff/Lake Louise Tourism** (☎ 403-762-8421; www.banfflakelouise.com) both maintain counters inside the historic **VIC** (224 Banff Ave; ☯ 8am-8pm summer, 9am-5pm winter). Before commencing any hiking in the area, check in here; Parks Canada publishes a detailed map, and the staff will tell you about current trail conditions and hazards. Anybody who plans on hiking overnight in the backcountry must sign in and purchase a wilderness permit. Free naturalist programs and guided hikes take place regularly, and every night in summer there is a lecture on some aspect of the area. There is even a handy drop box to pay your parking tickets.

To stay up to date with local events, tune into the Friends of Banff Park (www.friends ofbanff.com) radio station (101.1FM), which features park news, condition reports and other interesting features. The group also runs a good bookstore located in the information center.

Dangers & Annoyances

The police are strict in Banff, and it's a bad idea to drive after a night at the bar; not only are you putting yourself and others at risk, but police often spot-check cars for drunk drivers and drugs. The fines are heavy. You'll have to work to avoid a parking ticket; they're given out in such great quantity that there's a place to pay them in the VIC.

As for all those photogenic elk you may see wandering the streets, remember that they're wild animals and will charge at you if they feel threatened. Every year there are people who are attacked. It's advisable to stay at least 30m away, particularly during the autumn rutting and spring calving seasons.

Sights

The stretch of Banff Ave between Wolf and Buffalo Sts is just one long glitzy strip mall. Pause for air at the **World Heritage Park**, with displays about Unesco. Toward the south end of Banff Ave you'll find **Central Park**, where you can stroll alongside the mellow Bow River. Followed the signed **nature path** north along the river. Still further south across the Bow River Bridge is the **Park Administration Building**, a good place for a view and a photo of the town. Behind the building, the **Cascade Gardens** burst with flowers. A stream, ponds and a few benches dot the gardens. In summer the Siksiki Nation erects a **tepee** with displays of traditional culture and dance exhibitions. Inside the building is the idiosyncratic Canada Place (p290).

BANFF PARK MUSEUM

Be sure to join Babe Ruth as one of the visitors who've signed the guest book at the **park museum** (☎ 403-762-1558; 93 Banff Ave; adult/child $4/2; ☯ 10am-6pm summer, 1-5pm winter) – he did so in 1922. Near the Bow River Bridge at the southern end of town, this lodge-style wood building was built by the CPR in 1903. Check out the surprising inner atrium.

Before trails first led curious wildlife watchers into the bush, the museum housed a zoo and aviary, so Victorian visitors to Banff could catch a safe glimpse of the park's wildlife. The museum, a national historic site, contains a collection of animals, birds and plants found in the park, including two small stuffed grizzlies and a black bear, plus a tree carved with graffiti dating back to 1841. A visit here is just like stepping back 100 years.

THE ROCKIES

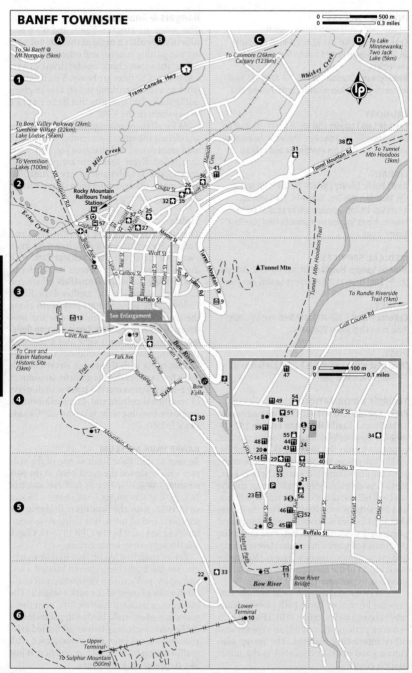

WHYTE MUSEUM OF THE CANADIAN ROCKIES

The **Whyte Museum complex** (☎ 403-762-2291; www
.whyte.org; 111 Bear St; adult/child $6/3.50; ☺ 10am-5pm)
features an art gallery and a vast collection of
photographs telling the history of early explorers, artists and the CPR. Many of the exhibits
rotate, but be sure to check out the Heritage
Gallery with its story of the unlikely romance
of Peter and Catherine Whyte, the museum's
founders. On the property are four log cabins
and two Banff heritage homes, one dating from
1907 and the other from 1931. The museum
conducts tours of the complex and walking
tours of the town year-round (p290).

BUFFALO NATIONS LUXTON MUSEUM

This **museum** (☎ 403-762-2388; 1 Birch Ave; adult/child
$6/4; ☺ 11am-6pm summer, 1-5pm winter) is in the
fort-like wooden building to the right as you
head south over the bridge. Popular with kids,
it mainly explores the history of the First Nations of the Northern Plains and the Rockies, but also covers indigenous groups from
all over Alberta. Through life-sized displays,
models and re-creations, it depicts traditions
such as buffalo hunts. The museum was
started by Norman Luxton in 1952; he had
lofty inclinations after years running a souvenir shop on the site.

CAVE & BASIN NATIONAL HISTORIC SITE

This historic site is the birthplace of Banff. The
discovery of hot sulfur springs in a cave here

led to the area being set aside from development in 1885. Like condo developments of
today, the idea spread rapidly and soon Banff
National Park and Canada's national park
system were created. The **complex** (☎ 403-762-
1557; adult/child $4/2; ☺ 9am-6pm May-Sep, 11am-4pm
Mon-Fri, 9:30am-5pm Sat & Sun Oct-Apr), southwest of
town at the end of Cave Ave, has been restored
to its 1914 appearance. Visitors can look at
(and smell) the cave and sulfurous waters, but
there's no bathing allowed. The **Middle Springs**
a little further down the hill are closed to visitors, to protect the delicate balance of waters.

You can stroll around the attractive
grounds, where you'll see both natural and
artificially made pools, for no charge. It's a
good place for picnics, as there are tables, a
fine view and a snack bar. Several pleasant
short walks begin here: the 400m Discovery
Trail, the 2.7km Marsh Loop and the 3.7km
Sundance Trail.

UPPER HOT SPRINGS

You'll find a soothing hot pool and steam
room at the **Upper Hot Springs spa** (☎ 403-762-
1515; adult/child $8/7; ☺ 9am-11pm May-Sep, 10am-
10pm Oct-Apr), 3km south of town on Mountain
Ave. Besides parboiling in the pool (where
water temperatures average 40°C), you can
also indulge in a massage or aromatherapy
treatment. You can rent bathing suits ($2),
stylish sulfur-colored towels ($2) and lockers
($1). Note the heated floors in the changing
rooms.

THE ROCKIES

THE ROCKIES

BANFF SPRINGS HOTEL

Since it was completed in the 1920s, the **Fairmont Banff Springs Hotel** (☎ 403-762-2211; 405 Spray Ave; public areas free), an 800-room baronial palace 2km south of downtown, has posed for thousands of postcards and millions of snapshots. The spectacular design includes towers, turrets and cornices, giving the impression that the hotel is full of hidden secrets. Many people come just to wander the gardens and absorb the views (is there a better one than the one down the valley, perfectly framed by granite bluffs?). See p292 for details on accommodations here.

BANFF GONDOLA

In less than 10 minutes, the **Banff Gondola** (☎ 403-762-2523; www.banffgondola.com; adult/child $23.50/11.75; ☽ approximately 10am-dusk) whisks you up to the 2281m summit for spectacular views over the surrounding mountains, Bow River and Banff town. The upper terminal looks like something from an old James Bond movie and has the expected restaurant.

Alternatively, you can hike up the steep east side of the mountain in about two hours one way. You will be aptly rewarded with great views. The trail starts from the Upper Hot Springs parking lot. Or just hike down.

The lower terminal is just over 3km south of Banff on Mountain Ave; it's adjacent to the Upper Hot Springs pool. A cab ride costs about $14.

LAKE MINNEWANKA

The largest reservoir in the national park, Lake Minnewanka is 11km east of the Banff town. Forests and mountains surround this scenic recreational area.

Lake Minnewanka Boat Tours (☎ 403-762-3473; www.minnewankaboattours.com; adult/child $37/18; ☽ 9am-5pm, mid-May–Sep) offers pricey yet popular 90-minute cruises on the lake to **Devil's Gap**. Unfortunately the boats are enclosed in order to protect the delicate sensibilities of the masses. To get to the lake from town, take Banff Ave east over the Trans-Canada Hwy to Minnewanka Rd and turn right.

OTHER MUSEUMS & GALLERIES

Banff has a thriving arts community thanks to the twin influences of money and lots of resident artists.

Banff Centre (☎ 403-762-6301; www.banffcentre.ca; 107 Tunnel Mountain Dr), off St Julien Rd east of downtown, contains one of Canada's best-known art schools, complete with facilities for dance, theater, music and the visual arts. Exhibits, concerts and various other events take place regularly. During the Banff Summer Arts Festival, which happens throughout the season, students and internationally recognized artists present pieces in workshops and performances. The **Walter Phillips Gallery** (admission free; ☽ noon-5pm Wed-Sun, noon-9pm Thu) shows changing displays of contemporary art that are often provocative.

A large private gallery that sells work by Canadian artists and those from the Rockies in particular, **Canada House Gallery** (☎ 403-762-3757; cnr Caribou & Bear Sts; ☽ 9am-7pm) is an excellent place to see recent trends and works.

Scattered throughout the Cascade Plaza Mall, **Canadian Ski Museum West** (☎ 403-762-8484; 317 Banff Ave; admission free; ☽ 7am-11pm) exhibits chronicle Banff's ski history through bronze statues of skiers and panels describing the evolution of the sport and its growth in Banff. If you can survive the smells of potpourri from the boutiques, you can learn about everyone from the charming Swiss guide Bruno Engler to modern national ski greats such as Ken Read and Karen Percy.

Activities

If you can do it outdoors, you can probably do it in and around Banff.

HIKING

You'll find many good short hikes and day walks around the Banff area that will get you out into some of the beauty that caused the creation of the park in the first place.

Parks Canada publishes an excellent brochure, *Day Hikes in Banff National Park*, outlining hikes accessible from the town. For longer, more remote hiking, pick up the useful brochure *Backcountry Visitors' Guide*, which contains a simple map showing trails throughout the whole park.

You can take a pleasant, quiet stroll by **Bow River**, just three blocks west of Banff Ave beside Bow Ave. The trail runs from the corner of Wolf St along the river under the Bow River Bridge and ends shortly after on Buffalo St. If you cross the bridge, you can continue southwest through the woods to nearby **Bow Falls**.

For a short (2.3km one way) climb (260m) to break in your legs and survey the area, walk up stubby **Tunnel Mountain**, east of downtown.

A trail leads up from St Julien Rd; you can drive here, but it's not a long walk from downtown to the start of the path. From the east end of Buffalo St, a 5.1km interpretive trail between Bow River and Tunnel Mountain heads north and east toward the **Tunnel Mountain Hoodoos**. The term 'hoodoo' refers to the distinctive vertical pillar shapes carved into the rock face by rainfall and glacial erosion.

Just west of downtown, off Mt Norquay Rd, is the 2km **Fenland Trail** loop, which goes through marsh and forest and connects the town with First Vermilion Lake.

Some excellent hiking trails meander off the Bow Valley Parkway (Hwy 1A), northwest of Banff. The Parkway branches off from, but finally rejoins, the Trans-Canada Hwy en route to Lake Louise. Waterfalls are the lure of a trail that follows the sparkling waters of **Johnston Creek**, which has creatively carved its way through the soft limestone of Johnston Canyon. The trail is paved as far as the **Lower Falls** (2.2km). The next 3.2km stretch to the **Upper Falls** is more challenging but worth it for the views. A further – and mostly untraveled – 6.2km brings you to the **Ink Pots**, five small springs of blue and green water surrounded by snowy peaks.

CANOEING

You can go canoeing on **Lake Minnewanka** and nearby **Two Jack Lake**, northeast of Banff. The **Vermilion Lakes**, three shallow lakes connected by narrow waterways, attract lots of wildlife and make excellent spots for canoeing. To get to the lakes, head northwest out of town along Lynx St and follow signs toward Hwy 1. Just before the highway, turn left onto Vermilion Lakes Dr, and you'll soon come to small parking areas for the lakes.

In town your best bet is the Bow River. **Blue Canoe Rentals** (☎ 403-762-5465; rentals per hr/day $25/50; ☻ 10am-6pm mid-May–Jun & mid-Sep–mid-Oct, 9am-9pm Jul & Aug) rents out canoes at the corner of Bow Ave and Wolf St near the river. From here you can paddle to the Vermilion Lakes in about 30 minutes.

CYCLING & MOUNTAIN BIKING

You can cycle on the highways and on most of the trails in and around town. Excursions of all varieties are possible, whether you're looking to ride for a few hours, a day or several days with overnight stops at campgrounds, hostels or lodges. Two good, short cycling

routes close to Banff run along **Vermilion Lakes Drive** and **Tunnel Mountain Drive**.

For something more challenging, go 1km past the Banff Springs Golf Course to the 14km **Rundle Riverside Trail**, which plunges into the backcountry with a lot of rough riding along the way.

Parks Canada publishes a brochure, *Mountain Biking and Cycling Guide Banff National Park*, that describes trails and regulations.

Ski Stop (☎ 403-760-1650; www.theskistop.com; 203A Bear St; 1-day bike rentals from $30; ☻ 9am-9pm summer, 7:30am-9pm winter) runs self-guided trips in the backcountry that include van shuttle, bike, gear and map.

Bactrax (☎ 403-762-8177; www.snowtips-bactrax.com; 225 Bear St; rentals from $30 per day; ☻ 8am-8pm) organizes two-hour rides from $40.

HORSEBACK RIDING

Why just imagine what the pioneers felt like? Hop on a horse and you can enjoy the same feel *and* smells. In Banff the most popular routes lie south of Bow River. **Holidays on Horseback** (☎ 403-762-4551; www.horseback.com), which operates out of the **Trail Rider Store** (132 Banff Ave; ☻ 9am-9pm), offers a variety of horseback-riding trips around the region. Among the choices: an hour-long ride along Spray River ($39) and a three-hour Bow Valley Loop ($84). Much longer multiday camping adventures in the backcountry start at $500 per person.

ROCK CLIMBING

The Banff area's rocky crags and limestone peaks present almost endless opportunities for good climbing. In fact many of the world's best climbers live in nearby Canmore so that they can enjoy easy access to this mountain playground. This is not terrain for unguided novice climbers; even experienced climbers should talk to locals, do research and check weather conditions before venturing out.

Mountain Magic (☎ 403-762-2591; www.mountainmagic.com; 224 Bear St; ☻ 9am-9pm) has an indoor climbing wall and staff are ready to share local expertise. **Banff Adventures Unlimited** (☎ 403-762-4554, 800-644-8888; www.banffadventures.com) offers lessons for all skill levels, beginning at $230 for a half-day.

SKIING & SNOWBOARDING

Three excellent mountain resorts with spectacular scenery are accessible from Banff; together they offer 248 trails.

THE ROCKIES

Ski Banff @ Norquay (☎ 403-522-3555, 800-258-7669; www.banffnorquay.com; 1-day lift pass adult/child $49/16), just 10 minutes from downtown Banff on Mt Norquay Rd, is the area's oldest resort. It has 77 hectares of skiable area, 28 trails and a drop of 503m.

Sunshine Village (☎ 403-762-6500, 877-542-2633; www.skibanff.com; 1-day lift pass adult/child $70/24), 22km southwest of Banff, has a drop of 1070m and 1282 hectares of skiable runs.

Near the Samson Mall, about 60km northwest of Banff, **Lake Louise Ski Area** (☎ 403-522-3555, 800-258-7669; www.skilouise.com; 1-day lift pass adult/child $69/22) ranks among Canada's largest ski areas, boasting a 1000m drop and 28.5 sq km of terrain spread over four mountain faces.

The three resorts work together (check out www.skibig3.com) and sell passes good at all three (adult/child $216/102 for a three-day pass).

Numerous stores in Banff and the various ski resorts rent equipment. Ski Stop and Bactrax (p289) are well regarded.

SPAS

Weary from a long day on the slopes, trails or shops? A spa is just the thing for you.

Among the many choices:

Pleiades Massage and Spa (☎ 403-760-2500; Upper Hot Springs; 1-hr massage $75; ☼ 11am-9pm) Enjoy the springs and then choose from many massages and treatments including aromatherapy.

Red Earth Spa (☎ 403-762-9292; Banff Caribou Lodge; 521 Banff Ave; treatments from $100; ☼ 9am-7pm) Upscale spa with lavish baths, all manner of treatments and plenty of private spaces for couples to revive.

Banff for Children

Almost everything in Banff can be a treat for kids – well, their eyes might glaze over in the gold shops, but then most adults' do as well. Above all else, the Banff Gondola (p288) scores high on the fun meter. Also in the running is the Banff Park Museum (p285) with its many stuffed critters. Then there are the silly exhibits in Canada Place (right).

The VIC can help with various short hikes aimed at kids, and in winter the area's three ski resorts each have children's programs – from special ski schools to play groups that let the adults romp off and do adult things.

As a treat for good behavior, stop by **Welch's Chocolate Shop** (☎ 403-762-3737; 126 Banff Ave; ☼ 9am-10pm), where the little darlings can truly behave like kids in a candy store.

Quirky Banff

You will want to wave a maple leaf – or perhaps rent the *South Park* movie with the 'Blame Canada' song – after you visit the unusual, almost jingoistic **Canada Place** (☎ 403-760-1338; Park Administration Bldg, 1 Cave Ave; admission free; ☼ 10am-6pm Apr-Oct, 1-4pm Wed-Sun Nov-Mar). Various exhibits and interactive displays celebrate all things Canuck. You can even sit yourself down in a birch-bark canoe but, try as we might, we could not find a Tim Hortons doughnut anywhere.

Tours

WALKING

The **Whyte Museum** (p287) in summer offers numerous daily guided walks and tours from $7 per person. Itineraries include Heritage Homes and Historic Banff. The tours have excellent and enthusiastic guides and are highly recommended.

Discover Banff Tours (☎ 403-760-5007; 215 Banff Ave) has a range of guided four- to six-hour hikes in the region for $70.

BUS

So that's who to blame! **Brewster** (☎ 403-762-6767, 877-791-5500; www.brewster.ca) has been a major player in developing tourism for more than 100 years. You may well find yourself stuck behind one of its ubiquitous buses throughout the Rockies and beyond. Among its myriad tours is a three-hour **Discover Banff tour** (adult/child $73/37), which includes a ride on the Banff Gondola. Other tours: Lake Louise (adult/child $58/29), a return trip to the Columbia Icefield ($106/53) and a one-way trip to Jasper ($106/53) that stops at the icefields. The tours depart from the **Banff Bus Station** (☎ 403-762-1092; 100 Gopher St) and various hotels.

Discover Banff Tours (☎ 403-760-5007; 215 Banff Ave) offers roughly the same lineup as Brewster and at similar prices, but uses much smaller buses. It also has tours aimed at spotting local critters.

Festivals & Events

Banff/Lake Louise Winter Festival (☎ 403-762-0270) Annual town-wide party held in late January and early February since 1919 with much mirth and merriment.

Banff Mountain Film & Book Festival (☎ 403-762-6301; www.banffmountainfestivals.ca) International stories and movies about mountain adventure are honored in early November.

Sleeping

Accommodations are varied; from the storied heights – literally – at the Fairmont Banff Springs Hotel, to the humble pleasures of a hostel, there is something for every taste and budget. Be sure to book ahead in summer. The staff at the VIC are good, but they may not be able to pull a room out of their hats on a sunny weekend evening.

Most places in town line Banff Ave or are very close by. Things are compact enough that you'll be able to walk about the center wherever you stay. Saunas and hot tubs are common. And it's not rare to find kitchen facilities.

B&Bs and vacation rentals are on the rise and Banff/Lake Louise Tourism shows more than 70 on its website (www.banfflakelouise.com).

There are hundreds more motel rooms in fast-food- and chain-store-bedeviled Canmore, 26km east of Banff on the Trans-Canada Hwy. It's the place held up as the worst case scenario by people arguing to rein in Banff's growth.

The rates listed here are for the peak summer season. Travelers in spring and fall will find bargains (but no crowds) everywhere. There are modest spikes in rates during the ski season coinciding with holidays.

BUDGET

Banff National Park contains 13 campgrounds, most of which lie right around the town or along the Bow Valley Parkway. Most are only open between May or June and September. They are all busy in July and August, and availability is on a first-come, first-served basis, so check in by noon or you may be turned away. Campgrounds with showers always fill up first.

Two Jack Main Campground (campsite $19; ✪ mid-May–Aug) Located 12km northeast of Banff on Lake Minnewanka Rd, it features 380 sites and flush toilets but no showers.

HI Banff Alpine Centre (☎ 403-670-7580, 866-762-4122; www.hihostels.ca; 801 Coyote Dr; dm/r from $23/75; 🖳) This large facility, off Tunnel Mountain Rd, consistently scores among the top HI hostels worldwide. There's a café, patios and decks, fireplaces and numerous activities. It also operates a rustic hostel on Castle Mountain west of Banff.

Tunnel Mountain Village Campground (☎ 877-737-3783 reservations; www.pccamping.ca; campsite $24) On Tunnel Mountain Rd, this campground

actually includes three separate campgrounds: two primarily cater to RVs needing electrical hookups and one, Village 1, accommodates only tents, with a whopping 618 tenting sites. Close to town, it has flush toilets and showers. The sites vary widely in quality. Some are secluded, some have views and some are only for the deluded. Village II remains open all year.

Two Jack Lakeside Campground (campsite $24; ✪ mid-May–Aug) About 1km south of Two Jack Main Campground, this place has 74 sites and showers.

Johnston Canyon Campground (campsite $24; ✪ Jun–mid-Sep) About 26km along the Bow Valley Parkway west of Banff, this campground is wooded and fairly secluded, with flush toilets and showers. It has 132 tent sites.

Banff Y Mountain Lodge (☎ 403-762-3560; www.ymountainlodge.com; 102 Spray Ave; dm/r from $30/60; 🖳) This unadorned dorm has a good central location. It accommodates both men and women in its 117 dorm beds and 45 private rooms. The facilities include a café and common cooking area.

SameSun Banff (☎ 403-762-5521, 877-562-2783; www.samesun.com; 449 Banff Ave; dm/r from $32/95; 🖳) Right on the motel strip, this hostel is actually an old motel that's never seen happier days. Pub crawls are a regular event – although some don't make it past the courtyard. There are four to nine beds per room, and free wi-fi.

MIDRANGE

In spring and fall you can get rates well under $150 at the following places. But in summer, things are more expensive. Check websites for deals. B&Bs and rentals average $60 to $120 per night.

Rocky Mountain B&B (☎ 403-762-4811; www.rockymtnbb.com; 223 Otter St; r from $75) This 1918 boarding house has been reborn as a modest guest house close to the center. The 10 rooms are basic, some share bathrooms and the TV is in the common area. It's a good deal for the location.

Squirrel's Nest B&B (☎ 403-762-4432; banffsquirrelsnest.com; 332 Squirrel St; r from $100) Each of the rooms in this family house has a queen bed and its own bathroom. Given the name and address, you might be tempted to bury your nuts here.

Red Carpet Inn (☎ 403-762-4184, 800-563-4609; www.banffredcarpet.com; 425 Banff Ave; r from $100; 🐾 🖳) One of the best deals on the strip, the

THE ROCKIES

52 rooms won't win any design awards (except maybe from the Institute of Institutions) but do come with fridges and free wi-fi. And you car will sleep almost as soundly as you: the garage is heated.

Banff Aspen Lodge (☎ 403-762-4401, 800-661-0227; www.banffaspenlodge.com; 401 Banff Ave; r from $130; 🖵) This older motel has been spiffed up with an inoffensive beige and deep green decor in all 89 rooms. There's parking underground and facilities include a hot tub, sauna and laundry. It often has the best deals of the Banff Ave motels.

Brewster's Mountain Lodge (☎ 403-762-2900, 888-213-1030; www.brewstermountainlodge.com; 208 Caribou St; r from $140; 🖵) A modest but comfortable place right in the center. Get one of the 77 rooms that includes a balcony; otherwise, all have a sort of inviting faux-cabin motif.

Banff Caribou Lodge (☎ 403-762-5887, 800-563-8764; www.bestofbanff.com; 521 Banff Ave; r from $145; 🖵) Another of the large chalet-style motels on Banff Ave, the Caribou horns in with 195 sizable and comfortable rooms with wi-fi over four floors. Guests can make lots of new friends in the 35-person hot tub.

TOP END

Most of the really luxe places are in the hills overlooking the valley. Most offer shuttles into town should you need to run out and buy fudge.

Spruce Grove Motel (☎ 403-762-3301, 800-879-1991; www.banffvoyagerinn.com; 545 Banff Ave; r from $150; 🖵 🐾) An attractive lodge-style inn with parking below. Guests in the 89 large and comfortable rooms here share facilities with the aesthetically challenged Banff Voyager Inn next door. Rooms have high-speed internet.

Banff Ptarmigan Inn (☎ 403-762-2207, 800-661-8310; www.bestofbanff.com; 337 Banff Ave; r from $150; 🖵) Post-and-beam construction sets off this otherwise modern and comfortable inn with 139 large rooms, most with balconies and some with whirlpools. It's a gracious place.

Rimrock Resort Hotel (☎ 403-762-3356, 800-661-1587; www.rimrockresort.com; Mountain Rd; r from $300; 🔀 🖵 🐾) Close to the Upper Hot Springs, this luxurious resort has 346 rooms spread over nine stories. Rooms with balconies and valley views are best, but all have extra large baths with plenty of complimentary potions, wi-fi and really deep carpet. There's a spa, indoor pool and ice rink.

Fairmont Banff Springs Hotel (☎ 403-762-2211, 800-441-1414; www.fairmont.com; 405 Spray Ave; r from $350; 🔀 🖵 🐾) Few of the 770 rooms here are alike and that's central to the charm of this legendary property, which no one ever calls the Fairmont (That's Banff Springs Hotel to you, mister). There's a good sense of history about the place and the staff are truly helpful – even as people who shouldn't be wearing shorts ask directions to the bathroom. Rooms with valley views are prized – despite their modern luxuries, don't take a room in one of the newer annexes. It's probably best to stay here in the spring or fall, when the tourist day-trippers are gone and the prices have fallen.

Eating

There's all manner of cafés and restaurants in Banff offering a range of cuisines and catering to all budgets. Beware of tourist joints luring in the unwary knowing they'll never return. For good tips, ask your bartender.

You can pick up some prepared deli foods and other picnic fixings at **Safeway** (☎ 403-723-3929; 318 Marten St; ⏱ 24hr), just off Banff Ave.

BUDGET

Evelyn's Coffee Bar (☎ 403-762-0352; 201 Banff Ave, Town Centre Mall; snacks $3; ⏱ 7am-11pm) Tightly packed with gossipers, Evelyn's dishes the dish – in this case sausage rolls, soups and excellent coffees.

Barpa Bill's (☎ 403-762-0377; 223 Bear St; meals $5; ⏱ 11am-9pm) Tantalizing smells waft out of this Greek fast-food place that does wonders stuffing a pita.

Wild Flower (☎ 403-760-5074; 211 Bear St; meals from $5; ⏱ 8am-8pm) From the coffee to the artisan bread, everything is organic at this bright bakery, which serves up yummy soups, sandwiches and gelato. Chill out at a patio table.

Bruno's Café & Grill (☎ 403-762-8115; 304 Caribou St; meals $5-10; ⏱ 8am-1am) This home to lavish burgers honors Swiss skier and longtime local Bruno Engler. Breakfast is served all day and there are lots of treats on the comfort menu, such as European-style sausages.

Natur'el (☎ 403-760-2511; 103 Banff Ave; meals $6-10; ⏱ 9am-9pm) The place for ladies – and everyone else – who tea. The odors wafting out of this cute pastel café-cum-shop will draw you right in for all sorts of organic breakfasts and lunches. There's a good wine list and Canada's best iced tea.

MIDRANGE

Coyotes (☎ 403-762-3963; 206 Caribou St; meals $6-25; ⓨ 8am-10pm) Southwestern cuisine is on stage in the open kitchen at this bustling favorite. Grab a counter spot for a front-row seat. Popular items include spicy black bean burritos, four chili pork chops and that heaven-sent hangover cure, huevos rancheros.

Nourish (☎ 403-760-3933; 2nd fl, 215 Banff Ave; meals $7-15; ⓨ 9am-9pm) Take your pick of meals at this healthy place that takes things so seriously it hasn't bothered to decorate: choose from wheat-free, gluten-free, vegan, raw, or plain old organic.

Wolf St Grill (☎ 403-760-6668; 204 Wolf St; meals $10-20; ⓨ 11am-9pm) A light and woodsy old house in the heart of Banff, this modern bistro has a global menu that ranges from burgers and salads at lunch to Asian-accented mains at dinner. Try the spicy curries on the big patio.

Grizzly House (☎ 403-762-4055; 207 Banff Ave; meals $15-30; ⓨ 11:30am-late) Another place that will take you back to the days when disco was cutting-edge, this old-time fondue house has timeless dark booths where you and your partner can do much dipping. Should you need to come up for air, there's a small patio out front that's good for watching street action.

Bison (☎ 403-762-5550; 211 Bear St; meals $15-40; ⓨ 11am-10pm) At street level this chic restaurant has an upscale deli serving exquisite little sandwiches and other gourmet treats (from $8). Upstairs the bright and airy dining room overlooks both the peaks and an open kitchen. Woodfired pizzas are tops, as are boldly flavored seafood and meat mains. Many specials.

TOP END

Bumper's Beef House (☎ 403-762-2622; 603 Banff Ave; meals $25-35; ⓨ 5-10pm) Northeast of the center, Bumper's remains a local institution. Prime rib in several sizes is the specialty, aged 21 days by the restaurant. Some steaks come with a pat of seasoned butter on top, just in case you're worried about your calories. But that shouldn't stop you from loading up at the throwback salad bar.

Le Beaujolais (☎ 403-762-2712; 101 Banff Ave; meals from $30; ⓨ 6-10pm) More exclusive than its mass-market namesake grape, this old-world restaurant has a classic French menu of the kind rarely seen anymore in a world of fusion this and global that. Think lobster vichyssoise and chateaubriand. Tables in the 2nd-floor dining room overlook the park and river.

Drinking

Nightlife in Banff easily goes past midnight in the peak seasons. Most bars also serve food.

St James Gate (☎ 403-762-9355; 205 Wolf St) An ersatz upscale English pub replete with lots of dark wood and snugs, this place packs 'em in for the 24 beers on tap, stiff drinks and tasty fish and chips. It gets crowded late as the pals of the staff drop by after the places they work close.

Rose & Crown (☎ 403-762-2121; 202 Banff Ave) A view that validates your existence in Banff is the reason to come to this pub, which has an amazing rooftop deck. Count the peaks when you arrive, then do so again after a few pints and see if the numbers agree. Inside it has live rock, darts and pool tables.

Pump & Tap (☎ 403-760-6610; lower level, 215 Banff Ave) This basement dive in the divey Sundance Mall is the place to go if you have a summer/winter job in Banff, are broke, or both. It's the place to chat up your hostel desk clerk; the drinks are cheap and there's always the hint of impending scandal.

Entertainment

Banff is the social and cultural center of the Rockies. You can find current entertainment listings in the 'Summit Up' section of the weekly *Banff Crag & Canyon* newspaper. Also check the schedule at the Banff Centre (p288), which has regular musical and artistic performances.

HooDoo (☎ 403-762-8434; 205 Caribou St; cover $5-10) is a downstairs dance bar with a bocce ball court – don't even ask how play goes after a few shots of Jägermeister. **Aurora Nightclub** (☎ 403-760-3343; lower level, 110 Banff Ave, Clock Tower Village Mall; cover $5-10) is all Eurotrash flash.

Getting There & Away

Banff is 138km west of Calgary and 90km east of Field. If you're going or coming from the former, note that the archaic Trans-Canada Hwy seems to be permanently clogged in Calgary. If you're going to the airport, you could find yourself stuck in traffic admiring the city's seedy strip of porn peddlers and loan shops while your flight flies off. Give yourself at least three hours to get inside the terminal.

THE ROCKIES

It's really a crime that VIA Rail no longer serves Banff, as the tracks from Calgary to Vancouver go right through town. There is an ongoing effort to rectify this, especially as the best way to traffic-clogged Calgary is by train.

BUS

Brewster (☎ 403-762-6767; www.brewster.ca; 100 Gopher St) Operates express buses to/from Lake Louise (adult/child $16/8, one hour, two daily), Jasper ($70/35, five hours, one daily May to mid-October) and Calgary ($50/25, two hours, two daily).

Greyhound buses (☎ 403-762-1092; 100 Gopher St) Buses operate from the spiffy Brewster terminal. Services east to Calgary ($26, two hours, five daily) and west to Vancouver ($119, 13 to 15 hours, four daily) via Golden, Revelstoke, Kelowna and more.

Mountain Connector (☎ 780-852-1575, 888-786-3641; www.mountainconnector.com; ☙ Dec-Apr) Winter and spring service between Banff and Jasper (adult/child $53/29, four hours, one daily) via Lake Louise.

Getting Around
TO/FROM THE AIRPORT
Banff Airporter (☎ 403-762-3330, 888-449-2901; www .banffairporter.com; adult/child $48/24) has frequent service to/from Calgary airport (two hours).

BUS
Banff Transit (☎ 403-762-1215; www.banff.ca; adult/ child $2/1; ☙ 7am-midnight) offers three routes. Rte 1 follows Spray and Banff Aves between the Fairmont Banff Springs Hotel and the RV parking lot north of town. Rte 2 follows Tunnel Mountain Rd to the HI Banff Alpine Centre and Tunnel Mountain Village Campgrounds. Rte 3 goes from the center and up Mountain Ave to the Upper Hot Springs. Service is good, every 30 minutes.

CAR
All of the major rental-car companies have branches in Banff.

TAXI
Banff Taxi (☎ 403-762-4444)
Legion Taxi (☎ 403-762-3353)

LAKE LOUISE
Some people love Lake Louise, some avoid it due to the incessant crowds in high season. Let's concentrate on the former. The first person to spy Lake Louise must have had some sort of word or exclamation for the vista that

presented itself: a huge glacier (now called Victoria after you know who) perched atop a mountain that backs a lake whose iridescent color changes with every movement of the sun. And all this framed by snowy peaks. Well damn!

So the buses, they come. And the people, they walk about 50m, take snapshot and go. And all this makes for something akin to the arteries of a bacon-cheeseburger addict: clogged. Yet amid the jam and the commercialism of iconic Fairmont Chateau Lake Louise on the north shore, there are hints of escape. You can enjoy the lake and not get trampled. Or, visit away from July or August, when you can drive right up and do whatever you want.

Orientation
The lake, known as the jewel of the Rockies, lies about 57km northwest of Banff, at the conjunction of Hwys 1 and 93. Before you get to the lake, you'll reach the uninspiring village of Lake Louise, which is essentially nothing more than the Samson Mall shopping center and a service station. Though small, the convenient strip of shops can provide you with everything from postal services to groceries and liquor, from restaurant meals to hiking boots (in case you left yours at home). The town is essentially a tourist attraction; few permanent residents actually live here except for those who staff the hotels.

The lake, named for Queen Victoria's daughter Louise (neither of whom ever came to the lake), is 5km uphill from the village. If you're walking, it takes about 45 minutes on the footpath.

Information
Parks Canada and Banff/Lake Louise Tourism offer information at the **VIC** (☎ 403-522-3833; ☙ 9am-7pm Jul & Aug, 9am-5pm Sep-Jun) beside the Samson Mall; the center also features a good exhibition on the geological and natural history of the Rocky Mountains.

Woodruff & Blum (☎ 403-522-3842; Samson Mall; ☙ 9am-8pm) carries general guides and maps to the Canadian Rockies; very helpful.

Sights
First you'll want to go and see **Lake Louise**. The vast parking lot is a five-minute drive from Hwy 1. Easy walks are 1.1km along the southeast side of the lake or 3.8km along the

north shore to a quartz cliff wall. There are no trails circling the entire lake. In summer avoid going from 11am to 4pm, when the crowds peak.

Overlooking the scene, the iconic Lake Louise Chalet opened in 1890 to alleviate some of the pressure on the Banff Springs Hotel. Renamed **Chateau Lake Louise** in 1925 (and Fairmont Chateau Lake Louise after the upscale chain absorbed it), the hotel features almost 500 rooms on eight floors, as well as six restaurants and three lounges. Though smaller and less fabled than its Banff counterpart, it enjoys a grand lakeside setting. You can join the other millions of tourists who wander through the hotel every summer on their own. At certain times, **tours** (☎ 403-522-3511) are offered; check for details.

If you're thinking of a dip, consider this: at 1731m above sea level, Lake Louise averages a chilly 4°C.

Mt Whitehorn and the Lake Louise ski area lie east of the village, 4.5km along Lake Louise Dr. In summer the **Lake Louise Gondola** (☎ 403-522-3555; www.lakelouisegondola.com; adult/child $23/11.50; ◷ 9am-5:30pm mid-May–Sep) takes you to the top, where you can hike the trails and enjoy views of Lake Louise and Victoria Glacier. The ticket price includes an array of excellent programs, including guided walks and hikes, and there is an interpretive center. The outings into the alpine meadows are highly recommended and are such a nice change from another chance to buy something. For slightly more money on your ticket (breakfast/lunch $2/4) you can enjoy a real deal on a buffet meal at the top.

Though lesser known than Lake Louise, **Moraine Lake** always astounds even the jaded. Surrounded by peaks and a deep teal in color, it is nothing less than stunning. If you get your hands on an old $20 bill (first produced in 1969), take a look at the picture on the back and you'll recognize the view of the lake. Look for an attractive lodge, gift shop and numerous trails. The lake sits in the gorgeous Valley of the Ten Peaks, 15km (mostly uphill) from the village. To get there, take Lake Louise Dr toward the chateau, turn left onto rugged Moraine Lake Rd and follow it to the end. If you're camping, you can also take the free shuttle from the campgrounds. A vendor often rents rowboats, so you can enjoy a 360° vista.

> **GETTING AWAY FROM IT ALL**
>
> Ask Parks Canada people the best way to get away from the crowds at Lake Louise and they suggest you go to Yoho National Park, which is only about 20km west on the Trans-Canada Hwy. Highly recommended is the walk to Sherbrooke Lake (see boxed text, p281), another spectacular glacial body of water.

Activities

Lake Louise boasts 75km of **hiking** trails, many of which lead to beautiful alpine meadows that fill up with colorful wildflowers in July and August. It is common to see pikas (plump furry animals also called conies) and the larger, more timid marmots along these trails. You often hear ice rumbling on the slopes too. Note that trails may be snowbound beyond the 'normal' winter season – often there are avalanche warnings well into July.

Note too that large numbers of trails are now only open to groups of six or more; this includes all those in Paradise and Larch Valleys and the area around Moraine Lake (the lake itself is still open to individuals). The idea behind group access is to bunch visitors together so that hikers have peaceful interludes and aren't tempted to make a snack of individual hikers. The affected area is one of three main grizzly bear breeding areas in Banff National Park. Consult with the hiking experts at the Parks Canada booth at the VIC for current conditions.

Many of the hiking trails become crosscountry ski trails in winter. For downhill types, Lake Louise boasts the largest **skiing** area in Canada. The resort operates in conjunction with Ski Banff at Mt Norquay and Sunshine Village. See p289 for details on all three areas.

Rock climbing on the Back of the Lake, a backwater crag, is popular, partly because it's easy to access. There are lots of different routes with interesting names like 'Wicked Gravity' and 'Chocolate Bunnies from Hell.' Other places to climb, of varying degrees of difficulty, include Fairview Mountain, Mt Bell and Eiffel Peak. But no one, not even very experienced climbers, should venture out to any of these spots without getting the full avalanche and trail conditions report from one of the Parks Canada information centers.

THE ROCKIES

Wilson Mountain Sports (☎ 403-522-3636; www
.lakelouisewilsons.com; Samson Mall; ski packages $33, moun-
tain bikes per day $40; ⊗ 9am-8pm) rents out a full
range of winter sports gear as well as fairer
weather gear such as mountain bikes, camping equipment and climbing gear.

Sleeping

Compared to Banff, Lake Louise has relatively
few places to stay. However, the ones that are
here tend to be of high quality.

Lake Louise Campgrounds (☎ 403-522-3980, reservations 877-737-3783; www.pccamping.ca) Parks Canada operates two campgrounds, both on the
Trans-Canada Hwy. The tenting campground
(campsite $24), off Moraine Lake Rd, contains
220 summer-only (May to September) sites,
while the RV campground, at the south end
of Fairview Rd off Lake Louise Drive, offers
189 sites ($28) year-round. Both have flush
toilets and showers.

HI Lake Louise Alpine Centre (☎ 403-522-2200,
866-762-4122; www.hihostels.ca; dm/r from $25/80; 🖳)
On Village Rd north of Samson Mall, this
huge lodge has all the charm of a mountain
chalet without requiring the big expenditure.
The 164 beds are split between two- to six-
bedrooms, many with private bathroom. Hikers note: the hostel is part-run by the Alpine
Club of Canada, so affairs of the foot are well
cared for.

Paradise Lodge & Bungalows (☎ 403-522-3595;
www.paradiselodge.com; 105 Lake Louise Dr; cabins from $160)
Bed down in your own stylish cabin at this
attractive resort on the road to Lake Louise.
Most units have decks and some have claw-
foot soaking tubs. The main lodge has large
suites, many with bedside Jacuzzis.

Fairmont Chateau Lake Louise (☎ 403-522-3511,
800-441-1414; www.fairmont.com; 111 Lake Louise Dr;
r from $350; 🖳 🖳 🖳) Like its sister in Banff, the
Chateau Lake Louise can get overrun by day-
trippers in the summer. However it is not of
the same grand baronial design and instead
is a very light stone that seems downright
reticent given the setting. The 486 rooms vary
greatly in size and price. Obviously if you're
going to go to the trouble of staying here you
don't want to be on the wrong side of the hall
– get a room with a view. Or go nuts and get
one with a terrace and a view.

Eating

Samson Mall has a small grocery and a couple
of uninspired café-bakeries.

Lake Louise Station (☎ 403-522-2386; meals $8-30;
⊗ 11am-9pm) One kilometer from the Samson
Mall on Sentinel Rd, here you get the chance
to eat in a historic 1884 train station, or on
its patio, or in one of two old dining cars. The
menu is casual at lunch; for dinner things
smarten up with complex preparations of
meat and seafood.

Fairmont Chateau Lake Louise (☎ 403-522-3511,
800-441-1414; 111 Lake Louise Dr; meals $10-50) You'll
find several places to eat at all price levels
here. Options range from the formal Fairview
Dining Room to the casual Poppy Brasserie
to the takeout Chateau Deli. Many wouldn't
miss afternoon tea, others take the plunge into
the Swiss fondue at Walliser Stube.

Getting There & Around

See p293 for transport details to/from Banff,
Jasper and Calgary.

The **bus terminal** (☎ 403-522-3870) is at Samson
Mall; Greyhound and Brewster Jasper shuttles
stop here.

ICEFIELDS PARKWAY

Let's see – you've got 230km of Unesco-
designated world heritage scenery that spans
two famous parks *and* it's traversed by a good
truck-free road *and* you'll probably see critters
such as mountain goats by the roadside *and*
there are lots of glaciers… Where do you sign
up? Well, you don't need to sign anything –
just hit the Icefields Parkway, which makes
vast parts of the stunning Canadian Rockies
accessible to one and all.

Opened in 1940, this 230km road (Hwy
93) links Lake Louise with Jasper, following a lake-lined valley between two chains
of the Eastern Main Ranges which make
up the Continental Divide. From here wa-
tershed rivers flow either eastward toward
the Atlantic Ocean or westward toward the
Pacific. The mountains here are the highest,
craggiest and maybe the most scenic in all
the Rockies.

The highway is in good condition, but it's
slow going nonetheless. In addition to the
gawking tourists (you'll be one of them), animals including goats, bighorn sheep and elk
often linger beside the road or even on it. If
you're on the bus, you'll see the best scenery if
you sit on the left-hand side going from Lake
Louise to Jasper.

You can drive the route in a couple of
hours, but stopping at the many viewpoints,

picnic spots and sights, or hiking on one of the trails, can require a full day or longer. You can take your time and camp along the way or stay at one of the several rustic hostels. Cycling the Icefields Parkway is so popular that often you'll see more bikes than cars on the road. Because of the terrain, it's easier to bike heading north.

Parks Canada publishes a worthwhile brochure, *The Icefields Parkway*, which includes a map and describes the sights along the way. It notes the seven major icefields – upland glaciers – and 25 smaller ones you'll pass along the way.

As is so often the case, the best time to see **Peyto Lake**, one of the world's most beautiful glacial lakes, is early in the morning. It's 40km north of the junction with the Trans-Canada Hwy near Lake Louise.

Some 17km further north, around **Waterfowl Lake**, moose are plentiful (as are duck!). After a long horseshoe curve around a small spring littered with amazing rocks, the **Bridal Veil Falls** overlook is almost at the road's halfway point, 113km north of the start. Other key points of interest include **Sunwapta Falls**, which surge through a canyon (176km north) and **Athabasca Falls** (200km north), which has a powerful 23m drop.

Athabasca Glacier

The Athabasca Glacier, a fat tongue of the vast Columbia Icefield, can be glimpsed from the road. And we say glimpsed, because it's in serious retreat. Each year global warming is melting this enormous pile of ice – note the huge lakes forming at its base. But while it may be in retreat the forces of commercialism are not.

The **Icefield Centre** (☎ 780-852-6288; ☻ 9am-5pm mid-Apr–May & Sep–mid-Oct, 9am-6pm Jun-Aug) is a vast facility across from the glacier that is run by überoperator Brewster. Much of the place is designed to get you to buy a glacier tour (there's ads in the inside of toilet stall doors, for goodness sakes), however there is a very helpful albeit politically constrained **Parks Canada information desk**. Staffers told us they have to be careful what they say about global warming given current politics in Canada (meanwhile you can see the glacier melting into the lakes outside the window…) but with a little talk, you might get a look at an annotated photo they have showing the glacier's rapid shrinkage year by year.

DETOUR: PARKWAY 93A

Starting at Athabasca Falls, Parkway 93A is the old highway that was replaced by the modern Icefields Parkway (Hwy 93). It's a meandering road that gives you a much more intimate feel for the park than the main road, and there are several picnic spots. After about 20km, it rejoins Hwy 93 10km south of Jasper.

It's the kind of information one would hope to find in the display area on the ground level but doesn't – although there is a good time-lapse video showing how ice can slowly but surely literally move mountains. (There is talk about improving the displays – let's hope they show the same initiative as the Brewster sales force.)

In addition to the obligatory gift shop, the center has several restaurants that fully enjoy their monopoly status.

You can take the walk to the toe of the glacier from the visitor center (1km and counting), or you can save yourself from slogging across a moonscape of gravel by driving part of the distance.

For an experience right on the ice, **Athabasca Glacier Icewalks** (☎ 800-565-7547; www.icewalks .com; Icefield Centre; ☻ Jun-Sep) offers a three- to four-hour **'Ice Cubed' trip** (adult/child $55/25; ☻ tours 10:30am Jun-Sep) up the glacier and a five- to six-hour **'Icewalk Deluxe' trip** (adult/child $65/30; ☻ tours 10:30am Thu & Sun Jun-Sep) to various destinations in the snowfields. Bring warm clothes. Gear is provided.

Should you fall for the hype of Brewster's **ice tours** (☎ 403-762-6735, 877-423-7433; www.brewster .ca; adult/child $34/17; ☻ 9am-5pm Apr-Sep, 10am-4pm Oct), you'll be joined by up to 5000 people on busy days. The 90-minute trip in a special bus takes you out on the ice and to vast areas of the glacier that can't be seen from the road.

The Icefield Centre is 123km north of the parkway's start and 103km south of Jasper. Note: if you really want to be amazed by glaciers, see p354 for details on the ones around Stewart, BC.

Sleeping

You will find a few Parks Canada campgrounds along the way, all with pit toilets and no showers. The Parkway is lined with a good batch of rustic HI hostels, most of which

THE ROCKIES

ICE DREAM

The Columbia Icefield contains about 30 glaciers and reaches the epic volume of 350m thick in places. This remnant of the last ice age covers 325 sq km – about the size of Vancouver – on the plateau between Mt Columbia (3747m) and Mt Athabasca (3491m) off the parkway connecting Lake Louise to Jasper. This mother of rivers straddling the Continental Divide is the largest icefield in the Rockies and feeds the North Saskatchewan, Columbia, Athabasca, Mackenzie and Fraser River systems with its meltwaters. They flow to three oceans: the Pacific, the Atlantic and the Arctic. The mountainous sides of this vast bowl of ice rise to some of the highest heights in the Rocky Mountains, with nine peaks over 3000m. The Athabasca Glacier, of which a mere tongue is seen from the Icefields Parkway, is one of these.

---

lie quite close to the highway in scenic locations. Though these small spots lack showers, there's usually a 'refreshing' stream nearby. Be sure to reserve through **HI hostels** (☎ 403-670-7580, 866-762-4122; www.hihostels.ca; ☺ Apr-Oct, call other times to confirm).

Columbia Icefield Campground (campsite $14; ☺ mid-May–early Oct) Close to the Icefield Centre, this campground has 33 tents-only sites, with picnic tables and firewood.

Wilcox Creek Campground (campsite $14; ☺ Jun–mid-Sep) Near Columbia Icefield Campground and with similar amenities, this place has 46 sites. Remember, you're in glacier territory and it gets mighty chilly at night.

HI Mosquito Creek Hostel (dm/r from $20/54) An excellent choice of the HI places, this hostel, on the Icefields Parkway about 27km north of Lake Louise, has a fireplace, sauna, and 32 beds in four cabins and private rooms.

HI Rampart Creek Hostel (dm from $20) Ice and rock climbers should head 11km north of the Saskatchewan River Crossing (88km north of Lake Louise) to this place with its sauna and 24 beds.

Closer to Jasper along the Icefields Parkway are two places managed by the **HI Jasper International Hostel** (☎ 780-852-3215, 877-852-0781; www.hihostels.ca; ☺ Apr-Oct, other times confirm):

HI Beauty Creek Wilderness Hostel (HI Jasper International Hostel ☎ 780-852-3215, 877-852-0781; www.hihostels.ca; dm from $20; ☺ Apr-Oct, call other times to confirm) Located 145km north of Lake Louise, and closer to Jasper, this 22-bed hostel is one of two places managed by the HI Jasper International Hostel.

HI Athabasca Falls Wilderness Hostel (HI Jasper International Hostel ☎ 780-852-3215, 877-852-0781; www.hihostels.ca; dm from $20; ☺ Apr-Oct, call other times to confirm) Also run by HI Jasper International Hostel, this place, 198km north of Lake Louise, has 40 beds.

Icefields Chalet (☎ 780-852-6550, 877-423-7433; www.brewster.ca; r $110-225; ☺ May-Sep) The Icefield Centre contains this humdrum Brewster-run place where some of the rooms lack glacier views.

JASPER NATIONAL PARK

Larger (10,878 sq km) than Banff National Park, wilder and less visited, Jasper National Park is the preferred destination for many in the Canadian Rockies. Glaciers link mountain peaks, waterfalls crash into rocky canyons, and rivers feather across wide valleys. Look for bear, mountain lions, elk, beaver, mountain goats and many more of the region's iconic critters.

Established in 1907, Jasper has a number of easily reached must-see sights such as Maligne Canyon and Lake. But there is much more here for you to discover – think about having a goal of finding your very own alpine lake.

The town of Jasper is a good place to base yourself – big enough to have nightlife and services but small enough not to induce urban headaches. Fires in 2003 charred many areas visible from the Yellowhead Hwy (Hwy 16) east of Jasper, but you can see the start of nature's recovery.

JASPER
pop 4400

On a wide plain near the Athabasca River, Jasper is a very appealing town. Yes it's totally devoted to tourism but not with the sense of desperation you find in other tourist towns. There's a good selection of restaurants and motels, plus plenty of services. From most parts of town, you can see a ring of snowy peaks, and trails will take you right into the wilderness from the center in 15 minutes. For these reasons, many people prefer Jasper to Banff.

The town, 369km southwest of Edmonton and 376km east of Prince George (p321), is a regional transportation hub. VIA Rail (p304) trains run east to Edmonton and west to both Vancouver and Prince Rupert (p338), while the Icefields Parkway travels 230km south towards the Trans-Canada Hwy and Lake Louise.

And in case you're not ready to go to the wildlife, it may come to you. Elk like to hang out downtown during the autumn rutting and spring calving seasons. Besides leaving poop pellets everywhere, they occasionally charge tourists and emit a haunting cry like a weasel caught in a wringer. Stay at least 30m away (as if you'd want to get any closer to a rutting elk?).

History

Archaeological evidence shows that First Nations people lived here as early as 12,000 years ago. It is believed that the First Nations came here seasonally, arriving with the snowmelt to gather food, then leaving again once everything iced over. Many groups used the area, including Shuswap, Sekani and Beaver from the west, Iroquois and Stoney from the east and Cree from throughout the area.

In the early 1800s David Thompson and the North West Company established a fur-trading route into the Kootenays over Athabasca Pass. Voyageurs soon intermarried with Iroquois and Cree, creating a Métis 'mixed-blood' group whose descendants shaped Jasper's history. Though the fur trade slowly died

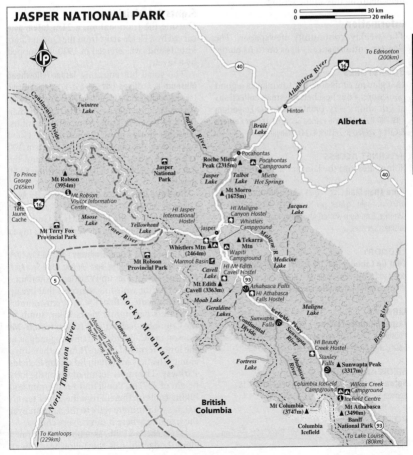

JASPER NATIONAL PARK

0 — 30 km
0 — 20 miles

THE ROCKIES

out, the steady flow of scientists and explorers did not. People were curious about the great glaciers, and soon adventurers and mountaineers were exploring the majestic peaks. In 1930 the National Parks Act was passed, fully protecting Jasper as a national park.

Orientation

The main street, Connaught Dr, has everything, including the train and bus station, banks, restaurants and souvenir shops. Patricia St, parallel to Connaught Dr, is also parallel in terms of the services it offers. Street numbers throughout town, when posted at all, are difficult to follow.

Off the main street, the town consists of small wooden houses, many with flower gardens befitting this alpine setting.

Information

The weekly community newspaper, *The Booster*, enthusiastically lives up to its name.

BOOKSTORES

In a glaring omission, the town lacks a good bookstore. Your best bets are small collections at gift shops. Try **Counter Clockwise Emporium** (☎ 780-852-3152; 616 Patricia St) and **Jasper Camera & Gift** (☎ 780-852-3165; 412 Connaught Dr).

INTERNET ACCESS

Some cafés and the laundry have internet.

More Than Mail (☎ 780-852-3151, 888-440-3151; 620 Connaught Sq Mall; per 10 mins $1; ⏰ 9am-9pm summer, 9am-6pm winter) Also stores luggage and offers business services.

LAUNDRY

Coin-Op Laundry (☎ 780-852-3852; 607 Patricia St; per load $5; ⏰ 8am-9pm; 🖥) Bright and airy, has showers, coffee bar and fast internet access (per hr $8).

LIBRARY

Jasper Municipal Library (☎ 780-852-3652; 500 Robson St; ⏰ 11am-9pm Mon-Thu, 11am-5pm Fri & Sat) Small, with limited internet access.

MEDICAL SERVICES

Seton General Hospital (☎ 780-852-3344; 518 Robson St; ⏰ 24hr)

POST

Post office (☎ 780-852-3041; 502 Patricia St; ⏰ 9am-5pm Mon-Fri)

TOURIST INFORMATION

Right in the heart of town, the **Jasper Information Centre** (500 Connaught Dr; ⏰ 8:30am-7pm Jun-Sep, 9am-5pm Oct-May) is easily one of Canada's most eye-pleasing tourist offices. Built in 1913 as the park office and superintendent's residence, the stone building is surrounded by flowers and plants. The large lawn is a popular meeting place that's often strewn with lounging travelers. It has three information desks: **Jasper Tourism & Commerce** (☎ 780-852-3858; www.discover jasper.com), **Parks Canada** (☎ 780-852-6176; www.parks canada.ca) and the **Friends of Jasper National Park** (☎ 780-852-4767; www.friendsofjasper.com), which has a store for guides and maps. See boxed text, p302 for details on the Friends of Jasper National Park group's Jasper Institute.

Sights & Activities

Outside the train station, a 21m **totem pole** carved by a Haida artist from the Queen Charlotte Islands was erected in 1920. It's topped by a raven.

The small but engaging **Jasper-Yellowhead Museum & Archives** (☎ 780-852-3013; 400 Pyramid Lake Rd; adult/child $4/3; ⏰ 10am-9pm Jun-Aug, 10am-5pm Sep-May) provides a context to the Canadian Rockies that's missing from other exhibits. Personal stories bring the past to life. Good ones cover the development of tourism 100 years ago, when swells swanned around the Rockies on the backs of laborers earning $3.50 per day.

Brushfire Gallery (☎ 780-852-3554; cnr Elm Ave & Patricia St; ⏰ 10am-10pm May-Sep, 10am-5pm Sat & Sun Oct-Apr) is run by the Jasper Artists Guild and has rotating showings of works by the many local artists.

The popular **Jasper Tramway** (☎ 780-852-3093; adult/child $24/12; ⏰ 10am-9pm Jun-Aug, 10am-5pm Apr & May, Sep–early-Oct) goes up Whistlers Mountain – named for the whistling marmots that live up top (How cute is that?) – in seven minutes and offers panoramic views 75km south to the Columbia Icefield and 100km west to Mt Robson in BC. Board the tramway gondolas at the lower terminal, about 7km south of town along Whistlers Mountain Rd off the Icefields Parkway. The upper terminal sits at the lofty height of 2277m. You'll find a restaurant and hiking trails up there. From the upper terminal, it's a 45-minute walk to the summit over the tree line, where it can be very chilly.

Lakes Annette & Edith, 3km northeast of town along Lodge Rd (off the Yellowhead Hwy),

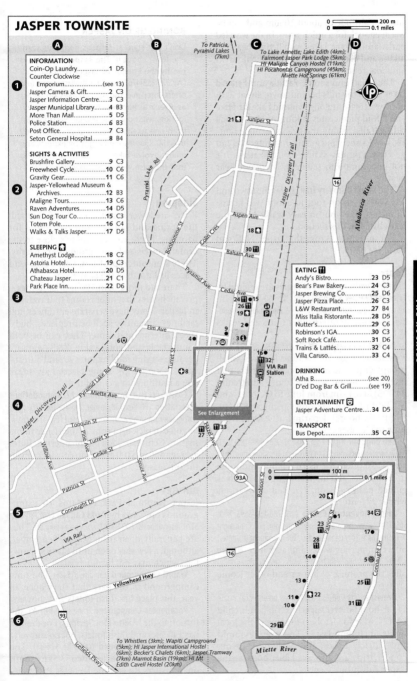

JASPER TOWNSITE

| 0 | 200 m |
| 0 | 0.1 miles |

INFORMATION
Coin-Op Laundry..................1 D5
Counter Clockwise
   Emporium.....................(see 13)
Jasper Camera & Gift............2 C3
Jasper Information Centre......3 C3
Jasper Municipal Library.......4 B3
More Than Mail..................5 D5
Police Station.....................6 B3
Post Office.........................7 C3
Seton General Hospital........8 B4

SIGHTS & ACTIVITIES
Brushfire Gallery..................9 C3
Freewheel Cycle................10 C6
Gravity Gear......................11 C6
Jasper-Yellowhead Museum &
   Archives........................12 B3
Maligne Tours....................13 C6
Raven Adventures..............14 D5
Sun Dog Tour Co................15 D5
Totem Pole........................16 C4
Walks & Talks Jasper..........17 D5

SLEEPING 🏠
Amethyst Lodge..................18 C2
Astoria Hotel......................19 C3
Athabasca Hotel.................20 D5
Chateau Jasper..................21 C1
Park Place Inn....................22 D6

EATING 🍴
Andy's Bistro......................23 D5
Bear's Paw Bakery..............24 C3
Jasper Brewing Co..............25 D6
Jasper Pizza Place..............26 C3
L&W Restaurant..................27 B4
Miss Italia Ristorante..........28 D5
Nutter's............................29 C6
Robinson's IGA...................30 C3
Soft Rock Café...................31 D6
Trains & Lattés...................32 C4
Villa Caruso.......................33 C4

DRINKING
Atha B..............................(see 20)
D'ed Dog Bar & Grill..........(see 19)

ENTERTAINMENT 🎭
Jasper Adventure Centre.....34 D5

TRANSPORT
Bus Depot.........................35 C4

To Patricia,
Pyramid Lakes
(7km)

To Lake Annette; Lake Edith (4km);
Fairmont Jasper Park Lodge (5km);
HI Maligne Canyon Hostel (11km);
HI Pocahontas Campground (45km);
Miette Hot Springs (61km)

Juniper St

Patricia Cir

Jasper Discovery Trail

Athabasca River

16

Pyramid Lake Rd

Aspen Ave

Balsam Ave

Bonhomme St

Colin Cres

Pyramid Ave

Cedar Ave

Elm Ave

Turret St

Patricia St

Maligne Ave

Pyramid Lake Rd

Miette Ave

Tonquin St

Pine Ave

Turret St

Geikie St

Willow Ave

Spruce Ave

Patricia St

Connaught Dr

VIA Rail

93A

16

Yellowhead Hwy

93

Icefields Pkwy

VIA Rail
Station

See Enlargement

Jasper Ave

Robson St

Miette Ave

Patricia St

Connaught Dr

0 | 100 m
0 | 0.1 miles

To Whistlers (3km); Wapiti Campground
(5km); HI Jasper International Hostel
(6km); Becker's Chalets (6km); Jasper Tramway
(7km) Marmot Basin (19km); HI Mt.
Edith Cavell Hostel (20km)

Miette River

THE ROCKIES

sit at an altitude of about 1000m and can be warm enough for a quick swim. In the wooded parks around the lakes, you'll find beaches, hiking and biking on paved trails, picnic areas and boat rentals.

The small and serene **Patricia** and **Pyramid Lakes** are in the hills behind town, about 7km northwest of town along Pyramid Lake Rd. Here you'll find picnic sites, hiking and horseback riding trails, fishing and beaches, canoe rentals, kayaks and windsurfers. In winter you can go cross-country skiing or ice skating. It's not uncommon to see deer, coyote or bear nearby.

The **Jasper Discovery Trail** circles the town and lets you do so on foot in about two hours. Branches take you on easy walks to all the lakes listed in this section.

For activities across the Jasper National Park, see p305.

Tours

Historic walking tours of Jasper are offered by **Friends of Jasper National Park** (☎ 780-852-4767; Jasper Information Centre; tours $2; ☒ 7:30pm mid-May–mid-Sep). The group offers other tours and walks as well.

Walks & Talks Jasper (☎ 780-852-4994, 888-242-3343; www.walksntalks.com; 626 Connaught Dr) leads small groups of people on personalized tours that include two-hour wildlife tours (adult/child $45/25) at 6:45am from June to October, and Mt Edith Cavell Meadows picnics ($70/40; five to six hours) departing at 9:30am from June to October).

Sun Dog Touring Co (☎ 780-852-9663, 888-786-3641; www.sundogtours.com; 414 Connaught Dr; tours adult/child from $50/35) offers the usual wildlife and tours to local icons, and interesting options such as guided train rides on VIA Rail and various winter adventures.

Jasper Adventure Centre (☎ 780-852-5595; 800-565-7547; www.jasperadventurecentre.com; 604 Connaught Dr in the Chaba Theatre in summer, 306 Connaught Dr winter) offers numerous walks and activities. **Nature walks** (adult/child $40/20; ☒ walks several times daily) offer the promise of beaver and other iconic critters.

Brewster (☎ 780-852-3332; www.brewster.ca) runs a four-hour **Discover Jasper** bus trip (adult/child $48/24, May to October) to some of the local sights, including Jasper Tramway, Pyramid and Patricia Lakes, and Maligne Canyon. Longer trips are also available; book at the Jasper Adventure Centre.

BONING UP ON JASPER

Don't just stare at Jasper's gorgeous scenery, learn about it. The **Jasper Institute** is run by the Friends of Jasper National Park (☎ 780-852-4767; www.friendsofjasper.com) and offers intensive summer courses on topics as diverse as bird-watching, wilderness navigation, wildflowers and bear. Sessions last from one to three days and cost from $60 to $150. Classes are taught by experts and many involve hikes for hands-on learning (not the case with bear, however…).

Sleeping

Prices are lower here than in Banff, but still the spring and fall are your best times for bargains. There are good motels close to the center; hostels and campgrounds are nearby. There's an outcrop of low-key higher-end places just north of the center.

There are more than 100 tourist homes – private homes that offer rooms to travelers – in Jasper. Many have separate entrances, full facilities, amenities such as fireplaces, high-speed internet and more. They can be both comfortable and good value. B&Bs are rare because serving food requires several bureaucratic hoop jumps. Some places may sneak you a muffin with a cup of tea.

Contact the **Jasper Home Accommodations Association** (PO Box 758, Jasper, Alberta T0E 1E0; www.stayinjasper.com) to receive its useful list of rooms, or you can pick up a copy at the Jasper Information Centre, or look on the internet. Rates average $60 to $100 and drop considerably in the off-season.

BUDGET

Jasper National Park contains 10 campgrounds operated by **Parks Canada** (☎ 780-852-6176, reservations 877-737-3783; www.pccamping.ca). They are generally open from May to September, although a few stay open until the first snowfall (which may not be much later).

Wapiti Campground (campsite $15-28) The only campground in the park that stays open all year, this place has flush toilets and showers.

Pocahontas Campground (campsite $19) At the turnoff to the Miette Hot Springs, Pocahontas has 140 sites and flush toilets, but no showers.

Whistlers Campground (campsite $24-33) The closest campground to town, 3.5km south on Whistlers Rd (off the Icefields Parkway), this gigantic place – which includes electricity, showers and flush toilets – can get crowded, despite having 781 sites. In summer, films and talks are presented nightly.

HI Jasper International Hostel (☎ 780-852-3215, 877-852-0781; www.hihostels.ca; dm/r from \$22/60; 🖵) On Whistlers Rd toward the Jasper Tramway, 6.3km south of Jasper, this 84-bed hostel runs a shuttle bus into town.

Also south of Jasper are two HI hostels that can be booked through the Jasper hostel:

HI Mt Edith Cavell Hostel (dm from \$20; 🕙 mid-Jun–mid-Oct) On Mt Edith Cavell Rd 13km from the junction with Hwy 93A, this 32-bed place sits below the Angel Glacier. It offers excellent access to hiking trails, including the gorgeous Tonquin Valley. The rustic accommodations include outhouses and creek water only.

HI Maligne Canyon Hostel (dm from \$20; 🕙 closed Wed Nov-Apr) Barebones but close to good hiking, this place 11.5km east of town on Maligne Canyon Rd, has 24 beds in two cabins.

MIDRANGE

Athabasca Hotel (☎ 780-852-3386, 877-542-8422; www.athabascahotel.com; 510 Patricia St; r \$75-160) Built in 1929, the historic Athabasca Hotel has been much remodeled through the years. The present room decor is frilly in a vibrant way that's not really appealing. Cheaper rooms share bathrooms and are great deals in summer. Avoid rooms over the legendary Atha B bar.

Becker's Chalets (☎ 780-852-3779; www.beckerschalets.com; Icefields Parkway; r \$80-180) Located on a beautiful bend of the Athabasca River, tidy Becker's Chalet resort is 6km south of town. There are 188 units here, some of them clumped together in buildings and others in cute little log cabin-style buildings down by the water. Styles vary greatly. The restaurant wins plaudits.

Astoria Hotel (☎ 780-852-3351, 800-661-7343; www.astoriahotel.com; 404 Connaught Dr; r from \$120; 🏵 🖵) Of the 35 rooms, those in the front are best as they have evocative views of passing trains with a backdrop of craggy mountains. There's wi-fi throughout.

Amethyst Lodge (☎ 780-852-3394, 888-852-7737; www.mtn-park-lodges.com; 200 Connaught Dr; r from \$130; 🏵 🖵) This is one of those places you want to be on the inside looking out. But it's what's inside that counts and here the 97 rooms are large, have wi-fi and some have balconies. Watch for frequent specials, even in summer.

TOP END

Chateau Jasper (☎ 780-852-5644, 800-661-9323; www.decorehotels.com; 96 Geikie St; r from \$180; 🏵 🖵 🖳) In a quiet neighborhood with a couple of other top-end places a 10-minute walk north of the center, this is a refined low-rise motel with 119 large rooms and an indoor pool, hot tub, pub and restaurant. There's wi-fi throughout.

Park Place Inn (☎ 780-852-9770, 866-852-9770; www.parkplaceinn.com; 623 Patricia St; r \$180-250; 🏵 🖵) It looks a bit modern and bland from the outside, but inside, the 12 rooms here are all decorated in different styles from the 1930s. Some have claw-foot tubs. It's a soothing, comfy place.

Fairmont Jasper Park Lodge (☎ 780-852-3301, 800-441-1414; www.fairmont.com; r \$450-750; 🅿 🏵 🖵 🖳) Close to town, except that the intervening Lac Beauvert and the Athabasca River make it a 5km drive northeast, this lodge has a massive stone and log cabin–style main building, and nine restaurants and bars. The resort features every possible amenity, including horseback riding and a world-class golf course. The 446 rooms are scattered about in low-rise buildings.

Eating & Drinking

The best supermarket is **Robinson's IGA** (☎ 780-852-3195; 218 Connaught Dr; 🕙 8am-6pm).

Nutter's (☎ 780-852-5844; 622 Patricia St; 🕙 9am-7pm) The name isn't a commentary on the people who flock here for all manner of organic, vegan and macrobiotic foods.

our pick **Trains & Lattés** (☎ 780-852-7444; Jasper Train Station; snacks from \$3; 🕙 8am-6pm) A real find! Enjoy fresh sandwiches on great bread, soups, smoothies, coffees and more at this stand, which also sells all manner of train-related mags and books, plus model trains. Enjoy your treats at tables trackside in the sun.

Bear's Paw Bakery (☎ 780-852-3233; 4 Cedar Ave; snacks from \$3; 🕙 6am-6pm Tue-Sun) Ever-expanding, this top-notch bakery and café has great coffee, drinks and treats that range from sinful to merely sweet. Sandwiches can sell out early at lunch.

Soft Rock Café (☎ 780-852-5850; 632 Connaught Dr; meals \$6-14; 🕙 7am-10pm; 🖵) This coffee and sandwich place by day does a paradigm shift and serves Thai food at night. Patrons can then do their own paradigm shift and after their Pad Thai go shoot pool in the back. Many prefer to lounge at the sidewalk tables.

THE ROCKIES

L&W Restaurant (☎ 852-4114; cnr Hazel Ave & Patricia St; meals $8-20) A classic Greek coffee shop with a huge menu of comfort food and faves that range from huge breakfasts to thick steaks. Dine in one of the atrium rooms or outside on the terrace.

Jasper Pizza Place (☎ 780-852-3225; 402 Connaught Dr; meals $10-20; ⏰ 11am-late) The thin and cracker-crisp pizza is excellent. There's also many specials, burgers, salads and pasta. For a real treat, grab a rooftop table and delight in the panorama. Kids always enjoy it here.

Miss Italia Ristorante (☎ 780-852-4002; 2nd fl, 610 Patricia St; meals $10-20; ⏰ 11:30am-9:30pm) Follow the scent of garlic up the stairs to get to this fun and friendly place where the collection of goofy and silly posters grows each year. The pasta is made fresh daily and there's a few terrace tables.

Jasper Brewing Co (☎ 780-852-4111; 624 Connaught Dr; meals $10-25; ⏰ 11am-11pm) Look for the large antelope out front of this tasty microbrewery that always has six kinds of beer on tap, from pilsner to stout. The light and open interior is a good place to enjoy burgers, ribs and more.

Villa Caruso (☎ 780-852-3920; 640 Connaught Dr; meals $20-35; ⏰ 11am-10pm) Bright, open and bustling, the 2nd-floor Villa Caruso has good casual lunches. Dinners center on fresh fish, excellent steaks and prime rib. Seasonal dishes use local ingredients. There are balcony tables outside in season and the owners are simply lovely.

Andy's Bistro (☎ 780-852-4559; 606 Patricia St; meals $20-35; ⏰ 5-10pm) Appropriately located next to a fine wine shop, Andy's has an ambitious and creative menu that changes regularly. Choices may include blackened rare tuna or pork chops filled with mushrooms. The small dining room has tables topped with white tablecloths and fresh flowers. The Swiss chef will make you a sublime fondue for two.

Entertainment

Except for the cries of rutting elk, Jasper can get quiet pretty early. Make your own noises at the places listed here, which can be lively quite late. Several of the places listed under Eating & Drinking in this section are good for a beer.

Atha B (☎ 403-852-3386; Athabasca Hotel, 510 Patricia St; ⏰ 5pm-late) In the Athabasca Hotel, this rowdy institution (!) regularly features live rock and country plus dancing.

De'd Dog Bar & Grill (☎ 780-852-3351; 404 Connaught Dr; ⏰ noon-late) Here you can see the summer temp workers forming new liaisons. Gets a fun local crowd who enjoy the good beer on tap and pondering the gallery of dog photos.

Getting There & Away

BUS
Brewster (☎ 780-852-3332; www.brewster.ca; 607 Connaught Dr) In the bus depot in the train station, operates buses to Banff ($70/35, five hours, one daily May to mid-October) via Lake Louise.

Greyhound (☎ 780-852-3926; 607 Connaught Dr) In the bus depot in the VIA Rail station. Services to Edmonton ($62, 4½ hours, four daily), Prince George ($64, four hours, three daily) and Vancouver ($125, 12 hours, two daily). Luggage-storage service.

Mountain Connector (☎ 780-852-1575, 888-786-3641; www.mountainconnector.com; ⏰ Dec-Apr) Has winter and spring service between Jasper and Banff (adult/child $53/29, four hours, one daily) via Lake Louise. Ask about trips to Calgary.

TRAIN
VIA Rail (☎ 780-852-4102; 607 Connaught Dr) has a minihub in Jasper. The *Canadian* stops at Jasper three times a week en route between Vancouver and Toronto. In addition, the *Skeena* runs three times a week to Prince George, where the train continues to Prince Rupert after an overnight stay.

Getting Around

TO/FROM THE AIRPORT
From May to October, **Brewster** (☎ 780-852-3332; www.brewster.ca) has a bus to Calgary International airport (adult/child $89/44.50, eight hours, one daily).

CAR
Three rental-car firms share space in the train station, at 607 Connaught Dr.
Dollar (☎ 780-852-4506)
Hertz (☎ 780-852-9640)
National (☎ 780-852-1117)

TAXI
Jasper Taxi (☎ 780-852-3600)

AROUND JASPER

About 12km east of Jasper on the way to Maligne (ma-*leen*) Lake on Maligne Lake Rd, you'll pass **Maligne Canyon**, a limestone gorge about 50m deep, with waterfalls and interesting rock formations. You can walk from the teahouse along the floor of the canyon. Continue 16km further up the road to **Medicine Lake**, the level of which rises and falls due to underground caverns; sometimes the lake disappears completely.

The largest glacier-fed lake in the Rockies and the second-largest in the world, **Maligne Lake** lies 48km southeast of Jasper at the end of Maligne Lake Rd. The lake is promoted as one of the most scenic of mountain lakes, but this will be difficult to understand if you only stay near the parking lots and chalet. A little effort, however, will be rewarded. A stroll down the **east side lake trail** takes under an hour and leaves 90% of the crowds behind.

Maligne Tours (ticket office ☎ 780-852-3370; Jasper Tour Center, 616 Patricia St; www.malignelake.com) has a lock on local activities. The Chalet offers a range of decent food. Nearby you can rent a canoe ($25 per hour) – recommended – at the historic Curly Philips Boathouse. **Boat cruises to Spirit Island** (adult/child $41/20; ☺ frequent boats, Jun-Aug) are necessary if you want the iconic shot of the lake, island and soaring peaks beyond. And don't forget to stop off a few times on your drive to and from the lake – there are a number of almost untouched trails alongside the rushing **Maligne River**.

If you don't have a car to get to the lake, Maligne Tours runs a **shuttle service** (one way $17; ☺ mid-May–Oct) from Jasper.

To rest your weary bones, stop at **Miette Hot Springs** (☎ 780-866-3939; adult/child $7/6; ☺ 10am-9pm May–mid-Oct), 61km northeast of Jasper off the Yellowhead Hwy (Hwy 16) near the park boundary. Miette has the warmest mineral waters in the Canadian Rockies. Left alone, the springs produce a scalding 53.9°C, but the water is cooled to a more reasonable 39°C. The modern spa includes three pools (hot, warm and freezing) and has a forest setting.

Activities
HIKING
Fewer hikers tramp through Jasper than Banff, but more wildlife scampers through the woods, which means that you stand a good chance of spotting some. In addition to the hikes around the lakes close to Jasper, many other paths meander through the terrain. Get Parks Canada's *Day Hikers' Guide to Jasper National Park*. It lists hikes lasting from a couple of hours to all day. If the weather has been wet, you may want to avoid the lower horse trails, which can become mud baths. Topographic maps are available for all routes; buy them at the Jasper Information Centre (p300).

If you're hiking overnight, pick up copies of Parks Canada's *Backcountry Visitors' Guide* and the *Summer Trails Jasper National Park*, which offers overnight trail descriptions along with a map. If you're camping in the back-country, you have to obtain a backcountry permit from Parks Canada.

Just one of many lightly used trails near Jasper, the 12km hike to **Jacques Lake** combines remote lakes and ponds, mountain vistas and the final goal, which shimmers with greens and blues through the day. The difficulty is moderate; there's an elevation change of 90m. Most people do this in one eight-hour stretch, but there are crude campsites at Jacques Lake you can use. The trailhead is at the Beaver Creek Picnic Area at Medicine Lake, 26km along Maligne Rd.

CYCLING & MOUNTAIN BIKING
As in Banff National Park, you can cycle on the highways and on most of the trails in the park. For more information, pick up the *Trail Bicycling Guide Jasper National Park* at the Jasper Information Centre. **Freewheel Cycle** (☎ 780-852-3898; www.freewheeljasper.com; 618 Patricia St; bike rentals per hr from $6; ☺ 8am-8pm) has rentals and advice.

ROCK CLIMBING
With all the rock around, it's no wonder climbers aren't sure where to climb first in Jasper. Experienced climbers like to head to the popular Mt Morro, Messner Ridge, Mt Athabasca, Mt Andromeda and Mt Edith Cavell. In winter you can ice climb on the frozen waterfalls. Stop by **Gravity Gear** (☎ 780-852-3155, 888-852-3155; www.gravitygearjasper.com; 618 Patricia St; ☺ 9am-8pm), where you can get good advice, leads on guides and rent equipment.

WHITE-WATER RAFTING
Calm to turbulent rafting can be found on the **Sunwapta River** and the **Athabasca River** near Athabasca Falls. Rafting (or any boat usage) is prohibited on the **Maligne River** to protect the habitat for threatened Harlequin ducks.

Numerous companies offer trips of varying lengths, including the tour companies in Jasper (p302). **Raven Adventures** (☎ 780-852-4292; 610 Patricia St; trips from $50) runs trips on the Athabasca and the Sunwapta. Look for its bright purple rafts on the water.

THE ROCKIES

SKIING & SNOWBOARDING

Jasper National Park's only ski area is **Marmot Basin** (☎ 780-852-3816, 800-473-8135; www.skimarmot .com; 1-day lift pass adult/child $59/21), which lies 19km southwest of town off Hwy 93A. It features 84 good trails for both beginners and experts, plenty of scenic cross-country trails, nine lifts and a chalet. The drop is 914m.

Near Maligne Lake, the **Moose Lake Loop** (8km) and the trail in the **Bald Hills** (11km) are easy introductions to the 200km of cross-country skiing in the park.

The skiing season usually runs from December to April. Numerous companies also offer snowshoe treks and other icy excitement.

MOUNT ROBSON PROVINCIAL PARK

The highest peak in the Canadian Rockies is not in one of the great national parks but sits majestically in its own BC provincial park to the west of Jasper National Park. The obvious high spot of a visit are the views of 3954m Mt Robson, a peak that has been awing folks for thousands of years. The Yellowhead Hwy (Hwy 16) follows some of the best scenery in the park. It also follows the mainline of the Canadian National Railroad, the second of the great trans-continental lines after that of the CPR (see boxed text, p250). Watch for roadside markers detailing the work of the interned Japanese laborers who built this stretch of road during WWII.

Ambitious climbers have been tackling Mt Robson since 1907, but the sharp-edged ice castle wasn't successfully tackled until 1913. Mountaineers from all over the world come every summer to try to repeat this feat on Robson, considered one of the world's most challenging climbs.

At the base of the mountain, the **Mount Robson VIC** (☎ 250-566-4325; 8am-5pm Jun & Sep, 8am-7pm Jul & Aug) offers information on the park and runs interpretive programs during summer.

One of the highlights of the park is the 22km hike to **Berg Lake**, a two-day hike that follows the base of Mt Robson and passes through the Valley of a Thousand Falls (that's water, not hikers). Along the way, you'll pass numerous glaciers, including the Berg Glacier, which clings to Robson's northwest face. Periodically, bits of glacier fall into the lake, filling it with icebergs. You need to register and pay at the park **visitor center** (☎ 800-689-9025; www.discover camping.ca; backcountry fee $5) at Mt Robson before venturing onto the Berg Lake Trail.

The Fraser River begins its long and sometimes tumultuous journey through British Columbia at its headwaters in the southwest corner of the park. (The Fraser spills into the Pacific Ocean near Vancouver after traveling some 1280km.) In August and September you can see salmon spawning in the river at Rearguard Falls. You also stand an excellent chance of seeing moose in the park.

Adjoining the park's western end is the tiny **Mount Terry Fox Provincial Park**, named after the runner who lost a leg to cancer then attempted to run what he called the 'Marathon of Hope' across Canada, aiming to raise $1 from every Canadian for cancer research. Fox averaged a remarkable 37km a day until a recurrence of cancer forced him to end his run after 144 days and 5376km.

Accommodations include three park-run campgrounds and two private spots. Close to the VIC, both **Robson Meadows Campground** and **Robson River Campground** offer showers, flush toilets and firewood (☎ 800-689-9025; www.discover camping.ca; campsite $17; mid-May–Sep). **Lucerne Campground** (campsite $14; mid-May–Sep) is 10km west of the Alberta border on the southern shore of Yellowhead Lake. The facilities include only pit toilets and pump water.

Mount Robson Lodge (☎ 250-566-4821, 888-566-4821; www.mountrobsonlodge.com; r $70-125; May-Sep) has 18 log cabins and rooms with fine views of the mountain and the Fraser River.

Cariboo-Chilcotin & Coast

This vast region in the heart of BC nicely encapsulates the diversity of beauty and culture found through the province. Inland, the Cariboo region is home to scores of ranches, many of which you can visit. It follows the 1858 Cariboo Wagon Rd (now known as the Gold Rush Trail), which starts at 'Mile 0' in Lillooet and heads north to the historic town of Barkerville. Towns named for their distance from Lillooet sprouted up along the route, which explains unlikely names such as 100 Mile House, 108 Mile House and 150 Mile House.

West of here, the Chilcotin region is one big open space with only a few little towns and one long paved road – Hwy 20. It's a place of solitude and has several almost-unvisited provincial parks. After the road takes a sudden drop down the infamous Hill you are suddenly transported to an entirely different BC – one of dramatic weather, enormous trees, sheer mountain faces and limitless wildlife.

The Bella Coola Valley is one of the few places in BC where you can penetrate deep into the legendary Great Bear Rainforest, the largest coastal temperate rain forest left on the planet. Almost entirely wild, you can use the quirky and delightful valley as your starting point to truly wild adventure.

Best of all, by using the BC Ferries Discovery Coast service to Port Hardy on Vancouver Island, you can tour the region in a circle, never once repeating yourself. It's one of the best itineraries in BC.

HIGHLIGHTS

- Heading out by boat to see the **Great Bear Rainforest** (p319) from Bella Coola
- Tackling the ultimate canoe circuit at **Bowron Lake** (p312)
- Beholding Helmcken Falls in **Wells Gray Provincial Park** (p314)
- Trekking in the footsteps of Alexander Mackenzie from the **Bella Coola Valley** (p317)
- Listening for echoes of the Gold Rush in **Barkerville** (p311)

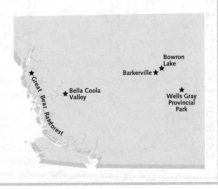

CARIBOO-CHILCOTIN & COAST

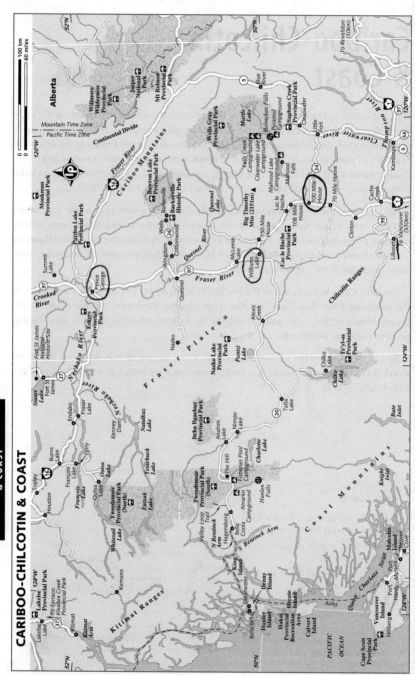

CARIBOO

Stretching from the namesake Cariboo Mountains in the east to the Fraser Valley in the west, the Cariboo Region of BC takes in vast ranchland, huge tracks of forest and several provincial parks. It's dominated by no one city, rather, places like Williams Lake provide travelers with a chance to recharge and continue their journeys. It's a place of cowboys and lumberjacks plus the visitor or two who knows there are some real gems here like Wells Gray Provincial Park and Bowron Lake.

Cariboo was the site of a gold rush in 1862, and when word spread that gold had been found, thousands of gold-diggers came rushing in from California and the east. For more, see p311.

GOLD RUSH TRAIL/CARIBOO HIGHWAY

With boundless open ranges and rolling grassy hills, the southern interior makes excellent territory for cattle raising. Working ranches are tucked into many folds of the Cariboo-Chilcotin landscape. The Cariboo alone boasts 500 cattle ranches, which produce 20% of the beef for the province.

Following the Gold Rush Trail (Hwy 97) north of Lillooet, you'll find **Clinton**, which in the 1860s had the evocative name Junction as numerous trails to the gold fields branched out from here. Its downtown streets feature western decor and some roaming dudes in cowboy boots.

The retail and service hub of the southern Cariboo region, **100 Mile House**, offers some good cross-country skiing.

Williams Lake
pop 11,900

Williams Lake is a major crossroads: you can follow Hwy 20 west 456km to the coastal town of Bella Coola (p317); or you can follow the Cariboo Hwy (Hwy 97) north to McLeese Lake, a small lakeside resort with log cabins, then on to Quesnel and Prince George (240km). To the south are Kamloops and Vancouver.

Williams Lake is all about extracting wealth from trees. Lumber yards, piles of logs and other evidence of the town's five mills surround the downtown area. About 65% of the population works in forestry. As such, the town is a rather bland supply hub known mostly for a huge cowboy party that is BC's answer to the Calgary Stampede.

RIDE 'EM COWBOY

There are some professions – say ditch-digging – where the idea of people paying good money to partake in the work would be hooted at. 'You want to pay good money to get sweaty and dirty?' would be a predictable gibe. However, this wouldn't be the case with cattle ranches where lots of people pay good money every year to get sweaty and dirty and love every minute of it.

The Cariboo region has scores of cattle ranches and many accept guests who revel at the chance to spend time in the iconic mountainous wilderness, the kind of tree-studded pasturelands that bring a tear to the eye while watching westerns and cause suburbanites to go and buy SUVs.

The guest ranches span the spectrum of experiences. Some are little more than luxury resorts, with golf courses, spas and maybe a bean or two mixed in with the salsa at the gourmet dinner. But others really are working ranches and guests do get a chance to experience the daily lives of ranchers – even if they are spared the constant concern about commodities prices, government regulation, mad cow disease and the like.

Many are found in the region around Clinton. Most charge about $150 to $250 per person per night (kids less) and that includes all meals and activities – and what activities they are! Lots of horse riding yes, but at many you can go right along on a cattle drive (where the cowboys often say it's easier to herd the cattle than the dudes) as well as learn more about the land on guided hikes and rides.

The **BC Guest Ranchers Association** (☎ 877-278-2922; www.bcgra.com) has detailed listings of ranches across the province. Two popular ones in the Cariboo are **Crystal Waters Guest Ranch** (☎ 604-465-9829; www.crystalwatersranch.com), which has log cabins at its lakeside location off Hwy 24 east of 100 Mile House, and **Wolf Valley Guest Ranch** (☎ 250-395-6694; www.wolfvalleyranch.com) where you can work the trail kinks out in a sauna or gather round a campfire.

INFORMATION

Discovery Centre (☎ 250-392-5025; www.williamslake chamber.com; 1660 Broadway S, off Hwy 97; ☺ 9am-5pm summer, 9am-4pm rest of year) is not your usual Visitor Information Centre. Opened late in 2006, it is a fantasy of wood constructed by two local log-home builders. The roof soars 17m and there are fascinating displays about the region. Best of all, the staff can help you plan trips throughout the Cariboo, Chilcotin and the coast. They have especially good information about driving Hwy 20 (p315).

SIGHTS & ACTIVITIES

In 1919 the Pacific Great Eastern Railway (later BC Rail and now the Canadian National) pushed its way into Williams Lake. People partied so much they decided to reenact the whole hootenanny again the following year. This marked the birth of the **Williams Lake Stampede** (☎ 250-398-8388, 800-717-6336; williamslakestampede.com), an annual four-day ho-down that happens on the Stampede Grounds in late June and/or early July, when the town's population more than doubles with cowpokes and cowpoke wannabes. It's serious business for the cowboys who come here from all over to compete in activities such as roping, barrel racing and the always exciting bull riding. Fringe events include the popular Stampede Queen Coronation and loggers' sports. Hotels fill up while the stampede takes over town, and the event keeps getting bigger. Tickets to festival events cost $15 to $50.

The small but interesting **Museum of the Cariboo Chilcotin** (☎ 250-392-7404; 113 4th Ave N; adult/child $2/free; ☺ 10am-4pm Mon-Sat Jun-Aug, 11am-4pm Tue-Sat Sep-May) features a very interesting exhibit on the history and paraphernalia of the Stampede, including photos of each 'Queen' from the annual pageant, dating back to 1933. Note how racial attitudes used to demand two queens. The museum also explores the history of ranching and logging in the area and includes the **BC Cowboy Hall of Fame**.

The old train station has been reborn as the **Station House Gallery** (☎ 250-392-6113; 1 Mackenzie Ave N; ☺ 10am-5pm Mon-Sat) and has exhibits on local, regional and touring artists. There're some talented folks in them thar hills.

SLEEPING & EATING

Being a crossroads, Williams Lake has several chain motels. Outside of Stampede season (short as it is), you'll be able to find a room at a good price. There are several modest but good places to eat in the center that are worth bypassing the crossroads chains to seek out.

Wildwood RV Park (☎ 250-989-4711; letscamp@wlbc .net; 4195 Wildwood Rd; campsite $15-23) Located 14km north of Williams Lake, off Hwy 97, the 36 sites here have good shade.

Drummond Lodge Motel (☎ 250-392-5334, 800-667-4555; www.drummondlodge.com; 1405 Hwy 97 S; r $75-100; ❄ ▢) The best bet of the non-chains, this 23-unit place near the Discovery Centre has great views of the lake as well as extensive gardens in the spacious grounds. There's high-speed internet access in the rooms – get one with a balcony.

Trattoria Pasta Shop (☎ 250-398-7170; 23A S 1st Ave; meals $10-20; ☺ 11am-8pm Mon-Sat) This pasta joint has surprisingly good Italian food. Many enjoy the create-your-own option where you pick the sauce, pasta and what goes in it.

GETTING THERE & AROUND

Buses run north to Prince George ($41, 3½ hours, three daily) and south to Vancouver ($86, nine hours, three daily) from the **Greyhound bus depot** (☎ 250-398-7733; 215 Donald Rd), just off Hwy 97.

Quesnel

pop 10,500

Neither Quesnel's picturesque setting at the confluence of the Fraser and Quesnel Rivers nor the carefully cultivated flowers along the riverfront trails can disguise the fact that this is first and foremost a logging town, similar to Williams Lake 124km south. However, it does make for a good pause on your journey; the downtown has several interesting cafés and shops.

The **Visitor Info Centre** (☎ 250-992-8716; www.north cariboo.com; 703 Carson Ave; ☺ 8am-6pm Jun-Sep, 9am-4pm Tue-Sat Oct-May) offers free internet access. From Quesnel, Hwy 26 leads east to the area's main attractions, Barkerville Historic Park (opposite) and Bowron Lake Provincial Park (p312).

SIGHTS & ACTIVITIES

The petite **Quesnel Museum** (703 Carson Ave; adult/child $3/1.50; ☺ 8am-6pm daily Jun-Sep, 9am-4pm Tue-Sat Oct-May), in the same building as the VIC, features a quirky array of antiques from the gold-rush days and a fascinating cache of historical photos of early residents.

An **observation tower** at the north end of town off Hwy 97 overlooks Two-Mile Flat, a large industrial area devoted to wood products. It's a vast, buzzing, humming and steaming place with action in all directions. There's action around the clock as beetle-killed trees (see the boxed text, p332) are brought in for processing at a record rate.

Feel like a walk in the woods? One of the great walks is northwest of Quesnel; the refurbished **Alexander Mackenzie Heritage Trail** follows ancient trails from the Fraser River west to Bella Coola, on the Pacific Ocean. In 1793 Alexander Mackenzie made the first recorded crossing of continental North America in his search to find a supply route to the Pacific Ocean. His carved graffiti can still be seen in a rock near Bella Coola (p319). This 420km trail winds its way through forest and mountains and makes for a tough 16-day walk. At least one food drop is required. You can do some of the more accessible segments for just a few days – eg the section through the southern end of Tweedsmuir Provincial Park. You can also take day hikes from Quesnel. To get to the trailhead, follow Blackwater Rd west from Quesnel. For trail guides, contact the **Alexander Mackenzie Trail Association** (☎ 250-762-3002; PO Box 425, Station A, Kelowna, BC V1Y 7P1). For more information about hiking in the area, contact the **Quesnel Forest Office** (☎ 250-992-4400; 322 Johnston Ave, Quesnel, BC, V2J 3M5).

SLEEPING & EATING

Quesnel has several place to eat worth checking out in the center.

Talisman Inn (☎ 250-992-7247, 800-663-8090; www .talismaninn.bc.ca; 753 Front St; r $60-110; 🎇 🖳) Just north of downtown off Hwy 97, the Talisman will bring broadband seekers good luck: every one of the 86 motel-style rooms is equipped. Some have in-floor Jacuzzis.

our pick **Granville's Coffee** (☎ 250-992-3667; 383 Reid St; meals $5-10; 🕑 7am-10pm Mon-Sat, 8am-5pm Sun) What a delightful place! From the water dish for dogs outside to the goofy movie posters inside, this café exudes whimsy. It also exudes great food. Homemade baked goods, chili, huge sandwiches and more. Oh, and the sign in the window: 'Sorry we're open.'

GETTING THERE & AWAY

Greyhound (☎ 250-992-2231; 365 Kinchant St) buses run south to Kamloops ($62, one daily, six hours) and Vancouver ($99, three daily, 10 hours), and north to Prince George ($21, three daily, two hours). Quesnel airport (YQZ) is just north of

town at the junction of Hwys 97 and 26. Air Canada Jazz flies to/from Vancouver.

BARKERVILLE & AROUND

BC's most authentic heritage town is well off the beaten path so you feel transported back into the past even before you get there.

Between 1858 and 1861, when the Cariboo Wagon Rd (now Hwy 97) edged north from Kamloops to Quesnel, ramshackle towns hastily built by gold prospectors, who had descended on the region from around the world, sprang up along the road. In 1862 one member of this new international population hit the jackpot, making $1000 in the first two days of his claim. Despite his luck, Cornishman Billy Barker probably had no clue that more than 100,000 salivating miners would leap into his footsteps, crossing rivers, creeks and lakes to storm the Cariboo Wagon Rd in search of gold. Soon Barkerville sprang up to become, for a brief time, the largest city west of Chicago and north of San Francisco. In its heyday, some 10,000 people resided in the muddy town, hoping to hit jackpots of their own.

Sights & Activities

BARKERVILLE HISTORIC PARK

If Billy was clueless about the gold rush, then he most certainly never predicted that people would still be flocking here to see Barkerville as it was, albeit with more fudge for sale than when the miners were here. Fortunately there is the odd bit of horse poop here and there to lend some authenticity.

The restored town, now called **Barkerville Historic Park** (☎ 888-994-3332 ext 29; www.barkerville .ca; adult/child $12.50/3.50; 🕑 8am-8pm mid-May–Sep), is 82km east of Quesnel at the end of Hwy 26. More than 125 buildings have been restored to their former glory, including a hotel, various

---

TOP FIVE PLACES TO GO BARE (NOT WITH A BEAR)

- In the hot tub at a **guest ranch** (p309)
- In the **hot springs** (p319) off Bella Coola
- In bracing **Turner Lake** (p316)
- On your own beach at **Bowron Lake Provincial Park** (p312)
- Anywhere you want in **Ts'yl-os Provincial Park** (see the boxed text, p315)

CARIBOO-CHILCOTIN & COAST

stores and a saloon. In summer, people dressed in period garb roam through town, and if you can tune out the crowds it actually manages to create a historical mood. (In the Theatre Royal, dancing shows are staged in a family-friendly manner that would have been pelted by the rough-and-tumble miners.) The free historic walking tours relate the history of the gold rush, the experience of the Chinese workers who built the Cariboo Hwy and the finer details of the art of panning for gold.

Outside of summer, the town site is open but most of the attractions are closed, which may actually make for a more evocative visit. Wind rustles the trees and as you walk the quiet streets you just might be able to take yourself back in time – until you step in that horse poop.

WELLS
Nearby Wells, 8km west of Barkerville, is also a historic town but without the paid folks in costume. The Wells **Visitor Info Centre** (☎ 250-994-2323, 877-451-9355; www.wellsbc.com; 4120 Pooley St; ☻ 9am-6pm Jun-Aug) runs an information center just off the highway in a small old general store. The town exists in two closely related parts: the older area up on the hill and the string of shops along the highway.

COTTONWOOD HOUSE HISTORIC SITE
This is a worthwhile stop, 26km east of Quesnel on Hwy 26, whether you are coming or going from Barkerville and/or Bowron Lake. **Cottonwood House Historic Site** (☎ summer 250-992-2071, winter 250-983-6911; www.cottonwoodhouse.ca; adult/child $4.50/free; ☻ 10am-5pm mid-May–Aug) is a classic roadhouse from the 1860s, restored so that it's now a faithful re-creation of the many places like this that lined routes throughout the north. Each was about a day's travel apart. This project, run in conjunction with local schools, is very well done. Aside from the roadhouse itself, there are trails that lead to other restored buildings, including a general store and barns. There are some interesting demonstration gardens and a café that sells homemade ice cream. You can also stay here (see right).

Sleeping & Eating
BC Parks (☎ 250-398-4414) runs three campgrounds around tiny Barkerville. Closest to the town site and mostly used by campers with tents (not recreational vehicles; RVs) is Government Hill Campground (campsite

$17). The 23 sites come with pit toilets but no showers.

St George Hotel (☎ 250-994-0008, 888-246-7690; www.stgeorgehotel.bc.ca; r $110-180) Inside historic Barkerville, the St George dates from the 1890s. The seven rooms are all filled with antiques. A stay here – it must be very quiet, even spooky, after the last day-trippers have left – includes your choice from a large breakfast.

Kelly House (☎ 250-994-3328, 866-994-0004; www.kellyhouse.ca; r $80-90) For something more intimate but equally authentic, try the three-room Kelly House in Barkerville. There are feather quilts and shared bathrooms.

Wells Hotel (☎ 250-994-3427, 800-860-2299; www.wellshotel.com; 2341 Pooley St, Wells; r $70-130) This is pretty much the hub of this small town. It's been popular since 1933 and is home to a good restaurant, pub and patio. Splash out in the new rooftop hot tub. Rates include a continental breakfast.

Bear's Paw Cafe (☎ 250-994-2346; meals $5-8; ☻ 11am-9pm May-Sep) The sign out front is almost as big as the building, so that should be reason enough not to miss this café right on Hwy 26 in Wells. The eclectic menu features a changing line-up of fresh and creative down-home items and there's a bakery. Choose from the good beer and wine list while out on the patio.

Cottonwood House (☎ summer 250-992-2071, winter 800-983-6911; www.cottonwoodhouse.ca; campsite $13, cabin for up to 6 people $35, r $40) It lets you really absorb the historic winds of the site (see left). Here you get both the fascinating setting and a good deal on basic accommodations that share a toilet and shower building.

BOWRON LAKE PROVINCIAL PARK
This circular chain of lakes is the ultimate string of pearls for people who love to canoe. The 116km circular canoe route passes through 10 lakes: Bowron, Kibbee, Indianpoint, Isaac, McLeary, Lanezi, Sandy, Babcock, Skoi and Swan, and over sections of the Isaac, Cariboo and Bowron Rivers. In between are eight portages, with the longest 2km over well-defined trails that can accommodate wheeled canoe carriers. The trip takes six to 10 days. You'll find backcountry campgrounds along the way; to make sure there are sites for everyone, the park service only allows a limited number of canoes to start the circuit each day. You must bring your own food (or catch it).

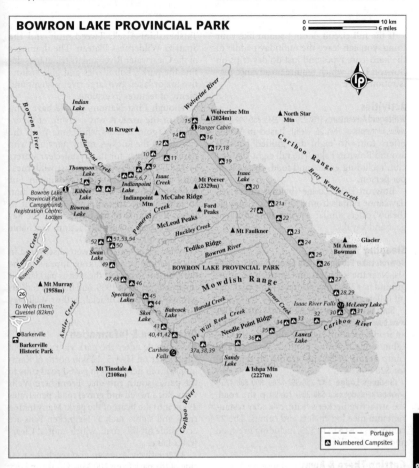

BOWRON LAKE PROVINCIAL PARK

The Mowdish Range runs right through the middle of the loop, while the Cariboo Range surrounds the perimeter of this amazing park, affording spectacular views no matter which direction you look in. With all of these mountains around, it's no wonder the park is often cool and wet. Wildlife abounds. You might see moose, black and grizzly bear, caribou and mountain goats. And, in late summer you stand a very good chance of spotting bears on the upper Bowron River, where they feed on the spawning sockeye salmon.

Weather will let you paddle this circuit anytime from mid-May to October. People generally choose to do the circuit in July and August, but September is also an excellent choice, since that's when the leaves change

color. Mosquitoes, which thrive in the wet, relatively windless environment, are at their worst in the spring.

Before planning your trip, visit **BC Parks** (www .env.gov.bc.ca/bcparks) and search for Bowron Lake. Follow the links and download the essential Bowron Lake Canoe Circuit Pre-Trip Information document. You will then need to make reservations with **BC Parks** (☎ 800-435-5622, outside North America 250-387-1642) to reserve your circuit. This can be done around January 2. The fee is $60 per person plus an $18 reservation fee. Once you get to the park, you must go to the **Registration Centre** (🕑 8am-6pm mid-May–Sep) at the time given to you when you make your reservation. Once there you can check in and undergo an orientation.

CARIBOO-CHILCOTIN & COAST

If the full circuit doesn't sound like your thing, you can leave the multiday paddle to the hard-core types and just do day trips on Bowron Lake, which require no advance registration or fee.

Activities

Whitegold Adventures (☎ 250-994-2345, 866-994-2345; www.whitegold.ca; Hwy 26, Wells), based in Wells, offers four- to eight-day guided paddles around Bowron Lake. The full eight-day circuit, including guides and food, costs $1500 per person.

Bowron Lake Lodge (below) offers 10-day canoe rentals from $130. Becker's Lodge (below) offers similar services. Both also rent gear and kayaks.

Sleeping

Bowron Lake Provincial Park Campground (campsite $14) Near the Registration Centre, this campground has 25 shady, nonreservable sites and pit toilets.

Bowron Lake Lodge (☎ 250-992-2733, 800-519-3399; www.bowronlakelodge.com; r $60-150; ✷ May-Sep) With an iconic location right on the lake, this 16-cabin lodge is always popular. You can also camp at one of 50 sites (some on the lake) for $20 to $24.

Becker's Lodge (☎ 250-992-8864, 800-808-4761; www.beckerslodge.ca; r $80-200) Just up the road, the attractive Becker's features a cozy restaurant and nice log chalets and cabins. The 25 campsites cost $15 to $25, including firewood and use of facilities.

Getting There & Away

By car turn off Hwy 26 just before Barkerville and follow the 28km-long gravel Bowron Lake Rd.

WELLS GRAY PROVINCIAL PARK

Thundering **Helmcken Falls** creates its own mist-laden clouds in its own tree- and moss-covered gorge, and at 141m is Canada's fourth-highest falls. Utterly remote, it is a perfect example of the allure of this isolated wonderland of lakes, peaks, wildlife and dozens of waterfalls.

In the Cariboo Mountains about halfway between Kamloops and Jasper, off the Southern Yellowhead Hwy (Hwy 5), the enormous 541,000-hectare Wells Gray wilderness park is a seldom-visited gem in the vast BC interior. It is the fourth-largest park in BC, after

Tatshenshini-Alsek, Tweedsmuir and the Spatsizi Wilderness Plateau. The drainages of the Clearwater River and its tributaries define the park's boundaries and give visitors five major lakes, two large river systems and plenty of features to explore.

Though First Nations people have long lived in the area, it was a group of Overlanders (gold seekers who came from the east side of the Rockies, many starving), who named the river for its crystal-clear waters in 1862. The area remained vast wilderness until various settlers started moving in. Fur trapper John Ray was the first white man to settle in the area and one of the last to leave. Remnants of his homestead, the **Ray Farm**, are now a park attraction, reachable by a 1km hike.

When giant waterfalls were discovered in 1913, people began making appeals to the government to protect the area as parkland. It finally happened in 1939, and the park took its name from a parks official, Arthur Wellesley Gray.

Orientation & Information

Most people enter the park via the town of Clearwater on Hwy 5, 123km north of Kamloops. From here a 36km paved road runs to the park's south entrance. From here Wells Gray Rd, a paved and gravel road, penetrates 29km into the heart of the park. Many hiking trails and sights such as Helmcken Falls are accessible off this road, which ends at Clearwater Lake.

Alternatively, you can also reach the west side of the park from 100 Mile House on Hwy 97 via an 86km gravel road that leads to Mahood Falls and the west end of Mahood Lake. From Blue River, 107km north of Clearwater on Hwy 5, a 24km gravel road and 2.5km track lead to Murtle Lake in the southeast part of the park.

Visitor Info Centre (☎ 250-674-2646; www.clear waterbcchamber.com; 425 E Yellowhead Hwy at Clearwater Valley Rd, Clearwater; ✷ 9am-5pm Jul & Aug, Mon-Fri Apr-Jun & Sep-Dec) Distributes loads of essential information and maps of the park.

Activities

You'll find opportunities for **hiking**, **cross-country skiing** and **horseback riding** along more than 20 trails of varying lengths. Another great way to explore the park is by **canoeing** on Clearwater, Azure, Murtle and Mahood

Lakes. Clearwater Lake lies at the north end of the Wells Gray Corridor. A narrow navigation channel from the north end of Clearwater Lake connects to the west end of Azure Lake; the two lakes form an upside-down 'L'. You can only reach the 6900-hectare Murtle Lake from the Blue River park entrance. You can reach Mahood Lake, on the southwest side of Wells Gray, from 100 Mile House (see Orientation & Information, opposite).

Rustic backcountry campgrounds dot the area around all four lakes. To rent canoes, contact **Clearwater Lake Tours** (☎ 250-674-2121; www.clearwaterlaketours.com; canoes per day from $35), which also leads treks.

The **Clearwater River** makes for some excellent, adrenaline-pumping white-water rafting. **Interior Whitewater Expeditions** (☎ 250-674-3727, 800-661-7238; www.interiorwhitewater.bc.ca; 3-hr trip adult/child $90/70) runs the river with a variety of trips.

Saying you can go backcountry hiking here is really an oxymoron as the entire place is backcountry, but among the dozens of hikes is a 15km one-way trek up to **Horseshoe Falls** on the Murtle River. Side trips lead to panoramas atop Pyramid Mountain and azure Pyramid Lakes.

Sleeping

There are no commercial operations in the park, but just outside of the south gate you'll find a couple of excellent accommodations options along Clearwater Valley Rd. Note that the BC government would like to have luxury accommodations built in the park; see the boxed text, p39.

Helmcken Falls Lodge (☎ 250-674-3657; www .helmckenfalls.com; 4373 Clearwater Valley Rd; r $125-160) A rustic delight – guests stay in 21 modern rooms in four buildings, with delicious meals served in the main lodge, which was built in 1948. The lodge rents canoes and offers horseback-riding trips. Cross-country skiers like to congregate here in winter. Campsites are $15 to $22.

Wells Gray Guest Ranch (☎ 250-674-2792, 866-467-4346; www.wellsgrayranch.com; campsites $15, r $75-130) This ranch has 12 rooms in cabins and the main lodge building. There's an old-west motif and you can camp in a tepee for $10 per person. It's 27km north of Clearwater.

There are three vehicle-accessible **campgrounds** (☎ 250-674-2194; campsite $14) in the park, all with pit toilets but no showers. One of the most bucolic, the 50-site **Pyramid Campground** (⊙ May-Oct), is just 5km north of the park's south entrance and close to Helmcken Falls.

Getting There & Away

For information on getting to the park, see Orientation & Information, opposite.

CHILCOTIN

Often lumped in with the Cariboo region to the east, the Chilcotin is really a distinct region of vast cattle ranches and forests. Thinly populated, many of those living here are the Tsilhqot'in First Nations people. The land is bisected by Highway 20 on its route to Bella Coola and the coast. For extensive information on the region, visit the Discovery Centre (p310) in Williams Lake.

HIGHWAY 20

Fabled and feared, this legendary road is really a pussycat. It's now paved for most of its 456km length and with the exception of the Hill (p316), is a modern and pleasant road that you should easily traverse in five to six hours.

Just west of Williams Lake, Hwy 20 crosses over the Fraser River, which marks the boundary between the Cariboo and the Chilcotin. Enjoy the wide open landscape dotted by lakes for much of the route before you reach the coast mountains, where the landscape makes a dramatic shift to craggy bluffs and rushing rivers before dropping down into the wet, lush central coast (p316).

Bella Coola is only accessible by car on Hwy 20 or by ferry (see p318) and there is no public transport on this route so you will definitely need your own vehicle. Success hitching is

---

DETOUR: TS'YL-OS PROVINCIAL PARK

You can get to the north end of 233,240-hectare **Ts'yl-os Provincial Park** (*sigh*-loss) by turning south off Hwy 20 at the town of Tatla Lake (219km west) and following the gravel road 63km to the rustic campground on the north tip of Chilko Lake, the largest high-altitude natural lake on the continent. Wildlife thrives here, and Chilko Lake is chock-full of fish.

unlikely and cycling would only be for the most determined and fit. Gas is limited, as are cafés, so you should bring a full tank of gas and a picnic from Williams Lake. All along the road you'll see evidence of beetle infestation (see the boxed text, p332).

From Hwy 20 you can take numerous side roads – most of which are gravel – to some of the province's most remote car-accessible provincial parks.

Excellent canoeing on its lake chain draws adventurers to **Nazko Lake Provincial Park**, which is reached by 32km of graveled Alexis Lakes Rd, off Hwy 20 117km west of Williams Lake. Some 54km further on, **Puntzi Lake** (171km west) is good for picnics and echoes to the calls of trumpeter swans in the fall.

After **Nimpo Lake** (295km west), Hwy 20 wanders through mountains, passing by small towns with limited services, such as **Anahim Lake** (313km west). From here there's new, paved road as far as the Hill (356km west).

THE HILL

Prior to 1953 the only way out of Bella Coola was by boat or packhorse through the Chilcotin. Then a group of locals decided that enough was enough and they took matters into their own hands. Ignoring government engineers who said it was impossible, they carved their way up the side of the mountain, creating what is sometimes called the 'Freedom Rd.' It was perilous then and it seems perilous now. Over the 30km gravel stretch from Heckman's Pass (elevation 1524m) to the base of the hill (nearly sea level) there are 10% to 18% grades and constant sharp switchbacks. But that's just the dramatic stuff. The reality is that the road is wide, and sight lines are good. Put you vehicle in low gear, take your time and you'll actually enjoy the view. To get an overview of what lies ahead, stop at the **viewpoint** right before the grade begins.

THE COAST

As you plunge (not literally of course) down the Hill from the dry plains of the Chilcotin to the coast you're in for a bit of a shock. Suddenly you're in the wet and wonderful world of the Great Bear Rainforest (see the boxed text, p319). Huge stands of trees line the steep

peaks, punctuated by sheer rock faces. Here and there is a trace of a glacier and everything is cleaved by wild river valleys surging with white water.

The waters empty out into deep ocean fjords that curl majestically through the coastal peaks and islands. It's all a bit of a jaw-dropper and the area in and around Bella Coola is one of the few easily accessible bits of this vast wilderness between Prince Rupert (p338) in the north and Powell River (p133) on the Sunshine Coast.

Once you're at the bottom of the Hill (386km west of Williams Lake), you are in Bella Coola Valley that stretches 53km to Bella Coola and the North Bentinck Arm, the fjord which runs 40km inland from the Pacific. There's really no limit on your activities here. You can hike into the hills and valleys starting from roads or at points only reachable by boat along the craggy shore.

And no matter what you do, you can enjoy the unique vibe of the valley, a delightful eccentricity common to end-of-the-road places everywhere. Artists, trekkers and dreamers abound.

TWEEDSMUIR PROVINCIAL PARK (SOUTH)

You are already in this gigantic, roughly arrowhead-shaped park when you drive the Hill. At 981,000 hectares, **Tweedsmuir** (☎ 250-398-4414) is the second-largest provincial park in BC (next to Tatshenshini-Alsek in the northwest corner of BC); the southern part is 506,000 hectares. The Dean River, roughly halfway up the park, divides Tweedsmuir into north and south. Hwy 20 is the only road through this mostly wilderness park, and it skirts the park's southern tip.

Tweedsmuir Provincial Park's features include the **Rainbow Range**, north of Hwy 20. The colorful dome of eroded rock and lava mountains appears, at certain lights, orange, red, yellow and purple. Most of the hiking in the park requires serious pre-planning. The **BC Parks website** (www.env.gov.bc.ca/bcparks/explore/parkpgs/tweedsmu.html) park has good information and links to some gear companies that can support travel in the park. Many people access areas via floatplanes chartered in Nimpo on Hwy 20.

The most popular trek is to **Hunlen Falls**, which plummet 260m into the Atnarko River at the north end of **Turner Lake**. Access starts at Tote Rd, an 11km 4WD-only road that starts at the base of the Hill. From the road's end, it's a 16.4km hike up the side of a hill (78 switchbacks) in an area where grizzly bears are common. The reward is the stunning falls and the start of the Turner Lake chain. Canoeists find the paddling here sublime; they gain access by floatplane.

Down in the Bella Coola Valley there's the enjoyable **Valley Loop Trail** that includes the trailhead of the Alexander Mackenzie Heritage Trail (p311). It runs up one side of Burnt Bridge Creek, across a small suspension bridge and down the other side for a total of 5km of raw nature and valley vistas. The start is 402km west of Williams Lake.

The most developed and pleasant camping in the park is at **Atnarko Campground** (campsite $14; ☽ Jun-Aug) on Hwy 20 at the start of Tote Rd. The 28 sites here are set in old-growth forest.

Tweedsmuir Provincial Park (North) is mostly reached by roads off the Yellowhead Hwy (see p333).

BELLA COOLA VALLEY

Alexander Mackenzie traveled through this area on his way to becoming the first white person to make it to the northwest coast, and indeed left his name written in grease and vermillion on a rock near Bella Coola on July 22, 1793 (see p319 and p21). Long before that, Bella Coola and Chilcotin peoples thrived along the rivers full of salmon.

GRIZZLIES & WHITE GUYS

Clayton Mack was a hunter, logger, tracker, guide and more during his life in the valley from 1910 to 1993. Late in life he was also a writer and penned *Grizzlies & White Guys,* a wonderfully readable book about his life in the Nuxalk nation and his hard-scrabble existence in the early days that gave way to something better after he started working as a hunting guide for wealthy Americans – who never quite realized that Mack was having the last laugh while they spouted arrogant nonsense and puffed their way up the trail. He also had amazing insight into the turbulent minds of bears and his experiences are fascinating. The book is available at **Kopas Store** (☎ 250-799-5553; Mackenzie St, Bella Coola).

DETOUR: ODEGAARD FALLS & PURGATORY POINT LOOKOUT

About 6km east of Hagensborg, Hwy 20 crosses the Nusatsum River Bridge. On the west side turn onto the forest service road and go 24km through rugged coast range forest until you reach an obvious clearing. Here there's a lookout over the river, and 1km further you'll find the trailhead for a 2km trail down to the river and on to crashing **Odegaard Falls.** Until this point the road is just accessible when it's dry for cars. If you have a 4WD, you can continue over a very crude abandoned loggers road another 8km to the **Purgatory Point Lookout.** It's the end of the road, but the view down into the vast valley extending to the Pacific is really a backcountry hiker's fantasy.

More than one-third of the population today is made up of First Nations people, descendants of the Nuxalk-Carriers. The Nuxalk (*new*-hawk) are well known for their carvings, paintings and trademark use of cobalt blue, which you'll see in artwork throughout the valley.

The two main towns, Bella Coola on the water and Hagensborg 15km east, almost seem as one, with most places of interest in or between the two.

Information

For information on the region, contact **Bella Coola Valley Tourism** (☎ 250-982-2212; www.bellacoola .ca; Co-op Store, cnr Mackenzie St & Burke Ave, Bella Coola; ☽ 9am-6pm Jun-Sep). This well-run place can help you navigate the mysteries and delights of the valley. Most places aimed at visitors are open May to September, but check for dates beyond that. Both the VIC and your accommodations can point you to guides and gear for skiing, mountain biking, fishing, rafting and much more.

Services like car repair, ATMs, laundry and the like are easily found. **Kopas Store** (☎ 250-799-5553; Mackenzie St, Bella Coola) has books, gifts, art and outdoor gear.

Sights & Activities

As you drive west on Hwy 20 from the Hill, you'll see the odd house here and there but little else in terms of development until you

CARIBOO-CHILCOTIN & COAST

reach **Hagensborg** (population 540; 432km west), settled in 1895 by a hardy group of Norwegians whose hand-hewn homes were built with crude saws and axes. Attracted to the area because it resembled their homeland, the Norwegians stayed and entrenched themselves in northern BC. Today the Scandinavian influence is still evident, and many residents still get cravings for lutefisk. Small, tidy farms line the road.

There's a good, short hike just west of Hagensborg at **Walker Island Park** on the edge of wide and rocky Bella Coola River floodplain. Upon leaving the parking area you are immediately in the middle of a grove of cedars that are 500 years old. To fully appreciate some of the sylvan vistas, saddle up for a horse ride with **Rolling Pigeon Ranch** (☎ 250-982-0010; trail rides per hr $38).

The local rivers are alive with salmon and you can buy succulent smoked variations at **Bella Coola Valley Seafoods** (☎ 250-982-2713; 🕑 8am-6pm), where the motto is 'Just say no to farmed salmon.' It's 5.7km off Hwy 20 on Salloompt River Rd. At **Barb's Pottery** (☎ 250-799-5380; 1090 Hwy 20), 8km east of Hagensborg, you can watch the genial Barb Gilbert work at her kiln and see some of the other excellent work of valley artisans.

Further east, at the **Petroglyph Gallery** (☎ 250-799-5673; Four Mile Reserve), you can marvel at the work of Nuxalk artists like Alvin Mack and Silyas Saunders.

The village of **Bella Coola** (population 890; 437km west) sits at the mouth of the Bella Coola River where it spills into the deep North Bentinck Arm. Like the rest of the valley, it is surrounded by the sharp, spectacular Coast Mountains. The **Bella Coola Museum** (☎ 250-799-5657), on Hwy 20 just west of Mackenzie St, provides lots of valley context (phone to check for opening hours).

About 2km west of town, **Government Dock** and the ferry terminal are an interesting stroll and viewpoint; just beyond is a brief walk to **Clayton Falls**.

Sleeping & Eating

There are dozens of B&Bs and small lodges in the valley. Many offer evening meals; otherwise, there are a couple of cafés and motels in Bella Coola.

Bailey Bridge Campsite & Cabins (☎ 250-982-2342; www.baileybridge.ca; Salloompt River Rd; campsite from $15, cabins from $55) Near the namesake bridge, has

nicely shaded campsites and cabins along the river bank. A small store has gear and supplies.

Eagle Lodge (☎ 250-799-5587, 866-799-5587; www.eaglelodgebc.com; 1103 Hwy 20, Bella Coola; r from $70; 🖳) Like a vacation retreat, Eagle Lodge is on a grassy spread and has seven rooms of varying sizes, wi-fi and good meals for guests at night. Ask Rosemary to give you her colorful history spiel.

Brockton House (☎ 250-982-2298, 866-982-2298; www.brocktonplace.com; 1900 Hwy 20, Hagensborg; r from $72; 🖳) This place is like a one-stop holiday. The 16 rooms are huge, and many have kitchen facilities and wi-fi. There's also a cute little coffee bar with an internet terminal. Finally, the charming owners also run Kynoch West Coast Adventures, which specializes in bear-filled float trips down local rivers (from $65).

Suntree Guest Cottages (☎ 250-982-2424, 877-982-2424; www.suntree.ca; cabins from $145; 🖳) Off Hwy 20 east of Hagensborg, Suntree has two large cottages that are nicely equipped and have a lovely hillside setting. As the owner was telling us about the birdlife a bald eagle flew over as if on cue.

ourpick **Talheo Cannery Inn B&B** (☎ 250-982-2344; www.centralcoastbc.com/tallheocannery; r from $100) One of the most extraordinary places you might stay in BC is across the water from Bella Coola. This is exactly what its name implies: an old cannery. As you boat with owner Jim Newkirk (a great ride in itself) you may have your doubts as you approach – large portions over the water are collapsing. But, rest easy, the rooms are in an old 1920s bunkhouse that's on solid ground. Staying here is not for everybody as conditions are basic, but for those with a real sense of adventure the views (stunning!), explorations (it's an entire village) and mystery (a rainbow of nets hang abandoned in one part of the old cannery) make this a fascinating change of pace.

Getting There & Away

You can combine a trip on BC Ferries with Hwy 20 for an unbeatable circle tour of the Bella Coola Valley and the Chilcotin. **BC Ferries** (☎ 888-223-3779; www.bcferries.com) runs the Discovery Coast ferry, which links Bella Coola and Port Hardy on Vancouver Island several times a week in summer (13 to 22 hours depending on stops, adult/child $120/60, car from $241). Best are the direct 13-hour trips as the usual boat, the *Queen of Chilliwack*, does

THE GREAT BEAR RAINFOREST

It's one of the last places like it on Earth. The Great Bear Rainforest is a wild region of islands, fjords and towering peaks on the BC coast. It stretches south from Alaska along the BC coast and Queen Charlotte Islands to roughly Campbell River on Vancouver Island (which isn't part of the forest). Covering 6.3 million hectares (or 7% of what's already a very large province), this is the last major tract of coastal temperate rain forest left anywhere. It's remarkably rich in life, from wild salmon, whales to eagles, elk and huge stands of ancient old-growth timber. It's also under huge threat.

As you survey the wilds around Bella Coola, which is roughly at the center of the Great Bear, you might not perceive the threat, but it's there. Remote river valleys are lined with forests of old Sitka spruce, Pacific silver fir and various cedars that are often 100m tall and 1500 years old. Logging companies eye the rest hungrily. Meantime conservation has produced some modest victories. A 2005 agreement gave permanent protection to 1.8 million hectares but also left the remaining 4.5 million hectares open to 'sustainable' logging.

Still it's a start, and as you gaze in rapt awe at this region's wild beauty from the deck of a ferry or on a backcountry hike, you can think about what you can do to help save the rest. See the boxed text, p57, for some of the environmental groups active in the Great Bear Rainforest.

And the name? That's in honor of the 'Spirit bears' or Kermode bears that live in the rain forest here. In tribal legend the raven turned one of every 10 bears white to show the people the earth's purity during the ice age. The bears, which are not albinos but rather a genetic variation of black bear with white fur, only number a few hundred and live exclusively in the Great Bear Rainforest.

not have cabins. This journey covers part of the Inside Passage – for more on this route see the boxed text, p400.

There is no transport along Hwy 20 to Williams Lake although you can get there by charter plane. **Pacific Coastal Airlines** (☎ 800-663-2872; www.pacificcoastal.com) has flight services to/from Vancouver. There are no 4WD rentals in the valley.

THE COAST & ISLANDS

The best way to appreciate the wild BC coast is from the deck of a BC Ferry on the Discovery Coast run to/from Bella Coola (see opposite). This is the heart of the Great Bear Rainforest and a place where even whales outnumber people. Small First Nations villages like **Bella Bella** are isolated and not visited by many. But for the intrepid who do their homework the opportunity to have your own ocean cove or entire driftwood-covered beach to yourself is unlimited.

Closer to Bella Coola, you should be able to arrange for a boat excursion if you ask around. Destinations can include hidden rivers where you might see a **Kermode bear** (see the boxed text, above), the **rock** signed by Alexander Mackenzie in 1793 (someone later replaced the paint with carving) or a small **beachside hot spring** on the South Bentinck Arm.

The North

The name says it all: the North. The very words, the concept, the idea evoke an image, one that will be different for each individual. An orca breaking the surface of a fjord captures the image of fresh, crisp water filled with fish, whales and otters, while an open road stretching into the distant horizon holds the promise of adventure, escape and another open road. Like the roads, the choices in the North seem endless.

Other images abound: a solitary totem pole, carved from a centuries-old cedar looks out to sea, its weather-beaten figures still animated with myth and belief; or maybe simply a nameless waterfall found tumbling over the rocks past a bend on a trail.

These are just a few of the images possible in the North, a region of British Columbia with so much promise for the traveler and a place where superlatives start out trite and end in clichés. Consider the Queen Charlottes – Haida Gwaii – the mist-shrouded islands that are home to the Haida, one of the world's great societies and one that is again thriving and welcoming visitors. Across the Hecate Straight, Prince Rupert is fun, dramatic and welcoming. And not far north is the Salmon Glacier, enveloping the surrounding peaks like a sheet.

Between all of the North's images are the roads. The Alaska, the Stewart-Cassiar and the Yellowhead Highways, avenues for discovery in yourself, the land, the culture, the beauty and more.

So come on, get up here and start forming your own images.

HIGHLIGHTS

- Letting the culture of the Haida on the **Queen Charlotte Islands** (p343) bowl you over
- Losing count of whales while riding a ferry on the **Inside Passage** (p343) to the Yukon
- Exploring the **Stewart-Cassiar Highway** (p353) north to the Yukon
- Watching the rain pound **Prince Rupert** (p338) from a cozy bar
- Plunging into the **Liard River Hotsprings** (p331) on the Alaska Hwy

★ Liard River Hotsprings

★ Stewart-Cassiar Hwy

★ Prince Rupert

★ Queen Charlotte Islands

★ Inside Passage

THE NORTH

PRINCE GEORGE

pop 77,200

No one really knows why Prince George is called Prince George. It was named by a predecessor railroad to the Canadian National (CN) in the early 1900s and surviving records give conflicting accounts – it's not even known if 'Prince George' was a real person. Sadly, the railroad folks missed the chance for a really appropriate name: Lheidli T'Enneh, the name of the First Nations people who lived here. Sure it's a mouthful for some, but the meaning – people of the confluence – couldn't be more appropriate. For Prince George is a junction of four major roads: the Yellowhead Hwy (Hwy 16) west to the coast and Prince Rupert (see p338 for details on *that* princely name), the John Hart Hwy (Hwy 97) northeast to the Alaska Hwy, the Yellowhead Hwy east to Jasper and the Rockies, and the Cariboo Hwy (Hwy 97) south to its namesake region and highways to Vancouver.

As a confluence, it's effective. Prince George is a good place to break your journey for a meal, a rest and maybe a diversion or two before you're on your way again. Beyond that, it's mostly a growing and sprawling lumber town and you are unlikely to linger.

ORIENTATION

Roads in this big confluence can be a confusing tangle. Hwy 97 from Quesnel becomes a commercial strip cutting across the edge of town as Central St before heading north to Dawson Creek (406km) and Mile 0 of the Alaska Hwy. The Yellowhead Hwy (Hwy 16) becomes Victoria St as it runs through town, coming to a dead end at 1st Ave. The Yellowhead turns east on 1st Ave and crosses the Yellowhead Bridge to Jasper (376km) and Edmonton. At the south end of town, Hwy 16 goes through a disheartening quadrant of big box stores and strip malls before it veers westward to become the long, scenic route to Prince Rupert (724km). The downtown area is compact, with little character.

INFORMATION
Bookstore

Stock up now as the selection as you go north does not get better until Whitehorse in the Yukon.

Books & Company (☎ 250-563-6637; 1685 3rd Ave; ⏰ 8am-6pm Mon, Wed & Sat, 8am-9pm Thu, 8am-10pm Fri, 10am-5pm Sun) In a beautiful building downtown with a huge selection, a good café and wi-fi.

Internet

There's internet access at the library (below), Books & Company (left) and the main Visitor Info Centre (VIC; below). Access is also common at motels.

Laundry

Just about every place to stay has a coin laundry.

Library

Prince George Library (Bob Harkins Branch; ☎ 250-563-9251; 887 Dominion St, Civic Centre Plaza; ⏰ 10am-9pm Mon-Thu, 10am-5:30pm Fri & Sat, 1-5pm Sun Sep-May) One-hour free internet access.

Medical Services

Prince George Regional Hospital (☎ 250-565-2000; 2000 15th Ave; ⏰ 24hr)

Money

Banks and ATMs abound in Prince George and you'll usually be very close to one, especially an ATM.

Post

Main post office (☎ 250-561-2568; 1323 5th Ave)

Tourist Information

Visitor Info Centre VIA train station (☎ 250-562-3700, 800-668-7446; www.tourismpg.com; 1300 1st Ave; ⏰ 8am-8pm May-Sep, 8:30am-5pm Oct-Apr); Hwy 97 (☎ 250-563-5493; cnr Hwys 97 & 16; ⏰ 8am-8pm May-Aug) The train station location is a beautiful facility that can make bookings like ferry tickets. Internet access per 30 minutes is $3.50.

SIGHTS

Exploration Place (☎ 250-562-1612; Fort George Park; adult/child $8.95/5.95; ⏰ 10am-5pm Jun-Aug, 10am-5pm Wed-Sun Sep-May) has a public atrium and 1115 sq m of exhibition space devoted to nature and history. Once you get past the gloss designed to attract people afraid of the word 'museum' the center is an engaging stop. There's lots of good historical stuff - especially on First Nations groups like those confluencers, the Lheidli T'Enneh - and it's fun to check out the Nature Exchange, where kids can trade rocks and other items they've found. Kids also

THE NORTH

THE NORTH

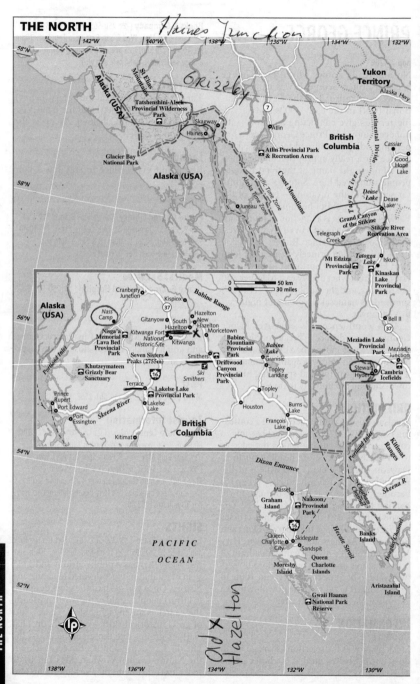

Haines Junction

Grizzly

Old × Hazelton

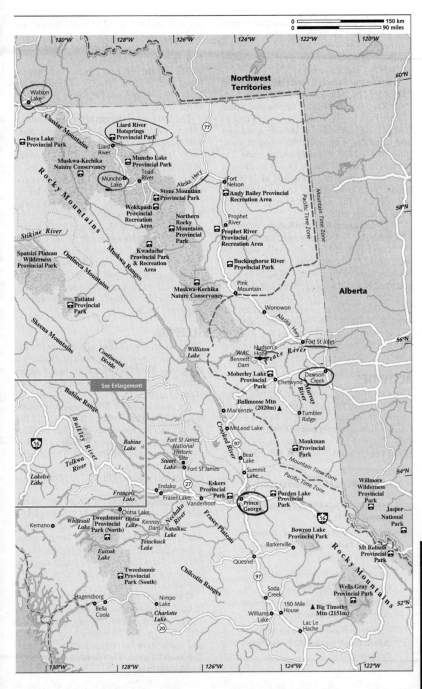

seem to love the SimEx ride simulator (where you get shaken up like a can of paint at the hardware store; no big chili lunches first). It's southeast of the downtown area on the corner of 20th Ave and Queensway.

Prince George Railway & Forest Industry Museum (☎ 250-563-7351; 850 River Rd; adult/child $6/5; ☺ 10am-5:30pm May 15-Oct 15) is beside Cottonwood Island Nature Park (right) and features a big collection of train memorabilia, including old cars and cabooses, a unique 1903 wooden snow plow and a 1913 steam-powered crane. On the forestry side of things, there's an antique chainsaw display and a logging arch truck, used to push around logs. And no, they can't tell you why the railroad named the place Prince George either.

The **Prince George Native Art Gallery** (☎ 250-614-7726; 1600 3rd Ave; ☺ 9am-5pm Mon-Fri, 10am-5pm Sat) in the Native Friendship Centre sells works by local artists. Myths and mythic beings form the basis for many of the works, which can be quite spiritual. It also has an excellent gift store.

Another excellent place to both view and buy works by local artists is the **Two Rivers Gallery** (☎ 250-614-7800; 725 Civic Centre Plaza; adult/child $5/2, admission free Thu; ☺ 10am-5pm Mon, Wed & Fri, 10am-9pm Thu, noon-5pm Sat & Sun). It has frequent special exhibitions and a striking design.

ACTIVITIES

There's something in the air in Prince George and its probably a pulp mill. Six companies operate them and one of the largest firms, Canfor, runs a **forestry tour** (admission free; ☺ Jun-Aug). This is a fascinating way to see where wood comes from. Note that the minimum

age is 12 and you need to book through the VIC (p321).

The 33-hectare **Cottonwood Island Nature Park**, north of downtown between the railway tracks and the river, is a protected riparian forest with a good network of trails. Many birds, beaver and moose thrive in the wet cottonwood forest.

The 130-hectare **Forests of the World** features 15km of easily navigable interpretive trails with plaques that tell about local flora and fauna. It lies at the north end of the University of Northern British Columbia campus west of town. To get there, follow 15th Ave west and turn right on Foothills Blvd. Then turn left on Cranbrook Hill Rd and left again on Kueng Rd, which you follow to the forest.

Tired of lugging that pack? Give it to a llama. **Strider Adventures** (☎ 250-963-9542, 800-665-7752; www.pgweb.com/strider) runs multi-day treks and half-day nature hikes (from $30 per person) where you do the walking and the llama does the work. No wonder they spit. Trips take place outside of town on various preserved lands.

SLEEPING

There are a few decent places downtown, but those closest to the train station are a tad grotty. Hwy 97/Central St makes an arc around the center and this is where you'll find scads of motels.

An association of B&B owners operates the **Bed & Breakfast Hotline** (☎ 250-562-2222, 877-562-2626; www.princegeorgebnb.com), a free booking service that will help you arrange a B&B in your price range ($50 to $100). The association also provides transportation from the train or bus station. The VIC (p321) also has B&B listings.

Bee Lazee Campground (☎ 250-963-7263, 866-679-6699; www.beelazee.ca; 15910 Hwy 97 S; campsite $15-23; ☺ May-Sep; ☙) A mere 10km south of town, this recreational vehicle (RV)–centric place features full facilities, including free hot showers, a pool and laundry. As the name suggests, the place also includes a honey farm, so go be lazy while they be busy.

97 Motor Inn (☎ 250-562-6010; 2713 Spruce St; r $60-70; ☒ ☒) No points for guessing that this new budget place is on Hwy 97, near the junction with Hwy 16. The 19 rooms have free wi-fi and some have balconies and/or kitchens. The noted Thanh Vu restaurant (opposite) is right out front.

TOP FIVE PLACES FOR SOLITUDE

- Your own rock overlooking the **Salmon Glacier** (p354)

- The beach at the end of the road in **Naikoon Park** (p349) on the Queen Charlotte Islands

- A random waterfall on wild Babine Mountain near **Smithers** (p334)

- Canoeing to one of dozens of deserted coves on **Eutsuk Lake** (p333)

- A shore with just you and an old totem pole in **Gwaii Haanas National Park Reserve** (p351)

THE NORTH

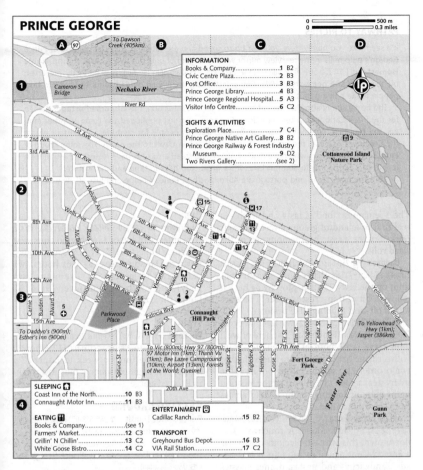

PRINCE GEORGE

INFORMATION	
Books & Company	1 B2
Civic Centre Plaza	2 B3
Post Office	3 B3
Prince George Library	4 B3
Prince George Regional Hospital	5 A3
Visitor Info Centre	6 C2

SIGHTS & ACTIVITIES	
Exploration Place	7 C4
Prince George Native Art Gallery	8 B2
Prince George Railway & Forest Industry Museum	9 D2
Two Rivers Gallery	(see 2)

SLEEPING	
Coast Inn of the North	10 B3
Connaught Motor Inn	11 B3

EATING	
Books & Company	(see 1)
Farmers' Market	12 C3
Grillin' N Chillin'	13 C2
White Goose Bistro	14 C2

ENTERTAINMENT	
Cadillac Ranch	15 B2

TRANSPORT	
Greyhound Bus Depot	16 B3
VIA Rail Station	17 C2

Connaught Motor Inn (☎ 250-562-4441, 800-663-6620; 1550 Victoria St; r $65-90; ✴ ▢ ⛱) This tidy 97-unit motel offers three good ways to relax: an indoor pool, a hot tub and a sauna. It's one of the best choices in the center.

Esther's Inn (☎ 250-562-4131, 800-663-6844; www.esthersinn.com; 1151 Commercial Cres; r $60-100; ✴ ▢ ⛱) Some people think Grama when they hear the name Esther (and oddly enough Grama's is an adjoining motel) but what they should be thinking is tiki-joy. The faux Polynesian theme in the atrium here extends through 120 rooms. There are three Jacuzzis for that tropical feel and a mega-cool pool slide.

Coast Inn of the North (☎ 250-563-0121, 800-663-114; www.coasthotels.com; 770 Brunswick St; r $135-180; ✴ ▢ ⛱) A multistory modern high-rise with 152 rooms, the Coast Inn is a good choice for business travelers. Rooms all have wi-fi and work desks. On a clear day you can see the pulp mills.

EATING & DRINKING

Look for locally brewed Pacific Western Brewing beers. The Prince George **farmers' market** (cnr George St & 3rd Ave; ☷ 8:30am-2pm Sat May-Sep) is a good place to sample some of the array of produce and foods produced locally. Books & Company, the topnotch bookstore (p321), has an excellent café with baked goods and other snacks ($2 to $6) and free wi-fi.

Thanh Vu (☎ 250-564-2255; 1778 Hwy 97 S; meals $8-15; ☷ 11am-9pm) This local favorite now has a larger location out on the Hwy 97 strip.

THE NORTH

PATHWAY TO RICHES

It'll seem like you barely have your car up to speed and are catching your last glimpse of Prince George's pulp mills in the rearview mirror when you get not one, but two excuses to stop. **Huble Homestead** (☎ 250-564-7033; admission by donation; ✆ 10am-5pm Jun-Aug) is a perfectly preserved pioneer farm and home from 1905. Enthusiastic volunteers lead guided tours and explain how people made a living off the land.

The home site is also the start of the area's second attraction, the **Giscome Portage**. Named for the Black Caribbean prospector John Giscome who first publicized the route to other miners, the trail had already been in use by First Nations people for centuries. A shortcut across the Continental Divide, the portage was a critical link in travel to the north. The same group of enthusiastic volunteers who have made Huble Homestead a success have restored the trail for a length of 7.5km north to Summit Lake. It's a great step back in time and into nature.

Both the homestead and portage are 40km north of Prince George and just off Hwy 97.

The Vietnamese food is tasty and fresh – a real find in a land of gloopy sweet and sour pork. Try the classic beef lemongrass or the salad rolls.

Daddyo's (☎ 250-563-2100; Anco Motel, 1636 Central St E; meals $9-18; ✆ 11am-11pm) A top pizza and ribs joint on the Hwy 97 strip. Stop by or have it deliver a bit of thin-crust wonder. There are lots of off-beat toppings like pesto.

Grillin' N Chillin' (☎ 250-612-0771; 1201 1st Ave; meals $10-30; ✆ 11:30am-11pm Mon-Sat) 'Eat here or we'll both starve' is the motto at this cool steak joint with a classic bar. Portions are huge whether you're ordering a salad, a burger or one of the many steaks. Don't be put off by the location in the dubious-looking National Hotel across from the train station.

White Goose Bistro (☎ 250-561-1002; 1205 3rd Ave; meals $8-25; ✆ 11:30am-10pm) A touch of class downtown, this white-tablecloth bistro has a French-Continental menu. Lunch sees salads, sandwiches and pastas; dinner classics such as beef *bourguignon* are warming on a cold night.

ENTERTAINMENT

Cadillac Ranch (☎ 250-563-7720; 1380 2nd Ave; cover varies; ✆ 8pm-3am Mon-Sat) For dancing, look for the parking lot of pick-ups at the bustling Cadillac Ranch, where the band or DJ plays mostly country music (classic rock does slip in) and you can two-step to your heart's content. The club gets many touring acts.

GETTING THERE & AWAY
Air
Prince George Airport (YXS; ☎ 250-963-2400; www.pg airport.ca) is on Airport Rd off Hwy 97. Air Canada Jazz and Westjet both serve Vancouver.

Bus
At **Greyhound** (☎ 250-564-5454; 1566 12th Ave) it's a convergence of buses. Greyhound runs west to Prince Rupert ($107, 11 hours, one daily), north to Dawson Creek ($71, six hours, two daily), east to Jasper ($64, five hours, two daily) and south to Vancouver ($116, 12 hours, three daily).

Train
VIA Rail's (1300 1st Ave) *Skeena* heads west three times a week to Prince Rupert (12½ hours) and east three times a week to Jasper (7½ hours). Through passengers must overnight in Prince George.

GETTING AROUND
Prince George Transit (☎ 250-563-0011; www.busonline .ca) operates local buses ($2).

Major car rental agencies have offices at the airport. For a cab, try **Prince George Taxi** (☎ 250-564-4444).

PRINCE GEORGE TO DAWSON CREEK
As you travel north from Prince George, the mountains and forests give way to gentle rolling hills and farmland as Hwy 97 (at times called the John Hart Hwy) follows the meandering 1923km-long Peace River.

Beginning in the mid-1700s, the Cree and Beaver First Nations lived along the river and called it the 'river of beavers' for its huge populations of these thick-furred rodents. The two tribes periodically warred over the boundaries of the river, finally coming to an agreement about 200 years ago, renaming the river the 'Peace'. The east-flowing Peace River carves the only sizable opening through the Rockies to Alberta, making the climate in this region more similar to the prairie climate in Alberta. The climate also affects the political and social slant of the northeast communities; people read Alberta newspapers, know more about Alberta politics and tend to get their city fix in Grand Prairie instead of, say, Prince George or Vancouver.

If you are making this drive, you're probably heading north to bigger and better things. Although there are a few diversions along the way to the start of the Alaska Hwy should you need them, there's really no reason to dawdle on your way to Dawson Creek.

For the first 150km north of Prince George, Hwy 97 passes Summit, Bear and MacLeod Lakes, with provincial parks and camping along the way. North of MacLeod Lake, Hwy 39 heads west for 29km to **Mackenzie** (population 5500), which sits on the southern shores of the 200km-long **Williston Lake**, the largest artificial reservoir in North America and the largest lake in BC. Mackenzie's claim to tourism fame is the 'world's largest tree crusher,' a mammoth piece of machinery that sits, ironically, beside a wooded area along the town's main street. The big yellow crusher was used to clear the floodplain under what is now Williston Lake.

The next stop off Hwy 97, **Chetwynd** (population 2800), 300km north of Prince George, is little more than a strip of services along the highway. This industrial town contains sawmills, a pulp mill and a gas plant; it's no surprise that such a gritty place has become known for its chainsaw art. More than 50 carvings of varying sizes are spread around town, including the bears under the 'Welcome to Chetwynd' sign.

From Chetwynd you can head north through Hudson's Hope along Hwy 29 and avoid Dawson Creek and Fort St John on your way north (something you should consider, see below). Otherwise, it's 102km straight on to Dawson Creek.

Highway 29 North

If you take this road to join the Alaska Hwy 12km north of Fort St John (p329) you'll not only save 47km of driving and avoid the congestion of the towns along Hwy 97 but you'll also enjoy some superb scenery.

Hudson's Hope (population 1200), 66km north of Chetwynd on Hwy 29, overlooks the Peace River. The town's economy revolves around livestock ranching, grain and forage crops. Wildlife in the area is abundant (10 of North America's big game species are found here), but the biggest spectacle is the **WAC Bennett Dam** (☎ 250-783-5048; admission free; ⏰ 9:30am-4:30pm mid-May–mid-Oct). One of the world's largest earth-filled structures, the hydroelectric dam is 24km west of Hudson's Hope. Tours take you 150m down inside the dam where you can learn about the wonders of electricity.

Continuing east on Hwy 29 the road parallels the beautiful, broad Peace River Valley.

ALASKA HIGHWAY

Just the name evokes wanderlust. The Alaska Hwy, the road of dreams, the road of escape, the road of new hope. It starts simply enough and for the first couple of hundred kilometers seems like just another rural BC highway, but then the terrain becomes more dramatic, the views more wild and you know you're on one of the world's great journeys.

This section covers the Alaska Hwy (Hwy 97) in BC. See p366 for the highway north from the Yukon border.

DETOUR: TUMBLER RIDGE & BEYOND

You can penetrate deep into the seldom-visited heart of BC by taking Hwy 29 94km south from Chetwynd to **Tumbler Ridge** (population 2500). From here you can continue another 45km along the dirt Murray River Rd to **Kinuseo Falls**. Located inside **Monkman Provincial Park**, the spectacular falls are 60m higher than Niagara Falls. You can walk along a five-minute trail to the upper lookout or carry on 20 minutes further to the Murray River and look up at the falls. **Kinuseo Falls Campground** (campsite $14) offers 42 wooded sites close to the river and falls.

As for Tumbler Ridge, it was born in the early 1980s to service the enormous Quintette Mine, the world's largest open-pit coal mine. But coal giveth and coal taketh away and the population here goes up and down like the surrounding hills. Right now its up again and new mines are opening.

DAWSON CREEK

pop 11,500

A typical Canadian plains town, Dawson Creek is primarily known for the road out of town. It's the starting point – Mile 0 – for the Alaska or Alcan (short for Alaska-Canada) Hwy. Beginning at Dawson Creek, the Alaska Hwy goes through Watson Lake and Whitehorse in the Yukon all the way to Fairbanks in Alaska, some 2237km (although progress in the form of road improvements keeps nibbling away at that total).

Known only as the 'Beaver Plains,' the immediate area saw no white settlement until the turn of the 20th century. In 1879, the town's namesake, Dr George Mercer Dawson, led a survey team through here in search of a route to bring the railway over the Alberta Rockies. Though the railway didn't happen until later, Dawson's studies aided settlement and prompted later exploration for oil and natural gas. Unlike many other explorers, Dawson studied Native communities and languages, which, along with his geological and botanical studies across Canada, earned him the title 'Father of Canadian Anthropology.'

When the Northern Alberta Railway (NAR) finally chugged into town in 1931, the city quickly became a thriving agricultural center.

The **Visitor Info Centre** (☎ 250-782-9595, 866-645-3022; www.tourismdawsoncreek.com; 900 Alaska Ave; ☯ 8am-7pm May-Aug, 9am-5pm Mon-Sat Sep-Apr) is in the NAR Park along the highway, which becomes Alaska Ave as it runs through town. The VIC also has a nice little museum. Dinosaur fans – meaning most kids – will enjoy the fossils on display. In fact they can ask for a guide to bones on display all over the region.

Sadly for Dawson Creek boosters, there is virtually no link to the popular TV show *Dawson's Creek* which ran from 1998 to 2003 and followed the lives of four teens (who looked well into their 20s by the show's end) in a town near Boston. So the closest you'll get to Dawson, Jen, Joey and the rest is with the boxed DVD collection for sale at the Wal-Mart, one of scads of new chain stores on the southeastern edge of town.

A signpost in the middle of the intersection of 102nd Ave and 10th St has become a highly photographed post that celebrates the start of the Alaska Hwy. The real **Mile 0** is actually at the east end of NAR Park but there's no longer a sign to mark the spot – reasons given for this historical omission vary but the consensus is that gawking tourists ('Look honey, a sign!') caused traffic problems.

Except to leave, there's little other reason to come to Dawson Creek. So scat!

Sleeping & Eating

If you're not clearing out of town in a hurry, there are many places to stay – some belonging to chains that will seem ubiquitous as you journey north.

Mile 0 RV Park & Campground (☎ 250-782-2590; milopark@pris.ca; campsites from $15) This should actually be called the Kilometer 2.5 RV Park & Campground as that's where it is on the Alaska Hwy. It's a full-service place with hot showers and a laundry.

Alaska Hotel (☎ 250-782-7998; www.alaskahotel.com; 10209 10th St; r $35-70; 🖵) The lovable Alaska is Dawson Creek's oldest hotel by far. The management's philosophy is 'deluxe evolutionary' which means 'always changing for the better'. The very clean, small rooms have furnishings that date to the building of the Alaska Hwy. Bathrooms are shared. Sadly, the café is closed

---

WHAT TIME IS IT ANYWAY?

Many of BC's northwestern communities share the same time zone as Alberta – Mountain Standard Time (MST) – while much of the rest of the province is on Pacific Standard Time (PST). However, there's a twist: these communities – which include Chetwynd, Hudson's Hope, Tumbler Ridge, Dawson Creek and Fort St John – do not observe Daylight Saving Time. This means that in winter those towns are one hour ahead of the rest of BC; but in summer are on the same time as the rest of BC as Pacific Daylight Saving Time is the same as Mountain Standard Time.

Whatever the time, daylight seems to last forever in summer, while winter is shrouded in darkness. In the more northerly reaches, in towns like Fort Nelson or Dease Lake, the summer sun might set at 1am and soon rise again at 5am. Come winter, the sun sets at 3pm, not rising again until 10am.

for now but the nutty, goofy bar is just as nutty and goofy as ever.

Inn on the Creek (☎ 250-782-8136, 888-782-8136; www.innonthecreek.bc.ca; 10600 8th St; r $70-90; ✕ 🖥) Among the non-chains, this is a good choice. Don't let the name fool you, the sylvan setting is on the motel strip but the 49 rooms are large and have fridges and free wi-fi. It's an especially friendly place.

There's a good **farmers' market** (❤ 8am-noon Sat May-Oct) by the VIC. Stock up for the road ahead with natural delights from farm country.

Getting There & Away

At the **Greyhound terminal** (☎ 250-782-3131; 1201 Alaska Ave) you'll find buses north to Whitehorse ($206, 21 hours, one daily) and the Yukon and southwest to Prince George ($71, six hours, two daily). Dawson Creek is 412km northeast of Prince George.

DAWSON CREEK TO FORT NELSON

As the Alaska Hwy heads northwest from Dawson Creek and crosses the Peace River into the foothills of the Rocky Mountains, the landscape again changes, with the flat wheat-growing prairies soon left behind.

Fort St John (population 17,800), 75km north of Dawson Creek on Hwy 97, mainly functions as a service center for the oil and gas industries; in fact, its slogan is 'the energetic city'. There is no compelling reason to stop here, but should you need a break the **Fort St John-North Peace Museum** (☎ 250-787-0430; 9323 100th St; adult/child $4/2; ❤ 9am-5pm Mon-Sat) is well done. Check out the giant stuffed polar bear, a vial filled with the first drops of oil extracted, and the story of the first fort, which was built in 1794 (sadly, there's nothing left).

Hwy 29, the scenic shortcut (p327) to/from Prince George, meets the Alaska Hwy 12km north of Fort St John.

As you continue up the Alaska Hwy, you will have plenty of time to marvel at the scenery as the road gradually leaves the foothills and begins a gentle climb into the Rocky Mountains. Most towns on the highway have only one or two service stations. **Wonowon** (One-o-One; 162km north) is cleverly named for its place at Mile 101 on the highway. During highway construction, soldiers were stationed here to search all cars at the Blueberry Checkpoint. If you didn't have enough provisions (and spare auto parts) to make it through the vast wil-

> **DETOUR: KISKATINAW BRIDGE ROUTE**
>
> Take a break from the monotony of this modern stretch of the Alaska Hwy by venturing off into the scenic countryside on some historic roads. About 28km north of Dawson Creek, look for signs and a road to the east that is a 10km remnant of the original Alaska Hwy. The highlight of this pretty little drive is the **Kiskatinaw Bridge**, a 163m curved wooden structure that you drive across. The north end of the road is 41km south from Fort St John.

derness that lay ahead you were turned back. These days kids in the car might seize upon this spot to determine if there are enough DVDs for the journey . If not, it's back to the Wal-Mart in Fort St John.

Like so many tales along the Alaska Hwy, no one can seem to get straight why **Pink Mountain** (226km north) is named Pink Mountain. The color of trees in fall, the sunlight reflecting off the mountain at sunrise, the color of the mayor's underwear, there are all sorts of stories.

Before hitting Fort Nelson, you'll pass by a few provincial parks. First, at 278km north, is the 34-site **Buckinghorse River Provincial Park** (campsite $14), where you might see moose grazing alongside the river. It has pit toilets and fresh water.

Prophet River Provincial Recreation Area (350km north) has access to another original section of the Alaska Hwy. At Km 430, you'll see signs to **Andy Bailey Provincial Recreation Area** (admission by donation), 11km off the highway on a gravel road and enjoying access to quiet Jackfish Lake. The scenery over this entire stretch is pleasant enough but ultimately rather dull. And there's a dearth of 'comfort' stops, which no doubt leads scores of harried drivers to proclaim each day: 'I told you to go before we left!'.

FORT NELSON

pop 4900

You can't help but think of the *Beverly Hill-billies* when you're in Fort Nelson. No, it's not because you'll see the Clampetts riding around in a jalopy with Granny on the back (the locals all have new pick-ups) but because of the classic line in the opening song about 'black gold,' the substance that made the Clampetts rich. Oil is big in Fort Nelson, and so is gas. It's at the center of Canada's fast-booming energy industry and new residents – often young and ready to buy their first fancy pick-up – arrive daily.

As you pass through on the Alaska Hwy, you'll definitely know that you are in a boom-town. New strip malls blot the landscape and you'll be forgiven if you think the town is host to every chain and franchise store on the planet – it is. In 2006, the government's leasing of oil and mineral rights in the area topped $600,000,000 in value, up over 10% from the year before. Home prices in this corner of BC once known for its brutal and long winters are up as well, shooting past an average $230,000 in 2006.

If you might suspect that there is a hidden cost to all this sudden wealth, you'd be right. Oil exploration is dirty business and drilling test holes has left the landscape quite scarred. Of course, any trees that get in the way can go to BC's largest wood products plant, as it's here too. Various First Nations groups have been trying to protest the rampant and destructive use of land for which they have been trying to negotiate as part of a settlement process. Added into the mix is the proposed Enbridge Gateway pipeline project that would take oil extracted from Alberta's tar sands and send it to the BC port of Kitimat, where tankers would take it to the US (see the boxed text, p337). It's intended to pass close to Fort Nelson.

Given that the town is 456km north of Dawson Creek, many people stop here for the night. That really should be your only reason.

The **Visitor Info Centre** (☎ 250-774-2541; www .northernrockies.org; 5500 50th Ave N; ✆ 8am-8pm Jun-Aug, 9am-4pm Mon-Fri Sep-May) has information about surrounding areas, including the scenic points east.

The **Fort Nelson Heritage Museum** (☎ 250-774-3536; adult/child $3/2; ✆ 8:30am-7:30pm May–mid-Sep), at the west end of town, has an old trapper's cabin and displays about the Alaska Hwy.

Sleeping & Eating

With the local boom, motels are often booked out by house-hunting new arrivals. Fortunately there are new motels arriving too.

FROM BOG TO SLOG TO AGOG

Northeastern British Columbia was once just a massive tract of wilderness, with a geography of squishy muskeg ground and vast prairies, so different from the rest of the province that no one really knew what to do with it. With harsh winters and short, hot summers, the massive area attracted few residents, which meant that people tapped into only a speck of its rich natural resources. While the rest of the province was settled and growing, the Peace region was 'that snowy place up there somewhere'. Finally, though, events totally unrelated to this big chunk of forest put the Peace on the proverbial map.

During WWII, the US feared for its unprotected Alaska coast. There was nothing except wind and snow to prevent a Japanese attack on this remote and barely populated territory. The only way there was by plane or by boat along the stormy, dangerous coast. Americans needed a land route through Canada to move troops and supplies to protect Alaska.

The engineering feat that ensued was remarkable by any measure. Under a wartime deadline, survey crews stormed through the vast forests, followed by more than 11,000 troops, 16,000 civilian workers and 7000 pieces of equipment. From the air, it looked like a massive razor had come along and shaved a thick strip of the forest's heavy beard. More than 8000 culverts and 133 bridges crossed rivers. A mere nine months and six days after work started, the 2453km-long route from Dawson Creek to Fairbanks, Alaska, officially opened on November 20, 1942. The cost? A then-astonishing and today still-remarkable US$135 million (that's US$1.7 billion in today's dollars).

Though no one ever attacked mainland Alaska, the highway was an integral part of settlement in the Peace and in the entire northern region of BC. The highway is a vital link between the USA and Canada – and the scenery isn't bad either. For a good idea of what the road was like in its early days, check out the historic segment north of Fort St John (p329).

For more on the Alaska Hwy, including its immensely difficult construction in the Yukon, see the boxed text, p367.

Most are southwest of the center along the highway.

Blue Bell Inn (☎ 250-774-6961, 800-663-5267; www .bluebellinn.ca; r $70-110; ✗ 🖵) This non-chain motel contains a restaurant, 24-hour convenience store, coin laundry and 57 comfortable rooms with kitchenettes and high-speed internet. It also has 42 campsites (from $20).

Dan's Neighbourhood Pub (☎ 250-774-3929; 4204 50th Ave N; meals $7-15; ☾ 11am-late) Always fun – unless you stand on the bar and rip the world's dependence on oil – Dan's has a relaxing patio and a long and interesting menu that rises above pub food.

FORT NELSON TO WATSON LAKE

After Fort Nelson, you can put drilling behind you. The 513km drive to Watson Lake passes through some truly under-appreciated scenery – you'll see more wildlife here than in any other part of western Canada. Be prepared for vistas, peaks, lakes and lots of atmospheric, lonely stretches of highway (that is until you come across a bear). Muncho Lake is an azure jewel among the Rockies.

At Km 484, 28km past Fort Nelson, the Liard Hwy (Hwy 77) heads north to the Northwest Territories, Fort Simpson and the remote Nahanni National Park.

At Km 594, 138km west of Fort Nelson, the highway passes through the north end of beautiful **Stone Mountain Provincial Park**, in the eastern Muskwa Ranges of the Rockies; the 'stone mountain' in question is Mt St Paul (2127m). From the top you see successions of tree- and snow-covered peaks in all directions. The park's 28-site **campground** (campsite $14; ☾ May-Oct) offers access to hiking trails and backcountry camping. Look for the dramatic hoodoos – eroded stone pillars – at **Wokkpash Creek**. Throughout this area you're likely to see stone sheep, which are darker, smaller versions of bighorn sheep.

At the tiny town of **Toad River**, a former hunting lodge, **Toad River Lodge** (☎ 250-232-5401; www.toadriverlodge.com; Km 648; r $60-75), is a classic roadside icon: its pub has a ceiling lined with hundreds of baseball caps from around the world. It also has six cabins, six basic rooms and a garage.

Muncho Lake Provincial Park

Spruce forests, vast rolling mountains and some truly breathtaking scenery surround Muncho Lake Provincial Park, which begins at Km 695.

This 88,412-hectare park lies along Muncho Lake, which seems to glow with an emerald-green brilliance. 'Muncho' means 'big lake' in the Tagish language (and 'bad junk food' in the English language); 12km long, it's one of the largest natural lakes in the Rockies. For the Alaska highway construction crews, cutting the rocky terrace along the lakeside was the most difficult and costly part of the construction in the region. Today, it's an unforgettable piece of road. Stone sheep often gather alongside the highway to lick the artificial accumulations of salt on the stones. The mountains are part of the Terminal Range, which mark the northernmost section of the Rocky Mountains, ending at Liard River (60km northwest). The mountains extending into the Yukon and Alaska are the Mackenzies, which are geologically different. Of Muncho Lake's two campgrounds, 15-site **Strawberry Flats Campground** (Km 700; campsite $14) is especially stunning. It's on a point overlooking the lake's turquoise waters.

There are a few lodges scattered along the highway through the park. **Northern Rockies Lodge** (☎ 250-776-3481, 800-663-5269; www.northern -rockies-lodge.com; Km 708; campsite from $25, r $60-80) is easily one of the nicest. It has 45 rooms in the main lodge and log-style chalets. There are 35 RV campsites along the water.

Liard River Hotsprings Provincial Park

Take time to smell the orchids (there are 14 varieties) at the divine mineral springs here, long favored by Natives, trappers, smelly explorers, and now travelers. The underground bubbling springs create a lush boreal marsh and tropical vegetation that seems very out of place this far north. A remarkable 250 species of plants grow in this unique ecosystem.

A 500m boardwalk from the parking lot leads to the large **Alpha pool** (day use adult/child $5/3), where you can sit and soak for hours. If you get tired of that, walk around and check out some of the strikingly green ferns or colorful wildflowers that thrive in the heat and humidity. From the Alpha pool, stroll five minutes further up the boardwalk to the deeper, slightly cooler 3m-deep **Beta pool** (day use adult/ child $5/3). Fewer people come here, so take the opportunity to jump in and swim over to the sides where it's shallower; be sure to let the warm bottom mud ooze through your toes. One of the great things about both pools is that they're natural – no concrete creations looking like motel refugees here.

DAMN BEETLES

The mountain pine beetle is the size of a grain of rice. Its favorite meal is mature lodgepole pines, the most common trees across a swath of Canada from northern BC east to Alberta and beyond. Beetles attack the trees, killing them by eating the insides and leaving a fungus that chokes off the water supply. Historically nature has held the beetles in check through long cold winters that killed the beetles. But now with global warming, the beetles are thriving to such an extent that they have killed millions of trees across BC's north, extending south through the Cariboo-Chilcotin and the Fraser-Thompson regions. For the bugs, their world has become a holiday in Florida.

The results are the swatches of brilliant red pine trees that look like an autumn dream which line the hills. But of course the trees should be green and efforts to stop the beetle have proven futile. This is environmental destruction on a vast scale. The one major consequence is that logging of the forests has more than doubled and the wood products industry has invoked this circular logic: if you'd let us log the forests in the first place, the beetle wouldn't have killed them. See the text, p371 for details of what the spruce beetle has done to the Yukon's forests.

Beware: the pools can get crowded in July and August. If you can't come in the spring or fall, try coming later at night, when the families have gone off to dreamland. The park gate is closed from 11pm to 6am; outside of these hours you can still go in the springs, but if you're not camping in the park, you need to leave your car outside the gate and walk in.

The park's **campground** (☎ 800-689-9025; www .discovercamping.ca; campsite $14-17) has 52 sites. Rangers run interpretive programs throughout the summer.

From here it is 220km to Watson Lake and the Yukon (p368). Look for **scenic overlooks** of the Liard and Dease Rivers all the way to the Yukon border.

YELLOWHEAD HIGHWAY

With its roots in the Canadian prairies and Winnipeg, the 3185km Yellowhead Hwy takes a long time building to reach this, its grand finale through beautiful mountain scenery and rivers ending at the Pacific Ocean. It is the only highway spanning northern BC: from Alberta's beautiful Jasper National Park in the east (p298) through the confluence of Prince George and on to surprising Prince Rupert, the Yellowhead can be a trip in itself.

From Prince George, the highway meanders into the heart of the Lakes District at Burns Lake, then through the alpine outdoor adventure town of Smithers to the Hazeltons, an area rich in First Nations history. From there, it cuts southwest to Terrace, passing the junction for Hwy 37, the Stewart-Cassiar

Hwy (p353), an increasingly popular route to the Yukon. The 147km drive from Terrace to Prince Rupert is consistently rated one of the most scenic in the province; the Skeena River flows alongside the highway as it meanders through verdant mountains rich in wildlife. From Prince Rupert, ferries cruise in every direction: north to Alaska, south to Vancouver Island or west to the Queen Charlotte Islands (where the Yellowhead Hwy technically begins again, but that's just a political gimmick).

VIA Rail's *Skeena* line parallels the Yellowhead from Jasper to Prince Rupert.

VANDERHOOF

Vanderhoof (population 4800) is 97km west of Prince George. It's the first town of any size that you'll encounter and is mainly a service center – you can get a cup of coffee at one of the several gas stations. Nestled in the fertile Nechako River Valley, the town occupies the geographical center of the province. Prime grazing lands – cattle, buffalo and dairy farming – along with forestry, provide the main sources of income here. Vanderhoof roughly means Dutch for 'of the farm', which is appropriate as this was the first permanent agricultural settlement in the province.

FORT ST JAMES NATIONAL HISTORIC SITE

Simon Fraser may have been searching for a navigable route to the Pacific Ocean when he founded this site, but you don't need to search at all. Just make the drive up to this highlight of the Yellowhead Hwy.

THE NORTH

Fraser used this outpost as a place to trade furs with the area's trappers, mostly Carrier people, who were a branch of the Dene First Nations. The Carriers got their literal name from the mourning ritual of widows, who carried the ashes of deceased husbands in pouches on their backs until a memorial potlatch could be held. Early French-speaking traders referred to them as 'Porteurs' (porters), which the English-speaking traders later changed to 'Carriers'.

Fraser's post became a commercial center and headquarters of the district of New Caledonia. In 1821 the fort became a Hudson's Bay Company outpost and operated until the early 20th century. Though the relationship between the fur traders and Carriers was an amicable one, it altered some of the hunter-gatherer instincts of the Carrier people and introduced a new kind of greed and materialism, all of which changed the Carriers forever.

Restored in 1971, the **Fort St James National Historic Site** (☎ 250-996-7191; adult/child $7/3.50; ◷ 9am-5pm May-Sep) closely resembles its 1896 appearance. The site gives visitors a fascinating glimpse into recent yet pivotal history. Docents in each of the six major buildings provide background on the structure's function and the people who lived there. Among the nuggets of information you'll learn is that people had to trap a lot of beaver to trade for one blanket. There is a good place to picnic and enjoy the views of the placid lake.

It is 66km on Hwy 27 to the fort from the Hwy 16 turnoff, 7km past Vanderhoof. The town has services and a couple of cafés.

BURNS LAKE
pop 2000

Burns Lake, 229km west of Prince George, serves as the center of the Lakes District and northern gateway to the north part of Tweedsmuir Provincial Park. It also hosts the popular **Burns Lake Bluegrass Festival**, which takes place in mid-July. Out in the middle of the lake is **Deadman's Island Provincial Park**, the province's smallest provincial park, named after an accident that killed two men working on the Grand Trunk Railway (today the CN).

The carved trout sign that welcomes you to Burns Lake is a testimony to the serious anglers who descend upon the area's many lakes in spring and summer to catch rainbow and cutthroat trout, char, kokanee, ling cod and salmon, among other fish.

Like other towns along the Yellowhead, Burns Lake experienced its population boom during the construction of the Grand Trunk Railway. Today, it's a lumber town that has a pretty location and services to speed travelers on their way.

For the best fishing holes, boat rentals and trail information, see the Burns Lake **Visitor Info Centre** (☎ 250-692-3773; www.bldchamber.ca; 540 Hwy 16; ◷ 9am-5pm Jun-Aug, Mon-Fri Sep-May).

One of the best spots for canoeing, kayaking and fishing is 177km-long **Babine Lake**, 34km north of Burns Lake on the Babine Lake Rd. The stunning lake is well worth the detour. You can also access the lake from Topley on Hwy 16.

Sleeping & Eating

There are a few chain motels lurking on the edges of town. The small and simple Burns Lake Municipal Campground is near the center in a pretty area by the lake in Len Radley Memorial Park. The sites are – get this – free. It's just south of the Yellowhead Hwy on Hwy 35; turn at the carved trout sign.

Lakeland Hotel (☎ 250-692-7771, 888-441-2999; lakelandinn@hotmail.com; 329 Hwy 16; r $50-125; ▨ ▯ ▨) Right in the center, with a good restaurant and 25 small but clean rooms with wi-fi. Have a few in the bar and then retire to a Jacuzzi suite.

New Leaf Caffe (☎ 250-692-7709; 425 Hwy 16; snacks $4; ◷ 9am-4pm Mon-Fri) In a health-food store New Leaf offers a tasty alternative to the usual road fare. There's a range of coffee and organic sandwiches.

TWEEDSMUIR PROVINCIAL PARK (NORTH)

Encompassing more than 446,000 hectares, **Tweedsmuir Provincial Park (North)** is part of the province's second-largest provincial park. It's a place renowned by self-sufficient backcountry boaters, who explore remote **Eutsuk Lake**.

On the north and northwest, the park is bordered by the Ootsa-Whitesail Lakes Reservoir, on the west and southwest by the Coast Mountains and on the east by the Interior Plateau. The park is divided by the Dean River; the minimal access possible to Tweedsmuir Provincial Park (South) is off Hwy 20 (see p316).

Unlike many parks named for British dignitaries, Tweedsmuir took its moniker from someone who actually saw the park. In fact,

John Buchan, Baron Tweedsmuir of Elsfield, and also Canada's 15th governor general, traveled extensively through the park on horseback and by floatplane before it took his name.

Wildlife abounds in this vast area and includes woodland caribou, goats, moose, black and grizzly bears and wolves. Up in the air, look for willow ptarmigans, gray-crowned rosy finches and golden-crowned sparrows. In the Nechako Reservoir, look for fish-hunting ospreys in the fallen logs.

Eutsuk Lake forms a system of joining waterways with **Ootsa**, **Whitesail** and **Tetachuck Lakes**. Except for Eutsuk, most lakes were dramatically raised in 1952 with the building of the Kenney Dam and the creation of the Nechako Reservoir. The raised waters were deemed necessary to generate enough power to serve the giant Alcan aluminum smelter in Kitimat. Eutsuk retains a natural purity the other lakes lack.

Anyone venturing into wild Tweedsmuir should plan carefully and be ready to experience full wilderness camping and boating. You will need to be totally self-sufficient and be prepared for any conditions.

Getting There & Away

From Burns Lake, access the park by following Hwy 35 23km south to the François Lake Ferry (free, every 50 minutes, 5:30am to 10:30pm) across François Lake. After about another 40km, you reach the **Little Andrews Bay Marine Park** (access fee $50), where there are eight simple campsites. From here you boat Whitesail Lake to Chikamin Bay, site of the staffed **park ranger station** (May-Oct) where you pay the access fee. All that's left is to use the boat winch ($50 each way) and you're on Eutsuk Lake.

SMITHERS
pop 5600

This is the most appealing town for those looking to take a break between Prince George and Prince Rupert. And it's a great destination in its own right owing to its great location in the heart of the pretty Bulkley Valley, surrounded by the stunning Hudson Bay, Bulkley and Babine Mountains. It offers lots of activities, both in the summer and winter (although it's not quite as frostbitten as it looked standing in for Antarctica in the hit 2006 movie *Eight Below*).

History

Smithers was chosen as the divisional headquarters of the Grand Trunk Railway and was the first village to be incorporated in BC (1921). It became a town in 1967 and today is a government and administrative center with a casual alpine feel that's epitomized by Alpine Al, a wooden statue standing at the head of Main St. Al, along with his 10ft-long alpenhorn, is the town's distinctive mascot.

Smithers has a progressive bent, which works to balance tourist money and development with the downsides of growth.

Information

The weekly *Interior News* is a good local newspaper that provides a real window into the community.

BC Web (250-877-7777; 3855 2nd Ave; per 10 min $1; 9am-6pm Mon-Sat) Has a small internet café and can fix your iPod or sell you a new one.

Mountain Eagle Books & Bistro (250-847-5245; 3775 3rd St; 9am-6pm Mon-Sat) Has a good range of new and used books and is an excellent spot for community information, including details on the area's thriving folk music scene. The tiny café has great soup and lunches.

Visitor Info Centre (250-847-5072, 800-542-6673; www.tourismsmithers.com; 1411 Court St; 9am-6pm May-Sep, 9am-5pm Mon-Fri Oct-Apr) Across the parking lot from the Bulkley Valley Museum, this center covers the region. It offers everything from postage stamps to internet access.

Wash the Works (250-847-4177; 4148 Hwy 16; load $5; 8am-9pm) The name says it all: you can get coin-operated cleaning for your clothes, your car and your body.

Sights

Smithers' **Main St** is a delightful place for a stroll, with a full range of shops and services. There are enjoyable walks along the **Bulkley River** just north of the center at **Riverside Park**.

In the 1925 former courthouse at the crossroads of Main St and Hwy 16, you'll find the **Bulkley Valley Museum** (250-847-5322; admission free; 10am-5pm), which features exhibits on Smithers' pioneer days. In the same building, the **Smithers Art Gallery** (250-847-3898; admission by donation; noon-4pm Mon-Sat) displays and sells works by local and regional artists.

The 1810m **Kathlyn Glacier**, an Ice Age survivor, carved a 1.6km-wide gulch into Hudson Bay Mountain and recedes more every year. Gushing waterfalls cascade off its back, providing spectacular views in summer and world-class ice climbing in winter. From the parking lot, a short, easy trail leads to a viewing platform at the base of the glacier's **Twin Falls**, which plunge for 90m. More adventurous types can do the steep three-hour climb to the toe of the glacier. The less adventurous can view the glacier from the highway, a little further west of town. To get there, drive 4km west of Smithers, then take Kathlyn Glacier Rd and follow the signs for 6.1km.

The small and historic town of **Telkwa** (population 1450), 8km west on Hwy 16, has some nice river walks. The **Old Ranger Station Gallery** (☎ 250-846-5454; Hwy 16) has art, books and more by local artists and writers.

Activities

Mountain biking is popular throughout the Bulkley Valley and you'll find some well-maintained trails for all levels of rider. There are numerous outdoor gear stores on Main St, including **McBike & Sport** (☎ 250-847-5009; www.mcbike.bc.ca; 1191 Main St; ☺ 9am-6pm Mon-Sat) for trail information. The shop rents bikes for $20/30 per half-/full day and leads guided tours. It also rents drift boats for fishing (from $150 per day).

Valhalla Pure Outfitters (☎ 250-847-0200; 1122 Main St) has gear, advice and organizes tours for hiking, backpacking and climbing. The VIC (opposite) can recommend guides and instructors for a range of activities. See p336 for two excellent nearby parks.

For an injection of pure adrenaline, join a white-water rafting trip on the Babine River to Hazelton in the Bulkley River Canyon. Several local companies offer trips, usually from about $100 per person. Kayaking is big, and the river and many lakes offer a lot opportunities for one day, or longer, trips. Contact **Babine Mountain Watersports** (☎ 250-847-2779; dfw@telus.net; kayaks per day from $65) for information on trips and renting gear. A popular place for kayakers is Tatlow Falls.

For skiing, **Ski Smithers** (☎ 250-847-2058; www.skismithers.com; one-day lift pass adult/child $37/20) is a low-key ski resort on Hudson Bay Mountain, with 34 mostly intermediate runs. The vertical drop is 533m. Most local sporting stores rent gear.

Festivals & Events

If you're around in late June, don't miss the legendary **Bulkley Valley Folk Music Society Midsummer Festival** (☎ 250-847-1971; www.bvfms.org; adult/child $40/30), which features lots of live music.

Mountain Eagle Books & Bistro (opposite) is a center of information for the event.

Sleeping

The VIC (opposite) makes free accommodations reservations and has lists of B&Bs and holiday homes. There are several motels on or near Hwy 16.

Riverside Park Municipal Campsite (☎ 250-847-1600; campsite $15-21) The sites have a bucolic location right on the river and there are lockers. You can drive or make the 10-minute walk up Queen St from the center.

Tyee Lake Provincial Park (☎ 800-689-9025; www.discovercamping.ca; Hwy 16; campsite $20) This is 8km east of Smithers off Hwy 16, and has 59 popular wooded sites and a playground.

Smithers Guesthouse & Hostel (☎ 250-847-4862; www.smithershostel.com; 1766 Main St; dm from $24, r $40-70; ☐) In a residential area close to both the center and Riverside Park. It has simple, clean rooms and high-speed internet access. It gets a lot of fan mail.

Fireweed Motor Inn (☎ 250-847-2208; fireweedmotorinn@hotmail.com; 1515 Main St N; r $54-70; ☒ ☐ ☐) Close to the center and stores, this two-story motel-style place has 20 decent rooms with wi-fi, fridges, microwaves and more.

Stork Nest Inn (☎ 250-847-3831; www.storknestinn.com; 1485 Main St; r $65-80; ☒ ☐) The 23 basic and fairly new rooms have doors off inside corridors. Guests receive a large breakfast and have access to high-speed internet access. The center is a brief walk.

Eating

Alpenhorn Pub & Bistro (☎ 250-847-5366; 1261 Main St; meals $7-12; ☺ 11am-late) The pub menu at this big place is a winner (the Caesar salad has a tangy garlic zing). The fireplace is cozy and there's a patio, and the Rickard's Red beer has gusto.

Ironhorse Café & Bar (☎ 250-877-7870; 3700 Railway Ave; meals $7-15; ☺ 9am-4pm Sun & Mon, 9am-9pm Tue-Sat; ☐) Located in a restored part of the old train station, this excellent café has a bakery, good omelets, burgers, salads, steaks and more. It also has a coffee bar and free wi-fi. Grab a table outside and watch the trains go by.

Getting There & Away

Four kilometers west of town off Hwy 16 is **Smithers Airport** (YYD; ☎ 250-847-3664). Air Canada Jazz serves Vancouver.

THE NORTH

Greyhound (☎ 250-847-2204; 4011 Hwy 16) serves Prince George ($60, five hours, two daily) and Prince Rupert ($55, five hours, two daily) along Hwy 16.

The VIA Rail's *Skeena* stops in Smithers; the station is at the south end of Main St. The tri-weekly service takes six hours to both Prince George and Prince Rupert.

AROUND SMITHERS

Babine Mountains Provincial Park (☎ 250-847-7329) is a 32,400-hectare park deep in the glorious backcountry wilderness of the Babine Range of the Skeena Mountains. Trails to glacier-fed lakes and sub-alpine meadows provide accessible hiking and mountain biking during summer, while during winter, the trails make excellent routes for snowshoeing and cross-country skiing. The recently renovated **Fletcher-Gardner Trail** is a 13km hike through gorgeous wilderness to Lower Reiseter Lake, and makes a great spot for some wilderness camping.

Look for healthy populations of moose, marmots and mountain goats. To reach the park, follow Hwy 16 for 3km east of Smithers, and then turn northeast onto Babine Lake Rd, then north onto McCabe Rd which zigs into Driftwood Rd. It's about 16km total. You can backcountry camp here.

Driftwood Canyon Provincial Park (☎ 250-638-8490) was created in 1976 to protect the rich fossil beds that were discovered along the Driftwood Creek around 1900. Formations found in the shale indicate that plants, insects and animals lived in the area some 50 million years ago. Over time, the running creek eroded through the sedimentation, finally exposing the fossil beds.

Today, you can walk to a viewing platform on the east bank of the creek, where interpretive panels describe the area's geological significance. It's on Driftwood Rd, 5km before Babine Mountains Provincial Park.

MORICETOWN

pop 660

Going 20km west of Smithers, the small burg of Moricetown was built near the **Bulkley River Gorge**. Here a centuries-old salmon trap is still used by local First Nations people to net salmon each summer. The view and the spectacle of the huge silvery fish leaping through the water makes this a mandatory stop. It's right on Hwy 16.

NEW HAZELTON & AROUND

If you haven't seen forests of totem poles yet, the towns of New Hazelton, Hazelton and South Hazelton (area population 6400) are the places to see 'em (opposite). Named for the hazelnut bushes growing along the river terraces, the three towns have large First Nations populations and sit within the walls of the rugged Rocher de Boule (Mountain of Rolling Rock), near the confluence of the Skeena and Bulkley Rivers.

The Skeena River (skeena means mist) has long been an integral part of the area. The Gitksan and Wet'suwet-en people, who have lived here for more than 7000 years, first navigated cedar canoes along the treacherous Skeena all the way out to the coast. Fur trappers arrived in the area around 1866.

The town became an active and boisterous commercial center in the early 1900s. Soon, the influx of people spread, scattering inland to find riches in the mines, to stake land claims and to build farms. When the Grand Trunk Railway construction crews rolled through in 1914, they brought more people, more rowdiness and some general confusion about the profusion of Hazeltons.

For the record: **Hazelton** (also called the Old Town) was the original settlement, established long before the train showed up. Once it did, Hazelton was slated to become a ghost town with the founding of the 'South' and 'New' Hazeltons. The new communities vied for the position of commercial center and remained in a bitter and ridiculous battle while the train went bankrupt. Today, **New Hazelton** is the commercial center along Hwy 16; South Hazelton is essentially tacked onto it. The original Hazelton has found new life as a pioneer town with shops and the 'Ksan Historical Village.

DETOUR: KISPIOX ROUTE

The small First Nations village of **Kispiox** (population 800) has a stunning line of 16 totem poles. Many are recent, a result of the continuing resurgence of First Nations culture and art. Stop by the **Community Centre** (Lac Seel St), where you may be able to arrange a detailed tour. Kispiox is reached by a 13km paved road of the same name which begins near Hazelton. Watch for farm stands as you drive.

PIPELINE TO TROUBLE?

The industrial town of Kitimat will be the endpoint of the proposed **Enbridge Gateway Pipeline**, a $4 billion project that would bring oil to the coast from the oil sands fields 1150km east in northern Alberta. A companion pipeline will take 'condensate', a by-product of natural gas, from Kitimat to Alberta where it will be blended with the crude oil to make it flow easier.

The project has stirred the expected controversy from communities – especially First Nations ones – along its entire path. But what has really worried environmental groups is, the new port in Kitimat that will see tankers carrying both crude oil and distillate. The consequences of an *Exxon Valdez*–style spill are unthinkable. So far the federal and provincial governments can barely hide their glee at the project, which will send oil to gas-ravenous California.

The area's **Visitor Info Centre** (☎ 250-842-6071; junction Hwys 16 & 62; ◴ 8am-8pm Jul & Aug, 9am-5pm mid-May, Jun & Sep) is an essential stop for sorting through the various local sights. The photo-copied 'Hazeltons Explorers Journey' is vital, but also spend $2 for the 'Tour of the Totems'. In the summer there's a weekend **farmers' market** in the VIC parking lot. Look for lots of produce – especially berries – from the fertile fields and prepared First Nations food.

There are motels, campgrounds and restaurants in each of the Hazeltons.

You can spend half a day or more exploring the Hazeltons and the totem poles in 'Ksan Historical Village (below), Kispiox (see the boxed text, opposite) and Gitanyow (p353).

Hazelton

Amidst the rolling hills, the dramatic **Hagwilget Bridge** stands out – literally. It soars 100m over the Skeena River and is 2km into the 7km drive to Hazelton from the VIC. You can stop and walk across for some vertigo-inspiring views. In Hazelton stroll the banks of the Skeena River and explore the historic buildings. Placards along the river detail local history.

'Ksan Historical Village & Museum (☎ 250-842-5544; www.ksan.org; admission $2; ◴ 9:30am-4:30pm Mon-Fri, 9am-5pm Apr-Sep) is a replicated Gitksan Native village. It is one of BC's best windows into the culture. For a complete experience take one of the **guided tours** (adult/child $10/8.50; ◴ every 30 min) which provide essential context. Tours take you through the Frog House of the Distant Past, the Wolf House of Feasts and the Fireweed House of Masks and Robes. Along the way, you'll learn about Gitksan arts, culture, totem poles and beliefs. Note that the village is very popular and can get mobbed in summer. The Eagle House sells aboriginal snacks.

NEW HAZELTON TO PRINCE RUPERT

The junction with the **Stewart-Cassiar Highway** (p353; Hwy 37), a rapidly improving route north to the Yukon which also gives access to splendid Stewart and Hyder (p354) and totem-pole-filled Gitanyow (p353), is 25km west of New Hazelton.

Terrace (population 12,700) is a logging, government, service and transportation center astride the Skeena River. There's little reason to linger, but you can get a good break on trail-filled **Ferry Island**, off Hwy 16 just east of the center. It's also the junction for the highway to the Nisga'a Lava Bed (below) and the alternate route to the Stewart-Cassiar Hwy (see the boxed text, p352).

Nestled in the pit of the Douglas Channel's Kitimat Arm 58km south of Terrace (at the southernmost point of Hwy 37), **Kitimat** (population 10,100) has great natural potential – towering mountains, a deep protected port, fresh- and salt-water fishing – but has sold its future to industry and is welcoming a controversial possible new oil pipeline (see the boxed text, above).

The 146km **Skeena River drive** between Terrace and Prince Rupert is one of the most scenic in BC. Hwy 16 runs right alongside the ever-widening river. At time there is barely enough room for the road and the parallel CN train tracks between the river and the sheer rock walls of the hillside.

Nisga'a Lava Bed

Nisga'a Memorial Lava Bed Provincial Park (☎ 250-798-2277, tour information 250-633-2991) is for anyone intrigued by volcanoes. Jointly managed by the Nisga'a Nation and the government, this 18,000-hectare park in the beautiful Nass Basin, 91km north of Terrace along the Nisga'a Hwy, is one of the most extraordinary parks in the province. About 250 years ago, a

THE NORTH

massive volcanic eruption spilled hot, heavy lava onto the Nass floodplain. Destroying entire villages, suffocating vegetation and killing more than 2000 Nisga'a ancestors, the lava covered an area 10km long and 3km wide. It even rerouted the Nass River to the north edge of the valley, where it still flows today.

The lava created various formations (depending on the speed at which it flowed), including lava tubes, chunks and ropelike Paahoehoe lava. The pale gray rocks look almost furry with the hardened ash; the effect is reminiscent of a lunar landscape. Most of the **trails** in the park are short and accessible from the highway. One of the best is about 4km south of the Visitor Interpretation Centre and goes to **Vetter Falls**. The short trail traverses a lava bed before plunging into thick forest, where you'll find the namesake waterfall. It's a serene, almost magical place.

At the edge of the main lava bed the **Visitor Interpretation Centre** (☎ 250-638-9589; ☾ 10am-6pm mid-Jun–Aug) is in a traditional Nisga'a longhouse. Here you can get information on the history of the Nisga'a and pick up the *Self-Guided Auto Tour* brochure ($1), which offers good descriptions of park highlights. You can also book **tours** (adult/child $25/15; ☾ 10am Sat mid-Jun–Aug). There's a pretty 16-site **campground** (campsite $14) beside the visitor center.

The Nisga'a village of **Nass Camp** is about 7km northwest of the Visitor Interpretation Centre. Near here is the junction with the logging road that connects to the Stewart-Cassiar Hwy at Cranberry Junction. See the boxed text, p352 for details.

PRINCE RUPERT

pop 15,100

Prince Rupert is an ideal starting point for trips to Alaska and the amazing Queen Charlotte Islands. It's a town with cultural attractions, good restaurants and an often slightly goofy charm that only adds to its beautiful waterside location. Ferries converge here from Vancouver Island and the south, and from Alaska to the north.

After Vancouver, 'Rupert', as it's known, is the largest city on the mainland BC coast; it's also the wettest. It rains 220 days a year, giving the city one of the highest precipitation rates in all of Canada. And even when it's raining, misty, foggy or cloudy, its rugged mountain beauty and fjord-like coastal setting near the mouth of the Skeena River shouldn't

be missed. A new waterfront casino – near the Crest Hotel – promises to attract more visitors.

History

If the reasons for Prince George's name are unknown (see p321), little more is known about why Prince Rupert came to be named for an obscure German prince who fought for the English monarchy in the 1600s.

Perhaps Charles Hays was a fan. He was the general manager of the Grand Trunk Railway who, in 1906, saw in the vast harbor setting the potential to build a town that would rival Vancouver. Serious financial problems plagued the railway when Hays, who was off touring, unwisely booked fatal passage home on the *Titanic*. To make matters worse, WWI came along, stripping the region of young men, and the railway eventually suffered the indignity of having its assets frozen by the courts. The town never developed into the vast metropolis Hays envisioned but instead became a fishing center for the Pacific Northwest.

The Grand Trunk Railway ultimately became part of the CN system which 100 years later may finally allow Hays' dream for the world's deepest natural ice-free port to be realized. Prince Rupert's sleepy grain port is being transformed into a modern container terminal which will handle the world's largest container ships. This, coupled with the fact that the CN line along the Skeena (which continues via downtown Jasper, p298) can cut days off the travel times of shipments of Chinese-made goods like TVs, toasters and T-shirts to the heart of the US, means that the port is expected to be very busy. By 2010 over 1000 new jobs will have been created in perennially job-poor Rupert and some of the Chinese stuff will be staying right here.

Orientation

Prince Rupert is on Kaien Island and is connected to the mainland by a bridge on Hwy 16. Cow Bay, named for a dairy farm that used to be located here, has become a historic waterfront area full of shops and restaurants and the increasingly busy cruise ship port, Atlin Terminal. Cow Bay is just north of the compact and somewhat hilly downtown which has that odd Canadian system of naming intersecting streets and avenues with the same number.

Information

BOOKSTORE

Eddie's News (☎ 250-624-4134; 611 2nd Ave W) Lots of magazines and a few books.

Rainforest Books (☎ 250-624-4195; 251 3rd Ave W) This place has a good selection of new releases and used books.

INTERNET ACCESS

Java Dot Cup (☎ 250-622-2822; 516 3rd Ave W; per hr $4; ⏲ 7:30am-9pm) Has numerous terminals plus a decent café in a heritage setting.

LAUNDRY

King Koin (☎ 250-624-2667; 745 2nd Ave W; ⏲ 8am-10pm) Self-serve or drop clothes off for royal treatment.

LIBRARY

Prince Rupert Library (☎ 250-627-1345; 101 6th Ave W; ⏲ 10am-9pm Mon-Thu, 10am-5pm Fri, 1-5pm Sat & Sun) Has wi-fi.

MEDICAL SERVICES

Prince Rupert Regional Hospital (☎ 250-624-2171; 1305 Summit Ave; ⏲ 24hr) In Roosevelt Park.

POST

Post office (☎ 250-627-3085; Rupert Sq Mall; ⏲ 8:30am-5pm Mon-Fri)

TOURIST INFORMATION

Visitor Info Centre (☎ 250-624-5637, 800-667-1994; www.tourismprincerupert.com; ⏲ 9am-8pm May-Sep, 9am-5pm Oct-Apr) In the Cow Bay Atlin Terminal.

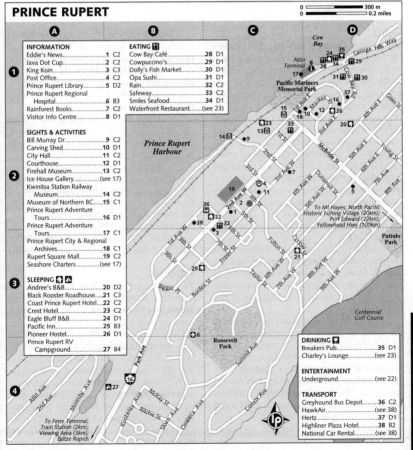

PRINCE RUPERT

INFORMATION	
Eddie's News	1 C2
Java Dot Cup	2 C2
King Koin	3 C3
Post Office	4 C2
Prince Rupert Library	5 D2
Prince Rupert Regional Hospital	6 B3
Rainforest Books	7 C2
Visitor Info Centre	8 D1

SIGHTS & ACTIVITIES	
Bill Murray Dr	9 C2
Carving Shed	10 D1
City Hall	11 D1
Courthouse	12 D1
Firehall Museum	13 C2
Ice House Gallery	(see 17)
Kwinitsa Station Railway Museum	14 C2
Museum of Northern BC	15 C1
Prince Rupert Adventure Tours	16 D1
Prince Rupert Adventure Tours	17 C1
Prince Rupert City & Regional Archives	18 C1
Rupert Square Mall	19 C2
Seashore Charters	(see 17)

SLEEPING	
Andree's B&B	20 D2
Black Rooster Roadhouse	21 C3
Coast Prince Rupert Hotel	22 C2
Crest Hotel	23 C2
Eagle Bluff B&B	24 D1
Pacific Inn	25 B3
Pioneer Hostel	26 D1
Prince Rupert RV Campground	27 B4

EATING	
Cow Bay Café	28 D1
Cowpuccino's	29 D1
Dolly's Fish Market	30 D1
Opa Sushi	31 D1
Rain	32 C2
Safeway	33 C2
Smiles Seafood	34 C2
Waterfront Restaurant	(see 23)

DRINKING	
Breakers Pub	35 D1
Charley's Lounge	(see 23)

ENTERTAINMENT	
Underground	(see 22)

TRANSPORT	
Greyhound Bus Depot	36 C2
HawkAir	(see 38)
Hertz	37 D1
Highliner Plaza Hotel	38 B2
National Car Rental	(see 38)

Cow Bay

George Hills Way

Atlin Terminal

Pacific Mariners Memorial Park

Prince Rupert Harbour

To Mt Hayes; North Pacific Historic Fishing Village (20km); Port Edward (22km); Yellowhead Hwy (100km)

Pattulo Park

Roosevelt Park

Centennial Golf Course

To Ferry Terminal, Train Station (2km); Viewing Area (3km); Butze Rapids

---

TSIMSHIANS & COUSINS

Various clans of northwest coast First Nations have inhabited this area for almost 10,000 years. Though more than 20 distinct native cultures lived here throughout history, the majority were (and still are) Tsimshian (poetically pronounced sim-*she*-an), as evidenced by the remains of 55 villages dotted around the harbor. Prior to the arrival of Europeans, this was one of the most populated areas in North America; archaeological digs have uncovered evidence of human habitation dating back thousands of years.

When the Europeans arrived in 1834, nearby Port Simpson (then called 'Fort' Simpson) became a Hudson's Bay Company trading post that eventually lured the Tsimshians away from their seclusion in Prince Rupert. The usual slew of diseases weakened the First Nations populations, and in 1884 the government banned the Natives from holding potlatches, one of the highest forms of celebration in First Nations culture. The failing population and cultural oppression hit hard, and decades of struggle to retain land and cultural freedom ensued.

Today, the Tsimshian population in Prince Rupert is doing better. Like the Haida on the Queen Charlotte Islands, the Tsimshians have a strong oral history and prodigious artistic ability, both of which have allowed them to recapture and build upon their cultural past, as you can see at the Museum of Northern British Columbia (below).

Sights

The amazing **Museum of Northern British Columbia** (☎ 250-624-3207; www.museumofnorthernbc.com; 100 1st Ave W; adult/child $5/1; ☯ 9am-8pm Mon-Sat, 9am-5pm Sun May-Sep, 9am-5pm Mon-Sat Oct-Apr) resides inside a post-and-beam building styled after a First Nations longhouse. This is something not to be missed. Through excellent exhibits and superb documentation, the museum shows how local civilizations enjoyed sustainable cultures that lasted for thousands of years. Using technologies based on steam, the people were able to make items as diverse as soup ladles (from goat horns) to canoes (from huge spruce logs). The displays include a wealth of excellent Haida, Gitksan and Tsimshian art. Special tours of the museum and walking tours of the town are excellent.

Included with the museum admission, the **Kwinitsa Station Railway Museum** (☯ 9am-5pm May-Sep), down the hill on Bill Murray Dr, is housed in an old train station. It documents the drama surrounding the building of the railway to Rupert.

You'll see **totems** all around town; two flank the statue of Charlie Hays beside City Hall on 3rd Ave. Many totems are replicas of very well-known traditional works. In summer, the Museum of Northern British Columbia offers guided **heritage** and **totem walking tours** around town ($2). Check for tour times. To witness totem-building in action, stop by the **Carving Shed**, next door to the courthouse. Often you'll see local artists there working on jewelry or cedar carvings.

A short walk from the center, **Cow Bay** is a delightful place for a stroll. The eponymous spotted decor is everywhere but somehow avoids being grating. There are shops, cafés and a good view of the waterfront where you can see both fishing boats and cruise ships unloading their catch.

The **Prince Rupert City & Regional Archives** (☎ 250-624-3326; 100 1st Ave E; ☯ 10am-3pm Mon-Fri) contains a huge collection of photographs, nautical charts and books.

Fire engine buffs – and addled rock fans – will enjoy the rebuilt 1925 REO Speedwagon fire engine at the small **Firehall Museum** (☎ 250-627-4475; 200 1st Ave W; admission by donation; ☯ 10am-4pm summer), beside the real fire hall.

See the bounty of Rupert's vibrant creative community at the artist-run **Ice House Gallery** (☎ 250-624-4546; Atlin Terminal; ☯ noon-5pm Tue-Sun).

Activities

You can picnic, swim, fish, hike or take out a canoe at **Diana Lake Provincial Park** and **Prudhomme Lake Provincial Park**, about 16km east of town on Hwy 16.

Dozens of charter-boat operators run **fishing** trips out of Prince Rupert, some just for the halibut, others for salmon and other fish. The VIC (p339) has a comprehensive list or you can wander Cow Bay and chat with the skippers.

Skeena Kayaking (☎ 250-624-5246; www.skeena kayaking.ca; rentals per 24hr $85) offers both rentals and custom tours of the area, which has a seemingly infinite variety of places to put into the water.

THE NORTH

Of the many **hiking** trails in and around town, one path goes up 732m **Mount Hays** from the Butze Rapids parking lot, east of town on Hwy 16. On a clear day, you can see local islands, the Queen Charlotte Islands and even Alaska.

Beginning at a parking lot on the Yellowhead Hwy, 3km south of town just past the industrial park, trails lead to Mt Oldfield, Tall Trees (you'll see some old cedars) and **Butze Rapids**. The rapids walk is a flat, 4km loop to Grassy Bay with interpretive signs; the others are more demanding. The VIC offers details on these and others.

Tours

Pike Island is a small island past Digby Island outside of the harbor. Thriving villages were based there as long as 2000 years ago, and remnants and evidence of these can still be seen today. **Seashore Charters** (☎ 250-624-5645, 800-667-4393; Atlin Terminal; tours adult/child from $50/40) runs half-day trips to Laxspa'aws, as the island is known, that include a 40-minute boat ride each way and the services of a First Nations guide. Seashore Charters also offers various harbor and wildlife tours. Phone ahead for times.

Prince Rupert Adventure Tours (☎ 250-627-9166; 207 3rd Ave E; adult/child from $45/35) offers harbor tours through the year. It also runs tours to

see whales and various other wildlife-related trips (adult/child $145/130). It's also at the Atlin Terminal.

Festivals & Events

In June, **Seafest** (☎ 250-624-9118) celebrates Rupert's seaside location with parties and events like arm-wrestling competitions. The **Udderfest** (☎ 250-624-3626) in August presents five days of fringe theater performed by local groups and national performers.

Sleeping

Rupert has a range of accommodations, but when all three ferries have pulled in (a sort of nautical 'triple witching night'), competition gets fierce; book ahead. Rupert has more than a dozen B&Bs, of which the VIC (p339) has lists.

Prince Rupert RV Campground (☎ 250-624-5861; 1750 Park Ave; campsite from $19) Near the ferry terminal, contains 88 sites, hot showers, laundry and flush toilets. Tent sites are on wooden platforms so your tent doesn't get soaked when (not if) it rains.

Pioneer Hostel (☎ 250-624-2334, 888-794-9998; www.citytel.net/pioneer; 167 3rd Ave E; dm $15-24, r $40-48; 🖳) The small rooms and bathrooms are spotless and accented with vibrant colors. There's a small kitchen, barbecue facilities out back, free bikes and wi-fi.

BEAR HAVEN

Like bears to, well, honey, many travelers are drawn to **Khutzeymateen Grizzly Bear Sanctuary**, a 45,000-hectare park 40km northeast of Prince Rupert. The area has long been important to First Nations people. The name is a Tsimshian word meaning 'confined space of salmon and bears.' Sounds like bear heaven really and today there are about 50 grizzlies thought to be happily living in the confines.

The remote valley is the traditional territory of the Gitsees people, who used the valley for fishing, hunting, trapping and growing food such as berries, crab apples and potatoes. It's rich with all forms of wildlife, which shelter and feed in the thick rain forest and along the river estuary at the mouth.

The park is jointly managed by BC Parks and the Tsimshian First Nations. It was permanently protected as parkland in 1992. In 1994, the area became officially designated as a 'grizzly bear sanctuary' to be jointly managed by the provincial government.

Because grizzlies are reclusive by nature and do better when left alone, the human presence in the park is heavily restricted, though you can join a boat tour or take a floatplane in for a peek. Both Seashore Charters and Prince Rupert Adventure Tours (see Tours, above) offer these types of tours.

The number of guides allowed to lead people into the sanctuary is extremely limited. One, Dan Wakeman of Prince Rupert, has written *Fortress of the Grizzlies: The Khutzeymateen Grizzly Bear Sanctuary*, a book about the preserve. His company, **Sun Chaser Charters** (☎ 250-624-5472; www .citytel.net/sunchaser), runs multi-day trips into the park from $1880 per person for four days.

Black Rooster Roadhouse (☎ 250-627-5337; www .blackrooster.ca; 501 6th Ave W; dm from $20; 🖳) A newish hostel in an oldish house, it's all sparkling here. Guests can enjoy lounging on the patio or in the bright common room. There's wi-fi throughout, free shuttle pick-up and a barbecue.

Eagle Bluff B&B (☎ 250-627-4955; www.citytel.net /eaglebluff; 201 Cow Bay Rd; r $50-90) Right on Cow Bay, this basic place is in a heritage building that has had a colorful restoration. The seven clean rooms vary greatly; some share bathrooms.

Andree's B&B (☎ 250-624-3666; 315 4th Ave E; r $60-95; 🖳) In a historic residential neighborhood close to the center, this three-room B&B is in a grand house that's got old nautical stuff out front and great views out back. It's cute and just a tad cluttered.

Pacific Inn (☎ 250-627-1711, 888-663-1999; www .pacificinn.bc.ca; 909 3rd Ave W; r $75-140; 🖳) Is a comfortable but flash-free place with 77 large and understated rooms. There's free wi-fi and an underground garage so you won't get caught in the rain…

Coast Prince Rupert Hotel (☎ 250-624-6711, 800-663-1144; www.coasthotels.com; 118 6th St; r $85-135; 🍴 🖳) This mid-rise has 92 rooms good for business travelers. All have high-speed internet and decent-sized desks. Some have great views. The hotel also has the popular Underground bar (right).

Crest Hotel (☎ 250-624-6771, 800-663-8150; www .cresthotel.bc.ca; 222 1st Ave W; r $100-180; 🍴 🖳) If you can't score one of the rooms with harbor views, don't bother. The 102 rooms are a bit tight otherwise but nicely appointed. There's also a hot tub with the view. The Crest is very popular locally for its excellent restaurant and bar (right).

Eating

All those fishing boats mean you can enjoy fresh seafood (halibut and salmon star) all over town.

Cowpuccino's (☎ 250-627-1395; 25 Cow Bay Rd; coffee $2; 🕑 7am-8pm) Locally beloved funky coffeehouse with folk music some days.

Dolly's Fish Market (☎ 250-624-6099; 7 Cow Bay Rd; 🕑 10am-5:30pm) This sparkling purveyor serves locally caught fish in many forms and has a lunch café area with daily chowder specials and other tasty seafood treats. If you catch something, get it smoked here.

Opa Sushi (☎ 250-627-4560; 34 Cow Bay Rd; meals $8-18; 🕑 noon-9pm Tue-Sat) With fish this fresh,

why cook it? This welcoming sushi place is in a historic net loft and has views of the harbor. For a treat order the spectacular sashimi on a hand-carved cedar plank. There's a tree-covered terrace out back.

Smiles Seafood (☎ 250-624-3072; 113 Cow Bay Rd; meals $8-25; 🕑 11am-9pm) Since 1934 Smiles has served classic seafood meals that include the 'House of Fish sandwich' and excellent shrimp chowder. Flip over the placemat for a look at the menu from 1945, when a sardine sandwich on toast cost 25¢. There's a patio.

Cow Bay Café (☎ 250-627-1212; 205 Cow Bay Rd; meals $10-20; 🕑 11:30am-9pm) The creative menu changes twice daily but there are always a half dozen mains and amazing desserts to choose from. Enjoy one of the deck tables overlooking the harbor or take time to smell the many pots where fresh herbs grow.

Rain (☎ 250-627-8272; 737 2nd Ave; meals $10-20; 🕑 5pm-2am Mon-Sat) A little bit of Vancouver has fallen on Rupert. This trendy lounge/bistro has a stylish interior, a rooftop deck and an open kitchen that sends out a steady stream of fresh seafood and other seasonal creations. It's all very fresh and artfully presented.

If you're on a tight budget, stock up on food for the ferry at the **Safeway supermarket** (☎ 250-624-5125; 200 2nd Ave W; 🕑 7am-10pm).

Drinking & Entertainment

Feeling like a dive? There's a few old seaman's joints along 2nd Ave W.

Breakers Pub (☎ 250-624-5990; 117 George Hills Way; meals $8; 🕑 11am-late; 🖳) Right on the water at Cow Bay, this fun place has darts, a good beer selection and other diversions like wi-fi and pub grub.

Charley's Lounge (☎ 250-624-6771; Crest Hotel, 222 1st Ave; meals $8-15; 🕑 noon-late) It seems like half the town comes here for the heated patio and its fantastic harbor views. Enjoy a basic pub menu and many choices of BC wines by the glass. It adjoins the excellent high-end Waterfront Restaurant.

Underground (☎ 250-624-6711; Coast Prince Rupert Hotel, 118 6th St; 🕑 5pm-late) Named for its location, this club is a techno vision of red and black with DJs playing dance mixes and occasional live music.

Getting There & Away

There's no shortage of modes of transit in Rupert.

DETOUR: NORTH PACIFIC CANNERY VILLAGE MUSEUM

The **North Pacific Historic Fishing Village** (☎ 250-628-3538; www.cannery.ca; 1889 Skeena Dr; adult/child $12/8; 🕒 10am-7pm mid-May–Sep but phone to confirm), near the town of Port Edward (22km from Prince Rupert), explores the history of fishing and canning along the Skeena River. The fascinating complex was used from 1889 to 1968. Today, exhibits document the miserable conditions of the workers, along with the workings of the industry that helped build the region. The museum should be high on your list of sights and can easily occupy half a day. Guides provide insight into working conditions; watch the restored canning line in action and think about what was required of the average worker to fill 14 trays of cans in four minutes. The complex includes a good café that often serves excellent homemade chowder and salmon. Ask about their B&B. If you're really intrigued, the booklet *Everlasting Memory* ($17) is a good purchase. **Prince Rupert Transit** (☎ 250-624-3343; www.busonline.ca) offers bus service to the site.

AIR
Prince Rupert Airport (YPR; ☎ 250-622-2222; www.ypr.ca) is on Digby Island, across the harbor from town. The entire process of getting to/from town and the airport is an adventure involving a bus and a ferry. Given the complexities, you must be ready to be picked up by the shuttle bus at the **Highliner Plaza Hotel** (815 1st Ave) two hours before flight time. Be sure to confirm all the details with your airline or the airport.

Air Canada Jazz serves Vancouver; check-in is at the airport. **HawkAir** (☎ 866-429-5247; www.hawkair.ca; check-in Highliner Plaza Hotel, 815 1st Ave W) also serves Vancouver.

BUS
Greyhound (☎ 250-624-5090; 112 6th St) buses depart to Prince George ($107, 10 hours, one daily).

FERRY
Ferries share the same general harbor area, although the Alaska Marine Highway terminal is behind large fences as it is considered a US border crossing. All the boats listed here have cafeterias and will let you pitch a tent on deck. For more on the Inside Passage journey, see the boxed text, p400.

The Inside Passage run to Port Hardy (adult/child $116/58, car from $275, cabin from $75, 15 to 25 hours, three per week summer, one per week winter), with **BC Ferries** (☎ 250-386-3431; www.bcferries.com), is justifiably hailed for its amazing, wild scenery. Is that a whale? Queen Charlotte Islands service goes to Skidegate (adult/child $28/14, car from $102, cabin from $55, eight hours, six per week summer, three per week winter).

Alaska Maritime Highway (☎ 250-627-1744, 800-642-0066; www.alaskaferry.com) is an excellent service going to Ketchikan, Wrangell, Petersburg, Juneau and, most importantly, the Yukon-connecting towns of Haines ($172, 33 hours, two to three per week) and Skagway ($184, 35 hours, two to three per week). Cabins cost from $270 and vehicles start at $775.

TRAIN
The western terminus VIA Rail station (at the BC Ferries Terminal south of downtown), operates the tri-weekly *Skeena* to/from Prince George (12½ hours) and after an overnight stop, Jasper in the Rockies.

Getting Around
Prince Rupert Transit (☎ 250-624-3343; www.busonline.ca) has service in the central area (adult/child $1.25/1); and infrequent service to the ferry port and North Pacific Historic Fishing Village ($2.50). The main downtown bus stop is at the Rupert Sq Mall on 2nd Ave.

Major car rental companies include **Hertz** (☎ 250-627-9166; 207 3rd Ave E) and **National** (☎ 250-624-5318; Highliner Plaza Hotel, 815 1st Ave W).

A one-way trip to the ferries or train with **Skeena Taxi** (☎ 250-624-5318) is about $10.

QUEEN CHARLOTTE ISLANDS

pop 6100

There really is no other place in BC like the Queen Charlotte Islands – otherwise known by their traditional name of Haida Gwaii. This wedge-shaped archipelago of some 154 islands lies 80km west of the BC coast and about 50km from the southern tip of Alaska. They might as well be 500 or 5000 miles away in

THE NORTH

QUEEN CHARLOTTE ISLANDS

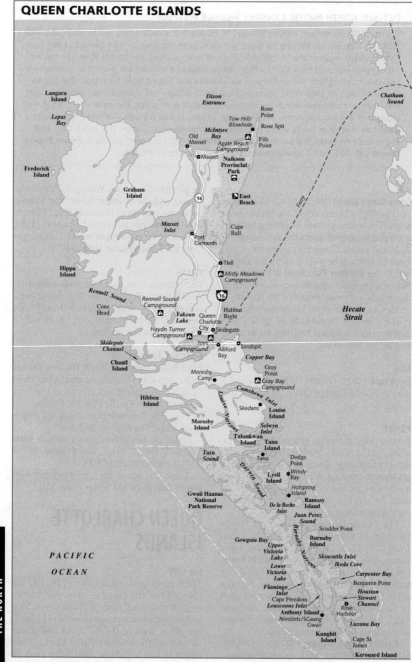

Langara Island
Lepas Bay
Frederick Island
Graham Island
Masset Inlet
Hippa Island
Rennell Sound
Cone Head
Chaatl Island
Hibben Island

Dixon Entrance
Tow Hill/ Blowhole
McIntyre Bay
Old Masset
Agate Beach Campground
Masset
Naikoon Provincial Park
East Beach
Port Clements
Tlell
Misty Meadows Campground
Rennell Sound Campground
Yakoun Lake
Halibut Bight
Queen Charlotte City
Skidegate
Haydn Turner Campground
Joys Campground
Alliford Bay
Sandspit
Skidegate Channel

Rose Point
Rose Spit
Fife Point
Cape Ball

Hecate Strait

Chatham Sound

16
16

Copper Bay
Gray Point
Gray Bay Campground
Moresby Camp
Cumshewa Inlet
Skedans
Louise Island
Louise Narrows
Selwyn Inlet
Moresby Island
Talunkwan Island
Tanu Island
Tasu Sound
Tanu
Dodge Point
Windy Bay
Lyell Island
Hotspring Island
Gwaii Haanas National Park Reserve
De la Beche Inlet
Ramsay Island
Juan Perez Sound
Scudder Point
Gowgaia Bay
Burnaby Island
Upper Victoria Lake
Skincuttle Inlet
Ikeda Cove
Lower Victoria Lake
Carpenter Bay
Benjamin Point
Flamingo Inlet
Cape Freedom
Houston Stewart Channel
Louscoone Inlet
Anthony Island
Ninstints/SGaang Gwaii
Rose Harbour
Luxana Bay
Kunghit Island
Cape St James
Kerouard Island

PACIFIC OCEAN

THE NORTH

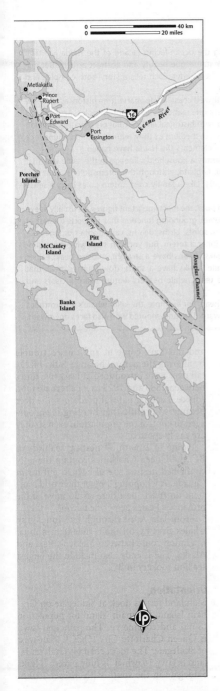

many respects. This sparsely populated, wild, rainy and almost magical place abounds with flora and fauna that are markedly different from those of the mainland.

The Queen Charlottes are warmed by an ocean current that rolls in from Japan, which means the islands get hit with 127cm of rain annually. All these factors combine to create a landscape filled with thousand-year-old spruce and cedar rain forests teeming with marine life. It's a place with hundreds of waterfalls, dozens of streams, and jagged, random peaks that top 1500m in height.

The arts of the Haida people – notably their totem poles and carvings in argillite (a dark, glass-like slate found only in southeast Alaska and on these islands) – are world renowned. You'll see evidence of the Haida's artistry throughout the islands.

A visit to the Charlottes will not reward those looking for another tick on their checklist of sights. Rather, the islands are for those who invest the time to be captivated by their allure, simple daily pleasures and wondrous culture.

No visit is complete without making the considerable effort necessary to see Gwaii Haanas National Park Reserve and Haida Heritage Site, a place that can feel like a lost world. But those who fall into the rhythms of the Charlottes may not escape their spell. Many come back year after year, others never leave.

History

Believed to be the only part of Canada that escaped the last Ice Age, the islands have been inhabited continuously for 10,000 years and are the traditional homeland (Haida Gwaii) of the Haida nation, generally acknowledged as the prime culture in the country at the time the Europeans arrived. Though they were fearsome warriors who dominated BC's west coast, they had few defenses against the diseases – primarily smallpox, tuberculosis and greed – that were introduced by European explorers. In 1835, the Haida population was estimated at 6000 people; in 1915, that number had shrunk to only 588.

Today, the Haida are proud, politically active and defiant people who make up one-third of the Charlottes' population. In the 1980s, they led an internationally publicized fight to preserve the islands from further logging. A bitter debate raged, but finally the

THE NORTH

YOUR LIFE, YOUR CULTURE, ON A LOG

Gazing at the row of totem poles punctuating the ocean-facing facade of the Haida Heritage Centre at Qay'llnagaay it's easy to admire their statuesque beauty and abstract artistry. But discerning the meaning of these creations is another matter. Each tells a story both complex and cultural, a record of a people and their beliefs.

Though most First Nations groups on the northwest coast lack formal written history as we know it, centuries of traditions manage to live on through creations such as totem poles. Art has long been a method of expression, intimately linked with historical and cultural preservation, religion and social ceremony, and the poles are the perfect medium as they require both an abundance of huge trees and extraordinary carving skills – elements the Haida have nailed.

Carved from a single cedar trunk, totems identify a household's lineage in the same way that a family crest might identify a group or clan in England, although the totem pole is more of a historical pictograph depicting the entire ancestry. Like a family crest, totem poles carry a sense of prestige and prosperity.

Despite the expression 'low man on the totem pole', the most important figures are usually at eye level; figures at the bottom usually serve an integral, grounding function that supports the rest of the pole. Totem figures can represent individuals, spirits, births, deaths, catastrophes or legends.

Unless you're an expert, it isn't easy to decipher a totem. But you can start with these simple paradigms: birds are identified by their beaks: ravens have a straight, midsize beak; eagles feature a short, sharp, down-turned beak; while hawks have a short, down-turned beak that curls inward. Bears usually show large, square teeth, while beavers feature sharp incisors and a cross-stitched tail.

A few animals appear as if viewed from overhead. For example, the killer whale's fin protrudes outward from the pole as if its head faces downward. The long-snouted wolf also faces downward,

federal government decided to save South Moresby and create South Moresby Gwaii Haanas National Park. (Logging – some of it quite destructive – still goes on in other parts of the Queen Charlottes.) More recently the Haida have successfully negotiated with institutions to have the remains of ancestors, once dug up by anthropologists, returned. And you're bound to see evidence of a campaign to stop rich bear hunters coming to the islands for trophies.

Flora & Fauna

The Queen Charlotte Islands boast a unique ecosystem. Poor drainage systems near the north end of Graham Island result in the growth of sphagnum moss and gentian, surrounded by lodgepole pine and yellow cedar. Elsewhere, mighty stands of western hemlock, Sitka spruce and western red cedar still cover the landscape in places not decimated by 20th-century clear-cutting. *Senecio newcombi*, a yellow flowering daisy, grows only here, as do some other flowers and mosses.

The islands also have their own unique versions of pine marten, deer mouse, black bear and short-tailed weasel. Unfortunately, introduced species like beavers, raccoons and rats have come in and caused trouble by altering the natural balance. Sitka blacktail deer were introduced at least five times between 1880 and 1925 as an alternate food source. Lacking natural predators, the deer became so prolific that hunting is encouraged to control the population; even so they are easily spotted.

Home to 15% of all nesting seabirds in BC, the Queen Charlottes contain the only confirmed nesting site of horned puffins in Canada. A whopping 30% of the world's ancient murrelets nest here, as do most of the province's Peales peregrine falcons.

From late April through late June, gray whales pass by on their 16,000km annual migration route between Mexico's Baja and Alaska. The islands also include the largest sea lion rookery in BC.

Orientation

Mainland ferries dock at Skidegate on Graham Island, the main island for population (80%) and commerce. The principal town is Queen Charlotte City (QCC), 7km west of Skidegate. The main road on Graham Island is Hwy 16, which is fully paved. It links Skidegate in the south with Masset 101km as does the frog. The pointy-headed shark (or dogfish), with a grimacing mouth full of sharp teeth, faces upward, as does the humpback whale.

See how many of these you can identify on the poles both inside and outside at the Haida Heritage Centre. Once you've got your bears sorted from your beavers, you can move on to figuring out the interconnected and complex relations between the creatures, which always have certain characteristics:

- black bear – serves as a protector, guardian and spiritual link between humans and animals
- beaver – symbolizes industriousness, wisdom and determined independence
- eagle – signifies intelligence and power
- frog – represents adaptability, the ability to live in both natural and supernatural worlds
- hummingbird – embodies love, beauty and unity with nature
- killer whale – symbolizes dignity and strength (often depicted as a reincarnated spirit of a great chief)
- raven – signifies mischievousness and cunning
- salmon – typifies dependable sustenance, longevity and perseverance
- shark – exemplifies an ominous and fierce solitude
- thunderbird – represents the wisdom of proud ancestors

For more background on totem poles see the boxed text, p29.

north, passing the small towns of Tlell and Port Clements.

Graham Island is linked to Moresby Island to the south by a small and frequent ferry from Skidegate. The airport is in Sandspit on Moresby Island, 12km east of the ferry landing at Alliford Bay. The only way to get to Gwaii Haanas National Park Reserve, which covers the south part of Moresby Island, is by boat or floatplane.

Information

The islands' relative remoteness, coupled with the lure of the land and Haida culture, has put the Charlottes on the traveler's map. While there are a number of hotels and services that meet the needs of the intrepid, it's still all but mandatory to make arrangements for accommodations in advance and understand that services are limited.

If you plan to visit the Gwaii Haanas National Park Reserve and Haida Heritage Site then you should understand that a visit takes several days (see p351). Don't be one of the boneheads who hop off the ferry expecting to see everything in a few hours and then depart. You won't. That said, don't be discouraged if you don't have time or money to do a long

boat or kayaking trip; you can always arrange a one-day paddle or boat trip and you can actually see a lot by car or bike. Regardless, take some time to go beachcombing along the windswept beaches, watch the sunset or chat with the locals, whose ideas and lifestyles are shaped by the salty fresh air and solitude.

Pick up a copy of the weekly **Queen Charlotte Islands Observer** (www.qciobserver.com; $1.50) which includes the *Islands This Week* supplement that covers just that.

BOOKSTORES
Northwest Coast Books (☎ 250-559-4681; 3205 Hwy 3rd Ave, QCC; 🕙 10am-4pm Mon-Fri) Great collection of QCI books, good recommendations; commentary by Buster, the profane parrot.

EMERGENCY
Ambulance (☎ 800-461-9911)
RCMP (☎ QCC 250-559-4421, Masset 250-626-3991)

INTERNET ACCESS
The main areas of the island are due to receive universal wi-fi coverage. Otherwise, ask around for places with computer terminals; the Purple Onion Deli (p348) in Queen Charlotte City has paid access.

LAUNDRY

Coin laundry (117 3rd Ave, City Centre Store complex, QCC; ☺ 8am-6pm) Also has locations in Port Clements and Masset.

MEDICAL SERVICES

Queen Charlotte Islands General Hospital
(☎ 250-559-4506, emergency ☎ 250-559-4300; 3209 3rd Ave, QCC; ☺ 24hr) Masset is getting a new facility to replace its small clinic (☎ emergency 250-626-4711). For major emergencies, patients are generally sent to Prince Rupert by air ambulance.

MONEY

ATMs are easily found in QCC, Masset and Sandspit.

POST

QCC post office (☎ 250-559-8349; 117 3rd Ave) In the City Centre Store complex.

TOURIST INFORMATION

Your first stop should be the excellent **Visitor Info Centre** (☎ 250-559-8316; www.qcinfo.com; 3220 Wharf St, QCC; ☺ 8am-noon & 4-9pm May-Sep, 9am-5pm Tue-Sat Oct-Apr). It occupies a nice building on the water on Wharf St, has good natural history displays, the island's best website and a small library. A second VIC at the airport opens for arriving flights in summer. Both carry marine and topographical charts.

In Masset, the **Visitor Info Centre** (☎ 250-626-3982; 1450 Christie St; ☺ 10am-4pm Jun-Aug) is near the entrance to town from the south.

At the VICs, ask about **Haida community feasts**. These events often welcome visitors, who for a modest fee can enjoy the dishes made from the plethora of local foods like crabs, salmon, mushrooms and berries. Also pick up a copy of *Art Route,* a guide to more than 40 studios and galleries.

A good website for information is www.haidagwaiitourism.ca.

QUEEN CHARLOTTE CITY

pop 1100

This small fishing village serves as the commercial center of the islands – the spot where you'll find the most restaurants and accommodations, plus the headquarters for most of the adventure outfitters on the islands. The community of permanent residents takes the massive summer influx of tourists in stride. People are friendly and eager to share tips about the islands' secret spots. Note that there is a movement to give a new unified name to the town's main road, which at present goes by Hwy 33, 3rd Ave and Cemetery Rd.

Sleeping

Haydn Turner Park Campground (campsites $10) Deeply shaded at the west end of town, there are pit toilets here. Three walk-in sites ($5) are on the beach. Follow 3rd Ave to the end.

Premier Creek Lodging (☎ 250-559-8415, 888-322-3388; www.qcislands.net/premier; 3101 3rd Ave; dm from $23, r $30-90; ▢) This pretty lodge has been just that since it opened in 1910. Often-renovated, it has 12 large rooms, some of which have great water views from the common porch. There's wi-fi, fridges and microwaves. Hostel rooms out back share a common kitchen.

Sea Raven Motel (☎ 250-559-4423, 800-665-9606; www.searaven.com; 3301 3rd Ave; r $45-95; ✷ ▢) Right by the VIC, this vaguely modern hotel has 31 rooms, some overlooking the bay. There are private balconies and kitchenettes with some rooms. Guests enjoy the Sea Raven's seafood café.

Hecate Inn (☎ 250-559-4543; www.qcislands.net/hecateinn; 321 3rd Ave; r $75-110; ▢) Neat as a pin, the 16 rooms here have high-speed internet and a cozy design highlighted by handmade oak and cedar furniture. Some have kitchens. You'll know you're here when you see the profusion of nasturtiums out front.

Eating & Drinking

Queen Charlotte has several places to eat. The three highly recommended places below are all within a salmon's jump of the VIC and each other.

Purple Onion Deli (☎ 250-559-4119; 3207 Wharf St; meals $5-8; ☺ 8am-5pm; ▢) A bright deli with a cute decor accented by little garlic heads and onions, where the sandwiches, salads, soups and burgers are fine. Sunny (on sunny days…) tables out front.

Queen B's (☎ 250-559-4463; 3201 Wharf St; meals $7-15; ☺ 9am-5pm Mon-Thu & Sat, 9am-9pm Fri, 10am-4pm Sun) Need a definition of funky? Come here. There are tables with water views outside and lots of local art inside. The spirited staff serves up homemade baked goods and organic treats like soup, quiche and pizza throughout the day. On Fridays, dinner is often delectable fresh salmon.

Sip's (☎ 250-559-4733; 3201 Wharf St; ☺ 10am-5:30pm Mon-Sat) The menus here have pages where patrons can share often hilarious thoughts on booze, life, poetry etc. The former Canadian Legion building has been turned into a gem of a bar that features martinis, live folk music and a great deck with a view. (And an upscale homewares shop to boot!)

SKIDEGATE
pop 740

Skidegate (pronounced 'skid-a-git'), a Haida community on the shores of Rooney Bay, is leading the revival of Haida culture and art. Its new museum is a stunner.

Haida Heritage Centre at Qay'llnagaay

One of the top attractions in the north is the marvelous new **Haida Heritage Centre at Qay'llnagaay** (☎ 250-559-4643; www.haidaheritagecentre.com; 10am-5pm Mon-Fri, 1-5pm Sat & Sun Jun-Aug, 10am-noon & 1-5pm Mon-Sat May & Sep, 10am-noon & 1-5pm Tue-Fri, 1-5pm Sat Oct-Apr). From its location to its architecture to its collection and programs, it's magnificent. The rich traditions of the Haida are fully explored in galleries, programs and work areas, where contemporary Haida artists create a new generation of art, such as totem poles (you won't miss the row right along the front of the building; see the boxed text, p346).

New canoes – more than 10m long – are being carved in the large and open carving shed. Exhibits will show how the Haida culture evolved into one ideally suited for their QCI – Haida Gwaii – homeland. One discovery is that bears usually ate their salmon under certain trees and these trees ended up being especially vigorous – the perfect candidate for a totem pole.

This new cultural gem is an amazing accomplishment and it's all the more fitting that as you enter the building, you see a traditional Haida copper-shield that symbolizes 'wealth among wealth'.

Parks Canada is using the center for its orientation sessions for visitors to Gwaii Haanas National Park Reserve (p351).

TLELL
pop 380

The 40km road from Skidegate north to Tlell follows the dramatic, rocky coast right at the water's edge. The village is barely definable as such – it's more a small collection of artsy places along the road. Look for little cafés such as the **Rising Tide Bakery** (8am-5pm Wed-Sun Jun-Aug), loved by locals and visitors alike for its sticky buns made with flour that's ground on-site.

Tlell is the southern gateway to **Naikoon Provincial Park** and home to the **park headquarters** (☎ 250-557-4390; 9am-4pm Jun-Aug). Here you can obtain information on the tides and check out the interpretive displays.

The beautiful 72,640-hectare park, extending to the northeast tip of Graham Island, is comprised mostly of sand dunes and low sphagnum bogs surrounded by stunted and gnarled lodgepole pine and red and yellow cedar. The word 'naikoon' is a corruption of 'nai-kun', meaning 'long nose' – the name for the 5km-long Rose Spit that separates the stormy Hecate Strait and Dixon Entrance. The park is loosely divided into North (at Masset) and South (at Tlell). You'll find campgrounds and interesting hikes at either end.

From Tlell, take the worthwhile **Pesuta Trail** to the wreck of the *Pesuta*, a timber-hauling ship that ran aground in 1928. The trail begins at the Tlell River Picnic Area, just off Hwy 16 past the park headquarters, and follows the river to East Beach. You then follow the high-tide line out to the wreck. Allow about seven hours to make the 10km round-trip.

See p350 for details on the north end of the Naikoon Provincial Park.

Just off Hwy 16, **Crystal Cabin Gallery** (☎ 250-557-4383; 778 Richardson Rd; 9am-6pm) is a shop filled with works by local artists, some of it quite exquisite. Outside there is a fascinating sculpture/installation, the **Tlell Stone Circle**.

Sleeping

Naikoon Provincial Park (☎ 250-557-4390) contains two excellent campgrounds. **Misty Meadows Campground** (campsite $14; mid-May–Sep), just off Hwy 16 at the south end of the park, features 30 shaded sites, some of which have platforms so your tent doesn't get soaked. A short trail leads to the beach. See p351 for information on Agate Beach Campground.

Cacilia's B&B (☎ 250-557-4664; www.qcislands.net /ceebysea; r $40-75) Let the surf lull you to sleep at this beechwood beach house surrounded by dunes just off Hwy 16 as it turns inland. There are six sizable rooms and serene isolation.

PORT CLEMENTS
pop 550

This logging and harbor town lies 21km north of Tlell on Hwy 16. For years it was known for the **Golden Spruce**, a huge genetically unique spruce that had a low chloroform count and thus a golden color. In 1997, Grant Hadwin, an anti-logging logger and zealot, cut it down to protest 'the hypocrisy of logging'. The act didn't just kill the tree, it traumatized the community as well. (Hadwin supposedly drowned while trying to return to the islands by kayak from Prince Rupert.) The entire affair is brilliantly chronicled in *The Golden Spruce* by John Vaillant.

Today, a 1m-tall tree sprouted from a golden spruce pinecone grows gamely behind a huge fence near the museum. The jury is still out as to whether it has inherited its parents' golden genes.

There are two good walks near Port Clements. About 1km south on Juskatla Rd is **Sunset Park**, which has a 2km boardwalk into the marshes and a tall watchtower from where you can see oodles of birds, otters and other critters. The **Golden Spruce Walk**, 5km further south, may now only feature the stump of its namesake but this actually lets you focus more on the amazing and verdant coastal rain forest along the 3km trail. Just after the start, bear to the right and you'll see a huge cedar growing on the side of a yet larger spruce.

The **Port Clements Museum** (☎ 250-557-4285; admission $2; ☉ 9am-1pm Jun-Aug, 2-4pm Sat & Sun Sep-May) on Bayview Dr has artifacts from the era of clear-cutting.

Golden Spruce Motel (☎ 250-557-4325, 877-801-4653; www.qcislands.net/golden; 2 Grouse St; r $42-62; ▣) is a rambling place with 12 rooms that have a basic brown decor and wi-fi. Owner Urs Thomas can set you up for all manner of QCI adventures on land and sea. There's a laundry and a good breakfast café.

MASSET & OLD MASSET
pop 1700

These two adjoining towns divide right along cultural lines: Haida live in Old Masset, others live in Masset, the commercial center of the north end of the island. There are a few artists with studios here and the setting, on broad and flat Masset Inlet, make it an interesting stop, especially for fishers and birders.

You'll see marinas and harbors here and the seafaring heritage is preserved at the **Dixon Entrance Maritime Museum** (☎ 250-626-6066; 2182 Collison Ave, Masset; adult/child $2/free; ☉ 1-4pm Jun-Aug, 2-4pm Sat & Sun Sep-May). It also has a good gallery of local art. In Old Masset, **Haida Rose Café** (☎ 250-626-3310; 415 Frog St; snacks $3-5; ☉ 8am-

5pm; ▣) is a community hangout and gallery. The coffee is excellent and there's wi-fi and internet access.

Sleeping & Eating

Shops, cafés and groceries are along Main St, Masset. There are also some interesting places along the north coast (below). There are a dozen or more B&Bs and vacation rentals here and along Tow Hill Rd east of town.

Hidden Island RV & Resort (☎ 250-626-5286, 866-303-5286; www.hidden-island-resort.ca; 1440 Tow Hill Rd; campsites from $15) About 1km from Masset on Tow Hill Rd this has 16 shady sites. It has a café (open 11am to 8pm Tuesday to Sunday) with superb fish and chips.

ourpick Copper Beech House (☎ 250-626-5441; www.copperbeechhouse.com; 1590 Delkatla Rd, Masset; r $75-150). Run by legendary chef and bon vivant David Phillips, this rambling old house backs onto the Masset harbor and features three unique rooms, all with private bathrooms. The 'Field General' room puts you almost in the middle of the boats. There's always something amazing cooking in the ever-expanding kitchen.

Masset's small airport (p352), 1km east of town, is also the site of the slightly notorious **HaidaBucks Lounge** (☎ 250-626-5548; meals $8-12; ☉ noon-late), which gained fame after Starbucks threatened legal action for trademark infringement (the name). After international condemnation, the coffee purveyor caved. Discuss the finer points of briefs on the patio or in the merry bar.

NORTH COAST

Tow Hill Rd runs 26km east of Masset along the beach. This is a definite must on your explorations as it follows the wild and woolly coast the entire way; parts are under a canopy of moss-draped trees arching overhead. Scattered all along here are funky little businesses and other attractions. The road goes from paved to graded but is fine, except possibly after one of the many massive winter storms.

Delkatla Wildlife Sanctuary, off Tow Hill Rd 4km east of Masset, is excellent for birdwatchers.

Rapid Richie's Rustic Rentals (☎ 250-626-5472; www.beachcabins.com; cabins $40-70), 10km east, is the perfect place to get away. Cabins come with views that are almost senselessly scenic and the rates are great.

Beachcomb until you drop at **Alaska View Lodge** (☎ 250-626-3333, 800-661-0019; www.alaskaview lodge.ca; r $70-110), right on the beach 12km east from Masset. The four warm and cozy rooms are the perfect counterpoint to the pounding surf.

Embodying the spirit of this road to the end of everything, **Moon Over Naikoon** (☎ 250-626-5064; ❤ 8am-5pm Jun-Aug), 16 km east of Masset, has a bakery and a kaleidoscopic collection of artworks and stuff found on the beach.

Bed down while tides driven from Asia hit the beach at Naikoon Provincial Park's **Agate Beach Campground** (☎ 250-557-4390; campsites $14; ❤ mid-May–mid-Sep), 23km east. The 43 sites sit right on the sand. On clear days, you can see Alaska. Named for the pretty glasslike stones found along the beaches, Agate Beach can get windy and downright cold after dark. Outside of the season, you can camp here for free but there are no pit toilets or firewood.

Near the end of the road lies **Tow Hill**, a columnar basalt outcropping an hour's hike from a parking lot. At the top, you'll enjoy incredible views of the north end of Naikoon Provincial Park as well as north to Alaska. Also worth checking out is the **Blowhole**, which spurts out ocean water on incoming tides.

For real adventure, hit the **Cape Fife Loop Trail**, a 21km loop that takes you over the Argonaut Plain to Fife Point and Rose Spit through the northern part of Naikoon Provincial Park.

At the very end of the road you can park on packed sand and see the **beach** stretching seemingly forever east into the mists. It's mystic, beautiful and a bit primordial.

SANDSPIT
pop 460

Sandspit is just that – a long sandy spit jutting out into Hecate Strait. The only community on Moresby Island, Sandspit is home to the airport and a couple of stores. It's also the major gateway into the Gwaii Haanas reserve, though if you're heading to the park from QCC, you can get off the ferry at Alliford Bay and bypass the town.

GWAII HAANAS NATIONAL PARK RESERVE & HAIDA HERITAGE SITE

Other-worldly and ethereal, this huge, wild park encompasses Moresby and 137 smaller islands at the south end of the Queen Charlottes. The 640km-long stretch of rugged coastline is true wilderness at its best. If you take out a kayak, you can paddle for days without seeing another human being. (Although you might find a few at the hot springs.)

Archaeological finds have documented more than 500 ancient Haida sites, including villages and burial caves dotted throughout the islands. The most famous (and photographed) village is Ninstints, on SGaang Gwaii (Anthony Island), where rows of totem poles stare eerily out to sea. This ancient village was declared a Unesco World Heritage site in 1981. Other major sights include Skedans on Louise Island and Hotspring Island, where you can soak away the bone-chilling cold in natural springs. The ancient sites are protected by the Haida Gwaii Watchmen, who live on the islands during summer.

The entire reserve only gained its protection in 1988 after the Haida and many others raised a multiyear ruckus over the clear-cutting that was destroying other parts of the QCI. Loggers were zeroing in on this unspoiled wonderland. It was named North America's top park destination in 2005 by *National Geographic Traveler* magazine for being 'beautiful and intact.'

Information

Access to the park is by boat or plane only. A visit demands a decent amount of advance planning and usually requires several days. If you want to travel independently, you need to reserve in advance, as only a limited number of people can be in the park at any given time (see Reservations & Fees, below).

Contact Parks Canada's **Gwaii Haanas office** (☎ 250-559-8818; www.pc.gc.ca/gwaiihaanas) with questions. The website is a thorough resource.

Anyone who has not visited the park during the previous three years must attend a free 90-minute orientation session. These are both informative and entertaining as they not only learn about the many do's and don'ts but also about the park, its culture and wildlife. Sessions are held at the new **Haida Heritage Centre at Qay'llnagaay** (☎ 250-559-4643) in Skidegate June to September (see p349). At times there may also be sessions held at the airport in Sandspit. Confirm times and locations when you reserve.

RESERVATIONS & FEES

For travel from May 1 through September 30 you must obtain one of a limited number of daily **reservations** (☎ 250-387-1642, 800-435-5622;

per person $15). In addition there are user fees (per night adult/child $15/7.50). Nightly fees are waived if you have a Parks Canada Season Excursion Pass. Each day from May 1 to September 30, six standby spaces are made available and demand for these can be fierce – call **Parks Canada** (☎ 250-559-8818; www.pc.gc .ca/gwaiihaanas) or check at the QCC **Visitor Info Centre** (☎ 250-559-8316; www.qcinfo.com; 3220 Wharf St; ☷ 8am-noon & 4-9pm May-Sep, 9am-5pm Tue-Sat Oct-Apr) for details.

Activities

The easiest way to get into the park is with a tour company. The QCC **Visitor Info Centre** (☎ 250-559-8316; www.qcinfo.com; 3220 Wharf St; ☷ 8am-noon & 4-9pm May-Sep, 9am-5pm Tue-Sat Oct-Apr) can provide lists of operators, many of whom are based in Vancouver and Victoria. They also can usually set independent up travelers with gear and other essentials such as kayaks (average per day/week $50/250).

Moresby Explorers (☎ 250-637-2215, 800-806-7633; www.moresbyexplorers.com) is Sandspit-based. It has one-day tours from $160 as well as much longer ones. It rents kayaks and gear.

Also QCI-based, **Queen Charlotte Adventures** (☎ 250-559-8990, 800-668-4288; www.queencharlotte adventures.com) offers one- to 10-day trips using power boats, kayaks or sailboats. It has a six-day kayak trip to the Unesco site for $1600.

Getting There & Away

AIR

The main airport for QCI is at **Sandspit** (YZP; ☎ 250-559-0052) on Moresby Island. Masset has a small airport (YMT) 1km east of town.

Air Canada Jazz (☎ 888-247-2262; www.aircanada .com) flies large plane services daily between Sandspit and Vancouver. **Pacific Coastal Airlines** (☎ 800-663-2872; www.pacific-coastal.com) flies between Masset and Vancouver several times each week. **North Pacific Seaplanes** (☎ 800-689-4234; www.northpacificseaplanes.com) offers a picturesque service between Prince Rupert and Masset, QCC and pretty much any place else a floatplane can land (one-way flights start from $225).

Note that reaching the airport from Graham Island is time-consuming: if your flight is at 3:30pm, you need to line up at the car ferry at Skidegate Landing at 12:30pm in order to make the 1pm ferry in order to have time to check in for your flight.

DETOUR: CRANBERRY JUNCTION ROUTE

At the mythical 'Cranberry Junction' (it's little more than a signpost) 82km north of Hwy 16, a logging road runs 51km east to the Nisga'a Lava Bed (p337). This is a great shortcut between Prince Rupert and the Stewart-Cassiar Hwy and it gives you an easy way to see the lava beds. One caveat: the logging road is unpaved for its length. During the late spring, summer and early fall when it's dry, cars should not have a problem but watch out for logging trucks. Another attraction is that it is a very pretty, quiet road. One October day we saw over a dozen bears.

FERRY

BC Ferries (☎ 250-386-3431) has a service between Prince Rupert and Skidegate Landing (adult/child $28/14, car from $102, cabin from $55, eight hours, six per week summer, three per week winter).

Getting Around

Once you leave Hwy 16, most of the roads are gravel or worse. Many are logging roads and you will have to contend with the very real hazard of encountering a speeding logging truck. If you plan on driving along these roads, contact **Western Forest Products** (☎ 250-557-6810; ☷ 6:30am-5:30pm Mon-Fri) to check out conditions.

BC Ferries operates a small **ferry** linking the two main islands at Skidegate Landing and Alliford Bay (adult/child $6/3, cars from $15, 20 minutes, hourly 7am to 10pm). This service can get jammed at busy times and you may have to wait one or more ferries for your turn.

Eagle Transit (☎ 877-747-4461; www.qcislands.net /eagle) meets flights and ferries. The fare from the airport to QCC is $15.

If you want to get around in a car, you are going to have to weigh the high cost of local car rental against the cost of bringing a vehicle on the ferry. **Budget** (☎ 250-637-5688; www.budget.com) has locations at both the airport and QCC. The slightly cheaper, **Rustic Car Rentals** (☎ 250-559-4641, 877-559-4641; citires@qcislands.net; 605 Hwy 33, QCC) operates out of a gas station and rents out cars from $39 per day plus $0.20 per kilometer.

STEWART-CASSIAR HIGHWAY

The remote Stewart-Cassiar Hwy (Hwy 37; 727 km) is Canada's most westerly road system linking BC to the Yukon and Alaska. It's been increasing in popularity in recent years as the province continually improves the road and it easily rivals the Alaska Hwy for scenery. The road starts and heads north from Hwy 16 at Kitwanga (right), 468km west of Prince George and 241km east of Prince Rupert. Officially it becomes the Stewart-Cassiar Hwy at Meziadin Junction.

No matter what your schedule is, don't miss the chance to revel in the incredible scenery and fun-filled vibe of Stewart, BC and Hyder, Alaska (p354). It's only a 65km trip off the Stewart-Cassiar.

Based on all the decades when it was a pretty crude road, the Stewart-Cassiar has something of a fearsome reputation. It shouldn't. Less than 10% is still not paved, and even these gravel stretches are kept in good shape. In summer, cars will have no problem.

Still, a lot of the road can be challenging to drivers not used to what is essentially a frontier road. Other drivers – especially those in over-sized RVs – can be menaces and storms and bad weather can make conditions tough. The solution is to take your time, enjoying the amazing scenery, river canyons, lakes, provincial parks and general desolation in parts.

Contact the following for **road condition reports** (☎ 250-771-3000, 250-771-4511; www.drivebc .ca). Note that many services and businesses are not open outside of summer and road conditions may be hopeless in winter.

KITWANGA

Kitwanga, along with nearby Gitanyow and Kispiox (see the boxed text, p336), is the traditional home of the Gitksan First Nations people, who traded along this section of the Skeena River for centuries. The area includes spectacular totems, as well as the small **Kitwanga Fort National Historic Site**. A path with interpretive signs follows a route up Battle Hill, where Canada's only Indian fort commanded the valley in pre-colonial days.

GITANYOW

Otherwise known as Kitwancool, this small First Nations town is home to more than a dozen stunning **totem poles** dating from over 100 years ago to the present (for more on the meaning of totem poles, see the boxed text, p346). Behind the array is a community center that is sometimes open and which has

---

HIGHWAY 37 QUICK REFERENCE

The Stewart-Cassiar Hwy becomes less of a challenge each year. There are now only three relatively short sections left unpaved. Here's a primer to conditions and services (confirm they're open outside June to September) with distances going north from the Hwy 16 junction (p337):

- Hwy 16 Junction–Meziadin Junction: Road is paved and modern for entire length. Meziadin Junction (156km north) has junction for Hwy 37A to Stewart & Hyder (p354) and gas, café and groceries.

- Meziadin Junction–Bell II: Road is modern and paved for the entire length. Bell II (250km north) has gas, a café, camping and a lodge.

- Bell II–Tatogga Lake: Road is paved except for one 20km stretch. Tatogga Lake (390km north) has gas, a restaurant (summer) and lodging.

- Tatogga Lake–Iskut: Road is paved. Iskut (405km north) has gas and lodging.

- Iskut–Dease Lake: Road has one unpaved 20km section. Dease Lake (488km) has gas, repairs, shops, cafés and lodging.

- Dease Lake–Good Hope Lake: Paved road has one short, unpaved portion along the lake. Good Hope Lake (626km) has gas.

- Good Hope Lake–Junction Hwy 37 & Alaska Hwy: The road is paved but narrow and curvy. Numerous warnings for animals. The junction with the Alaska Hwy (p366; 727km) has gas, repairs and cafés.

displays of local cultural items. The town is 21km north of Hwy 16 and well worth the detour even if you are not going any further on Hwy 37.

MEZIADIN JUNCTION

Meziadin Lake Provincial Park (☎ 250-638-8490), about 155km north of Kitwanga, has become a popular fishing spot and campground with pit toilets, a boat launch and 60 sites ($14), some of which are on the lake. Don't get gas here; instead, go a little further to Meziadin Junction, where the gas is cheaper and there are more services. This is the junction with Hwy 37A to Stewart and Hyder.

STEWART & HYDER

If you've come this far, don't miss the chance to take the 67km side trip west to the twin border towns of Stewart, BC, and Hyder, Alaska, which sit on the coast at the head of the Portland Inlet. You'll see breathtaking glaciers, waterfalls and other jaw-dropping scenery.

Stewart's **Visitor Info Centre** (☎ 250-636-9224, 888-366-5999; 222 5th Ave; ☽ 9am-6pm Jun-Sep, limited hr winter) covers the region and the Stewart-Cassiar Hwy all the way to the Yukon.

Sights

The ride in on Hwy 37A is a sight in itself: midway to Stewart you'll see more and more of **Bear Glacier** until you round a bend and there's a monstrous icefield flowing into a lake next to the road. It glows an ethereal blue. You've now already seen more glacial ice than people see all day on the Icefields Parkway in the Rockies (p296).

The long Portland Inlet, a steep ocean fjord that extends from the coast 90km into the mountains, finally stops at Stewart, Canada's most northerly ice-free port. The fjord cuts a natural border between Canada and the USA, which is why Hyder is only 3km away and is only connected to other parts of Alaska by water and air. For a good look at the isolated beauty of the area, watch *Insomnia*, a 2002 thriller with Robin Williams and Al Pacino.

Stewart (population 700) was once a bustling mining town where prospectors flocked after hearing about the discovery of gold. The boom, however, was short-lived, and when the riches ran dry, so did the population. Today, Stewart's port shuffles logs to southerly ports. Its center is historic **5th Avenue**.

Hyder (population 60, give or take a couple of dogs) ekes out an existence as a 'ghost town', although here the spooks sell knickknacks. Some 40,000 tourists come through every summer avoiding any border hassle from US customs officers – there aren't any (although going back to Stewart you'll pass through a Canadian customs post – keeping a beady eye out for guns and liquor smuggled into Hyder by boat). It has muddy streets and a long **pier** you can drive out on for great harbor views.

The towns collectively greet visitors to the area, and you'll barely know they're in separate countries. They say the postal code (V0T 1W0) sums it up: Very Old Town, One Way Out. You can use Canadian currency in both towns.

GLACIER HIGHWAY

The name is a bit of a misnomer – it's all rough gravel – but this road takes you through rich scenery and to what can best be described as a glacial orgasm.

Fish Creek, about 3km past Hyder, is a major run for pink and chum salmon. From late July through September, the salmon run and you can watch the drama from a long wooden elevated walkway. Spent fish lay their eggs and die in the shallows while bears, bald eagles, gulls and others feast. It all smells like a fish store three days after a power failure, but it's also riveting.

Continue on for 20km and slowly a vast icefield will come into view. Continue up the hill to a **viewpoint** (33km from Hyder) where the entire vast **Salmon Glacier** spreads in all directions. It's simply gigantic and you can't help but say something like 'wow!' The striated ice flows to the horizon through two series of peaks. Bring a picnic, settle back, sniff an alpine wildflower and just soak up the splendor. You might even want a cigarette afterwards.

Pick up the excellent *Salmon Glacier Self Guided Auto Tour* from the Stewart VIC.

Sleeping

Stewart's 5th Ave has a number of off-beat cafés, shops and places with internet access.

Rainey Creek Campground (☎ 250-636-2537; 8th Ave; campsites $10-20) Showers, kitchens, tent pads and flush toilets ensure the 98-site municipal Rainey Creek Campground is a good choice.

Ripley Creek Inn (☎ 250-636-2344; www.ripley creekinn.com; 306 5th Ave; r $50-120; 🖳) Spread across five historic buildings in Stewart's center, this inn is a real find. The 32 rooms are stylishly decorated with new and old items and range from simple rooms in an old brothel to large rooms with private decks overlooking the estuary. All have wi-fi. The inn also has a cool toaster museum of early kitchen conveniences.

King Edward Hotel & Motel (☎ 250-636-2244, 800-663-3126; www.kingedwardhotel.com; 405 5th Ave; r $60-100; 🗙 🖳) Of the two buildings here, the motel-style one has the nicest rooms. All 65 rooms have wi-fi and some have kitchens.

Eating & Drinking

Bitter Creek Café (☎ 250-636-2166; 311 5th Ave; meals $10-30; 🕙 5-10pm May-Sep) An artifact-filled pub run by the Ripley Creek Inn folks, the menu features excellent chowder, steaks, addictive biscuits and a little south-of-two-borders flair.

Glacier Inn (☎ 250-636-9248) Looks like hell from the outside and only a tad better inside. An authentic boozer, tourists get 'Hyderized' by slamming back a shot of '190-proof' something. Local characters lurk in the shadows.

NORTH OF MEZIADIN JUNCTION

At **Bell II**, an outpost 94km north of the Meziadin Junction, **Bell II Lodge** (☎ 604-639-8455, 800-530-2167; www.bell2lodge.com; r $100-150; 🖳) has 22 upscale chalets and 15 campsites (from $15). You can heli-ski from here in the winter.

North of here, the highway passes through some canyons with rushing white-water rivers.

At the Tahltan town of **Iskut**, the gateway to Spatsizi Plateau Wilderness Park (right), you'll find a grocery store, gas station and places to stay.

Just south of Iskut, the **Red Goat Lodge** (☎ 250-234-3261, 888-734-4628; www.karo-ent.com/redgoat.htm; dm/r from $20/60), on the shores of Eddontenajon Lake, is a haven for travelers, with hostel beds and upscale B&B rooms. There are campsites (from $15) and llamas wandering about.

Parks

On the Stewart-Cassiar Hwy, you'll come across pretty **Kinaskan Lake Provincial Park**. This park, excellent for trout fishing, offers 50 lakeside campsites ($14) with pit toilets (but no showers) and free wood.

Spatsizi Plateau Wilderness Provincial Park is a vast and wild place that is mostly inaccessible. The park entrance is 136km east of Hwy 37 at Tatogga along primitive roads, which pretty much end when you get to the park. The park's trails are often little more than vague notions across the untouched landscape.

Stikine River Recreation Area, a narrow park west of Dease Lake (below), connects the Spatsizi Plateau Wilderness Park with the Mt Edziza Provincial Park and serves as the pull-out for canoe trips starting in Spatsizi. Past the bridge, the river thrusts through the spectacular **Grand Canyon of the Stikine**, an 80km stretch through a steep-walled canyon that is completely unnavigable by boat.

The 230,000-hectare **Mount Edziza Provincial Park** protects a volcanic landscape featuring lava flows, basalt plateaus and cinder cones surrounding an extinct shield volcano. Though it's inaccessible by car, you can hike, horseback ride or fly into the park by making arrangements in Telegraph Creek or Dease Lake.

The stunning little **Boya Lake Provincial Park**, about 100km north of Dease Lake, surrounds the shockingly turquoise Boya Lake. Dotted with small tree-covered islets, this warm lake looks like something out of the tropics. You can camp right on the shore. The campground includes pit toilets, a boat launch and 45 campsites ($14).

Dease Lake & North

Although the area was once an important supply point for construction of the Alaska Hwy to the north, Dease Lake is today a small stop on the highway, a halfway point between Hwy 16 and Whitehorse. There are stores and motels. **Northway Motor Inn** (☎ 250-771-5341, 866-888-2588; r $70-90) has a restaurant and 44 basic rooms. Right on the Dease River, **Dease River Crossing Campground** (☎ 250-239-3646; campsites from $14) has 20 shady sites with fire pits and covered tent sites. There are also six cabins ($40 to $90).

West from Dease Lake is **Telegraph Creek**, a minute wilderness town 113km along Telegraph Creek Rd. The drive is rugged but scenic.

Hwy 37 is paved the rest of the way north to the Yukon (p366). The road becomes rather narrow but there are some pristine lakes along the way and lots of wildlife.

ATLIN
pop 460

Surrounded by the huge icefields and glaciers of the northern Coast Mountains, this remote town in the northwestern-most corner of BC sits alongside the 145km-long land-locked fjord known as Atlin Lake. Born in 1898 on the back of the Klondike Gold Rush, Atlin had gold of its own in nearby Pine Creek, which brought in a fast rush of prospectors. In town, colorful houses face the lake, with boats or floatplanes parked in front. Atlin served as the location for the 1983 film *Never Cry Wolf* about a government researcher who comes to love wolves.

GLACIER BAY NATIONAL PARK (ALASKA)

South of BC's Tatshenshini-Alsek Provincial Wilderness Park, this spectacular US park fits into the amazing jigsaw puzzle of borders and beauty here. Sixteen tidewater glaciers spill out from the mountains to the sea, making these unusual icefields some of the most renowned in the world. The glaciers here are in retreat, revealing plants and animals that fascinate naturalists. Most people prefer to kayak the small inlets and bays, particularly Muir, where cruise ships are not allowed. There are few trails except around the **park headquarters** (☎ 907-697-2627; www.nps.gov/glba) in Bartlett Cove. Lonely Planet's *Alaska* has extensive coverage of this wonderland.

At the southwest corner of the lake is the imposing **Llewellyn Glacier**, whose meltwater carries glacial sediment to the lake, making it a seemingly too-beautiful-not-to-be-fake turquoise. The glacier lies in the **Atlin Provincial Park & Recreation Area** – 271,134 hectares of icefields and glaciers, all of it only accessible by floatplane or boat.

The small **Atlin Museum** (☎ 250-651-7522; www.atlin.net; 🕑 10am-4pm summer; 🕑 mid-May–early Sep), housed in a 1902 schoolhouse, offers area information and the website is good.

The 98km partial-gravel to gravel road runs south from the Alaska Hwy in the Yukon. The junction is at **Jake's Corner** (p369) and is 346km west of the junction of Hwy 37 with the Alaska Hwy.

TATSHENSHINI-ALSEK PROVINCIAL WILDERNESS PARK

Jointly managed by BC Parks and the Champagne and Aishihik First Nations, this park on the northwest tip of BC is part of the Unesco World Heritage site that includes Kluane National Park and Reserve in the Yukon, and Glacier Bay and Wrangell-St Elias National Parks in Alaska. It is only accessible through the Yukon or Alaska, with Haines being a good starting point. At nearly a million hectares, the park superseded Tweedsmuir Provincial Park (981,000 hectares) as the largest park in the province. It's entirely wilderness although its two namesake rivers attract hardy and expert kayakers.

Yukon Territory

In 1897 word shot around the world about the discovery of gold near Dawson in the Yukon. Within weeks tens of thousands of people began heading for this remote place with visions of fabulous wealth blinding them to the perils that lay ahead. By the next year many had perished, others were ruined and the rest were heading home, tails between their legs. Those who got rich were either the very first miners or those who got rich off those with gold fever.

Today the Yukon is still a desolate and wild place but the only certainty now is that you'll have the time of your life here. Few places are so intrinsically linked with their history – the Klondike gold rush left old towns, travel routes and a whole lot of history you can enjoy today.

Visitors are often surprised by the territory's vibrancy. Whitehorse, the capital, has cutting-edge architecture, riverside developments and a thriving arts community. Dawson, the fabled gold rush town, has a delightful vibe beyond tourism. There's wilderness everywhere, headlined by Unesco-recognized Kluane National Park and Reserve.

And its no longer isolated. From the south you can come by ferry on the beautiful Inside Passage via Haines and Skagway, Alaska. By car there's the storied Alaska Hwy and the fascinating and remote Stewart-Cassiar Hwy. You can combine all for some amazing circle itineraries.

On your journey to the Yukon, you may not be blinded by gold but you may be blinded by beauty.

HIGHLIGHTS

- Finding your own lakeside spot in **Kluane National Park** (p370)
- Exploring the **Klondike Highway** (p373)
- Enjoying the scene in surprising **Dawson City** (p376)
- Canoeing the fast-flowing **Yukon River** (p359) or its tributaries
- Crossing the Arctic Circle on the 747km **Dempster Highway** (p384)

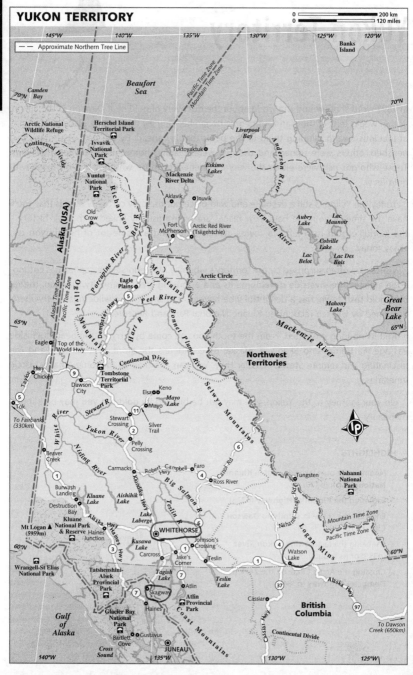

YUKON TERRITORY

--- Approximate Northern Tree Line

0 ——————— 200 km
0 ——————— 120 miles

145°W 140°W 135°W 130°W 125°W 120°W

Banks Island

Beaufort Sea

Camden Bay

70°N 70°N

Arctic National Wildlife Refuge

Herschel Island Territorial Park

Ivvavik National Park

Vuntut National Park

Old Crow

Liverpool Bay

Tuktoyaktuk

Eskimo Lakes

Mackenzie River Delta

Aklavik Inuvik

Fort McPherson Arctic Red River (Tsiigehtchie)

Aubry Lake Lac Maunoir

Colville Lake

Lac Belot Lac Des Bois

Arctic Circle

Eagle Plains

Mahony Lake

Great Bear Lake

65°N 65°N

Eagle Top of the World Hwy

Hwy Chicken

Tok

To Fairbanks (330km)

Tombstone Territorial Park

Continental Divide

Dawson City

Elsa Keno

Mayo Lake

Mayo

Stewart Crossing

Silver Trail

Pelly Crossing

Northwest Territories

Carmacks

Robert Campbell Hwy

Faro

Ross River

Carol Rd

Tungsten

Nahanni National Park

Beaver Creek

Burwash Landing

Kluane Lake

Destruction Bay

Kluane National Park & Reserve

Mt Logan (5959m)

Haines Junction

Aishihik Lake

Lake Laberge

WHITEHORSE

Big Salmon R

Mountain Time Zone

Pacific Time Zone

Nahanni Range Rd

Logan Mtns

Wrangell-St Elias National Park

Kusawa Lake

Carcross

Jake's Corner

Johnson's Crossing

Teslin

Watson Lake

60°N 60°N

Tatshenshini-Alsek Provincial Park

Tagish Lake

Atlin

Atlin Provincial Park

Teslin Lake

Cassiar

British Columbia

Skagway

Haines

Glacier Bay National Park

Bartlett Cove Gustavus

Cross Sound

Gulf of Alaska

JUNEAU

Continental Divide

To Dawson Creek (650km)

140°W 135°W 130°W 125°W

ORIENTATION

The Yukon is between the Northwest Territories and Alaska, with British Columbia to the south and the Beaufort Sea to the north. It's a sub-Arctic region about one-third the size of Alaska.

The Alaska Hwy is the main route across the Yukon, and there are a number of other scenic and demanding drives, including the Dempster Hwy, the only north–south road to cross the Arctic Circle. The Klondike Hwy follows the path of the gold rush from Klondike, Alaska, and links Whitehorse with Dawson City.

INFORMATION

The Yukon has six **visitor information centers** (VICs). Beaver Creek, Carcross, Dawson City, Haines Junction and Watson Lake are open in summer; Whitehorse is open all year. **Tourism Yukon** (☎ 800-661-0494; www .touryukon.com) will send free information, including the annual *Yukon* magazine with specifics on regional activities, events and accommodations. It also distributes an excellent road map. A number of other tourism publications are highly useful, including *Art Adventures on Yukon Time*, *Into the Yukon Wilderness*, *Yukon's Wildlife Viewing Guide* and many more.

It's also worth noting the extremes in daylight hours and temperatures. Whitehorse may experience long, 19-hour sunny days in July, but come January it's light for a mere six hours (actually, 'light' is the wrong term, think 'less dark') and the average temperature is -18.7°C. For all but the hardiest, the Yukon is truly a summer destination. In fact by September the birch trees will be turning a brilliant, glowing shade of yellow and the winds of winter will be blowing many south. Much of the territory is then closed until May or June.

ACTIVITIES

Yukon VICs can supply you with information and answer questions on hiking, canoeing, rafting, cycling, gold prospecting, skiing, fishing and various adventure trips. There are outfitters and tour companies to handle arrangements, but you really don't need an organized trip and you don't need to be wealthy to fully enjoy the Yukon.

Whitehorse (p363) is the place to get guides and gear for adventures across the territory.

ONLY IN THE YUKON

Certain details about the Yukon are different from British Columbia. Important ones are:

Police (☎ 867-667-5555)
Medical emergencies (☎ 867-667-5555, in Whitehorse 911)
Telephone area code (☎ 867; Alaska 907)
Road condition information (☎ 867-456-7623; www.gov.yk.ca/roadreport)
Government campgrounds Also known as territory campgrounds, they cannot be reserved. The fee at all campgrounds is $12 per tent/RV per night.

Hiking

The best known route is the Chilkoot Trail, which begins in Alaska, but Kluane National Park in the territory's southwest corner also has excellent hikes, from short and easy to long and demanding. The Tombstone Mountain area north of Dawson is also good, with the North Fork Pass considered the classic hike of the region. For Northern Alpine terrain, try MacMillan Pass at the Northwest Territories border, accessible by Canol Rd north from Ross River.

Canoeing & Kayaking

Canoeists and kayakers have many choices, from easy float trips down the waters of the Yukon River and its tributaries to challenging white-water adventures.

Gentle trips down the Yukon from Whitehorse range from a few hours to 16 days all the way to Dawson, and are popular. Many people start or end at Carmacks, the halfway point, making an eight-day trip. Boat rental and return charges for an eight-day, one-way trip are about $200 and transport can be arranged. See Whitehorse (p363) and Dawson City (p381) for more details. Also worthwhile is by Dan Maclean (www.publicationconsult ants.com/paddle.htm).

White-water Rafting

The Alsek and Tatshenshini Rivers are ranked among the best and wildest in North America. They're found in British Columbia, south of Kluane, and are accessible from Haines Junction. Other major areas are the Lapie (near Ross River) and Takhini (north of Whitehorse) Rivers.

Fishing

For anglers, www.yukonfishing.com provides regulations and a list of what's where as well as the best time and means to catch your prize salmon, trout or grayling.

Watching Wildlife

Yukon Tourism publishes a number of guides that detail the critters you can expect to see in the territory, many right along the highways. Bear, caribou and moose are just some of the larger animals commonly seen.

For an unforgettable introduction into the world of Yukon hunting, take a look at the government publication *Hunting Regulations Summary*. Besides telling you how to bag a moose, it has a section on determining the sex of caribou that will stay with you long after other memories of your trip fade.

FESTIVALS & EVENTS

The Yukon has a number of events that are important throughout the territory. When you have a total population of 31,600, it's easy to get everyone's attention.

February

Yukon Quest (www.yukonquest.com) This 1600km dog-sled race goes from Whitehorse to Fairbanks, Alaska.

June

International Storytelling Festival (www.yukon story.com) This Whitehorse festival features First Nations participants.
Kluane Chilkat International Bike Relay (www .kcibr.org) Bikers ride 238km from Haines Junction to Haines, Alaska.

TOP FIVE PLACES TO MAKE A DISCOVERY

- On the properly named **Top of the World Highway** (p383)

- In the barren recesses of the remote **Robert Campbell Highway** (see boxed text, p368)

- After a killer trek to the glaciers of **Kluane National Park** (p370)

- In the beautiful desolation of an **Arctic Park** (p385)

- In your own gold pan on a creek near **Dawson City** (p376)

August

Discovery Days Many, many folks head to Dawson (p382) to celebrate the discovery of gold or just to have a good time. Most of the territory shuts down to celebrate this, the third Monday of the month.

September

Klondike Trail '98 Road Relay Some 100 running teams of 10 each complete the overnight course from Skagway to Whitehorse.

WHITEHORSE

pop 23,700
The Yukon's capital will be a part of any trip to the territory. Its airport has good access and all the main roads pass through – the Alaska Hwy and the Klondike Hwy, the two most important, form an X with Whitehorse in the crosshairs. It's the place to get outfitted for your adventure and to stock up on whatever you need for your journey.

At first Whitehorse may not wow you – many of the buildings have the stark, utilitarian designs common in the north. But then down by the river you find a beautiful new development and you discover that there are some pretty good restaurants and you discern a surfeit of culture for a place this size, and pretty soon you're trying to stay an extra day. Or two.

HISTORY

Whitehorse has always been a transportation hub, first as a terminus for the White Pass & Yukon Route Railway from Skagway. Then during WWII it was a major center for work on the Alaska Hwy and its airport played an important strategic role. In 1953, Whitehorse was made the capital of the territory, to the continuing regret of the much smaller and more isolated Dawson City.

ORIENTATION

Whitehorse sits just off the Alaska Hwy between Dawson Creek in British Columbia (1430km to the east), where the highway starts, and Fairbanks in Alaska (970km west). The official city limits cover 421 sq km, making it one of the largest urban-designated areas in Canada. Despite this, the central core is quite small and it's easy to walk around. Downtown is designed on a grid system and the main traffic routes are 2nd and 4th Aves.

WHITEHORSE

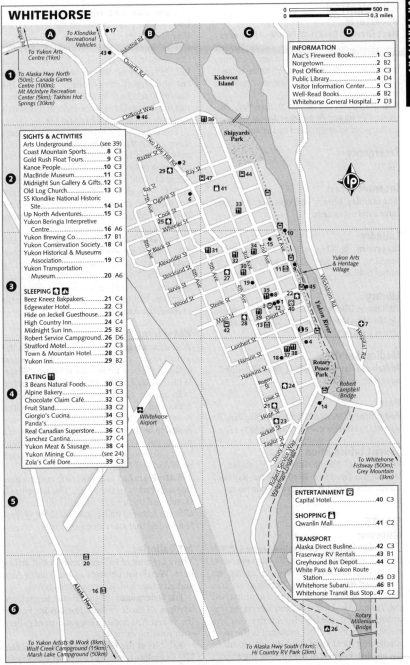

0 — 500 m
0 — 0.3 miles

To Klondike
Recreational
Vehicles

To Yukon Arts
Centre (1km)

To Alaska Hwy North
(50m); Canada Games
Centre (100m);
Mt McIntyre Recreation
Center (5km); Takhini Hot
Springs (30km)

Industrial Rd

Quartz Rd

Chilkoot Way

Kishwoot
Island

Two Mile Hill Rd

Baxter St

Ray St

Ray St

7th Ave

Ogilvie St

Cook St

Wheeler St

8th Ave

Black St

Alexander St

5th Ave

6th Ave

Strickland St

Jarvis St

Wood St

Steele St

Main St

Elliott St

Lambert St

Hanson St

Hawkins St

Rogers St

Lowe St

Hoge St

Jeckell St

Taylor St

Drum St

Robert Service Way

Waterfront Trail

1st Ave

2nd Ave

3rd Ave

4th Ave

Wickstrom Rd

Hospital Rd

Yukon River

Shipyards
Park

Yukon Arts
& Heritage
Village

Rotary
Peace
Park

Robert
Campbell
Bridge

Whitehorse
Airport

Alaska Hwy

To Yukon Artists @ Work (8km);
Wolf Creek Campground (15km);
Marsh Lake Campground (50km)

To Alaska Hwy South (1km);
Hi Country RV Park (2km)

To Whitehorse
Fishway (500m);
Grey Mountain
(3km)

Rotary
Millennium
Bridge

A   B   C   D

1   2   3   4   5   6

INFORMATION

Bookstores

Mac's Fireweed Books (☎ 867-668-2434; www.yu konbooks.com; 203 Main St; ⏱ 8am-midnight May-Sep, 8am-9pm Oct-Apr) Superb selection of history, geography and wildlife titles plus a section on First Nations culture. It also carries topographical maps, road maps, magazines and newspapers.

Well-Read Books (☎ 867-393-2987; wellreadbooks .yk.net; 4194 4th Ave; ⏱ 9am-6pm Mon-Sat, 10am-5pm Sun) Large and varied selection of used books.

Emergency

☎ 911

Internet Access

The laundry, library and several cafés (p365) have internet access.

Laundry

Norgetown (☎ 867-667-6113; 4213 4th Ave; per load from $3.50; ⏱ 8am-9pm; 🖳) Has a drop-off service and internet terminals.

Library

Whitehorse Library (☎ 867-667-5239; 2071 2nd Ave; ⏱ 10am-9pm Mon-Fri, 10am-6pm Sat, 1-9pm Sun) Free internet access for 15 minutes.

Medical Services

Whitehorse General Hospital (☎ 867-393-8700; 5 Hospital Rd; ⏱ 24hr)

Post

Post office (☎ 867-667-2485; Shoppers Drug Mart, 211 Main St; ⏱ 9am-6pm Mon-Fri, 11am-4pm Sat)

Tourist Information

VIC (☎ 867-667-3084; 100 Hanson St; ⏱ 8am-8pm May-mid-Sep, 9am-4:30pm Mon-Fri mid-Sep–May) Has territory-wide information, possibly more than you can carry.

SIGHTS

Museums

The **Yukon Beringia Interpretive Centre** (☎ 867-667-8855; www.beringia.com; Km1473 Alaska Hwy; adult/child $6/4; ⏱ 8:30am-7pm mid-May–mid-Sep, 9am-6pm mid-Sep–mid-May) focuses on Beringia, an area that, during the last Ice Age, encompassed the Yukon, Alaska and eastern Siberia yet was untouched by glaciers. Interactive displays re-create the time. This museum is the most interesting local sight, and it's just south of the airport. From downtown, take the airport

bus and then walk south for five minutes. Look for the giant beaver on the way in – it's Beringia life size.

The immaculately restored **SS Klondike** (☎ 867-667-4511; South Access Rd & 2nd Ave; adult/child $6/2; ⏱ 9am-5pm mid-May–mid-Sep) was one of the last and largest stern-wheelers used on the Yukon River. Built in 1937, it made its final run upriver to Dawson in 1955 and is now a museum and national historic site.

You'll find every iconic bit of the Yukon's story at the **MacBride Museum** (☎ 867-667-2709; cnr 1st Ave & Wood St; adult/child $6/3.50; ⏱ 9am-7pm mid-May–Sep, noon-4pm Tue-Sat Oct–mid-May). Mounties, the gold rush, First Nations, lots of stuffed critters – it's all here. At the entrance, check out the good camera shot of the old White-horse waterfront. The whole building looks like a log cabin – with a live sod roof.

The **Yukon Transportation Museum** (☎ 867-668-4792; 30 Electra Circle; adult/child $6/3; ⏱ 10am-6pm May-Aug) covers the perils and adventures of getting around the Yukon by plane, train, truck and dog sled. See what happened when thousands of troops had to mud-wrestle the very earth to build the Alaska Hwy.

Waterfront

Whitehorse is getting a new waterfront on the Yukon River, with parks as bookends. Central to this is the new **Yukon Arts and Heritage Village**. With the historic **White Pass & Yukon Route Station** as its anchor, the development will have new decks and plazas, some extending over the river's edge. New loft-style buildings are meant to be the home of many of the Yukon's plethora of cultural groups. As they say: stand by. It will be located along First Ave, bounded by Wood and Main Sts.

Rotary Peace Park is in the south and the new **Shipyards Park** is in the north. The latter has a skateboard track and toboggan hill. Linking it all is the restored **trolley** (adult/child $2/free; ⏱ 9am-9pm May-Sep) that runs along the river.

Art Galleries

There are a lot of galleries and a lot of artists here. Watch for changes as the Yukon Arts and Heritage Village opens (see above).

Arts Underground (☎ 867-667-4080; Hougen Centre lower level; 305 Main St; ⏱ 9am-5:30pm Mon-Sat), run by the Yukon Arts Society, is a good-sized gallery with rotating exhibits.

Exhibits at the **Yukon Arts Centre** (☎ 867-667-8484; www.yukonartscentre.org; Yukon College, 300 College Dr;

noon-5pm Tue-Sun) are well curated and rotate every few months. This is also a performing arts venue.

In a warehouse space 10km south of the airport, the artist-run collective **Yukon Artists @ Work** (☎ 867-393-4848; 3B Glacier Dr; noon-5pm Tue-Sun Jun-Aug, call for other times) has a wide variety. It may move to the new Yukon Arts and Heritage Village.

Don't be put off by the smell of fudge in the air (actually that might draw you right in) at **Midnight Sun Gallery & Gifts** (☎ 867-668-4350; 205C Main St; 9am-8pm) – it has good selections of Yukon arts, crafts and products.

Other Sights

Built by the town's first priest in 1900, the **old log church** (☎ 867-668-2555; 303 Elliott St; adult/child $3/free; 10am-6pm mid-May–Aug) is the only log cabin–style cathedral in the world, and the oldest building in town.

Yukon Brewing Co (☎ 867-668-4183; 102 Copper Rd; 11am-6pm, tours 11am & 3:30pm Jun-Aug), the maker of Yukon Gold, Arctic Red, Winter Lead Dog Ale and Cranberry Wheat, is based in Whitehorse. You'll find these fine products throughout the territory, so try some now!

Whitehorse Fishway (☎ 867-633-5965; admission free; 9am-9pm Jun-Aug) is one of the neatest sights in Whitehorse. The fishway is a 366m wooden fish ladder (the world's longest) that gives fish a road past the hydroelectric plant just south of town. The real attraction here is the large viewing window that lets you look eye to eye with returning salmon before they continue swimming. If they look weary it's because they've been swimming 2792km since they entered the Yukon River in west Alaska and they still have another 208km to go before finally reaching their spawning grounds. There's an excellent free booklet available. The fishway is on Nisultin Dr off 2nd Ave after it crosses the Robert Campbell Bridge.

About 10km off the Klondike Hwy (Hwy 2) north of town in a quiet wooded area are the **Takhini Hot Springs** (☎ 867-633-2706; Km10 Takhini Hot Springs Rd; adult/child $7/6.50; 8am-10pm Jun-Aug). The pools are almost suburban but it's a good place to avoid frostbite even in summer.

ACTIVITIES

There's no need to get lethargic in Whitehorse.

Coast Mountain Sports (☎ 867-667-4074; 208 Main St; 9:30am-6pm Mon-Sat, to 9pm Thu & Fri, noon-4pm

Sun) has a large selection of outdoor clothing and gear. Contact **There & Back Again** (☎ 867-633-5346; www.thereandbackagain.ca) backpacking and backcountry gear rentals.

Walking & Hiking

You can walk a scenic 5km loop around Whitehorse's waters that includes a stop at the fishway. From the SS *Klondike*, head south on the **waterfront footpath** until you reach the Robert Service Campground and the Rotary Centennial Footbridge over the river. The fishway (left) is just south. Otherwise, head north along the water and cross the Robert Campbell Bridge and you are back in the town center.

Around Whitehorse you can go hiking and biking, particularly at **Mt McIntyre Recreation Center**, up Two Mile Hill Rd, and at **Grey Mountain**, east of town. All along the **Ibex River Valley** west of Whitehorse is good for biking. The hiking trails become cross-country ski trails in winter.

Swimming

Canada Games Centre (☎ 867-668-7665; 200 Hamilton Blvd; adult/child $6.75/3.50; 7am-10pm) was renamed for the major national winter games held in Whitehorse in early 2007. It is a fantasyland of pools, skating rinks and other indoor activities.

Canoeing & Kayaking

Whitehorse is the starting place for popular canoe and kayak trips to Carmacks or on to Dawson City. It's an average of eight days to the former and 16 days to the latter.

Kanoe People (☎ 867-668-4899; www.kanoepeople.com; cnr 1st Ave & Strickland St), at the river's edge, can arrange any type of trip (canoe/kayak to Carmacks $195/275; to Dawson City $325/475). These prices for unguided trips

---

DETOUR: CHAMPAGNE

About 75km west of Whitehorse look for the turn to **Champagne**, a former popular stop on the old Alaska Hwy (the charmless modern stretch opened in 2002). A trading post during the gold rush, it now boasts a huge collection of hubcaps mounted on a fence. The entire detour lasts about 14km before you rejoin the new bit of the Alaska Hwy. Haines Junction is 60km west.

include an orientation session and transport. Bicycle rentals are also available. The store has a great view of the river and vast amounts of gear, maps and guides for sale. Custom trips can be arranged.

Up North Adventures (☎ 867-667-7035; www .upnorth.yk.ca; 103 Strickland St) offers similar services and competitive prices. Staff speak German.

TOURS

The **Yukon Historical & Museums Association** (☎ 867-667-4704; 3126 3rd Ave; admission $2; 10am-4pm Mon-Sat Jun-Aug) offers downtown walking tours four times daily. Meet at its office in the 1904 DonnEworth House. Guides dress like period swells.

The **Yukon Conservation Society** (☎ 867-668-5678; www.yukonconservation.org; 302 Hawkins St; 10am-4pm Mon-Fri Jul & Aug) arranges free nature hikes in the area, including fun children's programs and more serious six-hour hikes for adults.

Gold Rush Float Tours (☎ 867-668-4836; cnr 1st Ave & Wood St; adult/child $60/32; Jun-Aug) lets you feel like a prospector with 2½-hour trips on re-created gold rush rafts down the Yukon River. Of course, on these you don't starve to death and die penniless.

SLEEPING

Whitehorse can get almost full during the peak of summer, so book ahead. But as the sun goes down, so do the prices, and bargains abound in winter. The VIC has lists of B&Bs and holiday homes.

Wal-Mart has proven to be a disruptive influence. Steadfastly sticking to its policy of letting RVers (primarily from the US) park for free in its lot has put a real strain on local RV parks. And worse, there's been a real increase in RV discharging by the side of Yukon roads since people started sticking their $250,000 rigs in the Wal-Mart lot. No doubt a coincidence.

Budget

Yukon Government Campgrounds (☎ 867-667-5648; campite $12) South of Whitehorse on the Alaska Hwy are two campgrounds: Wolf Creek (16km from town), set in a wooded area, and Marsh Lake (50km) with nearby beach access. Sites include firewood.

Robert Service Campground (☎ 867-668-3721; sercamp@hotmail.com; Robert Service Way; campsite $14; May-Sep) This popular tents-only 69-site campground along the river is just 1km

south of town along the South Access Rd, with showers, fire pits, internet access and a small store.

Hi Country RV Park (☎ 867-667-7445; www.hicoun tryrvyukon.com; 91378 Alaska Hwy; campsite $16-30;) At the top of Robert Service Way, this camp-ground in a wooded setting offers hookups, showers, laundry and wi-fi.

Hide on Jeckell Guesthouse (☎ 867-633-4933; www .hide-on-jeckell.com; 410 Jeckell St; dm $20;) Rates include kitchen facilities, a fireplace and an outdoor hot tub. The book exchange is es-pecially large – like a library. Extra-strength fair trade coffee knocks sense into you in the morning.

Beez Kneez Bakpakers (☎ 867-456-2333; www .bzkneez.com; 408 Hoge St; dm/r $25/50;) A garden, deck, grill and free bikes are just some of the amenities here. There's no TV on purpose – make friends or read a book. It's all very friendly and in a house; free wi-fi and inter-net access.

Midrange

Stratford Motel (☎ 867-667-4243; www.thestratford motel.com; 401 Jarvis St; r $70-110;) Eleven of the 50 large motel-style rooms here have kitch-ens. The decor is inoffensive and this very tidy place has a profusion of floral accents in season.

Town & Mountain Hotel (☎ 867-668-7644, 800-661-0522; www.townmountain.com; 401 Main St; r $80-130;) Right downtown, this veteran has been kept up to date and all 30 rooms have wi-fi. Some rooms are aimed at families – less stuff to break, two double beds; others are aimed at couples and posher types – more stuff to steal, er, take home (you know, free toiletries and the like…).

Yukon Inn (☎ 867-667-2527, 800-661-0454; www.yukon inn.com; 4220 4th St; r $80-150;) There's no shortage of parking at this 95-room slightly older motel; the entire place sits behind a strip-mall-sized parking lot. All rooms are tidy and inoffensive and have wi-fi. The break-fast café is always busy.

Midnight Sun Inn (☎ 867-667-2255, 800-284-4448; www.midnightsunbb.com; 6188 6th Ave; r $85-125;) A modern B&B in an impressive building, the welcoming Midnight Sun Inn offers four themed rooms. Obviously whether you walk like one or not you will want to stay in the Egyptian room – with its amber walls and figures. There's high-speed internet and good work desks.

Edgewater Hotel (☎ 867-667-2572, 867-668-3014; www.edgewaterhotelwhitehorse.com; 101 Main St; r $80-180; 🐾 🖳) Right by the new riverfront heritage center, the Edgewater is a compact place with 30 rooms. Those in the slightly newer wing are a tad nicer. All have high-speed internet. The bar is popular.

Top End

High Country Inn (☎ 867-667-4471, 800-554-4471; www.highcountryinn.ca; 4051 4th Ave; r $90-200; 🐾 🖳) A minor high-rise (four stories!), the High Country is popular with business travelers and high-end groups. The 84 rooms are large – some have huge whirlpools right in the room – and there is wi-fi throughout the property.

EATING & DRINKING

Self-caterers will be spoiled for choice. Most restaurants are in the center – chains circle the edges.

Budget

Fruit Stand (☎ 867-393-3994; 208 Black St; ☾ 10am-7pm May-Sep) You can buy fresh fruit and veggies at this cross between a stand and a store, which sells lots of Yukon-grown produce (berries) and prepared items such as fireweed honey. Yum.

Real Canadian Superstore (☎ 867-456-6635; 2270 2nd Ave; ☾ 8am-9pm) Vast superstore with aisles of bulk-size foods. Stock up here for the expedition.

3 Beans Natural Foods (☎ 867-668-4908; 308 Wood St; ☾ 10am-5:30pm Tue-Sat) Good organic and bulk health foods, vitamins and juice; all the stuff that doesn't spell s'mores by the campfire.

Zola's Café Doré (☎ 867-668-5780; 305 Main St; coffee $2; ☾ 7am-10pm; 🖳) Bright, airy and open, this bustling coffee bar is a meeting place for many. You can grab a sandwich or a baked good, and ponder the community bulletin boards. There's internet access at terminals ($1 per 10 minutes).

our pick Yukon Meat & Sausage (☎ 867-667-6077; 203 Hanson St; sandwiches $6; ☾ 9am-5:30pm Mon-Sat) The smell of smoked meat wafts out to the street and you walk right in. This great deli has a huge selection of prepared items and sandwiches. Great for picnics, or eat in.

Midrange

Chocolate Claim Café (☎ 867-667-2202; 305 Strickland St; meals $5-15; ☾ 8am-6pm Mon-Sat) One of the better places to see Yukon art, there's always something new on the walls. The works set the tone for the cultured menu, which features organic granola in the morning and exquisite salads, soups and sandwiches later. As the name implies, plan on dessert.

Alpine Bakery (☎ 867-668-6871; 411 Alexander St; meals $6-14; ☾ 8am-6pm Tue-Sat) This bakery in a log building has great bread, rolls and pizza from organic ingredients. There's a patio and you can enjoy pita sandwiches and other veggie items.

Yukon Mining Co (☎ 867-667-6457; High Country Inn, 4051 4th Ave; meals $7-20; ☾ 11am-late Apr-Oct) The huge outdoor deck here is the perfect place to enjoy a Yukon Brewing Co brew. There's a long menu with excellent burgers and fresh seafood. TVs with sports abound and you can listen in while guides tell wide-eyed clients how they'll bag a moose.

Sanchez Cantina (☎ 867-668-5858; 211 Hanson St; meals $10-20; ☾ 11:30am-3pm, 5-9:30pm) An amazing breath of fresh Mexican air in the Yukon! This wonderfully authentic cantina has a kitchen with all manner of treats cooking up front. The molé is excellent and the guacamole piquant. There's a small and delightful patio.

Top End

Panda's (☎ 867-667-2632; 212 Main St; meals $15-30; ☾ 11:30am-2pm Tue-Fri, 5-9pm Mon-Sat) What with the iconic black-and-white panda on the logo you're thinking Chinese, right? Wrong! It's all German all the time at this bistro, where smoked pork chops are always on the menu and there're five kinds of schnitzel. It's both formal in its European service and casual in its ambience.

Giorgio's Cucina (☎ 867-668-4050; 206 Jarvis St; meals $15-35; ☾ 11:30am-2pm, 5-10pm) The best place in town for Italian has a long menu of standards plus inventive specials. The semi-open kitchen flames things up and the steaks are prime. Portions are mother lode size – make certain your room has a fridge. It's casual but stylish in a sort of vague Mediterranean way, and the wine list is long. Great service.

ENTERTAINMENT

There are a lot of local bands playing in Whitehorse. To find out who's playing where, check out the fliers that appear on poles and trash cans all over town. There are also lots of thespians about town. Look for shows throughout the year, especially at the Yukon Arts Centre (p362).

Capital Hotel (☎ 867-667-2565; 103 Main St; ☽ 3pm-late) This place has a lively bar scene and live music almost every night. It draws a large crowd who appreciate the many drink specials. It's the best of several slightly grungy places around Main St.

GETTING THERE & AWAY
Air
Whitehorse Airport (YXY; ☎ 867-667-8440; www.gov.yk.ca) is five minutes west of downtown off the Alaska Hwy.

Whitehorse-based **Air North** (☎ 800-661-0407; www.flyairnorth.com) serves Dawson City, Old Crow and Inuvik in the Yukon, Fairbanks in Alaska, and Vancouver, Edmonton and Calgary.

Air Canada (☎ 888-247-2262; www.aircanada.com) serves Vancouver.

Condor (USA & Canada ☎ 800-364-1667, all other countries 01805 707 202; www.condor.com) operates twice-weekly services to/from Frankfurt in summer.

First Air (☎ 800 267-1247; www.firstair.ca) flies to Yellowknife in the Northwest Territories.

Bus
Vital service to/from Dawson City is in flux. Check with the VIC for updates.

Alaska Direct Busline (☎ 867-668-4833, 800-770-6652; www.alaskadirectbusline.com; 509 Main St; ☽ mid-May–Sep) runs services two to three times per week from Whitehorse to Skagway (US$65, three hours), Haines Junction (US$65, three hours), Beaver Creek (US$100, seven hours) and on to Fairbanks (US$180, 14 hours) and Anchorage (US$165, 18 hours).

Greyhound (☎ 867-667-2223; 2191 2nd Ave) reaches the end of the line in Whitehorse. Service south along the Alaska Hwy to Dawson Creek ($205, 21 hours, three times per week, April to October) connects with buses for the rest of BC and Canada.

GETTING AROUND
To/From the Airport
Yellow Cab (☎ 867-668-4811) charges about $16 from the center for the 10-minute ride.

Bus
Whitehorse Transit System (☎ 867-668-7433; trips $2; ☽ Mon-Sat), with services every 30 to 70 minutes, has a transfer point at the Qwanlin Mall. Route 2 serves the airport, center and the Robert Service Campground. Route 5 serves Yukon College and the Yukon Arts Centre.

Car & RV
Hertz (☎ 867-668-4224; www.hertz.com), **Budget** (☎ 867-667-6200; www.budget.com) and **National/NorCan** (☎ 867-456-2277; www.national.com) can be found at the airport. Check your rate very carefully, as it is common for a mileage charge to be added after the first 100km, which will get you barely anywhere in the Yukon. Also understand your insurance coverage fully and who pays for a cracked windshield and other damage that can easily occur on gravel roads.

Fraserway RV Rentals (☎ 867-668-3438; www.fraserwayrvrentals.com; 9039 Quartz Rd) rents all shapes and sizes of RV, from $80 to $250 per day depending on size (it matters) and season.

Whitehorse Subaru (☎ 867-393-6550; www.whitehorsesubaru.com; 17 Chilkoot Way) can usually beat the big firms on price, but don't expect a Forester.

ALASKA HIGHWAY

For some an attraction, for others a way to get someplace, most visitors will enjoy this fabled road as a combination of both.

The Alaska Hwy, the main road in the Yukon, is 2451km long and starts in Dawson Creek, British Columbia (p328). It enters the Yukon in the southeast and passes through Watson Lake, Whitehorse, Haines Junction and Beaver Creek en route to Fairbanks, Alaska. The road is Hwy 97 in British Columbia, Hwy 1 in the Yukon and Hwy 2 in Alaska.

A joint project between the USA and Canada, the highway was begun in 1942 as part of the war effort. The highway is now paved and much tamer than the original, except for stretches torn up each year for construction as part of a continual process of improvements. Over its entire length the road is mostly in very good shape.

Along with the mythic lure of the Alaska Hwy is the tangible sense of adventure that comes from actually going on a real road trip. Throughout the Yukon the scenery is vast and dramatic; even just finding something as mundane as a gas station can seem like a real discovery after the long drives through wilderness.

A ROAD LIKE NO OTHER

The construction of the Alaska Hwy in 1942 is considered one of the major engineering feats of the 20th century. Canada and the US had originally agreed to build an all-weather highway to Fairbanks from the south as early as 1930, but nothing serious was done until WWII. Japan's attack on Pearl Harbor, then its bombing of Dutch Harbor in the Aleutians and occupation of the Aleutian islands of Attu and Kiska, increased Alaska's strategic importance. The US army was told to prepare for the highway's construction a month before Canada's prime minister, WL Mackenzie King, signed the agreement granting the US permission to do so.

The route chosen for the highway followed a series of existing airfields – Fort St John, Fort Nelson, Watson Lake and Whitehorse – known as the Northwest Staging Route.

Thousands of US soldiers and Canadian civilians, including First Nations people, built the 2450km gravel highway between Dawson Creek in British Columbia and Fairbanks in Alaska. They began work on March 9, 1942 and completed it before falling temperatures (in what was to be one of the worst winters in recorded history) could halt the work. Conditions were harsh: sheets of ice rammed the timber pilings; floods during the spring thaw tore down bridges; and bogs swallowed trucks, tractors and other heavy machinery. In the cold months the road crews suffered frostbite, while in the summer they were preyed on by mosquitoes, black flies and other pests.

The original road had many curves and slopes because, with the bulldozers right behind them, the surveyors didn't have much time to pick the best route. In April 1946 the Canadian portion of the road (1965km) was officially handed over to Canada. In the meantime, private contractors were busy widening, graveling and straightening the highway; leveling its steep grades; and replacing temporary bridges with permanent steel ones. In 1949 the Alaska Hwy was opened to full-time civilian traffic and for the first time year-round overland travel to Alaska from the south was possible.

The completion of the highway opened the northwest to exploitation of its natural resources, changed settlement patterns and altered the First Nations' way of life forever.

The name of the highway has gone through several incarnations. It has been called the Alaskan International Hwy, the Alaska Military Hwy and the Alcan (short for Alaska-Canada) Hwy. More irreverently, in the early days it was also known as the Oil Can Hwy and the Rd to Tokyo. Officially, it is now called the Alaska Hwy but many people still affectionately refer to it simply as the Alcan.

The Alaska Hwy begins at 'Mile 0' in Dawson Creek (p328) in northeastern British Columbia and goes to Fairbanks, Alaska, although the official end is at Delta Junction (Mile 1422) about 155km southeast of Fairbanks (Mile 1523).

Milepost signs were set up in the 1940s to help drivers calculate how far they had traveled along the road. Since then improvements, including the straightening of the road, mean that its length has been shortened and the mileposts can't be used literally. On the Canadian side the distance markers are in kilometers. Mileposts are still very much in evidence in Alaska, and communities on both sides of the border use the original mileposts for postal addresses and as reference points.

Until the mid-1970s conditions along the highway were difficult. The highway is now completely paved except for stretches where road crews are doing summer maintenance work on potholes and frost heaves (raised sections of pavement caused by water freezing below). Millions of dollars are spent annually on maintaining and upgrading the road.

As vital an artery as the Alaska Hwy is today, it's easy to forget how it changed the Yukon and actually – despite being an American project – served to more fully integrate the Yukon into Canada. Prior to the road's construction people had to go through American ports such as Skagway and Haines on sea voyages down the coast to British Columbia; the Yukon was effectively cut off by land from the rest of Canada. Now drives to Vancouver and Calgary are relatively easy, putting the territory within reach for any Canadian with a car.

You can get a sense of what building the road entailed (and why everybody took boats before 1942) at the VIC in Watson Lake (p368) and the Yukon Transportation Museum in Whitehorse (p362). For more on the logistics and challenges involved in building the road, see boxed text, p330.

BC TO WHITEHORSE

This section of the Alaska Hwy has a lot of rolling hills, and reasonably sedate scenery. It's pretty enough, but is not on the same scale as the highway west of Whitehorse. The road itself teases the Yukon before dropping back into BC. Then it crosses into the Yukon almost for good just southeast of Watson Lake (though, it does flirt with BC again west of Swift River).

Many people are now heading north via the much-improved Stewart-Cassiar Hwy (p353), which joins the Alaska Hwy 428km east of Whitehorse.

Watson Lake

pop 1550

Originally named after Frank Watson, a British trapper, Watson Lake is the first town you'll come to in the Yukon as you head northwest on the Alaska Hwy from British Columbia. It's a big rest stop but otherwise skippable.

The **VIC** (☎ 867-536-7469; www.watsonlake.ca; Km1021 Alaska Hwy; ☯ 8am-8pm May–mid-Oct), at the junction of the Alaska and Robert Campbell Hwys, is the place to go for information on the entire territory. It has a diverting little museum on the history of the Yukon and the Alaska Hwy.

The town has campgrounds, a passel of similar and unexceptional motels, gas, ATMs and a Greyhound station.

The town is famous for its **Signpost Forest** just outside the VIC. The first signpost was 'Danville, Illinois', nailed up in 1942 by Carl Lindlay, a homesick US soldier working on the Alaska Hwy. Others added their own signs and now there are more than 55,000. You can have your own sign made on the spot or find a way to bring one from home…

Twenty-six kilometers west of Watson Lake is the junction with the Stewart-Cassiar Hwy (Hwy 37), which heads south into British Columbia (p353).

Teslin

pop 420

Teslin, on the Nisutlin River 272km west of Watson Lake, began life as a trading post in 1903 to serve the Tlingits (pronounced 'lin-kits'). The arrival of the Alaska Hwy brought both prosperity and rapid change for this First Nations population. The **George Johnston Museum** (☎ 867-390-2550; Km1294 Alaska Hwy; adult/child $5/2.50; ☯ 9am-5pm mid-May–Aug) exhibits photographs, displays and artifacts on the Tlingits and the gold rush days. There's canoeing and camping at nearby Teslin Lake, and a few motels.

DETOUR: ROBERT CAMPBELL HIGHWAY

From Watson Lake, this 588km gravel road (Hwy 4) is an alternative route north to Dawson City; it meets the Klondike Hwy near Carmacks (p376). Named after Robert Campbell, a 19th-century explorer and trader with the Hudson's Bay Company, it's a scenic and less traveled route that parallels several major rivers; it has few services.

Ross River, 373km from Watson Lake at the junction with the Canol Rd (Hwy 6), is home to the Kaska First Nations and a supply center for the local mining industry. There's a campground and motels in town, and a government campground at **Lapie Canyon**.

Historic boondoggle the **Canol Road** runs 230km south from Ross River to Johnson's Crossing (opposite) on the Alaska Hwy. During WWII, the US army built the Canol pipeline at tremendous human and financial expense to pump oil from Norman Wells in the Northwest Territories to Whitehorse, and the Canol Rd was built alongside it. However, it was only used for a brief period and then abandoned. North of Ross River, the Canol Rd runs for about 240km before ending near the Northwest Territories border; to go any further you have to hike the demanding **Canol Heritage Trail**.

The only services on Canol Rd (Hwy 6) are in Ross River at the Robert Campbell Hwy (Hwy 4) junction.

Faro, 10km off the Robert Campbell Hwy on the Pelly River, was created in 1968 to support the huge copper, lead and zinc mine in the Anvil Mountains. Downtown, the **Campbell Region Interpretive Centre** offers advice on viewing the abundant wildlife, particularly Fannin sheep, which live only in the Yukon. Staff can direct you to trails, including ones that lead to a waterfall or Mt Mye. There are motels, a campground nearby and some trails around town.

Just west of Teslin, the **Teslin Tlingit Heritage Centre** (☎ 867-390-2526; 🕙 9am-5pm Jun-Sep) has a pretty lakeside spot. The focus here is on Tlingit culture and artwork, especially the rich tradition of carved masks.

Johnson's Crossing

The Alaska Hwy follows string-bean-shaped Teslin Lake for 51km northwest of Teslin. At **Johnson's Crossing** there is a gas station and the gravel Canol Rd, which goes 230km north to Ross River on the Robert Campbell Hwy (see boxed text, opposite)

Jake's Corner

The junction with the road to Atlin (p356) is at **Jake's Corner**, 47km west of Johnson's Crossing. The Tagish Rd here goes west 55km to Carcross (p375).

WHITEHORSE TO ALASKA

This is the most scenic portion of the Alaska Hwy, as you spend several hours driving past Unesco-recognized Kluane National Park and Reserve. Plan on going 'wow' a lot and pulling over to explore and experience.

From Whitehorse the road gets off slow in terms of scenery but fast in terms of speed. It's been heavily improved and the wide cuts and broad turns have obliterated a lot of scenery.

Haines Junction

pop 800

You'll know you've reached Haines Junction when you see a huge **sculpture** that looks like a nightmare cupcake at the intersection of the Alaska and Haines Hwys. After critics shot off the faces of the critters, a recent restoration has restored its hideous glory.

Haines Junction makes an excellent base for exploring Kluane National Park or to launch a serious mountaineering, backcountry or river trip. Edged by the Kluane Range and surrounding green belt, the views are dramatic and access is easy via the Alaska Hwy from Whitehorse (158km) or Tok, Alaska (498km); and also via the Haines Hwy (Hwy 3) from Haines, Alaska (238km). German travelers will hear their language spoken all over town.

Yukon Tourism and Parks Canada share the **VIC** (Yukon Tourism ☎ 867-634-2345; 🕙 8am-8pm Jun-Aug; Parks Canada ☎ 867-634-7250; www.parkscanada.gc.ca/kluane; 🕙 10am-6pm mid-May–Aug, 10am-4pm Sep–mid-May) in the Kluane National Park headquarters building on Logan St. There's lots of info from the two agencies, and a good model of the local terrain.

All shops, lodging and services, including a **Shell station** (☎ 867-634-2246), are clustered around the Alaska and Haines Hwys junction.

The post office, bank and ATM are inside **Madley's Store** (☎ 867-634-2200; Hwy 3; 🕙 8am-9pm; 🖳), which carries everything from fresh berries and never-fresh doughnuts to spark plugs and fishing tackle. It has internet access.

ACTIVITIES

The ridges looming over Haines Junction don't begin to hint at the beauty of Kluane National Park (p370). Although the park should be your focus, there are also some good activities in and around Haines Junction.

For a good way to stretch your legs after hours of driving, there's a pretty 5.5km **nature walk** along Dezadeash River where Hwy 3 crosses at the south end of town. At Pine Lake campground, 6km east of town on the Alaska Hwy, there's good **swimming**, picnic tables and a sandy beach with fire pits.

Paddlewheel Adventures (☎ 867-634-2683; www.paddlewheeladventures.com; 116 Kathleen St), opposite the VIC, has a fine deck where you can gaze at the nearby peaks. It arranges Tatshenshini rafting trips ($125 per person, includes lunch), scenic float trips and guided interpretive hikes ($45 to $80). It rents mountain bikes or canoes ($25 per day) and provides local transportation.

Owned by a longtime park warden and guide, **Kruda Ché Boat Tours** (☎ 867-634-2378; www.krudache.com) will arrange any number of custom tours by boat and foot within Kluane National Park. Wildlife, history and First Nations culture are just some of the themes.

On a clear day, consider a 40- to 120-minute flight over the icy heart of Kluane National Park with **Sifton Air** (☎ 867-634-2916; Km1632 Alaska Hwy), which charges $150 to $400 per person with three passengers. Call for schedules.

SLEEPING & EATING

There's a little thicket of motels in Haines Junction.

Pine Lake Campground (campsite $12) This territorial facility on the Alaska Hwy, 6km from town, is a good choice, with wooded sites and a day-use area.

Kluane RV Campground (☎ 867-634-2709, 866-634-6789; Km1635 Alaska Hwy; campsite from $16; 🖳) Away from the RV area, there are 45 sites in a nice wooded area.

Paddlewheel Cabins (☎ 867-634-2683; Auriol St; cabins $50) Opposite the Village Bakery, Paddlewheel Adventures (p369) has two convenient and cozy cabins with wood stoves, small kitchens and a shared bathroom.

Alcan Motor Inn (☎ 867-634-2371, 888-265-1018; www.yukonweb.com/tourism/alcan; s/d $95-130; 🏢) Alcan has 22 large, modern rooms with great views of jagged Auriol Range. It's a no-surprises kind of place and gets a lot of repeat customers who partake of the continental breakfast and a public coin laundry.

Raven Motel (☎ 867-634-2500; www.yukonweb.com/tourism/raven; 181 Alaska Hwy; s/d $120/135; 🏢 🖳) The Raven has 12 deluxe motel rooms with wi-fi. The restaurant, open for dinner (meals $35 to $50), is known across the Yukon for its fine-dining experience. There are French and Italian inspirations on the hearty menu, which also takes cues from Germany. Presentation is oh-so-correct and the wine list is expansive.

Village Bakery & Deli (☎ 867-634-2867; Logan St; meals $6-10; ⏰ 7am-9pm May-Aug; 🖳) Opposite the VIC, this laid-back place with an outdoor deck is a real find. Great baked goods and sandwiches; don't miss the salmon barbecue ($17) with live music at 7pm on summer Fridays. There's free wi-fi.

GETTING THERE & AWAY

Alaska Direct Busline (☎ 867-668-4833, 800-770-6652; www.alaskadirectbusline.com; ⏰ mid-May-Sep) Runs services two to three times per week to Whitehorse (US$65, three hours) and Skagway; west to Beaver Creek and Alaska.

Kluane National Park & Reserve

The Unesco-recognized Kluane National Park & Reserve looms south of the Alaska Hwy almost all the way to the Alaska border. This rugged and magnificent wilderness covers 22,015 sq km of the southwest corner of the territory. Kluane (kloo-wah-neee) gets its name from the Southern Tutchone word for 'lake with many fish.'

With British Columbia's Tatshenshini-Alsek Provincial Wilderness Park (p356) to the south and Alaska's Wrangell-St Elias National Park to the west, this is one of the largest protected wilderness areas in the world. You'll find numerous places where you can stop and enjoy the view, hike or blow a few million pixels on photos.

INFORMATION

There are two information centers operated by Parks Canada. See p369 for details on the main center in Haines Junction. A second center can be found at **Tachal Dhal** (Sheep Mountain; Km1706.8 Alaska Hwy; ⏰ 9am-4pm Jun-Aug) and covers visitors arriving from the west. It also serves as the starting point for hikes at the north end. Get a copy of the *Recreation Guide* which shows the scope of the park (and how little is actually easily accessible). The map also shows hiking opportunities, which range from 10 minutes to 11 days.

Winters are long and can be harsh, though some venture out on skis or snowshoes starting in February. Summers are short and temperatures are generally comfortable from mid-June to mid-September, which is the best time to visit. Note that freezing temperatures can occur at any time, especially in the high country, so bring appropriate clothing and rain gear.

SIGHTS

The park consists primarily of the still-growing **St Elias Mountains** and the world's largest nonpolar **ice fields**. Two-thirds of the park is glacier and interspersed are valleys, glacial lakes, alpine forest, meadows and tundra. The Kluane Ranges (averaging 2500m) are seen along the western edge of the Alaska Hwy. A green belt wraps around the base where most of the animals and vegetation live. Turquoise **Kluane Lake** is the Yukon's largest. Hidden are the immense ice fields and the towering peaks, including **Mount Logan** (5959m), Canada's highest mountain, and **Mount St Elias** (5488m), the second highest. Partial glimpses of the interior peaks can be found at the Km1622 viewpoint on the Alaska Hwy from Whitehorse and around the Donjek River Bridge, but the best views are definitely from the air. When you climb over the ridge and see that Kluane is literally a sea of glaciers stretching over the horizon you'll understand what all the Unesco fuss is about.

Parks Canada runs a range of **interpretive programs** through the summer from both visitor centers. Guided walks ($5, one to two hours) and the more ambitious guided hikes ($20, four to six hours) are recommended.

DEATH OF THE BEETLES?

You can't miss it as you drive the Alaska Hwy past Kluane National Park: millions upon millions of dead trees. Just as much of the park is covered in ice, so too is much of the park covered in a dead forest. The culprit is the spruce beetle.

In 1994 the first signs were noted that something was amiss. Huge swathes of yellowing and brown spruce began appearing. Normally the spruce beetles claim a tree here and there every year. It's part of nature's process that thins out weak and old trees so that new and healthy ones can thrive. But no one had seen vast areas where all the trees had fallen victim. The beetle population had exploded and they were burrowing in and killing every tree they encountered. It was easy for scientists to determine that the beetle population was benefiting from warmer temperatures. Normally the brutal, cold winters keep the numbers in check, but several mild winters in a row had let the little buggers go nuts.

By 2000 it was clear that most of Kluane's spruce forest was gone, more than 350,000 hectares in the park and much more in the surrounding region. Longtime residents and visitors could only look on sadly at a place they had remembered as being so green. But then a few things happened that prove that nature can find ways to balance even this kind of catastrophe. A really cold winter in 2006 provided the normal inhibition to the beetle population and the sheer size of the beetle population meant that eventually their predators caught up to the bounty at hand.

In the summer of 2006 researchers could say that new attacks on trees had plummeted towards historic levels. But that still leaves an enormous number of dead trees. Fears will continue every year for a while that they might go up in the forest fire of all time. Meantime, nature has opened the door to other trees; birch and alder, which grow quickly and are favored by moose, and other critters are thriving. Other parts of Canada are now having to contend with their own beetle infestations (see boxed text, p332.

To see the beetle destruction first hand, learn about how a tree is killed and witness the forest's early regeneration, stop off at the **Spruce Beetle Walk**. Just 18km past Haines Junction on the Alaska Hwy, Parks Canada has built this 1.7km loop trail into the forest. It has good explanatory signs on the phenomenon and is a worthwhile, if sobering, stop.

ACTIVITIES

The green-belt area of the park is a great place for **hiking**, either along marked trails or less-defined routes. There are about a dozen in each category, some following old mining roads, others traditional First Nations' paths. The Parks Canada hiking leaflet has a map and lists the trails with distances and starting points, including limited possibilities for **mountain biking**.

Detailed trail guides and topographical maps are available at the information centers. Talk to the rangers before setting out; they will help select a hike and provide updates on areas that may be closed due to bear activity. **Overnight hikes** require backcountry permits ($9 per person per night) and you must have a bear-proof food canister ($5 per night, $100 deposit). Haines Junction (p369) is a good place to organize gear and guides.

The Tachal Dhal information center is the starting point for **Slims West**, a popular 60km round-trip trek to **Kaskawulsh Glacier** – one of the few that can be reached on foot. This is a difficult and world-class route that takes from three to five days to complete. From the same trailhead, **Sheep Creek** is a moderate 10km day hike. The **Auriol** trail starts 7km south of Haines Junction and is a 15km loop above the tree line, providing some good views. From Kathleen Lake, **King's Throne** is a 5km one-way route with a steep 1220m elevation gain. Great views of the Alsek Valley are waiting at the top.

Fishing is good and wildlife abounds. You can't miss the thousands of Dall sheep that can be seen on the appropriately named **Sheep Mountain** in April, May and September. There's a large and diverse population of grizzly bears, as well as black bears, moose, caribou, goats and 150 varieties of birds, among them eagles and the rare peregrine falcon.

Famous among mountaineers, the internationally renowned **Icefield Ranges** provide excellent climbing on Mt Logan, Mt Kennedy and Mt Hubbard. April, May and June are considered the best months and climbers should contact the park well in advance for information and permits.

The only campground technically within the park is at **Kathleen Lake** (campsite $12, firewood $8), 24km south of Haines Junction off the Haines Hwy (right).

Destruction Bay
pop 60

This small village on the shore of Kluane Lake is 107km north of Haines Junction. Like Haines Junction and Beaver Creek, it started off as a camp and supply depot during the construction of the Alaska Hwy. It was given its present name after a storm tore through the area. There's boating and fishing on Kluane Lake and the village has a gas station.

Near the town, **Congdon Creek** (Km1723 Alaska Hwy; campsite $12) is a beautiful location with views across a sparkling mountain lake with snowy peaks in the background. It's cliché city! The campsites are well spaced and there's a playground. Read the warnings and don't become a Whitman sampler for a bear while you snooze in your tent.

Burwash Landing
pop 90

Burwash Landing, 19km north of Destruction Bay, pre-dates the Alaska Hwy with a brief gold strike on nearby 4th of July Creek. It's also home of the Kluane First Nations and noted for the excellent **Kluane Museum** (☎ 867-841-5561; Km1759 Alaska Hwy; adult/child $6/3; ☼ 9am-8pm mid-May–early Sep). The museum features a huge stuffed moose, ancient mammoth teeth and displays on natural and First Nations history. The little town has a gas station.

Beaver Creek
pop 110

Tiny Beaver Creek, Canada's westernmost town, is on the Alaska Hwy 457km northwest of Whitehorse and close to the Alaska border. Its main reason for existing is to give you somewhere to sleep.

The **VIC** (☎ 867-862-7321; Km1202 Alaska Hwy; ☼ 8am-8pm May-Sep) has a wildflower exhibit and information on the Yukon and Alaska. Just past the VIC is a silly life-sized **sculpture park** where you can get friendly with a beaver (p4) or stroke a Mountie. The Canadian customs checkpoint is just north of town and the US customs checkpoint is 27km further west. The border is open 24 hours.

Of the four motels in town, the literally named **1202 Motor Inn** (☎ 867-862-7600,

800-661-0540; 1202 Alaska Hwy; r from $50) has a log cabin motif inside and out. The 30 rooms are basic and functional. Get one away from the idling trucks, whose owners are in the café watching sports and chowing down on the decent pizza and big burgers.

Alaska

You'll soon note that the incredible scenery of the Alaska Hwy dims a bit once you cross into its namesake state. The Alaska Hwy department seems to have a 'bulldoze it and leave' philosophy, so the route is much more torn up and despoiled here than the pristine conditions in the Yukon.

From the US border, it's 63km (39 miles) to **Tetlin National Wildlife Refuge** on the Alaska Hwy. About 117km (73 miles) past Tetlin, you'll reach the junction with the Taylor Hwy (Hwy 5), which connects with the Top of the World Hwy (p383) to Dawson City. Another 19km (12 miles) on the Alaska Hwy west of the junction is **Tok** (population 1400), which has a slew of motels, restaurants and services.

HAINES HIGHWAY

Linking the important Yukon entry point of Haines Alaska with the Alaska Hwy at Haines Junction in the territory, this excellent road packs a lot in to a relatively short length.

In a mere 259km you get to visit Alaska, BC and the Yukon, as well as going from sea level to wind-blown passes high above the tree line where June snow is common. The route is popular with cyclists, many of whom compete in the annual Kluane Chilkat International Bike Relay.

There are myriad places to pull over and admire the beauty. The **Alaska Chilkat Bald Eagle Preserve**, from Mile 9 to Mile 32 along the Haines Hwy, has a local population of eagles that congregate by the thousands in November for the late salmon run. Near the Yukon border, **Million Dollar Falls** thunders through a narrow chasm; the surging water is a real jaw-dropper. All through the higher elevations are idyllic alpine meadows.

HAINES (ALASKA)
pop 2300

This pretty harbor town sits on the Lynn Canal. Surrounded by mountains and the always moody sea, mellow Haines is a good place to get your bearings if you're off a ferry. It is much more relaxed than Skagway – something easily seen as you sip a beer on a café deck watching the conga line of cruise ships steaming to that gold rush town. Haines is the departure point for longer raft trips on the Tatshenshini or Alsek Rivers in British Columbia (p356). By using the ferry to connect between Haines and Skagway, you can put together an interesting circle itinerary of the Yukon.

Prices for Haines are in US$. Alaska time is one hour earlier than Yukon time. For more coverage of Haines and southeast Alaska, see Lonely Planet's *Alaska*.

Information

Emergency ☎ 911

Haines Convention & Visitors Bureau (☎ 907-766-2234, 800-458-3579; www.haines.ak.us; 122 2nd Ave; ✆ 8am-7pm Mon-Fri, 9am-6pm Sat & Sun) Trail maps available, plus Yukon info.

Sights & Activities

Fort Seward, the first and for a time the only army post in Alaska, was established in the early 1900s and designated a national historical site in 1972. It also has native art galleries.

Chilkat Guides (☎ 907-766-2491; www.raftalaska .com) offers intense wilderness raft trips down the Tatshenshini and Alsek Rivers to the coast of Glacier Bay. Prices start at US$2895 per person for nine days. Local day trips to see bald eagles are also available.

American Bald Eagle Foundation (☎ 907-766-3094; www.baldeagles.org; Haines Hwy & 2nd Ave; adult/child US$3/1; ✆ 9am-5pm, May-Sep, by appointment other times) features an impressive display of more than 100 species of eagles and a video of the massive annual gathering of bald eagles at Chilkat River. Better yet is the live video of an eagle's nest (in season).

If you need more American icons, say a few thousand, the Alaska Chilkat Bald Eagle Preserve, from Mile 9 to Mile 32 along the Haines Hwy, has a local population of eagles that congregate by the thousands in November for the late salmon run.

Sleeping & Eating

Reserve rooms ahead in the summer.

Chilkat State Park Campground (Mud Bay Rd; campsite US$10) On the scenic Chilkat Peninsula 11km southeast of Haines, the 15 sites here have good views of Lynn Canal and of the Davidson and Rainbow Glaciers.

Captain's Choice Motel (☎ 907-766-3111, 800-478-2345; www.capchoice.com; 108 2nd Ave N; r US$85-160; ⚡) The cap'n offers the town's nicest lodging. The 39 motel-style rooms have wi-fi; aim for one with a private balcony. The motel's big flower-ringed sundeck overlooking Lynn Canal is a highlight.

Mountain Market & Café (☎ 907-766-3340; 151 3rd Ave; meals US$4-10; ✆ 7am-7pm Mon-Fri, 7am-6pm Sat & Sun) This groovy market has a café with bagels, big sandwiches and lots of organic prepared foods. It's where you should get your Haines Hwy picnic.

Fireweed (☎ 907-766-3838; Bldg 37 Blacksmith Rd; meals US$6-16; ✆ 11am-10pm) In Fort Seward, Fireweed has a great deck where you can enjoy its 'fine organic world cuisine.' The best place in town, it has pizza, sandwiches and salads. People swoon over the Haines Brewing Spruce Tip Ale.

Getting There & Away

If you use Haines as your entry into the Yukon, you should have your own vehicle.

The excellent **Alaska Maritime Highway** (☎ 800-642-0066; www.ferryalaska.com) service goes to Juneau, Petersburg, Wrangell, Ketchikan and, importantly, Prince Rupert in BC (per person US$172, vehicles from US$775, 33 hours, two to three per week) and Bellingham, Washington in the US (per person US$342, cabins from US$271, vehicles from US$772, 68 to 80 hours, one to two per week). To link up with Skagway (p374) for a circle route, you can take the ferry (per person US$30, vehicles from US$40, two hours, five to seven weekly). For more on the Inside Passage journey, see boxed text, p400.

The **Haines-Skagway Fast Ferry** (☎ 907-766-2100, 888-766-2103; www.chilkatcruises.com; ✆ Jun-Sep) carries passengers only (adult/child US$25/12.50, 35 minutes), three times per day.

KLONDIKE HIGHWAY

Covering this fabled 716km road – a route that in the past marked triumph and tragedy – is a highlight of the Yukon. It runs from Skagway in Alaska through the northwestern corner of British Columbia to Whitehorse and Dawson City, and more or less follows the Gold Rush Trail, the route some 40,000 gold seekers took in 1898. The highway, open year-round, is paved for its length. The stretch from Skagway to Carcross is a scenic marvel of lakes and mountains.

SKAGWAY (ALASKA)

pop 790

Skagway. Spat out with derision by some while sung with glee by others, this tiny gold-rush town can be over-run with day-trippers or offer a moody window to the past, all in the same day. Although it's in the US, it can only be reached by car using the Klondike Hwy from the Yukon through British Columbia. It's the starting point for the famed Chilkoot Trail and the White Pass & Yukon Route.

This is the last stop on the Alaska Marine Hwy ferry runs from Prince Rupert, BC (p338) and Bellingham, Washington in the US, making it an important entry point for the Yukon. Many people heading north take the ferry one way (which is spectacular) and drive either the Alaska or Stewart-Cassiar Hwys the other way.

Serene at night when you can stroll down the middle of the street, Skagway by day harkens back to the gold rush era when John Muir described it 'an anthill stirred with a stick.' Mammoth cruise ships disgorge up to 8000 day-trippers at once, who hit the streets with an inflamed passion for cheap T-shirts. If you are coming by ferry, you may wish to head into the Yukon via much more mellow Haines (p372). Lonely Planet's *Alaska* has extensive coverage of Skagway and the rest of Southeast Alaska. Prices in this section are in US$.

Orientation

From the ferry terminal, the foot and vehicle traffic spills onto Broadway St and the center of town. There's a post office, ATMs, campgrounds, hotels, restaurants and shops, including some selling non-T-shirt items such as fudge. The Klondike Hwy runs into the center from the opposite end of town.

Skagway is on Alaska time, which is one hour earlier than the Yukon. Most places close outside of summer.

Information

Chilkoot Trail Centre (☎ 907-983-3655, 800-661-0486; www.nps.gov/klgo; cnr Broadway & 2nd St; ☑ 8am-5pm summer) Run by Parks Canada and the US National Park Service; provides advice, permits, maps and a list of transportation options to/from the Chilkoot Trail.

Emergency ☎ 911

Skagway News Depot & Books (☎ 907-983-3354; 264 Broadway; ☑ 9am-6pm) Good selection of regional titles, guides and topographical maps.

Skagway Visitor Bureau (☎ 907-983-2854, 888-762-1898; www.skagway.org; 245 Broadway; ☑ 8am-6pm) In a stunning building with a driftwood facade.

US National Park Service (☎ 907-983-2921; cnr Broadway & 2nd St; ☑ 8am-6pm May-Sep) Offers free daily walking tours and the *Skagway Trail Map* for area hikes.

Sights

Skagway is filled with **historic buildings** restored to their gold rush appearance. Get a self-guiding map from the information centers and set off on your exploration.

At the southeastern end of 7th Ave is a 1900 granite building housing **Skagway Museum** (☎ 907-983-2420; 7th Ave at Spring St; adult/student US$2/1; ☑ 9am-5pm). The museum has sections devoted to various aspects of local history, including First Nations heritage and the Klondike gold rush. Look for the pistol that the notorious Soapy Smith kept up his sleeve.

The visually stunning **White Pass & Yukon Route** (WP&YR; ☎ 907-983-2217, 800-343-7373; www.wpyr.com; cnr 2nd Ave & Spring St; adult/child US$95/47.50; ☑ mid-May–late Sep) attracts most visitors in Skagway. It's a smart decision. The line twists up the tortuous route to the namesake White Pass, tracing the notorious White Pass trail used during the Klondike gold rush.

Sleeping & Eating

Reservations are strongly recommended during July and August. There are many places to eat and drink on or just off Broadway St.

Pullen Creek RV Park (☎ 907-983-2768, 800-936-3731; 501 Congress St; sites from US$20) There are 46 sites here, right near the ferry dock and State St.

Sergeant Preston's Lodge (☎ 907-983-2521; sgt prestons@usa.net; 370 6th Ave; r US$70-120; 🖳) The 37 rooms here are scattered among a few unassuming buildings right off Broadway. All are large and comfortable, even homey.

Bonanza Bar & Grill (☎ 907-983-6214; Broadway btwn 3rd & 4th Aves; meals US$7-15; ☑ 10am-midnight) A lively restaurant/sports bar with lots of good beers on tap.

Getting There & Away

From Skagway to Whitehorse on the Klondike Hwy (Hwy 2) is 177km. The road is modern and paved, and customs at the border usually moves fairly quickly.

BOAT

The excellent **Alaska Maritime Highway** (☎ 800-642-0066; www.ferryalaska.com) goes to Haines (US$30, vehicles from US$40, two hours, five to seven weekly), Juneau, Petersburg, Wrangell, Ketchikan and, importantly, Prince Rupert in BC (US$184, cabins from US$270, vehicles from $775, 35 hours, two to three per week); it also goes to Bellingham, Washington in the US (US$352, cabins from US$271, vehicles from US$795, 68 to 80 hours, one to two per week). For more on the Inside Passage journey, see boxed text p400.

The **Haines-Skagway Fast Ferry** (☎ 907-766-2100, 888-766-2103; www.chilkatcruises.com) carries passengers only (adult/child US$25/12.50, 35 minutes, June to September), three times per day.

BUS & TRAIN

Alaska Direct Busline (☎ 867-668-4833, 800-770-6652; www.alaskadirectbusline.com; ☻ mid-May–Sep) runs services two to three times per week from Skagway to Whitehorse (US$65, three hours), where you can connect to Haines Junction, Beaver Creek and then on to Fairbanks and Anchorage.

White Pass & Yukon Route (WP&YR; ☎ 907-983-2217, 800-343-7373; www.wpyr.com; cnr 2nd Ave & Spring St) offers a rail and bus connection to/from Whitehorse (adult/child US$95/47.50, four hours, one daily May to mid-September). The transfer point is Fraser, BC.

CHILKOOT TRAIL

Skagway was the landing point for many in the gold rush days of the late 1890s. From there began the long, slow, arduous and often deadly haul inland to the Klondike goldfields near Dawson City. One of the main routes from Skagway, the Chilkoot Trail over the Chilkoot Pass, is now extremely popular with hikers.

The well-marked 53km trail begins near Dyea, 14km northwest of Skagway, then heads northeast following the Taiya River to Lake Bennett in British Columbia, and takes three to five days to hike. It's considered a difficult route with good weather and can be treacherous in bad. You must be in good physical condition and come fully equipped. Layers of warm clothes and rain gear are essential.

Solo hikers will not have a problem finding company.

Along the trail you'll see hardware, tools and supplies dumped by the gold seekers. At several places there are wooden shacks where you can put up for the night, but these are usually full, so a tent and sleeping bag are required. There are 10 designated campgrounds along the route. The most strenuous part of the trail is over the Chilkoot Pass. The elevation gain on the trail is 1110m.

At the Canadian end you can either take the WP&YR train (left) from Bennett back to Skagway, or further up the line to Fraser, where you can connect with a bus for Whitehorse.

The Chilkoot Trail is a primary feature of the **Klondike Gold Rush International Historic Park**, a series of sites managed by both Parks Canada and the US National Park Service that stretches from Seattle, Washington to Dawson City. See (opposite) for details on the Chilkoot Trail Centre, which issues permits and required information.

Each hiker must obtain one of the 50 permits available each day and it's vital to reserve in advance. The permits cost $50 plus $10 for a reservation. Each day eight permits are issued on a first-come, first-served basis.

CARCROSS

pop 430

With the extension of White Pass & Yukon Route trains from Skagway in 2007, appealing little Carcross is ready for a boom – or at least a boomlet. Some 74km southeast of Whitehorse, it's the first settlement you reach in the Yukon from Skagway on the Klondike Hwy. The site was once a major seasonal hunting camp of the Tagish people, who called the area *Todezzane* (literally 'blowing all the time'). The present town name is an abbreviation of Caribou Crossing and refers to the local woodland caribou herds.

The **VIC** (☎ 867-821-4431; ☻ 8am-8pm May-Sep) is in the old train station and provides a top-notch walking tour booklet of the area's buildings. The station also has good displays on the local history and directly behind it there is a hall where local artists show their wares.

Two kilometres north of town, **Carcross Desert**, the world's smallest, is the exposed sandy bed of a glacial lake that retreated after the last Ice Age. Strong winds allow little vegetation to grow.

DETOUR: SILVER TRAIL

The Silver Trail heads northeast to three old mining and fur-trading towns: **Mayo**, **Elsa** and **Keno**. The road is paved as far as Mayo (52km). Elsa (50km from Mayo) and Keno (10km further) are almost ghost towns and are fascinating places to wander around. **Keno Hill** in Keno, with its signposts and distances to cities all over the world, offers more views of the mountains and valleys. There are hiking trails in the vicinity, ranging from 2km to 20km long, providing access to old mining areas and alpine meadows. Yukon Tourism publishes excellent walking tours to all three which can be found at VICs. Mayo has a couple of motels and a gold mining history. There are some interesting old buildings and historical displays along the banks of the Stewart River.

With its old buildings, picturesque railroad bridge over Lake Bennett and overall authentic heritage feel, Carcross is worth the extra 45km you'll drive detouring off the stretch of the Alaska Hwy between Whitehorse and Jake's Corner (p369).

WHITEHORSE TO CARMACKS

North of Whitehorse, between the Takhini Hot Springs Rd and Carmacks, the land is dry and scrubby, although there are some farms with cattle and horses. The Klondike Hwy skirts several lakes where you can go swimming, boating, fishing or camping. Near Carmacks the mountains become lower, more rounded hills and the land more forested. Between Whitehorse and Dawson City there are plenty of places to get gas – for your tank and your stomach. With one notable exception in Pelly Crossing, this might be a good time to pack a picnic from Whitehorse.

CARMACKS

pop 400

Perched on the banks of the Yukon River, Carmacks was once a fueling station for riverboats and a stopover on the overland trail from Whitehorse to Dawson City. Originally known as Tantalus, the town name was changed to Carmacks to honor George Washington Carmack, who, along with Skookum Jim and Tagish Charley, discovered gold at Bonanza Creek in 1896 and sparked the Klondike gold rush.

The town has gas stations, a campground, motels and the excellent **Tage Cho Hudan Interpretive Centre** (☎ 867-863-5830; admission by donation; ☷ 9am-4pm May-Sep). Here you can take a 15-minute interpretive walk by the river and learn answers to questions such as how did a First Nations girl become a woman, and were the America's Navajo tribe really Yukon refugees.

The junction for the Campbell Hwy (see boxed text, p368) is also here,

North of town about 25km, the **Five Finger Recreation Site** has excellent views of the legendary treacherous stretch of the rapids that tested the wits of riverboat captains. There's a 1.5km steep walk down to the rapids.

PELLY CROSSING

Look for **Penny's Place** (burgers $7; ☷ 9am-6pm Jun-Aug) along the road. There' are tasty shakes and famous burgers.

STEWART CROSSING

pop 50

Once a supply center between Dawson City and Whitehorse, Stewart Crossing sits at the junction of the Klondike Hwy (Hwy 2) and the Silver Trail (Hwy 11), another route taken by prospectors in search of silver.

Canoeists can put in here for the very good five-day **float trip** down the Stewart River to the Yukon River and on to Dawson City. Though you travel through wilderness, and wildlife is commonly seen, it is a trip suitable for the inexperienced. Canoeists should organize and outfit in Whitehorse (p363).

The tiny town has a café and gas station. At times there's a roadside visitor information hut that can supply useful information on the Silver Trail and its towns.

DAWSON CITY

pop 1800

The destination for tens of thousands in 1897 and 1898, Dawson – then little more then a muddy shoal at the confluence of the Yukon and Klondike Rivers – was a wild and woolly place where a miner would appear with a sack full of gold, and 24 hours later, wake up with but a dim memory of the bartenders, scammers, prostitutes and others who'd relieved him of it. (See boxed text, below for more on these characters.)

Summer sees a large influx of tourists and seasonal workers. RVs roam the streets like miners in search of a claim. But by September, 'flee sale' signs begin to appear all over town as seasonal residents (about half) head south. For those remaining, Dawson is a cold (average temperature in January is -27°C) and quiet place.

For many travelers, a summer visit to Dawson will be the highlight of their Yukon trip. Plan on staying at least two or three days.

HISTORY

The city grew up almost as fast as its boom faded. Once known as the 'Paris of the North,' by the early 20th century it was in slow, steady decline. Today, however, Dawson, while not exactly thriving, is healthy and has a thriving cultural life that extends beyond that derived from summer tourism. It's a place where you can still experience a tangible link to a storied past while making new contemporary discoveries.

Many buildings remain from the gold rush era. Parks Canada is involved in restoring or preserving those considered historically significant; regulations ensure that new buildings are built in sympathy with the old. With unpaved streets and board sidewalks, the town still has a gritty edge-of-the-world feel.

The town is built on permafrost, which begins just a few centimeters down. Buildings have foundations of planks resting on gravel and many show the seasonal effects of heaving. Outside of town are the eerie piles of tailings, which look like the work of mammoth gophers. These huge mounds are actually from gold dredges that sucked up the swampy earth at one end and left it behind sans gold at the other. Some 100 years after the original gold rush, dozens of enterprises are still mining for gold in the region around Dawson City.

TOUGH, FOOLHARDY & FUTILE

Some 40,000 dreamers traveled from Skagway to Dawson City in 1897 and 1898 in search of gold. Most didn't strike it rich and in fact most left the Yukon poorer than when they arrived – a consequence of overly optimistic claims, bad luck and the highly efficient apparatus in place to fleece even those few who did strike it rich.

It started when ships docked in Seattle and San Francisco in the summer of 1897 crammed with gold from the Yukon. Word that there was lots more spread quickly, and the fact that Canada would allow non-Canadians to stake claims and that the gold around Dawson City was placer gold – fairly easily mined without special tools – fueled the fire. Boats poured into Skagway that fall, turning it into the boomtown recalled today. That winter – could there have been a worse time for this? – thousands made their way up the Chilkoot Trail to the Canadian border. Only those with at least a thousand pounds of supplies were allowed into Canada; the country had enough problems without a bunch of starving miners dying all over the place. Consider this: the average miner had to walk, in the snow, the equivalent of 1800 miles to pack their supplies (few could afford animals or help to cover the 30 miles between Dyea and Bennett). And that was going uphill, loaded.

Once in Bennett, the prospective prospectors built boats out of whatever they could find. When the ice broke at the end of May, one of the motliest flotillas ever assembled set sail for Dawson on the Yukon. Of course, few of these people knew what to expect or had any experience with white-water rafting. Although the number is not known, it is guessed that far more people drowned during the summer of 1898 on the Yukon River and its tributaries than perished on the Chilkoot Trail. Those that made Dawson faced lawlessness, claim-jumpers, deprivation and a myriad other hardships. Adding an exclamation point to their futility, by the time word of the gold finds was reaching the world and setting off the gold rush, most of the valuable claims were already staked. Most of the would-be millionaires arrived a year too late.

The Klondike Hwy generally follows the Gold Rush Trail (as Parks Canada calls it) past Whitehorse as far north as Minto. If you want to stay on the route of the prospectors to Dawson City, you'll need a canoe from one of the outfitters in Whitehorse and you'll need several days to navigate the Yukon River.

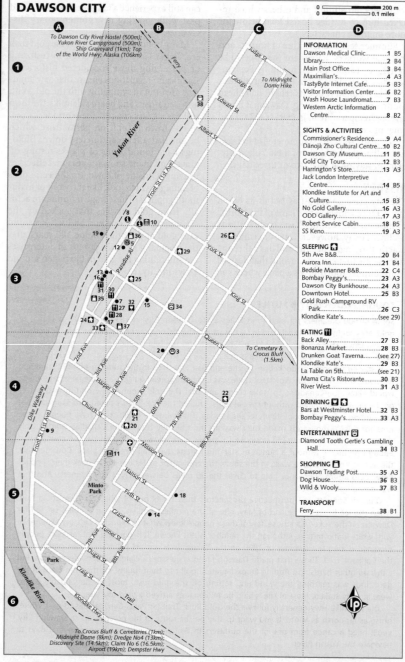

DAWSON CITY

0 — 200 m
0 — 0.1 miles

INFORMATION
Dawson Medical Clinic..............**1** B5
Library..**2** B4
Main Post Office.......................**3** B4
Maximilian's...............................**4** A3
TastyByte Internet Cafe..........**5** B3
Visitor Information Center.......**6** B2
Wash House Laundromat.........**7** B3
Western Arctic Information
 Centre......................................**8** B2

SIGHTS & ACTIVITIES
Commissioner's Residence........**9** A4
Dänojà Zho Cultural Centre....**10** B2
Dawson City Museum................**11** B5
Gold City Tours........................**12** B3
Harrington's Store....................**13** A3
Jack London Interpretive
 Centre.....................................**14** B5
Klondike Institute for Art and
 Culture...................................**15** B3
No Gold Gallery.......................**16** A3
ODD Gallery.............................**17** A3
Robert Service Cabin................**18** B5
SS Keno.....................................**19** A3

SLEEPING
5th Ave B&B..............................**20** B4
Aurora Inn.................................**21** B4
Bedside Manner B&B................**22** C4
Bombay Peggy's........................**23** A3
Dawson City Bunkhouse...........**24** A3
Downtown Hotel.......................**25** B3
Gold Rush Campground RV
 Park..**26** C3
Klondike Kate's.................(see 29)

EATING
Back Alley.................................**27** B3
Bonanza Market........................**28** B3
Drunken Goat Taverna.......(see 27)
Klondike Kate's.........................**29** B3
La Table on 5th.................(see 21)
Mama Cita's Ristorante............**30** B3
River West.................................**31** A3

DRINKING
Bars at Westminster Hotel.......**32** B3
Bombay Peggy's........................**33** A3

ENTERTAINMENT
Diamond Tooth Gertie's Gambling
 Hall..**34** B3

SHOPPING
Dawson Trading Post................**35** A3
Dog House.................................**36** B3
Wild & Wooly............................**37** B3

TRANSPORT
Ferry..**38** B1

Yukon River

To Dawson City River Hostel (500m);
Yukon River Campground (500m);
Ship Graveyard (1km); Top
of the World Hwy; Alaska (106km)

To Midnight
Dome Hike

To Cemetary &
Crocus Bluff
(1.5km)

Klondike River

Minto
Park

Park

To Crocus Bluff & Cemeteries (1km);
Midnight Dome (8km); Dredge No4 (13km);
Discovery Site (14.5km); Claim No 6 (16.5km);
Airport (19km); Dempster Hwy

ORIENTATION

The town is small enough to walk around in a few hours. The Klondike Hwy leads into Front St (also called 1st Ave) along the Yukon River. Just north of town, a free ferry crosses the Yukon River to the Top of the World Hwy (p383) and onward to Alaska. Dawson is 527km from Whitehorse and 240km south of the Arctic Circle.

Like a ray of sunshine in January, street numbers are a rarity in Dawson. Unless noted otherwise, opening hours and times given below cover the period mid-May to mid-September. For the rest of year, most sights, attractions and many businesses are closed.

INFORMATION

The weekly *Klondike Sun* has a good listing of special events and activities.

Bookstores

Maximilian's (☎ 867-993-6537; Front St; ☺ 8am-8pm) Excellent selection of regional books, magazines and out-of-town newspapers. Topographical and river maps.

Internet Access

Several places around town, including the library and laundry, have internet access.
TastyByte Internet Cafe (☎ 867-993-6105; Front St; per hr $6; ☺ 9:30-5:30pm) Good coffee, wi-fi access and computer services.

Laundry

Wash House Laundromat (☎ 867-993-6555; 2nd Ave & Queen St; per load $4; ☺ 9am-8pm; 💻) Has showers and internet access (per hr $5).

Library

Dawson City Community Library (☎ 867-993-5571; 5th Ave & Queen St; ☺ noon-7:30pm Tue-Thu, 10am-5:30pm Fri & Sat; 💻) Has internet access.

Medical Services

Dawson Medical Clinic (☎ 867-993-5744; Church St nr 6th Ave; ☺ 9am-noon, 1-5pm Mon-Fri) A private clinic; nurses are always on call at the adjoining government clinic (☎ 867-993-4444).

Post

Post office (☎ 867-993-5342; 5th Ave & Princess St; ☺ 8:30am-5:30pm Mon-Fri, 9am-noon Sat)

Tourist Information

VIC (☎ 867-993-5566; www.dawsoncity.ca; cnr Front & King Sts; ☺ 8am-8pm) Also has a Parks Canada desk.

Western Arctic Information Centre (☎ 867-993-6167; Front St, opposite the VIC; ☺ 10am-6:30pm) Maps and information on the Northwest Territories, Inuvik and Dempster Hwy including road updates (☎ 800-661-0750).

SIGHTS

In summer, if the historic heart of town feels mobbed, just wander off uphill for a few blocks, where you'll find timeless old houses and streets.

Klondike National Historic Sites

Dawson and its environs teem with places of historic interest. Parks Canada does an excellent job of providing information and tours. In addition to the individual sight fees listed below, there is a good-value **pass** (adult/child $28/14) valid for all the Parks Canada sites and tours. For information, go to the Parks Canada desk in the VIC. See p380 for details on Dredge No 4.

ROBERT SERVICE CABIN

Called the 'Bard of the Yukon,' Robert W Service lived in this typical gold rush **cabin** (cnr 8th Ave & Hanson St; admission free; ☺ 10am-4pm) from 1909 to 1912. Don't miss the readings of Service's poems (adult/child $6/3, 10am and 3pm) by a Parks Canada employee.

COMMISSIONER'S RESIDENCE

Built in 1901 to house the territorial commissioner, this proud **building** (adult/child $6/3; ☺ 10am-5pm, tour times vary) was designed to give potential civic investors confidence in the city. The building is also noted for being the long-time home of Martha Black, who came to the Yukon in 1898, owned a lumberyard and was elected to the Canadian Parliament at age 70.

SS KENO

The voyage from Whitehorse to Dawson was not an easy one. The season was short and there were perilous areas of white water to navigate on the way. The **SS Keno** (adult/child $6/3; ☺ 10am-6pm) was one of a fleet of paddle wheelers that worked the rivers for more than half a century. Moored along the river, the boat has many good displays about travel 100 years ago.

HARRINGTON'S STORE

This old mercantile has been converted to a **gallery** (cnr 3rd Ave & Queen St; admission free; ☺ 9am-4:30pm) of historic photos from Dawson's heyday.

Dänojà Zho Cultural Centre

Inside this beautiful wood building on the riverfront, this **cultural centre** (☎ 867-993-6768; www.trondek.com; Front St; adult/child $5/2.50; ☯ 10am-6pm) has displays and interpretive talks on the *Hän Hwëch'in* (River People), who were the first to inhabit the area. The collection includes traditional artifacts and a re-creation of a 19-century fishing camp. Locally made crafts are for sale. Check on the schedule of cultural tours and performances of authentic dances. The striking building was designed by noted Yukon architects KVA.

Jack London Interpretive Centre

In 1898 Jack London lived in the Yukon, the setting for his most popular animal stories, including *Call of the Wild* and *White Fang*. At the writer's **cabin** (8th Ave at Grant St; admission by donation; ☯ 10am-1pm & 2-6pm) there are daily interpretive talks. A labor of love by historian Dick North, Dawne Mitchell and others, this place is a treasure-trove. Read the stories about 'Jack,' a local dog, which Jack, the noted author, used as a model for Buck in *Call of the Wild*, and how North was able to locate a photo of London working in the Klondike.

Dawson City Museum

This **museum** (☎ 867-993-5291; 5th Ave; adult/child $7/5; ☯ 10am-6pm) houses a collection of 25,000 gold rush artifacts. Engaging exhibits walk you through the hard-scrabble lives of the miners. The museum is housed in the landmark 1901 Old Territorial Administration building. It was designed by noted architect Thomas W Fuller, who also designed the old post office and other buildings around town. Next door is an old locomotive barn with historic trains.

Midnight Dome

The quarried face of this hill overlooks the town to the north, but to reach the top you must travel south of town about 1km, turn left off the Klondike Hwy onto New Dome Rd, and continue for about 7km. The Midnight Dome, at 880m above sea level, offers great views of the Klondike Valley, Yukon River and Dawson City. From here on summer solstice, you can witness the midnight sun barely sink below the Ogilvie Mountains to the north before rising again. There's also a steep **trail** from Judge St in town; maps are available at the VIC.

Crocus Bluff & Cemeteries

A 15-minute walk up King St behind town leads to the historic cemeteries. Look for the parking area and the short path out to pretty Crocus Bluff, which has excellent views of Dawson and the Klondike and Yukon Rivers. Historic cemeteries are nearby. If you're driving, ignore the 'Local Traffic Only' signs coming up King St. On New Dome Rd, turn at Mary McLeod Rd (ignoring 'No Exit' signs).

Mine Sites

The scarred valleys around Dawson speak to the vast amounts of toil that went into the gold hunt. Most emblematic is Bonanza Creek, where gold was first found and still yields some today. **Dredge No 4** (Bonanza Creek Rd; adult/child $6/3; ☯ 10am-4pm, tour times vary), 13km off the Klondike Hwy, is a massive dredging machine that tore up the Klondike Valley and left the tailings, which remain as a blight on the landscape. Parks Canada offers fascinating tours of this huge machine that worked something like a freak worm in a science fiction novel.

Just 1.5km further up the valley, the **Discovery Site** is roughly where gold was first found in 1897. It's a quiet site today, with a little water rippling through the rubble. Another 2km brings you to **Claim No 6**, a site where you can pan for your own gold for free (ask at the VIC about sources for a pan).

Ship Graveyard

When the Klondike Hwy was completed, the paddlewheel ferries were abandoned. Several were sailed just downstream from town and left to rot on the bank. Now overgrown, the remains are a fascinating destination for a short hike. Take the ferry across the river, then walk north through the Yukon River Campground for 10 minutes and then another 10 minutes north along the beach.

Galleries

Dawson is another northern city with a thriving arts community – although like so many others, most artists head south in winter in search of not just better light but simply light. The **Klondike Institute for Art and Culture** (KIAC; ☎ 867-993-5005; www.kiac.org; cnr 3rd Ave & Queen St) has an impressive new studio building and offers artist in residence programs.

KIAC's exhibition space, the **ODD Gallery** (☎ 867-993-5005; cnr 2nd Ave & Princess St; ☯ 10am-8pm), shows local works.

LOCAL VOICES: A MODERN MINER

The more you learn about the early gold miners in the Dawson area, the more you learn about their unrelenting sacrifice in pursuit of gold. And this isn't just the thousands who lost everything trying to get there during the gold rush. But rather it's the miners who worked their claims during the long and brutal winters after 1897. Miners would build fires on the frozen ground to melt the ice below. Then they would dig down. They would repeat the process again and again until they were several meters down. At this point they would start tunneling along the seams of gold-laden dirt, scooping out gravel so it could be panned after the thaw. And they did this in the dark.

On a crisp fall morning, David Millar is thinking about just this kind of sacrifice. A modern-day miner, he's just run into a 100-year-old tunnel with his bulldozer. With the broken logs used to support the earth now sticking up into the daylight, he says 'I can't even imagine how hard they worked.'

Millar is a second-generation Dawson miner and he works a contiguous collection of 69 claims along GoldBottom and Hunker Creeks. It's hard work, but whereas the early guys had little more than their frostbitten fingers, Millar has a variety of backhoes and other modern equipment to do the heavy lifting. However, there's a contrast, he points out: 'The early miners were looking for gold nuggets the size of their toes, I'm looking for ones the size of sea salt.'

It's modern equipment that has allowed Millar and a few hundred others like him to continue placer (which means sand or gravel bank) mining in an area that has already been scoured once or twice or more. 'You work long days,' he notes, and 'you keep working until it just gets so cold, you have to do something else.'

Given that there's always the hope that the next scoopful of gravel will yield a truly huge nugget, there's a parallel to gambling in the work. When to quit?

'My dad got the gold bug in 1972,' says Miller, 'and he gave it to me.'

In order to bolster the family income as much as possible, Millar's wife Deborah works a job in town and the family runs a small business during the tourist season. They give daily tours of the open-air mining area and a chance to do some panning as well, with visitors keeping what they find. 'I tell them that if I'm doing well that day, they'll do well that day,' says Millar. Of course there's real art to panning so that the tiny grains don't end up sloshed away and Millar has it down. He's competed in several international gold-panning championships. 'A lot of people can't,' he says with a grin before going back to scooping out more promising gravel before winter sets in.

GoldBottom Tours (☎ 867-993-5750; www.goldbottom.com) runs daily tours during the summer at the site, 15km up Hunker Creek Rd, which meets Hwy 2 just north of the airport. Tours cost $20 (children free) or you can include transport to/from Dawson for $35. If you get bitten by the gold bug, the Millars have four cute cabins where you can stay for $100 per person per night and pan – and keep – to your heart's content.

No Gold Gallery (☎ 867-993-5203; cnr Front St & Queen St) is an enthusiastic supporter – and dealer – of local artists. Bombay Peggy's (p382) also displays and sells local works.

ACTIVITIES

One of the main do-it-yourself canoe float trips goes from Dawson three days and 168km downstream to Eagle City, Alaska. This popular trip is good for less-experienced canoeists.

Dawson Trading Post (☎ 867-993-5316; Front St; canoe per day $30) rents out canoes, with longer trips and transportation arranged. It hasn't changed its rental prices since 1987.

Dawson City River Hostel (☎ 867-993-6823; www .yukonhostels.com), across the river, can also rent you a canoe and help make arrangements.

The walks up to Crocus Bluff, Midnight Dome and the ship graveyard are popular, ask at the VIC for many more possibilities.

TOURS

Parks Canada docents, often in period garb, lead excellent **walking tours** (adult/child $6/3; ⓨ tours 9:30am, some days extra tours) of Dawson. Learn about individual buildings and Paradise Alley, which is demure today but which in its time was home to more than 400 prostitutes.

You can also take a self-guided **audio tour** (adult/child $6/3; ☺ 9:30am-4:30pm).

Gold City Tours (☎ 867-993-5175; Front St), opposite the SS *Keno*, is a longtime operator of tours in and around Dawson. In 2006 the owners retired, so check for the current situation. GoldBottom Tours runs daily tours to a family-run working gold mine south of Dawson (see boxed text, p381).

FESTIVALS & EVENTS

Dawson City Music Festival (☎ 867-993-5384; www.dcmf.com) Held in late July, this festival features well-known Canadian musicians. It's very popular – tickets sell out two months in advance and the city fills up – so reservations are a good idea.

Discovery Days The premier annual event in Dawson City celebrates you-know-what of 1896. On the third Monday in August there are parades and picnics. Events, including a very good art show, begin days before.

SLEEPING

Most places are open from May to September and fill up in July and August. The VIC will tirelessly search for vacant rooms on busy weekends. Many lodgings will pick you up at the airport, a not inconsiderable distance. Ask in advance.

As you approach Dawson from the south, you'll pass several large RV-style commercial campgrounds.

Budget

Yukon River Campground (campsite $12) On the western side of the river about 250m up the road to the right after you get off the ferry, this territorial campground has 98 wooded sites.

Gold Rush Campground RV Park (☎ 867-993-5247; 866-330-5006; www.goldrushcampground.com; cnr 5th Ave & York St; campsite $19-40; ☐) Literally one big parking lot downtown for RVs; 83 sites and wi-fi.

Dawson City River Hostel (☎ 867-993-6823 summer; www.yukonhostels.com; dm $16-20, r $42) This rustic, funky hostel is across the river from town and five minutes from the ferry landing. It has good views, cabins, platforms for tents, cooking shelter and a communal bathhouse. There's no electricity, and lockers are recommended for your gear. Owner Dieter Reinmuth has written many books on the Yukon.

Midrange

Dawson City Bunkhouse (☎ 867-993-6164; cnr 2nd Ave & Princess St r $50-120) Built not much different from building back during the gold rush, the bunkhouse has economy (small, shared bathroom) and larger rooms with bathrooms and TVs. It's all rather spare and the solid wood construction means that galoots coming home from the bars can be heard throughout.

Bedside Manner B&B (☎ 867-993-6948; cnr 8th Ave & Princess St; r $70-100; ☺ year-round; ☐) You don't have to be sick to enjoy the comfort of this simple place up in the residential part of town. The six rooms are comfy and there's a vast breakfast, hot tub and free laundry.

5th Ave B&B (☎ 867-993-5941; www.5thavebandb .com; 702 5th Ave; r $85-115; ☒ ☐) The place to learn about the community – the owners are politically active – this B&B is in a modern and comfortable building. Breakfasts are large and there's a lot of fresh fruit – important in the battle against scurvy. Open all year.

Downtown Hotel (☎ 867-993-5346, 800-661-0514; www.downtownhotel.ca; cnr Queen St & 2nd Ave; r $95-140; ☒ ☐) A landmark hotel on a prominent corner, the fittingly named Downtown has 34 rooms with wi-fi in its main, historic building (quality varies, so ask to see a couple) and 25 more in a modern annex across the street. It's open all year, as is the popular bar.

Klondike Kate's (☎ 867-993-6527; www.klondike kates.ca; cnr King St & 3rd Ave; cabins $120-140; ☐) The 16 cabins here behind the ever-popular restaurant of the same name are simply cute as buttons. Flowers decorate the porches and inside you'll find fridges, microwaves and wi-fi in a modern, faux-rustic setting (trust us, when you read about how the gold miners lived, you'll pick faux-rustic every time).

Aurora Inn (☎ 867-993-6860; www.aurorainn.ca; 5th Ave; r $110-160; ☐) All 18 rooms in this newish place are sizable and very comfortable. The service is European-style, with a continental breakfast. La Table on 5th Ave is one of Dawson's most creative restaurants.

Bombay Peggy's (☎ 867-993-6969; www.bombay peggys.com; cnr 2nd Ave & Princess St; r $75-180; ☒ ☐) The most interesting place to stay in town, Peggy's is a renovated old brothel that takes its theme from its past life. Ornate rooms are decorated with period furnishings. Budget 'snug' rooms share bathrooms. The bar is justifiably popular. Open most of the year.

EATING & DRINKING

There are a few places that cater mainly to tourists that are best avoided. Consider mud-covered pick-ups out front a solid local recommendation.

River West (☎ 867-993-6339; cnr Front & Queen Sts; meals $4-7; ☺ 7am-7pm Mar-Oct) A local morning hub, this café has excellent coffee, baked goods, soup and sandwiches. The tables outside are sunny and you can eat in or picnic out.

Bonanza Market (☎ 867-993-6567; 2nd Ave; sandwiches $6; ☺ 8am-6pm) A good market with interesting and some organic fresh foods. The deli makes tasty sandwiches.

Klondike Kate's (☎ 867-993-6527; cnr King St & 3rd Ave; meals $6-20; ☺ 8am-9pm) Locals know that spring has sprung when the much-loved Kate's reopens for the year. Every night there's a long list of specials – usually hearty meaty dishes and excellent fresh seafood. It's all creative, right down to the 'news' in the tabloids kept for your amusement. Nice patio out back.

Drunken Goat Taverna (☎ 867-993-5800; 2nd Ave; meals $7-20; ☺ noon-9pm) Even when it's closed the Greek music wafts out onto the street from this fun place with food from the Mediterranean. All the standards are here and taste spot-on thanks to a Greek owner and a Greek chef. A small café in the back alley has cheap and cheery pizzas.

Mama Cita's Ristorante (☎ 867-993-2370; 2nd Ave; meals $8-22; ☺ noon-9pm) Meals here can feed two. Vast plates of tasty pasta are the specialty. There's a nice deck on the side. The baked spaghetti and meatballs will restore even the most road-weary traveler.

La Table on 5th (☎ 867-993-6860; 5th Ave; meals $9-25; ☺ 5-9pm) Dawson's most eclectic restaurant is helmed by Antoinette Oliphant, who made her way to Dawson from her native Tobago via some top restaurants in Toronto. Flavors of the Caribbean spice the wide range of fresh and tasty dishes on the oft-changing menu.

our pick Bombay Peggy's (☎ 867-993-6969; cnr 2nd Ave & Princess St; ☺ 11am-11pm) Peggy's is always hopping with locals who appreciate the superior wine list, well-poured mixed drinks and good beer selection. The atmosphere often crackles with not-yet-realized tête-à-têtes inside or on the rear patio.

Bars at Westminster Hotel (3rd Ave; ☺ noon-late) These two bars carry the mostly affectionate monikers 'Snakepit,' 'Armpit' or simply 'Pit.' The one to your left as you face the pink building has a great old tin roof that matches the age of some of the timeless characters hanging out by the bar. The bar to the right has more of a '70s motif as well as live music many nights. Both get lively.

ENTERTAINMENT

A re-creation of an 1898 saloon, **Diamond Tooth Gertie's Gambling Hall** (☎ 867-993-5575; cnr Queen St & 4th Ave; cover $6; ☺ 7pm-2am) is complete with small-time gambling, a honky-tonk piano and dancing girls. The casino's winnings go toward town restoration, so go ahead, lose a bundle. On weekends it can get packed as locals jostle with tourists to support preservation. Each night there are three nightly floor shows that are heavy on schmaltz and kicking legs.

SHOPPING

Dawson Trading Post (☎ 867-993-5316; Front St; ☺ 9am-7pm) Sells interesting, old mining gadgets, antiques, books and stones, and old mammoth tusks so you can take up carving. It has a good bulletin board.

Dog House (☎ 867-993-5405; Front St; ☺ 10am-7pm) The local center for dog-sledding. Dress as a musher and get your picture taken.

Wild & Wooly (☎ 867-993-5170; cnr 3rd Ave & Princess St; ☺ 10am-7pm) This place has all sorts of lovely, locally made jewelry along with quite fashionable men's and women's clothes. This is the place to see some of the large nuggets still being found near Dawson.

GETTING THERE & AWAY

Dawson City airport (YDA) is 19km east of town off the Klondike Hwy. **Air North** (☎ 800-661-0407; www.flyairnorth.com) serves Whitehorse, Old Crow, Inuvik in the NWT and Fairbanks in Alaska.

Reaching Dawson by land can be problematic. Various operators have come and gone from the Whitehorse–Dawson route. But given the demand, it's worth checking with the VICs to check the current situation. There have also been buses from Dawson over the Top of the World Hwy to Fairbanks in Alaska, so it's worth checking this as well. Just to complicate things further, rental-car operators have proved impermanent as well. Whitehorse may be the closest source for a car.

DAWSON TO ALASKA

At the northern end of Dawson City's Front St the ferry crosses the Yukon River to the scenic **Top of the World Highway** (Hwy 9). Open only in summer, the road is mostly paved in Canada for the 106km to the US border along ridge tops.

You'll really feel on top of the world as you complete the border crossing: it's treeless and alpine. Note that the border crossing has very strict **hours** (☺ 9am-9pm Pacific (Yukon) Time, 8am-8pm Alaska Time May 15–Oct); don't be one minute late or you'll have to turn back and try the next day.

On the US side the road becomes all gravel, with stretches of dirt that are okay for cars in summer. After 19km (12 miles) you reach the Taylor Hwy (Hwy 5). The old gold mining town of **Eagle** on the Yukon River is 104km (65 miles) north of this junction.

South 46km (29 miles), you hit **Chicken**, a small idiosyncratic community of 40 which has a couple of shops and a bar that even at 11am is filled with a good percentage of the local population offering distinctly libertarian views on good government.

Another 124km (77 miles) south over mostly good roads and you reach the Alaska Hwy (p369) junction.

DEMPSTER HIGHWAY

This road should carry a parental guidance warning. The tortuous Dempster Hwy (Hwy 5 in the Yukon, Hwy 8 in the Northwest Territories) starts 40km southeast of Dawson City off the Klondike Hwy. It heads north over the Ogilvie and Richardson Mountains beyond the Arctic Circle and on to Inuvik in the Northwest Territories, near the shores of the Beaufort Sea.

The highway is a real adventure for most people who drive it. While Inuvik (right) is a long way from Dawson City – 747km of gravel road – the scenery is remarkable: mountains, valleys, rivers and vast open tundra. The highway is open most of the year but the best time to travel is between June and early September when the ferries over the Peel and Mackenzie Rivers operate. In the winter, ice forms a natural bridge over the rivers, which become ice roads.

The road is a test for drivers and cars. Travel with extra gas and tires, and expect to use them. For information, the **Western Arctic Information Centre** in Dawson (p379) is an excellent resource. It's always important to check **Road Information** (☎ 800-661-0750, 877-456-7623; www.hwy.dot.gov.nt.ca/highways/).

The Dempster is closed during the spring thaw and the winter freeze-up; these vary by the year and can occur from mid-April to June and mid-October to December respectively.

Accommodations and vehicle services along the route are scarce. There is a gas station at the southern start of the highway at **Klondike River Lodge** (☎ 867-993-6892). The lodge will rent jerry cans of gas you can take north and return on the way back.

The next services are 369km north in Eagle Plains. The **Eagle Plains Hotel** (☎ 867-993-2453; eagleplains@yknet.ca; r $100-130) is open year-round and offers 32 rooms. The next service station is 180km further at **Fort McPherson** in the Northwest Territories. From there it's 216km to Inuvik.

The Yukon government has three campgrounds – at **Tombstone Mountain** (73km from the start of the highway), **Engineer Creek** (194km) and **Rock River** (447km). There's also a Northwest Territories government campground at **Nitainlaii Territorial Park**, 9km south of Fort McPherson. Campsites at these campgrounds cost $12.

TOMBSTONE TERRITORIAL PARK

The Yukon's newest territorial park, Tombstone, is 73km up the Dempster Hwy, with the good **Dempster Highway Interpretive Centre** (☺ 9am-5pm Jun-Aug) and an adjoining campground with expansive views. The pointed shape of the prominent peak was a distinctive landmark on First Nations routes and is now an aerial guide for pilots. There are several good **day hikes** leading from the center, as well as longer, more rigorous backcountry trips for experienced wilderness hikers. With no established trails, these require skilled mapreading. Note that weather can change quickly, so bring appropriate gear even for day hikes. In mid-June there's hiking with some snow pack; July is best for wildflowers, balancing the annoyance of bug season.

It's possible to visit Tombstone as a day trip from Dawson City or to spend the night at the campground (sites $12; pit toilets, river water, firewood) to experience a bit of the Dempster and see the headwaters of the Klondike River. All hikers should check in at the center for updates.

INUVIK (NWT)
pop 3300

Inuvik is the reward at the end of the Dempster Hwy. Although it's in the Northwest Territories, its main access is from the Yukon. It is also the staging point for trips to Vuntut and Ivvavik National Parks and Herschel Island Territorial Park in the far north of the Yukon.

Inuvik lies on the East Channel of the Mackenzie River 97km south of the Arctic Coast. It was built in 1955 as an administrative post for the government. For 56 days from late June, Inuvik has 24 hours of daylight. In early December the sun sets and does not rise until January. The first snow falls in September. Although looking rough around the edges, it is an interesting place to visit – even if you are just passing through to the parks.

The **Western Arctic Visitors Centre** (☎ 867-777-4727, winter 867-777-7237; www.inuvik.ca; 284 Mackenzie Rd; ☯ 9am-7pm Jun–mid-Sep) has numerous displays about the area and its ecology.

Parks Canada (☎ 867-777-8800; www.parkscanada.ca; 187 Mackenzie Rd; ☯ 8:30am-5pm Jun-Aug, call other times) has information on northern Yukon national parks such as Vuntut and Ivvavik.

Several tour companies specialize in tours of varying duration to the Yukon parks. Other services include logistical work for independent travelers as well as gear rental.

Arctic Nature Tours (☎ 867-777-3300; fax 867-777-3400; www.arcticnaturetours.com; 65 Mackenzie Rd) has tours to places like Herschel Island ($480 per person).

Western Arctic Adventures (☎ 867-777-2594; www.inuvik.net/canoenwt; 38 Spruce Hill Dr) rents canoes and kayaks for about $200 per week, depending on the destination, and makes logistical arrangements for independent travelers.

Inuvik has several motels. **Arctic Chalet** (☎ 867-777-3535; www.arcticchalet.com; 25 Carn St; r from $110) has bright cabin-style rooms in a pretty setting. The energetic owners rent canoes, kayaks and cars, run dog-sledding tours and are good sources of local info.

Most people drive the Dempster to Inuvik, but flying can save you two days' traveling time and about four tires. Dawson City is 747km south. **Mike Zubko Airport** (YEV) has service by **Air North** (☎ 800-661-0407; www.flyairnorth .com), with flights to Whitehorse and Dawson City, some via Old Crow.

ARCTIC PARKS

Three parks are found in the very far north of the Yukon. These are places with virtually no services, just nature at its most raw. Parks Canada in Inuvik (right) has information on these national parks.

VUNTUT NATIONAL PARK

Vuntut, a Gwich'in word meaning 'among the lakes,' was declared a national park in 1993. It's north of the isolated village of **Old Crow** (population 300), the most northerly settlement in the Yukon. Each spring a porcupine caribou herd of 160,000 follows a migration route north across the plain to calving grounds near the Beaufort Sea. In Canada these calving grounds are protected within Ivvavik National Park and extend into Alaska where they are part of the Arctic National Wildlife Refuge.

With its many lakes and ponds, Vuntut National Park is visited by around 500,000 **water birds** each autumn. Archaeological sites contain fossils of ancient animals such as the mammoth, plus evidence of early humans. The only access to the 4345-sq-km park is by chartered plane from Old Crow, which itself is reachable only by air.

IVVAVIK NATIONAL PARK

Ivvavik, meaning 'a place for giving birth to and raising the young,' is situated along the Beaufort Sea and adjoining Alaska and covers 10,170 sq km. The park is dominated by the British Mountains and its vegetation is mainly tundra. It's on the migration route of the porcupine caribou and is also a major waterfowl habitat. There are no facilities or services.

The park holds one of the world's great white water rivers, the **Frith River**, which can be navigated for 130km from Margaret Lake near the Alaskan border north to the Alaska Sea. When the river meets Joe Creek, the valley narrows to a canyon and there are numerous areas of white water rated class II and III+.

Access is by charter plane from either Old Crow or Inuvik (opposite), where there is also an office for the park.

HERSCHEL ISLAND TERRITORIAL PARK

Herschel Island Territorial Park (www.environ mentyukon.gov.yk.ca/parks/herschel.html) is off the coast of Ivvavik in the Beaufort Sea, below the Arctic Ocean and about 90km south of the packed ice. Rich in plant, bird and marine life, particularly ringed seals and bowhead whales, it was an important area for the Thule. They called it 'Qikiqtaruk', or 'it is an island.' There have been several waves of people through the area, but the Thule, expert whale hunters, were thought to be the first to make a permanent settlement here, about 1000 years ago.

THE TOP OF THE WORLD HEATS UP

Visitors to **Herschel Island** (p385) are in for a macabre sight: coffins rising from the ground. That's because warming temperatures are causing long-buried coffins to float up through the melting permafrost. At the same time the sharp decline in Arctic ice means that the shoreline is now exposed to pounding ocean waves. The water itself in the north is no longer pristine and crystal clear; the thawing of the land and sea means that there's now vast amounts of run-off into the Arctic Ocean, filling the water with silt and debris.

Of course, some can always find a way to profit from any catastrophe. International shipping lines are making preliminary investigations into running tankers and freighters through the ice-free waters between Asia and Europe (the fabled Northwest Passage is no longer a myth) and the normally chummy US and Canada have been verbally sparring over who controls the Arctic Ocean.

Pauline Cove is deep enough for ocean vessels and protected from the northerly winds and drifting pack ice. As a haven for ships, it became a key port during the last days of the whaling industry when the whales were hunted first for lamp oil and then for baleen. Bowhead whales had the longest bones and were the most desirable for women's corsets. Fashion nearly drove them to extinction. Following the whalers and their families, who numbered about 1500, was an Anglican missionary in 1897, whose members tried to win converts among the Thule. The whaling station was abandoned around 1907, though the Canadian police continued to use the island as a post until 1964.

The flight across the Mackenzie Delta to reach the island is spectacular. At Pauline Cove, park rangers provide a tour of the historical buildings and lead a hike above the harbor to a hill carpeted with tiny wildflowers in July. The rangers are wonderful hosts and some have family connections to the island. Primitive camping during the short summer season (from late June to August) is possible. There are fire rings, wind shelters, pit toilets and limited water. Access is by chartered plane, usually from Inuvik (p384), 250km southeast. Most of the 500 annual visitors spend half a day.

For more on the island's tenuous future, see boxed text, above.

Directory

CONTENTS

ACCOMMODATIONS

Most areas of British Columbia have abundant accommodations options, available for a wide range of prices. The North and the Yukon are the only exceptions; these far-flung regions have few budget accommodations outside of the cities, and their relatively few (and generally spartan) motel rooms are priced higher than comparable establishments elsewhere.

British Columbia Approved Accommodation Guide, an annual directory published by **Tourism BC** (☎ 800-435-5622, outside North America 250-387-1642), is a detailed guide with options in all classes of lodgings. It's free and is available at visitor info centers or from Tourism BC.

In this book, accommodations are listed in order of ascending price. This means that, where applicable, campgrounds and hostels will be listed first.

Seasonal Rates

The prices given in this book are for the peak season, which is usually summer; in ski areas, like Whistler, high season is winter. Outside of summer, you can expect discounts of up to 50% off the high-season rates throughout most of British Columbia and the Yukon. Exceptions to this occur when there is a special event on.

Vancouver's accommodations rates ebb and flow depending on conventions, events and other factors. Often good deals are available for midrange accommodations on weekends, when the business travelers have left town. Rates listed do not include the various taxes (see p394).

Discounts

To look for deals, check out a place's website first and then cross-reference it with one of the large internet booking services (though, these services often do not list interesting, independent places). It is always worthwhile to call a place you are interested in staying at and ask about any special deals: we saved 50% and got a slew of normally costly extras free at one well-known resort just by asking: 'Do you have any specials?'

It's always good to reserve in advance. This is vital during the peak season and on busy weekends around holidays. Conversely, it's usually not necessary to reserve in a town like Fort Nelson in the north, which has a string of largely similar motels aimed at people bedding down for the night along the Alaska Highway.

BOOK ACCOMMODATIONS ONLINE

For more accommodations reviews and recommendations by Lonely Planet authors, check out the online booking service at www.lonelyplanet.com. You'll find the true, insider lowdown on the best places to stay. Reviews are thorough and independent. Best of all, you can book online.

DIRECTORY

B&Bs

With over 3000 Bed & Breakfasts in British Columbia and the Yukon, your choices are myriad. North American B&Bs are typically more upscale than the casual, family-style pensions found in Europe. Many (especially those catering to honeymooners and other romantic escapists) require reservations and have fairly strict policies on children, pets, smoking and so on. But there's a wide range of places and with a bit of investigation you can find somewhere that fits your needs and price range. Prices span the gamut, although basic places are generally in the $50 to $100 range.

The local visitors information center (VIC) usually has complete listings along with photos and descriptions. In the Rockies, B&Bs are prevalent in towns and can provide good basic and private lodging. Other B&Bs may be in wilderness settings that offer a range of activities. B&Bs can also be a good source of local information on activities, particularly in an area like the Queen Charlotte Islands.

Camping

Camping is one of the most popular activities enjoyed by residents and visitors and there are many places to camp, from primitive forest sites to deluxe campgrounds with resort-style amenities. Reservations are a good idea during the summer, but they're essential in the most popular places over long weekends.

Depending on the services (electricity, water, cable TV) your rig requires, private campground sites cost about $20 to $35 a night for two people. Campsites usually cost about $15 to $23.

British Columbia Parks manages hundreds of campgrounds with fees ranging from $12 per party for basic sites to $24 per party for the most highly developed campgrounds. About 70 popular parks offer **reserved sites** (☎ 800-689-9025; www.discovercamping.ca), however, most BC Parks' campgrounds are not reservable. At popular campgrounds, arrive early to avoid disappointment. Instructions at the entrance will tell you where to check in or otherwise register and pay your camping fee.

There are over a thousand Ministry of Forests campgrounds but, in a bid to save money, the ministry has deemed that most are 'user-managed' which means you stay there for free and take care of everything yourself.

The Yukon has scores of government campgrounds in scenic locations. All charge $12 per night and none of them accept reservations. *Camping on Yukon Time* is a good annual government publication that lists the territory's campgrounds.

Parks Canada campgrounds (☎ 877-737-3783, www.pccamping.ca) charge $14 to $28 a night and the very busiest (such as a few in the Rockies) take reservations.

The annual BC Tourism booklet *Super Camping Guide* (www.camping.bc.ca) is a good resource when looking for private, RV-oriented campgrounds, although it also lists BC Parks sites. Look for the guide at VICs. *Go Camping BC* lists British Columbia Parks campsites.

PRACTICALITIES

- For all emergencies in BC, dial ☎ 911; for emergency numbers in the Yukon Territory see p359.

- The electric current is 110 volts, 60 cycles; plugs have two flat parallel pins with an optional round grounding pin, the same as the US.

- The metric system is used throughout Canada, although popular references to the imperial system (as used in the US) still survive.

- Canada is in DVD region 1. Buy or watch videos on the NTSC system.

- Most towns have a daily or weekly newspaper. The *Vancouver Sun* provides good regional coverage.

- For radio listeners, signs at the entrances to towns provide local tuning information for the CBC Radio One network.

- Most places to stay have TVs with dozens of Canadian and US channels.

Guest Ranches

BC has dozens of guest ranches, the euphemism for dude ranches of *City Slickers* fame, where you can join a trail ride or sit by a mountain lake. Many are in the Caribou-Chilcotin region (p309).

Hostels

Hostels are common in tourist areas and most have beds for about $15 to $25 per person per night. These are usually in dorm-style rooms with four to six beds, although many hostels offer private rooms for an additional cost. Expect shared bathrooms, kitchen facilities and common areas. Amenities might include a variety of activity discounts, laundry facilities, internet access, game rooms, bike or other sporting gear rentals, and group outings to local pubs and attractions.

Some of the hostels listed in this book are affiliated with **Hostelling International** (HI; www.hihostels.ca). **SameSun** (www.samesun.com) also operates budget lodges and hostels. There are also many independent hostels in popular locations such as Vancouver.

Motels & Hotels

Rates vary tremendously around the province. Urban and resort locations have the highest prices; plan to spend close to $100 for a basic double room with a private bathroom during high season in Vancouver and Victoria. (In small, nonresort towns you can usually find a motel room for a little more than half that.)

The quality of hotels and motels varies greatly. A lovely roadside motel bedecked in flowers will often be next to a dingier establishment. Generally, however, the typical motel room includes private bathroom, one or two large beds, a tea and coffee maker, and a TV with dozens of channels. Truly luxurious places can be found in Vancouver, Victoria and the Rockies.

Many motels (and an increasing number of suite-style hotels) offer kitchenettes. As a happy compromise, quite a few midrange motels now include a small refrigerator and microwave in their standard-room price. Children can often stay free in the same room as their parents, but the age limit for free stays varies.

BUSINESS HOURS

Stores in downtown retail areas open at around 9am or 10am and close at 5pm or 6pm. Suburban shopping centers, discount stores and grocery stores typically stay open until 9pm; some groceries and pharmacies are open 24 hours. On Sunday, businesses follow more limited hours, with some shopping centers opening at noon and closing at 5pm. In small towns most businesses will be closed on Sundays.

At eating establishments breakfast hours are typically from 6am to 11am, lunch is served from 11:30am to 2pm and dinner from 5pm to 9pm, although in rural areas restaurants may close at 8pm. Pubs are usually open from 11am until after midnight and often serve food until 10pm or 11pm.

CHILDREN

British Columbia and the Yukon are excellent destinations for children. Parks and museums often have programs geared toward youngsters, all but the most extreme activities are suitable for children and, quite simply, kids are welcome everywhere. Vancouver for Children (p82) brims with ideas on where to take the little ones. See p36 for info on eating with kids.

Car rental firms offer child seats, most public restrooms have diaper-changing facilities and the better motels and hotels can suggest child-minding facilities. At ski resorts, there is usually a range of programs that will occupy children for hours, if not days. Bars and pubs will often have family rooms, since kids are not allowed in the main bar area. The one caveat relates to accommodations in rural and wilderness places – some do not cater for children. That said, there are other rural establishments that offer a full range of child-specific activities. When in doubt just ask before booking.

Lonely Planet's *Travel With Children* is a good resource for taking along the family.

CLIMATE

British Columbia has a varied climate influenced by latitude, mountainous terrain and distance from the moderating effects of the Pacific Ocean. Along the coast it's mild, with warm, mostly dry summers (June through September) and cool, very wet winters (December through March). The interior of the province is much drier, particularly in the south along the Okanagan Valley, which gets less than 347mm of rain each year (compared with 6550mm at Henderson Lake on Vancouver Island's Barkley Sound); summers

DIRECTORY

are generally hot and winters are cold. In the mountain regions summers are short with warm days and cool nights; winter snowfalls are heavy.

The Yukon has short mild summers which can be a true delight. But those other eight to 10 months of the year can be cold with winter temperatures well below freezing and little light.

See p12 for additional details.

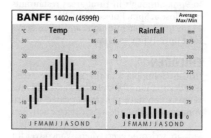

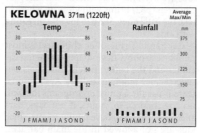

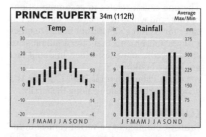

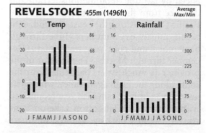

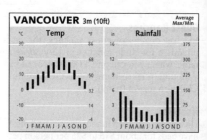

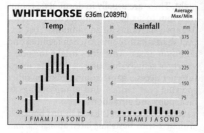

CUSTOMS

The duty-free allowance coming into Canada is 1.14L (40oz) of liquor, 1.5L (or two 750mL bottles) of wine or a case of beer, as well as up to 200 cigarettes, 50 cigars or 400g of tobacco. Only those at least 19 years old can bring in alcohol and tobacco products. You are allowed to bring in gifts up to a total value of $60. Gifts with a value higher than $60 are subject to duty and taxes on the over-limit value.

Sporting goods, including cameras, film and two days' worth of food, can be brought into the country. It's probably worthwhile to register excessive or expensive sporting goods and cameras with customs, as this will save you time and trouble when leaving, especially if you plan on crossing the Canada–US border.

If you are bringing a dog or cat into the country you will need proof that it has had a rabies shot in the past 36 months. For US citizens this is usually easy enough, but for residents of other countries there may well be more involved procedures. To avoid problems check with the **Canadian Food Inspection Agency** (www.inspection.gc.ca), which also handles plant and animal health, before leaving home.

Pleasure boats may enter Canada either on a trailer or in the water and can stay for up to one year. An entry permit is required and is obtainable from the customs office at or near the point of entry. All boats powered by motors over 10HP must be licensed.

Pistols, fully automatic weapons, any firearms less than 66cm (26in) in length and self-defense sprays (like pepper or mace) are not permitted into the country.

DANGERS & ANNOYANCES

British Columbia and the Yukon are generally very safe places. Violent crime is unusual, but theft can occur. See p73 for things you should consider in urban Vancouver.

Outdoor Hazards

We don't want to scare you, but there are some precautions you should take to fully enjoy the vast BC and Yukon great outdoors. For more information, see p406.

BEARS

Bear attacks, though rare, are a very real threat in BC and the Yukon. See p49 for tips on protecting yourself.

BLACK FLIES & MOSQUITOES

During spring and summer black flies and mosquitoes can be murder in the interior and northern reaches of BC and the Yukon. There are tales of lost hikers going insane from the bugs. This is no joke – they can make you miserable. The cumulative effects of scores of irritated, swollen bites can keep you up at night, itchy and grumpy.

Building a fire will help, and camping in a tent with a zippered screen is a necessity. In clearings, along shorelines or anywhere there's a breeze you'll be safe, which is why Vancouver and the coast are relatively bug-free.

Wherever you go, bring liquid or spray repellents. DEET, an ingredient often used in repellents, is very effective but is harmful to the environment and should not be used on young children.

FIRE

Campfires should be confined to fire rings at designated campgrounds or fire pans in the backcountry. Before turning in for the night or leaving an area, make sure fires (including cigarettes) are completely out. Special care must be taken during the summer months, when fire danger is at its highest. Forest fires often force temporary campfire bans (even far from the burning areas), so obey posted signs.

SWIMMERS ITCH

A tiny parasite found in some of BC's lakes can generate this pesky rash, however, warnings are usually posted at places where it's a problem. To help prevent itching, apply baby oil before you enter the water then dry yourself off completely with a towel after getting out.

TICKS

Wood ticks hop onto warm-blooded hosts from tall grasses and low shrubs throughout the region. They're most troublesome from March through June. Protect your legs by wearing gaiters or tucking your pants into socks. Give yourself, your children and pets a good going over after outdoor activities. If you find a tick burrowing into your skin it's most easily removed by grasping and pulling it, gently, straight up and out with a small pair of tweezers. Disinfect the bite site with rubbing alcohol. Save the tick in a small plastic or glass container if possible. That way, a doctor can inspect it if a fever develops or the area around the bite appears to be infected. See p407 for information on lyme disease.

WATER

Tap water in BC is safe to drink, but in the backcountry you'll need to purify water you collect before drinking it. The simplest way of purifying water is to boil it – vigorous boiling for five minutes should be satisfactory even at high altitude.

Simple filtering will not remove all dangerous organisms, so if you cannot boil water it should be treated chemically. Chlorine tablets (Puritabs, Steritabs or other brand names) will kill many pathogens, but not giardia or amoebic cysts. Iodine is very effective in purifying water and is available in tablet form (such as Potable Aqua), but follow the directions carefully – too much iodine can be harmful.

DISCOUNT CARDS

Seniors (generally those over 65) and students (those with a valid International Student Identity Card) will qualify for discounts on admissions to many of the museums, parks and other attractions listed in this book. The cost is usually somewhere between the low price given for children and the high price given for adults.

EMBASSIES & CONSULATES
Canadian Embassies, High Commissions & Consulates

Following are the embassies and consulates recommended for visa, immigration and travel matters in each country by **Citizenship and Immigration Canada** (www.cic.gc.ca).

Australia (☎ 02-9364 3050; http://geo.international .gc.ca/asia/australia; Level 5, 111 Harrington St, Quay West, Sydney, NSW 2000) Residents of New Zealand can also contact this office.

France (☎ 01-44 43 29 00; www.dfait-maeci.gc.ca /canada-europa/france/; 37 Ave Montaigne, 75008 Paris)

Germany (☎ 030 20 31 20; www.dfait-maeci.gc.ca /canada-europa/germany/; Leipziger Platz 17, 10117 Berlin) Citizens of the Netherlands can also contact this office.

UK (☎ 020-7258 6600; www.dfait-maeci.gc.ca/canada -europa/united_kingdom/; MacDonald House, Immigration Section, 38 Grosvenor St, London W1K 4AA) Irish citizens can also contact this office.

US (☎ 202-682 1740; geo.international.gc.ca/can-am; 501 Pennsylvania Ave NW, Washington, DC 20001); Seattle consulate (☎ 206-443 1777; geo.international.gc.ca/can -am/seattle/; Ste 600, 501 4th Ave, Seattle 98101)

Consulates in British Columbia

In Vancouver there are several dozen consulates but no embassies (these are located in Ottawa, Ontario). Consulates include the following:

Australia (Map pp64-5; ☎ 604-684-1177; Ste 1225, 888 Dunsmuir St)

France (Map pp64-5; ☎ 604-681-4345; Ste 1100, 1130 W Pender St)

Germany (Map pp64-5; ☎ 604-684-8377; Ste 704, 999 Canada Place)

Ireland (Map p69; ☎ 604-683-9233; Ste 401, 1385 W 8th St)

Netherlands (Map pp64-5; ☎ 604-684-6448; Ste 821, 475 Howe St)

New Zealand (Map pp64-5; ☎ 604-684-7388; Ste 1200, 888 Dunsmuir St)

UK (Map pp64-5; ☎ 604-683-4421; Ste 800, 1111 Melville St)

USA (Map pp64-5; ☎ 604-685-4311; 1095 W Pender St)

FESTIVALS & EVENTS

There are scores of regional and local festivals and events in BC. See the Getting Started chapter (p13) for a list of our favorites. BC Day (first Monday in August) is a cause for widespread celebration and parades.

The Yukon has a few events, like Discovery Day, that are celebrated throughout the territory. See p360.

FOOD

In places like Vancouver you'll find food in every price range. Elsewhere prices tend to be moderate so as to be affordable by locals. You'll always find pricey places in resort areas.

In the places to eat included in this book, you can have a meal at a budget place for under $10, spend between $10 and $20 at a midrange place and drop $20 or more at a top-end place.

For a full discussion of what to eat, how to eat and when to eat it, see the Food & Drink chapter, p34.

GAY & LESBIAN TRAVELERS

In BC the attitude toward gays and lesbians is open in urban areas like Vancouver (see p83) and Victoria. While you won't find as open a gay and lesbian culture in other parts of BC, throughout the province and the Yukon attitudes are tolerant. That said, the lack of prominent gay and lesbian communities outside urban areas centers tends to mean that most people keep their orientation to themselves.

In 2003, BC became the second province after Ontario to allow gay marriage. The BC Ministry of Health maintains a website with information for same sex couples who would like to marry (www.vs.gov.bc.ca/marriage /howto.html).

HOLIDAYS

National public holidays are celebrated throughout Canada. Banks, schools and government offices (including post offices) are closed and transportation, museums and other services operate on a Sunday schedule. Holidays falling on a weekend are usually observed the following Monday and long weekends are among the busiest on BC's roads and waterways. Either plan your visit for a different time or secure accommodations in advance. The following is a list of the main public holidays:

January
New Year's Day (January 1)

March/April
Easter (Good Friday, Easter Monday)

May
Victoria Day (Monday preceding May 25)

July
Canada Day (July 1)

August
BC Day (first Monday of the month; BC only)
Discovery Day (third Monday of August; Yukon only)

September
Labour Day (first Monday of the month)

October
Thanksgiving (second Monday of the month)

November
Remembrance Day (November 11)

December
Christmas Day (December 25)
Boxing Day (December 26; many stores open, other businesses closed)

INSURANCE

Residents of British Columbia are covered by the provincial health-care system, however, visitors to the province are not so it's smart to take out travel insurance before leaving home. Not only does it cover you for medical expenses and luggage theft or loss, but also for cancellations or delays in your travel arrangements under certain circumstances, such as becoming seriously ill on the day before your scheduled departure.

Before obtaining special travel insurance check what's already covered by your other insurance policies or credit card; you might find that you won't need to take out a separate policy. The critical questions to ask your current insurer and those offering coverage are: 'Who pays if I get sick in BC,' 'Who pays if my trip is canceled or delayed (assuming you would have a liability)?' or 'Who pays if my belongings are stolen?'

Worldwide coverage to travelers from over 44 countries is available online at www.lonely planet.com/travel_services.

INTERNET ACCESS

Wi-fi access to the internet is becoming commonplace throughout BC and the Yukon in places to stay and many cafés. There's a growing trend to have access over an entire town, with several BC and Yukon towns considering this.

Many places to stay also have high-speed access requiring an Ethernet connection, and, for the three people who still do it, dataports for dial-up access are common on motel phones.

You'll find internet computers in libraries, some cafés and internet cafés in larger towns, as well as in accommodations. Paid access usually costs about $1 per 10 minutes.

Because most people in BC and the Yukon have their own internet access, stores filled with terminals are not common, so there's little evidence of efforts to subvert travelers' internet security.

For useful and fun websites that can improve your trip, see p14.

LEGAL MATTERS

The Canadian federal government permits the use of marijuana for medicinal purposes, but official prescription cannabis is strictly regulated. It's illegal to consume alcohol anywhere other than a residence or licensed premises, which puts parks, beaches and other public spaces off limits.

You can incur stiff fines, jail time and penalties if caught driving under the influence of alcohol or any illegal substance. The blood-alcohol limit is 0.08%, which is reached after just two beers. Penalties include being thrown in jail overnight, followed by a court appearance, heavy fine and/or further incarceration.

If you are arrested, you have the right to remain silent, however, never walk away from law enforcement personnel without permission. After being arrested you have the right to an interpreter and one phone call. For free or low-cost legal advice, try contacting the **Legal Services Society** (☎ information 604-408-2172, appointments 604-601-6206; www.lss.bc.ca; Ste 820, 1140 W Pender St, East Vancouver).

MAPS

Members of the Canadian Automobile Association (CAA), American Automobile Association (AAA) or affiliated clubs can get

HOW OLD IS OLD ENOUGH?	
▪ Driving	16
▪ Voting	18
▪ Drinking	19
▪ Age of consent for sex (may be raised to 16)	14
▪ Age of homosexual consent (for males)	18

free road maps before leaving home or from offices throughout BC. Bookstores, gas stations and convenience stores usually sell a wide variety of maps ranging from regional overviews to detailed street atlases.

If you plan to do a bit of hiking or other land-based backcountry activities, you'll want to invest in good topographical maps. **Gem Trek Publishing** (www.gemtrek.com) offers some of the best Rocky Mountain maps in scales from 1:35,000 to 1:100,000. These can be widely purchased throughout the Rockies. Other topographical maps and marine charts are available at bookstores and sporting-goods shops.

Lonely Planet's *Vancouver City Map* has a full index and it's rain-proof. Free local and regional maps also are available from VICs in BC and the Yukon.

MONEY

The Canadian dollar ($) is divided into 100 cents (¢). Coins come in 1¢ (penny), 5¢ (nickel), 10¢ (dime), 25¢ (quarter), $1 (loonie) and $2 (toonie) pieces. The 50¢ coin is seldom seen. Notes come in $5, $10, $20, $50 and $100 denominations. Bills in larger denominations are produced but rarely used; $50 and $100 bills can prove difficult to cash. Canadian bills are all the same size but vary in their colors and images. Some denominations have two styles as older versions in good condition continue to circulate.

See p12 for information on costs and the inside front cover for exchange rates. Prices in this book are quoted in Canadian dollars except for a few places where US dollars (US$) are used.

ATMs

ATMs are common throughout BC and the larger towns of the Yukon. Using an ATM card to withdraw Canadian currency from your account is handy and usually a fiscally wise choice. Service fees are generally lower at bank ATMs than at machines found in restaurants, bars and stores. Near the US border, you may have a choice of Canadian or US currency.

Changing Money

Although some businesses in British Columbia, especially along the US border, accept a variety of currencies, it's best to exchange your money soon after arriving in the province.

There are several 24-hour currency exchange machines and counters placed throughout Vancouver International Airport. Currency exchange offices are abundant in Vancouver and Victoria, as well as other larger towns throughout the province. Note, however, that most charge a commission fee and give less favorable exchange rates than banks. If you are coming from the USA (or elsewhere for that matter), the best thing to do is use your ATM card to withdraw cash once you cross the border.

Taxes & Refunds

The federal Goods and Services Tax (GST) adds 7% to nearly every product, service or transaction, on top of which there is usually a 7% BC provincial sales tax (PST). Alcohol draws a 10% tax. Accommodations (aka 'cash cows' to revenue authorities) draw an 8% provincial tax plus local taxes that can range from 1% to 17%.

Visitors are eligible for refunds on GST paid for short-term accommodations and nonconsumable goods, although the refund process is inconvenient. To wit: your purchase amounts (before taxes) must total at least $200, and each individual receipt must show a minimum amount of $50 before taxes. You must have original receipts (credit-card slips and photocopies are not accepted), and the receipts are not returned. Receipts for goods (not accommodations) must be stamped by Canadian customs to be eligible for a refund: at the airport go to the Refund Office; at land borders go to the customs office or a refund-designated duty-free shop. Visitors departing Canada by commercial carrier (including air, rail, noncharter bus or ferry) must also include their original boarding pass or carrier ticket with the refund claim. You also have to know *all* the words to the *South Park* song 'Blame Canada.' Not really.

Once you've met all the criteria above it's time to fill out and mail in the rebate form, widely available at 'tourist' shops, hotels and tourist offices. You can also contact the **Canada Customs and Revenue Agency's Visitor Rebate Program** (☎ within Canada 800-668-4748, outside Canada 902-432-5608; www.ccra.gc.ca/visitors; Ste 104, 275 Pope Rd, Summerside, PE C1N 6C6). Expect to wait four to six weeks for your check, which is paid in Canadian dollars unless issued to a US address (in which case it will be in US dollars). Note you also can get on-the-spot refunds for amounts under $500 at land borders that have specially designated duty-free shops.

Tipping

Tips are expected by restaurant and bar servers, as well as by taxi drivers and anyone else rendering a personal service, such as a guide. In restaurants, bars and clubs, the staff are paid a minimum wage and rely on tips to make a reasonable living. Never, ever tip less than 10% of the total bill; leave 15% if the service was fine and up to 20% if it was exceptional. Some restaurants impose a service charge on the bill, in which case no tip should be given. You needn't tip in fast-food, take-out or buffet-style restaurants where you serve yourself.

For others, give 15% if their service is satisfactory. Baggage carriers in airports or hotels receive $1 per bag. Don't forget to leave a couple of dollars for the motel or hotel housekeeping staff for each night you stay.

Traveler's Checks

Traveler's checks are accepted at tourist places but their usage is becoming infrequent as travelers use ATMs for their cash needs.

POST

Canada Post (www.canadapost.ca) is reliable and easy to use. Postal service counters have been installed in convenience stores, groceries and even flower shops. Postal rates for postcards and letters to the US are 89¢, to the rest of the world $1.49.

SHOPPING

The best souvenirs and gifts from BC and the Yukon are items made by local artisans. We give numerous tips about where to find local treats and creations throughout the book. If in doubt, a bottle of Okanagan Valley wine always goes down well.

SOLO TRAVELERS

BC and the Yukon can be good to solo travelers. The people are generally friendly, so striking up conversations is easy, and many activities and other attractions lend themselves to meeting others. However, this is also the place to enjoy perfect solitude if that's what you're looking for. The one caveat is going out into the backcountry, where traveling alone can leave you more exposed to a bear attack or accident.

TELEPHONE

Pay phones are common in cities and towns, however, you'll need coins or a long-distance phone card (for domestic and international calls) to work them. Phone cards are available from myriad companies and are sold in myriad places (convenience stores, gas stations etc). Compare prices if you are going to buy one.

If you are calling another number in North America, you start with a ☎1 followed by the 10-digit number. Conversely, if you are calling a number within the same area code, drop the area code (the first three numbers) and dial only the last seven digits of the phone number.

For calling outside of North America dial ☎011 followed by the country code and the number. When calling North America from abroad the country code is ☎1.

TIME

Most of BC and the Yukon operate on Pacific Standard Time, which is eight hours behind Greenwich Mean Time. Both BC and the Yukon generally observe Daylight Saving Time; clocks are turned forward one hour on the second Sunday in March and are turned back one hour on the first Sunday in November. For exceptions to this, see p267 and p328.

TOURIST INFORMATION

With tourism being such a major part of the economy for both BC and the Yukon, it's no surprise that the tourism infrastructure is well-funded and easy to use.

Tourism BC (☎ 800-435-5622, outside North America 250-387-1642; www.hellobc.com) has over a 100 visitor information centers (VICs) in towns and cities throughout the province. These excellent local resources can assist you with planning, reservations, maps, activities information and much more. They are usually along major roads and are well-marked with blue, green and yellow signs. Hours vary, but larger offices are typically open from at least 8am to 6pm daily during summer and from 9am to 5pm on weekdays throughout the rest of the year.

Yukon Tourism and Culture (☎ 800-661-0494, outside North America 867-667-5340; www.touryukon.com) maintains six VICs at major entry points to the territory. See p359 for more information.

Besides providing gobs of excellent free literature that may satisfy your reading needs for the trip, the BC and Yukon tourist offices can be good places to buy specialist guidebooks and maps.

TOURS

BC and the Yukon have dozens of tour companies that can get you out into the wilds as well as make your time in towns and cities more meaningful. Tour options include white-water rafting and other water sports, whale-watching, scenic boat tours, hiking, mountain biking or simply seeing the sights by bus. You'll find tour operators listed throughout this book.

TRAVELERS WITH DISABILITIES

Guide dogs may legally be brought into restaurants, hotels and other businesses. Many public-service phone numbers and some payphones are adapted for the hearing impaired. Most public buildings are wheelchair accessible and many parks feature trails that are likewise accessible.

The federal government lists wheelchair-accessible transport throughout Canada at www.accesstotravel.gc.ca online. VIA Rail (p404) and long-distance bus companies (p402) can accommodate wheelchairs if given advance notice. Apply for disabled parking permits ($15) via **SPARC BC** (☎ 604-718-7744; www.sparc.bc.ca).

Other helpful resources include:

BC Coalition of People with Disabilities (☎ 604-875-0188, 604-875-8835; www.bccpd.bc.ca)

Canadian National Institute for the Blind (☎ 604-431-2121; www.cnib.ca)

Canadian Paraplegic Association of BC (☎ 604-324-3611; www.canparaplegic.org/bc)

Mobility International USA (☎ 541-343-1284; www.miusa.org)

Society for Accessible Travel & Hospitality (☎ 212-447-7284; www.sath.org)

VISAS

All visitors to Canada, except US citizens, must have a valid passport. Visitors from the US are required to have a driver's license and one other proof of identification (such as a valid birth certificate), however, this exception is meant to end by January 1, 2008 if not before. US citizens should check with

the **US Department of State** (www.travel.state.gov) for updates.

Short-term visitors from most Western countries, except parts of Eastern Europe, normally don't require visas, but citizens of another 130 countries do. As visa requirements change frequently it's a good idea to check with the **Canadian Immigration Centre** (☎ 416-973-4444; www.cic.gc.ca) or the Canadian embassy or consulate in your home country to see if you're exempt.

VOLUNTEERING

The omnibus www.volunteerbc.bc.ca is a good starting point for those who want to volunteer for programs (literacy, assisting the disabled, cleaning up the environment etc) while they're in BC. The 2010 Winter Olympics is a magnet for volunteers; learn how you can participate at www.vancouver2010.com.

WOMEN TRAVELERS

British Columbia is generally a safe place for women traveling alone, although the usual precautions apply. In Vancouver, the Main and Hastings Sts area is best avoided and it's probably not a good idea to go for a walk in Stanley Park on your own after dark. In more remote parts of the province, particularly in the North, women traveling alone will find themselves a distinct minority.

The more populated and frequently visited parts of BC are great for women travelers. Hostels usually have formal or informal group outings to pubs and local attractions, and many outfitters, ski areas and the like offer trips and classes geared to women. With these opportunities BC is an excellent place to experiment with new recreational activities and meet many like-minded women and men who enjoy adventure and active travel.

WORK

People able to work short-term jobs such as in restaurants and bars should be able to find seasonal work in popular tourist spots. Ski resorts always need people and the coming 2010 Olympics means that there are lots of opportunities around Whistler (see p121). Outside of the Rockies work will be harder to find, although if you have a mining degree, the open pits north of Fort Nelson are ready and waiting.

Transportation

THINGS CHANGE...

The information in this chapter is particularly vulnerable to change. Check directly with the airline or a travel agent to make sure you understand how a fare (and ticket you may buy) works, and be aware of the security requirements for international travel. Shop carefully. The details given in this chapter should be regarded as pointers and are not a substitute for your own careful, up-to-date research.

GETTING THERE & AWAY

British Columbia is easily reached from major international points as well as from the USA. Getting to the Yukon usually requires a simple plane connection, although getting there by car and boat can be half the fun. Flights, tours and rail tickets can be booked online at www.lonelyplanet.com/travel_services.

ENTERING THE COUNTRY

Entering Canada is normally a straightforward affair, assuming you have the proper documents such as visas (opposite). However, those crossing the border from the US may

get stuck in long lines. We've sat in endless lines at borders with but one agent on duty on Sunday night when scores of weekending BCers are simply trying to return home. More memorably, after word came that there was someone carrying a gun *in California*, the Canadian border agents in BC closed the border and walked off their jobs just in case the gun-toter should cross through two more states and try to cross into Canada. (Lines at Vancouver International Airport can also be long.)

AIR

Though many BC-bound travelers will fly into Vancouver, people who are most interested in the Rockies or the Kootenays may want to travel instead to Calgary, Alberta, just a short distance from Banff and the other national parks.

Airports

Vancouver International airport (YVR; ☎ 604-207-7077; www.yvr.ca) is 13km south of downtown Vancouver near the suburb of Richmond. It's Canada's second-busiest airport and likely to be your port of entry to BC if you fly. It has good connections throughout western Canada, and there is international service to the US, Europe and Asia.

The main airport has two terminals: international and domestic. It has some pretty features but also some annoying ones: poor signage and avaricious walkways right through the middle of duty-free shops. The smaller south airport terminal, off Inglis Dr, handles small regional airlines and seaplanes. There is a shuttle bus between the two terminals.

For Rockies-bound travelers, **Calgary International airport** (YYC; www.calgaryairport.com) has service from the USA and Europe. **Edmonton airport** (YEG; www.edmontonairports.com) has service from the USA.

Kelowna Airport (YLW; p241) has service to/from Seattle with Horizon Air, which makes the Okanagan Valley an easy connection for travel from the USA.

Whitehorse Airport (YXY; p366) in the Yukon has service to Alaska and summer flights to/from Germany.

TRANSPORTATION

Airlines

Airlines serving Vancouver's international airport include:

Air Canada & Air Canada Jazz (airline code AC; ☎ 888-247-2262; www.aircanada.ca)

Air China (airline code CA; ☎ 604-685-0921; www.airchina.com.cn)

Air North (airline code 4N; ☎ 800-661-0407; www.flyairnorth.com)

Air Transat (airline code TS; ☎ 866-847-1112; www.airtransat.com)

Alaska Airlines (airline code AS; ☎ 800-252-7522; www.alaskaair.com)

American Airlines (airline code AA; ☎ 800-433-7300; www.aa.com)

British Airways (airline code BA; ☎ 800-247-9297; www.britishairways.com)

Cathay Pacific (airline code CX; ☎ 604-606-8888, 888-338-1668; www.cathaypacific.com)

China Airlines (airline code CI; ☎ 604-682-6777; www.china-airlines.com)

Continental Airlines (airline code CO; ☎ 800-523-3273; www.continental.com)

Delta Air Lines (airline code DL; ☎ 800-221-1212; www.delta.com)

EVA Air (airline code BR; ☎ 800-695-1188; www.evaair.com)

Horizon Air (airline code QX; ☎ 800-547-9308; www.horizonair.com)

Japan Airlines (airline code JL; ☎ 800-525-3663; www.jal.co.jp/en/)

Lufthansa (airline code LH; ☎ 800-563-5954; www.lufthansa.com)

Northwest Airlines (airline code NW; ☎ 800-447-4747; www.nwa.com)

Pacific Coastal Airlines (airline code 8P; ☎ 604-273-8666; www.pacific-coastal.com)

Singapore Airlines (airline code SQ; ☎ 604-689-1223; www.singaporeair.com)

Thai Airways International (airline code TG; ☎ 800-426-5204; www.thaiair.com)

United Airlines (airline code UA; ☎ 800-241-6522; www.united.ca)

WestJet (airline code WS; ☎ 800-538-5696; www.westjet.com)

Airlines with service to Whitehorse (p360) in the Yukon include:

Air Canada & Air Canada Jazz (airline code AC; ☎ 888-247-2262; www.aircanada.ca)

Air North (airline code 4N; ☎ 800-661-0407; www.flyairnorth.com)

Condor (☎ 800-364-1667; www.condor.com)

First Air (☎ 800 267-1247; www.firstair.ca)

Tickets

With so many international airlines flying there, Vancouver is a great destination for

---

CLIMATE CHANGE & TRAVEL

Climate change is a serious threat to the ecosystems that humans rely upon, and air travel is the fastest-growing contributor to the problem. Lonely Planet regards travel, overall, as a global benefit, but believes we all have a responsibility to limit our personal impact on global warming.

FLYING & CLIMATE CHANGE

Pretty much every form of motorized travel generates carbon dioxide (the main cause of human-induced climate change) but planes are far and away the worst offenders, not just because of the sheer distances they allow us to travel, but because they release greenhouse gases high into the atmosphere. The statistics are frightening: two people taking a return flight between Europe and the US will contribute as much to climate change as an average household's gas and electricity consumption over a whole year.

CARBON OFFSET SCHEMES

Climatecare.org and other websites use 'carbon calculators' that allow travelers to offset the level of greenhouse gases they are responsible for with financial contributions to sustainable travel schemes that reduce global warming – including projects in India, Honduras, Kazakhstan and Uganda.

Lonely Planet, together with Rough Guides and other concerned partners in the travel industry, support the carbon offset scheme run by climatecare.org. Lonely Planet offsets all of its staff and author travel.

For more information check out our website: www.lonelyplanet.com.

competitive airfares. To get a good idea of what's being charged, check out websites like Expedia (www.expedia.com), Orbitz (www.orbitz.com) and Travelocity (www.travelocity.com). Individual airline websites often feature specials that apply only on that airline, so it's a good idea to check those operating from your part of the world as well. Note also that connections going on to various BC cities can add little to the airfare. The regional chapters list important airports, so it doesn't hurt to check fares to those as well, if you want to get close to your final destination by air.

Asia

There is nonstop service to Vancouver from major Asian capitals.

STA Travel proliferates in Asia, with branches in Bangkok (☎ 02-236 0262; www.statravel.co.th), Singapore (☎ 6737 7188; www.statravel.com.sg), Hong Kong (☎ 2736 1618; www.statravel.com.hk) and Japan (☎ 03 5391 2922; www.statravel.co.jp). Another resource in Japan is **No 1 Travel** (☎ 03 3205 6073; www.no1-travel.com); in Hong Kong try **Four Seas Tours** (☎ 2200 7760; www.fourseastravel.com/english).

Australia

Service from down under requires a stop in the US. Choices include:
Flight Centre (☎ 133 133; www.flightcentre.com.au)
STA Travel (☎ 1300 733 035; www.statravel.com.au)

France

Recommended agencies:
Lastminute (☎ 0892 705 000; www.lastminute.fr)
Nouvelles Frontières (☎ 0825 000 747; www.nouvelles-frontieres.fr)
OTU Voyages (www.otu.fr) This agency specializes in student and youth travelers.
Voyageurs du Monde (☎ 01 40 15 11 15; www.vdm.com)

Germany

Lufthansa flies to Vancouver, as do budget carriers. Recommended agencies:
Expedia (www.expedia.de)
Just Travel (☎ 089 747 3330; www.justtravel.de)
Lastminute (☎ 01805 284 366; www.lastminute.de)
STA Travel (☎ 01805 456 422; www.statravel.de) For travelers under the age of 26.

The Netherlands

One recommended agency is **Airfair** (☎ 020 620 5121; www.airfair.nl).

New Zealand

You'll have to go via the US from Kiwi land. Some choices:
Flight Centre (☎ 0800 243 544; www.flightcentre.co.nz)
STA Travel (☎ 0508 782 872; www.statravel.co.nz)

UK & Ireland

British Airways flies nonstop from London. Recommended travel agencies:
Flightbookers (☎ 0870 814 4001; www.ebookers.com)
Flight Centre (☎ 0870 890 8099; flightcentre.co.uk)
STA Travel (☎ 0870 160 0599; www.statravel.co.uk) For travelers under the age of 26.
Trailfinders (www.trailfinders.co.uk)

USA

Most American airlines have flights to Vancouver from one or more of their hub cities.

Websites recommended for making online bookings:
Expedia (www.expedia.com)
Orbitz (www.orbitz.com)
STA (www.sta.com) For travelers under the age of 26.
Travelocity (www.travelocity.com)

LAND
Border Crossings

Points of entry on the US–Canada border are open 24 hours except for some minor ones and those in the Yukon that have limited hours and/or close for the season.

Along the southern BC border, Friday and Sunday are especially busy at the major border crossings. Delays can be especially bad on the holiday weekends in summer, particularly at the Blaine, Washington (WA)–Douglas crossing south of Vancouver, where you may have to wait several hours. Either avoid crossing at these times, or drive to one of the other Lower Mainland crossings such as Aldergrove or Huntingdon. Note that minor border crossings may not be open 24 hours a day.

From the USA
BUS

You can travel to many places in BC (and Whitehorse in the Yukon) from the USA via **Greyhound** (☎ 800-661-8747; www.greyhound.com). Most routes require you to travel between Seattle and Vancouver, then transfer. See p102 for details.

Pacific Coach Lines (☎ 800-661-1725; www.pacificcoach.com) has services between Vancouver and Victoria and connections to Seattle.

TRANSPORTATION

CAR

The US highway system connects directly with Canadian highways at many points along the BC border. Gas is generally cheaper in the USA.

TRAIN

Amtrak (☎ 800-872-7245; www.amtrak.com) connects Vancouver to Bellingham and Seattle with one train and two buses daily that take four hours. See p102 for details. From Seattle, Amtrak trains go south to Portland, San Francisco and Los Angeles, and east to Minneapolis and Chicago.

From Canada
BUS

Greyhound Canada (☎ 800-661-8747; www.greyhound .ca) has routes into BC from Edmonton through Dawson Creek, as well as Jasper and in the south from Calgary through the Rockies.

TRAIN

VIA Rail (☎ 888-842-7245; www.viarail.ca) runs the *Canadian* between Vancouver and Toronto. Stops include Kamloops (p213), Jasper (p304), Edmonton, Saskatoon and Winnipeg. It's a scenic trip, but it only runs three times a week.

SEA
Alaska Cruises

The BC and Alaska coast is one of the world's most popular – and profitable – cruise destinations. In total, more than 35 vessels from over a dozen cruise lines make hundreds of sailings between the US West Coast, Vancouver and Alaska every year from May to October. **CruiseMates** (www.cruisemates.com) has a useful round-up of the many lines and boats now sailing the Inside Passage. Many include Vancouver in their itineraries. Some boats are now doing the run from US ports such as Seattle and San Francisco, making it possible to create a package where you can sail one way to/from BC or even the Yukon via Skagway in Alaska and travel by ground or air the other way. However a complex itinerary such as this would require the services of a travel agent.

Of the various lines, **Holland America Line** (☎ 877-724-5425; www.hollandamerica.com) is the largest through the Inside Passage. In addition, it operates numerous trips and tours throughout the Yukon that are at times open to non-cruise-ship passengers.

Ferry

The **Alaska Marine Highway ferry** (AMH; ☎ 800-642-0066; www.ferryalaska.com) sails from Bellingham, Washington, along the stunning Inside Passage to Haines (p372) and Skagway (p374) in Alaska, which are key entry ports to the Yukon. These trips take almost four days and run twice a week in summer and once a week in winter. It is one of the most spectacular voyages anywhere – note the number of cruise ships that do it – and the advantage of the ferry is that you can bring your car to the Yukon with you.

The AMH ships are comfortable, with decent cabins, good, fresh-cooked food and usually a park ranger offering commentary on the many sights that include scads of wildlife such as whales. Many people pitch tents on the deck. Reservations for this route are a must. One of their other great advantages is what they aren't: cruise ships. There's no planned fun, no endless buffets, no stupid games – just scenery and serenity.

Another AMH option is to take the boat from Prince Rupert (p338) in BC to Haines or Skagway and then on to the Yukon. This route is nearly the equal in terms of scenery

---

SAILING THE INSIDE PASSAGE

Taking an **Alaska Marine Highway ferry** (above) or **BC Ferries** boat (opposite) along the stunning Inside Passage and BC and Alaska coasts can be the highlight of any trip. Expect to see marine life from whales to dolphins to orcas. Look for eagles overhead and bears on the shore. The rugged coastline is largely part of the Great Bear Rainforest (see boxed text, p319) and you will spend hours passing deserted islands and rocky coasts with waterfalls as accents. On these runs the crews are friendly and captains will slow the ships when, say, a pod of dolphins swims past. On most of the boats (but sadly not BC Ferries to Bella Coola), you can get a cabin and just spend a day or more relaxing, reading and gazing. Note: none of the boats is flashy, although the Alaska boats have better food – lots of fresh seafood.

with the Bellingham run and it takes half as long. Both routes to Haines and Skagway stop at Southeast Alaska towns such as Juneau and Ketchikan.

You can get to Victoria by ferry (p153) from Seattle, Port Angeles and Anacortes, Washington.

GETTING AROUND

AIR

Air Canada is the country's main domestic airline and has flights to Vancouver from other major Canadian cities. Its regional affiliate Air Canada Jazz flies to numerous smaller cities in BC. The other major airline is WestJet, which flies to Vancouver, Victoria, Prince George, Kelowna and other cities.

See p366 for details of Yukon air links.

Airlines

Larger airlines providing regional service in BC and the Yukon are as follows:

Air Canada & Air Canada Jazz (airline code AC; ☎ 888-247-2262; www.aircanada.ca)

Air North (airline code 4N; ☎ 800-661-0407; www .flyairnorth.com)

Baxter Aviation (☎ 250-754-1066, 800-661-5599; www.baxterair.com)

Central Mountain Air (☎ 250-877-5000, 888-865-8585; www.flycma.com)

Pacific Coastal Airlines (airline code 8P; ☎ 604-273-8666; www.pacific-coastal.com)

West Coast Air (☎ 604-606-6800, 800-347-2222; www.westcoastair.com)

WestJet (airline code WS; ☎ 800-538-5696; www .westjet.com)

BICYCLE

British Columbia Cycling Coalition (www.bccc.bc.ca) is the best source of information on bicycling as transportation in BC. Bike rentals are widely available, and in the various regional chapters of this book you will find bicycle-rental listings for many towns. You can take your bike on most forms of public transportation. Call ahead to the air, ferry, bus and train companies listed to see what their rates and requirements are.

Rental

Mountain bikes usually rent for about $35 per day and are available in most larger towns and cities. A credit card will cover the deposit.

Purchase

The same places that rent bikes also sell them at prices similar to those in other developed areas.

BOAT

The blue-and-white BC Ferries are a symbol of coastal British Columbia as well as a mode of transportation. You'll find extensive details on BC Ferries service throughout the Vancouver & Around, the Vancouver Island and the Whistler & the Sunshine Coast chapters.

What follows is an overview of services, plus details on the long-distance Inside Passage and Discovery Coast Passage routes.

BC Ferries Corporation (☎ 888-223-3779; www.bc ferries.com) operates a fleet of 35 ferries on BC's coastal waters. Formerly a government-run operation, it has been part-privatized to much controversy. Fares have risen ('temporary' fuel surcharges never seem to go away even when the price of fuel drops), there are questions about the levels of service, and most disastrously, they sunk one of the prides of their fleet (see boxed text, p402).

Look for occasional specials. One popular package is SailPass, which gives you either four consecutive days of ferry travel for $169 or seven consecutive days for $199. The pass includes unlimited travel on the Southern Gulf Islands, Northern Gulf Islands and Brentwood Bay–Mill Bay routes, along with one round trip on each of the Mainland–Vancouver Island and Sunshine Coast crossings.

Another good package is CirclePac, a four-route travel package that gives you up to 15% off regular, one-way fares on each of the following routes: Horseshoe Bay–Langdale, Earls Cove–Saltery Bay, Powell River–Comox, and Vancouver Island–Mainland (your choice of Nanaimo–Horseshoe Bay, Nanaimo–Tsawwassen or Swartz Bay–Tsawwassen).

Vancouver Area Service

The two busiest routes are from Tsawwassen (about an hour's drive south of downtown Vancouver) to Swartz Bay (a half-hour drive north of Victoria), and from Horseshoe Bay (a half-hour drive north of downtown Vancouver) to Departure Bay near Nanaimo on Vancouver Island. From Tsawwassen, ferries also go to Duke Point near Nanaimo, and to the Southern Gulf Islands (Salt Spring, Galiano, Mayne, Saturna and the Pender Islands).

TRANSPORTATION

TRANSPORTATION

QUEEN OF THE NORTH GOES DOWN

On the night of March 22, 2006, the *Queen of the North*, the pride of the BC Ferries fleet, hit an island 135km south of Prince Rupert. The ferry soon filled with water and sank, while 99 of the 101 passengers (a very light load because of the season) clambered into lifeboats to await rescue. Two others were never seen again.

It was a shocking accident, especially for a company with a proud history like BC Ferries. And it happened to a boat and crew that had made the run scores of times before on a night when the weather wasn't bad. What happened? Canada's Transportation Board launched a lengthy investigation. Meanwhile it was obvious that the boat had failed to make a standard course change and simply ran straight ahead until it impacted rocky and diminutive Gil Island.

What was happening on the bridge while the unattended auto pilot sailed the boat onto the rocks is a focus of the investigation. Not surprisingly, it added to the voices that have been dubious of BC Ferries's partial privatization. Many asked whether profits had trumped safety. Meanwhile, BC Ferries has bought a used ferry from Europe (and renamed it *Northern Adventure*) to use on the route for the next several years.

From Horseshoe Bay, ferries also go to Bowen Island and the Sunshine Coast.

Other BC Ferries routes cover Gabriola Island, Thetis Island, Kuper Island, Texada Island and the Northern Gulf Islands (namely Denman, Hornby, Quadra, Cortes, Malcolm and Cormorant).

It's always much cheaper to travel on BC Ferries without a motorized vehicle. You can take bicycles, canoes or kayaks onboard.

Vehicle **reservations** (☎ 888-223-3779; www .bcferries.com) are recommended for weekends on the Tsawwassen–Swartz Bay, Horseshoe Bay–Departure Bay and Tsawwassen–Duke Point routes.

Inside Passage

The Inside Passage route between Port Hardy and Prince Rupert is among the most scenic boat trips in the world. Generally there's a northbound sailing from Port Hardy at 7:30am every other day in summer, arriving in Prince Rupert at 10:30pm. The southbound sailings have a similar schedule. There are sailings October through May, too. You must reserve space on Inside Passage sailings. See p343 for more details on schedules and fares, as well as p400 for more on the route and voyages.

Discovery Coast Passage

This route covers the lovely route between Port Hardy and Bella Coola (p317) on the central BC coast. It's shorter than the Inside Passage route, but just as scenic. Ships run only from mid-June through mid-September. Reservations are necessary.

There are no cabins on the *Queen of Chilliwack*, which usually sails the Discovery Coast Passage, but there are reclining lounge seats where you can sort of sleep. Some passengers even set up their tents on deck and sleep there.

Queen Charlotte Islands

For details on the Queen Charlotte Islands services from Prince Rupert, see p343.

BUS

Greyhound Canada (800-661-8747; www.greyhound .ca) covers most of BC and has service into the Yukon along the Alaska Hwy as far as Whitehorse. You can find various discounts by booking online. The fares listed in this book are full fare.

Pacific Coach Lines (☎ 800-661-1725; www.pacific coach.com) has services between Vancouver and Victoria and connections to Seattle.

Note that places off the main highways and much of the Yukon have no public bus service of any kind.

Backpackers Bus

There's a backpackers bus service run by **Moose Travel Network** (☎ 888-244-6673, outside North America 604-777-9905; www.moosenetwork.com; ☾ Jun-Sep, less often May & Oct), running small buses on a series of routes that includes Vancouver, Jasper, Banff, Revelstoke and Kelowna. For one fare ($229 to $869) you can get on and off between however many segments you've paid for. The buses stop at major (and minor) scenic highlights along the way and there are all sorts of group activities. The buses can be a lot of fun and each day's run ends with drop-offs at hostels.

CAR & MOTORCYCLE
British Columbia and the Yukon is a big place, and if you want to see a lot of it on your own timetable, a car or motorcycle is usually the way to go. In many ways, driving is the best way to travel in the region. You can go where and when you want, use secondary highways and roads, and get off the beaten track. You can use ferries to cover some segments and create interesting circular routes.

Automobile Association
With 24 offices throughout the province, the **British Columbia Automobile Association** (BCAA; ☎ 877-325-8888; www.bcaa.com; membership per year $81) provides its members, and the members of other auto clubs (such as AAA in the USA), with travel information, maps, travel insurance and hotel reservations. It also provides service in the Yukon. Many people join for the **emergency roadside assistance** (☎ 604-293-2222, Lower Mainland 800-222-4357).

Bring Your Own Vehicle
Cars licensed to drive in North America may be driven in BC and the Yukon.

Drivers License
Generally your drivers license from home is good in the BC and the Yukon.

Fuel & Spare Parts
At the time of writing, gasoline (petrol, usually just called gas in BC) costs from 90¢ in the competitive Vancouver area to $1.10 per liter in the uncompetitive north.

Places to purchase fuel are common throughout southern BC. In the north along major roads such as the Alaska Hwy, service stations are spaced at regular intervals. That said, on some side roads and out-of-the-way places don't expect to find a gas station. A good rule of thumb is to fill up your tank when your level is sitting on about half empty (or half full if you're feeling optimistic).

Auto parts and mechanics who have seen it all also exist at regular intervals on major roads in the north. But it is still a good idea to carry at least one full-service spare tire – especially if you will be driving on one of the gravel highways.

Insurance
Cars from North America usually have insurance coverage in BC and the Yukon. If in doubt ask your agent. Wherever you're from, if you are renting, check to see if your auto policy or credit card covers you while driving the rental. If so you can avoid buying the extortionate rental company's insurance. No matter what kind of insurance coverage you have, all bets may be off if you go off major roads – check in advance before you head north.

Rental
Major car-rental firms have offices at airports in BC and Whitehorse, as well as some city centers. In smaller towns there are often independent firms; these are listed through the book. It's again worth noting that you should clarify your insurance coverage for things like gravel damage if you will be driving off major paved roads.

By shopping around you can find some pretty good deals. Just watch out for deals that don't offer unlimited kilometers for driving. And never buy the rental-car company's gas if offered when you pick up your car – it's a bad deal. Buy your own and return it full. If you are considering a one-way rental, look out for high fees.

RENTAL-CAR FIRMS
Alamo (☎ 800-462-5266; www.alamo.com)
Avis (☎ 800-272-5871; www.avis.com)
Budget (☎ 800-268-8900; www.budget.com)
Hertz (☎ 800-263-0600; www.hertz.com)
National (☎ 800-227-7368; www.nationalcar.com)

RECREATIONAL VEHICLES
Recreational vehicles (RVs) are hugely popular in BC and the Yukon, and rentals must be booked well before the summer season. In high season, RVs cost $80 to $200 or more a day, including 100km per day. One-way rentals are possible but you'll pay a surcharge. Also budget plenty for fuel, because RVs typically get very poor gas mileage.

ROAD REPORTS

- Road Conditions BC: ☎ 800-550-4997, www.drivebc.ca

- Road Conditions Yukon: ☎ 877-456-7623, www.gov.yk.ca/roadreport

Large rental companies have offices in Vancouver, Calgary, Whitehorse and in large BC towns.

CanaDream (☎ 800-461-7368; www.canadream.travel)

Fraserway RV Rentals (☎ 867-668-3438; www.fraserwayrvrentals.com)

West Coast Mountain Campers (☎ 604-279-0550; www.wcmcampers.com)

Road Hazards

It's best to avoid driving in areas with heavy snow, but if you do, be sure your vehicle has snow tires or tire chains. Many Canadian cars have four-season radial tires. If you get stuck, don't stay in the car with the engine going; every year people die of carbon monoxide suffocation by doing this during big storms. A single candle burning in the car will keep it reasonably warm.

Make sure the vehicle you're driving is in good condition and take along some tools, spare parts, water and food.

Some additional precautions apply for off-the-beaten-track travel. Gravel logging roads tend to be particularly dangerous. Logging trucks have the right of way in every instance, and they'll often zoom past you, kicking up gravel and dust. It's best not to drive on logging roads at all during weekday working hours.

Gravel roads of all kinds – such as the many gravel highways in the Yukon – can take a toll on windshields, so if you're renting, sort out breakage coverage in advance. (Some rental companies prohibit customers from taking cars on gravel roads.) Keep a good distance from the vehicle in front of you, and when you see an oncoming vehicle (or a vehicle overtaking you), slow down and keep well to the right. Carry a spare tire.

Wild animals on the road are another potential hazard. Most run-ins with deer, moose and other critters occur at night when wildlife is active and visibility is poor. Many areas have roadside signs alerting drivers to possible animal crossings. Keep scanning both sides of the road and be prepared to stop or swerve. A vehicle's headlights often mesmerize an animal, leaving it frozen in the middle of the road. Try flashing the lights, as well as using the horn.

Road Rules

North Americans drive on the right side of the road. Speed limits, which are posted in kilometers, are generally 50km/h in built-up

areas and 90km/h on highways. A right turn is permitted at a red light after you have come to a complete stop, as is a left turn from a one-way street onto another one-way street; U-turns are not allowed. Traffic in both directions must stop when stationary school buses have their red lights flashing – this means children are getting off and on. In cities with pedestrian crosswalks, cars must stop to allow pedestrians to cross.

The use of seat belts is compulsory throughout Canada. Children under the age of five must be in a restraining seat. British Columbia law requires motorcyclists to drive with the lights on and for cyclists and passengers to wear helmets. The blood-alcohol limit when driving is 0.08% (about two drinks).

HITCHHIKING

Hitchhiking is not common in BC and the Yukon. It's never entirely safe in any country in the world, and is not recommended. Travelers who decide to hitchhike (or pick up hitchhikers) should understand that they are taking a risk. If you do choose to hitchhike, do it only in pairs. Hitching on the Trans-Canada Hwy is illegal until 40km past the Vancouver city limits.

LOCAL TRANSPORTATION

British Columbia has excellent, widespread local public transportation in the area around Vancouver and Victoria. Outside of these areas service can be sparse, erratic or infrequent. Look in the regional chapters for details on each town's offerings, or see the province-wide website (www.transitbc.com), which features links to the local bus systems. Most places have taxi companies.

In the Yukon, public transit in Whitehorse will suffice if you just need to get from the airport to town and hook up with a tour operator or gear-rental place. Like much of BC, you'll have a hard time getting around without a car.

TRAIN

Railroad service is limited in BC. The national carrier, **VIA Rail** (☎ 888-842-7245; www.viarail.ca), has only one route from Vancouver. The *Canadian* departs a paltry three times a week and makes few stops in BC, including outside of Kamloops before reaching Jasper. VIA Rail also runs the *Skeena* between Prince Rupert and Jasper thrice weekly. It's a daytime-only

TRANSPORTATION

trip with an overnight stay in Prince George, and stops in Terrace, New Hazelton, Smithers, Houston and Burns Lake. Passengers on the *Skeena* have a choice of service class and fare, and you find your own lodgings in Prince George.

One-way fares from Vancouver to Jasper are $200 or more; Prince Rupert to Jasper $150 or more. But like the airlines, VIA Rail offers various discounts for round trips and fares can change daily depending on demand, so it's worth checking often.

On Vancouver Island, VIA Rail runs the *Esquimalt & Nanaimo Railiner*, also known as the *Malahat*, a short, scenic trip from Victoria to Courtenay up the coast of Vancouver Island, with one train daily in each direction (p153) which is often threatened with a permanent shut-down.

Rocky Mountaineer Vacations (☎ 877-460-3200; www.rockymountaineer.com) runs cruise-train-type trips between Vancouver and Whistler (p127) as well as trains on the historic Canada Pacific Railway (CPR) line to Banff and the Canadian National (CN) line to Jasper. The latter two runs in particular are sold as part of packages and aren't aimed at independent travelers.

TRANSPORTATION

Health Dr David Goldberg

There's a high level of hygiene found in this region, so most common infectious diseases will not be a significant concern for travelers. Also, superb medical care is widely available.

BEFORE YOU GO

INSURANCE

The Canadian health-care system is one of the finest in the world. Excellent care is widely available. Benefits are generous for Canadian citizens, but foreigners aren't covered. Make sure you have travel-health insurance if your regular policy doesn't apply when you're abroad. Find out in advance if your insurance plan will make payments directly to providers or reimburse you later for overseas health expenditures.

ONLINE RESOURCES

There is a wealth of travel-health advice on the internet. The World Health Organization publishes a superb book, called *International Travel and Health*, which is revised annually and is available online at no cost at www.who .int/ith. Another website of general interest is **MD Travel Health** (www.mdtravelhealth.com), which provides complete travel-health recommendations for every country, is updated daily and is available at no cost.

It's usually a good idea to consult your government's travel-health website, if one is available, before departure:

Australia (www.smartraveller.gov.au)

United Kingdom (www.doh.gov.uk/traveladvice/index .htm)

United States (www.cdc.gov/travel)

IN CANADA

AVAILABILITY & COST OF HEALTH CARE

For immediate medical assistance anywhere in BC, call ☎ 911; in the Yukon, call ☎ 867-667-5555. In general, if you have a medical emergency, the best bet is to find the nearest hospital and go to its emergency room.

If you have a choice, a university hospital can be preferable to a community hospital, although you can often find superb medical care in small local hospitals and the waiting time is usually shorter. If the problem isn't urgent, you can call a nearby hospital and ask for a referral to a local physician, which is usually less expensive than a trip to the emergency room.

Pharmacies are abundantly supplied, however you may find that some medications which are available over-the-counter in your home country require a prescription in Canada.

INFECTIOUS DISEASES

There are several infectious diseases that are unknown or uncommon outside North America. Most are acquired by mosquito bites, tick bites or environmental exposure.

West Nile Virus

Infections were unknown in Canada until recently, but West Nile virus has now been observed in many provinces, including Saskatchewan, Alberta, Ontario, Québec and Manitoba. The virus is transmitted by Culex mosquitoes, which are active in late summer and early fall, and generally bite after dusk. Most infections are mild or asymptomatic, but the virus may infect the central nervous system, leading to fever, headache, confusion, lethargy, coma and sometimes death. There is no treatment for West Nile virus.

At the time of writing there was no evidence of the virus in British Columbia or the Yukon. For the latest update on the areas affected by West Nile, go to the Health Canada website at www.hc-sc.gc.ca/english/index_e.html. See also Mosquito Bites (p408).

RECOMMENDED VACCINATIONS

No special vaccines are required or recommended for travel to Canada. All travelers should be up-to-date on routine immunizations, listed below.

Vaccine	Recommended for	Dosage	Side effects
tetanus-diphtheria	all travelers who haven't had booster within 10 yrs	one dose lasts 10 years	soreness at injection site
measles	travelers born after 1956 who've had only one measles vaccination	one dose	fever; rash; joint pains; allergic reactions
chickenpox	travelers who've never had chickenpox	two doses one month apart	fever; mild case of chickenpox
influenza	all travelers during flu season (Nov-Mar)	one dose	soreness at the injection site; fever

Lyme Disease

This has been reported from the southern parts of the country. The infection is transmitted by deer ticks, which are only 1mm to 2mm long. Most cases occur in late spring and summer. The first symptom is usually an expanding red rash that is often pale in the center, known as a bull's eye rash. However, in many cases, no rash is observed. Flu-like symptoms are common, including fever, headache, joint pains, body aches and malaise. When the infection is treated promptly with an appropriate antibiotic, usually doxycycline or amoxicillin, the cure rate is high. For prevention tips, see Tick Bites (p408).

Giardiasis

This parasitic infection of the small intestine occurs throughout North America and the world. Known colloquially in BC as 'Beaver fever,' Giardiasis has symptoms that may include nausea, bloating, cramps, and diarrhea, and may last for weeks. Avoid drinking directly from lakes, ponds, streams and rivers, which may be contaminated by animal or human feces.

Rabies

Rabies is a viral infection of the brain and spinal cord that is almost always fatal. In Canada most cases of human rabies relate to exposure to bats. Rabies may also be contracted from raccoon, skunk, fox, and unvaccinated cats and dogs. All animal bites and scratches must be promptly and thoroughly cleansed with large amounts of soap and water, and local health authorities contacted to determine if there is a risk of rabies. If there is

any possibility, however small, that you have been exposed to rabies, you should seek preventative treatment, which consists of rabies-immune globulin and rabies vaccine, and is quite safe. In particular, any contact with a bat should be discussed with health authorities, as bats have small teeth and may not leave obvious bite marks.

HIV/AIDS

This infectious disease occurs throughout Canada.

ENVIRONMENTAL HAZARDS
Cold Exposure

Cold exposure may be a significant problem, especially in the northern parts of the country. To prevent hypothermia, keep all body surfaces covered, including the head and neck. Synthetic materials such as Gore-Tex and Thinsulate provide excellent insulation. Since the body loses heat faster when wet, stay dry at all times. Change inner garments promptly when they become moist. Keep active, but get enough rest. Consume plenty of food and water. Be especially sure not to have any alcohol. Caffeine and tobacco should also be avoided.

Watch out for the 'Umbles': stumbles, mumbles, fumbles and grumbles, important signs of impending hypothermia. If someone appears to be developing hypothermia, you should insulate them from the ground, protect them from the wind, remove wet clothing or cover with a vapor barrier such as a plastic bag, and transport immediately to a warm environment and a medical facility. Warm fluids (not

HEALTH

HEALTH

MEDICAL CHECKLIST

- Acetaminophen/paracetamol (Tylenol) or aspirin
- Anti-inflammatory drugs (eg ibuprofen)
- Antihistamines (for hay fever and allergic reactions)
- Antibacterial ointment (eg Neosporin or Bactroban) for cuts and abrasions
- Steroid cream or cortisone (for poison ivy and other allergic rashes)
- Bandages, gauze, gauze rolls
- Adhesive or paper tape
- Scissors, safety pins, tweezers
- Thermometer
- Pocket knife
- DEET-containing insect repellent for the skin
- Permethrin-containing insect spray for clothing, tents and bed nets

Bring medications in their original containers, clearly labeled. A signed, dated letter from your physician describing all medical conditions and medications, including generic names is also a good idea. If carrying syringes or needles be sure to have a physician's letter documenting their medical necessity.

---

coffee or tea) may be given if the person is alert enough to swallow.

Mosquito Bites

When traveling in areas where West Nile or other mosquito-borne illnesses have been reported, keep yourself covered (wear long sleeves, long pants, hats and shoes rather than sandals). Apply a good insect repellent, preferably one containing DEET, to exposed skin and clothing. Avoid contact with eyes, mouth, cuts, wounds or irritated skin. Products containing lower concentrations of DEET are as effective, but for shorter periods of time. In general, adults and children over 12 should use preparations containing 25% to 35% DEET, which lasts about six hours. Children aged between two and 12 years should use preparations containing no more than 10% DEET, applied sparingly, which will last about three hours. Neurologic toxicity has been reported from DEET, especially in children, but appears to be extremely uncommon and generally related to overuse. DEET-containing compounds should not be used on children under age two. Insect repellents containing certain botanical products, including oil of eucalyptus and soybean oil, are effective but last only 1½ to two hours. Products based on citronella are not effective.

For additional protection, you can apply permethrin to clothing, shoes, tents and bed nets. Permethrin treatments are safe and remain effective for at least two weeks, even when items are laundered. Permethrin should not be applied directly to skin.

Tick Bites

To protect yourself from tick bites, follow the same precautions as for mosquitoes, except that boots are preferable to shoes, and pants tucked in. Be sure to perform a thorough tick check at the end of each day, with the aid of a friend or mirror. Ticks should be removed with tweezers, grasping them firmly by the head. Insect repellents based on botanical products cannot be recommended to prevent tick bites.

Mammal Bites

Most animal injuries are directly related to a person's attempt to touch or feed the animal. Any bite or scratch by a mammal, including bats, should be promptly and thoroughly cleansed with large amounts of soap and water, followed by application of an antiseptic such as iodine or alcohol. The local health authorities should be contacted immediately for possible post-exposure rabies treatment.

Glossary

aurora borealis – charged particles from the sun that are trapped in the earth's magnetic field and appear as other-worldly, colored, waving beams; also called the northern lights

beaver fever – giardiasis; disease affecting the digestive tract caused by bacteria found in many freshwater streams and lakes; can be avoided by boiling drinking water
boreal – refers to the Canadian north and its character

Canadian Shield – a plateau of rock formed 2.5 billion years ago that covers much of the northern region of Canada; also known as the Precambrian or Laurentian Shield
clear-cut – an area where loggers have cut every tree, large and small, leaving nothing but stumps
coulees – gulches, usually dry
CN – Canadian National Railroad; one of two main railroads in Canada
CPR – Canadian Pacific Railway; the other main railroad in Canada

down-island – on Vancouver Island, anywhere south of where you are

First Nations – denotes Canada's aboriginal peoples; often used instead of Native Indians or Native people

gasoline – petrol, known as gasoline, fuel, or simply gas; mostly sold unleaded in Canada
GST – the 7% goods and services tax levied on most purchases throughout Canada

hoodoo – distinctive vertical pillar shape carved into a rock face by rainfall and glacial erosion

icefield – a large, level expanse of floating ice
Inside Passage – sea route from the Alaskan Panhandle to Washington state that runs between mainland BC and the chain of islands off the coast

Kermode bear – sometimes called Spirit Bears, have white fur and live in the Great Bear Rainforest

loon – aquatic bird
loonie – slang term for Canada's one-dollar coin, which depicts a loon on one side
Lower Mainland – common term for the southwestern part of BC, including metropolitan Vancouver

Métis – Canadians of mixed French and First Nations ancestry
Mounties – Royal Canadian Mounted Police (RCMP)
muskeg – undrained boggy land found in northern BC

névé – compacted snow that forms the surface of the upper part of a glacier
no-see-um – various tiny biting insects that are difficult to see and can annoy travelers in the woods or along beaches; can be kept out of tents with no-see-um netting, a very fine mesh screen
NWT – Northwest Territories, the part of Canada to the east of the Yukon.

Ogopogo – monster similar to the Loch Ness monster, thought to reside in Okanagan Lake; has never been photographed
oolichan – aka eulachon and candlefish; small, oil-rich fish important to First Nations people

portage – process of transporting boats and supplies overland between navigable waterways
petroglyphs – ancient paintings or carvings on rock
potlatch – competitive ceremonial activity among some BC First Nations people (usually coastal), involving the giving of lavish gifts to emphasize the wealth and status of a chief or clan; now often just refers to a wild party or revel
PST – Provincial Sales Tax; currently 7% in BC; when coupled with the GST, it can bring the tax on many purchases to 14%

quay – pronounced 'key'; a city's waterfront docks area, as in North Vancouver's Lonsdale Quay or Port Alberni's Harbour Quay

RCMP – Royal Canadian Mounted Police; the main law-enforcement agency throughout Canada

sourdough – a person who has completed one year's residency in northern Canada
spelunking – exploration and study of caves

taiga – coniferous forests extending across much of subarctic North America and Eurasia
toonie – slang name for a Canadian two-dollar coin
trailer – caravan or mobile home

up-island – on Vancouver Island, anywhere north of where you are

VIC – Visitor Information Centre

The Authors

RYAN VER BERKMOES

Ryan's been bouncing around British Columbia and the Yukon for more than two decades. One of his first forays was a jaunt around Stanley Park after midnight – he wouldn't try that in many places. Since then worthwhile jaunts have included a trip to the end of the road in the Queen Charlotte Islands, a trek to the middle of Kluane National Park and an encounter with the bottom of a bottle of Okanagan Valley wine. (Note that some of the preceding were accomplished more than once.) Along the way there's been adventures with moose, bears and Mounties. (He doesn't recommend any of these.) When not up north Ryan enjoys the slightly more temperate rain in Portland, Oregon.

My BC

Get me to the coast when I'm in British Columbia (unless, of course, I'm lost in the Yukon…a fate I regularly hope for). The **Alaska Marine Highway ferries** (p400) are superb – low-key but comfortable, with good bars (the bartender on the *M/S Columbia* may be the best on the planet) and not a hint of the cruise ship experience. Instead you're on deck watching the ship thread the **Inside Passage** (p400) while you spot orcas passing the bow. On shore it's my fab four: the remote **Bella Coola Valley** (p317), surprising **Prince Rupert** (p338), the captivating **Queen Charlotte Islands** (p343) and glaciated **Stewart** (p354). The first three are on ferry lines, the last is at the end of a killer drive.

LONELY PLANET AUTHORS

Why is our travel information the best in the world? It's simple: our authors are independent, dedicated travellers. They don't research using just the internet or phone, and they don't take freebies in exchange for positive coverage. They travel widely, to all the popular spots and off the beaten track. They personally visit thousands of hotels, restaurants, cafés, bars, galleries, palaces, museums and more – and they take pride in getting all the details right, and telling it how it is. For more, see the authors section on www.lonelyplanet.com.

JOHN LEE

Born in the UK, John first visited Vancouver for Expo '86, a world fair that he remembers chiefly for its endless sunny days, British-themed pub and floating McDonald's restaurant. Aiming to return to Canada as soon as possible, he became a graduate student at BC's University of Victoria a few years later. He eventually transformed his study visa into citizenship, following a ceremony where he had to pledge allegiance to the Queen. A Vancouver-based travel writer since 1999, John's work has appeared in 120 publications around the world, including the *Guardian*, *Los Angeles Times*, *Chicago Tribune* and *Russian Life*. Specializing in writing about Canada and the UK, his all-time favourite journey was on the Trans-Siberian Railway. Keep up-to-date with his travel journalism at www.johnleewriter.com.

My BC

What surprised me most about my trek around BC was how much I enjoyed the silence of the natural areas and the quirky camaraderie of the smaller communities. Ever the urbanite, I'm more used to city life, but soaring over **Pemberton** (p127) in a glider, boating over the **Skookumchuck tidal rapids** (p132), munching seaweed on the beach in **Sooke** (p158) and hanging-out with the trees in **Ronning's Garden** (p191) were enough to make me re-think my city-loving ways. As for drives, the best route was from **Campbell River** (p184) towards **Cape Scott Provincial Park** (p191) on Vancouver Island's northwestern tip. Via tiny **Sayward** (p188), charming **Telegraph Cove** (p188) and a couple of berry-eating black bears along the roadside, the deserted, achingly beautiful beaches up there would make an environmentalist of anyone.

Behind the Scenes

THIS BOOK

This guidebook was commissioned in Lonely Planet's Oakland office, and produced by the following:

Commissioning Editor Emily K Wolman
Coordinating Editor Lauren Rollheiser
Coordinating Cartographer Herman So
Coordinating Layout Designers Carol Jackson, Carlos Solarte
Managing Editor Melanie Dankel
Managing Cartographer Alison Lyall
Assisting Editors Elizabeth Anglin, Elisa Arduca, Louise Clarke, Kim Hutchins, Anne Mulvaney
Assisting Cartographers Anneka Imkamp, Jody Whiteoak
Assisting Layout Designers Wibowo Rusli
Cover Designer Pepi Bluck
Project Manager Glenn van der Knijff

Thanks to Sin Choo, Rebecca Dandens, Sally Darmody, Ryan Evans, Mark Germanchis, James Hardy, Craig Kilburn, Andrew Smith, Celia Wood

THANKS
RYAN VER BERKMOES

The number of folks to thank outnumber Kermode bears but here's a few: the generous Rosemary Smart and Sherry Fontaine in the Bella Coola Valley – where I'd always go to the end of the road with Fraser Koroluk and Holly Willgress. Jim Kemshead is the best thespian in a Yukon filled with characters (including the brave man who plunged from the piano in Dawson). Nathalie Macfarlane, of the beautiful new Haida Gwaii Heritage Centre in QCI is a star as is John Lee – and not just for buying me beer. And Erin and the DNC: I love one and thank the other.

JOHN LEE

Many thanks to photographer Dominic Schaefer for supplying the igloo camping image – it makes me look way cooler than I actually am. Thanks also to the sterling band of generous locals and tourism bureau staff who took the time to help me out while I was on the road – without you, my contribution to this book would not be nearly so colorful (or informed). Special thanks for their help on this and other projects to Janice (Tourism BC), Emily (Tourism Vancouver) and Kristine (Tourism Victoria).

Thanks also to my Vancouver friends (including the Friday breakfast crew) for hanging in there while my fingers were stapled to the keyboard during write-up – I know it was hard to remember what I looked like when I finally staggered out into the sunlight (okay, the rain) of a cold October day. Which reminds me: credit to my local Tim Hortons for being open 24/7 – doughnuts look pretty good at 5am but a toasted bagel with peanut butter always tastes better.

Finally, hearty thanks to my Dad, nephew Dominic and brother Michael for coming over from England to have fun here during my research period – Michael: we definitely need to hit more pubs next time.

THE LONELY PLANET STORY

The story begins with a classic travel adventure: Tony and Maureen Wheeler's 1972 journey across Europe and Asia to Australia. There was no useful information about the overland trail then, so Tony and Maureen published the first Lonely Planet guidebook to meet a growing need.

From a kitchen table, Lonely Planet has grown to become the largest independent travel publisher in the world, with offices in Melbourne (Australia), Oakland (USA) and London (UK). Today Lonely Planet guidebooks cover the globe. There is an ever-growing list of books and information in a variety of media. Some things haven't changed. The main aim is still to make it possible for adventurous travelers to get out there – to explore and better understand the world.

At Lonely Planet we believe travelers can make a positive contribution to the countries they visit – if they respect their host communities and spend their money wisely. Every year 5% of company profit is donated to charities around the world.

OUR READERS

Many thanks to the travelers who used the last edition and wrote to us with helpful hints, useful advice and interesting anecdotes:

Eric Anderson, Sam & Sarah Argov, Enrica Benedetto, Christine Bickson, Brendan Birkett, Melissa Bowerman, Harold Brand, Charlotte Burton, Jim Busby, Fiona Cannon, Helen Clark, Paula Davies, Cindy Dern, Dave Dorey, Christopher Drew, Adam Dunnett, Louise Edney, Tony Feeney, Patrick Fergusson, Crystal Flaman, Caroline Freitas, Godfrey Family, Tony Gordon, Colin Gore, Thomas Guerrero, Melissa Hayward, Sabina Heyde, J C Hokke, Frans Holla, Barbara Homewood, June Hornby, Natalie Horsfield, Graham & Katie Hunt, Alisha Jackson, Gillian Jeens, Pat & Terry Jefferies, Gemma Jones, Mary Keller, Irving Levinson, Jane Margulis, Linzi Martin, Erin McQauley, Mary McInerney, Dale McKinnon, Yvonne Megens, Ng Mei Yun, Neil Mercer, Peter Mieras, Ziver Miller, David Noel, Cathal O'Donnell, Kate O'Hara, Karen Olch, Kirsten Ostapowich, Dick Parsons, Robin Peterman, Ian Plumtree, Martin Pollock, Ann Pope, Stuart & Jone Riley, Norm & Nancy Rollheiser, Philippa Sanders, Debra & Alan Sayles, Dirk-Jan Scheffers, Karl Seyffer, Amina Shamsie, Doug Unsworth, Eliana Uretsky, Jetske van den Bijtel, Vyque White, Michael Williams, Paul Williamson, Salome & Stephan Wolf, Jill Zimonick

SEND US YOUR FEEDBACK

We love to hear from travelers – your comments keep us on our toes and help make our books better. Our well-traveled team reads every word on what you loved or loathed about this book. Although we cannot reply individually to postal submissions, we always guarantee that your feedback goes straight to the appropriate authors, in time for the next edition. Each person who sends us information is thanked in the next edition – and the most useful submissions are rewarded with a free book.

To send us your updates – and find out about Lonely Planet events, newsletters and travel news – visit our award-winning website: **www.lonelyplanet.com/contact**.

Note: we may edit, reproduce and incorporate your comments in Lonely Planet products such as guidebooks, websites and digital products, so let us know if you don't want your comments reproduced or your name acknowledged. For a copy of our privacy policy visit www.lonelyplanet.com/privacy.

TRAVEL WIDELY, TREAD LIGHTLY, GIVE SUSTAINABLY – THE LONELY PLANET FOUNDATION

The Lonely Planet Foundation proudly supports nimble nonprofit institutions working for change in the world. Each year the foundation donates 5% of Lonely Planet company profits to projects selected by staff and authors. Our partners range from Kabissa, which provides small nonprofits across Africa with access to technology, to the Foundation for Developing Cambodian Orphans, which supports girls at risk of falling victim to sex traffickers.

Our nonprofit partners are linked by a grass-roots approach to the areas of health, education or sustainable tourism. Many – such as Louis Sarno who works with BaAka (Pygmy) children in the forested areas of Central African Republic – choose to focus on women and children as one of the most effective ways to support the whole community. Louis is determined to give options to children who are discriminated against by the majority Bantu population.

Sometimes foundation assistance is as simple as restoring a local ruin like the Minaret of Jam in Afghanistan; this incredible monument now draws intrepid tourists to the area and its restoration has greatly improved options for local people.

Just as travel is often about learning to see with new eyes, so many of the groups we work with aim to change the way people see themselves and the future for their children and communities.

Index

Index

000 Map pages
000 Photograph pages

National Hockey League 28, 71
Nelson 258-63, **259**
New Denver 256-7
New Hazelton 336-8
New Pornographers 30
newspapers 31, 388
Nikkei Internment Memorial Centre
  256
Nimpo Lake 316
Nine O'Clock Gun 76
Nisga'a peoples 23-4
Nk'Mip Desert & Heritage Centre 222
Nlaka'pamux peoples 212
Nootka treaty 21
North Pacific Historic Fishing
  Village 343
North Pender Island 198-200
North Star Mine 270
North Vancouver 104-7
Nulth peoples 20
Nuxalk peoples 20, 29

O
Oceanside 169-72
Odegaard Falls 317
Ogopogo 233

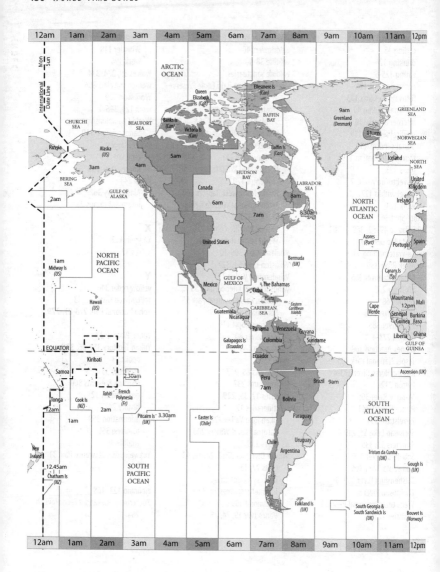

12pm 1pm 2pm 3pm 4pm 5pm 6pm 7pm 8pm 9pm 10pm 11pm 12am

Mon / Sun
International Date Line

Svalbard (Norway)

Zemlya Frantsa-Iosifa (Russia)

Severnaya Zemlya (Russia)

Novaya Zemlya (Russia)

KARA SEA

LAPTEV SEA

Novosibirskie Ostrovo (Russia)

EAST SIBERIAN SEA

BARENTS SEA

Sweden 1pm
Norway
Finland 2pm
3pm
Denmark
Germany Poland Latvia Belarus
France Austria Ukraine
Italy Romania
Tunisia Greece Turkey
MEDITERRANEAN SEA
Algeria Libya Egypt
Niger
Chad Sudan
Nigeria
Central African Republic
Gabon 1pm Congo (Zaire)
Angola
Namibia Zambia Zimbabwe
Botswana Mozambique
South Africa

4pm
5pm
6pm
Kazakhstan
Uzbekistan Kyrgyzstan
Turkmenistan
4pm
Syria Iraq Iran
3.30pm
Afghanistan 4.30pm
Pakistan 5pm
Saudi Arabia
4pm
Oman
Yemen
ARABIAN SEA
Ethiopia 3pm
Somalia
Kenya
Tanzania
Malawi
Madagascar
Mauritius
Reunion (Fr)

7pm

Russia

Mongolia

China
8pm

Tibet (China)
Nepal 5.45pm
India 5.30pm
6.30pm
Myanmar
Bangladesh
BAY OF BENGAL 5.30pm
Sri Lanka
Maldives

6pm Thailand
Vietnam
Malaysia
Indonesia

9pm

10pm

11pm

12am

SEA OF OKHOTSK

North Korea
South Korea Japan

EAST CHINA SEA

Taiwan

Philippines

Palau

9pm

Federated States of Micronesia 11am

BERING SEA

3am
2am

NORTH PACIFIC OCEAN

Northern Mariana Is (US)

Marshall Is (US)
12am

Kiribati

Nauru EQUATOR

Seychelles 4pm
6.30pm Cocos (Keeling) Is (Aust)

INDIAN OCEAN

East Timor

Papua New Guinea
Solomon Is

SOUTH PACIFIC OCEAN

Vanuatu

9.30 pm
Australia

New Caledonia (Fr)
10.30 pm Lord Howe Is (Aust)
11.30 pm Norfolk Is (Aust)

Fiji

New Zealand

Prince Edward Is (S. Africa)

French Southern & Antarctic Territories (Fr)
3u

Heard & McDonald Is (Aust)

TASMAN SEA

SOUTHERN OCEAN

12pm 1pm 2pm 3pm 4pm 5pm 6pm 7pm 8pm 9pm 10pm 11pm 12am

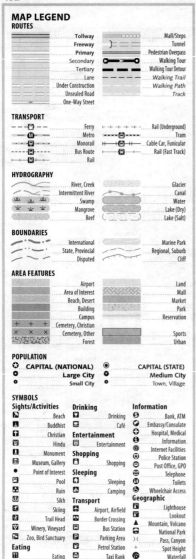

432

MAP LEGEND
ROUTES

Tollway	Mall/Steps
Freeway	Tunnel
Primary	Pedestrian Overpass
Secondary	Walking Tour
Tertiary	Walking Tour Detour
Lane	Walking Trail
Under Construction	Walking Path
Unsealed Road	Track
One-Way Street	

TRANSPORT

Ferry	Rail (Underground)
Metro	Tram
Monorail	Cable Car, Funicular
Bus Route	Rail (Fast Track)
Rail	

HYDROGRAPHY

River, Creek	Glacier
Intermittent River	Canal
Swamp	Water
Mangrove	Lake (Dry)
Reef	Lake (Salt)

BOUNDARIES

International	Marine Park
State, Provincial	Regional, Suburb
Disputed	Cliff

AREA FEATURES

Airport	Land
Area of Interest	Mall
Beach, Desert	Market
Building	Park
Campus	Reservation
Cemetery, Christian	
Cemetery, Other	Sports
Forest	Urban

POPULATION

○ CAPITAL (NATIONAL)	◉ CAPITAL (STATE)
● Large City	● Medium City
● Small City	○ Town, Village

SYMBOLS

Sights/Activities
- Beach
- Buddhist
- Christian
- Hindu
- Monument
- Museum, Gallery
- Point of Interest
- Pool
- Ruin
- Sikh
- Skiing
- Trail Head
- Winery, Vineyard
- Zoo, Bird Sanctuary

Eating
- Eating

Drinking
- Drinking
- Café

Entertainment
- Entertainment

Shopping
- Shopping

Sleeping
- Sleeping
- Camping

Transport
- Airport, Airfield
- Border Crossing
- Bus Station
- Parking Area
- Petrol Station
- Taxi Rank

Information
- Bank, ATM
- Embassy/Consulate
- Hospital, Medical
- Information
- Internet Facilities
- Police Station
- Post Office, GPO
- Telephone
- Toilets
- Wheelchair Access

Geographic
- Lighthouse
- Lookout
- Mountain, Volcano
- National Park
- Pass, Canyon
- Spot Height
- Waterfall

LONELY PLANET OFFICES

Australia
Head Office
Locked Bag 1, Footscray, Victoria 3011
☎ 03 8379 8000, fax 03 8379 8111
talk2us@lonelyplanet.com.au

USA
150 Linden St, Oakland, CA 94607
☎ 510 893 8555, toll free 800 275 8555
fax 510 893 8572
info@lonelyplanet.com

UK
72–82 Rosebery Ave,
Clerkenwell, London EC1R 4RW
☎ 020 7841 9000, fax 020 7841 9001
go@lonelyplanet.co.uk

Published by Lonely Planet Publications Pty Ltd
ABN 36 005 607 983

© Lonely Planet Publications Pty Ltd 2007

© photographers as indicated 2007

Cover photograph: Horses and birch trees, Ernest Manewal/Lonely Planet Images. Many of the images in this guide are available for licensing from Lonely Planet Images: www.lonelyplanetimages.com.

Although the authors and Lonely Planet have taken all reasonable care in preparing this book, we make no warranty about the accuracy or completeness of its content and, to the maximum extent permitted, disclaim all liability arising from its use.